HISTORY OF
POLITICAL
T H E O R Y
AN INTRODUCTION

Volume II

HISTORY OF POLITICAL THEORY
AN INTRODUCTION

Volume II
Modern Political
Theory

George Klosko
University of Virginia

THOMSON
———✦———™
WADSWORTH

Australia • Canada • Mexico • Singapore • Spain • United Kingdom • United States

Publisher	Ted Buchholz
Senior Acquisitions Editor	David C. Tatom
Developmental Editor	Cathlynn Richard
Project Editor	Erica Lazerow/Krystyn K. Freidlin
Production Manager	Melinda Esco
Book Designer	Sue Hart
Cover Designer	Michele Anderson

ISBN: 0-03-074014-2

Library of Congress Catalog Number: 92-53970

Wadsworth Group/Thomson Learning
10 Davis Drive
Belmont CA 94002-3098
USA

For information about our products, contact us:
Thomson Learning Academic Resource Center
1-800-423-0563
http://www.wadsworth.com

For permission to use material from this text, contact us by
Web: http://www.thomsonrights.com
Fax: 1-800-730-2215
Phone: 1-800-730-2214

Special acknowledgments of copyright ownership and of permission to reproduce works
(or excerpts thereof) included in this volume begin on page 469 and constitute an extension of this page.

Printed in the United States of America
10 9 8 7 6 5 4 3

To the memory of
Minnette Klosko

Eishet Hayil

Contents

2

PREFACE

"THE IDEAS OF ECONOMISTS AND political philosophers," said Lord Keynes, "both when they are right and when they are wrong, are more powerful than is commonly understood. Indeed the world is ruled by little else . . . Madmen in authority, who hear voices in the air, are distilling their frenzy from some academic scribbler of a few years back." The extent to which the ideas of political thinkers actually inspire political actors is a difficult question, and one addressed by various theorists discussed in this work. What is clear, however, is that the ideas that have been espoused by political leaders and around which major political movements have formed throughout Western history are classically expressed by the "academic scribblers" we examine. Whatever we ultimately decide about the influence of ideas, the political theorists we examine in this volume are the most important of the past three or four centuries and in many ways appear to rule us still.

This two-volume history of political theory traces a series of attempts to deal with fundamental questions of political association. The range of questions is impressive, varying over time. But many questions with which the great theorists wrestle are of great concern to contemporary citizens and must be confronted. The first volume covers the ancient and medieval periods and draws to a close with the Reformation, as *liberal* political theory began to emerge. In this volume, much discussion is focussed on liberal political theory and the different forms it has assumed in the hands of different authors. Though I address a range of additional concerns, many thinkers examined in this volume are great figures in the liberal tradition, or powerful critics of it.

In examining modern political theory, I assume that "our" political ideas are essentially liberal, though we may not be entirely aware of this. Accordingly, the "we" invoked is liberal citizens, myself included. Exactly what liberal ideas are is discussed briefly in the Introduction, and then throughout this volume. I should note, however, that liberal ideas exist in different forms and have been subjected to severe criticisms. In addition to presenting a clear definition of liberal theory and the different ways it has been developed, I am greatly concerned with presenting a balanced account. Because I assume the reader's approach to political matters is essentially liberal, I develop criticisms with particular care, notably in the chapters on Rousseau, Hegel, and Marx, in keeping with the great liberal value of open-mindedness (classically expressed in John Stuart Mill's *On Liberty*, discussed in Chapter 8).

As in Volume I, my main concern throughout this volume is providing clear, reliable accounts of the political theories under discussion and reasons for their continuing relevance. Because it is important to consider theorists' own expression of their ideas, I include an unusual amount of direct quotation. Collecting this material should give students small anthologies of the most important political passages of the theorists covered. Because much of this material takes on added meaning against the circumstances of thinkers' lives, I also provide essential intellectual and political background, though this seems more necessary in certain cases than others.

This textbook is aimed primarily at courses in which the instructor wants sustained, detailed attention to the ideas of the great thinkers but does not wish to assign only original texts. Because I do not assume student familiarity with works discussed, I am careful to explain and illustrate basic concepts. But I hope my discussions will be of interest to more advanced readers as well. The ideas of many thinkers discussed in this volume are difficult. Clear accounts of their central ideas should be helpful to a variety of audiences.

A work of this sort requires numerous choices about what to include and omit. Because my main concern is depth rather than breadth, I focus on small number of major thinkers, paying less attention to subsidiary figures. I also concentrate on central ideas, instead of attempting complete accounts of theorists' views. Because of the great importance of the concept of freedom in modern political theory, I examine many theorists in reference to this, especially the nature of freedom and the conditions necessary for its realization. Thus, in discussing Marx I pay greater attention to his view of ideology and his critique of liberal political theory as the ideology of a specific class than to other aspects of his thought, for example, his contributions to political economy or account of alienation. In discussing Hegel, I limit consideration to central ideas of the *Philosophy of Right* and *Philosophy of History*, especially Hegel's linked notions of freedom, the nature of the individual, and the state. Another notable theme in several chapters is the rise of reason and scientific method and its effects on our understanding of politics. Though other themes are obviously important, it seems advisable to limit the range of topics in order to be able to develop ideas carefully and clearly.

To make this work as useful as possible, I have attempted to use editions and translations that are widely available. For easy reference, primary sources are collected at the end of each chapter under the heading "Texts Cited." I also include brief lists of suggested secondary readings. Because spelling in seventeenth- and eighteenth-century works is often haphazard, I have taken some liberties with this, and with punctuation, in order to make material more accessible. References to primary sources are explained in the notes to each chapter. And to cut down on the number of footnotes, I often place citations, including those to frequently cited secondary sources, in parentheses in the text.

I am happy to acknowledge the assistance of many people who have helped make this a better book. My colleague, Dante Germino, kindly read the entire manuscript and provided valuable comments and criticisms. Specific chapters were read by Stephen White, Joshua Dienstag, and Tim Collins, for whose comments I am also grateful, as I am to the following readers for Harcourt Brace, for valuable criticisms and suggestions: Terence Boll, University of Minnesota; Marilyn A. Davis, Spellman College; Tom Horne, University of Tulsa; Christin di Stefano, University of Washington; Peter Stillman, Vassar College. Jeff Miller provided valuable research assistance and helped verify quotations. I am also grateful to the staff of Alderman Library at the University of Virginia, and Library Express on Grounds, which made the task of assembling material far less taxing than it might have been.

I owe a great debt to Julian Franklin and the late Herbert Deane, who taught me how to work in the history of political theory, and whose model of sound historical scholarship I have sought to emulate here. I am also greatly indebted to my students, undergraduate and graduate, at Columbia and Purdue Universities and the University of Virginia, to whom I have presented different versions of this material for the past seventeen years. Krys Freidlin of Harcourt Brace has patiently seen volume II of this work through the press. David Tatom and Cathlynn Richard of Harcourt Brace have been model editors in terms of suggestions, encouragement, and gentle guidance.

I thank my father, Emanuel Klosko, for building the room in which this work was written, and my brother Steve, for computer consultation. As always, I wish to thank my wife, Margaret, and daughters, Caroline, Susanna, and Deborah, for moral support.

"WORLD HISTORY IS THE PROGRESS of the consciousness of freedom—a progress whose necessity it is our business to comprehend."

G. W. F. Hegel

INTRODUCTION

PHILOSOPHICAL DISCIPLINES ARE DEFINED BY the questions they address. Political theory focuses on the nature and purpose of human association. Human beings are, as Aristotle says, "political animals."[1] Not only must we cooperate in order to survive, but our moral and intellectual faculties can develop only in association with other people. Problems of communal life have been apparent since society first arose. Some of these are obvious today: how to preserve order, to protect the weak from the strong, to provide for the common defense, to care for those unable to care for themselves. But more fundamental questions must also be addressed, including the overall goals communities should pursue.

In certain ways, the value of the history of political theory (or political philosophy—terms I will use more or less interchangeably)[2] is apparent. Among the authors who have contributed to the field are some of the greatest thinkers in our tradition. Prominent authors discussed in Volume I of this work include Plato, Aristotle, St. Augustine, and St. Thomas Aquinas. In this volume we examine great works of Hobbes, Locke, Hume, Rousseau, Hegel, Mill, Marx and others. To study their works is to come into contact with their individual visions of human life, and so immeasurably to enrich and broaden one's horizons. It is not surprising that many works we discuss are prominently included on standard lists of the "Great Books" of Western civilization.

But the history of political theory is important in other ways as well. As citizens of our countries, we confront in our own lives the questions it addresses. As citizens, we have responsibilities to our fellow citizens and governments as well as to our families and friends. It is imperative to think about these, about what they entail and why we have them. Because these requirements are so important, we cannot simply accept the accounts given by others. For one thing, their views often conflict, and it is not clear whose we should accept.

As citizens, we are constantly presented with particular questions bearing on our relationship to government. Should I pay such and such tax? Is it permissible to violate speed limit laws? Is it more permissible if most everyone else does so? If my country demands that I make myself available for military service, to fight and possibly to die, must I do so? While serving in my country's army, must I do whatever I am ordered to? Are there any limits here? If so, what are they, and how are they enforced? In attempting to answer these questions and others like them, one is inevitably drawn to more general and fundamental questions concerning political authority. What purposes does political authority serve? What are the individual's obligations to it? At what point do these obligations run out? What recourse does one have when they do?

Because of the dependence of specific questions on these more general ones, we might appear to have arrived at an impasse. If we cannot know whether we should pay our taxes until we sort out general questions of political authority, then we have a problem. The general questions are so abstract and complex that one hardly knows where to begin in attempting to answer them. One of political theory's great contributions is that it attempts to provide answers. In making clear our relationship to the state, political theory is of inestimable importance.

The fundamental questions we have noted are central to the main tradition of modern Western political theory, which is known as the "liberal" tradition. The liberal political theory discussed in this volume (commonly referred to as "classical liberalism") is liberalism with a small "l," as opposed to the views of the "Liberal" wing of the Democratic party in the United States, and similar parties in other countries. The liberal tradition views the political world in a distinctive way. The individual is conceived of as standing apart from society. She has interests fully formed and is endowed with moral claims against other people, with "rights" that do not depend on membership of a particular society. The central questions of liberal political theory concern her relationship to society. Basic liberal assumptions are apparent in major documents in our tradition. For instance, the *Declaration of Independence* begins with individuals and their rights: "We hold these Truths to be self-evident, that all Men are created equal, that they are endowed by their Creator with certain unalienable Rights, that among these are Life, Liberty, and the Pursuit of Happiness." Government arises from a union of individuals, intended to protect the rights they already have prior to its formation: "to secure these Rights Governments are instituted among Men, deriving their just Powers from the Consent of the Governed. . ." The central question of liberal political theory, often referred to as the question of "political obligation," concerns the bonds between individual and state. What does the individual rightfully owe society and government? From another point of view, we confront the opposite question: What do society and government owe the individual? Of course, it is not enough simply to specify the respective requirements. We must also explain why they hold.

The rise of liberal political theory, which began in the sixteenth and seventeenth centuries, was bound up with the emergence of both free individuals and political institutions from the tangled medieval world. With the rise of the state in roughly the sixteenth century, the individual took center stage in the great drama of Western history.

The theorists discussed in Volume I inhabited a world of prestate political institutions, and premodern modes of thought. Studying their works provides an essential corrective to the assumption—an easy, perhaps natural assumption—that people have always and everywhere thought about politics as we do. An important lesson the history of political theory teaches is the *variety* of views the Western tradition has brought forth, each associated with distinctive political forms then in existence: *polis*, empire, medieval monarchy. But from roughly the time of the Reformation, the individual and his rights have been the focus for theorizing about politics. As we will see especially in our discussion of Rousseau, premodern (or preliberal) ideas reappear in large part in critiques of and alternatives to the liberal tradition.

Central to modern political theory is the retreat of religion from medieval heights. In conjunction with a lessening of its influence on political affairs, religion's place in the intellectual world increasingly gave way before the growing prestige of reason. This was closely associated with development of the scientific method and science's great accomplishments in unraveling the mysteries of the natural world. Reason was—and is—the central intellectual force of the modern era. Among its profound implications for political theory is the requirement that authority be *justified*; political authority must be shown to benefit society, on the basis of reasoned arguments. Attempts to explain why we need the state are central to modern political theory, and along with these, exploration of important related questions, for example, the kind of state we need.

Throughout the liberal tradition, perhaps the central value theorists defend is individual freedom—a specific conception of freedom, as we shall see. The state is viewed as an infringement on freedom, and so to paraphrase Thomas Jefferson, the least government is the best government. Unless it can be shown convincingly that the individual needs the state, he is free to do without it, and to do away with it if it no longer serves its function. This conception of freedom is claimed for the individual against the state in the incendiary writings of John Locke, and against both society and the state in the eloquent appeals of John Stuart Mill. The central argument of Mill's *On Liberty* is a defense of the individual's freedom to do as she pleases, unless this harms other people.

Though in many ways the arguments of Locke and Mill are basic to our view of the political world, there is more to the concept of freedom than the liberal tradition has advanced. Though Locke and Mill present what we may well regard as timeless truths, their views are one-sided and so susceptible to criticism. Along with important proponents of the liberal view of freedom, we will examine major critiques. In many ways, modern political theory has centered on a great dialogue about the nature and meaning of freedom. As political and social institutions arose to provide unprecedented liberty to unprecedented numbers of people, critiques as well as defenses of freedom filled the air.

There is a great deal more to modern political theory than the notion of freedom, its defense, and its drawbacks. Throughout this volume, we will explore the writings of some of the greatest minds the Western tradition has produced. To draw upon a quotation presented in the Introduction to Volume I, these men whose works we explore "are bone of our bone, and their thought like the architecture of the Middle Ages, is so much our common heritage that its originators remain unknown."[3] By examining their central arguments and the assumptions on which they rest, we become aware of similar features of our own ideas as well. In this respect the intellectual distancing required in this volume is less than in Volume I. Because the liberal tradition is our own, the authors we discuss address concerns recognizably similar to those we still have, while the political institutions on which they theorize are the direct basis for those that are with us still. But though the material in this volume connects more directly with our own experience, the goals of the two volumes are in large part the same. By exploring the origin of our ideas, we discover how they fit together and the basic assumptions on which they rest. Studying the history of political theory allows us to begin to address fundamental questions for ourselves. Attaining clarity about the different components of our thought is a necessary step on the way towards being able to disentangle them and so to understand them.

The history of political theory is the intellectual root of our own political ideas, part of what makes us what we are. By coming to understand the theoretical foundations of our distinctive view of politics, we are able to move beyond conceiving of it as inevitable or given. Our political ideas are human creations and so subject to critical assessment. Only when we are conscious of the inner workings of our ideas are we able not only to understand and criticize them, but also to accept them.

NOTES

1. Aristotle, *Politics*, I.1, 1253a1–3; see Volume I, Chapter 5, Sec. 4. Unaccompanied references to Volume I are to volume I of this work, *History of Political Theory: An Introduction*, Volume I, *Ancient and Medieval Political Theory* (Fort Worth, 1993).

2. Conventional distinctions between "political philosophy," "political theory," and "political thought" are in regard to levels of abstraction. In regard to the last, theoretical reflection is directed at immediate controversial issues, as for example, in newspaper editorials. The "political thought" of people of the United States, England, or France concerns their ideas about political issues. "Political philosophy" and "political theory" are closer in meaning. Both combine theoretical reflection and some concern for political questions. In general, the former emphasizes the element of reflection rather more; the latter emphasizes the political dimension. But both "political philosophy" and "political theory" differ from "political thought" in having less immediate practical concerns.

3. J. N. Figgis, *Political Thought From Gerson to Grotius: 1414–1625* (1916; rpt. New York, 1960), pp. 2–3.

C h a p t e r

1

Niccolò Machiavelli

In the *Third Part* of Shakespeare's *Henry VI*, Richard, Duke of Gloucester and future King Richard III, plots to gain the throne:

> Why, I can smile, and murder whiles I smile,
> And cry "Content!" to that which grieves my heart,
> And wet my cheeks with artificial tears . . .
> And set the murderous Machiavel to school.
> (*3 Henry VI*, III, ii, 182–93)

We see in this passage Shakespeare's association of a certain kind of villainy with the name of Machiavelli. Richard is not only evil but rejoices in it, pursuing power with supreme duplicity.

Shakespeare was not alone in his view of Machiavelli. Some four hundred similar references appear in Elizabethan literature.[1] The combination of fraud, lack of morality, and lust for power embodied by Shakespeare's Richard III are attributes that have been associated with Machiavelli's name for hundreds of years. *The American Heritage Dictionary* defines Machiavellianism as a "political doctrine . . . which denies the relevance of morality in political affairs and holds that craft and deceit are justified in pursuing and maintaining political power."[2] In the Dedicatory Epistle to *The Prince*, a work much discussed in this chapter, Machiavelli asks Lorenzo de' Medici, a would-be benefactor, to "recognize the great and unmerited sufferings inflicted on me by a cruel fate."[3] Victim of many misfortunes in life, Machiavelli appears to be similarly afflicted even after his death.

In spite of his infamy, Machiavelli was a political theorist of the first importance. Though not a systematic thinker, he worked out and presented with great literary skill certain principles of political life that are—for better or worse—of permanent validity. In the *Discourses* he remarks his intention "to open a new route, which has not yet been followed by any one" (*Dis.*, Bk. I, Introduction). Writing at the emergence of the modern state system, Machiavelli remains one of its clearest observers. Though roughly a contemporary of Luther (Machiavelli 1469–1527; Luther 1483–1546), he broke sharply with major tendencies of medieval political thought and has been viewed as the first significant practitioner of the modern science of politics.

Among the qualities Richard III ascribes to Machiavelli is the ability to change colors like a chameleon. This is a quality Machiavelli himself possessed (though Shakespeare's anachronism should be noted, as Richard was dead for many years (1485) before Machiavelli began to gain a reputation). Though *The Prince* in particular is a brief book, written in lucid prose, it has been subject to a remarkable number of different, often conflicting, interpretations.[4] But as Isaiah Berlin says, according to the most common view, Machiavelli was "a man inspired by the Devil to lead good men to their doom, the great subverter, the teacher of evil."[5] Bertrand Russell viewed *The Prince* as "a handbook for gangsters," while, to quote Berlin once again, "Few would deny that Machiavelli's writings, more particularly *The Prince*, have scandalized mankind more deeply and continuously than any other political treatise."[6] Throughout this chapter, we will explore reasons for this assessment and the extent to which it is deserved.

MACHIAVELLI'S LIFE

Machiavelli was born in Florence in 1469 to a distinguished, though not wealthy, family.[7] At that time the government of Florence was under the control of the Medici, a prominent banking family. But with the French invasion of Italy in 1494, the Medici were overthrown and a republican government instituted. In 1498, Machiavelli was appointed to an important position in the Florentine chancery, which managed the republic's foreign affairs. Thus, at a relatively young age he was sent on diplomatic missions to some of the most important courts and rulers in Europe.

Machiavelli's political outlook was heavily influenced by direct experience of political affairs. Italy at that time was torn by conflict between city-states and with more powerful rising nation-states, especially France and Spain, which invaded repeatedly. Machiavelli concluded that political success depends on force and fraud. Successful leaders must violate the norms of Christian conduct, act decisively, and keep faith only when forced to. Machiavelli's surviving diplomatic reports reveal the distinctive outlook of *The Prince* several years before that work was written.

To take a notable example, in the career of Cesare Borgia, Duke of Romagna, a rising political and military figure, Machiavelli witnessed the importance of good fortune, but also its limits. The son of Pope Alexander VI, Borgia flourished along with the power of his father. But when his father died, his own ruin was not long in coming. Machiavelli saw in Borgia's deeds the importance of decisive action and of violence, carefully applied, but also the futility of attempting to maintain one's position without the necessary means. As Machiavelli's biographer says, when Borgia's time had passed, Machiavelli observed him "like an anatomist looking at a corpse." From his dissection of Borgia's career, Machiavelli drew political lessons, presented in his inimitable style. For instance, in regard to Borgia's increasingly empty threats, Machiavelli noted: "At one time he never said what he was going to do; now he says things which he is incapable of doing" (Ridolfi, p. 71).

While serving in the Florentine chancery, Machiavelli received an additional responsibility, to organize a militia unit, composed of citizen-soldiers. In Italy at that time, warfare was generally conducted by mercenary armies. On the basis of his experience, Machiavelli distrusted mercenaries, and excoriates them in his writings. To a large extent he attributes the weakness of Italian cities to their reliance on mercenaries. His units enjoyed some success, most notably in the conquest of Pisa, in 1509. However, they were routed by experienced Spanish troops in 1512.[8] Machiavelli presents a systematic account of the advantages of citizen militia and numerous matters bearing on the subject in *The Art of War*, which was published in 1521.

Machiavelli's political career came to a sudden end in 1512. As the Florentines and their French allies were defeated by Spanish armies, the republican government was ousted and the Medici were restored to power. Not only was Machiavelli removed from office, but he was soon implicated in a plot against the Medici. Though innocent, he was imprisoned and tortured. However, good fortune intervened. To celebrate the elevation to the papacy of a family member, the Medici declared an amnesty. Freed from prison, Machiavelli retreated to his small estate on the outskirts of Florence.

Machiavelli's famous works are the result of a combination of circumstances. Because the Florentines followed a practice of appointing humanists to government positions, Machiavelli was able to combine his overflowing literary talents with diplomatic experience. Then on top of this was enforced idleness. Because participation in government, the passion of his life, was closed to him, he turned to writing about politics, on the basis of both firsthand experience and the study of history and classical texts. As he says in a letter written in 1513, "Fortune has determined that since I don't know how to talk about the silk business or the wool business or about profits and losses, I must talk about the government; I must either make a vow of silence or discuss that."[9]

Machiavelli did not abandon hope of resuming a political career. His correspondence during his early years of exile is filled with schemes to effect his return.[10] He hoped to serve the Medici in some minor capacity, from which he could advance:

> [T]here is my wish that our present Medici lords will make use of me, even if they begin by making me roll a stone; because then if I could not gain their favor, I should complain of myself.[11]

At least in part, he wrote *The Prince* to gain the favor of Lorenzo de' Medici, to whom it is dedicated. This hope shows up in his treatment of his subject, especially concentration on the situation of a new prince, which corresponds to that of the Medici, recently returned to power.

The Prince did not achieve its intended purpose, and Machiavelli remained out of favor. In more leisurely fashion, he composed a second great political work, *Discourses on the First Ten Books of Titus Livius*, in which he analyzes and passionately defends republican government. The relationship between this work and *The Prince* will be discussed below. The two works remained unpublished during Machiavelli's lifetime. The *Discourses* was published only in 1531 and *The Prince* in 1532. Machiavelli's only significant political work published during his lifetime was *The Art of War*. But he published other works, most notably his ribald comic play, *Mandragola*, which modern audiences enjoy and is still widely performed. This has been called not only the greatest comic play in the Italian language but perhaps the greatest Italian play (Ridolfi, p. 175).

As Machiavelli's exile from politics continued, he received a commission from the Medici to write a history of Florence, which is his fourth major political work. The Medici also began to assign him minor tasks, some of which made use of his diplomatic skills (see Ridolfi, Chap. 18). But in 1527, news that a Spanish army had sacked Rome, striking a blow at the Medici pope, brought about the collapse of Medici government in Florence.

The republican constitution was reinstated, and along with this, Machiavelli's hope of returning to government service. But having curried favor with the Medici for years, receiving some slight favor in return, he was viewed with suspicion by the new government and passed over (Ridolfi, pp. 247–248). This new misfortune took its toll; within a few weeks Machiavelli fell ill and died (ibid., pp. 248–250).

Machiavelli's life, then, was one of disappointment. Barred from the political career he craved, he could only reflect and write upon the theory and practice of politics as he experienced and read about it in the works of classical authors. He continually hoped his study of politics would somehow effect his return to active practice, but was never successful. Ironically, then, Machiavelli's frustrated ambition was necessary for the immortality earned through his political works. But thinking and writing about politics was also a source of solace while he lived. In a famous letter, Machiavelli describes the mundane pursuits that filled his days, and then returning to his study:

> On the coming of evening, I return to my house and enter my study; and at the door
> I take off the day's clothing, covered with mud and dust, and put on garments regal
> and courtly; and reclothed appropriately, I enter the ancient courts of ancient men,
> where, received by them with affection, I feed on that food which only is mine and
> which I was born for, where I am not ashamed to speak with them and to ask them
> the reason for their actions; and they in their kindness answer me; and for four hours
> of time I do not feel boredom, I forget every trouble, I do not dread poverty, I am not
> frightened by death; entirely I give myself over to them.[12]

POLITICAL BACKGROUND

One reason Machiavelli stands at the beginning of modern political thought is because he was able to study the workings of a modern state system. Throughout the Middle Ages, European politics was heavily influenced by two great supra-national institutions, the Church and the Holy Roman Empire, which impinged upon the independence of other political bodies. Independence from such organizations was necessary for the development of modern states. In those parts of Europe where Church and Empire were most influential, mature states were late emerging. Italy and Germany were not unified under single governments until the mid-nineteenth century. The rise of the state much earlier elsewhere in Europe is indicated by the widespread use of the term "state" in the sixteenth century in something approaching its modern sense.

According to Max Weber's widely quoted definition, the state is "a human community that (successfully) claims the *monopoly of the legitimate use of physical force* within a given territory."[13] What is clear here is that incontestable power is the state's essence. The state is able to enforce its will—generally in the form of laws—against all other authorities in its territory. The unchallenged command Weber notes also presupposes absence of challenges from outside. If state *A* is under the control of an outer power—most likely Church or Empire—it is not able to enforce its will but must act at the behest of the higher power.

The development of the concept "state" ran hand in hand with the rise of unchallenged governments.[14] In the sixteenth century, recognizable states arose in England, France, and Spain, with the decline of the Empire and Church and the ascendancy of incipient national governments over feudal rivals. Emerging states pursued their interests against others like them, pushing aside the demands of morality, embodied in natural and international law. This revolution in political relationships opened the way for a similar change in political theory, as epitomized in the works of Machiavelli.

In the late Middle Ages, political conditions in Italy anticipated the later development of the system of states in Europe as a whole. By the fifteenth century, Italy was divided between a number of significant powers rooted in city-states—mainly Venice, Milan, Naples, the Papal States, and Florence—struggling for ascendancy. Though the Papal States were ruled over by the Pope, Machiavelli viewed them as little more than another monarchical government in competition with the others. As we shall see, this contributed to his low opinion of the Church. In order to pursue their interests, city-states developed bureaucratic mechanisms: foreign offices staffed by knowledgeable public officials, who maintained policies beyond the reigns of individual rulers. Similar mechanisms continued in operation throughout Europe and much of the world until World War I.[15] We have noted Machiavelli's involvement in Florentine diplomacy. In a sense, he was present at the creation of the modern international order.

Modern political theory, like any stage in the history of political theory, is heavily influenced by the forms of political organization with which it is concerned. As we see in Volume I of this work, ancient political theory is bound up with the *polis* or city-state. Hellenistic political theory is concerned above all with empires, and medieval political theory with the intertwined institutions of Church and State that constituted Christendom. With modern political theory we turn to the state and its relationships, internally with its subjects and externally with other states.

It follows, then, that one reason Machiavelli is a modern political theorist is because he presents a theory of the state—or at least certain aspects of it. Though he uses the term "state" (*stato*) frequently, this is generally not in the full Weberian sense.[16] But what shows through many of his writings is the idea of clearly defined territorial entities, pursuing their interests without regard to other considerations.

To some extent, Machiavelli's theoretical originality can be attributed to his experience. Indeed, according to one commentator, "all he did was to express the actual and existing assumptions on which the scramble of competition was carried out among Italian princes."[17] This is undoubtedly an exaggeration, as Machiavelli possessed a transforming imagination and wished to change his world as well as interpret it. But there is little doubt that what separates Machiavelli from many other thinkers of his time is the conviction that useful prescriptions depend on accurate assessment of the way things actually are, of how governments actually behave, behind their veil of moralistic illusions.

Machiavelli's political views were shaped by his own experience. An important example is his interest in war and insistence that a prince build up a powerful military establishment. Because it was unable to ward off foreign foes, Italy was repeatedly invaded, with disastrous consequences for political stability. Thus Machiavelli writes in *The Art of War*:

> [A]ll the arts that have been introduced into society for the common benefit of mankind, and all the ordinances that have been established to make them live in fear of God and in obedience to human laws, would be insignificant if they were not supported and defended by military force . . . [T]he best ordinances in the world will be despised and trampled under foot when they are not supported, as they ought to be, by a military power. . . . (*AW*, p. 4)

A second example is Machiavelli's low opinion of the Church, for which he blamed the weakness of Italy. He writes in the *Discourses*:

> [T]he sole cause why Italy is not in the same condition [as France and Spain] and is not governed by either one republic or one sovereign, is the Church. (I, 12, p. 152)

According to Machiavelli, though the Church was not powerful enough to unite all Italy in its own hands, it had sufficient strength to prevent any other power from doing so.

Along with these particular lessons came Machiavelli's overall view of the political world. Though his observations centered on Italian politics, in many ways developments in Italy foreshadowed the emerging state system, giving his observations extended relevance. As one commentator says, "what was true of the small despots of Italy was about to become true of the national monarchs of Europe."[18]

MORALITY AND POLITICS

Machiavelli puts his political experience and study into practice in *The Prince*, which is in the form of an advice book for princes, dedicated to Lorenzo de´ Medici. Machiavelli presents Lorenzo with his greatest gift, "knowledge of the deeds of great men which I have acquired through a long experience of modern events and a constant study of the past." This is intended to help Lorenzo achieve "that grandeur which fortune and [his] own merits" have in store for him (Preface, pp. 3–4). The advice book for princes was a traditional literary genre, referred to as the "mirror-for-princes." Machiavelli employs the genre's literary conventions. But his work differs from previous examples. It is intended to be "of use" in the world, as it actually is (*Pr.*, Chap. 15, p. 56).

The mirror-for-princes is a manual designed to inform the prince of how to succeed at the business of politics. A work of this sort makes use of a form of reasoning to which we can refer as "instrumental rationality." This is reasoning according to means and ends: if you want to achieve *X*, then you must do *Y*. The criterion of rationality is that the means must be effective in attaining the end. This form of reasoning is basic to the accomplishment of almost any goal. If you want to drive to the grocery store, then you must use a car. If the store is a good distance away, not to use the car would not be rational. If you want the car to work, then you must make sure it is in good repair and has gas in its tank. If you want to take the shortest route, then you must go down Main Street and make a left turn onto Park, etc. Again, to take a more roundabout route would not be rational. The efficacy of this sort of reasoning depends heavily on careful definition of the ends involved. In regard to going to the store or other aspects of our everyday lives, defining ends is usually not difficult. But there can be complications. Even if the store is far away, walking to it can be rational if you want the exercise. Even if Main Street is the shortest route, it can be rational to go another way if Main Street is under repair, or if you want to drive by beautiful gardens. Complexities are immeasurably greater in the political world, for political ends are subject to dispute. It is not immediately clear what specific goals a prince should pursue. And of course the means he should employ depend on what he wishes to accomplish.

Traditional medieval authors of mirrors-for-princes took it for granted that proper political goals were religious in nature. The prince should want to be a good Christian and to use his office to promote true religion. Beyond this, it was assumed that the prince should promote justice in his realm, and in order to do so, must be virtuous himself.[19] We encounter reasoning of this sort in a work discussed in Volume I, Luther's *Secular Authority: To What Extent It Should Be Obeyed*. This is especially useful for comparison with *The Prince*, because it was published only ten years after Machiavelli's work was written. Luther's overall argument need not be summarized here. An indication of its thrust is the following passage, which concerns how the prince should comport himself:

> He must consider his subjects and rightly dispose his heart toward them in this matter. He does this if he applies his whole mind to making himself useful and serviceable to them and does not think, "Land and people are mine; I will do as I please"; but thus, "I belong to land and people; I must do what is profitable and good for them. My concern must be, not how I may rule and be haughty, but how they may be protected and defended by a good peace." And he should picture Christ to himself, and say, "Behold, Christ the chief Ruler came and served me, sought not to have power, profit and honor from me, but only considered my need, and did all He could that I might have power, profit and honor from Him and through Him. I will do the same, not seek mine own advantage in my subjects, but their advantage, and thus serve them by my office, protect them, give them audience and support that they, and not I, may have the benefit and profit by it." Thus a prince should in his heart empty himself of his power and authority, and interest himself in the need of his subjects, dealing with it as though it were his own need. Thus Christ did unto us; and these are the proper works of Christian love.[20]

For Luther, who of course was primarily a religious figure, the duty of the ruler was to promote goodness and virtue. He should take Christ as his model and behave as a good Christian.

Humanist authors of mirrors-for-princes presented slightly different views. They deemphasized the ruler's religious responsibility, placing greater importance on the need to be virtuous. Thus such tracts are described as "catalogues of virtues."[21] For humanist authors, an important model was Cicero, who, especially in *De Officiis* (*On Moral Duties*), argued for continuity between virtue and expediency. According to Cicero, the ruler promotes his own interest by being virtuous; virtuous conduct and what is good for oneself coincide.[22]

Cicero and other Roman authors described a series of moral situations in which people should take the virtuous path. One should be generous rather than miserly; nothing "appeals more to human nature than this" (*DO*, I, xiv, p. 42). Similarly, in his work *De Clementia* (*On Clemency* or *On Mercy*), Seneca denounced the vice of cruelty and argued for its avoidance. In *De Officiis* Cicero argued along similar lines that to secure power over others, it is better to be loved than feared:

> [O]f all motives, none is better adapted to secure influence and hold it fast than love; nothing is more foreign to that end than fear. (*DO*, II, vii, p. 23)

Not surprisingly, Cicero also argued for the importance of keeping faith and performing one's promises, describing this as the "foundation of justice" (*DO*, I, vii, p. 23). In their desire to learn from and imitate classical texts, humanist authors drew much of their advice for princes from Cicero and Seneca and other similar figures. *De Officiis* was especially influential; it was read and copied more often than any other work of Latin prose during the Middle Ages and Renaissance.[23]

In view of the formidable existing literature on how princes should behave, one might wonder what Machiavelli had to add. His great originality lay in questioning a fundamental assumption of previous authors, that the good ruler must be a good man. In advising rulers, earlier authors had assumed that virtue for a ruler is an extension of the virtue of a private citizen. Thus the ruler should possess such qualities as justice, wisdom, and temperance, and be a good Christian. However, in both his experience of the political world and his study of ancient history, Machiavelli discovered that these qualities have little to do with political success. He places his advice book in opposition to those of other authors, who have not confronted the world as it actually is:

> [M]y intention being to write something of use to those who understand, it appears to me more proper to go to the real truth of the matter than to its imagination; and many have imagined republics and principalities which have never been seen or known to exist in reality; for how we live is so far removed from how we ought to live, that he who abandons what is done for what ought to be done will rather learn to bring about his own ruin than his preservation. (*Pr.*, Chap. 15, p. 56)

The tragic but simple fact of the matter is that people are not good. The ruler who behaves virtuously toward them, under the assumption that his goodness will be reciprocated, is not only deluding himself but jeopardizing his state. If people are not going to deal virtuously with you, then their *lack* of virtue must be reciprocated. In Machiavelli's famous words,

> A man who wishes to make a profession of goodness in everything must necessarily come to grief among so many who are not good. Therefore it is necessary for a prince, who wishes to maintain himself, to learn how not to be good, and to use this knowledge and not use it, according to the necessity of the case. (*Pr.*, Chap. 15, p. 56)

Return to instrumental rationality. A prince must act to achieve certain ends, and pursues them rationally only if he adopts the most effective means. To reconstruct Machiavelli's train of thought, he apparently believes that former writers of mirrors-for-princes had not been completely clear about the ends princes should pursue. Under the assumption that the proper goals are promotion of Christian religion and moral virtue among the citizenry, they believed the prince should be virtuous and practice true religion. Thus, in order to achieve his proper ends, a prince must be good. But Machiavelli believes there is something missing from this account of the prince's role, that is, the political dimension. Because his own political experience was of unending conflict between states, Machiavelli takes an unsentimental view of politics. In his eyes, the primary role of the prince is to preserve his state, and his own place in it. In order to achieve *these* ends, the prince must work in the world as it actually is. The main consideration here is of course human nature—people and how they can be expected to behave. From what we have seen of Machiavelli's study of history and politics, it is not surprising that he concludes that princes who have known *how not to be good* have prospered, while others have fallen by the wayside. On this basis the wise prince should proceed.

Machiavelli expresses his central teaching with a series of striking images. Experience shows that unscrupulous princes have prevailed over those who attempted to play fair. The prince must be beast as well as man:

> You must know, then, that there are two methods of fighting, the one by law, the other by force; the first method is that of men, the second of beasts; but as the first method is often insufficient, one must have recourse to the second. It is therefore necessary for a prince to know well how to use both the beast and the man. This was covertly taught to rulers by ancient writers, who relate how Achilles and many others of those ancient princes were given to Charon the centaur to be brought up and educated under his discipline. The parable of this semi-animal, semi-human teacher is meant to indicate that a prince must know how to use both natures, and that the one without the other is not durable. (*Pr.*, Chap. 18, p. 64)

Two particular animals Machiavelli invokes are the lion and the fox. The lion is powerful enough to fend off wolves but not sufficiently cunning to avoid traps. The fox is cunning but not powerful. The prince must therefore be both lion and fox: "One must therefore be a fox to recognize traps, and a lion to frighten wolves" (p. 64). This pair of animals is doubtless suggested by Cicero in *De Officiis*, who presents them as examples to avoid:

> [W]rong may be done . . . in either of two ways, that is, by force or by fraud, both are bestial: fraud seems to belong to the cunning fox, force to the lion; both are wholly unworthy of man, but fraud is the more contemptible. (*DO*, I, xiii, p. 41)

In Machiavelli's eyes, however, for a prince to follow Cicero's advice would court disaster. His use of Cicero's example is doubtless intentional. In *The Prince* Machiavelli pursues a twofold task. He not only presents his central moral/political teaching, but in the course of doing so, refutes other writers.

Specific examples Machiavelli discusses in *The Prince* show his intention to criticize previous authors. The moral questions he discusses in Chapters 16–18 were standard topics in traditional mirrors-for-princes. First (in Chap. 16) is whether the prince should be generous or thrifty; that is, whether or not he should spend a great deal of his state's revenue. The conventional answer, of course, is that he should be generous. As we have seen, Cicero argues that even the suspicion of cheapness must be avoided. Machiavelli takes a hard-nosed look at the question. If the prince wishes to be generous, he must have a source of revenue. But if he taxes his subjects, they will hate him. Thriftiness, on the other hand, brings security. Pursuing this policy does not incur hatred and allows the prince sufficient revenue for defense. Would-be recipients of the prince's generosity will resent this course, but they are few. Because thriftiness in the long run favors the many, it is the preferred course. One exception to this rule is that a prince can afford to be generous with other people's money. The fruits of sack, ransom, and plunder can be dispensed freely, without incurring resentment from one's own population.

In Chapter 17 Machiavelli turns to the subject of cruelty. He argues for its judicious use, and that it is better for a prince to be feared than loved. Though these conclusions appear paradoxical, Machiavelli regards them as obvious truths. Under certain circumstances violence is necessary to secure the state. This is especially true for a new prince.

By creating a few well-chosen examples, he can prevent civil disorders that would require much more violence to suppress. Consider the problem a new prince faces in dealing with surviving members of the former ruling family. He can kill them or let them live. Obviously, the latter would be the humane course; to kill them would be unjust and abhorrent to ordinary moral sentiments. But if he spares them, they will be a continuing focus for the aspirations of his opponents. Their presence could increase the chances of civil war, which would be ruinous to the entire state. And so letting the family members live is actually more cruel than putting them to death. For Machiavelli, then, it goes without saying that they must be killed. In Chapter 3, this is presented as a fundamental rule:

> Whoever obtains possession of such territories and wishes to retain them must bear in mind two things: the one, that the blood of their old rulers be extinct; the other, to make no alteration either in their laws or in their taxes. . . . (*Pr.*, Chap. 3, p. 8)

A similar point is supported by the example of Cesare Borgia, whose alleged cruelty brought peace and order to Romagna:

> If this is considered well, it will be seen that he was really much more merciful than the Florentine people, who, to avoid the name of cruelty, allowed Pistoria to be destroyed. A prince, therefore must not mind incurring the charge of cruelty for the purpose of keeping his subjects united and faithful; for, with a very few examples, he will be more merciful than those who, for excess of tenderness, allow disorder to arise, from whence spring bloodshed and rapine; for these as a rule injure the whole community, while the executions carried out by the prince injure only individuals. (*Pr.*, Chap. 17, p. 60)

Machiavelli's praise of executions runs directly counter to the traditional view, as presented by Seneca in *De Clementia*. But in his eyes politics is an inherently violent business. Not to use violence under certain circumstances can make it necessary to use much more in the future.

Machiavelli's teaching here has been referred to as the "economy of violence."[24] In Chapter 18 he distinguishes between cruelties that are well and badly committed. Well committed are those that lead to the need for fewer cruelties in the future; badly committed do not lessen the need. The clearest instances of the former are those committed by a new prince to secure his regime. If a new prince acts properly he can commit all the necessary cruelties at once and bring peace to his state. To refrain from violence at the beginning of one's reign can permanently strain relations between the prince and his subjects as the need for further violence persists:

> Whence is it to be noted, that in taking a state the conqueror must arrange to commit all his cruelties at once, so as not to have to recur to them every day, and so as to be able, by not making fresh changes, to reassure people and win them over by benefiting them. Whoever acts otherwise, either through timidity or bad counsels, is always obliged to stand with knife in hand, and can never depend on his subjects, because they, owing to continually fresh injuries, are unable to depend upon him. (*Pr.*, Chap. 18, p. 35)

Machiavelli's logic is analogous to what is commonly encountered in military situations. Under certain circumstances, it may be necessary for a commanding officer to sacrifice some of his men in order to save the rest. Thus a platoon may have to be sacrificed to save the company, a company to save the regiment, a regiment to save the brigade. In each of these cases, the commander faces a difficult choice. He must send people, perhaps many people, to their deaths, which is ordinarily a heinous thing to do. But war imposes difficult choices. Though it might appear harsh to make such sacrifices, Machiavelli believes that prudence often lies in regarding the least bad alternative as good (*Pr.*, Chap. 21, pp. 84–85). Not to make a necessary sacrifice could doom many more men, perhaps all. A commanding officer who is unwilling to order the necessary sacrifices is dangerous to his army and has no business being in command.

The close relationship between more or less normal politics and military affairs Machiavelli observes is supported by military examples. Consider the case of Hannibal, who kept a huge army together without dissension, though it was composed of men of many nations and fought in foreign countries. The secret of his success was his reputation for cruelty (*Pr.*, Chap. 17, p. 62). Cruelty, ordinarily a vice, can be an essential attribute for a military leader or prince.

Cruelty is necessary to keep people in line because of the essential baseness of their nature. Good deeds can earn people's loyalty, but this cannot be counted on:

> For it may be said of men in general that they are ungrateful, voluble, dissemblers, anxious to avoid danger, and covetous of gain; as long as you benefit them, they are entirely yours; they offer you their blood, their goods, their life, and their children, as I have before said, when the necessity is remote; but when it approaches, they revolt. (*Pr.*, Chap. 17, p. 61)

It follows from this view of human nature that it is better for a prince to be feared by his subjects than loved. Because "men love at their own free will, but fear at the will of the prince . . . a wise prince must rely on what is in his power and not on what is in the power of others" (p. 63). Once again, the traditional view, as presented by Cicero, is that it is better to be loved than feared. (*DO*, II, vii, p. 23) Effortlessly, Machiavelli brushes this aside.

Machiavelli's most striking excursion into morality concerns fidelity. It was commonly held by humanist writers that the prince must keep his promises; this goes almost without saying. But once again Machiavelli criticizes the traditional teaching. If men were good and one could rely on *their* keeping faith, then perhaps the prince should keep faith with them. But "as they are bad, and would not observe their faith with you, so you are not bound to keep faith with them" (*Pr.*, Chap. 18, p. 64). Strikingly, Machiavelli observes: "men will always be false to you unless they are compelled by necessity to be true" (*Pr.*, Chap. 23, p. 89). Recent history shows that successful princes "have had little regard for good faith." This has helped them to overcome "those who have made loyalty their foundation" (*Pr.*, Chap. 18, p. 63).

The essence of Machiavelli's political teaching, then, is that the prince must do what works. It is an unfortunate fact of political life that forsaking virtue is often more effective than behaving virtuously. The wise prince must face this fact and, once again, learn how *not* to be good. To complicate matters, Machiavelli recognizes the importance of *appearing to have* the traditional virtues, whether or not one actually has them. Though it may be dangerous *to be* virtuous, it is all to the good to *appear* so. People are more willing to follow a prince who appears to be honest, kind, generous, and faithful, though, once again, Machiavelli believes it is not good for the prince actually to have these qualities. Thus he sharply distinguishes the realms of appearance and reality. He believes traditional authors of advice books for princes have been deceived by appearances and so believed it is necessary to *be* virtuous. But for Machiavelli appearance alone must suffice. Though a prince must be prepared not to be "merciful, faithful, humane, sincere, [and] religious," he must take pains to appear to have these qualities. A measure of deceitfulness is important to political success. But deceiving the masses should be easy. Most men are easily deceived—almost eager to be deceived: "one who deceives will always find those who allow themselves to be deceived" (*Pr.*, Chap. 18, pp. 64–66).

MACHIAVELLI'S MESSAGE

If Machiavelli's main moral teaching is as presented in the last section, we can understand why he is viewed as subversive. His main concern is political success, and his main discovery that the means to this are far removed from those usually recommended.

The major reason for Machiavelli's teaching is the fact of human nature, as revealed in his own political experience in Italy, and in his reading of history. Because human nature is constant, Machiavelli believes the study of history is relevant to contemporary politics and teaches timeless truths.

In examining the works of classical authors for their political lessons, Machiavelli's practice is in keeping with major tendencies of the Italian Renaissance. The "rebirth" the term indicates is in regard to classical learning, but Machiavelli's specific practice is original. In the Introduction to Book I of the *Discourses*, he claims to have opened "a new route, which has not yet been followed by any one" (*Dis.*, p. 103). Students of other fields had learned from the ancients; his innovation is in extending their method to politics:

> The civil laws are in fact nothing but decisions given by their [the ancients'] jurisconsults, and which, reduced to a system, direct our modern jurists in their decisions. And what is the science of medicine, but the experience of ancient physicians, which their successors have taken for their guide? And yet to found a republic, maintain states, to govern a kingdom, organize an army, conduct a war, dispense justice, and extend empires, you will find neither prince, nor republic, nor captain nor citizen, who has recourse to the examples of antiquity! (*Dis.*, Intr., p. 104)

To some extent, Machiavelli's lack of appreciation for historical change is understandable because of similarities between the ancient world and his own. Both civilizations were dominated by city-states, constantly at war. More important, Machiavelli believes the lessons of history are permanently valid because human nature is a great constant factor that never changes. History is a record of how people have behaved in the past. Because those beings are similar to the people of the present world, the past provides permanently valid lessons about human conduct. In Book I of the *Discourses* Machiavelli writes:

> Whoever considers the past and present will readily observe that all cities and all peoples are and ever have been animated by the same desires and the same passions; so that it is easy, by diligent study of the past, to foresee what is likely to happen in the future in any republic, and to apply those remedies that were used by the ancients, or, not finding any that were employed by them, to devise new ones from the similarity of the events. (*Dis.*, I, 39, p. 216)

Viewing human nature as constant, Machiavelli believes history is a cyclical process. The great advantage of studying history is that as circumstances similar to those encountered in the past recur, people will behave similarly.

Unfortunately, the unchanging essence of human nature is a propensity towards evil. Any political leader who does not realize this simply requires more experience:

> All those who have written upon civil institutions demonstrate (and history is full of examples to support them) that whoever desires to found a state and give it laws, must start with assuming that all men are bad and ever ready to display their vicious nature, whenever they may find occasion for it. If their evil disposition remains concealed for a time, it must be attributed to some unknown reason; and we must assume that it lacked occasion to show itself; but time, which has been said to be the father of all truth, does not fail to bring it to light. (*Dis.*, I, 3, p. 117)

Given the realities of human nature, the successful politician must behave in ways that are not good, virtuous, and pure. This is necessary because of the basic facts of political life. To do otherwise might seem pure and noble, but it actually courts disaster.

Though this line of argument appears straightforward, it is so upsetting to some commentators that they have viewed Machiavelli's purpose as essentially satirical. While pretending to instruct his readers about how princes must behave, Machiavelli is really informing them of the despicable tactics evil princes employ. Armed with this knowledge, presumably, lovers of republican liberty will be able to take proper precautions.[25] Though this interpretation is not impossible, it is unlikely. Barring compelling evidence to the contrary, Machiavelli should be taken at his word. To some extent, what is disturbing about his presentation is the sardonic relish with which he writes. But probably more upsetting is the fact that much of what he writes is obviously true.

What is perhaps most scandalous in Machiavelli's view can be seen in his use of moral terms. As we recall, in Chapter 15 of *The Prince* he describes how the advice book he has written is intended to be "of use." Because how we live is far removed from how we ought to live, he addresses the real world rather than imagination (p. 56). He writes:

> A man who wishes to make a profession of *goodness* in everything must necessarily come to grief among so many who are not *good.* Therefore it is necessary for a prince, who wishes to maintain himself, to learn how not to be *good,* and to use this knowledge and not use it, according to the necessity of the case. (*Pr.*, Chap. 15, p. 56; my emphasis)

One will note the remarkable bluntness of this statement, as seen in Machiavelli's use of moral terms. He has the courage of his convictions. He does not pretend the political world is without pain or unpleasantness, that the successful prince can avoid being bad.

Machiavelli embraces these truths; being bad is a subject one must study. Consider another passage:

> [I]t must be understood that a prince, and especially a new prince, cannot observe all those things which are considered good in men, being often obliged in order to maintain the state, to act against faith, against charity, against humanity, and against religion. (*Pr.*, Chap. 18, p. 65)

The message here is similar, though Machiavelli qualifies his moral terms, speaking of "what is considered good" rather than simply what is good. Despite this difference in language, his overall message is consistent in the two passages, as is seen clearly if we return to a third passage, which is quoted above:

> [T]here are two methods of fighting, the one by law, the other by force: the first method is that of men, the second of beasts; but as the first method is often insufficient, one must have recourse to the second. (*Pr.*, Chap. 18, p. 64)

Though moral language is not used here, the message again is clear: the successful prince must forsake the norms of human society and behave like a beast.

Machiavelli's presentation in the three passages, as throughout *The Prince*, is notably straightforward—and the more disturbing for that. Other writers might sweeten the bitter message by using moral language somewhat differently. If political success requires cruelty and deceit, one might argue, such behavior *is not bad*. Political success is obviously desirable and good. Therefore, because what is necessary for success must also be good, *cruelty and deceit are good*. Machiavelli does not take this easy way out. He looks squarely at the fact that cruelty and deceit are not good, while still acknowledging they may be necessary to attain what we want.

In the three passages, moral terms are used in their conventional sense. By this I mean that their content corresponds to mainstream Christian (or Judeo-Christian) morality, the moral ideas that have dominated Western culture since the time of the Greeks. Mainstream moral imperatives center on not harming other people, not deceiving them, not stealing their property, in short, not taking advantage of them. For ease of reference, we can refer to these values (as in Volume I) as "traditional morality" or "traditional values," and behavior that is in accordance with them as embodying "traditional virtues."

According to an influential discussion of Isaiah Berlin, whom I follow here, Machiavelli's message undermines one of our cherished convictions about the moral world. We like to believe that problems have solutions. With sufficient ingenuity and goodwill, we can overcome any obstacle and achieve a satisfactory outcome. But Machiavelli says we cannot. In the words of Berlin, the conviction Machiavelli undermines is "belief in the ultimate compatibility of all genuine values."[26] Consider another approach to the problem. Another thinker (such as Callicles[27]) might agree with Machiavelli that the political world requires conduct opposed to traditional morality. Thus, according to Callicles, what men call justice is actually weakness and so bad. What is *actually right* is to follow the law of the jungle (or of the international arena) and take advantage of other people for self-aggrandizement and to satisfy one's appetites. Though shocking, this view is in a way less disturbing than Machiavelli's. For Callicles (according to the presentation here) still believes in the compatibility of all genuine values. Traditional morality is wrong about true values, but there is an alternative set to replace them. For Machiavelli, things are not so simple. Though people do not understand the values that are required for success in the political world, this is only part of the problem. Correcting their error does not make way for a different but still harmonious moral view, but rather to the realization that this is impossible. In short, Machiavelli's message is the *incompatibility* of important values—and so the necessity of choice, and the inescapability of paradox.

Thinkers before Machiavelli were aware of the conflict between different values. Perhaps the clearest example is Thucydides. In Book III of his *History of the Peloponnesian War*, which recounts the fifth-century B.C. war between Athens and Sparta and their allies, Cleon, the Athenian demagogue, expounds on the rules governing relations between an imperial state and its subjects. The rules of this relationship are different from those that hold within one's city. Subject states cannot be dealt with on the same terms as fellow citizens:

> To feel pity, to be carried away by the pleasure of hearing a clever argument, to listen to the claims of decency are three things that are entirely against the interests of an imperial power. Do not be guilty of them. As for compassion, it is proper to feel it in the case of people who are like ourselves and who will pity us in their turn, not in the case of those who, so far from having the same feelings towards us, must always and inevitably be our enemies. . . . And a sense of decency is only felt towards those who are going to be our friends in future, not towards those who remain just as they were and as much our enemies as they ever have been. (III, p. 40)

What Cleon says here is similar to Machiavelli's central teaching. It too is premised on a belief about how other people will behave. They cannot be dealt with humanely, because they will not respond in kind. If we take Cleon to express a general account of political morality, then it approaches the view of Machiavelli. But Cleon addresses only a narrow set of relationships—between master and subject states. He also contrasts these relations with those at home. Machiavelli drives a deeper wedge.

It was not (and still is not) uncommon for thinkers to hold that it is part of morality to help friends and harm enemies—and so, again, that there are different moral rules for different situations. But Machiavelli breaks down the distinction between friends and foes. The rules presented in *The Prince* pertain to fellow citizens. In addition, Machiavelli is often taken to be an early proponent of "reason of state" (*raison d'état*), the idea that the interests of the state take precedence over other moral considerations.[28] He clearly says this in regard to preserving the safety of the state:

> For where the very safety of the country depends upon the resolution to be taken, no considerations of justice or injustice, humanity or cruelty, nor of glory or of shame, should be allowed to prevail. But putting all other considerations aside, the only question should be, What course will save the life and liberty of the country? (*Dis.,* III, 11, p. 528)

However, this statement does not fully represent Machiavelli's view, since its scope is limited to cases where the state is threatened. More accurate perhaps is a statement in Chapter 18 of *The Prince*, in which he says the prince should pretend to have the traditional virtues and work to make people think he has them:

> With regard to all human actions, and especially those of rulers, who cannot be called to account, men pay attention to the outcome. (*Pr.*, Price trans., Chap. 18, p. 63)

To Machiavelli, in politics, considerations of success, the end to which people look, take precedence over traditional morality. This is of course true in regard to the safety of the state. But it is also a general rule of the political world.

By all accounts, in his personal life Machiavelli was a good man in the traditional sense. He was honest in personal dealings, a loving father, an affectionate husband (aside from the usual infidelities). He also appears to have been religious. In spite of the dislike for the Church which shows through many of his works, one of his sons, Guido, took vows.[29] But these factors are not relevant to the world of politics. Machiavelli's awareness of this truth is not without regret. In Book I of the *Discourses*, he describes the drastic measures a new prince should employ in order to secure his power. He should appoint new governors and overturn everything, making the poor rich and the rich poor. He should destroy old cities and build new ones. Taking Philip of Macedon as his model, he should move his subjects from province to province as a shepherd moves his flocks (Chap. 26, p. 184). Because these measures would cause severe suffering, their cruelty must be recognized. Thus, they can be looked at from two opposing points of view:

> Doubtless these means are cruel and destructive of all civilized life, and neither Christian nor even human, and should be avoided by every one. In fact, the life of a private citizen would be preferable to that of a king at the expense of the ruin of so many human beings. Nevertheless, whoever is unwilling to adopt the first and humane course must, if he wishes to maintain his power, follow the latter evil course. But men generally decide upon a middle course, which is most hazardous; for they know neither how to be entirely good or entirely bad, as we shall illustrate by examples in the next chapter. (*Dis.*, I, 26, p. 184)

One will note Machiavelli's refusal to flinch from the horrors of the recommended policies. They are not only harsh, but *evil*—in the traditional sense. But evil or not, they are necessary. If someone wishes to pursue a life of politics, he must be willing to make the necessary choices, in spite of other values. However, many leaders are unable to disregard traditional morality. Attempting to balance two sets of concerns that cannot be balanced, they take halfway measures that benefit no one.

It would not surprise Machiavelli to realize that many disastrous rulers have been decent and upstanding human beings. Two examples are Louis XVI, King of France during the outbreak of the French Revolution, and Nicholas II, Czar of Russia during the outbreak of the Russian Revolution. To preserve their states (and their lives, and those of their queens), harsh and decisive measures were necessary. But in spite of their admirable personal qualities, these rulers were unable to take the necessary steps. It is likely that their good qualities made them *less* able to act. The horrors of these two great European revolutions could conceivably have been avoided if Louis and Nicholas had known better how not to be good.

ADVICE TO RULERS

In addition to ensuring the survival of the state and one's power in it, Machiavelli believes the particular end political—and military—leaders should pursue is glory. This can be defined as "very great fame or honour that is generally recognized, acquired through extraordinary merits or talents, through valorous deeds or great enterprises."[30] In Chapter 21 of *The Prince*, Machiavelli praises King Ferdinand of Aragon for being at that time "for fame and glory the first king in Christendom" (p. 82). In Chapter 25, he describes riches and glory as "the end which everyone aims at" (Price trans., p. 85). To attain this end, certain means are necessary. But these do not include the traditional virtues—aside from the value of appearing to have them.

If one looks at history, one sees that the people who have achieved the greatest glory are founders of religions. After these come those who have established republics and kingdoms, followed by successful military leaders. Contrariwise, men who are "doomed to infamy and universal execration" are those who have undermined religions and helped to overturn republics and kingdoms (*Dis.*, I, 10, p. 141). Machiavelli takes it to be a truth of the political world that leaders—political and military—work to achieve glory. Towards this end, he recommends imitating great figures from the past:

> [A]s to exercise for the mind, the prince ought to read history and study the actions of eminent men, see how they acted in warfare, examine the causes of their victories and defeats in order to imitate the former and avoid the latter, and above all, do as some men have done in the past, who have imitated some one, who has been much praised and glorified, and have always kept his deeds and actions before them, as they say Alexander the Great imitated Achilles, Caesar Alexander, and Scipio Cyrus. (Chap. 14, p. 55)

Along similar lines, in order not to attain infamy one should avoid the crimes of subverters of states (*Dis.*, I, 10, p. 143).

The desire for glory limits the means a prince can employ. In spite of what is often said about him, Machiavelli does not advocate violence or ruthlessness for their own sakes. He always views these as necessary means to political success. Though a prince should cultivate his people's support, it is not enough to be loved. People cannot be counted on to do what they must of their own accord. As Machiavelli says, people love at their own discretion but fear at that of the prince. Consider the case of Savonarola, who in effect ruled Florence through moral and religious authority for four years but was doomed when he lost popular support. As Machiavelli says, while armed prophets have conquered, unarmed ones have failed (*Pr.*, Chap. 6, p. 22).

Though violence is an indispensable means, even successful princes can destroy their possibilities for lasting glory through its excessive use. Among the categories of rulers Machiavelli surveys are those who gained power through villainy (*Pr.*, Chap. 8). Most notable is Agathocles of Syracuse. The son of a potter, Agathocles rose through the ranks of the militia to become military leader of Syracuse. To hold his position, he gathered all the senators and richest men of the city for a conference and then had them killed. But though he was an able general with many admirable qualities, the infamy attached to his means of ascent can never be outlived:

It cannot be called virtue to kill one's fellow citizens, betray one's friends, be without faith, without pity, and without religion; by these methods one may indeed gain power, but not glory. . . . [H]is barbarous cruelty and inhumanity, together with his countless atrocities, do not permit of his being named among the most famous men. (*Pr.*, Chap. 8, p. 32)

To consider more recent examples, the twentieth century has unfortunately witnessed a series of dictators and tyrants who have committed atrocities on an enormous scale. Such figures as Hitler, Stalin, Mao, and Pol Pot have indulged in violence as if for its own sake. Despite whatever temporary successes they might have achieved, they have done little good and enormous harm to their countries. But even if their countries had benefited from their rule, so great were their crimes that they too could never achieve great names.

In order to establish a successful republic or kingdom, one must be given the opportunity. The best situation is a corrupt state, which one can work to reform:

[I]f a prince be anxious for glory and the good opinion of the world, he should rather wish to possess a corrupt city, not to ruin it wholly like Caesar, but to reorganize it like Romulus. For certainly, the heavens cannot afford a man a greater opportunity for glory, nor could men desire a better one. (*Dis.*, I, 10, p. 145)

Thus Machiavelli's main concern is the situation of a new prince, one recently risen to power. By reforming his state, such a figure can achieve great glory. In discussing new princes, Machiavelli undoubtedly has in view the situation of Lorenzo de' Medici in Florence. Machiavelli wishes to inspire him to great deeds, thereby revamping the fortunes of Italy. We will return to this theme later.

Particular models Machiavelli repeatedly refers to are Moses, Cyrus, Romulus, and Theseus. He describes them as princes who attained their positions through their own arms and ability, and so are worthy of imitation: "Not being always able to follow others exactly, nor attain to the excellence of those he imitates, a prudent man should always follow the path trodden by great men and imitate those who are most excellent, so that if he does not attain to their greatness, at any rate he will get some tinge of it" (*Pr.*, Chap. 6, pp. 19–20). The prudent man acts like an archer who aims much higher than his distant targets (ibid.). The figures Machiavelli names possessed surpassing abilities and owed nothing to fortune but the opportunity to exercise them (p. 20).

Machiavelli refers to the particular talents a leader requires as *virtù*. *Virtù* is the indispensable means to political success and glory. "Virtue" is the closest English correlate, though *virtù* is less moralistic and has strong connotations of skill and ability, as seen in the related adjective *virtuoso*. Because *virtù* has no precise English equivalent, it is best to leave the word untranslated.

The precise way in which Machiavelli uses the term *virtù* has been the subject of much academic discussion.[31] Because Machiavelli is neither a systematic nor a precise thinker, it is not surprising that there is a certain looseness to his usage. But one scholar exaggerates in saying that Machiavelli "is innocent of any systematic use of the word."[32] In certain contexts *virtù* is synonymous with "virtue" in the traditional sense. For example, in a passage just quoted: "it cannot be called virtue (*virtù*) to kill one's fellow citizens, betray one's friends, be without faith, without pity, and without religion . . ." (*Pr.*, Chap. 8, p. 32). But on the whole, *virtù* refers to the set of qualities necessary for political and military success. Exactly what qualities are necessary will vary from case to case. But these can be learned by studying historical figures who achieved the greatest success.[33] What stands out is the need to be forceful and decisive, courageous, and willing to take risks. One also requires insight into the distinctive features of particular situations and how to exploit them. In addition, *virtù* includes the ability to burst traditional moral constraints to do what is necessary for one's end. Because of his belief in the resemblance between political and military affairs, Machiavelli also views *virtù* as the qualities a successful general exhibits under battlefield conditions. To some extent, the essence of *virtù* is summed up in the saying of Danton, during the French Revolution: «*audace et audace et audace.*»

One reason for the close relationship between Machiavelli's political and military teachings is the successful prince's need to be a military leader. It is essential for him to develop a strong military establishment. Machiavelli believes all regimes are founded on "good laws and good arms." Because there cannot be good laws where there are not good arms (*Pr.*, Chap. 12, p. 44), the wise prince will constantly think of war: "A prince should . . . have no other aim or thought, nor take up any other thing for his study, but war and its organization and discipline, for that is the only art that is necessary to one who commands." (*Pr.,* Chap. 14, p. 53).

Machiavelli believes it is essential to base one's army on citizen soldiers. His own experience leaves its mark here. He is contemptuous of mercenaries. They are courageous and loyal until it is time to fight, but then they run away (*Pr.*, Chap. 12, p. 45). Similarly, it is dangerous to rely on the forces of one's allies: "These forces may be good in themselves, but they're always dangerous for those who borrow them, for if they lose you are defeated, and if they conquer you remain their prisoner" (*Pr.*, Chap. 13, p. 49). It is better to lose with your own men than to conquer with the forces of others (*Pr.*, Chap. 13, pp. 50–51).

Because of constant military demands, being a successful prince is not an easy life. We have seen that he must make difficult decisions, which will perhaps haunt his conscience: "the life of a private citizen would be preferable at the expense of the ruin of so many human beings" (*Dis.*, I, 26, p. 184). In addition, preoccupied with war and its demands, the prince must constantly engage in hunting, to come to know his country and accustom his body to hardship (*Pr.*, Chap. 14, p. 54). Temptations must be resisted. Though his people must fear him, they must not hate or despise him. Thus he must keep his hands off their property and women (*Pr.*, Chap. 17, p. 62). If he must kill someone, he should still leave his property alone: "men forget more easily the death of their father than the loss of their patrimony" (p. 62).

Though the prince need not—indeed must not—possess the traditional virtues, he should appear to possess them. Thus he must be "a great feigner and dissembler" (*Pr.*, Chap. 18, p. 64). In addition to the traditional virtues, he must contrive to show courage and resolution in all his actions (*Pr.*, Chap. 19, p. 67). In order to keep the people's favor, he should dispense rewards and favors himself, but assign unpopular duties to his subordinates (*Pr.*, Chap. 19, p. 70). Along similar lines, he should deal resolutely with his enemies and make sure they cannot harm him in the future: "men must either be caressed or else annihilated; they will revenge themselves for small injuries, but cannot do so for great ones; the injury therefore that we do to a man must be such that we need not fear his vengeance" (*Pr.*, Chap. 3, p. 9). This policy is essential for security from potential assassins. Against the "deliberate action of a determined man" who is not afraid to die, there is no defense (*Pr.*, Chap. 19, p. 74).

Through these and similar means, a prince can gradually win his people's favor. In spite of his low opinion of human nature, Machiavelli generally trusts the common people. A prince who governs in the state's interest and does not unduly harm his subjects will gradually win their allegiance. This is necessary for his self-preservation. If the state's army is made up of citizens, their goodwill is essential. In addition, in times of trouble, a prince must turn to the people for help: "the best fortress is to be found in the love of the people" (*Pr.*, Chap. 20, p. 81). Though this aspect of his view perhaps departs from Machiavelli's general opinion of people, we should bear in mind that the people's goodwill is gained through the means we have discussed, not through adherence to traditional virtues. In part the people will love their prince because he has deceived them. But more important is his avoidance of egregious abuses. He has not taxed them unduly, has otherwise left their property alone, and perhaps most important, through his rule, the state has become as strong as possible.

Machiavelli places great weight on the prince's abilities, virtually to the point of believing no obstacle cannot be overcome. In *The Prince* he places *virtù* in opposition to Fortune (*Fortuna*). This means good luck, but also the set of circumstances initially beyond one's control that must be mastered if an enterprise is to succeed. In his survey of different kinds of principalities, Machiavelli devotes Chapter 6 to those acquired through the prince's arms and abilities. The rulers discussed in this chapter include the great heroes noted above, who required from Fortune only the opportunity to exercise their powers. Chapter 7, in contrast, deals with rulers who came to power through the agency of other people or Fortune. Notable here is Cesare Borgia, who owed his power to being the son of Pope Alexander VI. Despite his great abilities, after his father died, he soon lost his position.

Chapter 25 is devoted to the subject of Fortune. Former writers had assigned responsibility for all human affairs to Fortune, viewed as an impersonal power analogous to Fate. But Machiavelli believes this can be opposed. Fortune rules half our actions, but allows people to control the other half. If people take proper precautions, they can master it:

> I would compare [Fortune] to an impetuous river that, when turbulent, inundates the plains, casts down trees and buildings, removes earth from this side and places it to the other; every one flees before it, and everything yields to its fury without being able to oppose it; and yet though it is of such a kind, still when it is quiet, men can make provision against it by dykes and banks, so that when it rises it will either go into a canal or its rush will not be so wild and dangerous. So it is with fortune, which shows her power where no measures have been taken to resist her, and directs her fury where she knows that no dykes or barriers have been made to hold her. (*Pr.*, Chap. 25, p. 91)

The able prince will perceive the distinctive features of different situations and adapt to them. If a particular situation demands caution and prudence, he will behave accordingly; if one requires bold action, he will take it. Machiavelli believes a significant cause of political failure has been inability to adapt to the times. A cautious ruler who has always succeeded through slow and deliberate action will have trouble when circumstances require impetuosity. The same is true of different rulers when caution is necessary. But success awaits the prince who is able to adapt: "if one could change one's nature with time and circumstances, Fortune would never change" (p. 93).

On the whole, Machiavelli believes in bold action. A man of *virtù* can master Fortune by seizing the initiative: "[F]ortune is a woman, and it is necessary, if you wish to master her, to conquer her by force." Thus Fortune favors the young, "because they are less cautious, fiercer, and master her with greater audacity" (p. 94).

The purpose of Machiavelli's paean to bold action becomes clear in the final chapter of *The Prince*, which is an "Exhortation to Liberate Italy from the Barbarians." The key to success is seizing the initiative. Machiavelli addresses Lorenzo de´ Medici and his "illustrious house" (p. 97). By imitating great leaders of the past, Lorenzo can make Italy great. Circumstances present a rare opportunity—comparable to those accorded to Moses, Theseus, and Cyrus. In order for the *virtù* of Moses to be displayed, he had to find the Israelites enslaved in Egypt. For Cyrus to achieve greatness, he had to find the Persians oppressed by the Medes. The *virtù* of Theseus depended on finding the Athenians dispersed. Conditions in Italy combine these afflictions. Italy is "more enslaved than the Hebrews, more oppressed than the Persians, and more scattered than the Athenians . . . beaten, despoiled, lacerated and overrun," suffering "ruin of every kind" (p. 95).

But with affliction comes opportunity. Italy is ready to follow a bold leader. "There is nothing now she can hope for but that your illustrious house may place itself at the head of this redemption, being by its power and fortune so exalted, and being favoured by God and the Church, of which it is now the ruler" (p. 95). Lorenzo should imitate great leaders of old. Above all he should raise an Italian army to defend Italy from barbarian invaders. "This barbarous domination stinks in the nostrils of every one. May your illustrious house therefore assume this task with that courage and those hopes which are inspired by a just cause" (p. 98).

THE *DISCOURSES*

As his hopes of returning to government service faded, Machiavelli began to focus more of his energies on a literary life. He became involved with a discussion group of humanists and literary figures that met in the gardens of Cosimo Rucellai on the outskirts of Florence. Machiavelli's most significant work growing out of these discussions is the *Discourses*, which he dedicated to Rucellai and Zanobi Buondelmonte (on whom, more below). The importance of this group is seen in the fact that *The Art of War* is presented in the form of a dialogue between Rucellai and some other figures, situated in the former's gardens. In his dedication to the *Discourses*, Machiavelli notes his departure from the usual custom of dedicating works to princes. Instead of actual princes, Machiavelli addresses himself to those who have infinite good qualities and so are fit to be princes, "not to those who could load me with honors, rank, and wealth, but rather to those who have the desire to do so, but have not the power" (*Dis.*, Dedication, p. 102). Focusing less on immediate advancement, Machiavelli composed a discursive work approximately four times the length of *The Prince*.

The *Discourses* is in part a commentary on the first ten books of Livy's *History* of Rome, in part a series of essays on Machiavelli's familiar themes; for example, how states rise and fall, how they can preserve their liberty, and the conditions necessary for political and military success. As we have seen, Machiavelli takes pride in his exploration of these themes through historical material. But immediate political concerns are never far from view, as he moves easily between ancient Rome and Renaissance Italy, in keeping with his view of historical constancy. Though less well-known than *The Prince*, the *Discourses* presents a much clearer view of Machiavelli's overall political themes. As one commentator notes, *The Prince* should be understood in the light of the *Discourses*, rather than vice versa. In fact, *The Prince* can be viewed as "a particular application to Italy of the principles" set forth in the *Discourses*.[34]

The claim that the two works present a consistent political view might appear improbable. The *Discourses* evinces a clear sympathy for republican government, while *The Prince* is often viewed as favoring monarchy and tyranny. But to a large extent, the apparent conflicts between the works are due to their different subject matters. *The Prince* discusses monarchy and tyranny, and the *Discourses* follow Livy in being concerned with the Roman republic. In Chapter 2 of *The Prince* Machiavelli mentions that he will not discuss republics, having treated them in another work (*Pr.*, Chap. 2, p. 15). This is obviously a reference to the *Discourses*, which suggests that at least portions of that work were in existence before *The Prince* was written in 1513.[35] In any event, despite some minor differences, the two works are generally in accord.

In the *Discourses*, Machiavelli does not present a systematic theory of politics. He does not work out the implications of his points to make sure they all fit together in a coherent framework. Rather, he constructs his arguments through accumulation of examples and illustrations. The *Prince* and *Discourses* can be viewed as complementary series of observations. Specific examples used in *The Prince* are repeated in the *Discourses*. For instance, in both works Machiavelli discusses the role of cruelty in the generalship of Hannibal (*Pr.*, Chap. 17, p. 62; *Dis.*, III, 21, pp. 475–476). Or consider the dangers of confiding one's conspiratorial plans to a discontented fellow citizen: "as soon as you have disclosed your intention to a malcontent, you give him the means of satisfying himself" (*Pr.*, Chap. 19, p. 68); "If you attempt to measure a man's good faith by the discontent which he manifests towards the prince, you will be easily deceived, for by the very fact of communicating to him your designs, you give him the means of putting an end to his discontent" (*Dis.*, III, 6, pp. 416–417). *The Prince* is referred to a number of times in the *Discourses* (e.g., III, 42, p. 529). Numerous themes are prominent in both works, for example, the importance of the military side of politics, contempt for mercenaries and extolling native troops, and lessons of the ancients, which can be imitated in one's own practice.

In both *The Prince* and the *Discourses*, Machiavelli moves easily between past and present, commenting on modes of behavior that remain ever constant. The fact that he perceives clear resemblances between Livy's Rome and his own Italy is obviously one reason for his interest in Livy. In both works, Machiavelli is deeply concerned with what can be learned from the ancients in regard to the corruption of Florence and possible means of renewal. As in *The Prince*, perhaps his central interest in the *Discourses* is factors that make for political success. Rome, which achieved unique grandeur, epitomizes the necessary qualities. Livy's account of Rome's rise is an assemblage of fact and example that Machiavelli mines for insight. As in *The Prince*, the necessary qualities are referred to as *virtù*. But whereas in *The Prince* Machiavelli's primary concern is what makes for successful rulers, in the *Discourses* he is more directly concerned with the *virtù* of a people. Great accomplishments are possible for a republic only if its people are free and politically active. Their participation in politics and military affairs depends on possession of certain attributes. Absence of these constitutes corruption and presages decline.

Machiavelli fleshes out the theme of virtue and corruption against the backdrop of a grand historical theory, taken over from the Greek historian Polybius.[36] Briefly, Polybius argues that forms of government are distinguished by the number of rulers, whether they are one, few, or many, with good and bad forms of each. This gives us six forms: monarchy and tyranny, the good and bad forms of rule by one man; aristocracy and oligarchy, good and bad forms of rule by the few; good and bad forms of democracy. In the good forms of state, rulers obey the law and rule in the interest of the state; in the bad forms, rulers rule in their own interest. Polybius postulates a natural movement from one form of state to the next in an endless cycle. The first government that arises is rule by a wise, just king. But when power is passed down to one of his children, who is pleasure loving, he abuses it for his own purposes. When the people rebel against their new ruler's abuses, they institute an aristocracy, a government of the best men ruling in the public interest. But when power is passed down to their children, who have never known the evils of bad government, it is abused and an oligarchy emerges. The people as a whole arise and overthrow this, and institute a popular government in the interest of all. But again, their children abuse their power and democracy degenerates, with this new government in turn overthrown by a prince, thus giving rise to monarchy once again.

Machiavelli credits this pattern with universal validity: "Such is the circle which all republics are destined to run through" (*Dis.*, I, 2, p. 114). However, he argues, it is rare for states to complete the entire cycle:

> Seldom, however, do they come back to the original form of government, which results from the fact that their duration is not sufficiently long to be able to undergo these repeated changes and preserve their existence. But it may well happen that a republic lacking strength and good counsel in its difficulties becomes subject after a while to some neighboring state, that is better organized than itself, and if such is not the case, then they will be apt to revolve indefinitely in the circle of revolutions. (*Dis.*, I, 2, p. 114)

Because of the specific defects of each simple form of constitution, the way out of the cycle of decay is found by constructing a constitution of disparate elements:

> Thus sagacious legislators, knowing the vices of each of these systems of government by themselves, have chosen one that should partake of all of them, judging that to be the most stable and solid. In fact, when there is combined under the same constitution a prince, a nobility, and the power of the people, then these three powers will watch and keep each other reciprocally in check. (*Dis.*, I, 2, pp. 114–115)

The necessary lesson was learned by Lycurgus, lawgiver of Sparta, who combined the three forms of government in Sparta, thereby creating a government that maintained itself for over 800 years. Rome too benefitted from such a constitution. Though she had no single lawgiver like Lycurgus, other factors compensated:

> [Y]et the disunion which existed between the Senate and the people produced such extraordinary events, that chance did for her what the laws had failed to do. Thus, if

Rome did not attain the first degree of happiness, she at least had the second. (*Dis.*, I, 2, pp. 115–116)

Though Machiavelli adopts Polybius's cycle of constitutions, it is not clear how much it influences him. Polybius himself took the cycle very seriously, in his analysis of the sweep of Roman history.[37] But Machiavelli is mainly interested in aspects of Roman history that yield immediate practical lessons. Thus, unlike Polybius, he prefers the Spartan constitution to the Roman, because it was legislated at a single stroke by a specific lawgiver, while the Roman evolved gradually over time (*Dis.*, I, 2, p. 116; cf. Polybius, *Histories*, VI, 10, pp. 12–14). Because a future lawgiver can imitate the actions of Lycurgus, though not the protracted sequence of events through which Rome developed, Machiavelli views the Spartan form as superior.

In Machiavelli's eyes the cycle seems mainly to represent the variability of historical forces. Though human nature is constant and the past recurs in the future, states are always "in a state of perpetual movement, always either ascending or declining" (*Dis.*, II, Introduction, p. 272). Though the cycle of six forms is foreordained, few states complete it. Machiavelli believes virtue and power are transferred throughout history from state to state. In the past, they moved from Assyria, to the Medes, then to the Persians, and to Italy and Rome (*Dis.*, II, Introduction, pp. 272–273). Struggle between states is a permanent fact of life. Thus the theory of the cycle provides a theoretical expression of the tumultuous political world Machiavelli observed in his own Italy and read about in ancient works. A central aim of political life is to slow the cycle as much as possible, to maintain one's state and build a glorious reputation. To succeed, the state must be stronger than its neighbors; it must dominate them rather than being dominated by them. Security depends on power, and so in a world of constant struggle, there exists the close relationship between political and military affairs on which Machiavelli focuses throughout his works.

Despite the cycle's concentration on constitutional forms, one of the great accomplishments of Machiavelli's political theory is penetrating beneath constitutions to analyze more substantial factors responsible for states' success and failure. His initial remarks on the subject are somewhat surprising. Noting that Rome did not have the benefit of a single lawgiver, he says this was compensated for by "the disunion which existed between the Senate and people," which "did for her what the laws had failed to do" (*Dis.*, I, 2, pp. 115–116). Machiavelli notes that his analysis departs from the opinions of previous authors, who believed strongly in the importance of harmony and lack of discord between the parts of states. In actuality, conflict between different economic elements is essential to a state's well-being:

> I maintain that those who blame the quarrels of the Senate and the people of Rome condemn that which was the very origin of liberty, and that they were probably more impressed by the cries and noise which these disturbances occasioned in the public places, than by the good effect which they produced; and that they do not consider that in every republic there are two parties, that of the nobles and that of the people; and all the laws that are favorable to liberty result from the opposition of these parties to each other, as may easily be seen from the events that occurred in Rome. (*Dis.*, I, 4, p. 119)

Machiavelli does not carefully develop a single line of argument, the pieces of which neatly coalesce. But a generally coherent view can be extracted from the *Discourses*.

Machiavelli's main argument follows from his conception of human nature. Given his low opinion of man, it is not surprising that he views conflict and strife as political constants, both between states and within them. Key to political success is controlling conflict as much as possible. People's baser inclinations must be channeled for the good of the state. This can be accomplished through good laws and good education, supported by proper customs and religion. Because human aggressiveness cannot be eradicated, it must be given legal outlets, to avoid the need for illegal ones (*Dis.*, I, Chaps. 7–8).

Machiavelli's preference for republican government follows from his military views. Given his strong belief in the need for native troops, he believes the citizenry must be armed. This implies that they must be free—which means, basically, they must accept their rulers, and so have opportunities to participate in government in order to express their views. Political liberty is a necessary condition for political success (*Dis.*, II, 2, pp. 282–283). Finally, if the citizenry is going to be armed, free, and participate in government, then it must possess an overriding concern for the public good, or *virtù*. In the *Discourses*, the *virtù* with which Machiavelli is primarily concerned is that of the people rather than their ruler—and so I will use "civic virtue" more or less interchangeably with *virtù* in this sense.

As in *The Prince*, Machiavelli does not spell out the specific qualities that constitute *virtù*. But here too they can be identified as the attributes that make for political and military success, as exemplified by the Roman republic during its rise to world ascendancy. Machiavelli is obviously attracted to the example of Rome because of its extraordinary citizens, who were courageous and willing to make severe sacrifices for the public good. The opposite of civic virtue is corruption, which centers on concern for one's own good, rather than that of the city. Throughout the *Discourses* Machiavelli contrasts the corruption of the Italian cities of his day with the virtue of republican Rome.

The public-spiritedness necessary for a successful army must dominate the citizen body of a powerful republic. Machiavelli is deeply interested in different factors that contribute to and detract from this virtue, and so help to preserve or undermine the state. Because of the likelihood (perhaps inevitability) of conflict between the rich and poor, or nobles and common people, Machiavelli takes his stand on the side of the poor. While the rich desire to dominate them, the poor only wish not to be dominated and so are greater lovers of liberty. In general a free people should be poor rather than rich, as riches breed weakness and irresolution. Equality promotes liberty, as does a simple way of life and strong religious beliefs. To substantiate these points, Machiavelli appeals to the virtue of the Roman republic, as contrasted with the vice and corruption of the Italian cities of his own day.

Machiavelli views religion as important for the maintenance of civic virtue. Though he might have been personally religious, throughout his political works he views religion from a purely instrumental perspective. It is a force that can make for social stability and civic virtue, or the reverse. As noted above, Machiavelli claims the greatest reputations for glory have been won by founders of religions (*Dis.*, I, 10, p. 141). Not only does he criticize Christianity for keeping Italy divided and so weak (*Dis.*, I, 12, p. 152), but he is similarly critical of the values Christianity fosters. He views Christianity as otherworldly; it locates supreme happiness in "humility, lowliness, and a contempt for worldly objects" (*Dis.*, II, 2, p. 285). It is thus perhaps fortunate that these values are largely ignored by the religious establishment: "the nearer people are to the Church of Rome, which is the head of our religion, the less religious are they" (*Dis.*, I, 12, p. 151). (It is worth noting that Machiavelli was writing at a low point for the Church; the *Discourses* was written on the very eve of the outbreak of the Protestant Reformation.) But other religions, if taken seriously, can be forces for great good. Machiavelli attributes a large part of Roman soldiers' courage to religious predictions they would triumph. Though Roman practices such as auguries and auspices are easily derided, they can have powerful effects (*Dis.*, III, 33, pp. 506–507). Roman religion, unlike Christianity, placed ultimate value on "grandeur of soul, strength of body, and all such qualities as render men formidable" (*Dis.*, II, 2, p. 285). For this reason, everything possible must be done to promote serious adherence to suitable religion—without regard to whether the beliefs in question are true:

> It is therefore the duty of princes and heads of republics to uphold the foundations of the religion of their countries, for then it is easy to keep their people religious, and consequently well conducted and united. And therefore everything that tends to favor religion (even though it were believed to be false) should be received and availed of to strengthen it; and this should be done the more, the wiser the rulers are, and the better they understand the natural course of things. (*Dis.*, I, 12, p. 150)

In view of religion's importance to the success of Rome, Machiavelli has high praise for Numa Pompilius, Rome's second king, who was responsible for establishing Roman religion. Machiavelli estimates Numa's contribution as more important than that of Romulus, who founded the city (*Dis.*, I, 11, p. 147). In large part, Numa owed his success to the ruse that he had received his teaching from a nymph. As a rule, according to Machiavelli, not only founders of religions but sagacious lawgivers must resort to divine authority:

> In truth, there never was any remarkable lawgiver amongst any people who did not resort to divine authority, as otherwise his laws would not have been accepted by the people; for there are many good laws, the importance of which is known to the sagacious lawgiver, but the reasons for which are not sufficiently evident to enable him to persuade others to submit to them; and therefore do wise men, for the purpose of removing this difficulty, resort to divine authority. (*Dis.*, I, 11, p. 147)

As one might expect, the subject receiving the greatest attention in the *Discourses* is military affairs. A city cannot be secure unless it is powerful (*Dis.*, I, 1, p. 108). Machiavelli takes it for granted that the environment in which a state exists is one of constant conflict with other states. It is a Darwinian struggle; any given state is either rising or falling. Security depends on being able to field a formidable citizen army. Accordingly, the greater part of the *Discourses* is fairly straightforward military history. This particular focus distinguishes Machiavelli from other writers of his time. While other political theorists were interested in questions concerning the grounds of the state's authority, reasons why the subject must obey it, and questions concerning when obligations run out and the subject's recourse when they do,[38] Machiavelli largely ignores these questions. Undoubtedly under the influence of his political situation, he focuses on conditions necessary for the state's existence in a hostile world, and so on external affairs—and their internal requisites.

The military analysis that dominates the *Discourses* is something of a mixed bag. Familiar themes are discussed at length, for example, the need for native troops, dislike of mercenaries, and qualities necessary for successful generalship. Roman history is plumbed for lessons. These range from the obvious—for example, that a general must attempt to anticipate the moves of his counterpart (*Dis.*, III, 18)—to the surprising and almost certainly incorrect. Most notable here are Machiavelli's preference for infantry over cavalry (*Dis.*, II, 18) and dismissal of the importance of artillery (*Dis.*, II, 17)—presumably, one is tempted to say, because the Romans did not use it. Some maxims appear to apply equally well to politics and war: for example, that battle must be joined if one's enemy is determined to fight (*Dis.*, III, 10), and that one should not risk one's entire fortune with only a portion of one's forces (*Dis.*, I, 22).

Machiavelli's intense interest in military affairs and lessons makes the *Discourses* in many ways an untheoretical work. Though he presents a pioneering account of the social prerequisites of military success,[39] much of this material must be reconstructed by the reader. The bulk of his presentation is discursive military and historical narrative, which can be likened to journalism.[40] But Machiavelli is a gifted observer; many of his conclusions profoundly influenced subsequent authors.

It could be argued that Machiavelli's concentration on the military side of political life is dictated by his desire to produce a commentary on Livy. The books of Livy on which he focuses concern the rise of Rome through incessant conflict with other states. And so it might seem natural that Machiavelli concentrates on this. But it is of course Machiavelli who chose to write on Livy rather than some other author. We can assume he did this because of Livy's subject matter, from which Machiavelli believed he could draw lessons directly applicable to his own political concerns.

In the *Discourses*, as in his other works, Machiavelli presents brilliant analyses of specific political situations. Especially striking is his account of conspiracies in Book III, Chapter 6. In direct contrast to *The Prince*, which advises the ruler about how to keep his throne, in this chapter Machiavelli lays out essential information about what must be done to deprive him of it. From an accumulation of cases from different cities and different historical periods Machiavelli distills maxims of betrayal that have apparently timeless validity. For instance, he observes that conspiracies against the prince generally arise among his friends and associates, and notes the need to limit the number of participants in order to preserve essential secrecy: "When the number of accomplices in a conspiracy exceeds three or four, it is almost impossible for it not to be discovered, either through treason, imprudence, or carelessness" (*Dis.*, III, 6, p. 418). Similarly, to avoid exposure, it is essential to act quickly. As one might expect, Machiavelli is deeply concerned about possible treachery: "treachery is so common that you cannot safely impart your project to any but such of your most trusted friends as are willing to risk their lives for your sake" (*Dis.*, III, 6, p. 416). Because of these factors, conspiracies against a single person rarely succeed, while the difficulties are multiplied many times over in plots that involve coordinated attacks against two or more, which almost always fail.

We have noted that Machiavelli was suspected by the Medici of involvement in a plot against them and that he paid a severe price. There is no evidence he ever conspired against them again—and indeed assiduously courted their favor for years. But it is striking that Zanobi Buondelmonte, one of the two people to whom the *Discourses* is dedicated, did organize a plot against the Medici. The plot was exposed and Buondelmonte fled into exile.[41] Though Machiavelli was not implicated, these events meant the end of the discussion group in which he was engaged. It is difficult to find a precise connection between Machiavelli's discussion of conspiracies and the one in which his friend took part, but the coincidence is striking.

Because of his belief in incessant conflict between states, Machiavelli holds that any given state confronts difficult choices. The question of how a state should be organized depends on the purposes it is intended to achieve. There are two main possibilities. If the state chooses to extend its borders, then the model to follow is Rome. If it wishes to preserve itself but not to grow, the examples are Sparta and Venice. The former type of state should have a popular government. We have seen that military success ultimately depends on popular involvement in government. The latter form, less dependent on a citizen army, should be governed by an aristocracy (*Dis.*, I, 6, pp. 227–228). Though in the best of all possible worlds Machiavelli would choose the latter course, he believes it is unrealistic to hope for long-term stability. Thus he argues that the state must be organized for expansion, and so for war:

> And I certainly think that if she could be kept in this equilibrium it would be the best political existence, and would insure to any state real tranquility. But as all human things are kept in a perpetual movement, and can never remain stable, states naturally either rise or decline, and necessity compels them to many acts to which reason will not influence them . . . Seeing then the impossibility of establishing in this respect a perfect equilibrium, and that a precise middle course cannot be maintained, it is proper in the organization of a republic to select the most honourable course, and to constitute her so that even if necessity should oblige her to expand, she may yet be able to preserve her acquisitions. (*Dis.*, I, 6, p. 129)

Once again, the need for perpetual warfare, and so the stark choice between expansion and decline, reflects Machiavelli's dim view of human nature. As we have noted, people's passions require outlets. The healthy republic is not tranquil, but its inevitable dissensions are channeled away from harmful directions (see, e.g., *Dis.*, I, 7–8). War with other states is the ultimate outlet. Civic virtue at home is thus inseparably linked with incessant conflict abroad. The need for civic virtue in part arises from the need to stand up against one's enemies. But the chain of influence also works in the other direction. Civic virtue centers on public concern for the good of the state rather than one's own good. Because people's passions require an outlet, in the final analysis only warfare can preserve virtue—and so the state must expand. The inseparable connection between these elements is illustrated by the history of Rome. The legendary virtue of Roman citizens was most clearly demonstrated in their heroic responses to the numerous setbacks encountered during Rome's rise to world hegemony. War, then, is not only the natural condition of states and an outlet for citizens' public passions, but it affords the opportunity for a virtuous citizen body to demonstrate its *virtù*.

Machiavelli's emphasis on the capabilities of a virtuous people does not rest entirely well with his dim view of human nature. But he makes clear in the *Discourses* that people become as they are shaped by the state. If hunger makes men industrious, laws make them good (*Dis.*, I, 3, p. 118). Thus, in the final analysis, the people's faults can be attributed entirely to their rulers (*Dis.*, III, 29). We have seen Machiavelli's ringing declaration that all would-be founders of states must begin with the assumption "that all men are bad and ever ready to display their vicious nature" (*Dis.*, I, 3, p. 117). But placing this statement in its overall context in the *Discourses*, we see that founders must begin with this awareness in order to counter it. Through properly designed institutions, a wise lawgiver can give the people civic virtue.

The main connections between *The Prince* and the *Discourses* lie in the conviction that political and social institutions can shape a people. Viewing his own society as deeply corrupt, Machiavelli is concerned with the potential of political reform to combat corruption. Machiavelli has few illusions that this will be easy, but he does believe it is possible. A necessary condition for success is that political reform must be the work of one man—a lawgiver such as Moses, Lycurgus, Cyrus, and Romulus, figures extolled in *The Prince*—who must possess unaccountable power:

> [W]e must assume, as a general rule, that it never or rarely happens that a republic or monarchy is well constituted, or its old institutions entirely reformed, unless it is done by only one individual; it is even necessary that he whose mind has conceived such a constitution should be alone in carrying it into effect. A sagacious legislator of a republic, therefore, whose object is to promote the public good, and not his private interests, and who prefers his country to his own successors, should concentrate all authority in himself; and a wise mind will never censure any one for having employed any extraordinary means for the purpose of establishing a kingdom or constituting a republic. (*Dis.*, I, 9, pp. 138–139)

Though it takes a single individual to reform a state, he should use his power to institute a republican government, and so pass it on to the many (*Dis.*, I, 9, p. 139).

The means the founder must pursue fall beyond conventional morality. As we have just seen "any extraordinary means" are acceptable—though we should note that in the continuation of the paragraph just quoted, Machiavelli adds:

> It is well that, when the act accuses him, the result should excuse him; and when the result is good, as in the case of Romulus, it will always absolve him from blame. For he is to be reprehended who commits violence for the purpose of destroying, and not he who employs it for beneficent purposes. (*Dis.*, I, 9, p. 139)

We noted above the reprehensible but necessary tactics of Philip of Macedon, who unfortunately presents a model to be imitated. Thus for founders of states, the precepts of conventional morality are cast aside. For instance, Machiavelli notes the need for new rulers to kill surviving members of the former ruling family, in order to pacify the state (*Dis.*, III, 4; cf. I, 9, p. 139).

Scattered throughout the *Discourses* is a veritable treatise on founding a new state, or restoring a corrupt one to its former *virtù*. Machiavelli's concern with this theme is palpable in this work, as in *The Prince*. Treatment of specific details is also similar, though as a more discursive work, the *Discourses* ranges far afield in filling in the outline presented in *The Prince*. Machiavelli speaks timelessly of problems inherent in political reform—and so of why the world has witnessed so few successful instances:

> And as the reformation of the political condition of a state presupposes a good man, whilst the making of himself prince of a republic by violence naturally presupposes a bad one, it will consequently be exceedingly rare that a good man should be found willing to employ wicked means to become prince, even though his final object be good; or that a bad man, after having been prince, should be willing to labor for good ends, and that it should enter his mind to use for good purposes that authority which he has acquired by evil means. From these combined causes arises the difficulty or

impossibility of maintaining liberty in a republic that has become corrupt, or to establish it there anew. . . . And to attempt to restore men to good conduct by any other means [than an almost regal power] would be either a most cruel or an impossible undertaking. (*Dis.*, I, 18, p. 171)

But if against all odds the founder should succeed, he will not only establish a state able to maintain itself—for a time—but win great glory for himself, second only to that of founders of religions. "For certainly, the heavens cannot afford a man a greater opportunity of glory, nor could men desire a better one" (*Dis.*, I, 10, p. 145).

MACHIAVELLI AND MODERN POLITICAL THEORY

In order fully to appreciate Machiavelli's accomplishments, it is necessary to look more closely at the "new route" he set out to develop. It is often said that Machiavelli is one of the founders of political science. As we will see in subsequent chapters, the attempt to be scientific—according to different conceptions of exactly what this entails—is a major theme in modern political theory. Though the claim that Machiavelli is a full-fledged political scientist (regardless of how good a thing this is to be) is clearly overblown, there can be little doubt concerning his originality, and his break with previous modes of inquiry.

In recounting respects in which Machiavelli is original, we must begin with his outlook, which is both secular and based on close examination of his subject matter. To appreciate the significance of this, compare Machiavelli and St. Augustine. The latter is a powerful political thinker who holds views of human nature and the political world similar to Machiavelli's. But Augustine's political theory is dominated by the conviction that the Bible contains God's revelation and so political wisdom can be discovered in its pages, which should be read allegorically. Something similar is true of St. Thomas Aquinas. Though St. Thomas is interested in the wisdom of Greek philosophy, especially Aristotle, as well as Biblical truth, his thought is shaped by the conviction that these two sources of wisdom coincide. Among Machiavelli's near predecessors, the most significant political thinker with a secular outlook, basing his search for knowledge on reason rather than revelation, is Marsilius of Padua, who is also heavily influenced by Aristotelian philosophy and reads the Bible as an historical work. In these senses Marsilius anticipates intellectual tendencies of the Renaissance—as he does in observing a political form that prefigured the modern state.[42]

Though Machiavelli too is interested in religion, he views this primarily as a social phenomenon, with political implications. People's religious beliefs affect their character as citizens, and so Machiavelli has various recommendations about how religion can best be treated. But as is not the case with medieval thinkers, he casts off virtually all vestiges of a religious point of view. This is one respect in which Machiavelli is modern, and "scientific." Along similar lines, an essential feature of the scientific method is that it deals with phenomena as they are. On the whole, it is not able directly to address questions of value. Employing two distinctions often referred to, we can say that science addresses what *is* rather than what *ought* to be; it studies *facts* rather than *values*. Not only does Machiavelli focus on the world he sees before him, but his values are closely associated with this. We have seen that Machiavelli's political thought is not devoid of values. Much of what he writes is directed towards the attainment of specific goals, mainly the restoration of

Florentine virtue and power. However, in comparison to most medieval political thinkers, his works evince a remarkable degree of concern for the world as it is. He does not view the laws of particular states as specific applications or emanations of higher laws authored by God. The notion of natural law is absent from his political theory.[43] Religious truth as a source of value in its own right is absent from Machiavelli's political works. Nor does he explore God's revelation or the interpretation of Scripture by previous authors. The values he brings to his subject matter are inherent in the practice of politics: success and failure, the rise and fall of states.

In addition to what he avoids, Machiavelli pursues a method that is in some respects scientific in a more specific sense, centering on rigorous examination of his subject matter. Machiavelli's work is based on systematic research, unfamiliar to political authors since the time of Aristotle. Experienced in practical politics, Machiavelli is a careful observer of the Italian political scene and bases his writings on this body of knowledge. In addition, he makes a detailed study of ancient texts to supplement his experience and so has a wide range of historical material and examples to draw upon. We saw in Volume I that Aristotle bases his political analysis in the *Politics* on detailed examination of the constitutions and histories of 158 Greek cities. Though Machiavelli's scope is not as wide, he makes a sustained effort to explore his subject matter—under the assumption that what held true of Rome is equally good for Florence.

Finally, from his range of observations, Machiavelli attempts to extract general regularities or tendencies, the "laws" of his subject matter. These general rules resemble scientific laws, which are in essence regular patterns of interaction among observed phenomena, though Machiavelli's examples are not sufficiently precise to merit the designation "laws." As we have seen, Machiavelli believes in a specific cycle of political change. In the *Discourses* he borrows the cycle of constitutions presented by Polybius. It is not clear how much weight he places on the specifics of this view. But as we have seen, because human nature is constant, history moves in a cycle, and what one learns about the past is applicable to the future. As far as the discovery of general rules is concerned, because people's behavior falls in regular patterns, it is subject to prediction. Knowing how people have behaved under specific circumstances allows one to anticipate their future behavior— along the lines of scientific predictions in the natural world. In a sense, then, *The Prince* and *Discourses* are intended to reveal laws of the political world.

Examples of political "laws" abound in Machiavelli's works. For instance, in Chapter 3 of *The Prince* he notes "a general rule, which never or very rarely fails, that whoever is the cause of another becoming powerful is ruined himself" (p. 14). Other rules depend on the observation of human behavior. In regard to the prevalence of greed, Machiavelli observes that the prince should abstain from seizing people's property, because "men forget more easily the death of their father than the loss of their patrimony" (*Pr.*, Chap. 17, p. 62). Similarly, as a rule, princes who have succeeded are whose who have been willing to cast aside traditional values: "[T]he experience of our times shows those princes to have done great things who have had little regard for good faith and have been able by astuteness to confuse men's brains, and who have ultimately overcome those who have made loyalty their foundation" (*Pr.*, Chap. 18, p. 63). Innumerable other instances from *The Prince* and *Discourses* could be indicated.

In view of the regularities he presents, it is not surprising that Machiavelli views the study of history and politics as "sciences," similar to others that are better established. This is clearly expressed in the Introduction to Book I of the *Discourses*. Previous authors combed ancient texts for insight into the sciences of medicine and law. Machiavelli intends to replicate their efforts in regard to the questions that interest him, concerning founding and governing states. The general rules he seeks are practical; they are to inform political practitioners of the means necessary for specific ends, most often political success, honor, and glory. A field analogous to politics is topography, the study of which Machiavelli recommends for rulers. This too has general rules which one can learn to one's advantage:

> [B]y means of the knowledge and experience gained in one locality, one can easily understand any other that it may be necessary to observe; for the hills and valleys, plains and rivers of Tuscany, for instance, have a certain resemblance to those of other provinces, so that from a knowledge of the country in one province one can easily arrive at a knowledge of others. (*Pr.*, Chap. 14, p. 54)

In spite of the undeniable achievements of Machiavelli's study of politics, it is possible to criticize him in various ways. For instance, though he uses a number of sources, he is rather credulous in regard to them. His acceptance of Livy is almost uncritical. In the words of one commentator, "He went to Livy expecting what he would find there, duly found what he wanted and asked no questions."[44] Machiavelli's credulousness is clearly seen in certain historical figures he discusses. As we have seen, he is greatly interested in the virtue of Moses, Lycurgus, Cyrus, Theseus, and Romulus, and views these founders of states as examples for princes to emulate. It must be noted, however, that all these possessors of overweening *virtù* are highly mythic. The sources from which Machiavelli draws his knowledge of them—the Old Testament, Plutarch, Xenophon's *Cyropaedia*—contain heavy overlays of myth, which he accepts. Many of his supreme examples of political excellence, then, are largely fictional characters.

Similarly, because he believes in the uniformity of human nature across history, Machiavelli has little historical sense. Though he labors to identify respects in which people are similar from age to age, he shows little awareness of how they are different. This prevents him from developing a real comparative method and contributes to his tendency to state overly general truths and to base conclusions on insufficient evidence. An especially clear instance of this is his disdain for artillery (see p. 27).

Finally, though he is a brilliant observer and analyst of specific aspects of the political world, Machiavelli has little interest in systematic examination of politics. A point along these lines has been made in reference to the *Discourses*. Though he constructs generalizations on the basis of his reading and experience, Machiavelli does not attempt to work these into a coherent system. More serious, he does not pursue the implications of his separate observations to see what they entail and to make sure they are consistent with one another. Scholars refer to problems like these in questioning Machiavelli's claim to be a full-fledged scientific theorist.

In the final analysis, it seems that Machiavelli's greatness lies in his observation of central moral dilemmas of political life. His observations of Italian affairs, which prefigured those of the emerging European state system, are presented with a combination of intellectual penetration and literary brilliance that have been rarely equalled—overlaid with mordant wit. Machiavelli possesses greater literary gifts than virtually any comparable figure in the history of political theory. A gifted poet and playwright, as well as perhaps the greatest prose writer Italy has produced, Machiavelli's imagination is that of a poet. This is doubtless responsible for certain of his shortcomings—for instance, that he presents anecdotes rather than precise scientific formulations, or that he does not use historical evidence to test his generalizations but rather to illustrate conclusions based on intuitive insight. But these faults fade against the power of his intuition. His works classically express a certain view of politics. In the political world, purity of heart counts for little, in comparison to success, while this in turn often requires unpalatable means. The good ruler must learn to be bad—though while hiding this from his credulous subjects. In large part, the evil aura surrounding Machiavelli's name stems from his merciless assault on what people like to believe—and what their rulers like them to believe. But as he classically argues, in order to prosper in political affairs, one must see things as they are. For the great light he sheds on these unsavory truths, Machiavelli's reward has been undeserved, undying infamy, but also a prominent place among the founders of modern political theory.

NOTES

1. C. Morris, "Machiavelli's Reputation in Tudor England," *Il pensiero politico,* 2, (1969).

2. *The American Heritage Dictionary of the English Language,* W. Morris, ed. (Boston, 1981).

3. *The Prince* and *Discourses on the First Ten Books of Titus Livius* are quoted from the Modern Library edition, unless noted otherwise. Full references for this and others of Machiavelli's works used are found under "Texts Cited," at the end of the chapter. *The Prince* (*Pr.*) is cited according to chapter number; the *Discourses* (*Dis.*) cited according to book and chapter number. For direct quotations and references to specific passages, I also include page numbers in the Modern Library edition, and other translations as noted. *The Art of War* (AW) is cited according to page number in N. Wood's edition. Machiavelli's letters are identified by letter number, date, recipient, and page number in *Machiavelli: The Chief Works and Others,* A. Gilbert, trans., Vol. II.

4. See I. Berlin, "The Originality of Machiavelli," in *Against the Current: Essays in the History of Ideas,* H. Hardy, ed. (Harmondsworth, 1982), pp. 26–36.

5. Berlin, "Originality," p. 35.

6. Berlin, "Originality," p. 73; Russell is quoted by Berlin, p. 35.

7. R. Ridolfi, *The Life of Niccolo Machiavelli,* C. Grayson, trans. (Chicago, 1963), pp. 1–2. Biographical details are from Ridolfi, cited as Ridolfi in text.

8. A good brief discussion of Machiavelli's military experience is given by N. Wood in his Introduction to *The Art of War* (Indianapolis, 1965), pp. ix–xviii.

9. Familiar Letter, No. 120; Machiavelli to F. Vettori, April 9, 1513; *Chief Works and Others,* II, pp. 900–901.

10. See Familiar Letters in *Chief Works and Others,* Vol. II.

11. Familiar Letter, No. 137; Machiavelli to Vettori, December 10, 1513; *Chief Works and Others,* II, p. 930.

12. Ibid., p. 929.

13. M. Weber, "Politics as a Vocation," In *From Max Weber: Essays in Sociology*, ed. and trans. H. Gerth and C. W. Mills (New York, 1946), p. 78 (Weber's emphasis).

14. Q. Skinner, *Foundations of Modern Political Thought*, 2 vols. (Cambridge, 1978), Vol. II, Conclusion.

15. G. Mattingly, *Renaissance Diplomacy* (Boston, 1971), Foreword.

16. J. H. Hexter, "The Loom of Language and the Fabric of Imperatives: The Case of *Il Principe* and *Utopia*," *American Historical Review*, 59 (1964), 952–954.

17. J. N. Figgis, *Political Thought From Gerson to Grotius: 1414–1625* (1916; rpt. New York, 1960), p. 95.

18. Ibid., p. 98.

19. See F. Gilbert, "The Humanist Concept of the Prince and *The Prince* of Machiavelli," *Journal of Modern History*, 11 (1939), esp. Sec. II.

20. *Secular Authority*, p. 394; full reference below, under "Texts Cited"; this work was published in 1523.

21. Gilbert, "Humanist Concept," pp. 461–462.

22. For discussion of Machiavelli's relationship to Cicero and other Roman authors I draw on Skinner's "Introduction" to his edition of *The Prince*; and M. Colish, "Cicero's *De Officiis* and Machiavelli's *Prince*," *Sixteenth Century Journal*, 9 (1978).

23. Colish, "Cicero's *De Officiis*," p. 81.

24. S. Wolin, *Politics and Vision* (Boston, 1960), Chap. 7.

25. For example, Mattingly, "Machiavelli," in *Renaissance Profiles*, J. H. Plumb, ed. (New York, 1961), pp. 32–33.

26. Berlin, "Originality," p. 71.

27. See Vol. I, 22–23.

28. F. Meinecke, *Machiavellism*, D. Scott, trans. (London, 1957).

29. On Machiavelli's character, see Ridolfi, *Life*, esp. Chaps. 15, 22–23; for his religiosity, see S. De Grazia, *Machiavelli in Hell* (Princeton, 1989), Chap. 3; for his son's orders, see Ridolfi, p. 326 n. 24.

30. R. Price, "The Theme of *Gloria* in Machiavelli," *Renaissance Quarterly*, 4 (1977), 621.

31. See Price, "The Senses of *Virtù* in Machiavelli," *European Studies Review*, 3 (1973); Hexter, "Loom of Language," pp. 954–958; Wood, "Machiavelli's Concept of *Virtù* Reconsidered," *Political Studies*, 15 (1967).

32. J. H. Whitfield, *Machiavelli* (1947; rpt. New York, 1966), p. 105.

33. See Wood, "Machiavelli's Concept of *Virtù*."

34. J. W. Allen, *A History of Political Thought in the Sixteenth Century* (London, 1957), pp. 469, 464.

35. See Gilbert, "The Composition and Structure of Machiavelli's *Discorsi*," *Journal of the History of Ideas*, 14 (1953); H. Baron, "Machiavelli: The Republican Citizen and the Author of 'The Prince,'" *English Historical Review*, 76 (1961).

36. Polybius, *History*, Book VI; see Vol. I, 160–165.

37. See Vol. I, 160–165.

38. For the importance of these questions at approximately the same time, in regard to the Protestant Reformation, see Vol. I, Chap. 11.

39. See esp. J. G. A. Pocock, *The Machiavellian Moment* (Princeton, 1975), Chaps. 6–7.

40. Allen describes *The Prince* as "all but a piece of journalism dealing with current politics" (*History of Political Thought*, p. 466).

41. For events here, see Ridolfi, *Life*, pp. 202–203.

42. See Vol. I, Chap. 10. For St. Augustine and St. Thomas, see Chaps. 8–9.

43. Allen, *History of Political Thought*, pp. 479–481; on natural law, see Vol. I, 154–156, 254–259.

44. Allen, *History of Political Thought*, p. 486.

TEXTS CITED

Cicero. *De Officiis* (*On Moral Duties*). W. Miller, trans. Cambridge, MA, 1913.

Luther, M. "Secular Authority: To What Extent It Should Be Obeyed." In *Martin Luther: Selections from His Writings*. J. Dillenberger, ed. Garden City, NY, 1961.

Machiavelli, N. *The Art of War*. N. Wood, ed. Wood, and E. Farneworth, trans. Indianapolis, 1965.

Machiavelli, N. *The Chief Works and Others*. A. Gilbert, trans. 3 vols. Durham, NC, 1965.

Machiavelli, N. *The Prince*. Q. Skinner, ed. R. Price, trans. Cambridge, 1988.

Machiavelli, N. *The Prince and The Discourses*. Modern Library ed. L. Ricci, E. R. P. Vincent, and C. E. Detmold, trans. New York, 1950.

Thucydides. *History of the Peloponnesian War*. R. Warner, trans. Harmondsworth, England, 1954.

FURTHER READING

Allen, J. W. *A History of Political Thought in the Sixteenth Century*. London, 1957.

Baron, H. "Machiavelli: The Republican Citizen and the Author of 'The Prince.' " *English Historical Review*, 76 (1961).

Berlin, I. "The Originality of Machiavelli." In *Against the Current: Essays in the History of Ideas*. H. Hardy, ed. Harmondsworth, England, 1982.

Chabod, F. *Machiavelli and the Renaissance*. D. Moore, trans. New York, 1958.

Colish, M. "Cicero's *De Officiis* and Machiavelli's *Prince*." *Sixteenth Century Journal*, 9 (1978).

De Grazia, S. *Machiavelli in Hell*. Princeton, 1989.

Figgis, J. N. *Political Thought From Gerson to Grotius: 1414–1625*. 1916; rpt. New York, 1960.

Gilbert, F. "The Humanist Concept of the Prince and *The Prince* of Machiavelli." *Journal of Modern History*, 11 (1939).

Gilbert, F. *Machiavelli and Guicciardini.* Princeton, 1965.

Pocock, J. G. A. *The Machiavellian Moment.* Princeton, 1975. Part II.

Ridolfi, R. *The Life of Niccolò Machiavelli.* C. Grayson, trans. Chicago, 1963.

Skinner, Q. *The Foundations of Modern Political Thought.* 2 vols. Cambridge, 1978.

Skinner, Q. *Machiavelli.* Oxford, 1981.

Whitfield, J. H. *Machiavelli.* 1947; rpt. New York, 1966.

Wood, N. "Machiavelli's Concept of *Virtù* Reconsidered." *Political Studies,* 15 (1967).

C h a p t e r

2

THOMAS HOBBES

THOMAS HOBBES, OFTEN REGARDED AS the greatest English political theorist, was born in 1588, the year of the Spanish Armada. In his brief autobiography he writes: "the famous enemy fleet, the Armada, soon destined to perish in our sea, was standing at anchor in the Spanish ports . . . when in early spring, the little worm that is myself was born in Malmesbury."[1] The tumultuous times of Hobbes's birth foreshadowed troubled political events throughout his life.

According to Hobbes, external events affected his character: He was born afraid. In the shadow of the Armada, "my mother was big with such fear that she brought twins to birth, myself and fear at the same time" (*Autobiography*, p. 24). Fear is ever a keynote in Hobbes's political philosophy. Accordingly, he views peace and order as supreme political goods, and supports a powerful state because only this can insure peace. Hobbes views fear as one of two passions that incline men to peace and make ordered commonwealths possible.

Hobbes's political theory is often called "absolutist," because of the relationship he posits between the state and its citizens. He supports unaccountable political power and, as we will see, does everything possible to remove traditional checks on rulers. The upshot of his position is that subjects have virtually no rights against the state. In a technical sense, the power of Hobbes's rulers is not absolute, as it is subject to certain constraints. But Hobbes strives mightily to limit these. Though as we shall see below, his position verges on "liberal" political theory in important respects and Hobbes is a pioneer in the liberal tradition, he tilts the balance of rights and powers so far in the direction of the sovereign and away from individual citizens that he is not a "liberal" theorist in the proper sense of the term.

After completing his formal education, in 1608, Hobbes was fortunate to secure a position in the service of the Cavendish family, one of the wealthiest families in England. He served as tutor to family members, as a financial adviser, and in secretarial capacities, and was maintained by the Cavendish family for virtually all the rest of his long life. The family, which included Dukes of Devonshire and Newcastle as well as other nobles, supported the royal cause as King Charles I battled Parliament for political supremacy. Full-scale civil war broke out in 1642, which culminated in the victory of Parliamentary forces and the trial and execution of Charles in 1649. The monarchy was abolished and a republic declared, but in effect England fell under the military rule of Oliver Cromwell. Hobbes spent this period in France. Characteristically, he describes himself as "the first of all that fled."[2] While in exile, he was for a time mathematics tutor to the future King Charles II, also in exile. But after the publication of *Leviathan*, his greatest work, in 1651, he was banished from Charles's court because of his heretical ideas. Hobbes returned to England in 1651, "not well assured of safety, but because there was nowhere else I could be safer" (*Autobiography*, p. 28). After submitting to the republican government, he was allowed to live unmolested.

It is often said that political theory thrives during times of political trouble. Ordinarily, people go about their lives with political beliefs and assumptions into which they have little reason to inquire. But when existing political institutions begin to crumble, people must search for others that can solve their problems. As part of this process, they can begin to doubt their existing assumptions and approach political questions from a new perspective. Hobbes is an excellent example of this phenomenon. He viewed the political upheavals in England with obvious horror. Regarding civil war as the death of a commonwealth (*Lev.*, Introduction, p. 9), he searched for a theoretical solution to the problem of disorder. In the final paragraph of *Leviathan*, he notes that the work was "occasioned by the disorders of the present time" (*Lev.*, Review and Conclusion, p. 491).[3]

In fact, *Leviathan* was the third statement of Hobbes's political philosophy. The first presentation was contained in *The Elements of Law*, written in 1640. This work was circulated only in manuscript, until a corrupt edition, broken into two parts, was printed in London in 1649–50, probably without Hobbes's permission.[4] *De Cive* (*The Citizen: Philosophical Rudiments Concerning Government and Society*) was published in Latin in 1642; an English translation appeared in 1651. *Leviathan* also was published in 1651. Thus as civil war loomed in England and finally erupted, Hobbes ruminated on the desultory situation. From his refuge in France he worked and reworked his political philosophy, which was intended at least in part to allay the conflict.

Throughout the three versions of Hobbes's theory the central points remain essentially unchanged. But Hobbes does make alterations, both to improve his argument and to adapt to political developments. The most obvious change is in the amount of attention accorded matters of religion. This subject receives a few chapters in *Elements of Law*. Only two years later, in *De Cive*, it is a more significant theme, to which Hobbes devotes approximately twice as much space. Fully half of *Leviathan* is given over to religious questions. Parts III and IV of the work, which are exclusively concerned with religion, are themselves as long as *Elements of Law*. The reason for Hobbes's development in this respect is not hard to identify. The English Civil War, which began as a conflict between King and Parliament, became wrapped up in questions of religion, which had to be dealt with as a necessary condition for peaceful settlement. Thus in all three works, but especially *Leviathan*, Hobbes argues that the conclusions of his political philosophy are not inconsistent with, indeed are supported by, truths of religious revelation. It is instructive to trace developments in particular aspects of Hobbes's argument between the three versions of his political theory, as these help make clear exactly what he hoped to accomplish. In certain cases we find successive attempts to overcome specific problems. Reviewing Hobbes's attacks on these from different angles makes the nature of the problems more apparent.

In addition to his immediate political intentions, Hobbes was motivated by concerns of a scientific nature. In the service of the Cavendish house, he made several tours of the European continent and became acquainted with important scientific figures of the age, most notably Galileo and Descartes, major figures in the scientific revolution. In his autobiography, Hobbes notes his growing scientific interest, especially his extreme materialism, his conviction "that in the whole world only one thing is real," motion, more properly, matter in motion. "This is the reason why anyone who wishes to learn natural philosophy must first master the laws of motion" (*Autobiography*, p. 25). Because he viewed only matter as real, Hobbes regarded noncorporeal entities as "fantasies, creatures of our brains and nothing more" (*Autobiography*, p. 25).

While in Paris, Hobbes discussed his developing views with various scientific figures, and says that from that time on he "began to be numbered among the philosophers" (*Autobiography*, p. 26). In order to work out the implications of his materialism, he became interested in the idea of a comprehensive philosophical system, encompassing three main subjects: Body, Man, and Citizen, which he identified as "the whole of philosophy." "I resolved to write three books on these subjects and gathered my material day by day" (*Autobiography*, p. 26).

HOBBES'S PHILOSOPHICAL METHOD

Hobbes is often identified as a pioneering figure in the development of "political science." Though, as we saw in the last chapter, a similar claim is made on Machiavelli's behalf, in Hobbes's case it is more appropriate. As the term indicates, political science, and the "social sciences" more generally, represent a commitment to explain the workings of the political and social worlds according to the same sorts of rules and principles that are used to explain the natural world. A political scientist's conception of what constitutes a good explanation for some political or social phenomenon is based on developed explanations in such fields as physics, chemistry, and biology. According to recent social scientists, then, acceptable political explanations must be in terms of laws that hold generally of a range of phenomena. These laws must have been confirmed by repeated tests, but are also subject to revision or rejection should the results of further tests go against them. Hobbes subscribed to a similar orientation. However, his views were influenced by important scientific figures of his day, who derived their models of explanatory adequacy from mathematics, especially geometry.

In his "Brief Life" of Hobbes, John Aubrey recounts Hobbes's discovery of geometry:

> He was 40 years old before he looked on Geometry; which happened accidentally. Being in a Gentleman's Library, Euclid's Elements lay open, and 'twas the 47 *El. libri* I. He read the Proposition. By G— said he . . . this is impossible! So he reads the Demonstration of it, which referred him back to such a Proposition; which proposition he read. That referred him back to another, which he also read. *Et sic deinceps* [and so on] that at last he was demonstratively convinced of that truth. This made him in love with Geometry.[5]

What attracted Hobbes to geometry is apparent in this incident. Through geometrical reasoning, one is able to prove improbable, even apparently impossible, contentions. Geometric reasoning is deductive, or truth-preserving. As long as one's premises are true, by employing accepted operations of geometrical reasoning, one can arrive at true conclusions. The ideal of a geometrical system is everywhere apparent in seventeenth-century philosophy, most notably in the works of Descartes, and in Spinoza's *Ethics*. In the latter, as in Euclid's geometry, lists of definitions and axioms are presented at the beginning of the work, from which a long series of propositions is deductively derived.

An important aim of Hobbes's political writings throughout his career is to provide a certain, geometrical demonstration of his political claims. He hopes to produce in his readers an experience similar to his own in encountering Euclid. Even if his conclusions might at first appear improbable, or even impossible, they can be traced back to subsidiary steps in the argument, which can in turn be traced back to previous steps, eventually leading to first principles which are firmly established. Thus the same degree of certainty we associate with a proof in Euclidian geometry can be won for Hobbes's political conclusions. In his autobiography Hobbes notes his intent to connect "into a whole the knowledge I had gained, so that the conclusions might shine bright in the light of the first principles and the whole argument might have the permanence of a strong chain" (*Autobiography*, p. 26).

In the Dedicatory Epistle to *De Cive*, Hobbes makes great claims for the power of geometrical reasoning. He says that whatever ways his own age differs from crude antiquity are owed "merely to geometry." Important contributions he notes include observation of the heavens and earth and the benefits of navigation. If moral philosophers had applied similar reasoning to their subject matter, the results would be similarly impressive: "I know not what could have been added by human industry to the completion of that happiness, which is consistent with human life" (*DC*, Ep. Ded., p. iv). Ongoing disagreements about moral questions indicate a lack of progress in these matters, the remedy for which is geometrical reasoning (*DC*, Ep. Ded., pp. v–vi).

Hobbes's presentation of his political theory in the form of a deductive system makes important demands of the reader. Hobbes is very good at the game of reasoning. Granted his premises, he is apparently able to derive his deeply unsettling conclusions. The course of argument appears smooth, and the reader is hard-pressed to find flaws in it. The main conclusion, the need for unchecked authority, goes against some of our deepest political convictions. But in Hobbes's works it is tied down with seemingly unbreakable chains of argument.

It is important, however, to realize that Hobbes's conclusions depend unavoidably on his initial premises. As in any deductive system, his reasoning proceeds from particular starting points which are themselves not argued for but taken for granted or assumed as given. If Hobbes's conclusions appear improbable, then, we should examine his premises with great care. Defects in the premises will be passed along through successive stages of argument to the conclusions, thereby calling the entire system into question.

The premises of Hobbes's political theory are derived from his understanding of nature as matter in motion. There are three separate stages in his argument, which are identified above as constituting the "whole of philosophy," Body, Man, and Citizen. Hobbes believes the state must be understood in terms of its component parts, citizens, and these in turn in terms of the matter of which they are constituted. A clear statement of his method is given in the Preface to *De Cive*:

> Concerning my method, I thought it not sufficient to use a plain and evident style in what I have to deliver, except I took my beginning from the very matter of civil government, and thence proceeded to its generation and form, and the first beginning of justice. For everything is best understood by its constitutive causes. For as in a watch,

or some such small engine, the matter, figure, and motion of the wheels cannot well be known, except it be taken insunder and viewed in parts; so to make a more curious search into the rights of states and duties of subjects, it is necessary, I say, not to take them insunder, but yet that they be so considered as if they were dissolved; that is, that we rightly understand what the quality of human nature is, in what matters it is, in what not, fit to make up a civil government, and how men must be agreed amongst themselves that intend to grow up into a well-grounded state. (*DC*, Preface, p. xiv)

The analogy of the watch is important. If you want to discover how such an object functions, in order to make or repair one in the future, it is necessary to take it apart and study its inner workings. Once disassembled, the watch can then be put back together. In Hobbes's eyes, the same is true of states. Though a state cannot actually be taken apart, it must be understood in terms of its constituent parts, its citizens, who must in turn be viewed in terms of their constituent parts, matter in motion. As a materialist, Hobbes views human beings as nothing more than complex machines. Human behavior can be understood according to physical principles, while the workings of a state can also be understood in terms of these principles, as embodied in its citizens.

Accordingly, Hobbes begins each of the three statements of his political philosophy with detailed discussions of human physiology. This occupies the opening chapters of *Elements of Law* and *Leviathan*. Similar material is not found in *De Cive*, but this is because this work was intended to be preceded by two others, one on body and one on man. Though *De Cive* was written before the others, Hobbes did eventually write them also. *De Corpore* (*The Body*) was published in 1655, and *De Homine* (*The Man*) in 1658. Faith in geometrical methods and arguing from body to man to political conclusions are constant features of Hobbes's political philosophy. In *Elements of Law*, speaking of relationships between sovereign and subject, Hobbes describes his work as "the true and only foundation of such science" (*EL*, Ep. Ded., p. 2). He was later to write that "civil philosophy" is "no older . . . than my own book *De Cive*."[6]

SOCIAL CONTRACT THEORY

The classic statement of Hobbes's political theory is *Leviathan*, on which we will concentrate. According to Michael Oakeshott, an important political theorist, "The *Leviathan* is the greatest, perhaps the sole, masterpiece of political philosophy written in the English language."[7] In accordance with his geometric method, Hobbes begins with a detailed discussion of human nature, explained in purely mechanistic terms. Once the nature of man has been laid out, Hobbes justifies his particular conception of political authority by showing that men in a position of association with one another but without political authority would leave this situation, referred to as the state of nature, to erect government. Hobbes's argument commits him to two specific conclusions which we must keep distinct: that men would leave the state of nature to erect *a government*; that they would leave the state of nature to erect *the particular form of government Hobbes advocates*. We will see that Hobbes has an easier time proving the first of these contentions than the second. Though the state of nature is obviously a terrible condition which makes the need for government apparent, it is far from obvious that the only form of government able to alleviate the difficulties is one as powerful as Hobbes recommends. In his attempt to prove the second claim, a good deal depends on the particular way Hobbes frames the state of nature, and so this must be examined in detail.

But before we work through the details of Hobbes's political theory, it is advisable to step back and examine his argumentative strategy. Because the state is erected through some semblance of contractual agreement among its inhabitants, Hobbes's approach is referred to as "social contract theory" (or "contract theory," for short). This approach is central to the Anglo-American tradition of political thought, embodied in such classic documents as *The Declaration of Independence*. Along with John Locke and Jean-Jacques Rousseau, Hobbes is generally viewed as the greatest social contract theorist, though as we shall see, there are significant differences between these thinkers' approaches and the political conclusions they support. In the hands of Hobbes, and later Locke, contract theory presents the distinctive liberal approach to political questions in an especially vivid fashion. In order fully to appreciate Hobbes's argument, we will look into the main features of social contract theory. The defining features of "liberal" political theory and Hobbes's relationship to it will be discussed below, after we have run through the details of his argument.

Social contract theorists appeal to a distinctive yet commonsensical method of justifying political authority. In order to demonstrate the need for political authority, they envision a situation in which it does not exist. The need for government becomes apparent because severe problems arise in its absence. A particular form of government is justified by showing it is the one best suited to solve these specific problems. Accordingly, a social contract argument is in two stages. In the first we envision the prepolitical situation, the "state of nature." There is a certain lack of clarity in many theorists in regard to the state of nature. Theorists tend not to make clear whether they view it as merely an analytical device to justify a particular form of government, or as an actual historical situation out of which our forefathers contracted. In this last case, the social contract (or contract of government) is not merely a hypothetical device. It provides actual historical justification for existing government, much as the Constitutional Convention of 1787 and subsequent ratification process justify the existing government of the United States. In the cases of both Hobbes and Locke, analytical interpretations of the state of nature tend to be intermixed with historical elements. But it seems safe to regard the situation as a purely analytical device. This makes the theorists' arguments much clearer—and sheds light on important tendencies in contemporary political theory—even if this is not entirely faithful to their own understandings of their arguments.[8]

The social contract argument has an additional important component. As we have noted, a specific government is justified by showing it is the best solution to the specific problems encountered in the state of nature. These problems can in turn be traced back to the individuals who inhabit this situation. Social contract theorists construct the state of nature by taking individuals and placing them in a situation without political authority. The problems that arise are therefore due to the nature of the people placed in the natural condition, or to human nature. The social contract argument is accordingly an extremely clear device for drawing connections between three different components of a political theory:

I. a specific view of human nature;
II. consequently, a specific view of the problems that would arise in the absence of political authority;
III. a specific form of government that is best suited to overcome the problems.

The contract argument lays bare the premises of a particular form of state, or contrariwise, the implications of a particular view of human nature. If thinker *A* views human nature in a certain light, he will be committed to uphold a certain form of state. Thinker *B*, with a somewhat different view of human nature, will support a somewhat different state, and so on.

For Hobbes, who wishes to justify a particularly powerful government, the problems that arise in the absence of government must be severe. Because these problems result from placing people alongside one another without benefit of government, the inherent defects in human nature must be similarly grave. As we will see in the next chapter, the case is somewhat different for Locke. Because he wishes to justify more limited government, the problems he depicts in the state of nature are less grievous than those of Hobbes. Accordingly, in his view, the defects in human nature are also less severe.

In regard to the fundamental question of political justification, social contract theory is of great relevance to contemporary readers. Once familiar with the approach, the reader can ask important questions about her own society. To ascertain the specific form of government she supports, the reader should attempt to envision the specific problems that would arise in the absence of political authority. Her preferred form of government can then be justified by showing it is the one best suited to deal with the problems. In order to test Hobbes's conclusions the reader should attempt to imagine what *she* would do in Hobbes's state of nature. She must decide whether, if she were in the state of nature Hobbes describes, *she* would contract out of it and set up a government. Again, two distinct questions must be kept in mind here: whether she would agree to set up *a government*; and whether she would agree to set up *the particular form of government Hobbes advocates*. As we have noted, for Hobbes's argument to be convincing the reader must not only accept the need for government but for Hobbes's recommended form. Because this conclusion is strongly at odds with the political beliefs of most Americans, and citizens of the other Western democracies, the reader should be careful about accepting Hobbes's arguments until they have been carefully scrutinized. But Hobbes would doubtless say that his method is intended to demonstrate improbable conclusions. Just as in geometry, what at first sight appears impossible can be rendered compelling through a series of convincing logical steps.

For Hobbes's argument to work, a great deal depends on his particular characterization of the state of nature—and so of human nature. If a contract theorist wishes to support a particular form of government, he can do so by showing it is best suited to overcome the problems of the state of nature, *as he describes it*. Obviously, he can strengthen his case by carefully constructing his state of nature to make sure his preferred government is especially well suited to deal with its problems. Thus in addition to examining the choice of government people in the state of nature would make, we must look into Hobbes's depiction of the state of nature and whether it corresponds to what *we* imagine conditions would be like in the absence of government. A contract argument can be used to justify any form of government including anarchism. Anarchism is a social-political theory that advocates an absence of government. To support this conclusion, a theorist must demonstrate that the problems in the state of nature can be dealt with satisfactorily without relying on government. Accordingly, for an anarchist, the defects in human nature must be relatively slight. Otherwise, without government, defective human beings would come into conflict, which government would then be required to resolve.

THE STATE OF NATURE

The main premises of Hobbes's political theory lie in his distinctive view of human nature, supported by his mechanistic view of the world. As we have noted, Hobbes views the world as constituted entirely of matter in motion. He gives a purely mechanistic account of human psychology. Sensation results from contact between the sense organs and outside matter, whether the result is sight, touch, taste, hearing, or smell. All contents of the mind originate through sense perception. This explains imagination, which Hobbes calls "decaying sense" (*Lev.*, Chap. 2, p. 15), memory, and dreams. Especially important is Hobbes's view of appetite. Men are naturally attracted to certain objects, as for example, food, and naturally repelled by others. According to Hobbes, that to which we are attracted we call "good"; that to which we are averse we refer to as "bad." Attraction to something is accompanied by pleasure, aversion by pain. Thus we have two trains of association: appetite, attraction, pleasure, and good; aversion, repulsion, pain, and bad. This explains the basic use of moral terms. "Good" and "bad" have their meaning not in reference to things themselves or their inherent qualities, but from how we respond to them, whether we are attracted to them or repelled, given pleasure or pain: "For these words of Good, Evil, and Contemptible, are ever used with relation to the person that useth them: there being nothing simply and absolutely so; nor any common Rule of Good and Evil, to be taken from the nature of the objects themselves" (*Lev.*, Chap. 6, p. 39).

There is no objective goodness or badness found in nature or the nature of things. Goodness and its opposite are qualities ascribed to entities by people who experience them. Though people are alike in certain respects and so tend to view particular entities similarly, they also differ, in which cases the same things are regarded by some people as good and others as bad: "Good and Evil are names that signify our Appetites and Aversions; which in different tempers, customs and doctrines of men are different . . ." (*Lev.*, Chap. 15, p. 110).

Hobbes holds that human beings are striving creatures, driven by their appetites. Accordingly, life is motion. Happiness lies in the satisfaction of appetites. But this is not a one-time occurrence. Appetites are incessant; once satisfied, they begin to rise again, demanding renewed satisfaction:

> Continual success in obtaining those things which a man from time to time desireth, this is to say, continual prospering, is that men call FELICITY; I mean the Felicity of this life. For there is no such thing as perpetual Tranquility of mind, while we live here; because Life it self is but Motion, and can never be without Desire, nor without Fear, no more than without Sense. (*Lev.*, Chap. 6, p. 46)

Therefore happiness is not a stable condition. It does not lie "in the repose of a mind satisfied," but in "a continuall progress" of desire, from one object to another, endlessly (*Lev.*, Chap., 11, p. 70).

Hobbes holds that thought is spurred by desire. Desire supplies the ends we wish for, but once an end is given, the mind seeks out the means to attain it: "Thoughts are to the Desires as Scouts and Spies, to range abroad and find the way to the things Desired" (*Lev.*, Chap. 8, p. 53). As deliberation is concerned with achieving what we want, the will is described as "the last Appetite in Deliberating" (*Lev.*, Chap. 6, p. 45). It too is determined by desires. Hobbes believes the reasoning faculty develops with experience; from following specific courses of action in order to attain desired objects, people develop expectations about the future course of events and how to attain them again. What is crucial here is that people come to understand that satisfaction of desires is always temporary. Thus while one is satisfying a given desire, he cannot enjoy the experience fully. For he is aware the desire will recur and demand satisfaction anew. In addition to worrying about securing the means to present satisfaction, he must also provide for future satisfaction:

> [T]he object of man's desire is not to enjoy once only and for one instant of time, but to assure for ever the way of his future desire. And therefore the voluntary actions and inclinations of all men tend not only to the procuring but also to the assuring of a contented life. (*Lev.*, Chap., 11, p. 70)

Hobbes holds that the means necessary to satisfy desires are scarce and so there is competition for them. Thus one must not only worry about securing means but also about protecting them from other people, which requires power. Power is relative to other people. If there is competition for a given good, John will be able to secure it only if he has more power than Jane. Therefore in addition to worrying about securing the means to the good, John must worry about being more powerful than Jane. Thus power is also a means to goods, and so there is competition for power as well. In the highly rhetorical style of *Leviathan*, Hobbes gives a classic account of the result:

> So that in the first place I put for a general inclination of all mankind a perpetual and restless desire of Power after power, that ceaseth only in Death. And the cause of this is not always that a man hopes for a more intensive delight than he has already attained to or that he cannot be content with a moderate power, but because he cannot assure the power and means to live well, which he hath present, without the acquisition of more. (*Lev.*, Chap. 11, p. 70)

The need for power arises because each individual will view other people primarily as obstacles to his own satisfaction. What people need to satisfy desires is, once again, scarce, so competition is inevitable. In this competition, all people enjoy similar advantages, in the fundamental respect that each has the ability to kill others and cannot be assured of not being killed by them (*Lev.*, Chap. 13, p. 87).

Under these circumstances full-scale conflict between people is inevitable, a war of all against all. There are three specific causes of conflict. First is competition. Things people need to satisfy their appetites are scarce, and so competed over. Because a person's power depends on what others think of him, people's opinions are important and so a second source of conflict. Hobbes refers to this as "glory." If *A* devalues *B*, *B* has an incentive to strike at *A*, to raise his standing in the eyes of his fellows, and so to improve his ability to get what he needs. The third source of strife is fear. Self-preservation is the supreme good in the Hobbesian moral system. Regardless of our other beliefs and values, we all wish to live. Life has no ultimate purpose beyond itself, while life is necessary for the achievement of all other purposes. Because *A* views other people as his enemies and fears they may attack him, and perhaps kill him, he has an incentive to strike at them first. From this combination of competition and uncertainty a truly hellish condition emerges, which is described by Hobbes in one of the most famous passages in all of political theory:

> Whatseover therefore is consequent to a time of War, where every man is Enemy to every man, the same is consequent to the time wherein men live without other security than what their own strength and their own invention shall furnish them withall. In such condition there is no place for Industry, because the fruit thereof is uncertain; and consequently no Culture of the Earth; no Navigation, nor use of the commodities that may be imported by Sea; no commodious Building; no Instruments of moving and removing such things as require much force; no Knowledge of the face of the Earth; no account of Time; no Arts; no Letters; no Society; and which is worst of all, continual fear and danger of violent death; and the life of man, solitary, poor, nasty, brutish, and short. (*Lev.*, Chap. 13, p. 89)

The essence of the state of nature for Hobbes is the absence of political authority, and so the factors we have noted are able to spiral toward wholesale conflict and chaos. Lest we doubt the plausibility of his account, Hobbes presents evidence of what happens "during the time men live without a common Power to keep them all in awe" (*Lev.*, Chap. 13, p. 88). When taking journeys, people arm themselves; when going to sleep, they lock their doors. They also lock their chests against servants. Such actions afford clear testimony of what people think about other people's reliability. Actual circumstances corresponding to the state of nature are also familiar. The "savage people in many places of America . . . live at this day in that brutish manner." The state of nature is found in so-called civilized Europe as well. This is especially apparent in interstate relations. States too exist without a common power to keep them all in awe. Accordingly, they "are in continual jealousies and in the state and posture of Gladiators, having their weapons pointing and their eyes fixed on one another, that is, their Forts, Garrisons, and Guns upon the Frontiers of their Kingdoms." But countries escape the horrors of the full-blown state of nature internally. Because their governments are able to keep order within their borders, the ongoing state of war with other countries is not accompanied by the same degree of misery as in Hobbes's classic description (*Lev.*, Chap. 13., pp. 89–90).

Hobbes's account of the state of nature is undoubtedly sobering, even shocking. It only makes matters worse for the reader to reflect on the causes of the condition. This situation is not brought about because man is *evil*, as for example according to the doctrine of original sin espoused by St. Augustine and other Christian thinkers. Hobbes does not believe people are evil or that they enjoy harming others or causing suffering for its own sake:

> *Contempt*, or little sense of the calamity of others, is that which men call CRUELTY, proceeding from Security of their own fortune. For that any man should take pleasure in other men's great harms without other end of his own, I do not conceive it possible. (*Lev.*, Chap. 6, pp. 43–44)

According to Hobbes's iron logic, people behave as they do in the state of nature because it is the only *rational* way to behave. Given a scarcity of necessary objects and fear of and competition with other people, to behave differently is to place oneself at a disadvantage, perhaps to engineer one's own destruction. If Miguel *wishes* to trust other people, he can perhaps behave differently. But Henry would be a fool to trust Miguel. What if Miguel is only pretending to be cooperative, waiting for Henry to let down his guard so he can then strike? Henry cannot afford to take this chance. It could after all cost him his life, and life is the supreme value. Thus, even if Miguel makes friendly overtures to other people, they would be fools to trust him—and so he would be foolish to be friendly. It only takes a few ruthless, untrustworthy people in the state of nature to force everyone else to be constantly on guard. People are able to learn from experience. One thing experience teaches is that if you let down your guard to the wrong person at the wrong time, the consequences could be disastrous.

We have seen something approximating Hobbes's state of nature in international relations. During the forty-year period of intense competition between the former Soviet Union and the Western powers, each side poured hundreds of billions of dollars into weapons that could not possibly be used. As the number of nuclear warheads climbed into the thousands, it became apparent to all concerned that nuclear war would have unimaginable consequences. But each side was afraid to begin the process of disarmament—or even to slow the pace of weapons construction—for fear this would leave it vulnerable. The example of Hitler showed the costs of trusting an opponent who had no intention of abiding by his agreements.

The central teaching of Machiavelli, discussed in the last chapter, is relevant here. You can afford to keep faith with others only if you are sure they will keep faith with you. But can you ever be sure? Even if they *wish* to keep faith with you, how can they trust you? Perhaps you and they can mutually pledge adherence. Hobbes refers to a promise that requires performance in the future as a covenant. But even if Barbara and Lara enter into a solemn covenant, how can they trust one another to keep it? "Covenants without the Sword are but Words, and of no strength to secure a man at all" (*Lev.*, Chap. 17, p. 117). Thus all parties in the state of nature must continue to arm, regardless of how they feel about this, even if this increases the likelihood of the ultimate destruction of everyone concerned. The only way out of the impasse is to change the overall situation so it becomes safe to make peace. Peaceful gestures put one at risk of being exploited. And so one needs a guarantee that this will not happen. In the meantime, however, the *rational* strategy is to prepare for war. Hobbes's reasoning is especially telling in the current international setting, because the consequences of nuclear war would indeed make life "nasty, brutish, and short."

Because Hobbes's method places so much weight on his initial starting points, we should pause and consider distinctive aspects of these. Hobbes's account of human psychology proceeds through a large number of small, precise accounts and descriptions of different faculties, many in the form of definitions. Reasoning for Hobbes is necessarily done by means of words and so he believes it is important to become clear on questions of definition (*Lev.*, Chap. 5). Even if we concede, however, that no single description or definition Hobbes presents is especially objectionable, the results of his accumulated contentions must strike us as unusual. The picture of human nature Hobbes provides is strikingly one-sided; it omits many familiar, important features of human life.

Two particular points bear mention. First, Hobbesian man is extremely self-interested. As Hobbes writes in Chapter 14 of *Leviathan*, "of the voluntary acts of every man, the object is *some Good to himself*" (p. 93). Accordingly, Hobbes's account of human motivation leaves little room for fellow-feeling, whether benevolence toward other people or stronger impulses of love and willingness to sacrifice for close family members. Indeed, as we will see below, Hobbes depicts relationships between parents and children and husbands and wives as based on the same combination of fear and contractual agreement that characterizes relationships between rulers and subjects in political society.

Hobbes's orientation is, in addition, exclusively towards this world. Faced with the spectre and then the reality of religious civil war, Hobbes views religious inclinations as destructive of human order and combats them in his writings. As we have noted, Hobbes paid increasing attention to this theme as political events unfolded. Approximately half of *Leviathan* is given over to devaluing religious motivations. Throughout the early chapters of the work, where human psychology is explored, Hobbes repeatedly criticizes religious beliefs as vain and absurd. The reason for this is clear. Motivated by fear for their preservation in the state of nature, people will be willing to enter into civil society. But religious considerations can immeasurably complicate matters. If Juan cares for the well-being of his soul as well as preserving his life—perhaps as much or more than self-preservation—then he is likely to attach religious conditions to a government he is willing to accept. If many people feel this way—as indeed many did during Hobbes's day—the result is likely to be the same civil war he sought to allay. Accordingly, Hobbes argues that such motivations are based on confusion, especially misunderstanding the meaning of words. But this is not enough if Hobbes's political argument is to be persuasive. His account of human motivation must correspond to the facts with which his readers are familiar. This is essential if he is to convince them that *they too* should accept the particular form of government he recommends, though they have not previously realized this.

If Hobbes's account of the state of nature is unconvincing, this will have severe consequences for his political project. If we believe his account of human beings is not plausible and so must be redrawn, this revised account of the state of nature will justify different political relations. A state of nature dramatically different from the one Hobbes depicts will justify a government to which he would undoubtedly be opposed.

THE LAWS OF NATURE

The state of nature Hobbes describes is obviously intolerable. Confronted with it, individuals would do everything possible to leave, including accepting a powerful government. To confirm this claim the reader has only to imagine what *he* would do in this situation. Obviously, Hobbes's grim characterization is intended to justify his preferred state. If the natural condition were less horrific, people would be less likely to accept the form of government Hobbes recommends.

If we grant that the state of nature is as Hobbes describes, then the obvious question is how we can escape it. Two human faculties are sources of hope: reason, which includes the ability to learn from experience, and fear of violent death.

Hobbes presents the way out of the state of nature in two stages. First, on the basis of reason and experience, inhabitants conclude that its problems result from the way people behave. Obsessed with the threat of others, people recognize no limits in pursuit of security and the objects of their desires. But in spite of this, there is a set of obvious rules, which, *if people would follow them*, would put an end to the state of nature and its horrors. Hobbes refers to these rules as "laws of nature."

The rules Hobbes has in mind are intended to be in general form. They identify courses of action which, if followed by everyone alike, would lead everyone beyond the state of nature. The main thrust of the rules is obvious, as the reader will recognize. The state of nature is intolerable because of its absence of security. If everyone would recognize limits and refrain from attacking other people, all would be better off. The laws of nature, then, are rules of self-preservation:

> A Law of nature (*Lex naturalis*) is a Precept or general Rule, found out by Reason, by which a man is forbidden to do that which is destructive of his life, or taketh away the means of preserving the same, and to omit that by which he thinketh it may be best preserved. (*Lev.*, Chap. 14, p. 91)

Though Hobbes refers to the precepts in question as "laws of nature," they differ from laws of nature as they were traditionally understood in crucial respects we will examine. But we should note that, like traditional laws of nature, they are conclusions people are able to arrive at through the unaided use of their reasoning powers.[9] In discussing these throughout the remainder of this chapter, I will use the terms "laws of nature" and "natural law" interchangeably.

Hobbes's laws of nature are in conditional form. They declare what must be done in order to ensure survival. Given the horrors of the state of nature, their content is apparent. The individual must be willing to make whatever sacrifices are necessary to leave this situation for the security of civil society. Accordingly, the first law of nature is that "every man ought to endeavor Peace, as far as he has hope of obtaining it; and when he cannot obtain it, that he may seek and use all helps and advantages of War" (*Lev.*, Chap. 14, p. 92). The second law follows from this. In order to achieve peace, people must be willing to give up some of the rights they enjoy in the state of nature:

> That a man be willing, when others are so too, as far-forth as for Peace and defense of himself he shall think it necessary, to lay down this right to all things, and be contented with so much liberty against other men as he would allow other men against himself. (*Lev.*, Chap. 14, p. 92)

We will discuss exactly what Hobbes means by the "right to all things" below.

Numerous specific injunctions follow from these general rules. In order to achieve and preserve peace, all people must abide by certain moral precepts, and so there are additional laws of nature (presented in *Leviathan*, Chapter 15). The third is the need to keep one's covenants, or in Hobbes's terms, to be just, as violating covenants is paradigmatically unjust (p. 100). The fourth law concerns gratitude; the fifth is that one should accommodate himself, or try to get along with other people. The sixth is the need to pardon offenses against one. Hobbes presents nineteen laws of nature in all, which he summarizes as the golden rule (in its negative formulation): "Do not that to another which thou wouldst not have done to thy self" (p. 109).

We can employ a thought experiment to test Hobbes's claim that his natural laws are theorems of reason conducive to self-preservation. Imagine *you* were in the state of nature as Hobbes describes it. Clearly, you would realize that if everyone were willing to abide by simple rules of conduct, everyone would be immeasurably better off. The rules in question are easily discovered. What must people do in order to get along? Clearly, they must refrain from taking advantage of one another and be willing to make peace. A number of specific attitudes and courses of conduct follow from these general precepts. As Hobbes indicates, these boil down to the golden rule: People should not treat others as they do not wish to be treated. Accordingly, Hobbes believes the content of the natural laws is easily accessible to reason.

The precise thrust of Hobbes's laws of nature can be clarified in the light of his intellectual context. At the time he was writing, there was great disagreement about the possibility of objective moral rules. People had discovered that moral precepts varied greatly from country to country, region to region. In his famous *Essays* Montaigne wrote: "What truth is that which these Mountains bound, and is a lie in the world beyond them?"[10] But in opposition to this view, Hobbes believes in the existence of one clear moral truth, the need for self-preservation, which is the basis for all other values. Hobbes says that the study of his laws of nature "is the true and only Moral Philosophy" (*Lev.*, Chap. 15, p. 110). The natural laws are true because they are not rooted in the beliefs or customs of particular countries, but hold in all countries. Everyone, no matter what his other beliefs, wants to live. This is a matter of nature, not custom. As peace is conducive to self-preservation, war is its deadly enemy and must be avoided. This too is not custom or local belief but demonstrable moral truth. As reason tells us we must avoid war, so it also tells us how to do so. Anyone who thinks carefully about the matter will realize that certain modes of conduct promote peace, and others war. Thus the need for the former conduct is clear: "The Laws of Nature are Immutable and Eternal . . . For it can never be that War shall preserve life and Peace destroy it" (*Lev.*, Chap. 15, p. 110).

Though the precepts in question promote peace and self-preservation, Hobbes believes they are not "laws" in the proper sense of the term. He holds that laws are necessarily supported by force. The maker of laws must have the power to compel obedience: "Law properly is the word of him that by right hath command over others" (*Lev.*, Chap. 15, p. 111). The laws of nature are theorems of reason rather than laws, properly speaking, because they merely tell us what we should do in order to survive. They are not commands of a superior power who can force us to obey them—except in the eyes of some people who view them as commands of God.[11]

The fact that the laws of nature are not laws, properly speaking, suggests why they cannot by themselves rescue people from the state of nature. Because they are not commanded by a power able to enforce them, the penalty for disobeying them is not clear. Keeping covenants, for instance, is necessary for peace. But we have noted the danger of keeping one's covenants without assurance other people will also keep theirs. If Luis keeps his covenants, this will make it easier for others to take advantage of him. Even if Bob has good feelings towards Luis and wishes to cooperate, Bob knows he cannot really trust Luis, that this would leave *him* vulnerable. Though the laws of nature are precepts of reason that promote peace, circumstances in the state of nature are such that one person cannot afford to obey them unless he is certain everyone else will also obey. Failing this, adherence to the precepts will bring about one's destruction rather than preservation. Hobbes argues, accordingly, that the laws of nature are not binding in the state of nature:

> The Laws of Nature oblige *in foro interno*; that is to say, they bind to a desire they should take place; but *in foro externo*, that is to the putting them in act, not always.

For he that should be modest and tractable and perform all he promises in such time and place where no man else should do so, should but make himself a prey to others and procure his own certain ruin, contrary to the ground of all Laws of Nature, which tend to Nature's preservation. (*Lev.*, Chap. 15, p. 110)

Before the laws of nature can bind, they must be transformed into laws in the proper sense of the term. They must be supported by a power strong enough to enforce obedience.

The fact that the laws of nature do not bind in the state of nature follows from their conditional character. In this sense they differ from traditional natural laws. Theories of natural law have been at the heart of Western political philosophy since the time of the ancient Greeks. Though different thinkers have presented somewhat different accounts of natural law, they have generally agreed on some central points. The heart of a traditional doctrine of natural law is a set of moral precepts, which are regarded as objectively true, discoverable by reason, and binding everywhere—at all times, in all places. This is the essence of the view as first propounded by Stoic philosophers in the third century B.C. This is also the view of St. Thomas Aquinas, the great thirteenth-century philosopher, who presents a classic discussion of natural law in his *Summa Theologiae*. During the medieval period, natural law came to be combined with important moral rules contained in the Bible, notably the Ten Commandments. Many (if not all) of the commandments struck people as obviously true and so were considered natural laws as well as divine commands. But note the form of the commandments: "Thou shalt not steal"; "Thou shalt not kill"; and so on. These are *unconditional* commands, binding everywhere and always. Presumably, the author of the commands is God, who has the power to enforce them. In contrast, Hobbes's laws of nature are *conditional*. As theorems of reason, they point out the means to a desired end, self-preservation. If properly filled out, a given Hobbesian natural law would say: "*if you would preserve yourself,* then seek peace," or "*if you would preserve yourself,* then keep your covenants." These are a far cry from traditional formulations of these precepts: "seek peace"; "perform your covenants." Because they are conditional, Hobbes's laws of nature do not bind in the state of nature. Following them would lead to destruction rather than self-preservation.

A good idea of traditional natural law can be gathered from one of its classic statements, as presented by Cicero in his *De Re Publica* (which was written around the year 50 B.C.):

There is in fact a true law—namely right reason—which is in accordance with nature, applies to all men, and is unchangeable and eternal. By its commands this law summons men to the performance of their duties; by its prohibitions it restrains them from doing wrong. Its commands and prohibitions always influence good men, but are without effect upon the bad. To invalidate this law by human legislation is never morally right, nor is it permissible ever to restrict its operation, and to annul it wholly is impossible. Neither the senate nor the people can absolve us from our obligation to obey this law, and it requires no Sextus Aelius [a noted legal scholar] to expound and interpret it. It will not lay down one rule at Rome and another at Athens, nor will it be one rule today and another tomorrow. But there will be one law, eternal and unchangeable, binding at all times upon all peoples; and there will be, as it were, one common master and ruler of men, namely God, who is the author of this law, its interpreter, and its sponsor. The man who will not obey it will abandon his better self, and, in denying the true nature of a man, will thereby suffer the severest of penalties, though he has escaped all the other consequences which men call punishment. (*De Re Publica*, III, p. 22)[12]

The idea that the law of nature is a transcendent principle, decreed and enforced by God, is absent from Hobbes's account. But, like Cicero, he believes laws of nature are discoverable by reason and bind everywhere, though only in conscience, not in action, when there is no power to enforce them.

It is not hard to ascertain Hobbes's motive for employing the traditional *language* of the laws of nature in his political writings while altering the doctrine in important ways. Hobbes believes people act on the basis of their beliefs. In order to ensure political tranquility, it is important to propagate an accurate understanding of the proper relationship between rulers and subjects. Hobbes holds that the lack of such understanding was an important cause of the English Civil War. People were misled by various writers, ancient and modern, who argued that the power of rulers is limited, that they can be resisted and even overthrown for improper conduct. In *Leviathan* and his other political works, Hobbes attempts to demonstrate that this view of political relationships is not only incorrect but dangerous. He believes political power must be, in effect, unlimited. In order to bolster his position, *he systematically reinterprets central components of the traditional arguments for limited authority.* According to many traditional theorists, natural law is an important limit on the ruler's power. Hobbes therefore reinterprets natural law to remove its limiting force. He believes traditional doctrines of natural law and related notions are unscientific and incorrect. One of his main purposes is to correct their errors, and so he presents what he believes is a correct account of natural law—and of other notions we will encounter below. By making natural laws conditional and arguing that they do not bind in the state of nature, Hobbes attempts to reduce their force, and so their ability to cause political mischief.

The political heart of a theory of natural law is the relationship between laws of nature and positive laws. The latter are those made by the appropriate authorities, which bind the subjects of a given territory. According to traditional natural law doctrine, positive laws must be in keeping with natural laws or else lose their binding force.[13] This is seen in the above quotation, as Cicero says that it is never right to invalidate nature's law by human operation, and that it cannot be annulled. The classic statement of the relationship between natural and positive laws is given by St. Thomas Aquinas. According to St. Thomas, natural laws are general precepts which are applied to the particular features of different territories through positive laws. For example, reason tells us we should not steal, but exactly what constitutes stealing and the specific circumstances under which one can and cannot take another person's property must be determined by a particular legislature.[14] It necessarily follows from this view that acceptable positive laws must be in accordance with natural laws. If they are not, then subjects are not obligated to follow them. To support this contention, St. Thomas quotes an injunction of St. Augustine: "that which is not just seems to be no law at all."[15] Hobbes clearly wishes to avoid this sort of check on the ruler's power. In addition to reformulating natural laws so they bind only conditionally, he argues that they are rightfully interpreted only by the ruler. Thus the possibility of conflict between natural and positive laws can be eliminated. We will return to this subject below, in connection with the powers of the ruler.

In addition to laws of nature, Hobbes discusses the "right of nature." His introduction to this subject is as follows:

> The Right of Nature . . . is the Liberty each man hath to use his own power as he will himself, for the preservation of his own Nature; that is to say, of his own Life; and consequently, of doing any thing, which in his own Judgment and Reason he shall conceive to be the aptest means thereunto. (*Lev.*, Chap. 14, p. 91)

As the quotation indicates, Hobbes believes people in the state of nature are not effectively bound by moral precepts. We have seen that self-preservation is the foundation of all morality. In the state of nature, with everyone constantly threatened, people must take drastic steps to preserve themselves, and under these circumstances each person must be the judge of what is necessary. Clearly, nobody can trust anyone else to decide these matters for him.

In this regard too the state of nature is a state of war. According to the familiar saying, "All's fair in love and war." Because people must attempt to preserve themselves by hook or by crook, in Hobbes's words, "Force and Fraud are in war the two Cardinal virtues" (*Lev.*, Chap. 13, p. 90). We have seen that the individual is able to discover natural laws through the use of his reason. But even if he knows that everyone would be better off if certain precepts were generally followed, he also realizes that he cannot afford to follow them, and the same is true of everyone else. Because the laws of nature, which are the sole basis of morality, do not bind in the state of nature, this condition is devoid of right and wrong. Hobbes says that in the war of all against all, "nothing can be Unjust. The notions of Right and Wrong, Justice and Injustice have there no place. Where there is no common Power, there is no Law; where no Law, no Injustice" (*Lev.*, Chap. 13, p. 90). In this condition, property is insecure, because there is no authority to enforce the rules. Thus "there be no Propriety, no Dominion, no Mine and Thine." Consequently, there can be no theft or stealing. The only "property" rule that does hold is "that to be every man's that he can get, and for so long as he can keep it" (*Lev.*, Chap. 13, p. 90). Even if there were rules of property, it follows from what we have seen that a person could not afford to respect them, unless everyone else did so as well. But of course, in the absence of authority, there are no rules everyone will respect. Because the right to all things allows whatever one thinks necessary for survival, it is without limits: "It followeth, that in such a condition every man has a Right to every thing, even to one another's body" (*Lev.*, Chap. 14, p. 91).

The problem, however, is that a right of this sort amounts to very little. If everyone has a right to all things, this in effect means that no one has any rights. In the state of nature, Philippe has a right to an apple he finds, because he is hungry and needs it to preserve himself. But there are no rules of property to which he can appeal to prevent other people from taking it. They too have rights to the apple, and so there will be a struggle for it. In a situation in which everyone has rights to everything, no one has *exclusive rights* to anything—including his own body. Our conception of property centers on the notion of exclusive rights. My car is mine not only because I can do what I want with it, but I can prevent other people from using it. Because it is mine, they must obtain my permission to use it. I can, in other words, exclude them from my property.

In the Hobbesian state of nature, there are no exclusive rights. Sally has a right to what she can get, but because she cannot prevent other people from exercising their similar rights, she can make use of her "property" only as long as she can keep it from them. A lack of secure property has severe implications. For example, it means there will be no farming. If someone grows a crop, what is to prevent other people from making off with it? Clearly, what is needed is an authority able to untangle conflicting rights. Each person must give up the right to *all* things, in exchange for exclusive rights to *certain* things. This would obviously be far better for all concerned. But again, no single person can afford to surrender his rights unless he is sure everyone else will do the same.

Thus the situation in regard to property and the right to all things is similar to that in regard to the laws of nature. Everyone can understand what must be done, but no one can afford to do it. Unless the overall situation is changed, the necessary precepts cannot be followed. Rules alone are not enough. Also required is a power strong enough to force people to abide by them. If there were such a power, Viktor could keep his covenants, because he would be assured everyone else would do the same. If he wished to farm, he could grow a crop, because under a stable property system, the fruit of his labor would belong to him. A stable set of rules would provide an environment in which the amenities of civilized life could begin to be produced.

This line of argument explains the need for government. According to Hobbes, government must perform two main functions. As we have seen, it must enforce obedience to the laws of nature, so that everyone can afford to follow them. Indeed, once a ruler is chosen, he will punish violations of these laws and so adherence will be not only possible but mandatory. In addition, the ruler must determine exactly what the laws of nature say. Hobbes views people as self-interested. Though the basic contents of natural law can be ascertained by all alike, each person will understand it in a way that favors himself. We have seen that Hobbes views the reasoning faculty as a servant to desire. Therefore a single authoritative interpretation of the laws of nature is necessary. Hobbes does not believe in the possibility of *neutral* reason that is able to give an objectively true, or even a generally acceptable, interpretation. He expresses this sentiment most clearly in *Elements of Law.*

> For in these things private judgments may differ, and beget controversy. This common measure, some say, is right reason, with whom I should consent, if there were any such thing to be found or known *in rerum natura* [in the nature of things]. But commonly they that call for right reason to decide any controversy do mean their own. (*EL*, 2.10.8)

Disagreement about the laws of nature is inevitable, because of self-interest. Confronted with controversy, each person naturally prefers his own interpretation. After all, it seems correct to him. Only with the erection of government can a single, generally accepted interpretation of the laws of nature be produced. This will be in the form of the civil laws, which Hobbes views as the ruler's interpretation of the natural laws. As long as the government has sufficient force, it can compel obedience to these laws, and so put an end to the horrors of the Hobbesian state of nature.

THE CONTRACT OF GOVERNMENT

Because of the factors we have discussed, individuals in the state of nature are willing to leave it for civil society. Though this requires renunciation of their right to all things, they are willing to trade this for the security the state of nature lacks. Once again, it is essential to Hobbes's argument that the state of nature be viewed as so terrible that people will accept virtually any form of government in its place, including an unlimited authority. But it is not enough to show that such a government is acceptable; it must also be shown to be the preferred political system.

In order to set up a government, people must make agreements with one another. But the situation is tricky. Without a power to enforce them, agreements in the state of nature are only words, with no power to bind a man at all. Hobbes's state of nature is beset with a chicken-and-egg problem. There cannot be binding agreements without a government to enforce them, but government cannot arise without binding agreements. In order to escape from this dilemma, all individuals in the state of nature must agree simultaneously to set up a government, while this very act creates an agency to enforce the agreements out of which it arises.

To erect a state, each individual must enter into a covenant with every other. As noted above, a covenant is a contractual agreement which binds at least one party to some future performance. The precise form the covenant takes is as if everyone says the following formula to every other man: "*I Authorize and give up my Right of Governing my self to this Man or to this Assembly of Men, on this condition, that thou give up thy Right to him and Authorize all his actions in like manner*" (*Lev.*, Chap. 17, p. 120). The agreement can be used to set up different types of governments. Though Hobbes prefers monarchy, political power can also be put in the hands of an assembly of men. But we can set this complication aside for the remainder of this chapter and speak of the ruler or monarch, under the assumption it is a king rather than an assembly.

The particular agreement through which government arises is the centerpiece of Hobbes's political theory in *Leviathan*. At first sight, its main features are extremely peculiar. But they can be understood in the light of Hobbes's intentions and his historical situation. Hobbes's intention is straightforward. The contract is designed to create the most powerful government possible. Its details are directed towards this end. Even if the form of this agreement strikes us as unusual, Hobbes's argument is that people in the state of nature would accept it, because they wish to create such a government, and this particular agreement is the best way to do so.

The details themselves are best explained in historical terms. In the previous section, we saw that unusual features of Hobbes's doctrine of natural law should be understood in the light of traditional doctrines of natural law, which Hobbes wishes to undermine. The situation is similar in regard to the agreement that creates government. As with natural law, Hobbes can be seen to appropriate traditional language of the contract of government. But because his intention is to empty the traditional doctrine of its substance, his account departs from this in important respects.

In this section, we will examine three particular components of the traditional contract and how Hobbes revises them. The three are: (i) the traditional contract of government; (ii) the role of the "people" in the contract; and (iii) traditional notions of consent. To close the section, we will also look briefly at Hobbes's important distinction between two ways political power is attained, through "institution" and "acquisition." We begin with the contract of government.

Hobbes defines a "contract" as "a mutual transferring of Right" (*Lev.*, Chap. 14, p. 94). A contract between Saul and Bill gives rise to mutual obligations. The obligation of each party is conditional upon performance by the other. For example, suppose Saul sells his car to Bill. Saul agrees to sign the car over, if Bill pays him $1,000. If Saul does not deliver the car, Bill has no obligation to pay; if Bill refuses to pay, Saul has no obligation to deliver the car. The doctrine of the social contract (or contract of government, terms I will generally use interchangeably) became a central feature of Western political theory, through extension of the notion of contract, familiar from private law, to public, political situations.[16] The relationship between ruler and subjects was conceived on the model of a contract like that between Saul and Bill. The central idea is that the power of the ruler is conditional; it holds only as long as the ruler meets certain requirements. In general, the contract of government was appealed to in order to limit rulers' power, in extreme cases to justify removing them from office.

An early proponent of the contract of government was Manegold of Lautenbach, a Saxon monk, who wrote in opposition to the German emperor, Henry IV, during the eleventh century. According to Manegold, the ruler's power is derived from the people, who elevated him to his position in order to combat evildoers and promote justice. When the ruler ceases to perform these tasks and becomes evil himself, "is it not clear that he deservedly falls from the dignity conceded to him and that the people are free from his lordship and from subjection to him since it is evident that he first broke the compact by virtue of which he was appointed?" Manegold supports this argument with a simple comparison:

> To take an example from a meaner sphere, if a man hired someone for a fair wage to look after his swine and then found that he was not caring for them but stealing, killing and destroying them, would not the man withhold the promised wage from him and remove him ignominiously from his task of caring for the swine? Now, if this is observed in base things, that a man who does not care for his swine but destroys them shall not be kept as a swineherd, are there not just and reasonable grounds for maintaining that, in proportion as humans differ from swine, so too it is more fitting that anyone who does not strive to rule his subjects but rather to lead them into error should be deprived of the power and authority over men that he has received?[17]

Manegold likens the position of a ruler to that of any employee of the people. A swineherd is hired conditionally. He keeps his job and enjoys its benefits only as long as he performs satisfactorily. The same is true of a gardener, a groundskeeper, a butler, or a maid. Viewing a king or emperor in a similar light can justify dismissing him as well. If he violates the terms of his office, he loses his authority. Taking the matter one step farther, if he attempts to cling to power through force, the contract argument will support using force against him.

In the period between the eleventh century and the time of Hobbes, contract arguments took on added sophistication and force. For our purposes, the most important developments occurred during the sixteenth century, spurred by religious conflicts of the Reformation.[18] Throughout the Middle Ages, the most common view of the relationship between ruler and subjects was that the ruler was put in place by God and could not be resisted by his subjects. This position receives strong Biblical support from Chapter 13 of St. Paul's Epistle to the Romans, probably the single most important text in medieval political theory. In part, the passage reads:

> Let every person be subject to the governing authorities. For there is no authority except from God, and those that exist have been instituted by God. Therefore he who resists

he will discuss contracts. But while using their language, he empties the doctrines in question of their traditional substance. His natural law and contract are intended *not* to bind the ruler. His use of traditional natural law and contract terminology should be viewed as a rhetorical device, intended to increase the plausibility of his arguments.

We find something similar in regard to the notion of consent. This is the third topic mentioned above. Theorists who wished to place limits on governmental power had long argued that legitimate political power must rest on the consent of the governed. According to common conceptions, consent was given through legislative institutions, such as Parliament in England or the Estates General in France, which were the people's representatives and served as checks on the ruler. Parliamentary consent was required, especially for new taxes, which was one of the precipitating causes of the English Civil War.

The notion of consent went hand in hand with the contract of government. It was widely argued that, in order to be binding, a contract of government must be voluntarily entered into. Traditional contract theorists argued that the contract creates reciprocal obligations between ruler and people only if the people *consent* to the agreement and so voluntarily subject themselves to the ruler. The most noted theorist who argues along these lines is John Locke, whose views are discussed in the next chapter. But we can note here Locke's influence on subsequent thinkers, including the authors of the *Declaration of Independence*, who describe governments as "deriving their just powers from the consent of the governed."

In order to understand Hobbes's maneuvers here, it is necessary to realize a central feature of contracts or promises. If Josef holds Robin up and threatens to shoot her unless she brings him her life savings the next day, we would ordinarily say that her promise is not binding. When a person makes a promise, she imposes an obligation on herself. It is generally held that this process works only if the obligation is voluntarily incurred. Now exactly where we should draw the line between voluntary and involuntary promises is a complex subject, widely debated by scholars. But wherever one places it, virtually all authorities agree that forced promises do not bind, and that the kind of promise Robin makes to save her life is paradigmatically forced and not binding.

The fact that promises must be voluntarily accepted raises problems for Hobbes. First, as we have repeatedly noted, he presents the state of nature as such an appalling situation that people are willing to accept an extremely powerful government as an alternative (or as Hobbes would say, the only alternative). The covenants into which people enter generate obligations for them to obey their rulers which it would be unjust for them to break. An immediate problem is that the covenants in question could easily be viewed as coerced and so not binding. The complexities cannot be discussed here. But even if we accept the covenants as voluntary and so binding, there is another problem. Hobbes wishes to justify obligations to existing governments. As a rule, these did not arise through contractual agreements but through force. Hobbes calls this sovereignty by *acquisition* (on which more shortly). There is little doubt that the covenants on which most governments actually rest are paradigmatically forced and so not binding—according to the usual understanding. So in order to defend obligations to existing governments, once again, Hobbes must show that the way people usually think is incorrect. He must explain how forced promises are binding (or at least, how certain forced promises bind).

In order to deal with this problem, Hobbes revises traditional notions concerning voluntary actions. The details of his argument need not detain us. Briefly, he argues that any action is free if the agent chooses to perform it: "a Voluntary Act is that which proceedeth from the Will, and no other" (*Lev.*, Chap. 6, p. 44). The will, as we have seen, is "the last appetite in deliberating." It follows that an action is voluntary if it is aimed at getting something the subject wants. Accordingly, faced with two terrible alternatives, the person who chooses the least bad chooses voluntarily:

> Fear and Liberty are consistent; as when a man throweth his goods into the Sea for fear the ship should sink, he doth it nevertheless very willingly, and may refuse to do it if he will. It is therefore the action of one that was free. (*Lev.*, Chap. 21, p. 146)

The same principle extends to covenants that are ordinarily viewed as forced. Though these too are choices between unpleasant alternatives, they are done to benefit subjects and so are free. Hobbes knows full well that his view will appear paradoxical. He takes the bull by the horns and directly addresses the notorious example of a promise extorted by an armed robber:

> Covenants entered into by fear in the condition of mere Nature are obligatory. For example, if I Covenant to pay a ransom or service for my life to an enemy, I am bound by it. For it is a Contract, wherein one receiveth the benefit of life; the other is to receive money or service for it, and consequently . . . the covenant is valid. Therefore Prisoners of war, if trusted with the payment of their Ransom, are obliged to pay it. . . . And even in Commonwealths, if I am forced to redeem my self from a Thief by promising him money, I am bound to pay it, till the Civil Law discharge me. (*Lev.*, Chap. 14, pp. 97–98)

The same is true of "covenants" with governments that rule by force. Faced with the threat of being killed, people are not generally viewed as making binding promises to such governments. But if they do not freely surrender their liberty, why are they obligated to obey? To compound the problem, at the time *Leviathan* was written, England was ruled by a military conqueror, Oliver Cromwell, and Hobbes argues for the importance of accepting subjection to his rule in order to put an end to civil war. In order to justify rule by force, Hobbes argues that dominion or rule over other people can be attained in two ways: through *institution* or *acquisition*. Hobbes argues that the relationships between ruler and subjects are the same, regardless of how the ruler gains his power (*Lev.*, Chap. 20, p. 142). Sovereignty by institution is through a contractual process like the one discussed in this section. Sovereignty by acquisition is by conquest. When *A* is conquered by *B*, he falls under *B*'s power:

> A Commonwealth by Acquisition is that where the Sovereign Power is acquired by Force. And it is acquired by force, when men singly or many together by plurality of voices, for fear of death or bonds, do authorize all the actions of that man or Assembly that hath their lives and liberty in his Power. (*Lev.*, Chap. 20, p. 138)

If Marie conquers James but allows him to live, under the condition that he accept her rule, then James has an obligation to obey her. What is striking is Hobbes's claim that this obligation rests on consent:

And this dominion is then acquired to the Victor, when the Vanquished, to avoid the present stroke of death, covenanteth either in express words or by other sufficient signs of the Will, that so long as his life, and the liberty of his body is allowed him, the victor shall have the use thereof at his pleasure. And after such Covenant made, the Vanquished is a Servant, and not before. . . .

It is not therefore the Victory that giveth the right of Dominion over the Vanquished, but his own Covenant. (*Lev.*, Chap. 20, p. 141)

After his exhaustive presentation of the contractual mechanism through which government is created, it is surprising to see Hobbes argue that an equivalent set of relationships arises from the brute force of conquest. But conquest must be discussed, because it is the source of virtually all, if not all, existing governments. If conquest did not generate obligations, there would perhaps be no obligations to rulers anywhere in the world.

If this line of argument is accepted, however, another question arises. If all regimes originate in conquest, why does Hobbes spend so much time discussing sovereignty by institution? To this too there is a clear answer. The complex contractual mechanism he discusses is that to which people *would consent* if they had the choice. It expresses the precise terms of the relationship between ruler and ruled in a properly governed commonwealth. In keeping with the analytical method discussed above, Hobbes reduces existing commonwealths to their constituent parts in order to see how they work. In a well-functioning commonwealth, relationships between ruler and subjects are along the lines of his contractual arrangement. As we saw above, the situation is analogous to taking a watch apart in order to see how it functions. If it is working well, the parts must be arranged in a certain order. Hobbes's contractual mechanism is intended to explain the proper arrangement of ruler and subjects in a properly working state. Thus even a government that rules by force must maintain these relationships with its subjects if it is to function effectively. But as we have seen, this is not enough for Hobbes. According to widespread opinion, a government that rules by force is not legitimate. A legitimate government must rule with the consent of the governed. In order to defuse this dangerous line of argument, Hobbes attempts to meet it head on. Through his distinctive interpretation of voluntary actions and consent, he argues that even rule by force—sovereignty by acquisition—is with the consent of the governed.

Before moving on to the details of the balance of rights and powers between rulers and subjects, we should note an additional striking aspect of Hobbes's discussion of sovereignty by acquisition. He holds that rights of conquest also explain relationships in the family. According to Hobbes, the child has an obligation to obey her parents because they have the power to preserve or end her life. The child's obligation too is grounded on consent:

Dominion is acquired in two ways: by Generation and by Conquest. The right of Dominion by Generation is that which the Parent hath over his Children and is called Paternal. And is not so derived from the Generation, as if therefore the Parent had Dominion over his Child because he begat him, but from the Child's Consent, either express or by other sufficient arguments declared. (*Lev.*, Chap. 20, p. 139)

Like a vanquished soldier, the child has an obligation to obey the person who preserves her, "because preservation of life being the end for which one man becomes subject to another, every man is supposed to promise obedience to him in whose power it is to save or destroy him" (*Lev.*, Chap. 20, p. 140). It follows, then, that the parent's prerogatives are the same as those of sovereignty by acquisition or conquest.

LEVIATHAN, THE "MORTALL GOD"

The contract of government is intended to set up a ruler, or to use Hobbes's term, a "sovereign," who is to be as powerful as possible. In working out the division of rights and powers between ruler and subjects, Hobbes attempts to give the ruler as many as possible, and the subjects as few.

The "Rights of the Sovereign" are discussed in Chapter 18 of *Leviathan*. We will focus on three main points. First, Hobbes gives the ruler all the normal attributes of sovereignty, which we will discuss. Second, it is important to Hobbes that these be held by a single ruler (or assembly) and not divided. Third, he also gives the ruler a number of additional powers, which greatly increase his might and sharply shift the balance of power in the state in his direction.

The concept of "sovereignty" achieved prominence in Western Europe during the late sixteenth and early seventeenth centuries, in conjunction with the emergence of independent nation-states. The concept connotes political or legal supremacy in two different senses. When ascribed to a political body, generally a state, it means, first, that the state is free from other, higher authorities. During medieval times, territorial units in Europe were frequently under the control of two great supranational organizations, the Church and the Holy Roman Empire. Both of these exercised power over lesser political bodies, as was seen, for instance, in the Pope's intervention in temporal affairs and his claim to be able to depose kings and other rulers.[22] The Emperor too impinged on the independence of territories. A good example was Charles V, who as noted above, attempted to stem the rise of Protestantism in Germany, which was part of his empire. A necessary condition for the rise of the modern nation-state was independence from these institutions. This came about when individual countries became strong enough to defend themselves from outside intervention. Early examples were England, France, and Spain, which, by the sixteenth century, achieved independence and became "sovereign states." Thus a *sovereign state* is one that is supreme in its own territory in regard to outside powers. When an outside power attempts to intervene in its affairs, its government will resist, and justify resistance with the claim that its sovereignty is being violated.

A second necessary condition for sovereign states is internal. The government must be supreme in its territory and over all inhabitants. Probably the most widely quoted definition of the state is Max Weber's: "a state is a human community that (successfully) claims the *monopoly of the legitimate use of physical force* within a given territory."[23] A monopoly of the use of force is necessary for a sovereign state. This means the state has the power to compel all other agencies and persons in the territory to do its bidding. In no state does the government actually monopolize the use of force. Criminals, for instance, use force to get what they want. But their force is not legitimate. If they are caught using force to rob or kill people, they will be punished. The state monopolizes *legitimate* force, in that only force it uses or sanctions is allowable. An example of force sanctioned by the state is that used by parents to discipline their children. But parents can use force only up to a certain point, which is set by the state. They cannot severely beat or kill their children. If they do so, they too will be punished by the state.

Before the modern state could emerge, it had to overcome competing centers of force within its territory.[24] During the feudal period, for instance, political power was decentralized. The king was little more than one noble among others, each of whom was supreme in his own territory. The modern state emerged, again during the sixteenth century, with the conquest of separate, local centers of power by the central power. Formerly independent bodies were brought under royal control, as the king came to monopolize legitimate force by attaining power over his entire country.

With the attainment of independence from external authorities and control over all persons and bodies within its territory, the modern state emerged. The concept of "sovereignty" was developed to express the state's relationship to external and internal authorities. The former can be set aside, as we will concentrate on the state's relationship to its citizens. Jean Bodin, a French political theorist (c. 1529–96) is generally credited with introducing the concept, in his major work, *Six Books of the Commonwealth* (1576). As described by Bodin and subsequent thinkers, the sovereign power in some political body occupies a position of supremacy. It is the highest or ultimate source of political power—meaning, obviously, that there is no higher power. Bodin was a proponent of monarchy, and so his sovereign was intended to be a king. Thus he believed everyone in the territory should answer to the king, while the king answers to no one else. In addition, the sovereign is the *final* authority. He has the last word. The decisions of other bodies can be appealed to him, but his decisions are appealed to no one else.[25]

The most important attribute of sovereignty is the ability to make law. As the ultimate power, the sovereign makes laws binding on everyone else in the territory. Thus Bodin writes: "[T]he main point of sovereign majesty and absolute power consists of giving the law to subjects in general without their consent."[26] Law is defined as "nothing but the command of a sovereign making use of his power" (Bodin, Book I, Chap. 8, p. 38). Because the sovereign is the ultimate power and makes the laws, he himself is above the laws. As the highest power, he cannot be subject to laws made by anyone else, while he cannot bind himself and so is not subject to his own commands. The sovereign is, however, below God and so subject to natural law, which can be taken to be God's commands. However, if we distinguish right and force, even this law does not bind the sovereign, because he cannot be held accountable for violating it (at least in this world).

Though the ability to make law is the chief attribute of sovereignty, it necessarily encompasses other attributes as well. The ability to make law alone does not provide sufficient power to rule. The sovereign must also have the power to enforce the law, which includes the power to adjudicate disputes between his subjects, the power to raise money, which is necessary to finance his government, and so on. In *Six Books of the Commonwealth* Bodin lists the following powers as necessary attributes of sovereignty: to make war and peace; to institute officers of state; to be the final appeal from all other courts; to coin money; to levy taxes; and some additional lesser powers (Book I, Chap. 10). It is central to Bodin's argument that the powers of sovereignty are necessarily inalienable and indivisible. They must exist in one man (or assembly). The king cannot set up another sovereign alongside himself:

> Just as God, the great sovereign, cannot make a God equal to Himself because He is infinite and by logical necessity two infinities cannot exist, so we can say that the prince, whom we have taken as the image of God, cannot make a subject equal to himself without annihilation of his power. (Bodin, Book I, Chap. 10, p. 50)

Political stability requires indivisible sovereignty. If powers are divided between two persons or bodies, disputes can arise. One power could wish to declare war and the other forbid it; similar problems could arise about levying taxes, oaths of obedience, or requirements to pay homage. Bodin's sobering conclusion: "it must always come to arms until such time as sovereignty resides in a prince, in the lesser part of the people, or in all the people" (Book II, Chap. 1, p. 104). If one body is not higher than all others—and so the ultimate or sovereign authority—conflict is inevitable.

Hobbes's view of sovereignty is similar to Bodin's. Though Bodin is not cited in *Leviathan*, Hobbes does refer to him in *Elements of Law*: "if there were a commonwealth, wherein the rights of sovereignty were divided, we must confess with Bodin, Bk. II, Chap. 1, of *Six Books of the Commonwealth*, that they are not rightly to be called commonwealths, but the corruption of commonwealths."[27] Like Bodin, he argues that the attributes of sovereignty are indivisible. They are "incommunicable and inseparable," "indivisible and inseparably annexed to the sovereignty" (*Lev.*, Chap. 18, pp. 127–128), whether the sovereign is an individual man or an assembly.

The attributes of sovereignty discussed by Hobbes appear to be similar to those Bodin presents. The seventh power Hobbes lists is that of making the rules that determine property holding. In the state of nature, everyone has a right to all things; in civil society, ownership is determined by the sovereign (*Lev.*, Chap. 18, p. 125). The eighth power is judicature, the right to hear and decide all controversies. The ninth is the power to make war and peace. Tenth is the power to choose government officials, "Counselors, Ministers, Magistrates, and Officers, both in Peace and War" (*Lev.*, Chap. 18, p. 126). Eleventh is the power to confer rewards and punishments. The final power is to set rules of honor, to help put an end to quarrels stemming from vainglory.

These attributes of sovereignty are straightforward and not controversial. As we have noted, they must be held by one body, thereby giving it enormous power. But, the reader will note, I began the list with the *seventh* power Hobbes indicates. One's thought naturally turns to the first six. These are unusual and set the Hobbesian sovereign apart from rulers of other commonwealths, whether real or imaginary constructions. A brief look at these additional powers leaves little doubt that Hobbes intends to make his sovereign as powerful as possible.

According to the first power of sovereignty, the subjects cannot change the form of government. All people are responsible for all actions the sovereign performs (on which, more shortly), and so, once they have covenanted their power to him, they cannot make alternative arrangements (*Lev.*, Chap. 18, pp. 121–122). Second, as we have noted, there is no contract between the sovereign and people. Therefore, the sovereign's power cannot be forfeited for breach of contract:

> Because the Right of bearing the Person of them all is given to him they make Sovereign by Covenant only of one to another and not of him to any of them, there can happen no breach of Covenant on the part of the Sovereign, and consequently none of his

Subjects, by any pretense of forfeiture can be freed from his Subjection. (*Lev.*, Chap. 18, p. 122)

The third power concerns people who have not covenanted away their power to the sovereign. As long as the majority has erected a sovereign, Hobbes holds that everyone else has similar obligations to him. Thus it makes no difference whether or not one accepts the sovereign oneself. If a given person refuses to submit to the sovereign, he remains in a state of war with it, and "he might without injustice be destroyed by any man whatsoever" (*Lev.*, Chap. 18, pp. 123–124).

According to the fourth power, no matter what he does, the sovereign cannot injure any of his subjects. Hobbes arranges things so subjects cannot possibly complain about their treatment by the sovereign. His reasoning here is complex. Recall the legal formula through which the sovereign is set up: "I authorize and give up my right of governing myself to this man . . . on this condition, that you give up your right to him and authorize all his actions in like manner" (*Lev.*, Chap. 17, p. 120). The resulting commonwealth is described by Hobbes as a multitude "united in one Person." The "Essence of the Commonwealth" is: "One Person, of whose Acts a great Multitude by mutual Covenants one with another have made themselves every one the Author, to the end he may use the strength and means of them all as he shall think expedient for the Peace and Common Defense" (*Lev.*, Chap. 17, pp. 120–121). The particular language of authorization here can be understood through the analogy of representation. If I want to buy a house, I can appoint another person to act for me, as my agent. Thus he can bid on a house and bind me to a contract to buy it. In this transaction, he acts for me. His action is tantamount to my own; I am as bound by his bid as if I had bid myself. But it should be noted that if I appoint Jean as my agent *in regard to purchasing a house*, his authority is limited to this task. He cannot bind me to buy a car, or a life insurance policy. He is designated for a specific task and given authority to accomplish that (and only that). We see something similar in representative government. When our legislators pass a bill, it binds us, because through our system of government we have given them power to bind us. Once again, the power of the representatives is limited. They can pass laws within the framework of the constitution, but their power to represent the citizens is limited by constitutional provisions.

Hobbes refers to this kind of representative power as that to "bear someone else's person." He holds that the sovereign is erected through a legal transaction through which everyone in the territory gives him power to bear their persons in regard to everything he thinks necessary for peace and common defense. Because the sovereign bears my person, whatever he does binds me; whatever *he* does that concerns me is as if I had done it myself. Accordingly, I cannot contest his actions, because his actions are as if I had performed them myself. The point here is clearly illustrated in the fact that I cannot sue myself, no matter how badly I botch or mishandle my own affairs. In Hobbes's terminology, my agent, in this case the sovereign, cannot "injure" me, as I cannot "injure" myself.

Hobbes's argument here will probably strike the reader as peculiar, especially because Hobbes claims that the precise powers under discussion are those the reader too would authorize were he in the state of nature. The reason Hobbes presents things in this way is not hard to identify. If the subjects "authorize" the sovereign's actions, it will be difficult for them to complain about him. Like the peculiar contractual mechanism that is not a contract, and his view of consent that is not consent, his doctrine of authorization limits the degree of mutual obligation between sovereign and subjects, and illustrates once again Hobbes's intention to free the sovereign from possible limits on his power.

The fifth power, related to the fourth, is the right to use whatever means the sovereign believes necessary to accomplish his ends. This is similar to the "enabling clause" of the United States Constitution (Art. 1, Sec. 8, No. 18), which gives Congress the power to make whatever laws that are necessary and proper to carry out its aims.

Finally, the sixth power is to control the thoughts and opinions of the subjects. Hobbes strongly believes in the power of ideas. Because men's actions follow from their opinions, the sovereign must propagate helpful opinions and combat dangerous ones. This is especially important in regard to questions of political obligations and rights. Hobbes believes that incorrect understandings of the proper relationship between sovereign and subject were largely responsible for the English Civil War. Thus the sovereign must determine who may and who may not address multitudes of people, and who should judge what books can be published.

This is an important theme in Hobbes's political philosophy. Because he believes incorrect doctrine has terrible effects, he "cannot imagine how anything could be more prejudicial to a Monarchy than the allowing of such books to be publicly read" (*Lev.*, Chap. 29, p. 226). It is incumbent on the sovereign not to permit the people to be ignorant of proper relations between their ruler and themselves. In order to allow proper principles "to be diligently and truly taught" (*Lev.*, Chap. 30, p. 232), special days should be set aside for this purpose:

> It is necessary that some such times be determined, wherein they may assemble together and (after prayers and praises given to God, the Sovereign of Sovereigns) hear those their Duties told them, and the Positive Laws, such as generally concern them all, read and expounded, and be put in mind of the Authority that maketh them Laws. (*Lev.*, Chap. 30, p. 235)

Hobbes's model here is the Jewish people's practice of assembling on the Sabbath to read their laws contained in the Torah. In Hobbes's case, the proposed readings would be something approximating *Leviathan.*

Hobbes believes it is essential that all attributes we have listed remain undivided in the sovereign's hands. For the sovereign to turn over any of these to someone else is a breach of his duty, and contrary to the "Defense, Peace, and Good of the people" (*Lev.*, Chap. 30, p. 231). With the package of powers left entire, the Sovereign is a mighty figure. Hobbes famously describes him as more than human:

> This done, the Multitude so united in one Person, is called a Common-wealth, in Latin Civitas. This last is the Generation of the great LEVIATHAN, or rather (to speak more reverently) of that *Mortall God*, to which we owe under the *Immortal God*, our peace and defense. (*Lev.*, Chap. 17, p. 120)

In addition to giving the sovereign the powers we have noted, Hobbes removes the traditional checks that bind rulers, according to other views. We have seen the steps Hobbes takes to show that the sovereign is not bound by a contract of government. We have also seen his argument that even sovereigns by acquisition rule with the consent of their subjects.

Hobbes takes similar steps to defuse natural law, which was an important check on rulers throughout the Middle Ages. We saw above that Hobbes presents a distinctive view of natural law, according to which it is conditional, theorems of reason that aid in self-preservation. Because it is conditional, natural law does not bind in the state of nature. There it binds in conscience but not in regard to actions, because to follow its dictates under those circumstances would be dangerous. In civil society, this excuse no longer holds, and so subjects are bound by the law of nature. According to traditional natural law doctrines, the sovereign is also bound by the law of nature in society. We have seen above that even so resolute a champion of undivided sovereignty as Bodin argues that the ruler is below natural law. Hobbes, too, places the ruler below natural law, but he takes steps to ensure that this will not limit the ruler's power.

As noted above, the political heart of a theory of natural law is the claim that positive laws must be in accord with it. Man-made laws that contravene the laws of nature are not binding; they are not "laws" in the true sense of the term. This is obviously a conclusion Hobbes wishes to avoid. He argues, accordingly, that the law of nature is not self-interpreting. Because people's reasoning power is influenced by their passions, they will disagree about exactly what the law of nature says. Because such disputes are detrimental to public order, an authoritative interpretation of the law of nature is necessary. This is provided by the sovereign. In authorizing the sovereign power, people give him the power to determine the contents of the law of nature. What is more, the form in which the sovereign presents his interpretation is the civil laws. Hobbes thereby rules out the possibility that the civil laws can conflict with the law of nature. Contradiction is impossible, because the law of nature is by definition what the civil law says it is. Thus Hobbes writes:

> The Law of Nature and the Civil Law contain each other and are of equal extent. For the Laws of Nature, which consist in Equity, Justice, Gratitude, and other moral Virtues, on these depending in the condition of mere Nature . . . are not properly Laws, but qualities that dispose men to peace and to obedience. . . . for in the difference of private men to declare what is Equity, what is Justice, and what is moral Virtue, and to make them binding, there is need of the Ordinances of Sovereign Power, and Punishments to be ordained for such as shall break them; which Ordinances are therefore part of the Civil Law. The law of Nature therefore is a part of the Civil Law in all Commonwealths of the world. Reciprocally also, the Civil Law is a part of the Dictates of Nature. (*Lev.*, Chap. 26, p. 185)

In all legal systems, ability to interpret what the law says is a crucial power. In *Leviathan*, of course, Hobbes argues that this belongs to the sovereign alone. To a large extent the sovereign's power is epistemic. *Episteme* is the Greek word for knowledge. In calling the sovereign's power epistemic, I refer to the fact that the subjects authorize him to think for them. He not only has the power to make the laws, but to interpret what they say. Because he is also the authoritative interpreter of natural laws, he can eliminate the possibility of clashes between them and civil laws.

In setting up the sovereign, subjects agree to authorize his actions "as he shall think expedient for their Peace and Common Defense" (*Lev.*, Chap. 17, p. 121). People will probably disagree about exactly what is necessary for peace and common defense, but it is the sovereign's opinion that counts. What he believes is necessary must be accepted by the subjects whose persons he bears. It seems, then, that subjects do not actually turn over *all* their power to the sovereign. Rather, they turn over what he believes is necessary. But the grant is effectively without limit (aside from the exceptions noted in the next section), because subjects must accept what the sovereign thinks is necessary.

The situation is similar in regard to conscience. It is often said in liberal societies that a subject should not obey a given law if he believes it is wrong, or in other words, if he believes it conflicts with his conscience. Conscientious objection to military service is a relevant example, as were protests against what were widely viewed as discriminatory laws during the struggle for civil rights. Hobbes predictably attempts to eliminate possible conflicts between conscience and law. In authorizing the sovereign, part of what people grant is the power to form moral judgments:

> In the second place, I observe the Diseases of a Commonwealth that proceed from the poison of seditious doctrines, whereof one is that every private man is Judge of Good and Evil actions. This is true in the condition of mere Nature, where there are no Civil Laws, and also under Civil Government, in such cases as are not determined by the Law. But otherwise it is manifest that the measure of Good and Evil actions is the Civil Law, and the Judge the Legislator, who is always the Representative of the Commonwealth. (*Lev.*, Chap. 29, p. 223)

Because the sovereign is the official source of moral judgment, subjects are not allowed to go against his edicts when these conflict with their consciences. Allowing this would undermine civil tranquility.

Hobbes presents a similar line of argument to defuse possible conflicts over matters of religion. As indicated above, these became of great concern to Hobbes as the Civil War in England became enmeshed in religious questions. Parts III and IV of *Leviathan*, which comprise almost half the work, are given over to such questions. For reasons of space, I will not discuss these aspects of Hobbes's view in detail. The main points are straightforward. Throughout *Leviathan*, Hobbes is deeply concerned with demonstrating that the conclusions he advances on the basis of reason, in accordance with his scientific method, are supported by God's revelation, which is contained in the Bible. Thus nothing in the Bible can be contrary to reason:

> For though there be many things in God's Word above Reason, that is to say, which cannot by natural reason be either demonstrated or confuted, yet there is nothing contrary to it. (*Lev.*, Chap. 32, p. 256)

To support this claim, Hobbes presents a detailed interpretation of numerous Biblical texts. In regard to substantive teaching, he attempts to eliminate possible conflicts between subjects' religious beliefs and sovereign authority. He argues that the sovereign must control all aspects of external religious observance, including authoritative interpretation of the Bible. Church and State comprise the same people and must be united under the same sovereign: "Temporal and Spiritual Government are but two words brought into the world to make men see double and mistake their Lawful Sovereign" (*Lev.*, Chap. 39, p. 322).

In addition, in following the sovereign's teaching rather than his own beliefs, the subject does not place himself at risk. Distinguishing between external observance and internal belief, Hobbes argues that only one precept must be believed to insure salvation, that "Jesus is the Christ" (*Lev.*, Chap. 43, p. 407). A Christian sovereign will always allow this, and even if he does not, the subject must obey nonetheless: "Faith and Obedience are both necessary to Salvation" (*Lev.*, Chap. 43, p. 413). Even the infidel ruler must be obeyed, in accordance with "the counsel of the Apostles that admonishes all Christians to obey their Princes, and all Children and Servants to obey their parents and Masters in all things" (*Lev.*, Chap. 43, p. 414).[28]

Other possible sources of conflict are also eliminated. In all societies a body of customary law grows up. These are enactments that attain their force through long use or habit, rather than by being enacted by the sovereign. According to Hobbes, because the sovereign is the source of all law, he has authority over customary law as well. Customary law is taken to have received the consent of the sovereign if he does not act to change it. But he can annul it at his pleasure. Contrariwise, through legislation, he can confer on it the status of unquestionable law (*Lev.*, Chap. 26, p. 184).

Having examined the powers of Hobbes's sovereign, once again we can see the main thrust of his argument. Hobbes goes to great lengths to make the sovereign as powerful as possible, both by giving him a raft of extraordinary powers and by removing possible limits to his power. Once again, these powers must all be held by a single sovereign of awesome might. Hobbes writes:

> Hitherto I have set forth the nature of Man, whose Pride and other Passions have compelled him to submit himself to Government, together with the great powers of his Governor, whom I compared to *Leviathan*, taking that comparison out of the two last verses of the one and fortieth of *Job* where God having set forth the great power of *Leviathan*, calleth him King of the Proud. *There is nothing*, saith he, *on earth to be compared with him. He is made so as not to be afraid. He seeth every high thing below him, and is King of all the children of pride.* (*Lev.*, Chap. 28, pp. 220–221)

THE RIGHTS OF SUBJECTS AND DUTIES OF SOVEREIGN

Having outlined the main powers of Hobbes's sovereign, we can devote less space to the rights of subjects, as these are relatively few. But closely related to these are important duties of the sovereign. We have seen that in the covenant through which government arises the sovereign receives power to bear each subject's person, in order to assure the peace and security of the commonwealth. This in effect gives the sovereign unlimited power. According to the agreement, the sovereign is judge of what he requires and can make demands accordingly. We saw in the last section that Hobbes carefully removes traditional checks on sovereign power. But in spite of this, there are limits. The sovereign cannot act in any way he pleases, while subjects have definite rights, some of which follow from specific features of Hobbes's contractual mechanism, and others from general features of political relationships.

The subject's main right, according to Hobbes, is the right to be left alone in certain areas. The sovereign is judge of these areas, and can interfere with all aspects of subjects' lives when he wishes. But significant freedom remains.

Hobbes defines liberty as "the absence of external Impediments" (*Lev.*, Chap. 14, p. 91). These can take the form of physical obstacles, which can interfere with the "liberty" of a river to flow downhill, or a stone to fall. Or liberty can be limited by moral obstacles. Most notable of these are rules, such as the laws of nature. The civil laws also limit liberty, as the subject has an obligation to obey them, and will be punished if he does not. Hobbes argues that when a person enters into a covenant, he restricts his future liberty. It is injustice under the laws of nature not to keep one's covenants, and a prior covenant always overrules a later one (*Lev.*, Chap. 14). We have seen that covenants do not bind in the state of nature. But the one erecting a sovereign does, and because this is an unrestricted grant of authority, the subject incurs an obligation to do whatever the sovereign commands. In addition, the civil law is an authoritative interpretation of the natural law, with which the subject should abide in civil society, because it is safe to do so. This is a substantial infringement of the subject's liberty, and is more than a moral impediment, in that violations will be punished by the sovereign's awesome might.

In practical terms, the sovereign's laws are the most significant restriction of the subject's liberty. But in commonwealths the laws cover only a portion of life. The subject is free to do what he wants when the law is silent, and so should enjoy a good deal of autonomy:

> For seeing there is no Commonwealth in the world wherein there be Rules enough set down for the regulation of all the actions and words of men (as being a thing impossible), it followeth necessarily that in all kinds of actions by the laws praetermitted, men have the Liberty of doing what their own reasons shall suggest for the most profitable to themselves. (*Lev.*, Chap. 21, p. 147)

In addition to the silence of the laws, the subject enjoys liberties because of the nature of human life. We have seen that the agreement creating government is not a contract and so does not give rise to mutual obligations between sovereign and subjects. We have also seen that it is a general grant of authority, which allows the sovereign to demand what he thinks necessary. Still, because of the supreme value of self-preservation, which is the basis for the laws of nature and of government, certain rights cannot be granted to the sovereign, and his powers are inherently limited.

Because of the importance of self-preservation, the subject must retain the right of self-defense, whatever covenant he enters. There could be no possible reason to give this up. The sovereign is erected to protect people from violent death. It makes no sense for them to give up the right to defend themselves when this is necessary—including cases in which the threat of death is from the sovereign:

> And therefore there be some Rights which no man can be understood by any words or other signs to have abandoned or transferred. As first a man cannot lay down the right of resisting them that assault him by force to take away his life, because he cannot be understood to aim thereby at any Good to himself. The same may be said of Wounds and Chains and Imprisonment, both because there is no benefit consequent to such patience as there is to the patience of suffering another to be wounded or imprisoned, as also because a man cannot tell, when he seeth men proceed against him by violence whether they intend his death or not. And lastly, the motive and end for which this renouncing and transferring of Right is introduced is nothing else but the security of a man's person in his life, and in the means of so preserving life as not to be weary of it. And therefore if a man by words or other signs seem to despoil himself

of the End for which those signs were intended, he is not to be understood as if he meant it or that it was his will, but that he was ignorant of how such words and actions were to be interpreted. (*Lev.*, Chap. 14, pp. 93–94)

Not only do subjects retain the right of self-defense, but as we see in this passage, Hobbes extends this right in two senses. First, it includes more than defense against mortal threats. When people proceed against Glenn with force, he can resist them, whether he believes they intend to kill him, or merely to wound him. Faced with the threat of force, Glenn *must* resist; the consequences of not resisting are too severe to take chances. If he believes only wounds are threatened, he should still resist, as the consequences of being wrong could be fatal.

One will also note a certain gray area in the passage. Throughout his political writings, Hobbes attempts to limit people's interests as much as possible. It is fair to say that he attempts to reduce self-interest to self-preservation. The state of nature is meant to be so terrible that one cannot think of anything but survival. Hobbes's strategy here is clear. He wishes to limit sources of potential conflict between subject and state. As long as the state preserves Sara, she is better off in it than in the state of nature. She should therefore be willing to tolerate it, regardless of other factors. For example, it is in her interest to support it regardless of how well its laws accord with her religious or moral beliefs. In exchange for security, the Hobbesian citizen surrenders among other rights the right to think for herself in regard to religion and morals, and is glad to do so. If everyone retained these rights, the result would be the same state of nature one attempted to leave. In the above passage, however, Hobbes speaks of more than mere life. He notes that the end of the agreement is life "as not to be weary of it." This could be interpreted as a significant concession. It could mean that subjects should defend all aspects of their lives they care deeply about, since failure to preserve might make life unpleasant. Hobbes uses similar language elsewhere in *Leviathan*. For instance, consider the following passage:

> The Office of the Sovereign (be it a Monarch, or an Assembly) consisteth in the end for which he was trusted with the Sovereign Power, namely the procuration of the safety of the people . . . But by Safety here is not meant a bare Preservation, but also all other Contentments of life, which every man by lawful Industry, without danger or hurt to the Commonwealth shall acquire to himself. (*Lev.*, Chap. 30, p. 231)

But it seems clear that this and other similar passages should be interpreted narrowly. Hobbes undoubtedly believes the specific form of government he advocates will lead to a happy and prosperous state. A situation in which people are protected but left in poverty, ignorance, filth, and misery is obviously not his intention. But it is also not his intention to have subjects resist the sovereign if their standard of living falls below a certain point. A broad interpretation of the passage goes against Hobbes's entire political theory. So we should interpret these concessions as minimal.

It is also worth noting that in the passage quoted above, Hobbes qualifies his account of binding contracts. We have seen that he regards an action as "voluntary" even if it is performed because of a severe threat of force. If a holdup man threatens to kill you unless you agree to bring him money, that is a valid promise and so binding. But in the passage he limits the scope of voluntary actions in a different direction. All actions are intended for the good of the agent. Thus actions detrimental to self-preservation are not regarded as intentional. A contract to kill yourself or not to preserve yourself is not intentional and so not binding. A person who grants away the right to preserve himself must be viewed as not knowing what he is doing, and so that contract does not bind.

These points are confirmed by an additional passage in Chapter 14:

> A Covenant not to defend myself from force by force is always void. For . . . no man can transfer or lay down his right to save himself from Death, Wounds, and Imprisonment (the avoiding whereof is the only End of laying down any Right), and therefore the promise of not resisting force in no Covenant transferreth any right, nor is obliging. For though a man may covenant thus, *Unless I do so or so, kill me,* he cannot Covenant thus, *Unless I do so or so, I will not resist you when you come to kill me.* For man by nature chooseth the lesser evil, which is danger of death in resisting, rather than the greater, which is certain and present death in not resisting.

Continuing this passage, Hobbes again expands the sphere of self-interest beyond mere self-preservation:

> A Covenant to accuse oneself without assurance of pardon is likewise invalid. For in the condition of Nature, where every man is Judge, there is no place for Accusation, and in the Civil State the Accusation is followed with Punishment, which being Force, a man is not obliged not to resist. The same is also true of the Accusation of those by whose Condemnation a man falls into misery; as of a Father, Wife, or Benefactor. (*Lev.,* Chap. 14, p. 98)

It is notable that in this passage Hobbes depicts people as closely tied to one another. People feel so strongly about close family members or benefactors that life is not worth living without them. This is one indication of Hobbes's recognition that there is more to familial relations than the combination of fear and contract noted above. It also suggests a more reasonable view of human nature than the extreme self-interest Hobbes explicitly presents. But in regard to rights of the subject, though the passages we have seen suggest more than mere self-preservation, once again Hobbes should be viewed as narrowly confining aspects of life for which one should be willing to fight. Anything more would undermine the entire political theory he so elaborately constructs.

Even with this narrow construal of self-preservation, however, the subjects' need to preserve themselves places important restrictions on the sovereign's power. Because of the close connections between protection and obedience on which Hobbes's political philosophy is founded, subjects are required to obey only as long as the sovereign can protect them. When he is no longer able to do so, his power runs out: "The Obligation of Subjects to the Sovereign is understood to last as long and no longer than the power lasteth by which he is able to protect them" (*Lev.,* Chap. 21, p. 153).

Hobbes subsumes different circumstances under this proviso. If a subject is a prisoner of war, his captors have the ability to kill him, while his sovereign cannot protect him. Thus his allegiance transfers. This is especially obvious when the subject's original allegiance stemmed from sovereignty by acquisition. As he was conquered once and became a subject of sovereign *A*, he has now been conquered by forces of sovereign *B*, whose subject he now becomes. The same thing happens if a subject is banished or travels abroad. He is subject to the sovereign who rules the territory he is in: "whosoever entereth into another's dominion is Subject to all the Laws thereof" (*Lev.*, Chap. 21, p. 154).

Obligations also cease when the sovereign loses his power. The principle is the same. Without sufficient power, the sovereign can no longer do what he was chosen to do, and so subjects recover their liberty. This is the case if the sovereign is conquered by another. For example, when Nazi Germany conquered France, Belgium, and the Netherlands during World War II, the allegiance of subjects of these countries transferred to Germany. The case is similar in regard to civil war. If the sovereign is overcome and replaced by some of his subjects, the allegiance of other subjects shifts accordingly, to those who can offer protection. This proviso is obviously important to Hobbes, in view of his own historical situation. *Leviathan* was interpreted as requiring general submission to the military government of Oliver Cromwell.

Though the subject retains no other significant rights, Hobbes believes they are not necessary. It is not in the sovereign's interest to exploit or oppress his subjects. His interest lies in developing a prosperous and happy commonwealth. We have seen that, no matter how he rules, the sovereign cannot "injure" the people in a technical sense. Because he bears their persons, what he does to them they do to themselves, and of this they cannot rightfully complain. But the sovereign is bound by the law of nature "to render an account thereof to God, the Author of that law" (*Lev.*, Chap. 30, p. 231). He is to promote the people's safety, the end for which he was appointed. This includes more than bare protection. As we have seen, the sovereign must foster "all other Contentments of life, which every man by lawfull Industry, without danger, or hurt to the Commonwealth, shall acquire to himselfe" (ibid.).

It is important to note that, though the sovereign is required to promote these ends, he is not *legally* bound to do so. The sovereign stands above the legal system as a whole and is accountable to no one—aside from God. But though the sovereign is not legally required to behave in this way, he should anyway, because it is in his interest to do so. Hobbes believes the interests of the sovereign and his subjects largely coincide. The sovereign can be counted on to do what is good for his realm, because this is also good for himself.

In order to promote the welfare of his subjects, the sovereign must pursue specific policies. These constitute his duties and are generally straightforward (as presented in Chapter 30). First, he must maintain sufficient power to perform his essential tasks. Thus he must not divide the attributes of sovereignty. Because people's behavior follows from their beliefs, he must make sure proper principles of political obligation are taught throughout the commonwealth, along with reasons why objections to these views are false. As we have seen, special days should be set aside so the people can assemble and receive instruction on these crucial matters. In addition, the sovereign must govern in a way that promotes the peace and prosperity of his realm. He must see that justice is administered equally. The burden of taxes must be distributed fairly, to rich and poor alike. The sovereign must make sure those unable to work are cared for, and not left to the mercy of private charity, and that idleness is discouraged. Towards this last end, he must promote industry and commerce, to make sure there is sufficient work. Other specific measures are mandated. Most important is that the sovereign should make good laws. This means more than merely just laws, for as we have seen, "no Law can be Unjust" (*Lev.*, Chap. 30, p. 239). Good laws promote the interests of the commonwealth: "A good Law is that, which is Needful, for the Good of the people, and withall Perspicuous" (ibid.).

In short, the sovereign should rule in the state's interest, which is also his own interest, because his power stems from his people:

> It is a weak Sovereign that has weak Subjects, and a weak People whose Sovereign wanteth Power to rule them at his will. (*Lev.*, Chap. 30, p. 240)

In the vigor of his subjects lies the sovereign's "own strength and glory" (*Lev.*, Chap. 18, pp. 128–129). This should allow subjects to trust the ruler, without benefit of legal rights against him.

There is an additional reason why it is in the sovereign's interest to rule well. Though the people have no right to rebel if he rules badly, they are more likely to do so if they feel aggrieved. By ruling badly, the sovereign creates enmity among his people and so endangers his position. A telling example cited by Hobbes is Tarquin, king of ancient Rome. Tarquin failed to take action against the crime of one of his sons. This provoked the anger of the multitude, who not only chased Tarquin from Rome but dissolved the monarchy (*Lev.*, Chap. 30, pp. 240–241).

In this respect, the teaching of Hobbes is like that of Machiavelli discussed in the last chapter. The interest of the sovereign lies in being feared and respected, but not hated, by his subjects. A sure way to lose their allegiance and run the risk of revolution is by ruthless oppression and tyrannical excess. As long as the sovereign rules with moderation and attempts to keep his domain peaceful and prosperous, he will have little to fear from his subjects. Though the sovereign, as the ultimate political authority, is not legally bound to behave this way, it is in his interest to do so.

Thus it is incorrect to view Hobbes as a proponent of absolute authority, as this concept is often understood. What he has in mind is far removed from unbridled dictatorship, seen perhaps most clearly in the twentieth-century regimes of Hitler and Stalin—or from oriental despotism, which Montesquieu castigates (see pp. 193–4, 198–9). Though Hobbes believes even an awful regime is preferable to no government at all, he views the sovereign's great power as a means rather than an end. Unless he possesses the attributes we have examined, the sovereign cannot be secure, and so the commonwealth as a whole will be at risk. But the sovereign's unaccountable power is intended to create the framework for a peaceful, prosperous society. In a world of chaotic disorder, Hobbes's great discovery is the might of the state. The essential peace and order it makes possible benefit all concerned, subjects and sovereign alike.

Assessing the Argument

Though Hobbes restricts the power of the sovereign by requiring that he promote the public interest, an obvious response to his argument is that these limits are not enough. Many modern citizens would propose as an alternative to the powerful state Hobbes defends a moderate government in which citizens are protected from one another, and so from the horrors of the state of nature, but also from government. Protection from government is commonly achieved by the familiar constitutional devices of separation of powers and checks and balances, which are found in contemporary democratic states. In *Federalist* 51, we find a classic defense of these devices:

> It may be a reflection on human nature, that such devices should be necessary to control the abuses of government. But what is government itself but the greatest of all reflections on human nature? If men were angels, no government would be necessary. If angels were to govern men, neither external nor internal controls on government would be necessary. In framing a government which is to be administered by men over men, the great difficulty lies in this: you must first enable the government to control the governed; and in the next place oblige it to control itself.[29]

We will discuss the ideas expressed in this passage in some detail in our chapter on Montesquieu. For now we should note that in Hobbes's system great pains are taken to allow the government to control the governed, but little is done to *oblige* it to control itself.

Accordingly, even if we grant that Hobbes convincingly demonstrates the need for government, we must examine his arguments for *his form of government* rather than others. At first sight, Hobbes's view appears to be obviously incorrect. The form of state he recommends is strikingly different from what has emerged in all the Western democracies—and so from what liberal citizens would be likely to recommend. But the fact that Hobbes's position appears improbable is not enough. He undoubtedly would argue that his philosophical method can provide convincing demonstrations of what seems unlikely. Thus we must see how convincing a case he could make.

Stepping back from Hobbes's text, we can present three main arguments in defense of his form of state. The main question is what government we would choose if we were in Hobbes's state of nature, whether this would be absolutism or a limited government, such as those in the United States and the other Western democracies. For present purposes we can grant that the state of nature would be as Hobbes indicates.

The first argument is that life with a sovereign of the kind Hobbes discusses should not be intolerable. We have noted the sovereign's duties toward his subjects. Though these are not legally binding, the sovereign's interests do not lie in oppressing his subjects. Because his power depends on having a peaceful and prosperous state, he should do everything possible to foster this. Nor does Hobbes believe this conduct is contrary to human nature. We have seen that people in the state of nature are competitive and will stop at nothing to preserve themselves and advance their ends. One reason for this competition is natural equality. Because people know they are vulnerable and can be killed by others, they must be extremely fearful and willing to take preemptive action. But the sovereign's position is different. Far from being equal to others, he is a "mortal God." Because of his overwhelming might, other people pose no threat to him and he can set aside immediate fear. Clearly, one of Hobbes's main purposes is to create a sovereign who is so powerful that his subjects will not think of challenging him. They will automatically defer, thereby contributing to the peace and stability of the realm, and so allow the sovereign to relax his reins.

Because we are aware of the horrors of twentieth-century dictatorships, in spite of Hobbes's intentions, our response to a Hobbesian sovereign is likely to be less optimistic. We have seen in the persons of Hitler, Stalin, Mao, and Pol Pot rulers who have murdered millions of their subjects. The thought of the state of nature is obviously grim. But living in Nazi Germany or Stalin's Soviet Union during the Great Purge is not much more attractive. We should note that at the time Hobbes wrote, the technological means of mass oppression had not attained their modern level of effectiveness. The seventeenth-century state was a pale shadow of what has since emerged. Means of communications and transportation differed little from those of the ancient world. The English king had a relatively small army at his disposal. And so the means of oppression necessary for twentieth-century horrors did not exist. One could perhaps respond that regimes committed terrible crimes before our own times. The Spanish Inquisition and the expulsion of the Jews and Moslems from Spain are two examples. Still, the full horrors of totalitarianism were unknown to Hobbes. This perhaps contributed to the little attention he gave this danger. Perhaps one reason Hobbes was relatively confident about the state is that he did not envision it as driven by a specific ideology. The great crimes of twentieth-century totalitarian regimes have largely resulted from the all-embracing worldviews they have attempted to implement. Nazi racism, Soviet, Chinese, and Cambodian Communism clearly fit the bill. At the time Hobbes wrote, churches were driven by ideological fervor. Hundreds of years of ruinous religious warfare testified to this. But because he viewed the state as lacking religious motivations, Hobbes had little reason to fear that it would attempt to impose its worldview on its subjects, at terrible human cost.[30]

Clearly, problems caused by an evil or out-of-control sovereign constitute a significant weakness in Hobbes's case. Hobbes obviously believed the sovereign would not behave in this way. But these considerations would cause contemporary citizens seriously to consider separation of powers and checks and balances to keep the ruler under control. But let us set this line of argument aside and consider Hobbes's main defense of his position.

Hobbes's main argument for his particular form of state is that nothing else could work. He believes separation of powers is ruinous. We have noted Bodin's argument that division of powers leads to conflict. If the king says one thing and the legislative body something else: "it must always come to arms" (Bodin, Book II, Chap. 1, p. 104). Hobbes entirely agrees. He traces the English Civil War to divided government:

> If there had not first been an opinion received of the greatest part of England that these Powers were divided between the King and the Lords and the House of Commons, the people had never been divided and fallen into this Civil War. . . . (*Lev.*, Chap. 18, p. 127)

Thus Hobbes's fundamental criticism of separation of powers and checks and balances is that it leads to the breakdown of order, to civil war, which he regards as the death of a body politic.

Obviously, the question, then, is whether Hobbes is right about this. Though this might be surprising to citizens of modern liberal states, there is a great deal to be said for his view. First, if subjects believe they have rights against their ruler, they are more likely to press them. If they believe force is justified, they are more likely to use it. Thus the results of divided power would often be more tumultuous than if subjects simply submitted. If different governmental institutions took sides with different parties to a conflict, the result could well be civil war.

Imagine Hobbes's reaction to a constitutional crisis. In the early 1970s Richard Nixon was widely believed to have abused his Presidential powers, and there was strong sentiment to remove him from office. Written into the United States Constitution is an impeachment procedure through which this task could be completed in an orderly manner. But in order to impeach Mr. Nixon, proof was necessary, which the President refused to turn over to investigating bodies. When Archibald Cox, who had been appointed to investigate the President, insisted on gaining access to the tape recordings Mr. Nixon had made of his own conversations, the President had him fired. The Attorney General and Assistant Attorney General, who refused to carry out this order, were also removed from office. Then the President called on the FBI to take possession of Cox's offices and files. The storm of criticism these acts inspired eventually led the President to comply with an investigation of his activities, and he resigned in order to avoid impeachment.

From Hobbes's perspective, the crucial question is what would have happened if the President had not backed down? What would have happened if he had declared a national emergency and, instead of sending in the FBI to occupy Cox's offices, sent in troops to do this, and also to occupy Capitol Hill? There was clearly widespread unwillingness to impeach the President without proof of his wrongdoing, without a so-called "smoking gun." What if Mr. Nixon had destroyed the incriminating tapes, or refused to comply with a Supreme Court order to turn them over? Because power is divided under the U.S. Constitution, there is no ultimate authority to settle such conflicts between the branches of government. Can they be settled, then, in any manner short of a resort to arms? These are Hobbes's questions. Writing during a wholesale breakdown of order, he was acutely conscious of how constitutional conflicts could lead to similar breakdowns.

Faced with Hobbes's fear of such conflicts, we could respond that he surely exaggerates. With the mathematical precision for which he is famous, Hobbes forces every possible disagreement to its logical conclusion. If clear procedures for resolving a dispute are not at hand, then it *must* give rise to conflict, and so civil war. But try as we might to dismiss Hobbes's concerns—he was after all famously fearful—history does not offer comfort. Though public order has not broken down in the United States because of clashes between the different branches of the federal government, Hobbes's fears have been realized in regard to conflict between the federal and state governments. The Civil War is the most ruinous conflict in which the United States has been involved. This clearly was occasioned by division of power. The federal government claimed powers over the states, which certain states denied. The Confederate States declared their right to leave the Union, and the result was an appeal to arms. I do not wish to suggest that constitutional arrangements were the only—or even the major—cause of the Civil War. The fact that Hobbes concentrates on such factors to the exclusion of all else indicates a shortcoming in his analysis of politics. But it is clear that if there had been an undivided, supreme power in the United States in the 1850s and 1860s, which all parties recognized and to the judgment of which they had to defer, the Civil War might well have been avoided. Protection from an absolute ruler is undoubtedly important. But Hobbes would say that the price of such protection is paid at places like Gettysburg, Antietam, Fredericksburg, and Shiloh.

Turning away from American examples, we see even more clearly the thrust of Hobbes's concerns. In Yugoslavia, Josip Broz Tito was a dictator with enormous power. That there is something to be said for unaccountable power is clear in the terrible conflicts that have erupted in the former Yugoslavia since his death. Throughout Eastern Europe, the joy one naturally feels at the demise of Soviet Communism is tempered by forebodings about what could erupt in the absence of incontestable power. Ethnic or tribal warfare in Georgia, Armenia, Azerbaijan, and elsewhere could be only foretastes of what is to come. In many ways Soviet dictatorship seems less unattractive in comparison.

Hobbes's grim lesson is the need for political security and what this entails. Once again, unaccountable political power is not an end in itself, but without it, no other ends are possible. To achieve security, certain political arrangements are necessary, and once again, many examples support his point of view. But from the perspective of more secure societies, it is possible to question his conclusions.

In accordance with *Federalist* 51, democratic citizens recognize *two* different threats to their liberties: other people and the government. In a situation analogous to the state of nature, in which there is no power to keep all men in awe, other people are a significant danger, and Hobbes of course depicts the outcome as a war of all against all. In this situation, government does not exist and so is not a threat. Because of the dangers of the state of nature, people are willing to erect a government to protect them from other people, though this of course gives rise to the new danger of abuse of governmental authority.

There are important trade-offs here which we must recognize. The two main values involved are often referred to as "liberty" and "security." In this context, "security" refers to being safe from other people; "liberty" refers to being free from governmental power. The two sources of danger may well strike people differently, depending on their situations. Consider the point of view of the inhabitant of an American inner city where crime is rampant. Drugs are openly used and sold and fought over. Drug gangs are constantly at war, engaged in gun battles every day. Ordinary citizens, worried about being caught in the crossfire, are afraid to go out on the streets. What is worse, threatened by drug addicts who are desperate for money for their habits, they are unsafe in their homes as well. To such people, increased police protection would be a great boon. Of course the police are liable to misuse their power to a certain extent. But the need for protection is so overwhelming that people would be willing to face increased risk of such abuse in order to combat the plague of crime. If this line of argument is convincing, take things one step farther, to Bosnia, or the civil war in former Soviet Georgia. Under these conditions, a police state poses risks that many people would gladly accept.

When circumstances are more secure, the Hobbesian argument may well seem less compelling. The particular trade-offs involved are seen perhaps most clearly in a settled legal system. Cherished aspects of the American legal system are constitutional rights and protections. Americans enjoy constitutional guarantees against self-incrimination, illegal searches and seizures, being tried twice for the same crime, and from "cruel and unusual punishments." Since the rulings of the Warren Court in the 1950s and 1960s other protections have been added. For instance, criminal suspects have been guaranteed legal counsel—free legal counsel, if they need it—and the right to be informed of their rights. Obviously, these measures provide important protections against abuse of governmental authority. However, there is an obvious problem with them, because they make it easier for criminals to escape conviction. Confronted with the values of liberty and security, which must be weighed against one another, we will recognize the need for some balance between them. However, exactly what balance we prefer may well depend on our particular circumstances. From the point of view of crime victims, constitutional guarantees are less important than to people who are less threatened by crime. Assume for the moment that suspension of civil liberties would make significant inroads against violent crime. People who do not live in inner cities might be horrified at this prospect. But to people who are constantly under siege, suspension of civil liberties might not seem like a bad idea.

This last is essentially the view of Hobbes. Writing from the perspective of the wholesale breakdown of law and order, he pays almost exclusive attention to this, with little regard for possible abuse of governmental authority. It is clear that he has good reasons for his position, which are not alien to contemporary concerns. It also bears repeating that these concerns are familiar to citizens of relatively secure, peaceful, liberal societies. To show the relevance of Hobbes, we need not invoke the chaotic horrors of regimes in collapse. However, it appears that the contrast between Yugoslavia and American inner cities carries considerable weight. Though besieged inhabitants of inner cities might wish to suspend civil liberties *to some extent*, it is unlikely they would take this to the extent of a full Hobbesian state. Unless, or until, modern societies come to mirror the state of nature more closely, citizens of contemporary states are likely to be concerned with dangers from abuse of governmental power as well as the threat of other people.

There is another respect in which Hobbes's view is extreme. We have seen that he depicts human beings as narrowly self-interested. The object of every action is some good to the actor himself. Hobbes also presents a narrow construal of self-interest. In effect, this boils down to self-preservation. In the state of nature especially, people are so concerned with protecting themselves that they have no other values. We have discussed Hobbes's position above. It is important to note that this understanding of human nature is necessary for Hobbes's defense of the absolute state. People are willing to surrender all rights to government in order to preserve themselves. Once again, their concern with security is so great that they care little for liberty. If people were different, however, they would be less willing to make this bargain. For instance, if they cared more deeply about freedom of conscience or religious matters, they would be less likely to enter into the particular agreement Hobbes presents. And once in civil society they would be more likely to fall into conflict with the ruler and so contribute to political disorder.

Thus Hobbes's particular depiction of human nature is important to his central argument. But it is not clear that exclusively self-interested people are able to constitute a successful commonwealth. In order to maintain itself, a commonwealth must be able to do certain things. These are the attributes of sovereignty, discussed above. It must be able to make laws, tax, judge disputes, coin money, and so on. Offhand, there is little reason to doubt that Hobbes's commonwealth could do these things. But a state must also be able to wage war. In this regard Hobbes runs into problems.

In part because he wrote during a civil war, questions of the citizen's obligations to fight for his sovereign were of deep concern to Hobbes. He discusses these obligations and their limits in his chapter on the rights of subjects (*Lev.*, Chap. 21). There is a problem with his argument here, as he undoubtedly recognizes. As we have repeatedly seen, Hobbes argues that people are motivated by the desire for self-preservation. This is the foundation of the laws of nature, the only true moral science, and also of civil society. Though people in the state of nature surrender their right to all things, the right to defend themselves cannot be surrendered, "because [a person] cannot be understood to aim thereby at any Good to himself" (*Lev.*, Chap. 14, p. 93). But serving in the military is dangerous. Hobbes writes that "man by nature chooseth the lesser evil" (*Lev.*, Chap. 14, p. 98). If the risk of death from military service is significant, it is not clear how a subject could accept this if other courses of action would endanger him less. Draft resistance or desertion are obvious alternatives. There is of course some risk in these courses of action. For instance, deserters might be captured and shot. But if the subject thinks he has a *smaller* chance of dying by attempting to avoid military service or deserting than by serving, it is not clear why he should incur the greater risk.

In Chapter 21 Hobbes provides some leeway. He says no one can be bound to kill himself or other people, unless this is necessary to maintain the sovereignty. Thus Walter can refuse military service under certain circumstances—for instance, if he hires a substitute soldier in his place. Or if he is naturally timorous, allowance should be made. If Walter runs from battle out of fear rather than treachery, this is not injustice but dishonor. But Hobbes says the sovereign can rightfully punish these actions with death (*Lev.*, Chap. 21, pp. 151–152). But of course, the sovereign is always the sole judge of what can and cannot be rightfully punished with death.

There are two cases in which soldiers must serve, even at the risk of their lives. First is when someone has signed up as a soldier. This "taketh away the excuse of a timorous nature," and the subject is obliged "not only to go to the battle but also not to run from it without his Captain's leave" (*Lev.*, Chap. 21, p. 152). The source of the obligation here is the agreement to serve, under the natural law to keep agreements. However, one could argue that natural law is a set of rules that tend towards one's preservation. If following them will increase the chances of one's ruin, should one follow? The answer would appear to be "no," as Hobbes suggests in making the laws of nature bind in conscience but not "to the putting them in act" in the state of nature. If the subject thinks he stands a better chance of surviving by running than by fighting, it is not clear why he should fight.

The second case is when the sovereign is in need. Hobbes writes:

> And when the Defense of the Commonwealth requireth at once the help of all that are able to bear Arms, every one is obliged; because otherwise the Institution of the Commonwealth, which they have not the purpose or courage to preserve, was in vain. (*Lev.*, Chap 21, p. 152)

Once again, Hobbes's reasoning is questionable. There are certain circumstances under which people obviously must fight. One case is a war of extermination. If the enemy wins they intend to kill everybody on Ramon's side, perhaps through slow torture. Under these circumstances, it is obviously in Ramon's interest to fight; little would be gained by surrendering. But even here, Ramon should desert if he thinks this increases his chances. A more serious problem for Hobbes is that wars of extermination are unusual. In most cases, if Ramon's side loses, he merely exchanges a former sovereign for a new one. Living conditions might change, but for a Hobbesian individual who cares primarily about self-preservation, this is of little concern, unless the new sovereign is intent on wholesale murder. Once again, because this is not often the case, it is not clear why Ramon should not surrender at the first opportunity. Hobbes responds that this will destroy the commonwealth. But a central weakness of his political theory is apparent in the fact that this will be of little concern to the subjects, as long as the new sovereign does not intend their deaths.

In order to make his sovereign as powerful as possible and to cut off sources of conflict with and resistance against him, Hobbes reduces all sources of human motivation to self-interest, which is further reduced to self-preservation. Hobbes says people care about life "as not to be weary of it." But this is intended to add relatively little to self-preservation. The problem here is clear. Hobbes's inability to explain why soldiers should fight for their country indicates the insufficiency of political ties based solely on self-interest. In order to survive, a commonwealth must be able to claim the allegiance of its citizens. They must be willing to sacrifice for it, perhaps to sacrifice their lives. This is most apparent in wartime. The sacrifice of a few is necessary for the welfare of the many. Thus countries honor heroism and pay homage to those who gave their lives. But once again, Hobbes is not able to account for heroism. People bent on self-preservation would not risk their lives for their countries.

Proof that Hobbes recognizes this problem is found in his "Review and Conclusion." This is the final section of *Leviathan*. It comes after forty-seven chapters (and 483 pages of the Cambridge edition) of argument. Hobbes writes:

> To the Laws of Nature declared in the 15. Chapter I would have this added, That every man is bound by Nature as much as in him lieth to protect in War the Authority by which he is himself protected in time of peace. For he that pretendeth a Right of Nature to preserve his own body cannot pretend a Right of Nature to destroy him by whose strength he is preserved. It is a manifest contradiction to himself. (*Lev.*, Rev. and Concl., p. 484)

But is this a contradiction? The laws of nature are conclusions drawn by reason about what is necessary for self-preservation. Once again, reason supports the position that if you want to preserve yourself and believe the chances are better if you run than if you fight, then you should run away. If self-preservation is the foundation of all morality, Hobbes is actually guilty of the contradiction here, in recommending a course of action that could work against self-preservation.

The problem is not confined to war. In different aspects of life, commonwealths require sacrifice, up to and including risk of life. Police officers must risk their lives to combat criminals; firefighters must risk their lives to rescue people from burning buildings. On the basis of Hobbes's premises, there is no way to explain why people would or should be willing to do this. Once again, the consequences of their not being willing to do so would be ruinous to the state. But the Hobbesian individual will calculate: "though I recognize the need for *someone* to fight crime, *I* am not going to be the one to do it." If everyone thinks like this, as reason indeed suggests they should, then the state of nature will recur. But Hobbes is hard-pressed to explain why people should think differently.

Hobbes's problem can be seen more clearly if we turn to Pericles' funeral oration in Thucydides' *History of the Peloponnesian War*. This is one of the greatest funeral speeches in our literature. It should be noted that Hobbes's first published work was a translation of Thucydides into English. So this, one of the most famous portions of the *History*, is a text he knew well. In this speech, Pericles explains why the dead soldiers in whose honor he speaks were willing to give their lives:

> To me it seems that the consummation which has overtaken these men shows us the meaning of manliness in its first revelation and in its final proof. Some of them, no

doubt, had their faults; but what we ought to remember first is their gallant conduct against the enemy in defense of their native land. They have blotted out evil with good and done more service to the commonwealth than they ever did harm in their private lives. No one of these men weakened because he wanted to go on enjoying his wealth; no one put off the awful day in the hope that he might live to escape his poverty and grow rich. More to be desired than such things, they chose to check the enemy's pride. This, to them, was a risk most glorious, and they accepted it, willing to strike down the enemy and relinquish everything else. As for success or failure, they left that in the doubtful hands of Hope, and when the reality of battle was before their faces, they put their trust in their own selves. In the fighting, they thought it more honorable to stand their ground and suffer death than to give in and save their lives. So they fled from the reproaches of men, abiding with life and limb the brunt of battle; and, in a small moment of time, the climax of their lives, a culmination of glory, not of fear, were swept away from us. (Thucydides, II, p. 42)

We have no way of knowing whether Pericles' assessment is accurate. But its account of heroic action differs little from what is found in other funeral speeches. Heroes fight and die for various reasons: love of country, honor, unwillingness to let down their friends and comrades in arms, glory. It is striking that all these are motives a Hobbesian individual could not respond to. Hobbes removes these from human psychology to make it easier for individuals in the state of nature to erect a powerful state. But without these motives to appeal to, Hobbes is unable to justify fighting for one's country. If a functioning state requires sacrifice from certain citizens, Hobbes's "Mortall God" fails because it cannot inspire such sacrifice.

Hobbes's problems here point beyond his own political theory. In *Leviathan* and his other works he attempts to account for the citizen's obligations to the state solely in terms of self-interest. But because states require sacrifice, self-interest is not a secure basis. If a political theory is based on individuals united in political society out of self-interest, it will have a hard time explaining why they should make sacrifices for their fellow citizens. But without such sacrifices, no state can survive.

HOBBES AND LIBERAL POLITICAL THEORY

To close this chapter, I will discuss Hobbes's place in the development of liberal political theory. I have noted above that Hobbes played an important role in the liberal tradition, though he is not a liberal theorist in the proper sense of the term. Elaborating on his relationship to the tradition should help to clarify both Hobbes's thought and the nature of liberal political theory. Throughout subsequent chapters we will return to this theme and examine other thinkers' relationships to the liberal tradition. We can begin with a rough sketch of liberal political theory.

"Liberal" political theory, as discussed throughout this volume, is often referred to as "classical liberalism." It is not the ideology of the "liberal" wing of the Democratic party in the United States, epitomized by Ted Kennedy. That view, often referred to as "welfare-state liberalism," stands opposed to the Conservative views of Republican politicians like Ronald Reagan. Throughout this book, the "liberalism" under discussion is generally classical liberalism.

Classical liberalism has been the central current of political discourse in the English-speaking world since roughly the seventeenth century. Scholars present somewhat different accounts of classical liberalism, depending on their views and interests. As I interpret the theory, its main concern is the individual and his rights. The theory's central aim is protecting these rights, so the individual is able to enjoy as much freedom as possible. There are a number of unclear terms in this capsule account, especially "rights" and "freedom." I will not give detailed accounts of these here. Throughout subsequent chapters, we will be examining how different thinkers construe these concepts, which will allow us to appreciate some of their complexity.

The central elements of liberal thought can be broken down into five main propositions. Once again, the list I present is subject to some variation; specific points are to some extent arbitrary, as liberal theory can be carved up differently to meet different concerns. But the following rough points should be widely acceptable and should provide a starting point for more detailed analysis in subsequent chapters.

I. The first point is the centrality of the individual. Historically, liberalism arose from the breakup of feudal society. With people's liberation from serfdom and other forms of servitude, they gradually became the central actors in Western politics, epitomized in the rise and extension of democratic institutions. Thus liberal theory and the free "individual" appeared on the historical stage together. The liberal individual is conceptualized apart from society in a number of important respects. The individual is viewed as having his own interests, which are not given to him or heavily influenced by society. Accordingly, we can say that these interests exist "prior to" society, which is often said to come into being through the union of such individuals. Along similar lines, the individual possesses rights, or moral claims against other people. Rights are discussed in more detail in the following chapter. For now, we can note that their main feature can be understood in territorial terms. The individual possesses a space into which other people are not permitted to enter. What is crucial is that these rights are not received from society. The individual has them as a consequence of being human.

II. The second point is that society is viewed as nothing but individuals. It has no substantive existence apart from the people who constitute it. The same is true of the state. State institutions are reducible to the people who staff them. Thus the community is nothing but a collection of individuals assembled together. The common good or the good of society is nothing but a numerical sum of the best interests of the people who constitute it.

III. Third is a distinctive view of politics as "instrumental." As noted in the previous chapter, instrumental reasoning is in terms of means and ends. Given a specific end, the question is how it can be most easily or efficiently achieved. These categories are central to liberal theory, because individuals are viewed as self-interested, with interests and rights fully developed "prior to" entering political society. The state is erected because it is needed to achieve people's ends. Thus the state is a *means* to the attainment of ends that exist apart from it, and has no interests of its own. Because it is created to advance the interests and protect the rights of the people who constitute it, the state should be assessed according to how well it accomplishes these tasks.

An instrumental view of politics can be contrasted with other views, according to which political activity is good in itself. Perhaps the clearest statement of this alternative view is found in Aristotle's *Politics.* Aristotle claims that man is a "political animal," because his moral and intellectual capacities can develop fully only in political association with his fellows. For Aristotle, the state (*polis*) has the crucial function of helping people to develop in these ways. Thus the end of life is "ruling and being ruled in turn." According to the Aristotelian view, the state plays an essential role in giving people their ends. Thus Aristotle argues that *the state* is prior to the individual.[31] This is a far cry from the view that the individual enters political society to advance interests he already has.

IV. In order to attain its ends, the liberal state has limited functions. In general these center on protecting rights, especially the right to property. Generally, an important assumption underlying this position—whether stated or unstated—is that without political society property would be insecure. Classic accounts of exactly why this is so are the arguments of Hobbes and Locke, as we will see in the following chapter. This circumscribed view of the state's responsibilities can be attributed to the historical period when classical liberalism took shape. In subsequent centuries, as Western societies developed and became more democratic, the state expanded and took on new functions, in order to meet the ever-increasing demands of the enfranchised population. Its new responsibilities included education, public health, and social welfare programs—such as old age, accident, and unemployment insurance. Especially important, the state became responsible for maintaining a stable, growing economy. The result was the so-called welfare state found in varying degrees in all the industrial democracies. Liberal theory evolved accordingly, becoming increasingly involved with justifying expanded state programs. Its arguments are now found in the views of Liberal Democratic politicians. Present-day "Conservatives," such as Reagan, wish to reduce the size and functions of the state. In many respects, especially their call for less state intervention in economic affairs, their views represent a return to classical liberalism.

Closely related to the functions of the state is its composition. The state we associate with classical liberalism is minimal. As its main function is protecting rights, its main institutions are suited to this task. These include a police force, judicial system, and prison system. In order to protect the population from outside aggression, the state is also responsible for national defense and so puts forth a suitable military establishment. These elements comprise the bulk of state institutions. The state plays little role in such areas as education and public health. There are no large-scale bureaucracies to manage the economy or redistribute income to provide for the poor and needy. As noted in the Introduction to Volume I, Hegel describes philosophy as "its own time apprehended in thoughts."[32] The main reason classical liberals view the state as having these institutions is that this is what the state *was* as it existed in their societies. In subsequent centuries as the social welfare state arose, theorists' conceptions of the state developed accordingly.

V. Last is the liberal conception of freedom. This view is commonly referred to as "negative" freedom, in contrast with "positive" freedom, which will be discussed in detail in Chapter 6. The central concern of liberal freedom is the absence of coercive interference by other people, especially the government, though freedom can be abridged by the actions of individuals as well. When we speak of different freedoms guaranteed by the U.S. Constitution and Bill of Rights, it is this conception that we have in mind. Freedom of speech means one can say what one likes without being punished by the government. Freedom of the press means one can print what one likes without government censorship. The same is true of freedom of religion. This of course means the state will not interfere with the practice of one's religious beliefs.

If we put these different elements together, we can grasp the main themes of liberal political theory. People have rights, because they are human beings. These rights are not secure unless there exists a government to protect them. Government, then, is set up as a means to attain this end. According to this line of argument, entry into civil society entails surrendering a certain amount of freedom. If freedom is the absence of interference, then the rise of government necessarily entails a diminution of freedom. But the justification for government is that the loss of freedom caused by government is *less* than without government. For in the absence of government the individual is not secure in her rights because of the threat posed by other people. In spite of the loss of freedom it entails, government increases people's security and so freedom.

This line of argument is well illustrated by social contract theory, as discussed above. In order to justify government, theorists depict the problems people would encounter without it, in the state of nature. To overcome the problems of the state of nature, the primary purpose and institutions of government center on protecting the individual from other people.

In many important respects Hobbes is a liberal theorist. He too begins with the individual, who holds a right to all things necessary for his preservation. Self-preservation is the individual's primary interest, which he does not derive from political society. As we saw at length, Hobbes argues vigorously that society is nothing but a collection of individuals. Because of the horrible conditions of the state of nature, individuals agree to form government, which has the purpose of advancing their preexisting ends. Once again, the state has limited, coercive purposes and so limited, coercive institutions. In all these respects Hobbes is a liberal. In fact he deserves a certain amount of credit for pioneering this distinctive approach to political questions. He is one of the first theorists in our tradition to begin with the individual. In this light it is instructive to contrast his view with that of the author of the *Vindiciae contra Tyrannos*. Arguing against resistance to government by private citizens, Mornay writes:

> Now we are not speaking here of private individuals, who are not to be regarded as the basic parts of a community any more than planks, nails, and pegs are taken as the parts of a ship; or stones, beams, and mortar as the parts of a house.[33]

Thus some sixty years before Hobbes wrote *Elements of Law*, it was widely believed that individuals are *not* the primary elements of society. Mornay appears to advance a remnant of the medieval view that, roughly, society is composed of territorial units to which individuals are attached. We have seen why Hobbes wished to combat the idea of a preexisting community or people. The point to note here is that in developing his position, he advanced the distinctive liberal view of political relationships.

In spite of all these points of similarity, Hobbes is not generally regarded as a liberal political theorist in the full sense of the term. Though his approach is distinctively liberal, his conclusions are not. We have seen that he views freedom as the absence of interference, and so coincides with the liberal position in this regard. In addition, he believes that the erection of government represents an increase of freedom. Though the all-powerful Leviathan state can impede freedom in innumerable ways, its interference is *less* than that of other individuals in the chaotic state of nature. Though the individual surrenders virtually all rights to the state, this still represents an increase in freedom. The main reason for excluding Hobbes from the liberal camp is that the individual is too tightly restricted by the state. Not only does classical liberalism have a distinctive view of freedom, but a central concern of the theory is guaranteeing a significant sphere of freedom *from the state.* Hobbes, clearly, does not do this. We have seen his reasoning that the sovereign, though legally unchecked, will act to promote his subjects' interests. But most liberal theorists would insist on legal, constitutional checks (along the lines of those discussed in Chapter 5). Though Hobbes undoubtedly believes entry into civil society represents an increase of freedom, his fear of constitutional devices such as separation of powers and checks and balances is not shared by liberal theorists. They fear the *absence* of constitutional government would mean tyranny and so believe unchecked government of the kind Hobbes suggests is incompatible with freedom. In order to make this case, they too would argue from a hypothetical state of nature. But in their view, man's condition in the state of nature is significantly better than Hobbes allows. In the following chapter we will examine a fully developed liberal alternative to Hobbes's social contract theory.

In conclusion, then, as we saw in our discussion of *Federalist* 51, liberal theorists are concerned with *two* main sources of danger to individual rights. The individual is threatened by other people and by the state. The state protects one from other people, but poses a danger itself, and so must be held in check by constitutional devices. Throughout this chapter, we have seen that Hobbes is not deeply concerned with protecting the individual from the state. He insists on undivided sovereignty and is adamantly opposed to constitutional checks on abuse of governmental power. For these reasons, in spite of his important contribution to the development of liberal political theory, he himself is not generally viewed as a liberal theorist.

NOTES

1. T. Hobbes, "The Autobiography of Thomas Hobbes," B. Farrington, trans., *The Rationalist Annual* (1958), p. 23; this work cited hereafter as "Autobiography," in text. For biographical details see A. Rogow, *Thomas Hobbes* (New York, 1986); for a valuable discussion of Hobbes's intellectual context, see J. Sommerville, *Thomas Hobbes: Political Ideas in Historical Context* (New York, 1992).

2. See Rogow, *Thomas Hobbes*, p. 124.

3. *Leviathan* (*Lev.*) is cited according to chapter number and page number, in R. Tuck's Cambridge edition; *Elements of Law* (*EL*) and *De Cive* (*DC*) are cited according to part, chapter, and section number (thus 1.3.3 in either work would be Part I, Chapter 1, Section 3). Complete references below under "Texts Cited." Unless otherwise indicated, unaccompanied chapter and page references are to *Leviathan*. Throughout this chapter I take slight liberties with spelling and punctuation, and remove the italicization of various words and phrases. Unless otherwise indicated all italicizations presented are from original texts.

4. M. M. Goldsmith, Introduction to *Elements of Law*, 2nd ed. (New York, 1969), pp. v–vi.

5. J. Aubrey, *Brief Lives*, O. Dick, ed. (London, 1950), p. 150.

6. *Elements of Philosophy, The First Section, Concerning Body,* in *The English Works of Thomas Hobbes*, I, ix; full reference below, under "Texts Cited."

7. M. Oakeshott, "Introduction" to Hobbes, *Leviathan* (Oxford, 1946), p. viii.

8. For recent uses of similar devices, see esp. J. Rawls, *A Theory of Justice* (Cambridge, MA, 1971); R. Nozick, *Anarchy, State*, and *Utopia* (New York, 1974).

9. For traditional laws of nature, see discussions of St. Thomas Aquinas and Hellenistic Political Theory in Volume I, Chaps. 6 and 9.

10. M. Montaigne, quoted by R. Tuck, *Hobbes* (Oxford, 1989), p. 8.

11. *Leviathan*, Chap. 15, p. 111. Important scholars have argued that the laws of nature are intended by Hobbes to be laws in the proper sense in that they are commanded by God. This would make Hobbes a traditional natural law theorist. See A. E. Taylor, "The Ethical Doctrine of Hobbes," in *Hobbes Studies*, K. Brown, ed. (Cambridge, MA, 1966); and H. Warrender, *The Political Philosophy of Hobbes* (Oxford, 1957). For discussion, see T. Nagel, "Hobbes's Concept of Obligation," Philosophical Review, 68 (1959); Q. Skinner, "Thomas Hobbes: Rhetoric and the Construction of Morality," *Proceedings of the British Academy*, 76 (1990); D. Johnston, *The Rhetoric of Leviathan* (Princeton, 1986).

12. Cicero, *De Re Publica*, III, 22; translation by G. H. Sabine and S. B. Smith, as *On the Commonwealth*; full reference below, under "Texts Cited."

13. See esp. Volume I, 251–257.

14. See Volume I, 253–255.

15. *Summa Theologiae*, I–II, Q. 95, Art. 2; see Vol. I, 256–257. Augustine's contention here is out of keeping with the general tenor of his political theory; see H. A. Deane, *The Political and Social Ideas of St. Augustine* (New York, 1963), pp. 88–89.

16. See B. Tierney, *Religion, Law, and the Growth of Constitutional Thought: 1050–1650* (Cambridge, 1982); also O. Gierke, *Political Theories of the Middle Age*, F. W. Maitland, trans. (1900; rpt. Boston, 1958); see also, Vol. I, 269–277.

17. Quoted in Tierney, *The Crisis of Church and State 1050–1300* (Englewood Cliffs, NJ, 1964) pp. 79–80.

18. For the development of the doctrine, see Tierney, *Religion, Law, and the Growth of Constitutional Thought*; also Vol. I, Chaps. 10 and 11.

19. J. Franklin, *Constitutionalism and Resistance in the Sixteenth Century* (New York, 1969), pp. 138–139; quotations from the *Vindiciae* are from Franklin's edition, cited as *Vindiciae* in text, with page numbers from this edition.

20. For corresponding arguments in *Elements of Law*, see 2.2.1–9; for discussion, see Goldsmith, *Hobbes's Science of Politics* (New York, 1966), pp. 155–161.

21. Goldsmith, *Hobbes's Science of Politics*, pp. 160–161.

22. See Vol. I, 232–240.

23. M. Weber, "Politics as a Vocation," in *From Max Weber: Essays in Sociology*, H. Gerth and C. W. Mills, eds. (Oxford, 1946), p. 78; Weber's emphasis.

24. See Q. Skinner, *The Foundations of Modern Political Thought*, 2 vols. (Cambridge, 1978), esp. II, pp. 349–358.

25. P. King, "Sovereignty," in *The Blackwell Encyclopedia of Political Thought*, D. Miller, ed. (Oxford, 1987), pp. 492–495.

26. J. Bodin, *Six Books of the Commonwealth*, Book I, Chap. 8 (p. 23); this work cited hereafter, as Bodin, in text, according to book and chapter number, and page number in translation of J. Franklin; full reference below under "Texts Cited."

27. I owe the reference to Bodin to Sommerville, *Thomas Hobbes*, p. 82; in the quotation, I translate Hobbes's reference to Bodin (Bk. II, Chap. 1, of *Six Books of the Commonwealth*) into English.

28. Two good recent discussions of Hobbes's treatment of religion in *Leviathan* are Sommerville, *Thomas Hobbes*; and Johnston, *Rhetoric of Leviathan*.

29. *The Federalist: A Commentary on the Constitution of the United States*, from the Original Text of Alexander Hamilton, John Jay, James Madison (New York, n. d.), #51.

30. Tuck, *Hobbes*, p. 74.

31. See Vol. I, 110–112.

32. G. W. F. Hegel, *Philosophy of Right*, T. M. Knox, trans. (Oxford, 1942), p. 11.

33. *Vindiciae contra Tyrannos*, p. 152.

TEXTS CITED

Bodin, J. *On Sovereignty: Four chapters from The Six Books of the Commonwealth*. J. Franklin, ed. and trans. Cambridge, 1992.

Cicero. *On the Commonwealth*. G. H. Sabine and S. B. Smith, eds. 1929; rpt. Indianapolis, 1976.

Hobbes, Thomas. "The Autobiography of Thomas Hobbes." B. Farrington, trans. *The Rationalist Annual*. 1958.

Hobbes, Thomas. *De Cive*. In *The English Works of Thomas Hobbes*. W. Molesworth, ed. 11 vols. London, 1839–45. Vol. 2.

Hobbes, Thomas. *The Elements of Law*. 2nd ed. M. M. Goldsmith, ed. New York, 1969.

Hobbes, Thomas. *Leviathan*. R. Tuck, ed. Cambridge, 1991.

Hobbes, Thomas. *The English Works of Thomas Hobbes*. W. Molesworth, ed. 11 vols. London, 1839–45.

Mornay, P. *Vindiciae contra Tyrannos*. In *Constitutionalism and Resistance in the Sixteenth Century*. J. H. Franklin, ed. and trans. New York, 1969.

The Oxford Annotated Bible. H. May and B. Metzger, eds. Oxford, 1962.

Thucydides. *History of the Peloponnesian War*. R. Warner, trans. Harmondsworth, England, 1954.

Tierney, B., ed. *The Crisis of Church and State: 1050–1300*. Englewood Cliffs, NJ, 1964.

FURTHER READING

Goldsmith, M. M. *Hobbes's Science of Politics*. New York, 1966.

Hampton, J. *Hobbes and the Social Contract Tradition*. Cambridge, 1986.

Johnston, D. *The Rhetoric of Leviathan.* Princeton, 1986.

Kavka, G. *Hobbesian Moral and Political Theory.* Princeton, 1986.

Macpherson, C. B. *The Political Theory of Possessive Individualism.* Oxford, 1964.

Nagel, T. "Hobbes's Concept of Obligation." *Philosophical Review,* 68 (1959).

Oakeshott, M. Introduction to Hobbes, *Leviathan.* Oxford, 1946.

Peters, R. *Hobbes.* Harmondsworth, England, 1956.

Rogow, A. *Thomas Hobbes.* New York, 1986.

Skinner, Q. "Thomas Hobbes: Rhetoric and the Construction of Morality." *Proceedings of the British Academy,* 76 (1990).

Sommerville, J. *Thomas Hobbes: Political Ideas in Historical Context.* New York, 1992.

Strauss, L. *The Political Philosophy of Hobbes.* K. Sinclair, trans. 1936; rpt. Chicago, 1952.

Taylor, A. E. "The Ethical Doctrine of Hobbes." In *Hobbes Studies,* K. Brown, ed., Cambridge, MA, 1966.

Tuck, R. *Hobbes.* Oxford, 1989.

Warrender, H. *The Political Philosophy of Hobbes.* Oxford, 1957.

C h a p t e r

3

JOHN LOCKE AND LIBERAL POLITICAL THEORY

Wᴿɪᴛᴛᴇɴ ɪɴ ᴛʜᴇ ʏᴇᴀʀꜱ ʙᴇꜰᴏʀᴇ the Glorious Revolution of 1688, John Locke's *Second Treatise of Government* defends the rights of the individual against unjust political authority. The work was published in 1689, though Locke only acknowledged its authorship in a codicil to his will, which was read after his death. Through the Glorious Revolution, James II was driven from the English throne, to be replaced by William of Orange (William III) and his wife Mary (Mary II), James's eldest daughter. Locke's stated purpose in the work is as follows:

> [T]o establish the Throne of our Great Restorer, Our present King William; to make good his Title, in the Consent of the People, which being the only one of all lawful Governments, he has more fully and clearly than any Prince in Christendom: And to justify to the World, the People of England, whose love of their Just and Natural Rights, with their Resolution to preserve them, saved the Nation when it was on the very brink of Slavery and Ruin.[1]

Locke's language indicates that the work was written to justify a successful revolution. In recent years, however, scholars have established that it was actually written several years before 1688, in order to help bring a revolution about.[2] The *Second Treatise* has been appealed to in order to justify revolutions ever since, including the American Revolution, as it exercised profound influence on the American founders.[3]

Because Locke makes his case by arguing from an artificial state of nature, out of which people contract in order to establish government, the *Second Treatise* is readily compared with the political thought of Hobbes. Locke differs from Hobbes on central points; his contract theory provides an important counter to Hobbesian defense of unbridled political power. But the *Two Treatises* was actually written in opposition to a different defender of royal absolutism, Robert Filmer, whose chief work, *Patriarcha*, was widely read and discussed during the period in which Locke wrote. The *First Treatise* is a detailed and devastating refutation of Filmer's position. The *Second Treatise*, beginning where the *First* leaves off, systematically treats specific questions Filmer raised, in order to support the right to resist unjust power. In the following sections, I will repeatedly discuss similarities and differences between Locke and Hobbes, as these deepen our understanding of both thinkers. This should not be misleading if the actual circumstances of the *Two Treatises'* composition are kept in mind. Filmer is remembered today mainly as the target of Locke's theoretical wrath. Though many of his arguments are implausible from our point of view, because he shaped Locke's intentions in the *Second Treatise* as well as the *First*, his views are essential for understanding both *Treatises*.

LOCKE'S LIFE AND INTELLECTUAL BACKGROUND

Locke was born in Somerset, in 1632, to a modest landed family.[4] His father served as an officer on the Parliamentary side in the English Civil War, which culminated in the trial and execution of Charles I, in 1649. Through the patronage of one of the elder Locke's fellow-officers, John Locke received unusual educational opportunities, including a place at Oxford, where he stayed on to study medicine, the main alternative at that time to a career in the Church. Locke's subsequent fortunes were decisively influenced by his association with Lord Ashley, later Earl of Shaftesbury, a prominent nobleman, who became an important figure in English politics. Seriously ill, Shaftesbury submitted to a difficult liver operation, which Locke supervised and guided to miraculous success. Afterwards, Locke enjoyed Shaftesbury's patronage, until the latter's death, in 1683, serving in various capacities, most notably as Shaftesbury's "assistant pen."[5] Under Shaftesbury's influence, Locke became an opponent of the Stuart monarchy, and deeply involved in plans to exclude the Catholic James, brother of Charles and heir to the throne, from the monarchy upon Charles's death. The *Two Treatises of Government* was written to support exclusion, some time between the years 1679 and 1683. More precise dating is difficult, and it is also not clear how much of the work was written during this period and how much added later, in connection with its publication in 1689. Because no original manuscript of the work remains, it is not possible to say exactly when different portions were written, or their order of composition. It seems likely, however, that substantial portions of the *Second Treatise* were written before the *First*, and can be dated before 1680.[6]

In the crisis atmosphere surrounding the issue of exclusion, Shaftesbury fled to Holland in 1682, where he died. Locke fled in 1683, and remained in Holland until James had been removed from the throne. As we will see below, in many ways the *Second Treatise* is a radical tract. This probably explains why Locke never acknowledged its authorship during his life. Locke published two other important works in 1689, *An Essay Concerning Human Understanding*, and *A Letter Concerning Toleration*. Because of the *Essay* especially, he achieved enormous renown and secured a premier place as a proponent of reason and science among the forefathers of the Enlightenment. During his last years Locke was employed by the English government in various capacities, working, for example, on reorganizing English coinage and establishing an effective system of credit for the state.

Of special interest to students of Locke's political theory are his close connections with revolutionary political organizations. The *Two Treatises* is not a pure academic exercise; Locke wrote the work in connection with an active political movement. Arguably, his involvement in political activity was greater than that of any comparable figure in the history of political theory. As we will see below, Locke's concern with his specific political circumstances shows up in central features of the *Two Treatises*. At points the work verges on a *livre de circonstances*, a document written to justify specific policies in a specific situation, rather than a more theoretical examination of central issues undertaken for its own sake.

As an opponent of royal absolutism, Locke attempted to counter the most important theoretical defense of royal power of his day, Robert Filmer's *Patriarcha*. Throughout the medieval period, the main argument in favor of absolute royal power was that God had placed rulers on their thrones and given them unchecked power. This view receives strong biblical support, especially in Chapter 13 of St. Paul's Epistle to the Romans:

> Let every person be subject to the governing authorities. For there is no authority except from God, and those that exist have been instituted by God. (Rom. 13:1)

Arguments of this type are commonly referred to as the "divine right of kings." But as we saw in the last chapter, by the seventeenth century this line of argument had been largely superseded by different theories of the social contract, according to which political power was held conditionally. The main claim here is that people are originally free. Political power derives from the people, and is given to the ruler only for the sake of certain ends, mainly to protect them from foreign enemies and from one another, and to promote the public welfare. As long as the ruler pursues these ends, his power is legitimate and he should be obeyed. But when he does not fulfill his function, or acts contrary to the people's interests, then they recover their original liberty and no longer have to obey.

Obviously, this brief statement of medieval absolutism and contractarian counter-arguments is overly simple. But these broad claims set the parameters for much political debate during the early seventeenth century. We saw in the last chapter that Hobbes attempted to counter contractual limits on royal authority by arguing that the purported contract had not been entered into. Before the rise of a sovereign, there is no "people", and because the sovereign is not a party to the contractual agreement from which his power derives, subjects' obligations to him are not conditional.

Filmer pursues a different tack. His main argument depends on identifying the power of fathers and kings. Like many medieval thinkers, he argues from an interpretation of the Bible. But rather than concentrating on the fact that God has placed rulers on their thrones, Filmer focuses on the description of Creation in the Book of Genesis. Adam was not only the first father but the first king. Subsequent generations of his descendants are not born free but in subjection to Adam and his successors, with the power of fathers derived from God alone. Contract theorists argue that people (or the people) are originally free of government until they voluntarily surrender their power to their rulers. Filmer counters that this is absurd. People are not born free but into families, and so naturally subject to the authority of their fathers. In Filmer's words,

> I see not then how the children of Adam, or of any man else, can be free from subjection to their parents. And this subjection of children is the only foundation of all regal authority, by the ordination of God himself.[7]

In the *First Treatise*, Locke describes Filmer's position as consisting of two claims: first, that "all Government is absolute," because, second, "no Man is born free" (I, 2). Filmer holds that the claim that paternal authority has always been absolute—"as large and ample as the absolutest dominion of any monarch"—is demonstrated by the fact that early patriarchs had power of life and death over their children, as illustrated in biblical texts (Filmer, p. 7).

According to Filmer, relationships of subordination are natural. People are not equal, as the son is obviously below the authority of his father. Thus, up to a point, Filmer's view rests on inescapable facts of family life. He argues that subjection to paternal power is mankind's natural and inevitable lot: "There is, and always shall be continued to the end of the world, a natural right of a supreme father over every multitude . . ." (Filmer, p. 11). Because people are not naturally free, they are not able to choose their own governments. The power of rulers is not derived from subjects but by descent from Adam, directly from God, and so it is not bound by contractual restrictions. In the *First Treatise*, Locke describes Filmer's developed position as follows:

> Men are not born free, and therefore could never have the liberty to choose either Governors, or Forms of Government. Princes have their Power Absolute, and by Divine Right, for Slaves could never have a Right to Compact or Consent. Adam was an absolute Monarch, and so are all Princes ever since. (I, 5)

A more elaborate statement is given in I, 9:

> This Fatherly Authority then, or Right of Fatherhood, in our [Author's] sense is a Divine unalterable Right of Sovereignty, whereby a Father or a Prince hath an Absolute, Arbitrary, Unlimited, and Unlimitable Power over the Lives, Liberties, and Estates of his Children and Subjects; so that he may take or alienate their Estates, sell, castrate, or use their Persons as he pleases, they being all his Slaves, and he Lord or Proprietor of every Thing, and his unbounded Will their Law.

The reader will note that the power of the father/king extends beyond the political domain to property as well. Included in absolute royal power is absolute ownership. The king owns all, as he rules all. Indeed, political power is a form of property, bequeathed by father to eldest son, along with all other property. Questions of ownership are therefore important to Filmer, and so also to Locke, and we will return to them below.

From a contemporary perspective, Filmer's arguments will probably seem singularly unconvincing. Many of his specific points, moreover, are poorly supported, based on misunderstanding or misquotation of Biblical texts. A good example is his citation of the biblical injunction, "Honor thy Father," to support the need to submit to paternal power. In Filmer's words:

> To confirm this natural right of regal power, we find in the decalogue that the law which enjoins obedience to kings is delivered in the terms of "honor thy father" as if all power were originally in the father. (Filmer, p. 12)

As Locke has no trouble showing in the *First Treatise*, this is a poor argument. The biblical passage is misquoted. Correctly stated, the commandment in question is of course "Honor thy father *and thy mother*." The passage does not pertain to the monarchical power of the father but to "what was due in common to both Father and Mother" (Locke, *First Treatise*, 60–61). Locke argues that what is due to one's parents is honor, rather than the obedience of subjects to their rulers.

Throughout the *First Treatise*, Locke argues against Filmer's central claims. He states his main conclusions at the opening of the *Second Treatise*. Locke recounts four main points: (1) That Adam was not given the relevant power by God; (2) that even if Adam had been granted this power, his heirs did not have a right to it; (3) that even if his heirs did have such a right, there are no clear rules of succession according to which rightful heirs can be named; (4) that even if there were such rules, it is impossible to identify Adam's actual heirs, because of the great length of time that has passed since God's original grant of power to him (II, 1). Thus even if political power actually were derived from the power of the original father, this would have no practical implications.

Though *Patriarcha* was probably written in the 1630s, it was not published until 1680,[8] long after Filmer's death (in 1653). But Filmer's ideas were taken seriously in the heated atmosphere of the exclusion crisis, and Locke felt the need to respond. An indication of how seriously Filmer was taken is the fact that Rousseau addresses his ideas in his *Social Contract* (published in 1762) more than one hundred years after Filmer's death. In Book I, Chapter 2 of the work Rousseau says that he is not going to discuss King Adam or other forefathers. But he does this out of modesty:

> I hope I will be appreciated for this moderation, for since I am a direct descendant of these princes, and perhaps of the eldest branch, how am I to know whether, after the verification of titles, I might not find myself the legitimate king of the human race?[9]

Though Rousseau treats Filmer with levity, it is interesting that he treats him at all. As for Locke, though he has little trouble dismantling Filmer's arguments in the *First Treatise*, Filmer's influence is apparent in the *Second* as well. Having criticized Filmer in the *First Treatise*, Locke goes on to develop his own account of the nature and origin of political authority, to show there are alternatives to patriarchal power other than "perpetual Disorder and Mischief, Tumult, Sedition, and Rebellion,"(II, 1) as Filmer had claimed. But because Locke's view is intended as a counter to Filmer's, he feels impelled to provide correct accounts of matters Filmer discusses. Because Filmer argues that man is born in subjection to paternal authority, Locke must explain exactly how man is born free. Because Filmer conflates paternal and political power, Locke carefully distinguishes them. In the course of doing so, he presents a classic account of the liberal view of the respective rights and obligations of parents and children. An additional instance we will discuss is Locke's treatment of the origin of property in the state of nature, which is also required to clear up problems Filmer raises. Though Locke's *First Treatise* is not often read and Filmer is generally remembered, if at all, only as the unfortunate target of that work, there is strong continuity between the two *Treatises*. The influence of Filmer is necessary for understanding Locke's intentions in his greatest political work.

STATE OF NATURE AND LAW OF NATURE

Like Hobbes, Locke justifies political power through the device of the social contract. As we saw in the last chapter, a social contract argument proceeds in two stages. The theorist begins by positing a situation without political authority, generally referred to as the state of nature. This approach calls attention to the problems government must solve. The state of nature is constructed by placing people, as they are in existing society, in a condition without government—in other words, imagining how things would be if government disappeared. Under these circumstances, certain problems would arise. And so government is justified by showing it is necessary to solve them.

The specific form of government one endorses will depend on the problems in the state of nature. A particular conception is justified by showing it is best suited to solve the particular problems that arise, and so that individuals in the state of nature would choose to erect it rather than some other political form. Because the problems government must overcome depend on the theorist's conception of human nature, arguing from the state of nature provides an especially clear means of tracing connections between the nature of individuals, the problems to which they give rise, and the specific form of government needed to solve them.

In order to be convincing, a contract argument must give persuasive answers to two different questions. The first concerns the choice of government in the state of nature. If a theorist wishes to justify limited monarchy, for example, he must show that people in the state of nature would have strong reasons to choose it rather than possible alternatives. The other question concerns the state of nature itself. The theorist must show that it plausibly represents what things would be like without government, and so that choices its inhabitants make have some relevance to actual political affairs. The contract argument is open to manipulation. If a theorist wishes to justify a specific form of state, he can argue backwards to a particular account of the state of nature from which it would emerge. For instance, if he wished to justify a Communist utopia, he could argue that people in the state of nature would be staunch Communists and so would choose Communism to solve their problems. This is obviously a weak argument, because we would probably question the starting point. There is little reason to believe people are naturally (or by nature) Communists. In order to convince us of the need for a specific state, a theorist must present a state of nature we find plausible. In other words, his account must resemble what *we* imagine would take place if government disappeared.

Locke's political theory has had enormous influence in Western society, on citizens and political theorists alike. In many respects we are Lockeans; our conceptions of the nature and purpose of political authority are similar to those presented by Locke. It is therefore likely that if *we* were to argue backwards to the specific state of nature that justifies our form of state, this would also be similar to Locke's. Reading Locke is instructive, because he helps reveal the initial premises of our political theory. To a large extent, the problems with which Locke grapples are our problems; the nature of the human beings who cause these problems should coincide with our general conception of human nature.

The specific political form Locke wishes to justify is limited government. Government is necessary to perform certain functions, but it must not take over people's lives. They must still be free to do what they want in most aspects of their activities, though not in all. Obviously, then, the problems government is erected to solve must be limited as well. The contrast with Hobbes should be clear here. In order to justify a form of government that is effectively unlimited, Hobbes presents a state of nature that is so ridden with conflict that people would willingly surrender virtually all their rights in exchange for security. If circumstances in the state of nature were less grievous, Hobbes's solution would not be acceptable. Locke's task, then, is to construct a state of nature with *less* conflict than that envisioned by Hobbes. But this cannot be so devoid of conflict that people would be willing to stay in it. Though limited, the problems in the state of nature must be real. It cannot be a war of all against all, but it also cannot be a situation of harmony and peace. As noted in the last chapter, arguing from a social contract perspective, one could justify anarchism, i.e., a situation without government, as it is possible to justify other forms of political organization. The key to anarchism is that the state of nature must be tolerable. It can have problems, but these must be solvable without appeal to government. Thus if a theorist presents a peaceful, harmonious state of nature, the form of organization this would support is anarchism.

In contrast to Hobbes, Locke presents a state of nature that is immediately different from a state of war. Far from being the horrific condition Hobbes depicts, Locke's natural condition is described as "a state of peace, good-will, mutual assistance, and preservation" (II, 19). Yet this condition must also degenerate into something approaching a Hobbesian state of war, the "inconveniencies" of which government must be erected to solve.

In opposition to Filmer, Locke argues that man in the state of nature is naturally free. Though he is born into a family and must live for a time under the authority of his parents, this is only a temporary condition to be distinguished from political subjection. Details here will be discussed in subsequent sections.

Though man is naturally free, he exists in a state of liberty rather than license (II, 6). There are natural limits to his freedom. Because subjection to one's father is not the only bar to freedom, the absence of patriarchal authority does not mean complete absence of restrictions. As a reasoning creature, man is born under the law of nature, which sets limits to his relationships to other people and to himself. In Locke's words,

> The State of Nature has a Law of Nature to govern it, which obliges every one; And Reason, which is that law, teaches all Mankind who will but consult it, that being all equal and independent, no one ought to harm another in his Life, Health, Liberty, or Possessions. (II, 6)

The Law of Nature depends on God, its author and man's creator. It requires that men treat other people and themselves with a certain respect. Men do not belong to themselves but to God:

> For Men being all the Workmanship of one Omnipotent and infinitely wise Maker; All the Servants of one Sovereign Master, sent into the World by his order and about his business, they are his Property, whose Workmanship they are, made to last during his, not one another's Pleasure. (II, 6)

Because we are all God's creatures, we must strive to preserve ourselves and bear responsibility for the preservation of mankind. Other people can be harmed only "to do Justice on an Offender" (II, 6).

Because of the important role natural law plays in his political theory, Locke is in many ways similar to traditional medieval thinkers like St. Thomas Aquinas. Like many of these theorists, he argues that natural law is promulgated to man through his reason, and directs him to "his proper Interest" (II, 57). Locke's specific account of the law of nature leads him to place great weight on man's rights, or natural rights. Though the concepts of natural law and natural rights are often used interchangeably, they are actually quite different and must be kept distinct. While the idea of natural law can be traced back as far as Stoic philosophers of roughly the third century B.C. (see Vol. I, Chap. 6), the idea of natural rights came into its own only in the sixteenth century. Hobbes and Locke are the first prominent political philosophers in our tradition to speak extensively of natural rights (though they do not always call it this). One reason natural law and natural rights are obviously distinct, then, is their different origins. A fuller discussion of the nature of rights in general and natural rights in particular can be postponed until the next section.

As we saw in the last chapter (and throughout Volume I), as traditionally understood, the notion of natural law refers to an objective moral standard, discoverable by reason, binding on all rational beings, at all times and all places. God is believed to be author of this law, and generally its enforcer as well. Locke's view of natural law is traditional in most respects. This sets him apart from Hobbes. As we saw in the last chapter, though Hobbes uses language of traditional natural law, his own view departs from this in fundamental respects, and should probably be interpreted as intentionally subversive of traditional doctrines. The above quotations reveal the conventional character of Locke's view of natural law. Reason tells us we are God's creatures, and have duties toward one another. The content of these duties is also conventional. We are not permitted to injure one another (or ourselves). This coincides roughly with the Golden Rule (see p. 49).

The fact that Locke blandly asserts reason's ability to discover these moral precepts in the *Second Treatise* is widely regarded as a serious problem in his philosophy. In his *Essay Concerning Human Understanding*, he argues that the human mind contains no "innate ideas," that is, that everything we know can be traced back to experience. Proof that there are no universal, necessary moral truths to which the mind has access is the fact that moral precepts differ throughout the world. Moral precepts "have not an actual universal assent from all mankind . . . and I think it will be hard to instance any one moral rule" that is universally subscribed to.[10] In one of his early, unpublished works, *Essays on the Law of Nature*, Locke attempted to demonstrate the existence of God, and so also of divinely grounded moral precepts, on the basis of reason. But these *Essays* were left incomplete, and it seems that Locke despaired of ever bringing this project to a close.[11] But even if reason could not support these precepts, Locke believed religious faith could. There is little doubt about his firm belief in the existence of objective moral truth enshrined in natural law. And it is to this that he appeals in the *Second Treatise*.

It is notable that Locke does not feel pressed to argue for his moral views in this work. Though substantial portions of his other works are devoted to moral questions, and views put forth in them might appear to undermine his claims in the *Second Treatise*, in this work Locke argues *from* rather than *to* moral truth. The *Second Treatise* is a political work; because of the questions in which he is interested, Locke simply sets aside philosophical problems concerning the adequacy of his moral views. In this sense he is like the authors of the *Declaration of Independence*, who declare:

> We hold these Truths to be self-evident, that all Men are created equal, that they are endowed by their Creator with certain unalienable Rights, that among these are Life, Liberty, and the Pursuit of Happiness. . . .

The authors of the Declaration of Independence have clear political objectives, on which they focus. In actuality, it is not at all self-evident that all men (or all people) have the rights in question. Or even if this is self-evident to Americans or other inhabitants of the industrial democracies, it is not self-evident to other people in different societies in other parts of the world. This lack of agreement on purportedly self-evident precepts suggests that these are not rooted in man's reason, but in certain features of Western society, and differ in different societies. Though considerations along these lines led Locke to reject the idea of self-evident moral truths in the *Essay Concerning Human Understanding*, in the *Second Treatise* he has other fish to fry. He is interested in making a specific political case and so pursues this end without much attention to problems with his philosophical foundations.

NATURAL RIGHTS

In addition to his appeal to the law of nature, Locke rests important elements of his political theory on the idea of natural rights. As already indicated, this doctrine must be distinguished from natural law, though the two are closely related (especially in the precise form presented by Locke). Locke never gives a detailed account of exactly what he means by natural rights, though he uses language of rights throughout the *Second Treatise*. For instance, in the section following his discussion of natural law, he shifts easily to language of rights: "And that all Men may be restrained from invading others' Rights, and from doing hurt to one another . . ." (II, 7).

The concept "right" is used in different ways by different theorists, and scholars have distinguished a number of precise senses. For our purposes, much of this complexity can be set aside. As most commonly discussed by contemporary theorists, and by Locke as well, "rights" are viewed as important moral claims, inhering in individuals, which promote the protection of certain values, such as equality or autonomy.[12] We generally understand rights as a protected space or territory surrounding each individual, within which he should be secure to pursue his own ends. To say the space is protected indicates that it is protected *from* other parties. In our case, these are both other individuals and governments. If I have a right to worship as I please, this means that neither other people nor government can justifiably interfere with this. To say this claim is important means it should not be interfered with unless there is pressing reason to do so. Many theorists believe rights are so important that they take precedence over other moral claims. Thus my right to say what I like should not be interfered with unless there are very good reasons to do so. The fact that you may disagree with what I am saying or would prefer that I say something else would not ordinarily be considered sufficient grounds. But on the other hand, if my saying what I pleased would jeopardize public safety, that would be sufficient reason to curb my speech. A familiar example is that the right to say what one likes does not allow one to shout "Fire" in a crowded theater. Similarly, I have a right to move my arms as I please. But it is commonly held that my right to swing my arms ends where they will strike or harm other people.

Theorists commonly distinguish "natural" rights and "legal" rights. The former are held by all people, by virtue of the fact they are human. They do not depend on being Frenchmen or Englishmen, or on the enactments of some legal system, but on important characteristics human beings share. In Locke's case, natural rights stem from the fact we are God's creatures, created by him to do his bidding. Legal rights, on the other hand, depend on the laws of a given state. Familiar examples are rights to free speech and freedom of the press contained in the Bill of Rights to the United States Constitution. These rights are guaranteed by the U.S. political system, rather than by God. They are guaranteed to inhabitants of the United States rather than to mankind in general. For Locke, the distinction between these two kinds of rights is not as important as it might be, because he believes legal rights must stem from natural rights. Because God gives people certain rights, any legitimate political system must respect them. To fail to do so would cause a political system to lose its legitimacy.

Throughout the *Second Treatise*, Locke argues that man's natural freedom is bound up with the fact that people are the workmanship of God, who has placed us here for his purposes. As we are enjoined by the law of nature not to harm other people, people can be viewed as having rights not to be harmed. As with contemporary theorists, Locke's basic view is territorial. A recent scholar describes his conception of rights as follows: "a moral space for our own activities, free from the interference of others." Alternatively: "a zone of protected liberty that others are duty-bound to respect."[13]

Though Locke does not consistently use the language of rights, or natural rights, the language he does use can be understood in this sense. In the *Second Treatise* he speaks of men in the state of nature having "perfect Freedom to order their Actions, and dispose of their Possessions, and Persons, as they think fit" (II, 4). Similarly, he notes a person's "uncontrollable Liberty, to dispose of . . . his Person or Possessions" (II, 6). Each person has naturally "a Right of Freedom to his Person, which no other Man has a Power over, but the free Disposal of it lies in himself" (II, 190). In his *Letter on Toleration*, he writes: "[E]very man may consider what suits his own convenience, and follow what course he likes best."[14]

Though people have rights to do as they please, these are curtailed by God's purposes. Locke says that men in the state of nature are free "to order their Actions, and dispose of their Possessions and Persons as they think fit, *within the bounds of the Law of Nature*" (II, 4; emphasis added). As we have seen, the main requirement is that they not harm themselves or other people. In other words, each person's rights are limited by those of others. In including the proviso that each person must not harm himself, Locke in effect says that each person must respect his own rights as well as those of others. Each person has a fundamental right of self-preservation not to be damaged by anyone, including himself.

If people in the state of nature are bound by moral restrictions, the question naturally arises as to how these are enforced. This is a pressing problem, because it is precisely the absence of an effective enforcement mechanism that defines the state of nature: "Men living together according to reason, without a common Superior on Earth, with Authority to judge between them, is properly the State of Nature" (II, 19). The state of nature is distinct from civil society in that the latter condition contains a common judge between all parties:

> Those who are united into one Body, and have a common established Law and Judicature to appeal to, with Authority to decide Controversies between them, and punish Offenders, are in Civil Society one with another; but those who have no such common Appeal, I mean on Earth, are still in the state of Nature, each being, where there is no other Judge for himself and Executioner, which is, as I have before shew'd it, the perfect state of Nature. (II, 87)

As we will see, it is the need for a common judge that makes people willing to leave the state of nature.

The fact that there is no common judge in the state of nature renders the problem of enforcement acute. We have seen that each person is surrounded by a sphere of protected space, within which he can pursue his projects. But what is to prevent other people from interfering with him nevertheless? If the law of nature is truly a *law* there must be a means of enforcing it: "For the Law of Nature would, as all other Laws that concern Men in this World, be in vain, if there were no body that in the State of Nature had a Power to Execute that Law" (II, 7). The traditional medieval doctrine is that natural law is enforced by God. But if it is to have immediate effects in this world, there must be human enforcers as well.

Locke's solution to this problem is the "strange Doctrine" (II, 13) that in the state of nature all men are enforcers of natural law. This contention follows from the fact that people in the state of nature are equal. In contrast to Filmer, Locke argues against relationships of natural subordination (among adults). No one can have an exclusive right to enforce the law of nature, because that would make him naturally superior:

> [I]f any one in the State of Nature may punish another, for any evil he has done, every one may do so. For in that State of perfect Equality, where naturally there is no superiority or jurisdiction of one over another, what any may do in Prosecution of that Law, every one must needs have a Right to do. (II, 7)

All people therefore have the power of enforcement:

> And that all Men may be restrained from invading others' Rights, and from doing hurt to one another, and the Law of Nature be observed, which willeth the Peace and Preservation of all Mankind, the Execution of the Law of Nature is in that State put into every Man's hands, whereby every one has a right to punish the transgressors of that Law to such a Degree, as may hinder its violation. (II, 7)

Each person not only has the right to punish violations of natural law that directly concern himself, but those that affect others as well. In transgressing the law of nature, an offender declares himself an enemy to all men. Because reason binds mankind into a natural community, a violation of reason is "a trespass against the whole Species, and the Peace and Safety of it, provided for by the Law of Nature" (II, 8).

> And thus it is that every Man in the State of Nature has a Power to kill a Murderer, both to deter others from doing the like Injury . . . by the Example of the punishment that attends it from every body, and also to secure Men from the attempts of a Criminal, who having renounced Reason, the common Rule and Measure God hath given to Mankind, hath by the unjust Violence and Slaughter he hath committed upon one, declared War against all Mankind, and therefore may be destroyed as a Lion or Tiger, one of those wild Savage Beasts, with whom Men can have no Society nor Security. (II, 11)

The need to preserve the law of nature from violations justifies the practice of punishment, which has two distinct aspects. Punishment is necessary, first, to bring the perpetrator to account. As we have seen, the right to do this is held by all people. In addition, if some violation of natural law damages a specific individual, then she has a particular right to recompense. This right is not held by all people (II, 9). If Pierre breaks Luanne's window, she has a right against him to have it repaired. Other people, whose windows were not broken, obviously do not share in this right. The contrast between these two aspects of punishment indicates how equally the right to punish is held. If Kurt breaks Stacy's arm, she has a right to recompense. But her right to punish him for violating the law of nature and causing her pain is no greater than the similar rights held by all other people. In Locke's state of nature, people constitute a natural community, in that all are collectively enjoined to uphold the law of nature and punish violations.

There are limits to the right to punishment. People who violate the law of nature deserve to be punished, but they are still human beings with rights of their own. Legitimate punishment must be in proportion to the offense: "Each transgression may be punished to the degree and with so much Severity as will suffice to make it an ill bargain to the Offender, give him cause to repent, and terrify others from doing the like" (II, 12). But more than this is illicit.

If we step back for a moment from Locke's account of the state of nature, we can see that it is quite different from Hobbes's and has many attractive features. Like Hobbes, Locke argues that the state of nature is a condition of equality. All men are free, according to Hobbes, in the fundamental respect of their mortality. Each can be killed by others. In contrast, Locke's view centers on moral equality. There are no natural relations of subordination and superordination, and so all alike are not only under the law of nature but of equal status as its enforcers. Unlike Hobbes's state of nature, Locke's possesses binding natural law, enforced by all alike. Mutual subjection to natural law and mutual power to enforce it unite people in a natural community, in which the rights of one person are to be protected by all others. As we will see, Locke argues that government is necessary because the law of nature will not be properly enforced through the mechanism described. Government will provide adequate enforcement, and so protect everyone's rights.

The moral framework of the state of nature permeates Locke's entire political theory. Because the purpose of government is to enforce natural law, it too is bound by natural law. Even after men leave the state of nature for civil society, the law of nature must continue to be adhered to. Individual violators must be dealt with by government, but governments too cannot violate natural law:

> The Obligations of the Law of Nature cease not in Society, but only in many Cases are drawn closer and have by Human Laws known Penalties annexed to them, to enforce their observation. Thus the Law of Nature stands as an Eternal Rule to all Men, Legislators as well as others. The Rules that they make for other Men's Actions must, as well as their own and other Men's Actions, be conformable to the law of Nature, i.e., to the Will of God, of which that is a declaration, and the fundamental Law of Nature being the preservation of mankind, no Human Sanction can be good or valid against it. (II, 135)

THE STATE OF WAR

According to Locke, the state of nature and the state of war are distinct, but the former will degenerate into the latter, making government necessary. As already noted, the state of nature is devised by taking people as they are in society and placing them in a situation without government. What characterizes the state of nature, then, is equal individuals under the law of nature but without political power. Locke defines political power as follows:

> [A] Right of making Laws with Penalties of Death, and consequently all less Penalties, for the Regulating and Preserving of Property, and employing the force of the Community, in the Execution of such laws, and in the defense of the Commonwealth from Foreign Injury, and all this only for the Public Good. (II, 3)

In the absence of political power, each person has an obligation to uphold the law of nature and to make sure other people uphold it as well. Towards this end, as we have seen, each person has a right to punish violators of natural law, but only to the extent necessary to right wrongs and to make sure natural law is adhered to in the future. Locke believes the common right of punishment cannot function smoothly. It will cause "Inconveniencies," which make government necessary.

Unlike—and probably in direct allusion to—Hobbes, Locke distinguishes the states of nature and of war. Though the former is "a State of Peace, Good Will, Mutual Assistance, and Preservation," the latter is described as "a State of Enmity, Malice, Violence, and Mutual Destruction" (II, 19). More precisely, the essence of the state of war is force. Any time an individual's preservation is threatened by someone else there exists a state of war. In Locke's words, "force, or a declared design of force upon the Person of another, where there is no common Superior on Earth to appeal to for relief, is the State of War" (II, 19).

A state of war can exist in civil society, where there is a common judge between parties, as well as in the state of nature. In the state of nature the situation is clear. If Cordelia is attacked by James, she obviously has a right to defend herself. James's use of force makes him her enemy and gives her the right to use force against him. Because Locke argues that the law of nature requires that people help one another, James's use of force against Cordelia requires that other people come to her aid and use force against him as well. In society, a state of war exists when one person is threatened by force and cannot appeal to government for help. If Mary comes after Emilio to kill him, he must defend himself. The harm in this case would be immediate and irreparable. Because God intends that people be preserved, Emilio's need to fend for himself is clear. But under different circumstances, if the threat is not immediate and irreparable, he must appeal to government to punish the perpetrator:

> Thus a Thief, whom I cannot harm but by appeal to the Law, for having stolen all that I am worth, I may kill, when he sets on me to rob me, but of my Horse or Coat, because the Law, which was made for my Preservation, where it cannot interpose to secure my Life from present force, which if lost, is capable of no reparation, permits me my own Defense, and the Right of War, a liberty to kill the aggressor, because the aggressor allows not time to appeal to our common Judge. . . . (II, 19)

Locke's view here is familiar legal doctrine. Many legal systems recognize self-defense as an adequate justification for harming another person under certain circumstances. Again, the key idea is that one must be threatened with immediate harm and so unable to call in the police. If Mustafa has assaulted May or committed some other heinous act, she cannot take revenge herself but must leave this to the law. But if she has the opportunity to fend off the assault, then she can take whatever measures necessary, including killing him.

There is an important difference between the state of war as found in the state of nature and in civil society. The latter is far easier to leave. The state of nature is characterized by an absence of a common power. Thus if Kathy wrongs Juan, he must take matters into his own hands. Even if the threat of force no longer exists, she and Juan remain in a state of war, until Kathy offers reconciliation and makes right whatever her wrongs. In civil society, the state of war ceases with the actual threat of force, because the two parties "are equally on both sides Subjected to the fair determination of the Law," which will judge their disputes (II, 20).

Without appeal to an impartial authority, things are likely to develop badly. Though Locke does not view people as grievously flawed, he believes they are self-interested, and so not impartial judges of their own case. If Juan has wronged Boris, Boris has the right to punish him, but only in proportion to the offense. However, because Boris is not impartial, he is liable to punish too much. This would constitute a wrong on his part, which would justify Juan in punishing *him*.

To make matters more complex, it is not possible to say whether Boris has punished Juan properly unless we are able to identify proper punishment under the circumstances. Presumably, this is a matter that can be determined by reason. All people have access to the law of nature through their reason and so can judge proper punishment. But in the case at hand, Boris and Juan are likely to disagree about the extent of proper punishment. Boris is likely to think harsher measures are in order, and so when he attempts to apply them, Juan will likely believe his rights are being violated. If other people have obligations to punish violators of the law of nature, the question arises as to what *they* will view as proper punishment, and so whose side they will take. Will they support Boris because he was wronged, or Juan, who is now the victim of Boris's revenge? In the absence of clear standards and impartial judges to apply them, these determinations are difficult, and likely to give rise to conflict:

> I doubt not but it will be objected that it is unreasonable for Men to be Judges in their own Cases, that Self-love will make Men partial to themselves and their Friends. And on the other side, that Ill Nature, Passion and Revenge will carry them too far in punishing others. And hence nothing but Confusion and Disorder will follow, and that therefore God hath certainly appointed Government to restrain the partiality and violence of Men. (II, 13)

Thus government is to provide a neutral umpire to mediate disputes. Without government, the state of nature will be plagued by a cycle of escalating acts of revenge and counter-revenge, until Locke's initially peaceful situation comes to resemble a war of all against all.

The main flaw in human nature is clear. Though people have reasoning faculties, they are self-interested and so influenced by passion when their interests are at stake. It follows that mutual renunciation of the right of enforcement is in everyone's interest. Even if I believe I am able to exercise this right impartially, I still must worry about the judgment of others. Thus everyone should be willing to surrender the right of enforcement to government, which is a fair and neutral authority. Once government is set up, disputes can be put to rest and chaos avoided. Though everyone must cede certain rights, their other rights should be more secure.

To test Locke's view, each of us can imagine what we would do if placed in Locke's state of nature. We might argue that surrendering the right to enforce the law of nature is a real renunciation. But, on the other hand, a great deal is gained. If each of us retained this right, the outcome would probably be as indicated. Thus it pays to surrender this right in the interest of peace and security. This exchange is beneficial, however, only if it includes certain safeguards. Once government is erected it will have the power to do more than arbitrate disputes. Though we authorize it to serve as a neutral judge, the people who make up government are themselves self-interested and so likely to attempt to extend their power. Beyond a certain point, the threat of tyrannical government might appear worse than the "inconveniencies" of the state of nature. In setting up government, accordingly, people should include the proviso that government lose its power if it oversteps the prescribed limits. People will no longer have obligations to obey it, and will in fact have the right to use force to protect themselves from it.

Locke's state of nature, then, dictates the erection of limited government. Government should be limited in two ways. First, it is set up in order to perform limited functions. People authorize it to serve as a neutral judge, and so give it their own rights to enforce the law of nature. But this is essentially all government is set up to do. Unlike the situation recommended by Hobbes, people surrender only some of their rights, and do so in order to protect the rest. In addition, the relationship between individuals and government is explicitly contractual. Obligations are created on both sides. People surrender their rights to enforce the law of nature and are obligated to obey government as long as it fulfills this function. For its part, government claims obedience only as long as it fulfills its function. If it violates people's rights, it loses its power and its claim to be obeyed.

The right to enforce the law of nature is comprised of three separate rights: to interpret the law of nature, to apply it to specific cases, and to use force to support one's judgment. In order to remedy the defects of the state of nature, all three rights must be surrendered to government. Locke describes reasons to surrender them, in successive paragraphs in Chapter 9:

> First, there wants an established, settled, known Law, received and allowed by common consent to be the Standard of Right and Wrong, and the common measure to decide all Controversies between them. For though the Law of Nature be plain and intelligible to all rational Creatures, yet Men being biased by their Interests as well as ignorant for want of study of it, are not apt to allow of it as a Law binding to them in the application of it to their particular Cases.
>
> Secondly, in the State of Nature there wants a known and indifferent Judge, with Authority to determine all differences according to the established Law. For every one in that state being both Judge and Executioner of the Law of Nature, Men being partial to themselves, Passion and Revenge is very apt to carry them too far, and with too much heat, in their own Cases, as well as negligence and unconcernedness, to make them too remiss, in other Men's.
>
> Thirdly, in the state of Nature there often wants Power to back and support the Sentence when right, and to give it due Execution. They who by any Injustice offended, will seldom fail where they are able, by force to make good their Injustice; such resistance many times makes the punishment dangerous, and frequently destructive, to those who attempt it. (II, 124–126)

Thus in spite of the great advantages of living free under the law of nature, people will see that they would be better off in civil society, under government. The main impediment to peace and safety in the state of nature is an absence of clear standards of conduct, which can be applied impartially, and effectively enforced. Each person will accordingly agree to surrender the right to enforce the law of nature. Though this is a renunciation, it actually increases everyone's rights. Without this renunciation, no rights are secure in a conflict-ridden, precarious state of nature.

CIVIL SOCIETY

In moving from the state of nature to civil society, people set up a government to judge their disputes and so to remedy the inconveniences of the state of nature. The move to civil society takes place in two stages. First, individuals unite to form a community by ceding the three specific rights that constitute the natural right to enforce the law of nature. In the second step, the community sets up a government to act as judge. Locke describes the first stage as follows:

> Whosoever therefore out of a state of Nature unite into a Community must be understood to give up all the power necessary to the ends for which they unite into Society . . . And this is done by barely agreeing to unite into one Political Society, which is all the Compact that is, or needs be, between the Individuals that enter into or make up a Commonwealth. And thus that which begins and actually constitutes any Political Society is nothing but the consent of any number of Freemen capable of a majority to unite and incorporate into such a society. And this is that, and that only, which did or could give beginning to any lawful Government in the world. (II, 99)

Through this action, each individual surrenders his right to enforce the law of nature to the community. If the community is to act, it must designate specific people to perform this function. The community's decisions will naturally be made by majority rule, unless the members expressly agree to a number greater than the majority (II, 99)—which would make it more difficult to take any action. If we assume that decisions are made by the majority, the community's first act is choosing a legislative power, into the hands of which is placed the power to enforce the law of nature (II, 134). The community as a whole can continue to wield the legislative power, but this too must be decided by the community through majority rule.

In describing the process through which the legislature is erected, Locke does not use the language of contract. But if we view the essence of contract as the creation of mutual obligations, it is clear that the legislature enters into such a relationship with the community. That this amounts to a contract is clearly seen. Assume that Sean hires a painter to paint his house. The nature of their agreement is that the painter agrees to paint the house, while Sean agrees to pay him a certain amount of money. Clearly, if the painter does the job, Sean should pay, while if he does not, Sean does not owe him the money. Contrariwise, if Sean indicates his intention not to pay, the painter is not obligated to paint the house. In a relationship of this sort, the performance of each party is necessary to create obligations for the other.

The contractual nature of the community's grant of power to the legislature is seen in Locke's description of it as a "fiduciary" trust:

> [T]he Legislative being only a Fiduciary Power to act for certain ends, there remains still in the People a Supreme Power to remove or alter the Legislative, when they find the Legislative act contrary to the trust reposed in them. (II, 149)

What Locke means here is that the people give the legislative power certain responsibilities, but they always retain supreme power. The legislative has the ability to make laws, which makes it the supreme power *within* the political system (II, 150), but the people retain an essential right to judge the legislature's performance. Thus the people are the supreme power, while the legislature is only appointed to perform certain tasks. If the people find that the legislature does not function properly, they can remove it, and place its power in other hands. Similarly, to return to the example of the painter, if Sean finds that the painter is doing a poor job, he can dismiss him and give the assignment to someone else.

In most cases, the legislature will appoint another body, an executive, to enforce the laws. Because it is an assembly of men, the legislature will find it difficult to remain in session for protracted periods. This will not interfere greatly with its ability to make laws, which can be done in relatively short periods of time. But proper enforcement of the laws requires a body that meets continuously. Thus the executive power is generally placed in the hands of a single person, a king. In most cases, the executive will also control what Locke calls the "federative" power, which pertains to dealing with foreign governments, including making treaties and alliances, and war and peace (II, 146–147). But in spite of the executive's enormous power, he is subordinate to the legislature. His power is received from this body and can be withdrawn if it judges that he has not used it properly (II, 152–153).

Locke's insistence on the conditional nature of governmental power can be attributed in part to the circumstances in which he wrote. Faced with the spectre of an absolute monarch in England, on the model of Louis XIV of France, Locke joined in a political movement opposed to this possibility and wrote the *Two Treatises* for this cause. Throughout the work he returns repeatedly to the dreaded possibility of arbitrary power. This fear can be justified from the point of view of the inhabitants of the state of nature.

As we have seen, the main problem with the state of nature is that people are not impartial judges in their own cases. This situation would not be improved by setting up an absolute ruler. Like other men, such a ruler can be presumed to be self-interested and so will not be impartial in cases concerning himself. In the absence of an impartial judge to oversee disputes between the ruler and his subjects, he stands to them in a state of nature. From the subjects' point of view, this represents a worsening of their condition. The state of nature lacks an impartial judge, but each person has the right to defend himself. In society under an absolute ruler, the subjects are disarmed. The ruler is vastly more powerful than any of them and so able to enforce his will despite their opposition. If people give "themselves to the absolute Arbitrary Power and will of a Legislator, they have disarmed themselves and armed him, to make a prey of them when he pleases" (II, 137). People in the state of nature would not agree to such a bargain, and so arbitrary power cannot be justified.

It is interesting to compare the views of Locke and Hobbes in this regard. As we have seen, in setting up a government, people confront *two* problems. They must make sure the government protects them from other people, but they also require protection from it. As we saw in the last chapter, Hobbes views the first of these problems as so severe that he gives little attention to the second. But Locke worries primarily about the second. Though government is needed to protect us from other people, the danger they pose is *not* so great that other factors cannot also be considered. Because Locke is concerned with both sources of danger, he is far more demanding in regard to acceptable forms of government, and so rules out arbitrary power.

To avoid the possibility of arbitrary rule, power must be granted on a contractual basis, to be used for the community's benefit. In order to ensure that government's actions are not arbitrary, it must rule through standing laws, which are promulgated and made known to the people. These laws bind the rulers as well. Locke adds additional provisos— that the laws must promote the good of the people, and secure their property. This disallows taxation without their consent—a subject to which we will return. In order to avoid the uncertainty that plagues the state of nature, a fixed framework of rules must be established, thereby allowing people to pursue their lives in peace and security (II, 131, 137–142).

The major concession people make on entering civil society concerns their judgment. In many respects, the movement to civil society does not diminish their freedom. In the state of nature, their freedom is restricted by the law of nature. In civil society, they are bound by laws made by government. But because these laws must be consistent with natural law, their condition should not be greatly different. Their situation changes, however, in a significant respect. For though the law of nature is revealed to people in the state of nature through their reason, it still must be interpreted, while people's interpretations will differ—so giving rise to conflicts. Thus freedom in the state of nature is for each man to follow *his own interpretation* of the law of nature. Civil society is different in having a single accepted interpretation, embodied in the laws of the community. In entering civil society, each person agrees to follow these laws, and so in effect to *substitute* the community's interpretation of natural law for his own. The individual also substitutes the community's views in regard to particular cases under the law of nature, and agrees to help enforce the community's determinations, rather than his own. Thus for Locke, the core of a citizen's obligation to the state is to act according to its point of view rather than his own.

The elevation of common reason over each individual's reason is apparent in the appointment of a legislative body. Each person grants his rights to enforce the law of nature to the community, but how is this body to act? Ideally, all people would unite and enact legislation, with each person assenting to each law. But this is not only impractical; it goes against the problems of the state of nature. The state of nature erupts in conflict because self-interested people disagree. And so if unanimous assent is required for every law, nothing will ever be enacted. People must agree to follow the will of the majority—or of a greater number, if this is demanded (II, 99).

In order for a political body to act, everyone must be bound by majority rule. As Locke says, "the Majority have a Right to act and conclude the rest" (II, 95). To demand unanimous consent for every action would in effect return people to the state of nature:

> And thus every Man, by consenting with others to make one Body Politick under one Government, puts himself under an Obligation to every one of that Society, to submit to the determination of the majority, and to be concluded by it; or else this original Compact, whereby he with others incorporates into one Society, would signify nothing,

and be no Compact, if he be left free, and under no other ties, than he was in before in the State of Nature. (II, 97)

Thus people must accept decisions with which they disagree. All have equal voice in regard to where the legislative power is lodged, but once it is established, its determinations bind all members of society. Otherwise "the coming into Society upon such terms, would be only like Cato's coming into the Theatre, only to go out again. Such a Constitution as this would make the mighty *Leviathan* of a shorter duration than the feeblest Creature's, and not let it outlast the day it was born in" (II, 98).

Though private judgments are "excluded" by the legislature's determinations (II, 87), surrender of this faculty is not complete. Though in making laws, the legislature attains the right to substitute its opinion for that of each individual, it must legislate in accordance with natural law. We have seen that natural law continues to bind after people enter civil society. But in civil society, government's interpretation of natural law takes precedence over theirs. The crucial exception lies in the fact that government is created to advance the community's good. Because people's opinions will likely differ as to whether or not government is promoting this, it is important to decide whose opinion should be accepted. Locke insists that each person always retains a right to assess the government's performance. Though people grant the legislature power to make law, they always retain a residual right to judge whether it is behaving according to its charge—and to take appropriate steps if it is not. This is the heart of Locke's theory of resistance to unjust political power, a subject to which we will return.

Locke's position in regard to these questions of judgment is confirmed from the point of view of the state of nature. We have seen that the state of nature has severe inconveniences, which make it necessary that government be set up. But people in the state of nature know about the dangers of arbitrary power, which would make their condition worse than the state of nature. In order to avoid this, as we have seen, they insist that government have limited powers and rule according to settled, known law, and some additional measures. The contract between the community and government is not self-enforcing. It will work only if there is a means to make sure its terms are kept. In the absence of other alternatives, each person retains the right to judge this for himself, and to take appropriate action if the contract has been violated. People in the state of nature would clearly include this stipulation in their agreement, and would not enter into an agreement without it.

GOVERNMENT BY CONSENT

Because people are free in the state of nature, they come under the sway of governmental power only through their own consent. In the state of nature, people can join together and erect appropriate authorities. But if a person does not choose to join a given group, it has no power over him. We have seen that each person in the state of nature has a natural right to enforce the law of nature as he believes necessary. Though *everyone else* in the state of nature might join together in a community, Enrique will retain his right to enforce the law of nature, unless he joins as well. The awkward implication of Locke's position is that Enrique will exist as an independent entity alongside the association, retaining the right to punish violations of the law of nature as he sees fit. Consent is crucial for Locke, because only by consenting to join civil society does an individual cede his right to punish violations of the law of nature.

Locke's concern with consent stems from his desire to refute Filmer. As we have seen, Filmer argues that man is not born free but as part of a family. Thus people do not choose to join political society; they come into the world as subjects of specific societies and always remain so. In order to refute this argument, Locke must explain how free people can become members of political society (see II, 100). That people become members only through their own consent is a basic tenet of his theory, asserted repeatedly. For instance, "Men being, as has been said, by Nature, all free, equal and independent, no one can be put out of this Estate and subjected to the Political Power of another, without his own consent" (II, 95). To account for a person's obligations to obey government, moreover, it is not enough to show that his ancestors consented. Each person is born free and remains free, unless *he* consents, regardless of the actions of his forebears. Locke sharply distinguishes his position from Filmer's in insisting that the consent of the father does not bind the son (II, 116–118).

Even with these conditions attached, accounting for political subjection would not be difficult if all—or most—people could be shown to have consented. But this is not the case. No one doubts that "an express consent, of any Man entering into any Society makes him a perfect Member of that Society, a Subject of that Government" (II, 119). But because few people expressly consent, Locke places great weight on what he calls "tacit consent." He searches for actions performed by most people, which, though falling short of expressly consenting to government, still constitute consent and so generate obligations. Locke holds, basically, that if one enjoys benefits provided by civil society, then he consents to it:

> And to this I say that every Man, that hath any Possession, or Enjoyment of any part of the Dominions of any Government, doth thereby give his tacit Consent, and is as far forth obliged to Obedience to the Laws of that Government, during such Enjoyment, as any one under it; whether this his Possession be of Land, to him and his Heirs for ever, or a Lodging only for a Week; or whether it be barely traveling freely on the Highway; and in Effect, it reaches as far as the very being of any one within the Territories of that Government. (II, 119)

In fleshing out this position, Locke emphasizes that possessing property in a country constitutes consent to its government. Because it is impossible to remove one's land from a country, accepting ownership of land requires membership in a society and so consent to obey its laws. But if an individual gives up his property, he casts off this obligation and recovers his natural freedom (II, 121). The obligation to obey laws also extends to people who do not own property. Locke appears to argue that, because they benefit from civil society, these people too consent to obey its laws. He distinguishes this tacit consent from express consent, which makes one a "perfect member" of a society. If someone expressly consents to a commonwealth, he "is perpetually and indispensably obliged to be and remain unalterably subject to it, and can never be again in the liberty of the state of Nature" (II, 121). Tacit consent is less binding. If someone leaves a territory that has afforded him protection, he recovers his liberty. But more interesting than the distinction between perfect and less-than-perfect membership of a commonwealth is Locke's claim that "the very being of any one within the Territories" of a government constitutes tacit consent to obey its laws. In this sense express and tacit consent are alike, as both oblige one to obey the law.

In arguing that men are born free under natural law, Locke sets himself a difficult problem. If people are born free, they can lose their natural freedom only through consent. Thus a great deal depends on how one characterizes "consent." In general, the notion is understood on the model of a promise. For a promise to be binding, the subject must intend to make it. Some conditions generally appealed to are that she must be competent to make the promise (i.e., sober, sane, sufficiently old to be responsible for her actions, etc.). She must also be aware of what she is doing, and not forced into it. The same holds for consent. If Jane consents to something, she must do so voluntarily, in awareness of what she is doing. An act of consent, like a promise, is something one does *intentionally.* If I consent to let you use my car, I intentionally give you a right you did not have previously. It makes a great deal of difference if you simply take my car without asking or after receiving my consent. In the former case, you can be arrested for stealing, while in the latter, what you are doing is proper. Once again, in order for you to have a right to use my car, I must *intend* to give you the right. If you hear me say in my sleep that you can borrow my car, you do not have a right to take it (assuming you are aware I am sleeping, etc.).

If we carry this sense of consent to Locke's political theory, we run up against a simple fact of political life: most people do not consent to their governments. In this regard, Filmer is correct. Most people do not choose to join their societies; they are born into them, and continue in them until they die. (The main exceptions are naturalized citizens, who leave country X for country Y.) In order to account for the clear need for people to obey the law, Locke introduces the notion of tacit consent, and says in effect that for the majority of people, simply being within the borders of a given society constitutes consent to its government. However, a moment's reflection shows that simply being in a given territory is far removed from intentionally agreeing to obey its laws.

Locke's position on consent has been severely criticized by scholars, at least since the time of Hume (whose view we will discuss in the next chapter). As one recent theorist writes, "we are likely to feel cheated by Locke's argument: . . . why go through the whole social contract argument if it turns out in the end that everyone is automatically obligated?"[15]

Locke's problems with consent suggest a whole host of difficulties rooted in his initial premises. In order to justify revolution, he argues that man is born free under natural law and so that political relationships can be terminated when their conditions are violated. But as Filmer notes, this point of view is strikingly at odds with the facts. In discussing consent and tacit consent, Locke does not try to present a fully worked theory of political obligation. He simply attempts to meet the obvious need to account for how free people incur obligations to their governments. Consent is an attractive solution, but though intuitively appealing, it loses much of its force if one looks beneath the surface.

Locke's difficulties here are revealing. If we do not attain political obligations through express consent, one must wonder how we do attain them. For hundreds of years, different answers to this question have been suggested. In particular, various actions citizens perform have been viewed as entailing tacit consent to government. Some of these actions are voting in elections, engaging in political debate, or simply deciding not to leave one's country and go elsewhere. But careful scrutiny of these actions indicates that they too are not undertaken with the intention of incurring obligations to obey the law.

In spite of Locke's problems, consent is probably still the most common answer to the question of political obligation in Western societies. If one were to ask citizens why they are required to obey their governments, it is likely that their most common single answer would be, because they have consented to do so. This is reflected in basic documents of the Western tradition. To quote the *Declaration of Independence* once again, "it is to secure these rights that governments are instituted among men, deriving their just power from the consent of the governed." But if legitimate governments must actually be rooted in the consent of their citizens, few existing governments can be called legitimate. Locke's problems with consent raise severe difficulties, which have plagued political theorists ever since.

PARENTAL AND PATRIARCHAL AUTHORITY

As part of his overall argument that political obligations can be rooted only in consent, Locke criticizes alternative bases. Most notable are his criticisms of the view of Filmer which presents political power as an extension of patriarchal power. Locke carefully analyzes relationships between parents and children and distinguishes these from political relations. The result is a magisterially clear account of parental authority, which is one of the classic treatments of this subject in the liberal tradition.

Locke presents a battery of arguments to distinguish patriarchal and political power. First, as we have seen, Filmer's espousal of paternal power is in part based on misinterpretation of the Bible. His insistence on the father's absolute power flies in the face of repeated biblical injunctions to honor the mother as well. Because the Bible frequently places the mother on a par with the father (*First Treatise*, 61–62), authority is clearly not the father's alone. Indeed, Locke notes that the proper term for the power in question is *parental* rather than *paternal* (II, 52). This is especially damaging to Filmer, because one of his arguments in support of the father's unchecked power is any political system's need for a single, unchallenged locus of power. With power in the hands of the mother as well as the father, this need appears not to be met by Filmer's own biblical theory (II, 53).

Locke's account of the true nature of parental authority begins with the basic premise that all people are naturally free and equal. Locke means equal in a precise sense, the absence of natural relations of subordination, "that equal Right that every Man hath to his Natural Freedom, without being subjected to the Will or Authority of any other Man" (II, 54). But though all people are naturally equal and free, freedom must be exercised within the confines of natural law. This, as we have seen, is promulgated to man through his reason. Accordingly, freedom requires proper development of the individual's reasoning power. In Locke's words:

> [N]o Body can be under a Law which is not promulgated to him; and this Law being promulgated or made known by Reason only, he that is not come to the Use of his Reason, cannot be said to be under this Law. . . . (II, 57)

Thus children must be under their parents' direction until they are sufficiently mature to be guided by their own reason. This subordination, though natural and unavoidable, is also temporary. Locke likens it to swaddling clothes in which children are wrapped during "the weakness of their Infancy. Age and Reason, as they grow up, loosen them till at length they drop quite off, and leave a man at his own free Disposal" (II, 55).

A range of considerations support this position. That the son attains independence with maturity and the development of reason is seen by looking at the father. He too underwent a similar period of subordination, until, with maturity, he achieved independence from his father. "If this made the Father free, it shall make the Son free too" (II, 59). With mature reason required for freedom, in those cases in which it is not able to develop fully, people do not attain independence: "And so Lunatics and Idiots are never set free from the Government of their Parents" (II, 60).

That freedom under natural law and subjection to one's parents can coincide is seen most clearly in certain monarchs. According to Filmer, kings possess absolute, unlimited power. Yet consider what ensues if a king dies and passes his power on to an heir who is below the age of reason. The future monarch, though rightful sovereign and master, remains in subjection "to his Mother and Nurse, to Tutors and Governors, till Age and Education brought him Reason and Ability to govern himself and others" (II, 61). From this case Locke extrapolates the age at which a typical individual attains freedom under the law of nature: "If any body should ask me, When my Son is of Age to be free? I shall answer, Just when his Monarch is of Age to govern" (II, 61).

Because of Locke's basic assumption that people are not their own masters but belong to God, parents have obligations under natural law to care for their children. It is God's intention that people be preserved. Because care and education are necessary for the preservation and development of the child, its parents are bound to comply (II, 56). God's intention that things be so ordered is revealed in the tender sentiments he has infused in parents' breasts, which make them care for their children and so willing to raise them to reasoning independence (II, 64).

Locke presents some additional arguments, but his overall position should be clear. Parents have obligations to care for and nurture their children. Until they reach the age of reason, children are bound to obey. But their subjection is temporary, lasting only until they achieve freedom under natural law. Children are not, however, entirely without obligations to their parents. In return for their parents' efforts, children owe them honor, and are bidden never to harm, disturb, or affront them (II, 66). Parents attain an additional influence over their children through the power of inheritance. Because parents can do with their property as they please, children can be led to do their parents' bidding (II, 72). But this is a far cry from the absolute political subjection Filmer reads into parent-child relationships. In the final analysis, Locke takes the biblical injunction "Honor thy father and thy mother" far more literally than Filmer.

Locke's account of the relationship between husband and wife is also close to contemporary common sense. This relationship, like that which constitutes political society, is a voluntary union between free individuals. Man and woman become husband and wife out of willingness to do so, supported by common interest in nurture and care for their offspring (II, 78). The natural basis of marriage is children's lengthy dependency. Nature has ordained that man and woman should live together longer than in other species (II, 79–80). But when a couple's children have been raised, Locke suggests that marriage bonds can be dissolved. As they are made voluntarily, so can they be unmade (II, 81–82).

Locke believes it is natural that men should have authority over women, "as the abler and stronger" (II, 82). But this authority is distinctly limited:

[T]his reaching but to the things of their common Interest and Property, leaves the Wife in the full and free possession of what by Contract is her peculiar Right and gives the Husband no more power over her Life than she has over his.

The power of the husband is so far from that of an absolute monarch that the wife has the liberty to separate from him under certain circumstances (II, 82).

In discussing relationships within the family, Locke works from the same premises as in his account of political relationships. People are free and equal below natural law. They are bidden by God to preserve one another and so have obligations. Within the confines of these injunctions, however, they are free to live and to establish relationships with others as they prefer. Though recognizing natural functions of procreation and education the family fulfills, in responding to Filmer, Locke emphasizes the extent to which family relationships are voluntary or contractual, rather than mandated by a higher power.

THE RIGHT TO PROPERTY

One of the most original and influential aspects of the *Second Treatise* is Locke's discussion of property in Chapter 5. Locke presents a classic account of the origin of property in the state of nature, calling attention to the crucial role of labor in creating value and conferring rights of ownership. Locke's discussion of labor pioneered the "labor theory of value," developed in nineteenth-century political economy, most notably by Karl Marx.

Questions concerning rights to property were of great practical importance in Locke's England. Whether or not the King could rightfully take his subjects' property was a pressing issue. If he had this right, he could tax his subjects at will, without their consent. Proponents of limited royal power insisted the King required his subjects' consent—generally exercised through Parliament—in order to raise taxes. The implications of this dispute were apparent in the contrast between the French and English monarchies. Across the English Channel, Louis XIV exercised absolute power because of his ability to raise revenues without consent. Louis argued that kings have "the full and free disposition of all the goods possessed by ecclesiastics as well as laymen," to use for the needs of the state.[16] Of course Louis also claimed the right to say what was for the good of the state and so was able to pursue his aims unchecked. The Estates-General in France went 175 years without meeting. After breaking up in 1614, they were not called back into session until the fateful year, 1789, when Louis XVI, desperate for revenue, had no other recourse.

In England as well, Charles I had attempted to rule without Parliamentary consent. During the period 1629–40, he attempted to finance his government without the co--operation of Parliament, through a variety of unusual means, most notably "ship-money." This was a special tax ports were traditionally required to pay, which Charles attempted to extend throughout the kingdom. Though he succeeded for a time, trouble with Scotland eventually forced him to summon Parliament in order to finance an army. Once summoned, Parliament demanded attention to its concerns and entered into a furious struggle with the King. This led to civil war, which culminated in Charles's being tried before a High Court established by Parliament and executed, in 1649.

Defending royal prerogatives, Filmer argued that the king has absolute title to his subjects' property, as one component of the patriarchal power granted originally by God to King Adam. In his words:

> The first government in the world was monarchical, in the father of all flesh, Adam, being commanded to multiply, and people the earth, and to subdue it, and having dominion given him over all the creatures, was thereby the monarch of the whole world. None of his posterity had any right to possess anything but by his grant or permission, or by succession from him. The "earth," saith the Psalmist, "hath he given to the children of men"—which shows the title comes from the fatherhood. (Filmer, p. 236)

One of Filmer's arguments was that royal ownership is the only reasonable arrangement. If property is not given to the King, it must belong to all mankind in common. But if this is the case, then it cannot be used. If one person wishes to make use of any piece of property, he must first receive the permission of everyone else. This of course is absurd. The consequences, then, of kings' not owning everything make no sense (Filmer, pp. 219, 233–234).

In responding to this line of argument, Locke faces a dilemma. As we shall see, he is able to justify individual property holdings through appeal to natural law. His basic position is that, through natural law, people acquire property rights in the state of nature. Because people leave this condition and its inconveniences mainly to protect their property, safeguarding property is the chief function of government: "The great and chief end therefore, of Men's uniting into commonwealths, and putting themselves under government is the Preservation of their Property" (II, 124). The problem, however, is that natural law is inherently egalitarian. It holds that all people have equal rights, and so appears to imply that they have rights to equal property. Because the civil laws of any legitimate society must be consistent with natural law, a natural law defense of property might appear to require equal distribution of property in civil society. Seventeenth century England came nowhere close to that ideal, and Locke had no wish to uphold it.

Since the English Civil War, propertied classes feared that equal natural rights could be turned against unequal property. Their concerns are illustrated by the arguments of Henry Ireton, a leader of Cromwell's parliamentary forces, who engaged in a debate with more radical elements of the army, at Putney, in 1647. In response to democratic demands, based on the Law of God and the Law of Nature, Ireton argued as follows:

> If you will hold forth that as your ground, then I think you must deny all property too, and this is my reason. For thus: by the same right of nature (whatever it be) that you pretend, by which you can say, one man hath an equal right with another to the choosing of him that shall govern him—by the same right of nature, he hath the same [equal] right in any goods he sees—meat, drink, clothes—to take and use them for his sustenance.[17]

During the political debates of the 1670s and 1680s, similar claims were in the air. Tories, the defenders of monarchical authority, accused their opponents, the Whigs, of undermining property rights. Thus, according to a recent historian, Locke's treatment of property is so prominent a theme in the *Two Treatises* because the Whigs "needed some means of reconciling the language of equality, natural rights, and the view that all property was originally given to mankind 'in common' with a justification of individual property rights in order to defend themselves against the accusation of a design to level men's estates, which the Tories repeatedly hurled at them."[18]

Locke's discussion of property should be understood in this context. In arguing for natural rights to property under natural law, he attempts to hedge these rights in such a way that they are compatible with radically unequal distribution of property in society.

In discussing "property" in connection with Locke's political theory, it is important to realize that he uses the concept in two different ways, a broad sense as well as the more common narrow sense. In the narrow sense, property is what a person owns. It generally refers to someone's house, car, clothes, and so on, which she has "exclusive right to possess, enjoy, and dispose of" (to use a dictionary definition).[19] It is in this sense that Locke is concerned with political implications of property, especially in the government's right to infringe upon it without the owner's consent. But he also uses the term in a broader sense, in which it encompasses not only rights of ownership, but all of a person's rights. Two passages in which this broader usage is clear are as follows:

> And 'tis not without reason that [man] seeks out, and is willing to join in Society with others who are already united . . . for the mutual Preservation of their Lives, Liberties and Estates, which I call by the general Name, Property. (II, 123)

> By Property I must be understood here, as in other places, to mean that Property which Men have in their Persons as well as Goods. (II, 173)

Thus when Locke says that government's main function is protecting property, this is equivalent to protecting rights in general. But despite this, there is no denying that protection of property in the narrow sense as well is an essential function of government.

Locke justifies acquisition of property in the state of nature by appeal to man's natural right to preserve himself. In order to survive, people must eat and drink, and make use of other things they find in nature. Natural reason tells us "that being once born," men "have a right to their Preservation, and consequently to Meat and Drink, and such other things as nature affords for their Subsistence." This is confirmed by revelation. For instance, in the Book of Psalms, God gives the Earth "to the Children of Men," or Mankind in common (II, 25). But, Filmer argues, if natural things are given to men in common, then no one can make use of them without receiving the consent of everyone else. To do so without their consent would be to deprive other people of their rights.

To respond to this argument, Locke introduces the concept of labor. If Sasha had to receive everyone else's permission before he could use anything from the state of nature as food, he would die, which is of course counter to God's wishes, and the reason God gave men natural things in the first place. "If such a consent as that was necessary, man had starved, notwithstanding the Plenty God had given him" (II, 28). Because people must be able to survive, there must be a means through which they can appropriate natural things. The necessary means is labor. Locke argues that "every Man has a Property in his own Person," which no one else has a right to. "The Labor of his Body, and the Work of his Hands . . . are properly his" (II, 27). Because each person owns his own labor, he acquires rights to property by mixing his labor with natural things. Thus, if I pick an apple from a tree, as long as the tree does not belong to anyone else, the apple is mine. If I draw water from a stream, once again, by virtue of the fact that I have worked to attain it—or mixed my labor with it—it becomes mine.

In the cases just mentioned, Locke discusses conditions in the state of nature, in which all things belong to mankind in common. Thus the tree from which I pick the apple and the stream from which I draw water belong to everyone. My rights to these things are the same as other people's. If they had mixed their labor with them, they would have rights to them. But because it was I who labored, these things belong to me. The situation is obviously quite different in civil society, where there are legally established rights of ownership. If my neighbor owns an apple tree, she alone has the right to pick its fruit. If I pick an apple, it is stealing. But the state of nature is without legal rights to property. In the cases Locke discusses, a person's labor removes things from the state of nature. Analogous cases in civil society concern things that are viewed as commonly owned. Thus when people fish in the ocean, "that great and still remaining Common of Mankind," it is clear that a person who catches a fish owns it (II, 30).

Locke's position is strongly supported by common sense. Once again, there must be a way for people to establish property rights in the state of nature, or they would die. If Sasha catches and eats a rabbit, clearly, at some point it leaves the natural condition to become his. What is this point? Is it when he digests it? Perhaps it is when he begins to eat it. Or is this when he begins to skin it, or cook it? (II, 28). For Locke, the obvious moment it becomes his is when he mixes his labor with it by catching it. This creates a distinction between this particular rabbit and the commons, and so signifies the transition from the state of nature to Sasha's property.

We should note that Locke carefully chooses examples that support his position. His cases concern removing things from the common natural condition: picking fruit, catching fish or game, filling a pitcher with water. The idea is less clear as it bears on acquiring property in land. But here too Locke argues for a similar phenomenon. By mixing one's labor with a parcel of land, it becomes one's property: "As much Land as a Man Tills, Plants, Improves, Cultivates, and can use the Product of, so much is his Property. He by his Labor does, as it were, enclose it from the Common" (II, 32). Mixing labor with land is less clear-cut than catching a fish, but here too it seems reasonable to claim that someone owns crops grown through his labor.

These examples support the emphasis Locke places on the role of labor in property acquisition. According to Locke, labor creates value. Things in their natural condition are of no use to man, and so have no value. A fish in the sea is worth nothing, until someone catches it. Uncultivated land in the state of nature is worth little; it would take a large tract of land to support a few people, as they foraged for roots and berries, hunted, and fished. But if someone takes this same piece of land and improves it, by clearing it and planting crops, it becomes vastly more productive and able to support many more people. Clearly, a preponderant part of the land's value comes from the labor expended on it (II, 37). In Locke's words,

> For 'tis Labor indeed that puts the difference of value on every thing . . . I think it will
> be but a very modest Computation to say that of the Products of the Earth useful to

the Life of Man $\frac{9}{10}$ are the effects of labor; nay, if we will rightly estimate things as they come to our use, and cast up the several Expences about them, what in them is purely owing to Nature and what to labor, we shall find that in most of them $\frac{99}{100}$ are wholly to be put on the account of labor. (II, 40)

Because of the far greater amount of labor expended in developed societies, life there is incomparably better than in societies closer to man's natural condition: "a King of a large and fruitful Territory there [in America] feeds, lodges, and is clad worse than a day laborer in England" (II, 41).

The claim that labor creates rights to property in the state of nature receives strong support from Locke's view that labor is the primary source of value. Because labor is so important, it makes sense to say that by mixing it with some object in the state of nature one confers value on it, and so comes to own it. Once again, mixing labor with land is more complicated, as this has *some* value before it is cultivated, but the situations are sufficiently similar to satisfy Locke.

Even if we grant that Locke is able to account for property rights in the state of nature, it remains to be seen how he can avoid the spectre of radical egalitarianism. If all people have rights to property under natural law, then it appears that property distribution in civil society must also be equal. Locke recognizes that natural law places specific limits on what one can accumulate in the state of nature. There are two main limits.[20] First, because God gave the world to all mankind, if someone appropriates more goods than he can use, he takes them away from other people and so violates their rights. We can refer to this as the "spoilage" limitation. In Locke's words,

As much as any one can make use of to any advantage of life before it spoils, so much he may by his labor fix a Property in. Whatever is beyond this, is more than his share and belongs to others. Nothing was made by God for Man to spoil or destroy. (II, 31)

Natural law commands individuals not only to preserve themselves but also not to interfere with the preservation of others. Because all people have rights, the requirement not to waste natural goods they might use is clearly reasonable.

But the spoilage limitation is not enough. If Glenn has an enormous appetite, he could still take *and use* so much natural goods that this would damage other people. Not only must he not waste things, but he must not take more than his share. In general, we can assume that the state of nature is thinly populated, and so there is more than enough of everything to go around. But Glenn cannot simply take whatever he wants. He must make sure "enough and as good" is left for other people (II, 27).

Taken together the two limitations imply a degree of equal property in the state of nature. Locke recognizes that some people will be more industrious than others. God gave the earth "to the use of the Industrious and Rational" (II, 34), while "different degrees of Industry were apt to give Men Possessions in different Proportions" (II, 48). But however large these differences might be, each person can take no more than she can use and must make sure to leave as much and as good for others.

In the state of nature, the two limitations would not appear to have radical or undesirable effects. But things become more complex as we move to civil society. In the

England of Locke's day, there was a sharp division between rich and poor, between some who had more than they could use and many who had less than they needed. Because property distribution in civil society is subject to civil law rather than natural law, it might appear that such arrangements are acceptable, and Locke had no wish to argue for radical redistribution of property. But once again, in a legitimate society, the civil laws must be consistent with natural law. If natural law demands that no one take more than he can use, and leave "enough and as good" for others, then radically unequal property distributions are illegitimate, regardless of what civil law allows. We have seen that equal natural rights were widely believed to undermine property rights in civil society. To dissociate himself from such conclusions, Locke attempts to defuse the natural limits on property acquisition in the state of nature.

Locke argues that the two limitations are subject to important qualifications. He claims that the spoilage limitation is effectively repealed in the state of nature through the introduction of money. Through common consent, people in the state of nature "agreed that a little piece of yellow Metal, which would keep without wasting or decay, should be worth a great piece of Flesh, or a whole heap of Corn" (II, 37). By trading surplus produce, which would spoil, for money, which is valuable precisely because it does not spoil, people are rightfully able to accumulate large amounts of property. What is more, Locke holds that the unequal distribution of property that money allows was accepted by people when they agreed to put a value on money:

> [S]ince Gold and Silver, being little useful to the Life of Man in proportion to Food, Raiment, and Carriage, has its value only from the consent of Men, whereof Labor yet makes in great part the measure, it is plain that Men have agreed to the disproportionate and unequal Possession of the Earth, they having by a tacit and voluntary consent found out a way, how a man may fairly possess more land than he himself can use the product of, by receiving in exchange for the overplus Gold and Silver, which may be hoarded up without injury to any one, these metals not spoiling or decaying in the hands of the possessor. (II, 50)

Before proceeding, we should note how strained Locke's reasoning is. It is true that the introduction of money makes it possible for people to amass large amounts of property without wasting anything. It is also true that the value of money depends on general consent to take it in exchange for other things, as a measure of value. But Locke is clearly stretching things to say that, in placing a value on money, people in the state of nature have *consented* to unequal distribution of property. As we saw above, if Tom gives his consent to a certain state of affairs, he must knowingly and intentionally accept it. If I consent to your wish to live in my house, I give you a right to do so, which you did not previously have. Obviously, at minimum, my consent will create this right only if I knowingly and intentionally accept your request. Locke, however, makes no attempt to show that people knowingly and intentionally gave other people a right (which they would not have had otherwise) to accumulate large amounts of property when they began to use money as a medium of exchange. It is hard to imagine why people in the state of nature would do this. Locke certainly presents no convincing reasons.

The second limitation is that, in the state of nature, each man can appropriate property as long as he leaves "enough and as good" for other people. While the spoilage limitation is easily circumvented through the invention of money, this appears more intractable. Especially in regard to land, the most important form of property, there is not enough to go around. People who take land for themselves, even if they cultivate it assiduously, appear obviously to violate this limitation when there is not enough left for everyone else. This limitation bears especially clearly on civil society, in that Locke's England was beset with enormous inequalities in land ownership. If these are not sanctioned by the law of nature, the implications could upset society as a whole.

In order to circumvent this limitation, Locke appeals to two considerations. His main argument rests on the productivity of labor. God gave men land for them to use. In order to make use of it, it must be enclosed, and so God intended there to be property in land. Were there no such property, land would be far less productive and able to support fewer people. Those who appropriate land, in other words, do not lessen the store of goods available in the state of nature but increase it. Their appropriation represents an increase rather than a decrease of nature's bounty:

> [H]e who appropriates land to himself by his labor does not lessen but increase the common stock of mankind. For the provisions serving to the support of humane life produced by one acre of enclosed and cultivated land are . . . ten times more than those which are yielded by an acre of land, of an equal richness, lying waste in common. (II, 37)

This argument, of course, requires that the land in question be used properly, and so leaves the way open for criticism of vast estates in civil society, large percentages of which are not worked.

It is not clear that Locke's response defuses the objection. It is difficult to argue that Jacques leaves enough and as good for others when he takes the last available land, even if he farms it. Through his labor, the store of available commodities is increased. But it is not clear how other people can gain access to these. Locke's repeated emphasis on the contribution of money suggests they are to buy them. But where they are to get the necessary money is not clear. It appears that, far from leaving all people enough and as good, the enclosure of land Locke advocates would lead to a deep division in natural society between those with land and those without.

In response to this problem, it has been argued that landless people are intended to constitute a laboring class, and so to work for the landed.[21] This arrangement would solve the problem of explaining how the landless can afford to buy property-holders' surplus. But, obviously, a situation in which one group works for another because the latter have appropriated all the land does not rest well with the requirement that they leave "enough and as good" for others.

In the *First Treatise*, Locke recognizes that people without property can be at the mercy of the propertied and so forced to work for them. He argues that this situation would be in violation of natural law, which requires charity to one's fellows and forbids exploiting them:

> And therefore no Man could ever have a just Power over the Life of another, by Right of property in Land or Possessions; since 'twould always be a Sin in any Man of Estate, to let his Brother perish for want of affording him Relief out of his Plenty. As Justice

gives every Man a Title to the product of his honest Industry, and the fair Acquisitions of his Ancestors descended to him, so Charity gives every Man a Title to so much out of another's Plenty, as will keep him from extreme want, where he has no means to subsist otherwise; and a Man can no more justly make use of another's necessity, to force him to become his Vassal, by withholding that Relief God requires him to afford to the wants of his Brother, than he that has more strength can seize upon a weaker, master him to his Obedience, and with a Dagger at his Throat offer him Death or Slavery. (I, 42)

In this passage, Locke does not argue that charity requires equal property. The requirement is, rather, that the rich make sure the poor are able to survive. This clearly follows from the main requirement of natural law—to ensure everyone's preservation. Demands of charity would seem to allow the poor to work for the rich, as long as the terms of their employment are not unduly harsh. But this does little to alleviate the fact that, in appropriating all available land, one group does not leave "enough and as good" for others.

Perhaps to remedy this situation, Locke suggests there are places, for example, America, with land to spare. If there is no free land where Clare is, perhaps she should go to America. Once again, one can ask whether land in America is actually as good as land in England. To gain access to it, one must leave friends, family, and home and undertake an arduous journey. To make matters worse, the land in America would not appear to be lying waste, as it is used by Native Americans. But Locke argues that Native Americans can be expropriated. The fact that they do not use money signifies their lack of intention to cultivate their land fully. It therefore lies in common:

[T]here are still great Tracts of Ground to be found, which (the Inhabitants thereof not having joined with the rest of Mankind in the consent of the Use of their common Money) lie waste and are more than the People who dwell on it do, or can make use of, and so still lie in common. Though this can scarce happen amongst that part of Mankind that have consented to the Use of Money. (II, 45)

Thus the greater productivity of societies with money justifies forceful appropriation of areas that do not employ money. One could perhaps reply that the American Indians did have their own forms of money, most notably wampum. But if one looks at Locke's passage carefully, one can make out a possible response. The use of money alone is not enough; people must consent to use "common Money." It is not clear what Locke means by this. Perhaps he would argue that the money in question must be gold or silver, in other words, that which is in use in most places. Only if a society uses gold will it be able to find large markets for its surplus produce.

In justifying seizing the lands of people who do not use common money, Locke obviously strays from the spirit (if not the letter) of natural law. This indicates the depth of his problem. Natural law is an inherently radical, egalitarian notion. Locke has specific political purposes which make it convenient for him to employ it. It is especially valuable in justifying resistance to unjust authority. But natural law has other radical implications which Locke must scramble to defuse. We have seen this pattern in regard to the question of consent. Locke says that governments have power over people only if the latter consent. But as we have also seen, he is forced to retreat from this position, arguing that mere

residence in a territory constitutes consent to its government. We see something similar in regard to natural rights to property. Locke needs a means to account for natural appropriation, in order to respond to Filmer. But here, too, the implications of his position are unpalatable, and he retreats. As we will see in the next section, a similar pattern recurs in regard to the circumstances under which people can rightfully resist unjust authority.

RESISTANCE TO UNJUST AUTHORITY

Locke's doctrine of the social contract bears fruit in his justification of resistance to unjust authority. This view is the logical culmination of everything that has gone before. Demonstrating it is obviously one of his main purposes in the *Two Treatises*.

According to Locke, people in the state of nature leave it for civil society to improve their condition. Thus government must be impartial and protect their rights and liberties. Not only would submission to arbitrary government worsen people's situation, but Locke does not believe they have the *right* to place themselves under arbitrary government. People are not their own masters; they are the workmanship of God, who demands that they preserve themselves. Submitting to the "inconstant, uncertain, unknown, Arbitrary Will of another Man" conflicts with self-preservation and so is forbidden (II, 22–23):

> For no Body can transfer to another more power than he has in himself; and no Body has an absolute Arbitrary Power over himself, or over any other, to destroy his own Life, or take away the Life or Property of another. (II, 135)

Central to Locke's doctrine of resistance is fear of and desire to avoid arbitrary government.

The question of arbitrary power is complicated by Locke's realization that any government must have flexibility to act. Not all exigencies can be provided for by law. In emergency circumstances, governments must be free to take measures in accordance with the "Fundamental Law of Nature and of Government," the preservation of all members of society (II, 159). Locke calls this power "prerogative." He defines it as: "Power to act according to discretion, for the public good, without the prescription of the Law, and sometimes even against it" (II, 160).

We have encountered a similar concept in Machiavelli's notion of "reason of state." When the safety of the country is threatened, moral considerations should give way to what will save the country (see pp. 15–6). In contemporary American society, a similar doctrine is frequently referred to as "national security." Claims of national security are generally made in response to perceived foreign threats. They justify the president in taking emergency measures to provide for public safety. The doctrine was especially important during the presidency of Richard Nixon, who used it to justify criminal behavior, and to attempt to cover up evidence of his administration's wrongdoing.

As the example of Nixon indicates, the notion of prerogative raises fundamental questions. In order to preserve the country, the king must take emergency measures, some of which could violate the law and the rights of citizens. During the Civil War, Abraham Lincoln suspended the writ of habeus corpus and so jailed political opponents without normal legal procedures. The Civil War was obviously an emergency situation, and Lincoln is generally viewed as a great president, because he preserved the Union. But even if, in

retrospect, we view Lincoln's actions as justified, the example of Nixon shows that presidents can also abuse their power. Rulers can *always* say extra-legal behavior is justified by emergency conditions. "Necessity" is "the tyrant's plea."[22] Thus it is essential to be able to decide if a particular employment of extra-legal power is justified.

To complicate matters further, a central theme of Locke's political theory is that people are not entirely rational. Their self-interest clouds their reason and so they are likely to disagree when their interests are at stake. In a case of executive prerogative, the ruler and the people are likely to view the situation differently, and so whose judgment should be accepted? We have seen that, for Locke, political authority is mainly a matter of each individual person's substituting the judgment of the government, sanctioned by the majority, for his own. But what if he believes the government is abusing its power? Under these conditions, it is not necessary for the government to have malign intent. Richard Nixon might have actually believed his measures were justified by national security. But this would not have lessened his threat to the American people.

To some extent these difficulties can be addressed by the separation of powers in a properly constituted government. According to Locke, because human beings are self-interested, to unite legislative and executive powers in the same hands would tempt rulers to abuse their power and become tyrants (II, 143). Thus in all "well-framed Governments" the two powers should be separated (II, 159). We have noted Locke's belief that the legislative power is the more fundamental. The executive is erected mainly for reasons of convenience, because the legislature cannot easily remain in constant session. Thus if the executive abuses his power, he can be removed from office. To remedy problems caused by the executive's use of his prerogative power, it would appear that when the legislature reconvenes it can decide if his emergency measures were justified. This is a reasonable interpretation of Locke's view, and is also consistent with the behavior of legislative bodies. Traditionally, such bodies served as checks on the power of kings. This was fundamental to the "checks and balances" that characterized many constitutional systems. For instance, the power of impeachment, written into the United States Constitution, gives Congress ultimate authority to decide if the President has acted in accordance with his responsibilities. In the case of Richard Nixon, Congress decided that his actions were not acceptable, and he resigned rather than be impeached.

Though Locke undoubtedly views the legislature as superior to the executive, his discussion of the respective powers of the two bodies is complicated by specific facts of the English political system of his time. In seventeenth-century England, as in many countries at that time, the King had the power to call the legislature into session. Locke views this as a royal prerogative (II, 167), which he defends on grounds of convenience, because it is advantageous for the king to summon Parliament when the need arises (II, 156).

As we have seen above, the power to summon the legislature was significant. It was greatly to the King's advantage to rule without the legislature, if he could. In France, the Bourbon monarchs went many years without assembling the Estates-General, and were able to avoid calling them until 1789. In England, as we have seen, this was also a contentious issue. Locke argues that if the executive prevents the legislature from meeting, this is grounds for resisting him (II, 155). Throughout Locke's discussion of resistance to unjust authority, questions concerning the working of the legislature receive considerable attention. Tampering with the legislature is, along with abuse of power, one of the two main grounds for resistance.

If the legislative is not assembled, obviously, it cannot sit in judgment on the executive. This causes problems in determining whether royal prerogative has been used properly.

Locke's response to the legislature's inability to meet is radical. Though the people cede their rights to interpret, judge, and enforce the law of nature on entering civil society, they always retain a residual right to make sure this function is exercised properly. We have seen that they retain a right to judge the performance of the legislature itself. Similarly, the people retain a right to judge the use of royal prerogative, when this cannot be done by the legislature:

> [T]hey have, by a Law antecedent and paramount to all positive Laws of men, reserved that ultimate determination to themselves, which belongs to all Mankind, where there lies no Appeal on Earth, viz. to judge whether they have just Cause to make their Appeal to Heaven. And this Judgment they cannot part with, it being out of a Man's power so to submit himself to another as to give him a liberty to destroy him, God and Nature never allowing a man so to abandon himself as to neglect his own preservation. (II, 168)

The phrase "Appeal to Heaven" is Locke's euphemism for civil war. If the people must use force to defend their rights, Locke is willing to accept this.

Locke's radicalism is apparent in his view that the people may act when they do not receive justice elsewhere. This contention represents a significant break from traditional medieval doctrine, according to which people may never resist unjust authority. The standard medieval view is that an unjust king is God's punishment, visited upon the people for their transgressions. During the Reformation, opinions began to change. Luther, Calvin, and various other religious-political figures advocated the use of force against unjust rulers, largely for the sake of protecting Protestantism and Protestant populations in regions where it had been established. Because of biblical prohibitions against resisting rulers, these theorists generally framed their arguments in terms of natural law, especially the natural right of self-defense.[23] But because they feared the anarchical implications of allowing *everyone* to resist, they generally introduced a distinction between private citizens and public persons or magistrates and were careful to limit rights of resistance only to magistrates. Thus in his *Institutes of the Christian Religion*, Calvin discusses the evils of tyranny, but argues that these should be viewed as divine chastisement for the people's sins.[24] Accordingly, the people's only recourse is "to obey and suffer." The situation is different in regard to magistrates. Calvin writes: "This observation I always apply to private persons." Certain magistrates, acting in official capacities, are permitted to take action against unjust rulers in order to protect their subjects" (*Institutes*, IV, Chap. 20, Sec. 31).

With Locke, the distinction between private and public persons is eliminated. As an essential aspect of the fundamental right of self-preservation, each person has a right to judge public officials and to take action when he believes power has been misused. This is, again, a radical notion. Even more extreme, Locke argues that each person can take up arms against government when he believes *he alone* has been treated unjustly, regardless of the government's overall performance:

> [W]here the Body of the People, or any single Man, is deprived of their Right, or is under the Exercise of a power without right, and have no Appeal on Earth, there they have a liberty to appeal to Heaven, whenever they judge the Cause of sufficient moment. (II, 168)

As we shall see, however, Locke takes steps to limit the potentially anarchistic consequences of this doctrine.

In addition to Locke's views on who can resist the state, we should note his position on the form resistance should take. Locke's claims were not original; thinkers had advanced similar views since the Reformation (see Vol. I, Chapter 11). But this still represents a considerable departure from the standard medieval position. Throughout the medieval period, theorists generally argued that subjects have strong obligations to obey their rulers. These obligations are limited in one respect, by stronger obligations owed to God. If a command of the ruler directly contravenes the subject's religious duty, then he should not obey, which frequently means accepting martyrdom. He should "obey God rather than man" and accept the consequences.[25] Thus subjects were allowed to disobey, but not to resist.

The distinction between nonobedience and resistance is of great importance in the history of political theory. Throughout the medieval period, it was generally argued that subjects could not resist their rulers, though under certain circumstances they were allowed to disobey. In this light we should note how strongly Locke supports the right to take up arms against unjust rulers. By behaving unjustly, a ruler in effect loses his authority and can be opposed with force, as can any other man. The unjust ruler places himself in a state of war with his subjects. In response, subjects can resort to war themselves:

> [W]hosoever in Authority exceeds the Power given him by the Law and makes use of the Force he has under his Command to compass that upon the Subject, which the Law allows not, ceases in that to be a Magistrate, and acting without Authority, may be opposed as any other Man, who by force invades the Right of another. (II, 202)

We have seen that Locke is at his most radical in arguing that any single individual can resist government when he has been treated unjustly. To compound this position, Locke argues that each person must decide for himself how he has been treated, and whether the sovereign has initiated a state of war with him:

> [E]very Man is Judge for himself, as in all other Cases, so in this, whether another hath put himself into a State of War with him. (II, 241)

Because force is the necessary response to a state of war, Locke clearly holds that any single man can take up arms against his ruler, *when he finds cause*. One commentator describes this doctrine as "Locke at his most anarchistic."[26]

In spite of his radical position, Locke realizes the futility of resistance by isolated individuals. The state is vastly more powerful than any single man. For one or a few persons to assert the right to resist will "engage them in a Contest wherein they are sure to perish." It is "impossible for one or a few oppressed Men to disturb the Government," unless a large body of others believe themselves similarly aggrieved and are willing to act accordingly (II, 208). But in spite of the practical difficulties a single person would face in resisting, it is notable that he has a right to do so. All people are property of God. If government abuses a single person, it violates its trust, and so that person can take up arms against it. Because Locke views all people as constituting a natural community under the law of nature, it appears that all other people have obligations to come to the victim's aid. But Locke does not pursue the implications here, no doubt shying away from such incendiary themes. In addition, people are self-interested in their interpretations of natural law. (Even in civil society, they still interpret natural law in regard to the conduct of the government.) Thus they are likely not to judge the injustice of isolated cases as severely as the victims do. Resistance is unlikely "till the mischief be grown general, and the ill designs of the Rulers become visible, or their attempts sensible to the greater part. "[Th]e People, who are more disposed to suffer than right themselves by Resistance, are not apt to stir" (II, 230). Thus particular injustices are not likely to cause revolution. But when government causes general discontent, the great mass of men could rise up.

Locke discusses two main sets of circumstances under which resistance is justified. In these cases, government loses its power, in effect dissolving itself and allowing subjects to recover their natural liberty. Because of the two-stage contractual mechanism through which government arises, we should distinguish the dissolution of government and of society. When government violates the terms of the agreement through which it is set up, it loses its power, and subjects no longer have to obey (II, 222, 237, 243). But this does not return them to the state of nature. The agreement through which society was originally set up remains in effect. Governmental power reverts to society, which is free to place it in new, and hopefully better, hands. The "usual and almost only way" society can be dissolved is through foreign conquest, which, in overturning everything, frees people from all societal bonds to fend for themselves (II, 211).

The first set of circumstances that dissolve government are when the legislative power is altered. In light of his specific political circumstances, Locke was greatly concerned to protect the sanctity of the legislature, which he viewed as an essential defense against arbitrary, absolute monarchy. But because the King had the power to summon the legislature, it was largely at his mercy.

In discussing alteration of the legislature, Locke clearly turns from general questions of political theory to conditions in England. He focuses on a specific kind of legislative body consisting of two assemblies (obviously the Houses of Lords and Commons), and a "single hereditary Person having the constant supreme executive power," and also the "Power of Convoking and Dissolving the other two within certain Periods of Time" (II, 213). This person is obviously the King. A legislature of this kind is altered in four ways. First is when the ruler substitutes his own arbitrary will for the laws it makes, which are the true expression of the will of the community (II, 214). Second is when the prince prevents the legislature from meeting or fulfilling the function for which it was set up. This, too, obviously prevents the legislative power from expressing the will of the people (II, 215). Third is if the prince unjustifiably tampers with the means of choosing the legislators. Beyond a certain point, abuses of this sort would enable him to stack the legislature, once again preventing it from fulfilling its proper function (II, 216). Finally, delivery of the people into the hands of a foreign power alters the legislature (II, 217). Though Locke does not say exactly what he has in mind here, it is likely that he intends to disallow a Catholic ruler's subordination to the Pope.

Aside from his immediate political situation, Locke's concern for the sanctity of the legislature follows from central aspects of his theory. In leaving the state of nature, people surrender their rights to enforce the law of nature to government, subject to the conditions we have noted. Everyone agrees to accept the particular legislature that is chosen by majority rule, and so to be "concluded by the majority." Erection of the legislative body is "the first and fundamental positive Law of all Commonwealths" and "sacred and unalterable in the hands where the Community have once placed it" (II, 134). By tampering with this arrangement, the executive violates the people's consent. The terms under which they entered civil society no longer obtain, and so they recover their liberty.

The second set of conditions that dissolve government concern abuse of power. In Locke's words, "that is when the Legislative, or the Prince, either of them act contrary to their Trust" (II, 221). Locke defines tyranny as "the exercise of Power beyond Right, which no Body can have a Right to" (II, 199). People enter into civil society to protect their property and other rights from the inconveniences of the state of nature. The relationship between people and government rests on mutual obligations. The people must obey only as long as government fulfills its function. If it does not, it loses the right to be obeyed. To this basic idea, Locke adds that if the government violates subjects' rights, it places itself in a state of war with them and can be opposed with force:

> [W]henever the Legislators endeavor to take away and destroy the Property of the People, or to reduce them to Slavery under Arbitrary Power, they put themselves into a state of War with the People, who are thereupon absolved from any farther Obedience, and are left to the common Refuge which God hath provided for all Men against force and violence. (II, 222)

What is true of the legislature holds for the executive as well. He can also be resisted when he violates his trust (II, 222). In either case, those who break the agreements are the actual rebels and should be blamed for any troubles that ensue (II, 230).

In all the circumstances we have reviewed, government dissolves and people fend for themselves. Power reverts to the community, which can place it in new hands.[27] Central elements of Locke's view are highly inflammatory. These include the right of each individual to resist, the idea that dissolution of government empowers the people, and the permissibility of forcible resistance. Locke is, however, greatly concerned with countering the incendiary implications of his view—as he retreats from his doctrine's implications in regard to natural rights to property and government by consent. If the people are justified in opposing government every time it violates their rights, society will constantly be ridden with strife. Because government is imperfect, the contract will constantly be broken, thus inviting civil war, revolution, and chaos. These "desperate inconveniences" of government by consent were cited by Filmer in support of absolute monarchy (Filmer, pp. 224–225). Accordingly, Locke holds that revolution is justified only when it is "worth the trouble and cost of the Appeal" (II, 176). Such circumstances will be rare, as "open and visible rebellion" will have devastating effects (II, 218).

To counter the view that his doctrine invites frequent rebellion, Locke argues that the people are long-suffering. They fear revolution and the chaos it entails and so will not rebel for light and transient causes. "Great mistakes in the ruling part, many wrong and inconvenient laws, and all the slips of human frailty will be borne by the People, without mutiny or murmur" (II, 225). As we have seen, they will not be moved by particular injustices, until "the mischief be grown general," which will cause them to rise (II, 230). Thus people will be stirred to revolution only by a pattern of consistent, tyrannical action. In a famous passage, echoed in the *Declaration of Independence*, Locke refers to this as "a long train of Abuses, Prevarications, and Artifices, all tending the same way," which make the ruler's tyrannical intentions apparent (II, 225). When the many see the direction in which things are heading, they are likely to rebel. But these extraordinary measures are justified by the tyrannical conduct of the ruler. In causing revolution, a ruler is "guilty of the greatest Crime . . . a Man is capable of" (II, 230).

Locke's attempt to limit the right to resist is dictated by common sense as well as his particular political purposes. Writing in order to justify revolution, he places clear limits on royal authority, which he believes have obviously been violated in his own situation. But once again, he fears his argument might prove too much. Because people are naturally free and can be governed only by their own consent, he confronts a range of circumstances in which resistance is justified, including resistance by aggrieved individuals. Because such anarchistic doctrines are far from his intentions, he attempts to retreat. In the passages quoted above, one will note that Locke switches from what people are justified in doing to what they are likely to do. Though the view that political relations are derived from the free consent of people living under natural law in a state of nature is attractive in many ways, it also has radical implications, which Locke wishes to avoid.

LOCKE AND LIBERAL POLITICAL THEORY

For good reasons, Locke is widely viewed as the archetypal representative of liberal political theory. As discussed in the last chapter, liberal political theory is the mainstream of political discourse in the Western democracies since roughly the seventeenth century. The main features of this political philosophy have been discussed in the previous chapter, but I will briefly review them here for convenience.

Though different theorists use the term "liberal" in different senses, for our purposes a rough outline of the theory will do. Though the points presented here are not entirely without controversy, I believe, they would be accepted by most political theorists as representative of liberalism. As I view the theory, it centers on five main claims:

First, liberal theory has as its main concern the individual. The individual is conceived of as the basic building block of society. He is viewed as "prior" to society, in that he possesses rights by virtue of his humanity, rather than by having received them from society. He also has his ends or goals prior to his entry into society. Typically, as we see in both Locke and Hobbes, these aspects of the individual are conceptualized in a state of nature, which is a situation without government, prior to people's entry into society.

Second, according to liberal theory, the community or society is nothing but the individuals who compose it. This is closely related to the first point, but it has an added moral dimension. Liberals view the interest of the community as reducible to the interests of the people who compose it. Thus the community does not have ends or goals of its own apart from those of its members. This holds for the state as well. The interest of the state does not exist apart from the interests of its citizens. As with the community, what is good for the state is nothing more than what is good for the people who comprise it.

Third, liberals hold an "instrumental" view of politics. As we have seen, instrumental reasoning is according to the categories of means and ends. Instrumental rationality assesses policies according to how efficiently they serve as means to the attainment of given ends. In regard to liberal political theory, individuals are conceived of as having rights and interests apart from society, for the advancement of which they erect the state. Thus the purpose of political activity is to promote these values. Government does not create or define people's interests; it exists to serve interests they already have. The instrumental view of politics is seen clearly in the state of nature arguments of both Hobbes and Locke. Because of the inconveniences of living without government, people enter civil society. Because the interest of the community is reducible to the interests of the people who comprise it, government has no other end than advancing the interests of its members and should be assessed according to how well it does this.

The fourth point concerns the limited purposes of political activity, mainly the protection of rights and property. This is in opposition to other views of politics, for example, those of the classical Greeks, according to which the state exists to pursue more exalted aims, including the education and moral reform of its members. Liberals hold what is referred to as a "negative" view of the state. The state's main functions are coercive. It punishes people and threatens to punish others in order to deter them from invading other people's rights. Liberals are especially concerned with protecting rights to property. As we see in Locke, property exists in the state of nature, and it is mainly to protect property (though in a broad sense) that people enter civil society. The makeup of the state reflects these functions. Its main institutions are coercive: a police force, judiciary, prison system, an army, etc. As noted in the last chapter, the states that actually existed in the seventeenth century, when liberal theory arose, centered on these functions, and were comprised of these institutions. Liberal theorists worked from the political facts of their times.

Last is the liberal conception of freedom, which is generally referred to as "negative" freedom. This is absence of coercive interference by other people. There are two possible sources of interference that must be avoided, from other people and from government. Reflecting the circumstances under which their doctrine arose, liberals are generally more concerned with the threat to freedom posed by government. Historically, liberal political theory expressed the goals of opponents of monarchical governments, who conceived of freedom in opposition to this. Thus freedom of speech means that government does not punish people for saying what they please. The same is true of freedom of assembly, or of conscience. In these spheres and others, the individual enjoys an area of protected space free from governmental interference.

Governmental interference is not, however, the only threat to freedom. As is clear in Locke's and Hobbes's arguments from the state of nature, government is necessary to protect people from the encroachment of others. Because one's property, security, and very life can be threatened by the behavior of other people, individuals are willing to surrender some of their rights to government in order to protect the rest. Though this might appear to diminish their freedom, it actually enlarges it. Though people lose certain freedoms they once had, their gains in security from other people outweigh these.

If we assess Locke's political theory against these five points, we can see that he is a pure liberal in almost all senses. Like Hobbes, he begins with individuals in the state of nature. Clearly, the starting point of his political theory is the individual, rather than society or the state. Individuals in the state of nature have their rights from God, whose workmanship they are. They also labor in the state of nature and accumulate property. To protect their rights and property from the vagaries of this natural condition, they enter society and erect government. Both their rights and their ends exist prior to their entry into civil society.

Not only does Locke begin his political theory with the individual, but in doing so he presents the classic liberal account of the nature of the individual—and, as we have seen, of such related topics as the relationship between parents and children. Throughout this and the preceding chapters, we have seen that the state of nature argument provides a valuable means of illuminating the connections between a specific view of the state and its functions and the specific conception of human nature on which it rests. Because Locke provides a classic defense of the liberal ideal of limited government, his theory also uncovers the conception of human nature on which this political ideal rests. The Lockean individual, though self-interested, is not excessively so. He is, for instance, bound to his children by tender sentiments and is naturally associated with other people in a community under natural law. He is also a reasoning creature, and so able to comport his conduct with the dictates of natural law. His main flaw is that his passions can interfere with his apprehension of natural law, causing him to be partial to his own interests. Thus government's main role is to serve as a neutral arbiter. In depicting man as a basically decent but flawed creature, Locke presents the standard liberal view, generally encountered in major works of liberal political theory.

Because Locke views individuals as prior to society and the state, both of these situations are brought about by agreements between people. Locke argues that the move to political society is in two stages. The first step sets up society, the second government. In both cases, the conditions in question are brought about by the actions of individuals and have no substantial existence apart from the people who comprise them. Thus the interests of both society and the state are reducible to those of their individual members.

Because the state of nature has inconveniences, individuals erect government as a remedy. Government is a means to this end. It provides security by interpreting the law of nature, judging and enforcing cases under it. Its primary institutions are coercive, reflecting the political institutions that existed during Locke's own time. In all of these respects, Locke falls squarely within the liberal camp.

Locke's conception of freedom is also liberal. As we have seen, he argues that people in the state of nature are in a condition of liberty, not license. They are not free to do whatever they please but must abide by the law of nature as promulgated through their reason. The main content of this law is the obligation to preserve oneself and others. Thus freedom for Locke is to live within the law of nature. His main objection to arbitrary power is its threat to self-preservation, and so to one's obligations under natural law.

In the *Second Treatise*, Locke is concerned mainly with freedom from arbitrary power of government. Thus he argues that government must arise through a contract, with restrictions. Because of their obligations to God, people cannot enter into unrestricted agreements with government. To do so would make the power of government arbitrary, which is unacceptable. Properly constituted government is charged to enforce the law of nature. If it fails to fulfill this responsibility, it loses its power, and the people are free to place it elsewhere. Locke's concern with individual freedom is seen in his view that well-ordered governments place legislative and executive powers in separate hands, to prevent a single holder of both from misusing them. The doctrine of resistance in which the *Second Treatise* culminates is also obviously intended to limit government's power over the individual.

Locke is aware of the apparent paradox that the renunciation of rights to government increases rather than decreases people's freedom. The state of nature is a situation without government, but freedom there is threatened by the actions of other people. We have seen that self-interest leads people astray, and so causes them to infringe upon the rights of others. A proper government will insure that the laws of nature are observed throughout society. The laws made by the legislature will be in accordance with natural law, and effective because of their coercive sanction. Such laws no more limit freedom than natural law itself. In Locke's words,

> For Law in its true Notion is not so much the Limitation as the direction of a free and intelligent Agent to his proper Interest, and prescribes no farther than is for the general Good of those under that Law . . . [A]nd that ill deserves the Name of Confinement which hedges us in only from Bogs and Precipices. So that, however it may be mistaken, the end of Law is not to abolish or restrain, but to preserve and enlarge Freedom. For in all the states of created beings capable of Laws, where there is no Law there is no Freedom. For Liberty is to be free from restraint and violence from others, which cannot be where there is no Law. (II, 57)

This would not be true if liberty were for everyone to do as they wished. But liberty is always limited by natural law. With the existence of government people are more likely to be "safe and secure within the limits of the Law" (II, 137) than without it.

The expansion of freedom under government of course depends on government's adhering to the law of nature and not abusing its power. Locke was greatly concerned with insuring this. Undoubtedly because of his political experiences, he viewed arbitrary and tyrannical government as a serious threat to liberty. But this does not gainsay the fact that without government there is less liberty than in properly constituted civil society.

Locke's central place in the liberal tradition can be attributed largely to his concentration on the individual and his rights. As a political philosophy, liberalism is deeply concerned with protecting the individual from unjustified authority. Locke's concern with the individual shows up in—and is perhaps responsible for—the most radical aspects of his theory. It arises in the view that each individual must consent to government, and that each has the right to judge governmental performance and to take up arms if he finds cause. We have seen respects in which Locke attempts to retreat from radical implications of his theory. In this regard, he presents central problems of liberal political theory along with its great strengths.

The individual in the state of nature, not bound to political institutions and intent on securing his rights, is the ideal starting point for a political theory intended to limit certain kinds of political authority. But once this premise is developed, theorists confront the problem of excessive individualism. Self-interested individuals may be willing to enter political society, but they have little reason to sacrifice their interests for other people or the state. In subsequent years, implications that Locke refused to draw were eagerly seized upon by other thinkers. In the last chapter, we encountered a problem along these lines with Hobbes—in spite of his departures from liberal theory in other respects. Beginning with the individual, as Locke does, liberal theorists express the great value of each person. But excessive emphasis on this threatens other values that make community possible.

In his account, as we have seen, Locke attempts to skirt these problems. In carefully working out the implications of liberal individualism, he makes a permanent contribution to the defense of a certain conception of freedom. In subsequent chapters, we will incorporate Locke's view of freedom into a wider philosophical context. Criticisms of a Lockean view will reveal where liberal theory is vulnerable. Still, there is no question about the importance of the values Locke defends, or the power of his defense. In crucial respects, subsequent liberal theorists have retraced his steps.

NOTES

1. Preface to *Two Treatises of Government*. I will refer to this work as a whole as the *Two Treatises of Government*, or *Two Treatises* for short. The individual treatises will be referred to as the *First* and *Second* and cited according to Treatise (I, for the *First* and II, for the *Second*), and section number. Full references are found below, under "Texts Cited." I have modernized much of Locke's spelling and punctuation, while generally retaining his capitalization. Though I eliminate much of Locke's italicization, unless otherwise noted, that which remains is Locke's.

2. P. Laslett, "Introduction," to *Two Treatises of Government* by Locke, student edition (Cambridge, 1988); see also R. Ashcraft, *Revolutionary Politics and Locke's Two Treatises of Government* (Princeton, 1986).

3. S. Dworetz, *The Unvarnished Doctrine* (Durham, NC, 1990).

4. For biographical details, see M. Cranston, *John Locke: A Biography* (London, 1957).

5. See Laslett, "Introduction," p. 27.

6. Laslett, "Introduction," pp. 54–61.

7. R. Filmer, *Patriarcha and Other Writings*, J. Sommerville, ed. (Cambridge, 1991), p. 7; this work cited hereafter as "Filmer" in text.

8. Sommerville, "Introduction," to Filmer, *Patriarcha and Other Writings*, pp. xxxii–xxxiv.

9. J. J. Rousseau, *The Social Contract*, I, 2; in Rousseau, *The Basic Political Writings*, D. A. Cress, ed. and trans. (Indianapolis, 1987), p. 143.

10. Locke, *An Essay Concerning Human Understanding*, Bk. I, Chap. ii, Sec. 1; full reference below, under "Texts Cited."

11. Locke, *Essays on the Law of Nature*, W. Von Leyden, ed. (Oxford, 1954).

12. For a good brief account, see J. Waldron, "Rights," in *The Blackwell Encyclopedia of Political Thought*, D. Miller, ed. (Oxford, 1987), on which I draw here. An excellent recent discussion of Locke's view of rights is A. J. Simmons, *The Lockean Theory of Rights* (Princeton, 1992).

13. Simmons, *Lockean Theory of Rights*, p. 76.

14. Locke, *A Letter Concerning Toleration*, pp. 28–29; full reference below, under "Texts Cited." I am indebted to Simmons (*Lockean Theory of Rights*, p. 77), for references to the quotations in this paragraph.

15. H. Pitkin, "Obligation and Consent, I," *American Political Science Review* 59 (1965), 995; for a brilliant critique of Locke's view of political obligation, see Simmons, *Moral Principles and Political Obligations* (Princeton, 1979), Chaps. 3, 4.

16. Sommerville, "Absolutism and Revolution in the Seventeenth Century," in *The Cambridge History of Political Thought, 1450-1700*," J. H. Burns, ed. (Cambridge, 1991), p. 368.

17. In *Puritanism and Liberty*, A. S. P. Woodhouse, ed. (Chicago, 1951), pp. 56–58.

18. Ashcraft, *Revolutionary Politics*, p. 251. For good brief discussion of Locke's intentions, see T. Horne, *Property Rights and Poverty* (Chapel Hill, NC, 1990), Chap. 2.

19. *Webster's Third New International Dictionary*, P. B. Gove, ed. (Springfield, MA, 1971), q.v.

20. The classic discussion of these limits and how they are overcome is C. B. Macpherson, *The Political Theory of Possessive Individualism* (Oxford, 1962), Chap. 5, to whom I am indebted.

21. Macpherson brilliantly develops this line of argument, though his conclusions are obviously exaggerated (*Political Theory of Possessive Individualism*, Chap. 5). Cf. J. Tully, *A Discourse on Property* (Cambridge, 1980).

22. J. Milton, *Paradise Lost*, Book 4, 1. 393.

23. See Vol. I, 316–326.

24. Calvin, *Inst.*, IV, Chap. 20, Sec. 29; translation in McNeill, ed., *On God and Political Duty*, full reference below, under "Texts Cited." See Vol. I, 319–320.

25. See Vol. I, Chap. 7.

26. Laslett, Introduction, p. 379n.

27. An excellent account of Locke's doctrine in this regard and its originality is J. Franklin, *John Locke and the Theory of Sovereignty* (Cambridge, 1978).

TEXTS CITED

Calvin, J. *On God and Political Duty*. J. McNeill, ed. Indianapolis, 1956.

Filmer, R. *Patriarcha and Other Writings*. J. Sommerville, ed. Cambridge, 1991.

Locke, J. *An Essay Concerning Human Understanding*. A. C. Fraser, ed. 2 vols. Toronto; rpt. New York, 1959.

Locke, J. *A Letter Concerning Toleration*. P. Romanell, ed. 2nd ed. Indianapolis, 1955.

Locke, J. *Two Treatises of Government*. P. Laslett, ed. Student edition. Cambridge, 1988.

Mornay, P. *Vindiciae contra Tyrannos*. In J. H. Franklin, ed. and trans. *Constitutionalism and Resistance in the Sixteenth Century*. New York, 1969.

The Oxford Annotated Bible. H. May and B. Metzger, eds. Oxford, 1962.

FURTHER READING

Ashcraft, R. *Revolutionary Politics and Locke's Two Treatises of Government*. Princeton, 1986.

Burns, J. H., ed. *The Cambridge History of Political Thought, 1450–1700*. Cambridge, 1991.

Cranston, M. *John Locke: A Biography*. Oxford, 1985.

Dunn, J. *Locke*. Oxford, 1984.

Dunn, J. *The Political Thought of John Locke*. Cambridge, 1969.

Franklin, J. *John Locke and the Theory of Sovereignty*. Cambridge, 1978.

Gough, J. *John Locke's Political Philosophy: Eight Studies.* London, 1950.

Horne, T. *Property Rights and Poverty.* Chapel Hill, NC, 1990.

Laslett, P. Introduction to *Two Treatises of Government* by Locke. Laslett, ed. Student edition. Cambridge, 1988.

Locke, J. *Essays on the Law of Nature.* W. Von Leyden, ed. Oxford, 1954.

Macpherson, C. B. *The Political Theory of Possessive Individualism.* Oxford, 1962.

Parry, G. *John Locke.* London, 1978.

Pitkin, H. "Obligation and Consent." *American Political Science Review* 59 (1965); 60 (1966).

Simmons, A. J. *The Lockean Theory of Rights.* Princeton, 1992.

Simmons, A. J. *Moral Principles and Political Obligations.* Princeton, 1979. Chaps. 3–4.

Simmons, A. J. *On the Edge of Anarchy.* Princeton, 1993.

Tully, J. *A Discourse on Property.* Cambridge, 1980.

C h a p t e r
4

DAVID HUME

HUME'S SKEPTICISM

AMONG THE GREAT PHILOSOPHERS, THERE are "breakers" as well as "makers."[1] Some thinkers have contributed more by tearing down argumentative structures erected by others than by developing systems of their own. David Hume is often called "the greatest of all British philosophers."[2] According to even an unsympathetic scholar, "David Hume is beyond all question the ablest British philosopher."[3] While these judgments are perhaps controversial, there is little doubt that Hume is the greatest *critical* philosopher to have written in English—or perhaps in any language. If we measure philosophical achievement by quantity of faulty reasoning laid to rest, Hume is without peer. In a series of devastating arguments, conceived in his youth and presented in various forms throughout his life, Hume raises doubts about cherished beliefs in field after field. Many of his arguments are of great contemporary relevance; in raising questions with which philosophers still deal, Hume is very much a contemporary thinker.

We will see that Hume is far more than a destroyer. His great critical accomplishments have distracted attention from other aspects of his thought. Hume's German contemporary, Johann Georg Hamann, described him as "a spirit for tearing down, not building up."[4] But in moral and political philosophy, he develops powerful responses to important issues that he raises.

In order to appreciate Hume's accomplishments, we will pay considerable attention to his critical arguments, and so, unavoidably, to somewhat technical problems in epistemology (philosophy of knowledge) and moral philosophy. As a skeptical philosopher, Hume's recurrent demand is that philosophical claims be justified at the bar of reason. His view of reason, as we will see, is associated with developments in the natural sciences. It is a faculty for uncovering relationships and drawing connections between entities, and little more. With almost clinical detachment, Hume lays bare relationships underlying proposed claims to knowledge, in order to show why we actually assent to them.

Hume's relentless argumentation presents a central tendency of modern thought— and so of modern political theory. A problem he inescapably raises is where reason is to stop. Each time a claim to knowledge is brought forth, reason can reduce it to its components and uncover the undemonstrable assumptions on which it rests. Hume's merciless scrutiny brings down claims to knowledge of the natural world, while moral and religious truths are hit especially hard. Because there is no obvious end to the process of

136

questioning, reason naturally tends toward corrosive doubt. Accordingly, the need somehow to defend moral standards from the results of critical examination is a central theme in modern moral and political theory. In Hume's hands, reason emerges as a universal solvent, which no container can hold.

By temperament, Hume is not a complete skeptic and, as we will see, seeks refuge in habit and common sense. But as he no doubt would have admitted, his position too is vulnerable to skeptical criticism. In spite of Hume's positive accomplishments, then, the general opinion of him is as expressed by Isaiah Berlin: "No man has influenced the history of philosophy to a deeper and more disturbing degree."[5]

HUME'S LIFE AND LITERARY PURSUITS

Hume was born in Scotland in 1711 to a modest landowning family. As a younger son, he had to prepare to make a living and accordingly began to study law. But as he relates in "My Own Life," a brief autobiographical statement,[6] "I . . . was seized very early with a passion for Literature, which has been the ruling Passion of my Life and the great Source of my Enjoyments" (p. 1). With only a few interruptions, Hume pursued this passion throughout his life. "My Own Life" is extremely brief (some seven pages), but in it Hume recounts little more than the history of his writings, "as, indeed, almost all my Life has been spent in literary Pursuits and Occupations" (p. 1). He describes himself as "a man of mild Dispositions, of Command of Temper, of an open, social, and cheerful Humor, capable of Attachment but little susceptible of Enmity, and of great Moderation in all my Passions" (p. 7). "Love of literary Fame" is identified as his "ruling passion" (ibid.).

Hume's life was outwardly devoid of drama.[7] To supplement his modest income, he attained a variety of appointments, including a brief term as secretary to a mad young nobleman, and military and diplomatic posts. He acted as secretary to General James St. Clair, and as an aide-de-camp to St. Clair, serving, in uniform, in military embassies to Vienna and Turin. Clerical opposition prevented Hume from receiving academic appointments at the Universities of Edinburgh and Glasgow. But a term as Librarian to the Faculty of Advocates at Edinburgh gave him access to the research materials he required to write a six-volume *History of England*, on which his reputation rested for many years. Service with the British Ambassador to France took Hume to Paris, where he was a considerable literary celebrity. While in Paris, he befriended the difficult Jean-Jacques Rousseau, and brought him back to England. Rousseau soon turned on Hume, despite the latter's kindness, and the two engaged in a famous quarrel.[8] Hume eventually returned to Edinburgh and built a house, where he remained until his death. In his honor, the street on which he lived has been called St. David's Street ever since (see Mossner, pp. 566, 620).

Though Hume achieved literary fame, this was on the whole not for his greatest or most important works. At approximately the age of eighteen, he made the momentous philosophical discoveries on which his *Treatise of Human Nature* is based (*Letters*, I, 13). In a later letter, he describes this work as "plan'd before I was one and twenty, & compos'd before twenty five" (*Letters*, I, 158). The bulk of the work was written in France between the years 1734 and 1737. The first two parts, "Of the Understanding" and "Of the Passions," were published in 1739, and the third, "Of Morals," in 1740. But in spite of the work's brilliance, it was a disappointment to its author:

> Never literary Attempt was more unfortunate than my *Treatise of Human Nature*. It fell
> *deadborn from the Press*. . . . ("Life," p. 2)

Hume exaggerates here, as the work received some attention, though this was mainly hostile
(see Mossner, Chap. 10). Hume felt that the work's lack of success stemmed "more from
the manner than the matter." Believing he had published it too early ("Life," p. 3), he was
to lament his haste "a hundred & a hundred times" (*Letters*, I, 158). He spent much of the
rest of his life refining the matter of the *Treatise* to make it more palatable.

Hume's main endeavors in this direction are the two *Enquiries*, which were published
in 1748. The *Enquiry Concerning Human Understanding* was intended to supersede the first
Part of the *Treatise* and the *Enquiry Concerning the Principles of Morals* took the place of the
third. In his "Advertisement" to the posthumous 1777 edition of the two *Enquiries*, Hume
writes: "Henceforth, the Author desires that the following Pieces may alone be regarded as
containing his philosophical sentiments and principles."[9] Though lacking various matters
discussed in the *Treatise*, and without much of the earlier work's thorny argumentation, the
two *Enquiries* are indeed beautifully written presentations of Hume's main ideas. He says
of the *Enquiry Concerning the Principles of Morals* that it is, in his opinion, "of all my
writings, historical, philosophical, or literary, incomparably the best" ("Life," p. 4). But
revision was little help. This *Enquiry*, along with its companion, "came unnoticed and
unobserved into the World" ("Life," p. 4).

In spite of these setbacks, Hume's other efforts were more successful. He published
a number of volumes of essays on moral, political, and literary subjects, which were well-
received.[10] Some of these, as we will see, contain important components of his political
theory. In addition, his *History of England* was an enormous popular success. For instance,
Voltaire wrote: "Nothing can be added to the fame of this *History*, perhaps the best ever
written in any language. . . ."[11] This work was reprinted many times and was the standard
work on the subject until well into the following century. Thus it was the success of his
essays and *History* that brought Hume cherished fame. Through his royalties, he became
"not only independent but opulent" ("Life," p. 5). According to Ernest C. Mossner, his
biographer, by 1757, Hume was widely viewed as the leading man of letters in Britain. In
1762 James Boswell, later famous for his biography of Samuel Johnson, identified Hume
as "the greatest Writer in Britain" (Mossner, p. 223).

Because of the relentless critical edge to his philosophizing, Hume's character has
been much maligned. He is often accused of being more interested in fame than truth, of
philosophizing frivolously, solely as a means to this end.[12] Regardless of the merits of these
charges, it appears that Hume's character and philosophy are unusually closely interrelated.
The sustained, utterly dispassionate argumentation for which he is known was possible only
to someone who could keep his emotions in check—"of great Moderation in all my
Passions" ("Life," p. 7). Throughout his life, Hume displayed a remarkable ability to face
up to unpleasant truths. His posthumously published *Dialogues Concerning Natural Religion*
present a withering critique of purported religious truths founded on reason. Stricken with
a fatal illness, Hume contemplated his end with notable calm. Mossner provides an
amusing account of a deathbed conversation between Hume and Boswell. The latter,
morbidly preoccupied with death, was disturbed by Hume's cheerful discussion of his own
pending annihilation. When Boswell asked about the possibility of a future state, "He

answered It was possible that a piece of coal put upon the fire would not burn; and he added that it was a most unreasonable fancy that we should exist for ever . . ." (Boswell, quoted by Mossner, pp. 597–598). Hume's wry acceptance of things is seen in his autobiography, which was written a few months before he died.

> To conclude historically with my own Character—I am, or rather was (for that is the Style I must now use in speaking of myself, which emboldens me the more to speak my Sentiments). . . . ("Life," p. 7)

A glowing account of Hume's character is contained in a letter by his close friend, Adam Smith:

> Thus died our most excellent, and never to be forgotten friend; concerning whose philosophical opinions men will, no doubt, judge variously, every one approving, or condemning them, according as they happen to coincide or disagree with his own; but concerning whose character and conduct there can scarce be a difference of opinion. His temper, indeed, seemed to be more happily balanced, if I may be allowed such an expression, than that perhaps of any other man I have ever known. . . . Upon the whole, I have always considered him, both in his lifetime and since his death, as approaching as nearly to the idea of the perfectly wise and virtuous man, as perhaps the nature of human frailty will permit.[13]

THE EXPERIMENTAL METHOD

The subtitle of Hume's *Treatise of Human Nature* is "An Attempt to introduce the experimental Method of Reasoning into Moral Subjects." Hume's goal is associated with the great movement of thought known as the Enlightenment, which dominated the eighteenth century. Thinkers were deeply impressed with the accomplishments of Isaac Newton and other theorists who had cast new light on the workings of the natural world. Processes formerly shrouded in mystery were seen to be governed by simple mechanical laws. Figures such as Copernicus, Kepler, and Galileo, along with Newton, had uncovered the laws of planetary motion and shown that physical processes on earth behave according to the same principles. The following couplet by Alexander Pope expresses a view that was widely felt:

> Nature and Nature's laws lay hid in Night,
> God said, Let Newton be, and all was light.[14]

Many thinkers felt that discoveries in natural science were a prelude to new discoveries to come. As the working of the natural world had been laid bare, so similar laws must operate in society, though these awaited another Newton to discover them.

The desire to extend scientific methods into additional fields was a guiding principle of the Enlightenment. In the following chapter we will chart Montesquieu's pioneering efforts to develop scientific explanations of the laws and customs of different societies. A whole raft of thinkers are important in large part because of their contributions to understanding different fields according to methods and principles similar to those of the natural sciences. For instance, Adam Smith sought a scientific understanding of economic phenomena. Jeremy Bentham pioneered a scientific understanding of morals; Karl Marx developed a scientific understanding of historical processes. The list can be extended into the twentieth century. Sigmund Freud, for instance, viewed his great discoveries in psychoanalysis as an extension of scientific methods into the study of the workings of the unconscious mind. However, as we will also see, the great advances of Enlightenment thought evoked critical reactions, from Jean-Jacques Rousseau and Edmund Burke, among other thinkers.

As we have noted, the commitment to scientific understanding of the social world is seen in the very term "social sciences." Most academic departments that study politics in the English-speaking world are departments of "political science." This name reflects a commitment to explain political phenomena according to methods, laws, and principles similar to those at work in the natural world, though once again, both the feasibility and desirability of this goal are subjects of intense controversy.

In Hume's case, the aspiration to be scientific was intended in a specific sense. Hume believed he could shed new light on an important range of subjects by carefully examining the mental processes through which we come to know about them. Because knowledge of all subjects is necessarily influenced by these mental processes, studying them teaches us a great deal about the subjects as well. In Hume's words,

> 'Tis evident, that all the sciences have a relation, greater or less, to human nature; and that however wide any of them may seem to run from it, they still return back by one passage or another. Even Mathematics, Natural Philosophy, and Natural Religion, are in some measure dependent on the science of Man; since they lie under the cognizance of men, and are judged of by their powers and faculties. 'Tis impossible to tell what changes and improvements we might make in these sciences were we thoroughly acquainted with the extent and force of human understanding, and could explain the nature of the ideas we employ, and of the operations we perform in our reasonings. (*Treatise*, Introduction, p. 42)

Previous scholars had attacked isolated castles or villages on the frontiers of knowledge. Hume's plan was to strike boldly at its heart, "to march up directly to the capital or center of these sciences, to human nature itself" (Introduction, p. 43).

Hume's method was intended to contribute to a range of fields. The three Books of the *Treatise* are devoted to human understanding, the passions, and morals. In the "Introduction" to the *Treatise* he notes his intent to tackle issues in Mathematics, Natural Philosophy, Natural Religion, Logic, Morals, Criticism, and Politics. His aim is "a compleat system of the sciences built on a foundation almost entirely new, and the only one upon which they can stand with any security" (Introduction, p. 43).

The audacity of Hume's youthful plan is apparent. More striking yet is the fact that he succeeded in contributing to many of these fields. In each area, he made important critical advances, and also helped rebuild the wreckage his arguments left in their wake.

Hume's science of human nature is based on his belief that the mind works according to simple laws, analogous to those that govern the natural world. Newton, through careful observation, uncovered a small number of principles that explain the workings of numerous phenomena. Included among these laws are his principles of gravitation and his famous laws of motion. Hume believed similar laws are at work in human understanding. As scientists had uncovered the laws of natural phenomena, Hume thought he could make similar progress in regard to the mind: "[T]here is no reason to despair of equal success in our enquiries concerning the mental powers and economy, if prosecuted with equal capacity and caution" (*Human Understanding*, Sec. I, p. 14).

Hume argues that all contents of the mind arise through experience. Whatever is in our minds comes through sensations, which are in turn worked on and combined by mental processes such as memory, imagination, and dreams. In all its operations, the mind works according to rules of association, principles to which Hume refers as "the association of ideas." The three basic rules of association are resemblance, contiguity in time or place, and cause and effect (*Treatise* I, i, 4, p. 58) Briefly, from thinking about one thing, the mind will move to another that resembles it. Or it will move to a second entity that is associated with the first through physical or temporal closeness. Finally, the mind will move from one thing to another that causes it, or that it causes. According to Hume, these are the processes at work in all our thought. Proof that they are the only principles the mind follows can be gained through experimentation. In studying our minds, we do not have a laboratory for experiments. What we can do is scrutinize our train of thought and try to understand the principles it embodies:

> All we can do, in such cases, is to run over several instances, and examine carefully the principle which binds the different thoughts to each other, never stopping till we render the principle as general as possible. The more instances we examine, and the more care we employ, the more assurance shall we acquire, that the enumeration, which we form from the whole, is complete and entire. (*Human Understanding*, Sec. III, p. 24)

Observing our own thoughts, we are able to identify no principles other than those Hume names. These principles then, can be likened to the "laws" of the mind. The evidence of observation is able to establish that these principles exist and how they work. But we cannot go beyond experience to explain where they come from or why they hold (*Treatise*, Introduction, p. 45). Hume's careful attention to exactly what can and cannot be known is a central feature of his enterprise.

The irresistible implication of Hume's analysis of mental processes is sharply to limit the purview of what people can claim to know. In particular, Hume distinguishes knowledge of the world and of relationships between ideas.

As we have noted, all contents of the mind are derived from experience. But what is experience? According to Hume, experience is a series of perceptions encountered sequentially, one after another. These are the raw material for mental processes, combined, for instance, by the imagination. Proof of this is that we can identify no contents of the mind not derived from experience. All ideas we have are based on perceptions, which Hume calls "impressions." Complex ideas arise from combining simple ones. Thus we imagine a golden mountain by combining the simple ideas, gold and mountain (*Human Understanding*, Sec. II, p. 19). Even the idea of an imaginary creature, a chimera, for instance, is a combination of simple ideas: a lion's head, a goat's body, a serpent's tail, and so on. What is crucial for Hume is that relationships between these original impressions are created by the mind's mechanisms or propensities—mechanisms which the *Treatise* and other works examine.[15]

As noted above, Hume views reason as a faculty that draws relationships between ideas:

> All kinds of reasoning consist in nothing but a comparison and a discovery of those
> relations, either constant or inconstant, which two or more objects bear to each other.
> (*Treatise*, I, iii, 2, p. 121)

Particular relationships drawn by reason afford our only certain knowledge. These truths by
definition, which do not depend on experience, include mathematical propositions. For
instance, we are certain that 2 + 2 = 4, because this is what the terms mean. Similarly, we
have certain knowledge that a triangle has three sides, and that the three angles of a triangle
equal 180 degrees. It is self-contradictory to deny the truth of these or similar propositions.
Hume does not devote much attention to truths of this kind. But it is important to bear
in mind their *lack of relationship* with experience:

> Propositions of this kind are discoverable by the mere operation of thought, without
> dependence on what is anywhere existent in the universe. (*Human Understanding*, Sec.
> 4, p. 25)

Perhaps Hume's greatest contribution to philosophy is his claim that certainty is
limited to constructions of reason and does not depend on experience. Experience provides
only a series of impressions. Relationships between these and between the ideas they evoke
are created by the mind, not derived from impressions themselves. Our grasp of experience
depends heavily on relationships of cause and effect. Hume argues that experience does not
provide us with certain assurance of causal relationships. Rather what we *mistakenly believe*
is certain knowledge is actually the result of particular feelings we experience because of the
natural propensities. A closer examination of Hume's account of causation can be postponed until later.

For now we should note the crucial skeptical implications of his experimental
method. Reflecting carefully on the process through which people make causal inferences,
he believes he detects the work of faculties other than reason. By carefully pointing these
out, he is able to deflate much of what we take for knowledge of the world.

It seems that Hume came to this conclusion through an analysis of the processes at
work in aesthetic judgments.[16] At the time Hume wrote, there was a raging debate in the
philosophical community about whether aesthetic judgments are based on reason or
sentiment. Certain theorists of the former camp argued that an aesthetic judgment, for
instance, that a piece of sculpture is beautiful, is made by reason, which perceives specific
qualities in the object. Other thinkers had declared that the "judgment" that the sculpture
is beautiful is actually based on sentiment or feeling rather than reason. According to these
thinkers, the observer declares that the object is beautiful because of the way he responds
to it. The experience of beauty is a certain pleasure. The precise nature of the feeling will
vary according to what is experienced: a beautiful sculpture, a great novel or poem, a
beautiful sonata. But in each case there is a certain pleasure underlying the observer's
judgment that the object is beautiful. Thus the "beauty" of the object is not a quality
inherent in the object itself but stems from the response it evokes in the spectator. Hume
supports this second position. "Till such a spectator appear, there is nothing but a figure
of such particular dimension and proportions: from his sentiments alone arise its elegance
and beauty" (*Morals*, Appendix I, p. 291).

Hume's striking claim is that similar processes are at work in what we take to be knowledge of the world. In making causal judgments, people believe they are following reason, which has perceived relationships existing in the world. But according to Hume, these judgments too are based on sentiment rather than reason. Causal claims, like judgments of beauty, are made by the spectator *on the basis of how he responds to what he is observing.* Hume made this discovery when he was approximately eighteen years old. In a letter, written in 1734, he describes the tremendous excitement it evoked, and then notes its enormous critical potential in regard to morals. Morals always occupied a prominent place in his thought. Once again, the *Treatise of Human Nature* is "An Attempt to introduce the experimental Method of Reasoning into Moral Subjects." In this letter, Hume writes:

> I found that the moral Philosophy transmitted to us by Antiquity, labor'd under the same Inconvenience that has been found in their natural Philosophy, of being entirely Hypothetical, & depending more upon INVENTION than Experience. Every one consulted his Fancy in erecting schemes of Virtue & of Happiness, without regarding human Nature, upon which every moral Conclusion must depend. This therefore I resolved to make my principal Study, & the Source from which I wou'd derive every Truth in criticism as well as Morality. (*Letters*, I, 16)

THE CONTRACT OF GOVERNMENT

The implications of Hume's method are seen in his criticisms of a central feature of liberal political theory, the idea of the social contract (or contract of government). We will discuss this briefly before returning to Hume's analysis of knowledge based on experience. His account of the contract illustrates a central characteristic of his thought. Hume remarks that the contract supports a position in regard to the extent and limits of political authority that is basically correct. But these conclusions rest on faulty reasoning. His task, then, is to preserve the conclusions while replacing their flawed basis with sound reasoning. Hume writes:

> This conclusion is just, tho' the principles be erroneous; and I flatter myself, that I can establish the same conclusion on more reasonable principles. (*Treatise* III, ii, 9, p. 601)

Hume's purpose is in part—but only in part—destructive. He attempts to show that traditional political arguments and beliefs are gravely flawed. Indeed, his criticisms of the social contract are so severe the doctrine has never recovered. But that is not the end of the matter. Having refuted traditional grounds for our beliefs, he attempts to preserve some of their central aspects, but on the basis of reasoning that is not subject to his severe criticisms.

According to the theory of the social contract, as classically espoused by Locke (and discussed in Chapter 3), governments arise from the consent of the governed. People in a natural condition devoid of government, the state of nature, discover their need for government and so erect it. But they also realize the dangers government poses and are unwilling to surrender their natural liberty without assurance against abuse. Fearful of arbitrary power, they include limits to their allegiance to government in the agreement through which it is set up. Allegiance is conditional. The people agree to obey as long as government performs its tasks and respects its limits. But if it fails to live up to its end of the bargain, it loses its right to command, and the people can replace it. The central feature of the contract of government is the conditional nature of obedience, the fact that government is subject to limits and loses its authority if it does not respect them.

Hume's main criticisms of the contract are contained in his essay, "Of the Original Contract."[17] He believes government is clearly necessary to enforce adherence to rules on which the maintenance of society depends. But even though government is necessary, Hume does not believe it arose through the kind of historical act contract theory depicts. An element of consent was required for the original establishment of government. How else could men who were basically equal be subjected to the authority of others? But evidence of a formal agreement is not to be found:

> In vain, are we asked in what records this charter of our liberties is registered. It was not written on parchment, nor yet on leaves or barks of trees. It preceded the use of writing and all the other civilized arts of life. (*Essays*, p. 468)

To make matters worse, according to contract theory, even after government was founded, it continues to rest on a contractual basis. Subsequent generations of people are born free and would not surrender their natural liberty without contractual protection. But once again, evidence is lacking. Though all people are supposed to consent to government, they are not aware of doing so:

> Were you to preach, in most parts of the world, that political connexions are founded altogether on voluntary consent or a mutual promise, the magistrate would soon imprison you, as seditious, for loosening the ties of obedience; if your friends did not before shut you up as delirious, for advancing such absurdities. (*Essays*, p. 470)

In keeping with his basic principle that claims to knowledge must be tested according to the evidence of how people attained it, Hume finds contract theory in glaring opposition to the facts:

> It is strange, that an act of the mind, which every individual is supposed to have formed, and after he came to the use of reason too, otherwise it could have no authority; that this act, I say, should be so much unknown to all of them, that, over the face of the whole earth, there scarcely remain any traces or memory of it. (*Essays*, p. 470)

In principle, Hume has no objection to government based on consent. Government so established "is surely the best and most sacred of any" (p. 474). But governments can rarely if ever be shown to be so founded. Examination of the historical records of virtually all governments yields original acts of conquest or usurpation. Governments were not founded by consent but by force (p. 474). Though at first people chafe under an unfamiliar regime, in time they become used to it and obey out of habit. "Obedience or subjection becomes so familiar, that most men never make any enquiry about its origin or cause, more than about the principle of gravity, resistance, or the most universal laws of nature" (p. 470).

Instead of contractual agreement, the legitimacy of an existing regime rests on custom and habit. What was at first unfamiliar and called into question becomes familiar over time. People get used to a certain ruler or system of government and obey nonreflectively. Hume believes it is well that people's minds function in this way. As we will see in subsequent sections, his overall orientation to politics is conservative. He views political stability as precarious and is deeply fearful of revolution: "In reality, there is not a more terrible event, than a total dissolution of government" (p. 472).

As contract theory's claims concerning the origin of government are without foundation, the same is true of the contention that each individual voluntarily consents. People are born into political societies; they do not live outside them and then at some point choose to join them. The doctrine might make more sense if one generation of men went "off the stage at once, and another succeed, as is the case with silk-worms and butterflies" (p. 476). But of course people are born, individually, into existing societies.

As we saw in the last chapter, Locke has a counter to the obvious fact that most people do not expressly consent to government in the same way they voluntarily join professional societies and social clubs. Locke argues that consent to government can be given in either of two ways, either expressly or tacitly. Whereas express consent alone makes one a "perfect member" of his society, through tacit consent one attains an obligation to obey. And so Locke's question is: "what ought to be look'd upon as a tacit Consent, and how far it binds"?[18] Locke's answer is that, in the final analysis, residence constitutes consent. If someone stays in a certain territory and enjoys benefits provided by its government, he acquires an obligation to obey its laws. Thus for Locke, the means through which the bulk of people consent to government is through their presence in a given territory (see pp. 111–12).

Hume believes this position will not bear scrutiny. Consent to government is a kind of promise, and so must be given voluntarily. As he classically argues,

> Can we really say that a poor man's residence in a particular country is voluntary? Can we seriously say that a poor peasant or artizan has a free choice to leave his country, when he knows no foreign language or manners, and lives from day to day, by the small wages which he acquires? We may as well assert, that a man, by remaining in a vessel, freely consents to the dominion of the master, though he was carried on board while asleep, and must leap into the ocean, and perish, the moment he leaves her. (*Essays*, p. 475)

This argument in particular has proved difficult for defenders of the social contract. They claim that political obligation rests on voluntary consent to obey government, but most people have not expressly made the necessary agreements. They were born into their societies and did not voluntarily join them. Upon reflection, we can identify certain exceptions, mainly naturalized citizens, who do voluntarily emigrate to and join their chosen countries. But the vast majority of people are not naturalized citizens. If people have not expressly consented to their governments, proponents of consent must fall back on a doctrine of tacit consent. Though people consent to government, they do this through actions other than expressly consenting. But the only suitable action most people perform is staying in the countries where they are born. As Hume shows, in most cases this can hardly be viewed as voluntary consent.

In response to Hume's criticisms, subsequent defenders of consent theories of political obligation have attempted to identify actions that are (i) voluntary, (ii) performed by large numbers of citizens, and (iii) appear to constitute consent to government. A large variety of actions (e.g., voting, saying the pledge of allegiance, accepting benefits from government) have been proposed. But as things presently stand, none of these is able to bear scrutiny.[19] And so the doctrine of tacit consent appears to be without foundation.

Because neither express nor tacit consent is the basis for obligations to obey given governments, Hume attempts to locate a more plausible foundation. Briefly, his overall position is that government has been found to be necessary, and has therefore been established. As we will see in more detail below, government arose through something resembling agreement, though the formalized agreements posited by contract theorists were never entered into. Rather, governments emerged through extended processes of trial and error, and gradually attained legitimacy through custom. On the individual level, the doctrine of consent is a myth. We obey because we have been taught to. Once governments are securely established, they are obeyed out of custom and habit. But does this mean contract theory is entirely without merit? Hume responds, "No." The core of the doctrine is that governmental power exists under certain limitations. It is established to perform particular tasks and if it fails to do so, or if it becomes arbitrary and threatens the citizenry, it loses its authority. Hume believes this commonsensical position can be explained without reference to contract:

> A small degree of experience and observation suffices to teach us that society cannot possibly be maintained without the authority of magistrates, and that this authority must soon fall into contempt where exact obedience is not payed to it. The observation of these general and obvious interests is the source of all allegiance, and of that moral obligation which we attribute to it. (*Essays*, p. 480)

But the fact that government is necessary does not mean its authority is unlimited. "[O]bvious and general interests" impose limits. As Hume writes in the *Treatise*, government is necessary because of people's need for security and protection. When governmental oppression becomes so severe that provision of these benefits is impeded, the basis for its authority no longer holds, and people lose their reasons for obeying:

> As interest, therefore, is the immediate sanction of government, the one can have no longer being than the other; and whenever the civil magistrate carries his oppression so far as to render his authority perfectly intolerable, we are no longer bound to submit to it. The cause ceases; the effect must cease also. (*Treatise*, III, ii, 9, p. 602)

If government becomes tyrannical or extremely oppressive, people need no longer obey. But the reason for this is not that government has violated a formal contractual agreement but pure common sense. Cooperating with an oppressive regime has no point; people would be better off without it.

Thus common sense supports a view concerning the limits of political obedience similar to that of contract theory, but without the need to invoke the contract or explain away its problems. Though people habitually obey their governments, they do not believe they must obey without qualification. "'Tis certain . . . that in all our notions of morals we never entertain such an absurdity as that of passive obedience, but make allowances for resistance in the more flagrant instances of tyranny and oppression. The general opinion of mankind has some authority in all cases; but in this of morals 'tis perfectly infallible" (*Treatise*, III, ii, 9, p. 603).

In subsequent sections we will see that this basic pattern is replicated in other areas of knowledge. Through careful examination of what people actually think, Hume is able to dispense with much specious reasoning. But that does not end the matter. With important questions thrown open, common sense, experience, and attention to what people think can be marshalled to develop new answers. However, we should also note that overthrow of the social contract has left a void in contemporary political theory that is still felt. Many contemporary political theorists do not believe it is possible to justify obligations to the state upon the basic liberal premises of free, equal human beings.[20] Though Hume attempts to do so on the basis of habit and common sense, it is not clear that his position can withstand careful critical scrutiny—and at the present time, it is not widely held. In this regard, rational criticism resembles Pandora's box and may have to be curbed if necessary moral and political doctrines are to be preserved. As we will see in a subsequent chapter, the dangers of rational scrutiny are an important theme in the works of the greatest British conservative theorist, Edmund Burke, who writes: "what would become of the World if the practice of all moral duties, and the foundations of society, rested on having their reasons made clear and demonstrative to every individual?"[21]

CAUSE AND EFFECT

Hume's criticism of knowledge based on experience follows the pattern seen in the last section. Knowledge of the world stems from experience and depends on relationships of cause and effect. "All reasonings concerning matters of fact seem to be founded on the relation of Causes and Effect. By means of that relation alone we can go beyond the evidence of our memory and sense" (*Human Understanding*, Sec. III, p. 26). For good reasons, people put great store in knowledge gained from experience. They view it as *certain* knowledge. From a series of specific instances of cause A bringing about effect B, they believe it is certain that similar relationships will obtain in the future. They do not clearly distinguish this knowledge from that based on reason alone, seen for example in mathematics. But as we have noted, Hume holds that certainty is possible only in the realm of reason alone. In believing experience provides certain knowledge, people can be shown to be mistaken.

Hume's argument here, a central element of the *Treatise* and of his philosophy as a whole, is designed to accomplish several ends. First, he is deeply interested in undermining claims to certain knowledge based on experience. Application of the experimental method to our judgments of cause and effect shows the limits of causal knowledge. What is more, Hume moves beyond the *logical* mistakes people make and explains the *psychological* processes involved in mistaken judgments of causation. According to the pattern we saw in the last section, criticism of causal knowledge is not the last word. Hume does not argue in order to induce skepticism as an end in itself. To some extent he is a committed skeptic. He believes that puncturing knowledge claims has salutary effects, especially in regard to questionable metaphysical views, most notably religious views. Hume believes false claims to certainty breed zealotry, which threatens social and political stability. But he does not wish to leave a situation of doubt. Once false reasoning has been discarded, new foundations can be provided. Though claims of certainty must be rejected, new beliefs can be accepted as reasonable and necessary for normal life.

In criticizing certain knowledge based on experience, Hume reinforces his claim that certainty is found only in systems based on reason alone. Throughout his philosophy, the contrast between these two forms of knowledge is a central concern. On the one hand are mathematical truths, such as 2 + 2 = 4. These are apprehended through reason alone, without reference to experience, and afford certainty. To deny that 2 + 2 = 4 makes no sense; this is what the elements of the proposition mean. Knowledge of the other realm is gained from experience. For instance, the proposition that water freezes at 32 degrees is not garnered from reason alone and not known with certainty. It arises from repeated experience of what happens to water at this temperature.

Hume's analysis of causal knowledge is complex and can only be sketched here. We will concentrate on two aspects of his argument: (a) why such knowledge cannot be certain; (b) why people believe it is certain, though they are mistaken. More important for our purposes than the details of Hume's argument is its overall thrust, especially its bearing on the contrast between certain knowledge based on reason and less secure knowledge based on habit and experience.

As noted above, Hume holds that the contents of the mind are derived from experience, which in turn amounts to a series of sensations. These are the raw material for the mind's operations. Hume believes cause-and-effect relationships are derived from specific mental operations, but of habit or custom rather than reason.

Consider a simple instance of causal knowledge, the fact that water freezes at 32 degrees. This causal law has been learned from past experience. Going outside when it is less than 32 degrees, we see water frozen—frozen puddles, ice on car windshields, and so on—and no water in liquid form. According to Hume, our knowledge of the world amounts to a series of sensations. From repeated experiences, we have derived the law that water freezes at 32 degrees and have confidence it will also hold in the future. Hume's method is to examine the precise nature of these experiences. If we look into the matter, we can see that a specific experience of low temperature has been followed by another specific experience of frozen water. We can search our experience for the fact of *causation* but all we discover are numerous occasions on which one fact has been followed by the other. Because we can find nothing else in this causal relationship, Hume argues that *our judgment* that the low temperature causes the water to freeze is no more than a generalization of past experience. All judgments of causation have three components: spacial contiguity, the fact that cause and effect occur near each other; the fact that the cause is followed in time by the effect; and that the pattern recurs repeatedly (*Treatise*, I, iii, 6). Hume refers to this last as constant conjunction. *A has always been* followed by *B*; low temperature *has always been* followed by frozen water. The question, then, is whether these three constituents of a causal judgment provide certain knowledge.

Hume's reason for denying certainty is simple. Causal judgments amount to summations of past experience. But can we ever be sure similar patterns will always hold in the future? In the last paragraph, I indicate that Hume's idea of constant conjunction is in reference to what *has always been* true in the past. The simple problem is that we have no guarantee similar constancy will be observed in the future. No matter how many times we experience the relationship between temperature below 32 degrees and frozen water, there is no guarantee the next time the temperature falls beyond this point it will continue to hold. If the relationship constitutes certain knowledge, then the next time the temperature is below 32 degrees, I can be *certain* water has frozen. I can only be certain of this if I can be certain the relationship will continue to hold. But I cannot know that all factors affecting the relationship will remain constant. Perhaps the water I have always seen frozen is a particular kind of water, while the water I encounter next time will be importantly different. Though I believe this is unlikely, I cannot rule it out. In all cases, claims of causal knowledge can be called into question, because we cannot *know* circumstances will not change. Just because they have not changed in the past, we cannot *know* they will not change in the future. In Hume's words,

> [W]hy this experience should be extended to future time, and to other objects, which for aught we know, may be only in appearance similar; this is the main question on which I would insist. The bread, which I formerly eat, nourished me; that is, a body of such sensible qualities was, at that time, endued with such secret powers: but does it follow that other bread must also nourish me at another time, and that like sensible qualities must always be attended with like secret powers? (*Human Understanding*, Sec. IV, pp. 33–34)

Proponents of causal knowledge have a response. Nature is regular, they can assert. Therefore, what has held true in the past must continue to hold true, because that is the way nature works. Thus if water has always frozen at temperatures lower than 32 degrees in the past, we can be certain it will continue to do so in the future. For it not to freeze would violate the regularity of nature.

But to this Hume has a response of his own. The proponent of causal knowledge grounds his causal claim about water freezing on a broader causal claim concerning the workings of nature as a whole. The problem is why we should accept this broader claim. How do we *know* nature works according to regular patterns? To this the proponent can respond only on the basis of past experience. Throughout recorded experience, nature has displayed regular causal relationships. But if we attempt to move beyond this to the further claim that nature will *continue* to work in the same way in the future, we come up against the very objection we are attempting to dispel. We cannot *know* nature as a whole will continue to work as it always has. Our knowledge of nature as a whole derives entirely from experience. We simply cannot know that past experience will be replicated in the future.

Having undermined our confidence in the *certain* status of causal inferences, Hume turns to the closely related question of why we view them as certain, even if they are not. His analysis rests on the inner workings of the mind, the association of ideas. As noted above, the three basic patterns of association are resemblance, contiguity, and cause and effect. Here we are concerned primarily with the last of these. According to the normal workings of the mind, the idea of cause X will naturally give rise to the idea of its effect, Y. Thus when we think of lightning, the mind will easily move to thinking about thunder, or vice versa. A mental association of this sort has been developed through repeated experiences of X followed by Y. On numerous occasions, the experience of X has been followed by the experience of Y, until they have come to be associated by the mind. Thus the next time I encounter X, my mind naturally moves to the idea of Y as well. The experience of X gives rise to an *expectation* that I will also experience Y. Subsequent experience of *Y* is confirmation of that expectation, which strengthens the relationship between *X* and *Y*, and so strengthens the expectation the next time I encounter *X*. For example, from repeated experience of lightning followed by thunder, our minds naturally turn to the idea of thunder when we experience lightning. The experience of lightning gives rise to an expectation that thunder is coming. When it indeed follows, this fulfills the expectation.

According to Hume, it is this *feeling of fulfilled expectation* that we mistake for certain knowledge. The person with certain knowledge (or who thinks she has certain knowledge) that lightning causes thunder has a particular feeling in her mind. Hume contends that the person mistakes her feeling of fulfilled expectation when lightning is in fact followed by thunder for that of confirmation of certain knowledge.

The logical and psychological sides of Hume's analysis go hand in hand. The subject who believes she has certain knowledge that *X* causes *Y* has no reason to inquire into the nature of the feeling that constitutes her certainty. But once the logical basis of her knowledge claim has been undermined, the identity of the feeling is also called into question.

Thus Hume's analysis of causation rests heavily on the distinction between certain knowledge and knowledge based on experience, custom, and habit. The pattern is similar to what we find in aesthetic judgments. Encountering a given object, Marina regards it as beautiful. She believes some quality—beauty—is in the object. But according to Hume, her judgment that the object is beautiful is because of how she responds to it, how it makes her feel. Similarly, people mistakenly believe that causal laws are discovered by reason in the objects they observe. Instead, Hume argues, causal relationships are imposed on phenomena by the propensities of the mind. As beauty is not a relationship between the elements of some work of art, so causal laws are not present in phenomena. In each case, the subject's judgment is due to the way her mind works. According to Mossner, Hume's great discovery is the similarity between aesthetic and other kinds of judgments. In each area, what theorists view as reason's discovery of relationships is actually the mind's response to its experience. To quote Mossner, Hume's "unique contribution to philosophy" is "the extension of sentiment or feeling beyond ethics and aesthetics . . . to include the entire realm of belief covering all relations of matter-of-fact" (Mossner, pp. 76–77; his emphasis removed). In Hume's words,

> Thus all probable reasoning is nothing but a species of sensation. 'Tis not solely in poetry and music, we must follow our taste and sentiment, but likewise in philosophy. (*Treatise*, I, iii, 8, p. 153)

Because of his radical critique of causal knowledge, Hume is often regarded as a skeptic, as a destructive philosophical spirit. This assessment is obviously fair to some extent. Hume's critique of causal knowledge is certainly more tearing down than building up. But both temperamentally and philosophically, Hume draws back from extreme skepticism. There is a strong practical streak to Hume's philosophy, which causes him to ignore the far-reaching implications of his arguments when they come into conflict with the need to live in the world. One can imagine how a pure skeptic might function. Because he does not *know* for certain that he is walking off a cliff, he might as well keep walking.

Because he does not *know* the car he sees is about to hit him, he might as well not try to avoid it. When it comes time to get out of bed in the morning, how can he be certain the floor is still there? Though it was there the night before, how can he *know* he won't fall through the earth? The unfortunate fact is that he cannot know for certain. Just because the floor has always been there, that does not guarantee it will be there in five minutes. But according to Hume, we must act anyway. Life must go on, even if it does so without the benefits of certainty. For Hume, the choice between life without certainty or certainty without life is easy. Extreme skepticism is not a practical possibility, because it cannot guide us in the world. The pure skeptic must acknowledge that "all human life must perish, were his principles universally and steadily to prevail. Of course all action would immediately cease; and men remain in total lethargy, till the necessities of nature unsatisfied put an end to their miserable existence" (*Human Understanding*, Sec. XII, p. 160). As he writes elsewhere, "Philosophy would render us entirely Pyrrhonian [skeptical], were not nature too strong for it."[22]

Though certainty is not possible in the world, Hume believes it is unnecessary. Habit and experience, though falling short of certainty, are adequate guides through life. Though we cannot *know* the world will continue in the future as it has in the past, habit and experience tell us it will. What is more, we have a strong interest in taking this for granted, or else we would not be able to function. Though Hume's criticisms of knowledge from experience are profoundly troubling, they have few practical implications. Skeptical doubt cannot be proved wrong by philosophical arguments. But there is more to life than arguments. Fortunately, when we set our arguments aside, our skepticism leaves as well:

> Carelessness and in-attention alone can afford us any remedy. For this reason I rely entirely upon them; and take it for granted, whatever may be the reader's opinion at this present moment, that an hour hence he will be persuaded there is both an external and internal world. . . . (*Treatise* I, iv, 3, p. 268)

For Hume himself, moderation in his passions extends to philosophy as well. He is able to leave philosophical doubt behind as he turns to other pursuits:

> Most fortunately it happens, that since reason is incapable of dispelling these clouds, nature herself suffices to that purpose, and cures me of this philosophical melancholy and delirium, either by relaxing this bent of mind, or by some avocation, and lively impression of my senses, which obliterate all these chimeras. I dine, I play a game of backgammon, I converse, and am merry with my friends; and when after three or four hour's amusement, I wou'd return to these speculations, they appear so cold, and strain'd, and ridiculous, that I cannot find in my heart to enter into them any farther. (*Treatise*, I, iv, 7, p. 316)

CRITIQUE OF MORALITY BASED ON REASON

Hume criticizes moral arguments along similar lines. Once again, the distinction between two kinds of knowledge—certain knowledge derived from reason alone and noncertain knowledge from experience—is of fundamental importance. The distinction is indicated in the opening pages of the *Enquiry Concerning the Principles of Morals:*

> There has been a controversy started of late, much better worth examination, concerning the general foundation of Morals; whether they be derived from Reason, or from Sentiment; whether we attain the knowledge of them by a chain of argument and induction, or by an immediate feeling and finer internal sense; whether, like all sound judgement of truth and falsehood, they should be the same to every rational intelligent being; or whether, like the perceptions of beauty and deformity, they be founded entirely on the particular fabric and constitution of the human species. (*Morals*, Sec I, p. 170)

One of Hume's main purposes is to affirm the latter view. Moral judgments are like aesthetic judgments, based on habit and sentiment, rather than rational apprehension of relationships in the object. In a passage included in early editions of the *Enquiry* but later deleted, Hume presents his position clearly:

> That Faculty by which we discern Truth and Falsehood, and that by which we perceive Vice and Virtue had long been confounded with each other, and all Morality was suppos'd to be built on eternal and immutable Relations, which to every intelligent Mind, were equally invariable as any Proposition concerning Quantity or Number. But a late Philosopher [Francis Hutcheson] has taught us, by the most convincing Arguments that Morality is nothing in the abstract Nature of Things, but is entirely relative to the Sentiment or mental Taste of each particular [i.e., species of] Being; in the same Manner as the Distinctions of sweet and bitter, hot and cold, arise from the particular feeling of each Sense or Organ. Moral Perceptions, therefore, ought not to be class'd with the Operations of the Understanding, but with the Tastes or Sentiments.[23]

Hume's project, then, has two components. He must show what is wrong with the claim that moral qualities are apprehended directly by reason. And then he must explain the nature of the particular sentiments through which they are actually discerned.

Hume presents a series of arguments against the view that morality is based on relationships analogous to mathematical relationships perceived directly by reason. In order to appreciate the force of his arguments, it is necessary to have some idea of the views he is criticizing. The core of this doctrine, as presented by such late seventeenth- and early eighteenth-century thinkers as Ralph Cudworth and Samuel Clarke, is as I have described it. Moral qualities are said to be objectively grounded in nature, or "the nature and reason of things," to use Clarke's phrase. These qualities are perceived by reason, along the lines of mathematical qualities, and are able to influence the will of a rational creature. In his *Discourse Concerning the Unchangeable Obligations of Natural Religion*, Clarke presents the core of the doctrine as follows:

> There Are . . . certain necessary and eternal difference of things, and certain consequent fitnesses or unfitnesses of the application of different Things or different Relations one to another, not depending on any positive Constitutions, but founded unchangeably in the nature and reason of things, and unavoidably arising from the differences of the things themselves.[24]

The eternal moral laws assume the form of relationships and are as certain as mathematical truths, such as $2 + 2 = 4$, or the relationships between the angles of a triangle.

A prominent political theorist who presents this kind of view is Montesquieu (whom Hume lumps with Cudworth, Clarke, and Father Malebranche, and criticizes in a footnote to the *Enquiry* [Sec. III, p. 197 n. 1]). In Book I of *The Spirit of the Laws*, Montesquieu writes as follows:

> Before laws were made, there were possible relations of justice. To say that there is nothing just or unjust but what the positive laws ordain or prohibit is to say that before a circle was drawn, all its radii were not equal. (*Spirit of the Laws*, I, 1)

Though the view that morality rests on natural law is somewhat different from the specific doctrines Hume criticizes, it is similar in important respects. Natural law theory, too, presents morality as objectively rooted in nature and discoverable through reason alone. For instance, Locke argues that justice is comprised of essential moral commandments, rooted in natural law, which are promulgated by God to rational creatures through their reason. Through the use of reason alone, moral truth is apprehended, and presents dictates which people should follow in their actions (see pp. 98–101).

Though the idea of objective moral relationships discoverable by reason might appear attractive, Hume presents three distinct lines of criticism. First, in keeping with his overall critical stance, he wants to learn more about the relationships in question. Proponents of the views he examines declare that such relationships exist but say little more about them. He challenges them to present an action that is clearly wrong and to explain precisely where the relations in question lie. "Crime indeed consists not in a particular *fact*, of whose reality we are assured by reason; but it consists in certain *moral relations*, discovered by reason, in the same manner as we discover by reason the truths of geometry or algebra. But what are the relations, I ask, of which you here talk?" (*Morals*, Appendix I, p. 288). If we examine an instance of ingratitude, all we can find are particular feelings and actions. Where the relationships in question figure in is impossible to say. In this sense moral relationships are different from mathematical. In the case of a triangle or circle, relationships between lines or points can be clearly explained. But the analogy between mathematics and morality is no more than a suggestion until the moral relationships can be made equally clear (*Morals*, App. I, p. 288).

To make matters worse, in particular cases we can identify a specific relationship that appears to lie at the heart of a moral judgment. Consider parricide, a particularly heinous crime. The child kills the parent who gave him life, which is obviously reprehensible. The relationships in question are clearly identifiable. A creates B, and then B kills A. But, argues Hume, substitute inanimate objects. Consider an oak or elm tree, which "by the dropping of its seed, it produces a sapling below it, which springing up by degrees, at last overtops and destroys the parent tree." Here we have the same relationships: A creates B, and then B kills A. But do we view this as odious on the part of the sapling? (*Treatise*, III, i, 1, p. 518).

In addition to their problems specifying moral relationships, Hume believes proponents of the argument are deficient in regard to moral psychology. Morality is a subject about which people have strong feelings. We are excited and pleased by good behavior; we are appalled at bad. Who can think of the atrocities committed by the Nazis without a strong emotional response? Hume believes proponents of reason-based moral relationships cannot explain this aspect of the subject. He views reason as a passive mental faculty. It is able to discover and compare relationships between phenomena, but it cannot excite people to action. Mathematical reasoning is similar. It is able to discern relationships between different aspects of geometrical figures, but not to get people to care about them. According to supporters of reason-based morality, to believe murder is acceptable is analogous to making a mathematical error. But we are shocked and appalled by a person who makes the first sort of error in a way we are not by someone who makes the second.

Reason has practical effect on our actions by informing us about relationships between ends and means. If I want to make a great deal of money, reason can tell me what it is necessary to do. Reason in this sense is an *instrumental* faculty. As noted above (see p. 6), instrumental reasoning is in terms of ends and means. The faculty of reason is able to ascertain these relationships, like others. But beyond analyzing relationships it cannot go. It can tell me what I must do to gain a certain end, say, an amount of money. But my desire for the end must inspire action. Reason can tell me how to get the money, but not make me *care* about getting it. One will note that in an example of this sort the end exists already. The desire to make money comes before reason is assigned the task of discovering appropriate means. In the *Enquiry*, Hume makes a similar point in regard to the desire for health:

> Ask a man why he uses exercise; he will answer, because he desires to keep his health. If you then enquire why he desires health, he will readily reply, because sickness is painful. If you push your enquiries farther and desire a reason why he hates pain, it is impossible he can ever give any. This is an ultimate end, and is never referred to any other object. (*Morals*, App. I, p. 293)

Accordingly, Hume argues that any course of action can ultimately be traced back to a desire for something desirable of its own account. Because reason does not inspire desire or passion, it cannot cause action. In addition to postulating quasi-mathematical relationships perceived by reason, the moral view Hume criticizes must account for the strong element of desire or passion involved. Reason alone is not enough:

> Since morals . . . have an influence on the actions and affections, it follows, that they cannot be deriv'd from reason; and that because reason alone, as we have already prov'd, can never have any such influence. Morals excite passions and produce or prevent actions. Reason of itself is utterly impotent in this particular. The rules of morality, therefore, are not conclusions of our reason. (*Treatise*, III, iii, 1, p. 509)

Hume's analysis of the relationship between reason and passion has been widely discussed. It follows from his view that reason lacks motivational force. It can be influential only under certain circumstances. In supplying information about the means to a given end, reason can influence the form action will assume. But the subject will act at all only if he desires to attain the end. Reason is ultimately subordinate to the dictates of desire. Hume expresses this idea in dramatic terms:

> Reason is, and ought only to be the slave of the passion, and can never pretend to any other office than to serve and obey them. (*Treatise*, II, iii, 3, p. 462)

A passion is "an original existence," not grounded in reason (*Treatise*, II, iii, 3, p. 462). Because reason cannot generate preferences, these cannot be consistent or inconsistent with reason. Under certain circumstances reason can influence preferences. For instance, my desire to have a unicorn for a pet will be affected by the knowledge unicorns do not exist. Or my desire to hunt polar bears might be lessened by the knowledge that it is against the law to do so, or that in order to do so I must travel to the Arctic Circle. But outside questions of the existence of or means to desired ends, when reason is confronted with a given passion, it must give way. Hume expresses this idea too in dramatic fashion:

> 'Tis not contrary to reason to prefer the destruction of the whole world to the scratching of my finger. 'Tis not contrary to reason for me to chuse my total ruin, to prevent the least uneasiness of an Indian or person wholly unknown to me. 'Tis as little contrary to reason to prefer even my own acknowledge'd lesser good to my greater, and have a more ardent affection for the former than the latter. (*Treatise*, II, iii, 3, p. 463)

Obviously, Hume is not saying it *is* reasonable to prefer the destruction of the universe to scratching one's finger. Preference judgments are not the domain of reason at all. They are not based on intellectual perception of relationships but on emotion or sentiment. A preference is a feeling, rooted, in the final analysis, in what the subject wants, and so what makes him happy. Obviously, most people would be happier scratching their fingers than seeing everything destroyed. But this is not a conclusion of reason in the sense that 2 + 2 = 4 is. As Hume says: "Morality . . . is more properly felt than judg'd of" (*Treatise* III, i, 2, p. 522).

Hume has an additional related argument against reason-based morality. The main passage is lengthy, but I will quote it in full. It is one of the most influential passages in the history of moral philosophy.

> I cannot forbear adding to these reasonings an observation, which may, perhaps, be found of some importance. In every system of morality, which I have hitherto met with, I have always remark'd that the author proceeds for some time in the ordinary way of reasoning, and establishes the being of a God, or makes observations concerning human affairs; when of a sudden I am surpriz'd to find, that instead of the usual copulations of propositions, *is* and *is not*, I meet with no proposition that is not connected with an *ought* or an *ought not*. The change is imperceptible; but is, however, of the last consequence. For as this *ought* or *ought not* expresses some new relation or affirmation, 'tis necessary that it shou'd be observ'd and explain'd; and at the same time that a reason should be given for what seems altogether inconceivable, how this new relation can be a deduction from others, which are entirely different from it. But as authors do not commonly use this precaution, I shall presume to recommend it to the readers; and am persuaded, that this small attention wou'd subvert all the vulgar systems of morality. . . . (*Treatise*, III, i, 1, p. 521)

Hume's point is, to begin with, a simple point of logic. A typical theorist begins with factual observations. From these he makes moral recommendations. His initial propositions are of the form:

    X is the case.

From these he concludes:

    You ought to do *Z*.

Thus his argument is in the following form:

(1) *X* is the case.

(2) Therefore you ought to do *Z*.

We can see immediately that (2) does not follow from (1). If you wish to end up with an *ought* proposition, a prescription, in the conclusion, there must be an *ought* proposition among the premises. As is often the case, Hume's careful examination of how we reason calls attention to a problem previous thinkers had overlooked. At least in the form in which they are presented, many previous moral theories ("all the vulgar systems of morality") can be seen to contain serious logical flaws.

There is a possible response to Hume's point. A theorist can respond that he derives (2) from (1) with the aid of an additional premise:

(1A) If *X* is the case, then you ought to do *Z*.

The introduction of (1A) makes the argument logically valid.

Let us consider an example. A common moral argument is:

(i) God says, "Thou shalt not kill."

(ii) Therefore, you ought not to kill.

(i) is a factual statement, concerning what God is purported to have said; (ii) is the moral conclusion derived from (i). Though this argument is not formally valid, the problem can be corrected if we introduce an additional premise: (ia) If God tells you to do something, you should do it.

From Hume's point of view, the problem is the status of the additional premise. In regard to (ia), we can ask, why should we do something simply because God tells us to? Is this an additional command of God? If this is the answer, then the argument is circular. It says to do something because God tells us to. But the only reason it can give to obey God is because God tells us to.

To take another example, we can substitute an argument based on moral relations for the one based on God. Here we have

(iii) There is a relationship in the nature and reason of things according to which people should not kill.

(iv) Therefore, you ought not to kill.

Once again, we have the *ought* statement, (iv), derived from the *is* statement, (iii). Once again, the deduction is formally invalid, unless we appeal to an additional premise, such as the following:

(iiia) If there is a relationship of the specified type, you should behave in accordance with it.

The question once again is why. Is there a relationship in the nature and reason of things that says we should behave in accordance with such relationships? Then the question is why we should behave in accordance with this further relationship. It will not do to say that the answer is still a further relationship. There is no easy way out of this process as long as we attempt to base what we ought to do on moral facts discovered by reason.

Consider a different argument.

(v) Killing causes great unhappiness.

(vi) Therefore, you ought not to kill.

Once again, the argument is not valid logically. To make it valid we have to introduce an additional premise along the lines of

(va) If something causes great unhappiness, you ought not to do it.

Once again, the problem is the status of the additional premise. But here a better answer can be provided. In this case (va) is different from the added premises discussed above, because it rests on something we want. Because of the basic facts of human nature, we *want* to avoid great unhappiness. Thus we have strong reasons to behave in ways that help avoid it. These reasons do not depend on abstruse facts discovered in "the very nature of things" but on basic facts of human experience.

Hume's alternative to morality based on relationships discovered by reason is moral rules as means to the attainment of things we want.

His criticism of the motivational force of reason and his *is-ought* argument fit together neatly. The former indicates that something other than reason must be at work to explain our feelings about morality and to induce us to act morally. Similarly, the *is-ought* argument shows the need for basic moral rules in the form of *ought* rather than *is* to help attain the objects of our desire. In both cases, the need to move beyond the capabilities of reason is apparent.

Though Hume's arguments are directed at fairly specific views, they have wider implications. They present difficult challenges to the entire tradition of natural law. According to natural law theories, morality is based on law-like principles, which bind everywhere and at all times, and are discoverable through reason. But beyond this, the view does not easily proceed. The starting point of the *Declaration of Independence* is "self-evident truths" concerning human equality and rights. One can imagine how Hume would respond to a claim of self-evident moral truth. Along similar lines, Locke, a major proponent of natural law, has a good deal of trouble explaining the grounds for his moral views, and in the final analysis appears to fall back on religious faith (see pp. 99–100). One of Hume's main lessons is to scrutinize moral claims carefully. If theorist *A* says that people are able to know that *X* is good, we should look carefully at exactly how they are supposed to know this. Chances are good such claims will not survive scrutiny.

Hume's criticisms of morality based on reason are extended to questions concerning our access to religious truths through reason. As noted above, *The Dialogues Concerning Natural Religion* present incisive criticisms of traditional views. For example, Hume is extremely hard on the "argument from design."[25] According to this view, we can prove the existence of God from the beauty and intricacy of the natural world. Look at the complexity and wonder of the human eye. How could such a marvel be designed by chance? There must be a creative intelligence behind it, and so God. But if one looks at this argument carefully, one will see that it does not prove much. By "God" people traditionally mean a great deal more than a creative intelligence. They also mean an all-wise, all-knowing, merciful spirit, which rewards the just and punishes the unjust, forgives our sins and grants us eternal life. Even if we were to concede the existence of an ordering intelligence, that is a far cry from all the implications commonly drawn, which are without rational defense.

To make matters worse, Hume contends that we can use an analogous argument from design to infer God's moral qualities from the nature of His creation. Unfortunately, claims of God's justice and benevolence run up against the misery and injustice that fill the world. After cataloguing some of the afflictions of human life, Philo, Hume's spokesperson in the *Dialogues*, says:

> It must, I think, be allowed that, if a very limited intelligence whom we shall suppose
> utterly unacquainted with the universe were assured that it were the production of a

very good, wise, and powerful being, however finite, he would, from his conjectures form *beforehand* a different notion of it from what we find it to be by experience; nor would he ever imagine merely from these attributes of the cause, of which he is informed, that the effect could be so full of vice and misery and disorder as it appears in this life. (*Dialogues*, Part XI, pp. 67–68)

Look round the universe. What an immense profusion of beings, animated and organized, sensible and active! You admire this prodigious variety and fecundity. But inspect a little more narrowly these living existences, the only beings worth regarding. How hostile and destructive to each other! How insufficient all of them for their own happiness! How contemptible or odious to the spectator! The whole presents nothing but the idea of a blind nature, impregnated by a great vivifying principle, and pouring forth from her lap, without discernment or parental care, her maimed and abortive children. (*Dialogues*, Part XI, p. 74)

The implication of the *Dialogues* is that rational arguments cannot establish traditional religious truths. And so an attempt to ground rational morality in religion will not succeed.

To close this section, we can briefly note important political implications of Hume's criticisms of reason-based morality and religion. As indicated above, Hume was temperamentally conservative. Though he lived in relatively placid times, he viewed the political order as fragile. He believed its stability could be attributed largely to chance. Thus he was eager to deflate the claims to moral certainty of "zealots," whom he viewed as threats to the established order. Religion in his eyes was especially to be feared. Seized with religious enthusiasm, people were likely to throw off moral constraints and behave abominably. Among groups Hume castigates for such conduct in his *History* are sixteenth- and seventeenth-century Puritans and the medieval Catholic Church.[26] According to Hume, "Generally speaking, the errors in religion are dangerous; those in philosophy only ridiculous" (*Treatise*, I, iv, 7, p. 319).

In his moral thought, as in his view of political obligation, Hume attempts to establish conclusions similar to those that already exist "on more reasonable principles" (*Treatise*, III, ii, 9, p. 601). We will see in the next section that his moral conclusions are little different from Locke's, or those of the typical British citizen of his day. But one respect in which they do differ is in their solid grounding in common sense. To the extent that zealotry requires religious fervor or moral certainty, Hume's critical methods rule this out, while still leaving the way open for a serviceable moral view that does not depend entirely on reason.

MORAL JUDGMENTS

If reason is not the sole source of our moral judgments, Hume must explain exactly how they arise. He holds that reason plays a role, but it is supplemented by—and subordinate to—the passions. As indicated in previous sections, Hume believes that a moral judgment stems from a subject's response to a situation. We have seen that Helene will judge a painting on the basis of how she responds to it. If the painting gives her a certain pleasure, she will view it as beautiful; if it causes a certain displeasure, she will view it as not-beautiful, perhaps ugly. The particular feelings evoked by different objects or situations are themselves different and cannot be reduced to a common denominator. Thus the feelings evoked by a beautiful sculpture are distinctive, as are those from a good novel or musical composition. What is common to all these feelings is that they are forms of pleasure.

The situation is similar in regard to moral judgments. If a spectator views an act, he will experience a particular feeling. The responses on which moral judgments rest are, again, different from those of aesthetic judgments, and no doubt also differ with different kinds of actions. But once again, what is common to all actions we judge virtuous is that viewing them is pleasurable. Hume refers to the specific pleasure evoked by virtuous actions as "approbation," or approval; the corresponding feeling evoked by a nonvirtuous action is "disapprobation," disapproval. But these are clearly species of pleasure and pain. Depending on whether our response to a given action is approbation/pleasure or disapprobation/pain, we will judge it virtuous or the reverse.

Hume's theory avoids the problems with reason-based morality discussed in the last section. As we have seen, theorists claim that moral judgments are based on the perception of particular relationships in the nature and reason of things analogous to mathematical relationships. This view falls before the facts that the precise relationships in question remain mysterious and that their connection with the passions remains obscure. According to Hume, the viewer's moral assessment of an action is based on how viewing it makes him feel. Hume has little trouble explaining either the precise features of the action to which the viewer responds or how the mental faculties making the judgment connect up with the passions.

Hume's position is constructed on a basic fact of our emotional nature, which he calls "sympathy." He believes people naturally communicate feelings to one another. The mechanism at work is a form of identification or empathy. When we are with other people, at least to some extent, we naturally see things from their point of view and feel something of what they feel. Viewing someone who is happy makes us happy; if we see someone suffering or in pain, we feel an element of that pain. This fact of our mental makeup is easily confirmed by examination of our own feelings: "No man is absolutely indifferent to the happiness and misery of others. The first has a natural tendency to give pleasure; the second, pain. This every one may find in himself" (*Morals*, Sec. V, p. 220 n.). The sentiments evoked by the sight of another person's situation are reflected back upon the spectator, giving rise to a series of reverberating emotions. As Hume says, "the minds of men are mirrors to one another" (*Treatise*, II, ii, 5, p. 414). For instance, when one views a wealthy man, a certain pleasure is transmitted between the parties:

> [T]he pleasure which a rich man receives from his possessions, being thrown upon the beholder, causes a pleasure and esteem; which sentiments, again, being perceiv'd and sympathiz'd with, encrease the pleasure of the possessor; and being once more reflected, become a new foundation for pleasure and esteem in the beholder. . . . [T]he possessor has also a secondary satisfaction in riches arising from the love and esteem he acquires by them, and this satisfaction is nothing but a second reflexion of that original pleasure, which proceeded from himself. (*Treatise*, II, ii, 5, p. 414)

Communication of emotion between oneself and others greatly enhances one's emotional life. This is basic to man's natural sociability. "Reduce a person to solitude and he loses all enjoyment, except either of the sensual or speculative kind" (*Morals*, Sec. V, p. 220). Because of sympathy with the feelings of others, people are naturally interested in others' well-being—though additional factors can interfere with this, for example, jealousy or self-interest.

If we observe how our minds work, we will see that the degree of sympathy we experience varies according to our resemblance to or relationships with other people. An American will identify more strongly with a fellow-American who is suffering than with someone from a foreign country, with a different culture and religion, perhaps with different physical characteristics. Seeing a stranger in agony may not affect him as deeply as seeing his own child with a headache. But in either case, there is a natural reflection of unpleasant feeling.

Seeing a beating, then, makes one uncomfortable, because one feels something of the victim's pain. Moral judgments are based on the viewer's experiences when he contemplates different actions. The fact that viewing a beating is unpleasant is the basis of the moral judgment it is wrong. Hume believes this rubric of factors satisfactorily explains moral judgment:

> Take any action allow'd to be vicious: Wilful murder, for instance. Examine it in all lights, and see if you can find that matter of fact, or real existence, which you call *vice*. In which-ever way you take it, you find only certain passions, motives, volitions and thoughts. There is no other matter of fact in the case. The vice entirely escapes you, as long as you consider the object. You never can find it, till you turn your reflection into your own breast, and find a sentiment of disapprobation, which arises in you, towards this action. Here is a matter of fact; but 'tis the object of feeling not of reason. It lies in yourself, not in the object. So that when you pronounce any action or character to be vicious, you mean nothing but that from the constitution of your nature you have a feeling or sentiment of blame from the contemplation of it. (*Treatise*, III, i, 1, p. 520)

Once again, a great advantage of Hume's view is that it does not depend on strange or inexplicable phenomena in either the action being viewed or the mind of the viewer.

In viewing other people's actions, the spectator will respond pleasurably to actions that give *them* pleasure or make them happy. Thus Hume is a utilitarian of sorts—actually one of the forerunners of the utilitarian tradition. Briefly, a utilitarian believes an action is *right* if it brings about the greatest possible *good* under given circumstances. The good is generally identified as pleasure, and so most utilitarians argue that the right action in some situation is the one that produces the greatest amount of pleasure, or the least pain. Utilitarianism exists in many different forms, and we need not attempt to sort them out or discuss them here. This can be put off until our discussion of Jeremy Bentham, James Mill, and John Stuart Mill in Chapter 8. Here it is enough to note that Hume's position is roughly utilitarian, though the mechanism at work is complex.

Like utilitarians, Hume believes the actions we view as virtuous are those that produce pleasure. If a spectator witnesses an act of kindness, this act will evoke a pleasurable response in its recipient, which will be communicated to the spectator through sympathy. The spectator will view the act with approbation and so judge it virtuous. The reverse will be the case for an act that causes pain. Hume therefore posits a correlation between virtuous actions and the production of pleasure, and nonvirtuous acts and the reverse.

Things become more complex through the intervention of reason. The mechanism of sympathy is capable of a certain degree of refinement and focusing. Because of our interest in pleasure, we come to assess actions according to the motives of actors, rather than their actual effects. If a person attempts to bring other people pleasure, but because of circumstances beyond his control ends up harming them, we do not blame him. Our praise and blame are focused on the kinds of actions that cause the greatest pleasure to society over the long run. Such actions are performed for virtuous reasons. The virtues are qualities of character that dispose people to perform beneficial actions. Thus a courageous person will face danger for good reason. A charitable person will attempt to alleviate others' distress. An honest person will not deceive others, and so on. Though reason plays a role in identifying certain qualities as virtues, moral judgments still rest primarily on the passions. We would not feel the necessary approbation or disapprobation unless we *cared* about other people's pleasure or pain—which we do because of sympathy.

Hume refers to kinds of motives for actions that produce pleasure each time they cause actions as natural virtues. For instance, a generous action is beneficial to the recipient. Assume that a wealthy man gives a poor man money to buy food. A spectator viewing this action will feel some of the pleasure the action creates and judge it virtuous. An instance of vice will have the opposite effect. For instance, if the rich man gratuitously insults the poor man, the spectator will feel disapprobation and consider this an instance of vice. Mental traits such as generosity and cruelty will have their natural effects each time they give rise to actions.

Thus Hume is able to account for moral judgments without appealing to mysterious relationships between the elements of actions, or unclear means through which reason perceives them. His position is notably straightforward:

> The hypothesis which we embrace is plain. It maintains that morality is determined by sentiment. It defines virtue to be *whatever mental action or quality gives to a spectator the pleasing sentiment of approbation*; and vice the contrary. (*Morals*, App. I, p. 289)

Hume's explanations are intended to rest on simple mental processes familiar to everyone. Examination of the way we respond to different kinds of actions should convince us of the accuracy of his analysis.

HUME'S THEORY OF JUSTICE

Moral judgments in other cases are more complex. These involve what Hume calls the "artificial" virtues, the most important of which is justice. In these cases, reason makes a more significant contribution, and our natural faculties of sympathy are focused to a larger extent. Actions of this kind differ from those we have discussed in that not every instance of virtuous conduct will create pleasure or be beneficial. Moral judgment in such cases is complex, in that a spectator would view such actions as good through identification with the needs of society rather than the immediate effects on the people involved.

Central to the artificial virtues is the emergence of a network of rules, on which the maintenance of society depends. Hume's argument here is like that of traditional social contract theorists in important respects. Human beings are social creatures. They cannot satisfy their needs or be protected from natural dangers without the cooperation of others. Society in turn requires certain rules. Most important are rules of three main kinds: (a) rules of property; (b) rules of transferring property by consent, that is, through trading or buying and selling; (c) rules of promising. Because these rules were long ago found to be necessary to the preservation of society and its members, they were instituted.

Hume believes there was a time when people attempted to live together without rules of justice. They discovered this was impossible, and over time the necessary rules were devised. But though the rules in question are human contrivances, devised to solve specific problems, they were not the product of an explicit agreement. Indeed, one of the rules Hume discusses is that of promising, through which agreements are made. One of his criticisms of the contract of government is that it rests on a circular argument. People could not have entered into a contractual agreement to set up and obey government unless they could employ the rules of the institution of promising. But Hume believes the rules of promising are explained by the same factors that explain the origin of government. Thus it is not helpful to explain the former by the latter:

> It has been asserted by some, that Justice arises from Human Conventions and proceeds from the voluntary choice, consent, or combination of mankind. If by *convention* be here meant a *promise* (which is the most usual sense of the word) nothing can be more absurd than this position. The observance of promises is itself one of the most considerable parts of justice, and we are not surely bound to keep our word because we have given our word to keep it. (*Morals*, App. III, p. 306)[27]

The necessary rules, instead, arose through a gradual process of trial and error. Hume does not provide details here, nor are they necessary. We can presume that as people attempted to live together, they came into conflict with one another until clear rules of property were established. Over time, they became aware of specific difficulties they confronted and devised solutions. Though the process was gradual instead of a one-time agreement endorsed by everyone, it gave rise to a convention nonetheless:

> Two men who pull the oars of a boat do it by an agreement or convention, tho' they have never given promises to each other. Nor is the rule concerning the stability of possession the less deriv'd from human conventions, that it arises gradually and acquires force by a slow progression, and by our repeated experience of the inconveniences of transgressing it. (*Treatise*, I, ii, 2, p. 542)

The process through which rules of property, buying and selling, and promising came into existence are analogous to those through which other important human institutions arise. Two that Hume lists are language and the use of money:

> In like manner are languages gradually establish'd by human conventions without any promise. In like manner do gold and silver become the common measures of exchange, and are esteem'd sufficient payment for what is of a hundred times their value. (*Treatise*, I, ii, 2, p. 542)

Though money and language are inventions, intended to remedy specific problems and so improve the community's lot, neither was introduced all at once, of a piece. Similarly, the rules of justice came into use over time and were shaped to meet the needs of their inventors.

Hume calls justice an "artificial" virtue because it is not rooted in a "natural" human faculty. In referring to justice as "artificial," Hume means that it is not "natural" in a specific sense: it is not rooted in a particular psychological response human beings have by birth. In judging an instance of justice to be virtuous, the spectator feels approbation that someone follows a specific rule. Because the rule in question is a human invention, there is no doubt that the spectator's response had to be taught. In this sense judgments concerning justice are different from those concerning the natural virtues or vices. The spectator's response to an act of generosity is "natural," in that he responds to the pleasure created by the act, and does so through psychological propensities present in his mind since birth. There is some degree of education involved here as well, in that the spectator responds to the *motives* of the actor, rather than the effects of his action. But Hume believes the degree of training is far less than with the artificial virtues.

A second important difference between the natural and artificial virtues is that, while each single instance of the former is beneficial to the parties involved—and so gives rise to the pleasure to which the spectator responds—this is not true of the latter. The benefits of the artificial virtues of justice are enjoyed by society as a whole, and so all of its members. These arise from *general* adherence to the rules. Society cannot survive without the property system. Thus it is essential that the institution be observed, on the whole. But the property system is also ridden with particular features that are not directly beneficial to society. The rich have enormous wealth, while others live in poverty. Greater pleasure overall would be created by taking some of the former class's goods and distributing them among the latter. But Hume believes the benefits particular individuals would derive from actions of this sort are far outweighed by the damage they would do to the stability of the property system, on which the welfare of all depends. Thus his account of justice depends on a basic distinction between the immediate interests of particular people and the interests of society as a whole:

> Public utility requires that property should be regulated by general inflexible rules; and though such rules are adopted as best serve the same end of public utility, it is impossible for them to prevent all particular hardships, or make beneficial consequences result from every individual case. It is sufficient, if the whole plan or scheme be necessary to the support of civil society, and if the balance of good, in the main, do thereby preponderate much above that of evil. (*Morals*, App. III, p. 305)

To illustrate the distinction, consider what would happen if a poor man found a purse a rich man had dropped. Because he can put the money to good use, while it means little to the rich man, the poor man would benefit from keeping it more than the owner would from its return. In a case of this sort, we could also argue that *society* benefits more if the poor man keeps it, as the interest of society is simply that of all its members, and in this case the members appear to be better off. But Hume argues that this is not actually the case. A stable property system is indispensable to society and all its members. Therefore it actually benefits society more if the poor man returns the money. For him to keep it would jeopardize the stability of the property system, and so the welfare of all. (We should note the strong possibility that Hume exaggerates the damage to the property system caused by the poor man's action. A stable property system depends on *most* people's compliance with its rules most of the time. It is perfectly compatible with occasional violations of the rules by a percentage of the population.)

Hume employs a striking image to illustrate the difference between natural and artificial virtues in an appendix to the *Enquiry Concerning the Principles of Morals*. Acts in keeping with the former are like the stones in a stone wall. Each action contributes to society's good, in combining with others in an additive manner. The case is different in regard to the artificial virtues. Here individual acts contribute to an overall structure from which benefit is derived:

> The happiness and prosperity of mankind, arising from the social virtue of benevolence and its subdivisions, may be compared to a wall, built by many hands, which still rises by each stone that is heaped upon it, and receives increase proportional to the diligence and care of each workman. The same happiness, raised by the social virtue of justice and its subdivisions, may be compared to the building of a vault, where each individual stone would, of itself, fall to the ground; nor is the whole fabric supported but by the mutual assistance and combination of its corresponding parts. (*Morals*, App. III, p. 305)

Despite the fact that particular actions are not beneficial to society, Hume believes their disadvantages are outweighed by the indispensable benefits the institutions of justice provide. As people are trained to believe this, they are able to focus their capacity for sympathy on the interest of society as a whole, and so feel approbation or blame for actions that keep or violate rules of justice. Thus a spectator would feel disapprobation if the poor man kept the purse. He would realize that this action undermines the institution of property, on which the welfare of all depends. Though he would naturally feel an element of the poor man's pleasure at finding the purse, this would be outweighed by discomfort at violation of property rules. In a case of this sort, then, moral judgment is complex, because the immediate and long-range effects of the action are in conflict. But Hume believes that through training, we can be taught to feel approbation at just acts and disapprobation at the unjust.

To close out this section, we should note a somewhat different sense in which the artificial virtues can be said to be "natural." The word "natural" can be used in many different senses. We have seen that the virtues associated with justice are not "natural," because they are not rooted in innate psychological faculties, but must be inculcated through training. The word "natural" can also refer to what is always associated with human society. Because people cannot live together without rules of justice, there is a clear sense in which the rules of justice are "natural" (even though, in a different sense of the word, they are not "natural"). By employing similar reasoning, we could say that the use of language and money is "natural" to human beings, though both of these are clearly invented. In Hume's words:

> Tho' the rules of justice be *artificial*, they are not *arbitrary*. Nor is the expression improper to call them *Laws of Nature*, if by natural we understand what is common to any species, or even if we confine it to mean what is inseparable from the species. (*Treatise*, III, ii, 1, p. 536)

THE CIRCUMSTANCES OF JUSTICE

Hume presents strong evidence that the rules of justice are intended to advance people's interests. These rules can be seen to have been devised to solve particular problems, rooted in particular circumstances, which correspond to those of ordinary human society. If circumstances were to change, the rules of justice would lose their value. Hume's discussion is the classic account of the circumstances of justice in the philosophical literature.

Hume believes that the main circumstances of justice are *limited scarcity* and *limited benevolence*. Let us begin with the former. As we have seen, the major rules of justice concern property, exchange of property by consent, and promising. Rules of property were devised with limited scarcity in mind. Consider what human beings need most in order to survive. The answer here is clearly air, as without oxygen, people would begin to die in a matter of minutes. People could live without water for several days, while without food, they could survive for a number of months. Even though air is so important, human societies do not have rules governing its use. The reason for this is clear, because there is so much of it. The same is true of water—or at least was true when Hume wrote. In his words,

> We see, even in the present necessitous condition of mankind, that, wherever any benefit is bestowed by nature in an unlimited abundance, we leave it always in common among the whole human race, and make no subdivision of right and property. Water and air, though the most necessary of all objects, are not challenged as the property of individuals nor can any man commit injustice by the most lavish use and enjoyment of these blessings. (*Morals*, Sec. III, p. 184)

Consider what happens when circumstances differ. With shortages of air or water, rules of property would come into play. For instance, we are familiar with movies about men trapped in the desert, who are willing to trade all their belongings for a canteen of water. Less dramatically, in areas in which agriculture depends on irrigation, disputes often arise between needy farmers and the people whose water resources they invade. Were the earth's atmosphere to become so polluted as to have limited clean air, similar rules would doubtless be devised.

Thus as we move from abundance to limited scarcity, rules of property must be introduced. Now imagine that this progression continues, from limited to unlimited scarcity. Once again, the ordinary rules of justice would lose their point. Under conditions of famine, for example, when people face starvation, ordinary rules of property are suspended. Imagine that ten people are on the brink of starvation while their wealthy neighbor has an orchard overflowing with apples, more than enough for himself and his family. The ten would not be condemned for taking some of the apples to save their lives. In a situation of mass starvation, would the population of a city do wrong if they broke into a granary (public or private) to feed themselves? Again, these examples indicate the specific circumstances for which the rules of justice were constructed.

In addition to limited scarcity, the normal condition of society is limited benevolence. People may not love one another, but they are not generally at each other's throats. If we imagine circumstances of unlimited love and goodwill between people, we can see that rules of property again lose their force. The clearest example concerns relationships in a family. At least ideally, husband and wife have joint property. They give freely to their children, not charging them for meals. There is a Greek proverb: "Friends have all things in common." This is illustrated by the practice of religious communities in which, as an expression of mutual love, goods are held in common—perhaps as attempts to replicate family relationships. Thus if society were to move to a situation of general benevolence, property rules would no longer be needed:

> [S]uppose that, though the necessities of human race continue the same as at present, yet the mind is so enlarged and so replete with friendship and generosity that every man has the utmost tenderness for every man, and feels no more concern for his own interest than for that of his fellows, it seems evident that the use of justice would in that case be suspended by such an extensive benevolence, nor would the divisions and barriers of property and obligation have ever been thought of. . . . Every man, upon this supposition, being a second self to another, would trust all his interests to the discretion of every man, without jealousy, without partition, without distinction. And the whole human race would form only one family. . . . (*Morals*, Sec. III, pp. 184–185)

Again, reverse the circumstances. Imagine a situation of general hatred, rather than mutual love. The clearest instance is war, a situation in which people naturally help themselves to the weapons of their foes, without regard to rights of property. According to Hume, in circumstances of such enmity, all other considerations give way to self-preservation (*Morals*, Sec. III, p. 187). Along similar lines, in dealing with a criminal who has committed deeds obnoxious to the public, society inflicts punishments that would not be allowed by the rules of justice that ordinarily hold between people (p. 187).

Hume notes additional circumstances of justice. Equality between parties bears mention. Rules of justice were devised for dealings between equals. Imagine two species, one of which is markedly superior to the other and able to deal with it as it pleases, while the weaker does not have the capacity to make the stronger "feel the effects of their resentment." Rules of justice will not hold between the two. Their relationship will be on a different basis. Hume holds that it is against "the laws of humanity" for the stronger to exploit the weaker, but this is not injustice. He believes this is the situation between men and animals. Animals, inferior to men in the relevant respects, are exploited without injustice (*Morals*, Sec. III, pp. 190–191).

Thus, in regard to limited scarcity and benevolence, and rough equality, the rules of justice can be seen to have been devised to remedy the problems of our situation.

> [T]he rules of equity or justice depend entirely on the particular state and condition in which men are placed, and owe their origin and existence to that utility, which results to the public from their strict and regular observance. Reverse in any considerable circumstance the condition of men: Produce extreme abundance, or extreme necessity; Implant in the human breast perfect moderation and humanity, or perfect rapaciousness and malice; by rendering justice totally *useless*, you thereby totally destroy its essence, and suspend its obligation upon mankind. (*Morals*, Sec. III, p. 188)

This indicates that the rules are human inventions, devised for human purposes. Justice is to advance the social good, rather than based on eternal relationships which reason discovers. If justice were like truths of mathematics, eternal and invariable, we would not expect it to give way as circumstances changed.

Similar reasoning holds in regard to other social rules. Like rules of justice, they too are devised to advance people's interests. Specific rules of property are due in part to connections people naturally make through association of ideas (e.g., between a crop and the farmer who grew it), and in part to chance. Similar principles hold in regard to etiquette, or "rules of good manners, a kind of lesser morality calculated for the ease of company and conversation" (*Morals*, Sec. IV, p. 209). In order to get on with each other in society, Hume believes, people must have rules. These in general are explained by their contribution to the good of the parties involved:

> To carry the matter farther, we may observe that it is impossible for men so much as to murder each other without statutes, and maxims, and an idea of justice and honour. War has its laws as well as peace; and even that sportive kind of war, carried on among wrestlers, boxers, cudgel-players, gladiators, is regulated by fixed principles. Common interest and utility beget infallibly a standard of right and wrong among the parties concerned. (*Morals*, Sec. IV, pp. 210–211)

GOVERNMENT

Though rules of justice are necessary for society, they are not sufficient to provide peace and security. In addition to rules, it is necessary to have means through which they are enforced. Without a power to ensure compliance, the rules of justice would be broken, and life would become insupportable. To meet this need, governments are instituted. Though they too arose through a kind of convention, they were not put in place all at once through formal agreements. As is true of the rules of justice, governments arose gradually, through a process of trial and error, as the need for them became evident.

The flaw in human nature that makes government necessary is a form of self-interest. Hume argues that maintenance of the rules of justice is in everyone's interest. Without them, society would degenerate, and human association would be impossible. Thus if Ramon has the opportunity to violate the necessary rules, it is not in his interest to do so. Let us assume that Ramon is the poor man who finds a rich man's purse. Should he return it or not? He could make good use of the money—better than the rich man could. But Hume holds that if Ramon kept the purse he would threaten to plunge society into anarchy and terror. (Once again, Hume probably overstates the effects of single instances of injustice, though this does not substantially affect his argument. We will return to this subject below.)

Though Hume believes it is in Ramon's interest to return the purse, he also believes that Ramon might not realize this. The problem is that for Hume, as for Locke (see p. 105), passion often interferes with reason. Hume believes this takes a specific form. The benefits of absconding with the rich man's money are close at hand. Ramon can take the money and buy new clothes, perhaps toys for his children as well. The harms this causes are more remote. His keeping the money will not *immediately* bring about anarchy, though Hume holds that these effects are real nonetheless. Because the benefits of keeping the money are near at hand, Ramon is liable to overestimate their magnitude and so do what is not actually in his interest. The problem, then, is that people are misled by appearances and make errors:

> This is the reason why men so often act in contradiction to their known interest, and in particular why they prefer any trivial advantage that is present to the maintenance of order in society, which so much depends on the observance of justice. The

consequences of every breach of equity seem to lie very remote and are not able to counter-ballance any immediate advantage that may be reap'd from it. They are, however, never the less real for being remote, and as all men are in some degree subject to the same weakness, it necessarily happens that the violations of equity must become very frequent in society, and the commerce of men by that means be render'd very dangerous and uncertain. (*Treatise*, III, ii, 8, pp. 586–587)

The problems caused by self-interest can be remedied by government. Because of the pull of self-interest, people tend to miscalculate their near and long-term interests. The main task of government is to attach penalties to and punish violations of the rules of justice. Doing this will alter the costs and benefits of different courses of conduct and so affect people's calculations. If a law is passed against keeping other people's property and violators are subject to severe penalties, Ramon will think twice about keeping the money. Before the advent of the law, he was faced with a choice between his real advantage, which was remote, and an immediate and lesser good if he kept the money. With the law in place, his calculations must be importantly different. In addition to calculating the advantages of keeping or returning the money, he must now take into account being punished if he keeps it. This adds significant disadvantages to that course of conduct and so should lead him to respect the rules of property. With everyone else affected similarly, violations of equity will become less frequent. Because the stability of the property system and the other rules of justice are essential for everyone, in shoring this up, government plays an essential role.

Government is structured to uphold the rules of justice. People in political office are given various benefits, so they wish to keep their positions. They are then led to understand that if they do not enforce the rules they will lose their jobs. Thus, their short-term interest lies in supporting the framework of rules that are in the long-term interest of all members of society (*Treatise* III, ii, 8, pp. 588–589).

As I have suggested, it appears that there is an error in Hume's argument for justice. It is clear that Ramon and other members of society benefit enormously from rules of property and other rules of justice, which are essential for social life. It is also clear that *if, by keeping the purse, he would significantly damage these rules*, Ramon should return it, even if the damage in question is in the remote future. In a large society, however, it is not clear that his keeping the purse would have this effect. Maintenance of social rules depends on large-scale adherence: again, most members of society must obey them most of the time. But unless he is an especially prominent member of society or it could be shown that his violation would inspire similar violations by many other people, it is probably in Ramon's interest to break the rules. It is unlikely his conduct would have this effect, and so Hume probably errs in identifying his long-term interest.

On one level, this apparent error in Hume's reasoning does not significantly affect his political theory. Its main effect might even be to strengthen his argument for government. If the criticism of Hume is correct, people will be tempted to break the rules, not because they miscalculate, but because it pays to do so. The human condition is not plagued by widespread confusion about the relationship between individual and social interests but by conflict between them. Only by instituting government and penalizing rule violations can this more serious situation be remedied. Even if Ramon would gain in the long run as well as the short by keeping the money, with government in place, there is a possibility he will be punished severely if he keeps it. This should alter the cost-benefit calculations to make it pay for him to return the money. If Ramon realizes this, he will behave accordingly. But there is also a problem with this reasoning, to which we will return.

A mechanism of sympathy similar to that associated with justice yields moral judgments that support government. Once again, through education, sympathy can be focused. People can be taught that justice is essential to their own well-being as well as society's. Eventually, they will come to associate their own good with adherence to essential rules. They will feel disapprobation at violations, even if these immediately benefit their perpetrators. Through similar education, they can be taught that government too is necessary to their well-being, and so also maintenance of its power. When people associate their own good with adherence to the dictates of government, they will feel disapprobation at violations, even if single acts are more beneficial than harmful.

To test this argument, we can reflect on our own responses to various situations. Imagine that Lorna runs through a red light, without slowing down. As long as no one is harmed by her action, this is in her interest—if she is in a hurry—and society's too. After all, she is happier and no harm is done. But if one were to observe such an action, one would probably feel uncomfortable and that what Lorna did is wrong, even if the specific action caused more good than harm. Similarly, imagine that Ralph does not pay his taxes. Because he lives in a large country, his nonpayment does not make a detectable difference in the government's budget, while he and his family derive real enjoyment from the extra money. But once again, though no one appears to be harmed by this action, it will probably make us feel uncomfortable.

Hume would account for the moral judgments in these cases according to familiar mental mechanisms. The spectator, who has been taught to associate adherence to government's rules with the preservation of society, feels disapprobation at violations. He realizes that if many other people behaved similarly the results would be undesirable. Government would lose authority, which means that more people would break more laws, setting off a spiral into social collapse. The spectator's feeling of disapprobation comes from his concern with the well-being of society, which is in turn rooted in concern for his own interest.

Once it is in place, government is able to take on additional tasks. Especially important is coordinating many people's activity. Society would benefit from the successful completion of certain projects, for example, the building of roads. But constructing a road is too much for one person or a small group to accomplish, while it is difficult to combine the efforts of large numbers of people. Through devices such as forced levies and taxation, government is able to do this. It proclaims that people must pay such and such amount, or show up for work at such and such time and place, and the necessary labor can be organized. Because of its ability to provide benefits such as these—to which scholars refer as "public goods"—Hume views government as a great boon to mankind—at least under certain circumstances:

> Two neighbours may agree to drain a meadow, which they possess in common; because 'tis easy for them to know each other's mind, and each must perceive that the immediate consequences of his failing in his part is the abandoning the whole project. But 'tis very difficult, and indeed impossible, that a thousand persons shou'd agree in any such action, it being difficult for them to concert so complicated a design, and still more difficult for them to execute it, while each seeks a pretext to free himself of the

trouble and expence, and wou'd lay the whole burden on others. Political society easily remedies both these inconveniences. Magistrates find an immediate interest in the interest of any considerable part of their subjects. They need consult no body but themselves to form any scheme for the promoting of that interest. And as the failure of any one piece in the execution is connected, though not immediately, with the failure of the whole, they prevent that failure, because they find no interest in it, either immediate or remote. Thus bridges are built, harbours open'd, ramparts rais'd, canals form'd, fleets equip'd, and armies disciplin'd every where, by the care of government, which, tho' compos'd of men subject to all human infirmities, becomes by one of the finest and most subtle inventions imaginable, a composition which is, in some measure, exempted from all these infirmities. (*Treatise* III, ii, 8, p. 590)

As Hume indicates in this passage, though government is subject to human infirmities, these can be avoided. But the possibility of infirmities defines the limits of obedience. Hume clearly explains the need for government and how everyone in society benefits from placing power in the magistrate's hands. The problem, however, is that, being human, the magistrate is liable to misuse this power for his own ends. The subjects' recourse has been discussed above. Traditional theories hold that government's power is from the consent of the governed. In misusing his authority, the magistrate violates the terms of the agreement and so loses his power. We have seen that Hume finds much to criticize in this account. The original contract through which government was supposedly erected never took place, and individuals give their consent neither expressly nor tacitly. But though the contract of government is a fiction, Hume believes the conclusions it suggests are basically accurate. The power of government is conditional, though the terms depend on society's interests rather than a formal contract. Government is erected to advance these interests; when it abuses its power, it is no longer in people's interest to obey. Should government greatly abuse its power, the people will rise against it, and rightly so. Government has no warrant but the good it does; when it ceases to do good, its warrant expires. Because of the disorders rebellion incurs, Hume believes government must be extremely oppressive before this is justified, but if the requisite conditions exist, rebellion is in order (*Treatise*, III, ii, 9).

HUME'S CONSERVATISM

We have seen that Hume's criticism of the contract of government is similar to other aspects of his philosophy. Though he subjects the contract itself to withering objections, his intention is to preserve much of its content. Hume's recurrent task is to reestablish the substance of existing beliefs but on more defensible grounds. Once again, as he says of the contract argument, "The conclusion is just, tho' the principle be erroneous; and I flatter myself, that I can establish the same conclusions on more reasonable principles" (*Treatise*, III, ii, 9, p. 601). We have also noted, however, that there is a problem with this enterprise. Once unleashed, the power of critical reason is not easily contained. In the spheres of morals and politics, undermining the bases of existing points of view raises problems that are not easily put to rest.

By temperament, Hume is both philosophically and politically conservative.[28] His desire to preserve the substance of existing beliefs is sincere. It seems that his boundless skepticism extends to the very faculty of critical scrutiny he so effectively wields. Having cleared away the dross of defective arguments, Hume is able to ground his own convictions in other areas of experience. Though there is no necessary connection between his conservatism and his skepticism, it is often said that Hume represents a type of conservative thinker frequently encountered. If all moral arguments are defective, then we might as well accept the ones we have, with which we are comfortable. John Stuart Mill interprets Hume along these lines:

> [Hume's] absolute skepticism in speculation very naturally brought him round to Toryism in practice; for if no faith can be had in the operations of human intellect, and one side of every question is about as likely as another to be true, a man will commonly be inclined to prefer that order of things which, being no more wrong than every other, he has hitherto found compatible with his private comforts.[29]

Mill's analysis can be criticized. Hume's adherence to existing institutions is not because of the accidental fact that they rather than other institutions exist, but because of the legitimizing force of custom. Because of his concern for the public good, Hume believes in preserving the existing order, not because it exists but because it is stable. Like other conservative thinkers, his support is contingent on existing institutions not being egregiously oppressive. But with this qualification, he prefers them over alternatives. Institutions gain strength over time. As people become accustomed to them, they command greater authority. To destabilize existing arrangements is dangerous, because their replacements will take a long time to become as firmly established. Accordingly, a more accurate assessment of Hume's view is that his conservatism is based on the force of custom and directed toward the public good. The absence of transcendental moral principles leads him to emphasize less grand but still important considerations. But Mill is to some extent correct, in that these considerations have less obvious force than firmly held moral principles.

But in spite of Hume's defense of the existing moral and political order, his preferred conclusions by no means inevitably follow from the critical side of his philosophy. Undermining traditional moral arguments can cause more resolute skepticism to take root. The same critical faculty that dispenses with existing moral principles may not be satisfied with new ones that are brought forth. Extreme skepticism can promote unsettling conclusions. If traditional moral arguments are defective, why should we be moral, especially if demands of morality and self-interest do not coincide? If skeptical criticisms refute all claims but self-interest, is there ever reason to make sacrifices for other people? Even if such sacrifices are necessary for the social good, whether or not one individual makes such sacrifices will hardly be noticed, so why should any particular individual sacrifice? We have seen that rules of justice will be enforced by the state. But if one can violate these without being caught, is there any reason to comply? Questions along these lines are with us still, once again indicating Hume's contemporary relevance.

Hume's political conservatism does not necessarily follow from his skepticism either. Once again, refutation of additional moral considerations makes the legitimizing force of custom an important consideration, and so leaving things as they are appears attractive. We have also seen that Hume's assault on moral certainty had a political purpose. He sought to weaken the destructive zeal of political and religious fanatics by undermining their convictions. To leave such assaults unchallenged could be dangerous. As Sheldon Wolin puts this, "the attack on the authority of accepted ideas was soon accompanied by an attack on the legitimacy of accepted institutions."[30] If the arguments of his opponents could be left in ruins, Hume believed his favored institutions would triumph—almost by default.

But along with criticizing the arguments of his opponents, Hume himself also did a great deal to undermine traditional beliefs. Throughout the eighteenth century, many thinkers assailed existing moral and political doctrines, and the objectionable political and social order they upheld. Severe attacks on the religious basis of traditional authority were a central theme of the Enlightenment. To a large extent, Hume's purposes coincided with those of other critics, though as a conservative, he stopped far short of desiring wholesale political reform. But it is not difficult to see how his powerful criticisms of existing moral and religious beliefs could advance the ends of revolutionaries. By sweeping away grounds on which the existing order rested, Hume called increased attention to the question of its legitimacy.

Scholars note that Hume's moderate conservatism was made possible by the relatively placid times in which he lived.[31] Before the outbreak of the French Revolution, conservative parties and parties of reform agreed on many issues, and so the stakes of political debate were lower than they would become. This was especially true in England, which was relatively stable and prosperous throughout the eighteenth century. But as the French Revolution heralded a categorical assault on the existing order—in England and elsewhere in Europe, as well as France—the need to combat revolutionary ideas assumed pressing importance. Confronted with categorical critiques, conservative thinkers felt the need to move beyond refutation and develop sophisticated defenses, as we will see in our discussion of Burke (in Chapter 7). Toward this end, they frequently turned to religion. In Wolin's words, after the French Revolution, "conservatives were irresistibly drawn to some form of political supernaturalism" (Wolin, p. 1000). In this regard, Burke is typical. Though as we will see, he develops a series of powerful philosophical arguments, many of his claims require religious support. Something similar is true of Hegel, who, as we will see, relies on an elaborate, quasi-religious theory of history. Because many arguments of these and other conservative thinkers do not withstand philosophical scrutiny, there is something attractive about Hume's "conservatism without benefit of mystery" (Wolin, p. 1001).

But one must wonder how successful Hume ultimately was. If political allegiance rests on habit and custom, undermining existing beliefs can only be destructive. In his essay on Bentham, Mill describes certain harmful thinkers:

> negative, or destructive philosophers; those who can perceive what is false, but not what is true; who awaken the human mind to the inconsistencies and absurdities of time-sanctioned opinions and institutions, but substitute nothing in the place of what they take away.[32]

Hume is a primary target of Mill's reproach. Mill refers to him as "the profoundest negative thinker on record," and describes him in unflattering terms: "the prince of *dilettanti*, from whose writings one will hardly learn that there is such a thing as truth, far less that it is attainable; but only that the *pro* and *con* of everything may be argued with infinite ingenuity, and furnishes a fine intellectual exercise."[33] Though highly complimentary of Hume's abilities, the thrust of Mill's critique is, once again, unfair. In spite of the delight he takes in following arguments to their conclusions, Hume attempts to reconstruct the doctrines he pulls down.

Still, it is not clear that Hume escaped the consequences of his powerful destructive arguments. In regard to political theory, a fundamental problem his philosophy presents is the basis of allegiance when traditional beliefs have been undermined. Though Hume himself turned to custom, this too is readily criticized. Though established institutions are valuable because of their familiarity, other factors can override this. In particular, why should we defer to customs when they seem to conflict with the public good? Single-minded pursuit of the public good, on the other hand, is not a conservative force and can lead to wholesale rejection of what exists.[34] To his great credit, in wiping away specious moral and religious principles, Hume helped prepare the ground for government in the public interest. In this regard, his skeptical criticisms were a natural precursor of utilitarianism.[35] But in defusing grounds of allegiance other than self-interest, Hume presented future theorists with a host of problems. Though he sought to preserve the substance of existing beliefs on more defensible grounds, in many areas in which he worked, theorists are still searching for convincing replacements for the beliefs he swept away.

NOTES

1. D. C. Stove, "Hume, Kemp Smith, and Carnap," *Australasian Journal of Philosophy*, 55 (1977), 189.

2. A. J. Ayer, *Hume* (Oxford, 1980), p. 1; similarly, E. C. Mossner, "Introduction" to *Treatise of Human Nature*, Mossner, ed. (Harmondsworth, England, 1969), p. 7. The *Treatise* will be cited according to book, part, and section number, and page number in the Mossner edition. I leave out some of Hume's italicization. Unless otherwise noted, all italics are Hume's. I also modernize some of his punctuation; all changes in this regard are slight.

3. J. H. Randall, quoted by Mossner, "Philosophy and Biography: The Case of David Hume," in *Hume*, V. C. Chappel, ed. (Garden City, NY, 1966), p. 11.

4. Quoted by I. Berlin, "Hume and the Sources of German Anti-Rationalism," in *David Hume: Bicentennary Papers*, G. P. Morice, ed. (Edinburgh, 1977), p. 104.

5. Quoted by Mossner, "Introduction," p. 7.

6. "My Own Life" is cited in the text as "Life"; page references are to Vol. I of *The Letters of David Hume*, J. Greig, ed., 2 vols. (Oxford, 1932), where it is reprinted. Hume's letters are cited below as *Letters*, with page references to Greig's edition.

7. Biographical details are from Mossner, *The Life of David Hume*, 2nd ed. (Oxford, 1980) (this work cited in the text as "Mossner"); a good brief account is given in Ayer, *Hume*, Chap. 1.

8. On their relationship, see Mossner, *Life*, Chap. 35. For Hume's opinion of Rousseau, see p. 213.

9. The two *Enquiries* are cited as *Human Understanding* and *Morals*, respectively, by section number and page number. Full references below, under "Texts Cited." The contents of the *Enquiries* are conveniently collated with those of the *Treatise* by L. A. Selby-Bigge in the "Introduction" to the edition cited.

10. These are collected in Hume, *Essays: Moral, Political and Literary*, E. Miller, ed., revised ed. (Indianapolis, 1985). These are cited in the text as *Essays*, with page numbers

in this edition. For a history of the numerous editions of Hume's essays, see Miller's "Foreword," pp. xi–xviii.

11. Quoted in Mossner, *Life*, p. 318.

12. See essays by Mossner and Jessop, in *Hume*, Chappel, ed.

13. A. Smith, letter to William Strahan, Nov. 9, 1776; rpt. in Miller, ed., *Essays*, pp. xlviii–xlix.

14. Quoted by E. Nagel, "The Development of Modern Science," in *Chapters in Western Civilization*, edited by the Contemporary Civilization Staff of Columbia College, Columbia University, 3rd ed., 2 vols. (New York, 1961), I, 517.

15. A brilliant study of Hume's view of the mind's mechanisms is R. P. Wolff, "Hume's Theory of Mental Activity," in *Hume*, Chappel, ed.

16. See N. K. Smith, *The Philosophy of David Hume* (London, 1941).

17. Rpt. in *Essays: Moral, Political and Literary*.

18. J. Locke, *Second Treatise of Government*, in *Two Treatises of Government*, P. Laslett, ed. (Cambridge, 1988), Sec. 119.

19. A brilliant analysis and criticism of possible actions that constitute tacit consent is given in A. J. Simmons, *Moral Principles and Political Obligations* (Princeton, 1979), chaps. 3–4.

20. Some important examples are Simmons, *Moral Principles and Political Obligations*; C. Pateman, *The Problem of Political Obligation* (New York, 1979); J. Raz, *The Authority of Law* (Oxford, 1979), Chap. 12; M. B. E. Smith, "Is There a Prima Facie Obligation to Obey the Law?" *Yale Law Journal*, 82 (1973).

21. E. Burke, *A Vindication of Natural Society*, in *Prerevolutionary Writings*, I. Harrison, ed. (Cambridge, 1993), p. 11.

22. Hume, "An Abstract of a Treatise of Human Nature," ed. J. M. Keynes and P. Sraffa (Cambridge, 1938), p. 24.

23. Quoted by Smith, *Philosophy of David Hume*, p. 19.

24. Rpt. in L. A. Selby-Bigge, ed., *The British Moralists*, two vols. in one (1897; rpt. Indianapolis, 1964), II, 11.

25. Especially trenchant criticisms of the argument from design are found in Part X of the *Dialogues Concerning Natural Religion*; this work is cited in the text as *Dialogues*, according to part and page; full reference below under "Texts Cited."

26. See D. Miller, *Philosophy and Ideology in Hume's Political Thought* (Oxford, 1981), pp. 116–117.

27. For criticisms of the contract of government along these lines, see "Of the Original Contract," *Essays*, pp. 480–482.

28. For the nature of conservative political theory, see below, Chapter 7.

29. J. S. Mill, "Bentham," in *Essays on Politics and Culture*, G. Himmelfarb, ed. (Garden City, NY, 1962), p. 80; for a similar pattern of skepticism and conservatism, see the discussion of Protagoras, in Volume I, 17–18.

30. S. Wolin, "Hume and Conservatism," *American Political Science Review*, 48 (1954), p. 1000 (this work is cited in the text as Wolin).

31. Miller, *Philosophy and Ideology*, pp. 187–205.

32. Mill, "Bentham," pp. 79–80.

33. Mill, "Bentham," p. 80.

34. For this approach, see the discussion of Bentham in Chapter 8.

35. See below, Chapter 8.

TEXTS CITED

Clarke, S. *Discourse Concerning the Unchangeable Obligations of Natural Religion.* In *The British Moralists.* L. A. Selby-Bigge, ed. Two vols in one. 1897. Rpt. Indianapolis, 1964.

Greig, J., ed. *The Letters of David Hume*, 2 vols. Oxford, 1932.

Hume, D. *An Abstract of a Treatise of Human Nature.* J. M. Keynes and P. Sraffa, eds. Cambridge, 1938.

Hume, D. *Dialogues Concerning Natural Religion.* R. Popkin, ed. Indianapolis, 1980.

Hume, D. *Enquiries Concerning Human Understanding and Concerning the Principles of Morals.* L. A. Selby-Bigge, ed. 3rd ed. Revised by P. H. Nidditch. Oxford, 1975.

Hume, D. *Essays: Moral, Political and Literary.* E. Miller, ed. Revised ed. Indianapolis, 1985.

Hume, D. "My Own Life." In *The Letters of David Hume.* J. Greig, ed. 2 vols. Oxford, 1932.

Hume, D. *A Treatise of Human Nature.* E. Mossner, ed. Harmondsworth, England, 1969.

Montesquieu. *The Spirit of the Laws.* A. Cohler, B. C. Miller, H. S. Stone, eds. and trans. Cambridge, 1989.

FURTHER READING

Ayer, A.J. *Hume.* Oxford, 1980.

Chappel, V. C., ed. *Hume.* Garden City, NY, 1966.

Miller, D. *Philosophy and Ideology in Hume's Political Thought.* Oxford, 1981.

Mossner, E. C. *The Life of David Hume.* 2nd ed. Oxford, 1980.

Norton, D. F. *David Hume: Common-Sense Moralist, Sceptical Metaphysician.* Princeton, 1982.

Passmore, J. *Hume's Intentions.* Cambridge, 1952.

Smith, N. K. *The Philosophy of David Hume.* London, 1941.

Stewart, J. B. *The Moral and Political Philosophy of David Hume.* New York, 1963.

Whelan, F. G. *Order and Artifice in Hume's Political Philosophy.* Princeton, 1985.

Wolff, R. P. "Hume's Theory of Mental Activity." In *Hume.* V. C. Chappel, ed. Garden City, NY, 1966.

Wolin, S. "Hume and Conservatism." *American Political Science Review*, 48 (1954).

Chapter

5

Montesquieu

Charles Louis Secondat, Baron de la Brede et de Montesquieu, was born in 1689 to a noble family.[1] His education was mainly in the law, as he prepared to assume a hereditary seat on the *parlement* of Bordeaux. The parlements were judicial institutions. Montesquieu's responsibilities centered on the administration of criminal justice, including interrogating suspects under torture, sentencing convicted criminals to the galleys and penal colonies, and executions. He was also active in the Academy of Bordeaux, displaying interest in scientific research, and doing original work in different fields, though on a somewhat amateur level. With the publication of *The Persian Letters* in 1721, he achieved enormous literary success. The combination of literary renown and noble ancestry gave Montesquieu entree into the literary salons of the French aristocracy. He spent considerable time in Parisian society, and then traveled abroad to Germany, Italy, and England, where he spent two years, and came to know many important political leaders. His *Considerations on the Causes of the Greatness of the Romans and their Decline* was published in 1734, and his greatest work, *The Spirit of the Laws*, in 1748, with the former work examining on a smaller scale important themes of the latter. *Spirit of the Laws* was, again, an enormous success. It was printed in numerous editions, and earned its author international renown. The work was, however, attacked on religious grounds. Montesquieu responded with his *Defense of the Spirit of the Laws*, which, like his other works, was published anonymously. But despite his efforts, *Spirit of the Laws* was placed on the Index in 1751.

It is upon *Spirit of the Laws* that Montesquieu's reputation as a political theorist primarily rests. The product of twenty years' labor, the work is, as we shall see, sprawling and somewhat unfocused, but Montesquieu's genius is apparent throughout its thirty-one books and hundreds of chapters. From the work's welter of materials emerge two immensely important contributions to political theory, on which we will concentrate: Montesquieu's pioneering efforts in social science, and his classic analysis of the British Constitution, and more broadly, of the conditions necessary for political liberty. Inklings of both themes are apparent in *The Persian Letters*. Despite this work's sensational tale of harems and eunuchs, *The Persian Letters* is far more than an entertainment. With it we will begin.

THE PERSIAN LETTERS

The Persian Letters was published anonymously in Amsterdam in 1721, though Montesquieu's authorship was well known. It is an epistolary novel, which recounts the extended journey of two wealthy Persians, Usbek and Rica, through the Middle East and to Paris. The two exchange letters with friends back home, and with another friend, Rhedi, who is also traveling in Europe. The epistolary device affords Montesquieu the satirical opportunity to observe aspects of French society from an outsider's point of view. More than this, Usbek possesses a harem, housed in a seraglio. In his correspondence with and about the wives he has left behind and the eunuchs charged with guarding them, Montesquieu opens a highly entertaining but disturbing window into Oriental society. The different elements are combined with great literary skill. A cleric to whom Montesquieu showed the manuscript remarked that it would "sell like bread." The work was such a sensation that booksellers in Holland were reported to have pulled passersby by the sleeve, saying, "Monsieur, get me *The Persian Letters*" (Shackleton, pp. 27–28).

Assuming the perspective of foreign travellers allows Montesquieu to scrutinize and poke fun at French society. Rica especially is presented as young and curious, remarking on everything he sees. In one letter he describes the theater and opera from the point of view of someone who has little idea what is going on and has trouble distinguishing between actors on stage and the audience watching them (*PL*, 28).[2] Other letters present similar, lighthearted looks at Parisian society, for instance satirizing aristocratic salons and barely concealed marital infidelity. Religion is a central concern. In the Persians' eyes, monks are "dervishes"; the Pope is "a magician" (e.g., *PL*, 24). Christian and Moslem religious beliefs and practices are frequently contrasted, with a strong suggestion of the relativity of religious truth. Rica observes that if triangles were able to invent gods, they would have three sides (*PL*, 59). Usbek, who is less lighthearted, reflects on such topics as declining population, French politics, and theological questions. It is said that Usbek is something of a stand-in for Montesquieu, that Montesquieu was frequently addressed as Usbek after publication of the work.[3] It is not unlikely that many of Usbek's ruminations on religion and politics express Montesquieu's own views.

Aspects of European society are criticized more severely, for instance religious intolerance. A central theme of many of Montesquieu's works is the oppressive effects of different social and political institutions. In *The Persian Letters*, in commenting on different forms of government, Usbek notes that he prefers the one "that leads men in the manner most appropriate to their leanings and inclinations" (*PL*, 80). But his observations turn up numerous cases in which institutions squelch natural inclinations. The inhumanity of Christian practices is illustrated by certain dervishes in Spain and Portugal "who stand for no nonsense and will have a man burned as if he were straw" (*PL*, 29). In the same letter, Rica notes that, in the eyes of these judges, the accused is always assumed to be guilty and must prove himself innocent. The French reader cannot take comfort that such disreputable practices are confined to Spain and Portugal. Usbek makes clear references to Louis XIV's revocation of the Edict of Nantes, in 1685, which had provided religious toleration for Protestants, and so to the revival of religious persecution in France (*PL*, 85). Though the French monarchy is generally criticized only indirectly, at one point Usbek reports Louis XIV's remark that of all the governments in the world, he prefers those of Persia and the Turkish sultan (*PL*, 37). The comparison between French monarchy and Oriental despotism is not flattering. We will see below exactly what Montesquieu thinks of despotism, which casts a dark shadow across his political theory in *Spirit of the Laws*.

Throughout *The Persian Letters*, one of Montesquieu's central concerns is ethical relativism. In Volume I, we distinguished between two different claims, both of which are commonly referred to as "ethical relativism."[4] First, "factual relativism" is the observation that moral beliefs and customs are widely different in different societies. This discovery does not necessarily entail any specific view as to which—if any—of these conflicting beliefs is objectively valid. "Moral relativism," the second view, frequently[5] follows from factual relativism. Briefly, this is the claim that there *are no* absolute moral truths. What *is* right varies from society to society. For instance, a typical argument of this type might be that if people practice cannibalism in country *A* and abhor cannibalism in country *B*, this indicates the fact that killing and eating people is right in *A* and wrong in *B*. In objective terms, then, it is neither right nor wrong. There is no right or wrong beyond people's practices.

A major theme of *The Persian Letters* is factual relativism. Fundamental to Montesquieu's social theorizing is the discovery that different countries have different customs and moral and religious beliefs. His concern with the relativity of religious truth has been noted. This undoubtedly contributed to his commitment to religious toleration. The fact that religions vary from country to country suggests—at least in *The Persian Letters*—that no single religion is true. And so it makes no sense for adherents of one religion to persecute adherents of others.

From the relativity of religious views, it is a short step to moral views. If people believe one thing in Paris and quite the opposite in Persia, one is led to ask which belief is correct. Through the observations of his Persian travelers, Montesquieu presents a foreign perspective on French beliefs and customs, and so skillfully juxtaposes the conflicting views of East and West. But it is unlikely that he believes all moral views are equally true (or false). Speaking through Usbek, Montesquieu addresses the question of moral relativism. Usbek expresses his faith in the existence of a true moral standard that is unaffected by the variety of beliefs in the world:

> Justice is a true relationship of appropriateness which exists between two things, and this relationship is always the same, no matter by whom considered, whether it be god, or an angel, or finally a man. (*PL*, 83)

We will return to the idea that justice is a particular kind of relationship when we examine *The Spirit of the Laws*. For now we should note that if justice is real—if it is "eternal and not dependent on the conventions of men" (*PL*, 83)—then it must be pursued. Important political problems inevitably emerge, especially how we can seek justice in our political lives, and the particular institutions most suited to this task.

Even at this early stage of his career, Montesquieu displays strong interest in political questions. For instance, he uses the outsider's perspective to comment on the strengths and weaknesses of different forms of government (*PL*, 102–104). More important, his concern with the relationship between morality and politics is expressed in a series of Usbek's letters which recount the story of a small Arabian tribe, the Troglodytes.[5] The story is in three parts. The first concerns the consequences of living without virtue. The Troglodytes live without moral scruples. They elect magistrates but then ignore them. When they submit disputes to mediation, they refuse to obey if they do not like the decisions. When others are in need, they refuse to help, and so no one comes to their aid when they are in need. Rather than working, they steal from those who do work, but then fall into vicious conflict over the spoils. When they are ravaged by a cruel plague, a physician from outside comes to their aid. But once they have recovered, they refuse to pay him for his services. Their viciousness has consequences. When the plague returns, they appeal to the physician to help them once again. But he responds: "Be off . . . be off, evil men. You have in your souls a poison more fatal than the disease you seek to cure. You do not deserve to occupy a place on the earth, for you have no humanity, and the rules of justice are unknown to you" (*PL*, 11). Left to their own devices, the Troglodytes perish miserably.

Montesquieu's tale of the Troglodytes is obviously presented in reference to Hobbes's account of life in the state of nature. According to Hobbes, in a natural situation in which adherence to norms is impossible, human life is "solitary, poor, nasty, brutish, and short." Montesquieu was greatly interested in Hobbes's political theory, and waged a lifelong struggle against it.[6] Like Hobbes, Montesquieu believed life would be insupportable if people did not follow moral rules, and so the Troglodytes perish.

Of the tribe of Troglodytes, two members survive. They are men of extraordinary virtue, and because of their virtue they prosper. They love their families, are loved in return, and see their children grow into virtuous citizens. They worship the gods and live in joyful frugality, celebrating the bounty of nature and the gifts of fellowship with one another. As each works more for the benefit of others than himself, all exert themselves and all prosper. When savages attack them, each is willing to make the supreme sacrifice for friends and family, and the savages are put to flight. Thus the rewards of virtue are clearly seen, as the fruits of injustice are revealed in the first part of the tale.

But eventually, these Troglodytes grow weary of virtue's exertions. They choose an upright man to be their king. But the designated leader is taken aback and rebukes them: "Your virtue is beginning to weigh upon you. In the present state of affairs, with no chief, you must be virtuous in spite of yourselves. Otherwise you couldn't subsist and would fall into the misfortunes of your forefathers. But this yoke seems too hard to you. You prefer to be subjects of a prince and obey his laws, for they are less restrictive than your customs." As Usbek's narrative ends, the unwilling leader laments the day the Troglodytes came to require any ruler other than virtue.

As we will see in subsequent sections, central themes of Montesquieu's political theory are clearly touched on here. For instance, in the course of development of the virtuous Troglodytes, we detect foreshadowings of Montesquieu's eventual dissatisfaction with the republic as a form of state. In requiring virtue from its citizens, a republic makes demands that can be satisfied only under unusual conditions. *The Spirit of the Laws* is said to represent the labor of twenty years—as Montesquieu says in its "Preface" (*SL*, p. xlv). But he notes in a letter written soon after its publication that he had worked on the book for his entire life. (*Oeuvres*, III, 1200). This is certainly borne out by his treatment of some of the work's central themes in *The Persian Letters*.

Throughout his works, Montesquieu approaches moral questions—including questions of moral relativism—in a distinctive fashion, primarily through their relationship to social and political institutions. If justice is real, then it should be promoted by social practices. Among the many institutions examined in *The Persian Letters*, perhaps the most important is the treatment of women. Montesquieu's presentation of the practices of different societies calls attention to the question of how women *should* be treated, and by extension, proper treatment of all people.

One of Usbek and Rica's main discoveries is the variance of women's treatment between East and West. Arriving in Leghorn, Usbek remarks on the great liberty women there enjoy. They can look at men from a kind of window and go out wearing only one veil—in contrast to Persian women, who wear four (*PL*, 23). This liberty is of course insignificant in comparison to that of women in France. Encountering the freedom of European women prompts Rica to ask whether this is natural:

> It is quite another question to know whether the natural law subjects women to men. 'No,' a philosopher with a great penchant for the ladies told me the other day. 'Nature never dictated such a law. The dominion we hold over them is a veritable tyranny.' (*PL*, 38)

Whether the Asiatic system is domestic tyranny or sanctioned by nature is a central concern of the work.

Though Usbek's reflections on conditions in France, and on morality, religion, and politics, probably express Montesquieu's own views, Usbek is very much a Persian rather than a Frenchman in his domestic affairs. As noted above, he has a harem and several wives, of whom he is absolute master. Though he is absent from Persia for many years, he administers his domestic domain from afar, and is tormented by its slide into anarchy. Discussion of the seraglio is far more than Montesquieu's means of injecting an element of exotic titillation into a work of social theory. The harem theme provides the work's moral center. Though Usbek is a worldly observer of foreign customs, his letters reveal a less acute understanding of his own affairs. He believes his wives love him and live only for him. The unfolding of the novel reveals how wrong he is. In the final letters, the treachery of Roxane is revealed. This wife, whose virtue he extols (*PL*, 20), is found to have despised him, and deceived him at every turn. She has given herself to a lover, and in a final act of defiance poisons herself, declaring her hatred for Usbek even as she dies.

The seraglio is an institution that stands in defiance of nature, frustrating natural inclinations at every turn. For the sake of love, Usbek's wives are imprisoned, transformed into instruments for his enjoyment. The absurdity of the institution is seen in countless episodes. For instance, though Usbek travels outside of Persia for years, the wives' imprisonment continues. One wife, Fatima, describes her misery, having violent desires while deprived of the only man who can satisfy them (*PL*, 7). Two unfortunate passersby are murdered by the eunuchs, for having stumbled upon the wives on an outing and so seen what exists for Usbek's eyes alone (*PL*, 47). The institution's deforming effects are physically embodied in the eunuchs' mutilation.

The epistolary form of the novel allows the seraglio's psychological consequences to be communicated in an especially vivid manner as different characters reflect upon their situations. The reader is not merely *told* what the seraglio does to people. By identifying with different characters, the reader experiences something of its restraints. (Thus, reading the novel is far more powerful than being told about it.)

As the harem theme unfolds, illusions are stripped away. In the same manner that the outsider's perspective sheds new light on aspects of French society, Usbek is driven to see himself—and one wonders if he is really more capable of this than the absurd Europeans he observes. Regardless of the degree of his self-knowledge, however, by the end of the work he stands bare before the reader. At the end of the novel, the reader reflects back upon the relationship between Usbek and Roxane—and so also, by extension, his relationships with his other wives as well. The reader will likely recall Usbek's account of how he eventually won Roxane over after their marriage, though she resisted his advances for two months and on one occasion seized a knife and threatened to kill him. According to Usbek, "You looked upon me as an enemy who had outraged you and not as a husband who had loved you." But things eventually changed:

> When you enhance the beauty of your complexion with the most beautiful of colors, when you perfume your whole body with the most precious of essences, when you embellish yourself in your finest raiment, when you seek to make yourself stand out from your companions by the grace of your dancing or the sweetness of your voice . . . I cannot imagine that you have any other motive save that of pleasing me. And when I see you blush modestly, when your eyes seek mine, when you steal your way into my heart with your sweet and flattering words, then, Roxane, I could not possibly doubt your love. (*PL*, 26)

Observations along these lines strike the reader very differently in the light of Roxane's final letter:

> How could you have thought that I was naive enough to imagine that I was put into the world only to adore your whims? That while you pampered yourself with everything, you should have the right to mortify all my desires? No! I might have lived in servitude, but I have always been free. I have rewritten your laws after the laws of nature, and my spirit has ever sustained itself in independence. (*PL*, 161)

But in order to affirm her freedom, Roxane must end her life.

The world of the seraglio is eventually revealed as a domestic tyranny, with Usbek its tyrant. It is for his sake that so much suffering exists. To enhance and gratify his appetites, the desires of many others are thwarted. As one eunuch writes, "Great God! How much must be done to keep just one man happy!" (*PL*, 22). Thus it is a sad irony that the seraglio causes Usbek as much misery as happiness, as he is tormented by the thought that other men might also enjoy what is his alone. As one of his wives writes to him,

> Even in this very prison where you hold me, I am freer than you. You could not possibly redouble your concern for guarding me without my drawing pleasure from your worry. Your suspicions, your jealousy, and your heartaches are all so many proofs of your dependency. (*PL*, 62)

To enforce his will, he orders ferocious measures against his errant wives and others who have deceived him, emerging as "cruel Usbek" (*PL* 156, 158). Though others actually wield the sword, they are his instruments, servants of "what is now most precious to [him] in the world," his vengeance (*PL*, 153).

Even when he is in his harem, Usbek is surrounded by slaves. A striking lesson of the contrast between relatively open French society and the world of the seraglio is that a person can be free only if the people with whom he deals are also free. Usbek can be truly loved by his wives only if they love him freely. But the seraglio makes this impossible. It forces him "to live with slaves whose hearts and minds always reflect the baseness of their social position," whose feelings of baseness destroy the master's own feelings of virtue (*PL*, 34). In a despotism, the despot too is a victim.

The dehumanizing effects of the harem are manifested most clearly in the physical deformation of the eunuchs, who are deprived of manhood in order to serve the master. To the wives they guard and discipline, they appear as less than human (*PL*, 20). Not surprising is their overpowering jealousy of their master. The chief eunuch writes of his youth as follows:

> The effect of passion was snuffed out in me without extinguishing the cause, and far from being comforted, I found myself surrounded by objects that provoked my passion without cease. . . . As the crowning stroke to my misery, I had ever before my eyes a happy man. During these troubled times, I never led a woman to my master's bed, I never undressed her without returning to my room with rage in my heart and horrible desolation in my soul. (*PL*, 9)

The eunuch's suffering takes on an especially bitter tinge in the light of how little pleasure the harem gives Usbek.

The seraglio mutilates the eunuchs' souls as well as their bodies. As his other passions have subsided, the chief eunuch has come to find joy only in degrading the wives he serves:

> I remember always that I was born to command them, and it seems to me that I become a man again when I can still do so . . . The pleasure of making myself obeyed gives me a secret joy. When I deprive them of everything, I feel I do so for my own benefit, and indirectly, I always receive great satisfaction from it. In the seraglio it is as if I were in a small empire, and my ambition, the sole passion left to me, is satisfied a little. (*PL*, 9)

Not surprisingly, the wives retaliate by humiliating the eunuchs in return (*PL*, 9). The domestic empire is locked in psychological struggle, which degrades and causes misery for all concerned.

Thus, the seraglio emerges as a despotic social system, along the lines of the despotic political systems Montesquieu rails against in *Spirit of the Laws*. In his depiction of this institution and its effects in *The Persian Letters*, Montesquieu foreshadows the unnatural evils of despotic politics described in his greatest work.

MONTESQUIEU'S SOCIAL SCIENCE

Though Montesquieu is ever aware of the relativity of moral and religious beliefs, the mores of society, and political ideas, his relativism runs out in regard to science.[7] At one point Usbek remarks about the great accomplishments of Western theorists, who have explained the workings of the natural world according to "five or six truths," the laws of mechanics: "They have untangled chaos and have explained, by simple mechanisms, the order of divine architecture" (*PL*, 97). It was Montesquieu's lifelong goal to do something similar in regard to the workings of the social world.

In previous chapters, we have repeatedly seen the importance different thinkers placed on extending the methods of science to the social world, to provide the same illumination natural scientists had won in their areas of research. Fields such as physics, mechanics, astronomy, and physiology had experienced monumental advances. Therefore, it was widely believed that similar results were possible in the study of society. In the realm of nature, diverse phenomena—for example, the behavior of different mechanical bodies—had been seen to flow from a few simple principles. For instance, the surprisingly non-circular movement of the planets had been explained by Kepler's laws of planetary motion. The motion of bodies in both the heavens and on earth had been accounted for by Newton's laws of mechanics. Yet in the social world, variation reigned. Generations of travel writers had recorded different customs and practices throughout the world. Montesquieu's deep concern with this situation permeates *The Persian Letters*, with its theme of clashing cultures.

If such differences exist, how can they be accounted for? This question lies at the heart of Montesquieu's social inquiries. In the "Preface" to *Spirit of the Laws*, he remarks:

> I began by examining men, and I believed that amidst the infinite diversity of laws and mores, they were not led by their fancies alone. (p. xliii)

But if men's fancies have not given rise to the bewildering variety of existing laws, what has? In attempting to explain the factors responsible for the laws and mores of different societies, Montesquieu does pioneering work in the scientific study of society. *Spirit of the Laws* is regarded as a classic work in such fields as sociology, political science, and comparative jurisprudence. According to Émile Durkheim, one of the great figures in the history of sociology, "It was Montesquieu who first laid down the fundamental principles of social science."[8]

Montesquieu believed he had discovered the underlying factors responsible for the laws and customs of different societies. His meaning becomes clear if we distinguish two levels of causal analysis. Consider, for example, the outbreak of World War I, which erupted about 160 years after Montesquieu's death. One could say that the war was precipitated by the assassination of the Austrian Archduke, Francis Ferdinand, by a Serbian nationalist. As a result of this event, the European powers entered upon a series of specific steps that led to war. But to say this assassination was the *cause* of war is obviously superficial. Much more important was the complex of factors responsible for the strained relationships between the countries of Europe during that period. In preceding years, war had *almost* broken out several times. If we concentrate on this deeper level, we will see that the assassination was only the *occasion* for the outbreak of war. Because of the more fundamental causes of the strained international situation, war was likely to break out on *some* occasion. If it had not been this event, some other event would have set it off.

Analysis along these lines distinguishes between immediate and more fundamental causes. A distinction along these lines is central to Montesquieu's analysis of the fall of the Roman Republic in his *Considerations*. On a superficial level, one could say that the Republic's downfall was caused by the actions of particular people. Because Julius Caesar lusted for power and turned his army against Rome, the Republic was overthrown. But once again, if we study the matter more carefully, we may conclude that Caesar's conduct was only the *occasion* for the Republic's downfall. Rather than focusing on the particular actions of particular human beings, we should look at the more fundamental, underlying factors that made it possible for these actions to have far-reaching effects. In the *Considerations*, Montesquieu seeks out the underlying factors. While previous historians had emphasized the actions of particular people, Montesquieu argues that if their conduct had not brought about the Republic's collapse, the conduct of others would have: "If Caesar and Pompey had thought like Cato, others would have thought like Caesar and Pompey; and the republic, destined to perish, would have been dragged to the precipice by another hand" (Chap. 11, p. 108).

Concentrating on underlying causes lays bare the inner logic of events. It follows from the assumptions of previous historians that if particular people had acted differently, the outcome would have been fundamentally different as well. Thus this view implies that historical events, even critically important events of the magnitude of World War I and the fall of the Roman Republic, are subject to contingency and chance. Montesquieu contests this view. Even if the behavior of particular people might have been different, this was only the *occasion* for an important event. If we examine underlying factors, we can see that something like the event was bound to happen. If one specific occasion did not trigger it, another would have. Important events are not contingent; they follow an underlying logic. A general statement of Montesquieu's view is presented in Chapter 18 of the *Considerations*:

> It is not chance that rules the world. Ask the Romans, who had a continuous sequence of successes when they were guided by a certain plan, and an uninterrupted sequence of reverses when they followed another. There are general causes, moral and physical, which act in every monarchy, elevating it, maintaining it, or hurling it to the ground. All accidents are controlled by these causes. And if the chance of one battle—that is, a particular cause—has brought a state to ruin, some general cause made it necessary for that state to perish from a single battle. In a word, the main trend draws with it all particular accidents. (Chap. 18, p. 169)

In *Spirit of the Laws* Montesquieu argues along similar lines. Early in the eighteenth century, Charles XII of Sweden fought the Northern War against Russia, Denmark, and Poland. After winning a number of stunning victories, his army was decisively defeated at the Battle of Poltava (1709), and he was forced to flee. Again, for Montesquieu, to attribute the course of the war to particular events misses the point. More fundamental principles were at work:

> It was not Poltava that ruined Charles; had he not been destroyed at that place, he would have been destroyed at another. Accidents of fortune are easily rectified; one cannot avert events that continuously arise from the nature of things. (*SL*, 10.13)

The central task of Montesquieu's scientific research is to unearth the fundamental factors underlying the laws and customs of different peoples. To the ordinary observer, laws assume their form because of the actions of particular people. On a given day, a certain lawgiver or assembly makes one particular decision rather than another. But for Montesquieu, this analysis is superficial. The actions of lawmaking authorities are determined by deep-seated factors, of which they themselves might not be fully aware. It is not chance that rules the social world; what strikes the uninformed observer as an "infinite diversity of laws and mores" can be traced to a few fundamental principles, which it is Montesquieu's aim to bring to light.

A clear understanding of Montesquieu's task is impeded by an ambiguity in the word "law." The term has prescriptive and descriptive senses.[9] In the former, a law is an edict or command made by an appropriate authority, which is backed by force. Laws in this sense tell subjects what they *ought* to do, or are required to do, with the understanding that they will be punished if they do not comply. The word has another sense, as in the "laws of nature" discussed by scientists. These are descriptive rather than prescriptive. Kepler's laws of planetary motion explain how a body of observed phenomena *do* behave. These laws do not rest on the commands of authorities—unless we say that God issued commands to natural phenomena in the process of creating the universe.

Montesquieu moves between these senses of "law" without attempting to distinguish them. In the title of the work, *Spirit of the Laws*, the word "laws" refers to the laws and customs of different societies, and so to the commands of appropriate authorities— prescriptive laws. As we will see, the "spirit" of these laws is the network of factors that make them work, and so also explain how they came to be. But in the famous first sentence of the work, Montesquieu uses "laws" in the descriptive sense:

> Laws, taken in the broadest meaning are the necessary relations deriving from the nature of things; in this sense, all beings have their laws: the divinity has its laws, the material world has its laws, the intelligences superior to man have their laws, the beasts have their laws, man has his laws. (*SL*, 1.1)

According to Montesquieu, these different kinds of laws explain how different entities *do* behave. They are descriptive laws. As his definition indicates, Montesquieu views the conduct of these entities in terms of relationships, of the form: "if *A*, then *B*." As examples of laws of the physical world, he mentions mechanical laws discovered by natural scientists. What appears to the uninformed observer as random motion is actually determined by a few simple principles, which can be expressed as relationships:

> These rules are a consistently established relation. Between one moving body and another moving body, it is in accord with relations of mass and velocity that all motions are received, increased, diminished, or lost; every diversity is *uniformity*, every change is *consistency*. (*SL*, 1.1)

Montesquieu believes in the fundamental rationality of the world, that it is governed by reason, and so that there are laws of the different orders of existence, the behavior of each of which is according to discoverable relationships. We will return to these relationships, especially in regard to those that hold in the moral world (*SL*, 1.1), below.

Montesquieu's central task is to add to this list of (descriptive) laws an additional kind, which explain the nature of human enactments. The explanatory relationships that interest him are between the laws of a given society and a range of causal factors. In Book I, Chapter 3, he notes the following factors:

> [Laws] should be related to the *physical aspects* of the country; to the climate, be it freezing, torrid, or temperate; to the properties of the terrain, its location and extent; to the way of life of the people, be they plowmen, hunters, or herdsmen; they should

relate to the degree of liberty that the constitution can sustain, to the religion of the
inhabitants, their inclinations, their wealth, their number, their commerce, their mores,
and their manners; finally, the laws are related to one another, to their origin, to the
purpose of the legislator, and to the order of things on which they are established. They
must be considered from all these points of view. (*SL*, 1.3)

Montesquieu is interested in relationships between this range of factors and the eventual
laws a society will have. These underlying factors shape the laws of different societies more
profoundly than the actions of individual legislators (which Montesquieu includes as one
causal factor among many). His aim is to establish the (descriptive) laws that explain the
workings of the laws and customs (and so prescriptive laws) of particular societies.

His great discovery is that (man-made) laws and customs function as parts of overall
social systems. They serve specific functions in their societies and differ in accordance with
a society's fundamental characteristics. Like Aristotle before him, Montesquieu discovered
that laws are not good or bad in general; a law that is good in country X can be harmful
to Y, as circumstances differ. In different contexts, Montesquieu presents slightly different
lists of the specific factors that shape societies. In Book 19 of *Spirit of the Laws* he lists
climate, religion, laws, maxims of government, precedents, morals, and customs (*SL*, 19.4).
Together these factors give rise to a nation's "general spirit" (*esprit général*), a vital force with
which all effective laws should be in accord. For various reasons, both conscious and
unconscious, the legislation of different societies has been shaped by these factors. Though
Montesquieu is never entirely clear on the causal processes at work,[10] a likely mechanism
is as follows.

The basic characteristics of a society place clear limits on the laws that will work in
it. Through trial and error suitable laws are discovered and enacted. Thus if a given rule
of property transactions does more harm than good, it will be altered until a proper rule
is found. Over time, proper rules will be adopted—and so are explained by the underlying
characteristics.

Thus Montesquieu observes numerous striking correlations between specific (man-
made) laws and other elements of societies. To cite only one of many famous examples, he
notes a general relationship between the size of a country and the form of government it
will have. Hence it is natural for a republic to have a small territory (*SL*, 8.16), while a
monarchy tends to be of moderate extent (*SL*, 8.17), and a despotism tends to arise in a
large territory (*SL*, 8.19). As analyzed by Montesquieu, these relationships correspond to
modern sociological laws. He believes they are analogous to, though less perfect than, laws
of natural science. Within his lifetime Montesquieu was afforded at least some recognition
as the Newton of the social world (*Oeuvres*, III, 1478).

Montesquieu's scientific analysis is often crude. He is somewhat credulous in regard
to his use of sources. He read voraciously and tended to believe much of what he read. As
one commentator remarks, if he had something of Aristotle in him, he also had something
of Herodotus.[11] Montesquieu's analysis is often sloppy—as in his use of the concept "law."
He does not present clear definitions, and does not always abide by the ones he presents.
In composing *Spirit of the Laws* he tries too hard for literary brilliance, preferring aphorisms
to sustained analysis. These and other similar problems will be encountered below, in regard
to his political theory.

Montesquieu is also frequently criticized for paying too much attention to certain causal factors, especially climate and terrain. Thus one commentator writes:

> Instead of explaining [the history of different nations and cultures] by reference to human reason, he thought of it as due to differences in climate and geography. Man, in other words, is regarded as a part of nature, and the explanation of historical events is sought in the facts of the natural world.[12]

Though there is an element of truth to this criticism, on the whole it misrepresents Montesquieu's view. There can be no doubt about his interest in climate: "The empire of climate is the first of all empires" (*SL*, 19.14). In some parts of *Spirit of the Laws*, climate and geography are put forth as the major (if not only) causal factors behind the subjects under discussion. Two examples are the treatment of slaves and women in different societies, discussed in Books 15 and 16, respectively. In regard to climate, Montesquieu's analysis falls notably short of scientific exactitude. He argues that differences in climate produce essentially different character types. Central to his argument are climate's observable physiological effects, which he claims to have documented by examining a sheep's tongue under a microscope (*SL*, 14.2)

But in spite of these problems, Montesquieu's analysis accommodates a range of causal factors. In Book 19, after listing the different factors quoted above ("climate, religion, laws, the maxims of the government, examples of past things, mores, and manners"), he discusses their interaction as follows:

> To the extent that, in each nation, one of these causes acts more forcefully, the others yield to it. Nature and climate almost alone dominate savages; manners govern the Chinese; laws tyrannize Japan; in former times mores set the tone in Lacadaemonia; in Rome it was set by the maxims of government and the ancient mores. (*SL*, 19.4)

Thus in less developed societies, climate plays a larger role than in more developed societies. A good case could be made for the truth of this claim. In less developed societies, comparatively more energy is given to satisfying subsistence needs. With relatively undeveloped technology available, climate and geography decisively affect the way people live. But Montesquieu indicates that the preeminence of climate is not a universal truth. As societies become more developed, a wider range of factors come into play. In fact, among important causal factors he lists are existing laws and customs. Thus the laws and customs put into effect during a given period will affect (in some cases, decisively affect) the general spirit of the society, and so the laws and customs it will have at a later stage. Montesquieu's analysis is flexible, taking into account a wide range of possible causal factors.

Though thinkers before Montesquieu had attempted to extend the methods of science to the social world, and some had anticipated certain of his findings, none of his predecessors attempted this on so grand a scale, or with the enormous learning Montesquieu brought to the task. Though much of his analysis would be improved if it were less literary and more precise, the brilliance of his literary style undoubtedly served him well in increasing the size of his audience. In spite of the very real shortcomings of his social science, one must conclude that Montesquieu's exalted place at the beginning of modern social science is justified. As a noted commentator says: "I do not consider Montesquieu a precursor of sociology, but rather one of its great theorists."[13]

TYPES OF GOVERNMENTS

The centerpiece of Montesquieu's social science is his classification of governments. He presents three main forms: the republic, monarchy, and despotism. A distinction between two kinds of republics—democracy and aristocracy—yields four forms in all. Montesquieu was undoubtedly familiar with the traditional six-form classification of constitutions (see p. 23). According to this scheme, constitutions are distinguished according to two factors, number of rulers and quality of their rule. Thus we have good and bad forms of rule by one man, by the few, and by the many.[14] Montesquieu obviously breaks from this classification in the specific forms he presents. More important, however, is the basis for his classification.

In classifying different forms of government, Montesquieu focuses on two variables which he calls a government's "nature" and "principle." The nature of a government is determined by the major institutions in which political power is lodged. The principle of a government is the spiritual quality that animates its laws.

In discussing types of states, Montesquieu has in mind complete political organisms, comprised of a form of government and society, situated in a certain environment, with a particular climate, and so on. As we have seen, in each state, this network of factors determines the government that will arise. For the republic Montesquieu envisions an ancient political form, especially Rome or Sparta. He views this as a small unit, a city-state. The republic is relatively poor and uncultured, with little attention given to economic or family matters. The citizens are relatively equal economically as well as politically. Their lives are largely given over to military affairs and the state. Montesquieu's main model of monarchy is the France of his own day. He views this as a larger entity, with social and political systems characterized by vestiges of feudalism. There are developed social and political hierarchies. Each person has his place and his rank, and there is relatively little community between ranks. The despotism is Montesquieu's political nightmare. He sees this as a system of absolute inequality: one man rules, with all others his slaves. Montesquieu's model here is vast in size, most likely a desert empire, in which women are chattel, and the entire realm is subject to the despot's whim.

The nature of each kind of state is inextricably bound up with these overall types. The nature of a republic is that power is in the hands of the people, in either of two different ways. In a democracy the people rule directly; in an aristocracy a portion of the people holds power. The nature of each of these forms centers on the institutions through which either the whole or part of the people wields power, for example, the means through which they make decisions and through which officials are chosen.

The nature of monarchy is rule by one man, with his power checked in various ways. Most important is the existence of fundamental laws, binding on the king as well as the people, and what Montesquieu calls "intermediate" powers, especially the nobility. In a monarchy the king is part of a relatively stable, fixed political system. His power is limited by independent sources of power, especially the nobility: "In a way, the nobility is of the essence of monarchy, whose fundamental maxim is: *no monarch, no nobility; no nobility, no monarch*" (*SL*, 2.4). In order to persist, these other power centers must be protected: "If you abolish the prerogatives of the lords, clergy, nobility, and towns in a monarchy," the government will change to either a popular state or a despotism (ibid.).

In a despotism, like a monarchy, power is in the hands of one man. But this government is characterized by an absence of checks. The ruler is the source of all power. He makes the laws; in fact, his will is law. According to Montesquieu, in this form of state, the ruler gives himself up to debauchery and so cannot wield power himself. Thus the appointment of a chief minister, or vizir, is a basic characteristic of despotism (*SL*, 2.5).

To this point, it might appear that Montesquieu's classification of constitutions does not differ greatly from the traditional one, aside from the fact that he presents fewer forms and connects them up with overall social systems. But Montesquieu's classification is original in focusing on psychological features of the different states that are essential for the proper functioning of their laws. Montesquieu refers to these as *principles*:

> There is this difference between the nature of the government and its principle; its nature is that which make it what it is, and its principle, that which make it act. The one is its particular structure, and the other is the human passions that set it in motion. (*SL*, 3.1)

The principle of a government is its vital spirit. It gives the laws life and ideally should permeate all aspects of the state.

The principle of a republic is virtue. Montesquieu is careful to distinguish this "political virtue" from Christian virtue. The virtue of a republic is "love of the homeland, that is, love of equality" (*SL*, "Author's foreword," p. xli). For people successfully to govern themselves, they must be willing to set aside their own interests in favor of the public interest. What Montesquieu has in mind is most clearly seen in ancient Rome and Sparta. Both of these were inhabited by citizen-soldiers, who willingly sacrificed everything for their cities, with little regard for wealth or personal advancement. In describing the republic, Montesquieu looks backward through time. Virtue is the characteristic of the citizens of the two most successful ancient republics.

In an aristocracy, power is in the hands of a part of the people. This ruling group confronts few institutional limits on their power. To make sure they do not abuse it, they must possess moderation, which is the governing passion, or principle, of this form of state. As in the republic, the necessary characteristic is a patriotic virtue, not "one that comes from faintheartedness and from laziness of soul" (*SL*, 3.4).

In a monarchy the principle is honor. The stability of this form of state depends on maintaining the prerogatives of the intermediate ranks. Honor is self-interest attached to citizens' particular positions. "The nature of *honor* is to demand preferences and distinctions" (*SL*, 3.7). As each person demands the prerogatives of his rank, he acts to protect the system as a whole. Thus monarchy is maintained in spite of the self-interest of its members:

> You could say that it is like the system of the universe, where there is a force constantly repelling all bodies from the center and a force of gravitation attracting them to it. Honor makes all the parts of the body politic move; its very action binds them, and each person works for the common good, believing he works for his individual interests. (*SL*, 3.7)

The principle of a despotism is fear. In this state, the power of the ruler is without limit. All others are subject to his commands. For them to obey, they must be afraid not to:

> [W]hen in a despotic government the prince ceases for a moment to raise his arm, when he cannot instantly destroy those in the highest places, all is lost, for when the spring of the government, which is *fear*, no longer exists, the people no longer have a protector. (*SL*, 3.9)

Throughout *Spirit of the Laws*, Montesquieu describes this government in the blackest terms. With its absence of redeeming features, despotism verges on a caricature of itself. Montesquieu says that he "cannot speak of these monstrous governments without shuddering" (*SL*, 3.9).

The principles of the different states is central to Montesquieu's analysis. Because it gives life to the state as a whole, and so to all its laws, a state's principle is responsible for the proper functioning of the particular laws. As maintenance of the principle is central to a state's preservation, corruption always begins with its principle (*SL*, 8.1). If the principle is infected, it will spoil all the laws: "the best laws become bad and turn against the state." On the other hand, when the principle is secure, "bad laws have the effect of good ones; the force of the principle pulls everything along" (*SL*, 8.11).

Montesquieu took great pride in his discovery of the principles of different states. In the "Preface" to *Spirit of the Laws*, he describes his struggle with his material, until he discovered them:

> Many times I began this work and many times abandoned it; a thousand times I cast to the wind the pages I had written . . . I followed my object without forming a design; I knew neither rules nor exceptions; I found the truth only to lose it. But when I discovered my principles, all that I had sought came to me, and in the course of twenty years, I saw my work begin, grow, move ahead, and end. (*SL*, Preface, p. xlv)

He notes the principles' central place in his thought. The histories of all nations are "but their consequences," and they are responsible for all particular laws (*SL*, Preface, p. xliii).

THE SPIRIT OF THE LAWS

The principle of a government provides its vital force, its "spirit," in the sense of what distinguishes an animate being from an inanimate one. The spirit of a state infuses all its laws, giving them life if they are in accord with it, sapping their strength if they are not. In a properly constituted state, there is a relationship of mutual reinforcement between the principle and particular laws. It invigorates the laws, enabling them to function properly. Properly constituted laws, in turn, strengthen the principle and so increase the state's vitality.

The relationship between laws and principles explains why no law is good or bad in itself. As noted above, laws and customs exist as parts of overall systems. A law that is in accordance with the principle of one state will conflict with that of another. Thus a particular law that works well in a republic would damage a monarchy; what is good for a despotism is not good for other forms of state.

This line of argument is supported with countless examples throughout *Spirit of the Laws*. To the extent the work has a systematic theme, this centers upon the relationships between different kinds of laws and the principles of different states. Having discussed laws in general in Book 1, and then the nature and principles of the different states in Books 2 and 3, Montesquieu discusses different kinds of particular laws. A glance at the work's table of contents indicates the extent of his grasp. Book 4 discusses laws of education. Book 5 deals with the relationship between particular laws and a state's fundamental laws. Book 6 addresses civil and criminal laws. Book 7 deals with sumptuary laws (concerning extravagant expenditure) and the treatment of women. Military matters are discussed in Books 9 and 10. Criminal laws and punishments are discussed in Book 12. Taxes, climate, slavery, domestic slavery, and political servitude are discussed in Books 13 through 17. Additional subjects are treated in other books.

Throughout these (and other) portions of the work, Montesquieu's plan of analysis is apparent. He shows how particular laws of each kind are suited to different regimes. His main scientific argument is that the fit (or to use his term, relationship) between a law and its state explains how the former arose. To some extent, however, this argument is lost in a welter of details and illustrations. Extraneous matter is presented—often it appears for its own sake. Montesquieu appears to be unable to resist a striking image, anecdote, or turn of phrase. More seriously, he runs together causes and effects. We have seen that he is flexible in his analysis of causal factors. Not only are laws caused by the particular factors that give a state its distinctive characteristics, but once enacted, they too become causes and influence the course of future development. Presumably, because laws can play both roles, Montesquieu does not carefully distinguish between causes and effects. Intermixed in his discussion of particular laws that are shaped by, but also help shape, the principles of different states is discussion of basic geographical and climatic factors, which are not the work of human beings, and so are causes only, never effects. If we carefully sort out the different components of Montesquieu's analysis, his main argument would look something like this:

(1) The country's major features which are predetermined and so given (geography, climate, and to a lesser extent, means of subsistence, etc.) and (2) basic man-made features (especially religion and important customs)

determine (3) the government it has, defined by its nature,

which also entails (4) the government's principle,

which in turn determines (5) the particular laws the country will have, in regard to the range of subjects discussed throughout the work.

An argument along these lines constitutes the centerpiece of *Spirit of the Laws*. But it is more rigid than what Montesquieu presents. To some extent this is because of the work's shortage of careful analysis. But also, because of his vast knowledge and experience of different countries, Montesquieu is highly sensitive to the differences between peoples and governments and is reluctant to reduce their development to rigid formulas. To cite one example, as we have noted, as well as being shaped by the factors already in existence, the laws of a given country help shape subsequent laws. Because he is aware of the reciprocal interaction of causal factors, Montesquieu resists clear lines of causation. Accordingly, he would probably view this schema as objectionably rigid, in some respects verging on the crude geographical and climatic determinism he is often believed to uphold.

The relationship between principles and particular laws can be illustrated with a few examples. To begin with the republic, as we have noted, Montesquieu's models for this state are generally taken from the past, especially Rome and Sparta. In the republic, everything depends on the people's ability to govern themselves without external restraints, and so on their virtue. Virtue in turn requires a small state and relative economic equality. With wealth equally divided, there can be no luxury, which in turn contributes to virtue, while luxury fosters self-interest and so undermines this spirit:

> So far as luxury is established in a republic, so far does the spirit turn to the interest of the individual. For people who have to have nothing but the necessities, there is left to desire only the glory of the homeland and one's own glory. But a soul corrupted by luxury has many other desires; soon it becomes an enemy of the laws that hamper it. (*SL*, 7.2)

For virtue to take hold, a republic must have a powerful system of education. The reason for this is clear: "political virtue is a renunciation of oneself, which is always a very painful thing" (*SL*, 4.5). Education should promote "love of the laws and the homeland." In such a state, an important role is played by the force of example:

> [I]n a republic, everything depends on establishing this love, and education should attend to inspiring it. But there is a sure way for children to have it; it is for the fathers themselves to have it. (*SL*, 4.5)

The example of Sparta suggests that education should be run by the state (*SL*, 4.6), and supported by other institutions, such as community of property. These institutions can work only in a small state, "where one can educate the general populace and raise a whole people like a family" (*SL*, 4.6–7).

In such a state, virtuous citizens should willingly obey the laws. Incentives for extraordinary virtue must be in accordance with the spirit of the state, glory rather than financial rewards or luxuries. Because of the premium placed on virtue, "the state rewards only with testimonies to that virtue" (*SL*, 5.18). Similarly, the penalties for violating the laws should center on a loss of public esteem, which is central to the citizen's life (*SL*, 6.9).

These examples should illustrate the nature of a republic. Because of the great difference between this form of state and monarchy and despotism, it is necessary that the particular laws of these states differ as well. To illustrate this, I will briefly discuss the laws bearing on similar subjects in these two states.

The maintenance of monarchy depends on preservation of its graduated series of ranks. Particular laws should contribute to this, and to the principle of honor which allows the state to function smoothly. In order to preserve the nobility and its privileges, laws of inheritance should encourage estates to be left undivided, to one child (*SL*, 5.9). Because of the nobility's distinctiveness, luxuries should be encouraged: "luxury is singularly appropriate in monarchies and . . . they do not have to have sumptuary laws" (*SL*, 7.4). Accordingly, commerce should be encouraged, to satisfy the nobility's ever-increasing needs (*SL*, 5.9).

In the monarchical state, education is not state business but can be left to the world. It should encourage the development of nobility in the virtues, frankness in the mores, and politeness in manners (*SL*, 4.2). Courtly airs bear little resemblance to the virtue of republican citizens:

> At court one finds a delicacy of taste in all things, which comes from continual use of the excesses of a great fortune, from the variety, and especially the weariness, of pleasures, from the multiplicity, even the confusion, of fancies, which, when they are pleasing, are always accepted. (*SL*, 4.2)

Education in a monarchy pays great attention to preparing for war, as this is the nobility's main function, and making sure that people do not behave below their stations.

Because of the great importance of honor, penalties for crimes should focus on this. Depriving people of "their fortune, their credit, their habits, and their pleasures" is penalty enough. Further punishment would serve no purpose, and so clemency is "the distinctive quality of monarchs" (*SL*, 6.21). In a monarchy, as one would expect, the king rewards his subjects "only with distinctions," thereby increasing their honor. Presents are not in keeping with the spirit of this state, though the nobility requires luxuries, and so the honors the prince confers should also promote wealth (*SL*, 5.18).

Montesquieu sketches despotism in bleak terms. In such a state all are subject to the one who rules, who is himself ruled by his whims. Education in such a state is intended to promote fear. Because extreme obedience is furthered by ignorance, education in a despotism should promote ignorance as well, "even in the one who commands; he does not have to deliberate, to doubt, or to reason; he has only to want" (*SL*, 4.3). In such a state, education is a lowering process: "One must take everything away in order to give something and begin by making a bad subject in order to make a good slave" (*SL*, 4.3).

Montesquieu depicts despotism as virtually without law: "Despotic government has fear as its principle; and not many laws are needed for timid, ignorant, beaten-down people" (*SL*, 5.14). Because the ruler owns everything, there are no laws of ownership. Because of his right to inherit everything, there are no laws of inheritance. Because trade belongs exclusively to the ruler, there are no laws of commerce. Given the low condition of women, there are few laws concerning the privileges of wives or dowries. "Despotism is self-sufficient; everything around it is empty" (*SL*, 6.1). The criminal justice system is similarly arbitrary. "The pasha is no sooner informed than he has the pleaders bastinadoed according to his fancy, and sent back home" (*SL*, 6.2). "Each man should know that the magistrate must not hear of him and that he owes his safety only to his nothingness" (*SL*, 6.2). As one can imagine, penalties in such a state must be severe. "There is equal cruelty among savage people, who lead a hard life, and among the people of despotic governments where fortune favors only one man exorbitantly and abuses all the rest" (*SL*, 6.9). Because moral considerations have so little force, the administration of justice requires the giving of presents (*SL*, 5.17). Similarly, with nothing else to give by way of rewards, the sovereign can give only money (*SL*, 5.18).

As one can see from this brief survey, the different states are quite different in all aspects. Their overall characteristics obviously determine the laws that will work well in each, and so those that will be adopted. Laws that promote the virtue of the citizen would undermine the honor of a monarchy's citizens and the fear required in a despotism.

Courageous, self-sacrificing citizens would be dangerous to a despotism, as the craven, ignorant citizens of a despotism would be out of place in the other forms.

To illustrate this fundamental point, Montesquieu addresses general policy questions, answering them differently for each kind of state (*SL*, 5.12). For instance, "Should the laws force a citizen to accept public employments?" Obviously, the answer to this question depends on exactly what kind of citizens one wants, and what else is necessary for the laws to accomplish. The same is true of his other questions (e.g., Should a government have censors? Should offices be sold?). The answers to these and other questions will obviously vary in different social systems.

Thus one of Montesquieu's central lessons is the *particularity* of social and political forms. There is no such thing as a good law, without reference to the overall system in which it must function. Similarly, there is no such thing as man as such. Human beings differ in different countries with widely varying laws. The same is obviously true of government and all its features. All of these will differ in different regimes.

Montesquieu is well aware that the three (or four) political forms he presents are exaggerations, what later theorists refer to as "ideal types." They are perfect models that do not correspond entirely to reality. No republic is as virtuous as what he sketches; no despotism is so bleak. In regard to this last, it should be noted that Montesquieu lumps a dizzying assortment of countries under this single classificatory category: Turkey, Persia, China, Japan, Russia, Sweden under Charles XII, and others. Obviously, not all of these conform in all respects. In addition, though each regime has its particular principle, this does not mean that the principles of other regimes are not present as well. The republic is characterized by virtue. But of course it will also contain elements of honor and fear. Similarly, though (political) virtue is not the principle of a monarchy, monarchies are not entirely devoid of this. They obviously possess some virtue, though it is not their animating characteristic. (*SL*, Author's Foreword, p. xli). Montesquieu indicates his awareness that he is dealing with exaggerated types at the end of Book 3:

> Such are the principles of the three governments: this does not mean that in a certain republic one is virtuous, but that one ought to be; nor does this prove that in a certain monarchy, there is honor or that in a particular despotic state, there is fear, but that unless it is there, the government is imperfect. (*SL*, 3.11)

PRACTICAL POLITICAL REFORM

On the basis of our discussion in the previous sections, it seems that Montesquieu not only subscribed to factual relativism but established this position on a scientific basis. Not only do different countries have different moral beliefs and customs, but Montesquieu's pioneering endeavors in social science were in large part an attempt to explain why this is so. The conflicting beliefs and customs depicted in *The Persian Letters* are accounted for in *Spirit of the Laws*. But as we have seen, Montesquieu's investigations into differing moral beliefs did little to undermine his faith in objectively true moral values. We have seen that, in *The Persian Letters*, Usbek discusses true justice, "a true relationship of appropriateness which exists between two things," which holds regardless of who observes it (*PL*, 83). Similar faith in objective values is expressed in different ways throughout *Spirit of the Laws*. In Book 1,

Montesquieu presents a series of moral beliefs that do not rest on the laws or customs of particular societies:

> Before laws were made, there were possible relations of justice. To say that there is nothing just or unjust but what positive laws ordain or prohibit is to say that before a circle was drawn, all its radii were not equal.
>
> Therefore, one must admit that there are relations of fairness prior to the positive law that establishes them, so that, for example, assuming that there were societies of men, it would be just to conform to their laws; so that, if there were intelligent beings that had received some kindness from another being, they ought to be grateful for it; so that, if one intelligent being had created another intelligent being, the created one ought to remain in its original dependency; so that one intelligent being who has done harm to another intelligent being deserves the same harm in return, and so forth. (*SL*, 1.1)

Again, these moral truths hold without reference to positive laws, with the same degree of truth as mathematical relationships.

The analogy between moral truths and truths of mathematics should be familiar from our discussion of Hume in the previous chapter. As we have seen, in the *Enquiry Concerning the Principles of Morals*, Hume includes Montesquieu, along with Father Malebranche, Ralph Cudworth, and Samuel Clarke, as proponents of the rationalist moral views he criticizes.[15] But assuming that this identification is correct, the fact that Montesquieu subscribes to rationalist moral views does not rest well with the fact that he is also a pioneering figure in modern social science.

The conflict is seen in regard to the movement from factual relativism to moral relativism. Montesquieu clearly believes that moral views not only vary from society to society but that this variance can be explained by causal factors. His discovery that the beliefs of different people are determined by these factors should lead naturally to the main conclusion of moral relativism, that no set of moral beliefs is objectively true. It is therefore surprising that Montesquieu (like Usbek) displays less insight into his own situation. If the values of *other* people are the result of causal factors, he should realize the likelihood that this is true of *his own moral views* as well. But he never takes this step. He presents the list of moral precepts quoted above as objectively true, without inquiring into the causal factors that might have led him to hold them. In other words, Montesquieu's search for causal explanations runs out in regard to the factors responsible for his own beliefs. This is a notorious difficulty in interpreting his thought. According to Isaiah Berlin, the student of Montesquieu is hard put to thread his way through "a kind of continuous dialectic . . . between absolute values which seem to correspond to the permanent interests of men as such, and those which depend upon time and place in a concrete situation."[16] As Berlin notes, there is probably no strictly logical contradiction between Montesquieu's two attitudes.[17] But still, the belief that positive laws and morals are a function of natural and social conditions, on the one hand, and faith in a rigid standard of justice against which these social laws and mores must be measured, on the other, are strange bedfellows. Berlin, for one, is unable to reconcile Montesquieu's "genuine disparity of attitude."[18]

Montesquieu's conflicted attitude towards moral truth is essential for understanding the nature and purpose of the social science he developed. It appears that Montesquieu is more a potential moral relativist than an actual one. The worldview to which he subscribes (which is rooted in the scientific views of René Descartes)[19] allows for the existence of moral laws alongside those of the physical world. Descartes is a metaphysical dualist. He posits a rigid separation between matter and spirit, body and soul. Accordingly, though he views the physical world as governed by (descriptive) scientific laws, he does not extend these principles to the moral sphere, and so does not decisively break with traditional moral theories. Montesquieu follows in this path, and so does not realize the potentially damaging implications of his social science researches for his faith in objective moral values.

In Book 1, Chapter 1 of *Spirit of the Laws*, Montesquieu runs through a catalogue of different entities with their different laws. The (descriptive) physical principles previously noted (p. 185) are laws of the natural world, while in the next paragraph Montesquieu discusses the moral principles quoted on page 195 as laws of the "intelligent world." These too are descriptive laws, in that the "intelligences superior to man" always obey them. But human beings do not. Because man is a finite being, his conduct is not always in accord with these moral principles. Thus for men—as opposed to intelligences superior to men— these laws are prescriptive (presumably prescribed by God) but not descriptive.

Regardless of how successful we are in reconciling Montesquieu's faith in objective moral truth and his efforts in social science, the former is necessary for understanding Montesquieu's own conception of the latter. For he does not believe his science is in opposition to his moral views. Rather, he feels it is necessary in order to put his moral views successfully into practice. Montesquieu wishes to place his scientific study of laws and morals in the service of the traditional moral science of legislation.

Throughout *Spirit of the Laws*, Montesquieu's moral views show up in numerous contexts in different ways. Most noticeable is the large number of value judgments that permeate the work. Thus many customs and practices are condemned as being against "nature." A prominent example is torture. Perhaps because of his own experience with the practice, Montesquieu notes torture's usefulness, but then breaks off: "But I hear the voice of nature crying out against me" (*SL*, 6.17). Many of Montesquieu's criticisms of social and political institutions could be anticipated on the basis of what we have seen of *The Persian Letters*. In general, Montesquieu has a strong regard for human dignity and criticizes practices that assault it. For example, he bitterly satirizes a possible defense of the treatment of African slaves:

> It is impossible for us to assume that these people are men because if we assumed they were men one would begin to believe we ourselves are not Christians. (*SL*, 15.5)

Religious persecution receives similar criticism. In Book 25, Montesquieu presents what purports to be a remonstrance, written by an eighteen-year-old Jewish woman burned in an auto-da-fé in Lisbon, which takes issue with the reasoning of her persecutors (*SL*, 25.13). In certain cases, Montesquieu's complaints are based on deductive arguments. Most notable of these is criticism of the slaughter of captives in war (*SL*, 10.3). Other cases are based on utilitarian considerations, including his criticisms of slavery and despotism, practices which he believes benefit nobody. Though many of these criticisms are not based on systematic arguments, they reveal a consistent turn of mind, which was undoubtedly common in enlightened French society at that time.

A more significant respect in which Montesquieu's absolute values manifest themselves throughout *Spirit of the Laws* is in his discussion of the applied science of legislation. For this is a moral science. Montesquieu attempts to put traditional natural law political theory on a new footing. The basis for the great natural law tradition lay in deducing the best laws for society in general from the nature of the abstract individual. As we have seen in discussing Hobbes and Locke in previous chapters, man is depicted in a state of nature, and then the preferred form of government is defended as the one best able to alleviate the specific problems that arise. Montesquieu moves beyond this point of view, arguing that the laws of any society must be adapted to its particular conditions. Because people's characters vary from society to society, there is no such thing as man as such, or good laws as such. Because laws suitable for a specific people will depend on the rubric of factors we have discussed, the legislator must be a sociologist as well as a moralist. But granted this important difference, there is a fundamental element of continuity between *Spirit of the Laws* and the natural law tradition. As Montesquieu says in one of his *Pensées*,

> I give thanks to Messieurs Grotius and Puffendorf for having so well executed a part
> of the work required of me, with a level of genius I could never have attained.[20]

In *Spirit of the Laws*, Montesquieu offers generally consistent advice to the legislator. Like Hobbes, he believes that man is by nature passionately self-interested. The key to a good form of government is some means of channeling the destructive passions of individuals to work for the good of the state. This can be done by transforming passion into virtue in a republic, or through a more complex—but less utopian—system of social engineering in a monarchy (on which, more in the following section). Regardless of the details, both of these kinds of states are inestimably superior to despotism, in which passion reigns unchecked.

Because of his awareness of the complexity of political forms, Montesquieu's science of politics is more concerned with the real than the ideal. In particular, he prefers piecemeal improvement to any program of radical reform. If society is a complex system in which all parts are interrelated, then only piecemeal reform is possible. Laws must be in accord with a society's fundamental features. To legislate in opposition to these is a recipe for failure— which is why particular laws *have* attained their form over time. Montesquieu of course believes that laws can make a difference. Thus the wise legislator should combat the effects of climate: "The more the physical causes incline men to rest, the more the moral causes should divert them from it" (*SL*, 14.5). But on the whole, the legislator must work in accordance with the country's general spirit, and so with the principle of its government. The spirit in which *Spirit of the Laws* is written is one of moderate reform:

> I do not write to censure that which is established in any country whatsoever. Each
> nation will find here the reasons for its maxims, and the consequence will naturally be
> drawn from them that changes can be proposed only by those who are born fortunate
> enough to fathom by a stroke of genius the whole of a state's constitution. (*SL*, Preface,
> p. xliv)

Similarly, in *The Persian Letters*, Usbek writes: "[I]t is sometimes necessary to change certain laws. But the case is a rare one, and when it does happen, the laws should be touched only with trembling hand" (*PL*, 129). The attitude Montesquieu is most anxious to instill in his lawgiver is expressed clearly in the first sentence of the twenty-ninth Book, "On the way to compose the laws:

> I say it, and it seems to me that I have written this work only to prove that the spirit
> of moderation should be that of the legislator. (*SL*, 29.1)

It is important to note that this Book was originally intended to be the conclusion of *Spirit of the Laws* as a whole.[21]

Montesquieu's advocacy of "moderation" in regard to political reform is similar to the view of Edmund Burke—who was influenced by Montesquieu—discussed in Chapter 7. His basic orientation is towards preserving the good things one has attained, rather than hoping for dramatic improvements. Undoubtedly in large part because of his feeling that the French monarchy could degenerate into despotism, he believed it was important to combat this, and other forms of political instability that could unleash destructive passions.

In Montesquieu's practical political theory, despotism serves as a negative ideal, on which putative reformers should fix their eyes. Rather than believing in the possibility of an ideal form of government to which one should aspire, Montesquieu is appalled at the horrors of despotism, which must be avoided at all costs. As we have seen, despotism is characterized by a complete absence of institutional stability. Whatever slight stability despotic rule exhibits is a result of factors external to the government, such as religion or customs (*SL*, 3.10, 8.10): "For in these states, there are no laws, so to speak; there are only mores and manners, and if you overturn them, you overturn everything" (*SL*, 19.12). And so a despotism cannot be corrupted; by definition it is already corrupt (*SL*, 8.10). In such a state, chaos reigns. All men are alike in being nothing (*SL*, 6.12). They live like beasts, blindly submitting to the will of a savage (*SL*, 3.10). Montesquieu believes that despotic governments have produced the most dreadful calamities ever visited on man (*SL*, 11.4), and he cannot speak of them without shuddering (*SL*, 3.9). One famous chapter, entitled "The idea of despotism" (in its entirety) reads as follows:

> When the savages of Louisiana want fruit, they cut down the tree and gather the fruit.
> There you have despotic government. (*SL*, 5.13)

Fear of this form of government is an essential feature of Montesquieu's analysis of French politics: "Rivers run together into the sea; monarchies are lost in despotism" (*SL*, 8.17).

Accordingly, Montesquieu's advice to the legislator is largely concerned with fear of the corruption of a monarchy or republic that might lead to tyranny. Because the corruption of every government begins with the corruption of its principle (*SL*, 8.1), he is constantly pleading and exhorting, pointing out means through which a legislator may be able to strengthen the principle of his government. As well as being directed towards perfect forms of each state, such prescriptions have a moral value. Since adherence to the principles of different governments is a preservative against corruption, it is a good in itself.[22] For the most part, Montesquieu's prescriptive political theory manifests itself in concrete directives, giving advice about the steps that should be taken and the conditions under which they could succeed.

In regard to French politics, Montesquieu's fear of despotism leads him to support the prerogatives of the nobility—the all important intermediate powers. In his eyes, since the time of Louis XIV in the seventeenth century, the monarch has been dangerously concentrating power in his own hands, at the expense of the nobility. As noted above, in *The Persian Letters*, Louis is said to have preferred Oriental despotism to other political forms (see p. 177). Fearing this possibility for France, Montesquieu exerts himself on the nobility's behalf. He devotes the final two Books of *Spirit of the Laws* to an attempt to demonstrate the nobility's historical independence from the crown, and so the legitimacy of its prerogatives. He goes so far as to defend even so questionable a practice as venality of offices. Allowing the nobility to sell their offices strengthens them as a bulwark against the monarchy:

> Venality is good in monarchical states, because it provides for performing as a family vocation what one would not want to undertake for virtue, and because it destines each to his duty and renders the orders of the state more permanent. (*SL*, 5.19)

The fact that Montesquieu was a member of the class whose privileges he defended was not lost on his critics, who dismissed the political recommendations of *Spirit of the Laws* out of hand. Throughout the second half of the eighteenth century, the work was repeatedly appealed to in struggles between king and nobility. One prominent historian describes it as "the single greatest statement of the aristocratic position." But because Montesquieu upheld what was essentially a return to the political system of an earlier era, another historian describes him as "a reactionary, very representative of the nobility of the robe [the judicial nobility]."[23] Regardless of the merits of this charge, in Montesquieu's eyes, the nobility had to be protected. The alternative was too terrible to contemplate.

POLITICAL LIBERTY AND ITS PRECONDITIONS

Montesquieu's humanistic values and concern for political stability gave rise to extended examination of the conditions necessary for political liberty, in Books 11 and 12 of *Spirit of the Laws*. This is probably the most influential part of Montesquieu's political theory. His account of the English Constitution in Book 11 influenced the authors of the United States Constitution, among others, and is a classic contribution to constitutional theory.

Of the political forms in existence during his time, Montesquieu preferred that of England. Though *Spirit of the Laws* contains an idealized account of the republic and its virtue, Montesquieu apparently realized that this was an ancient political form, out of keeping with the modern world. The conditions necessary for a successful republic no longer existed, though Montesquieu does discuss the possibility of a federative republic, which would combine the advantages of small size and ability to defend itself against larger modern states (*SL*, 9.1; see below). In practical terms, then, the most one can hope for is a stable government that protects its subjects against abuse. Important values can be secured through properly constituted laws, along the lines of what Montesquieu had seen in England. He had spent an extended time in England and knew its government and political leaders well. He viewed England as the "one nation in the world whose constitution has political liberty for its direct purpose" (*SL*, 11.5).

In view of the central role liberty plays in his political theory, Montesquieu's discussion of the concept is surprisingly confused. This is perhaps another result of his lack of concern for precise analysis. But charitable interpretation allows his central meaning to emerge.

Montesquieu presents a definition of liberty in Book 11, Chapter 3, which is called "What liberty is":

> In a state, that is, in a society where there are laws, liberty can consist only in having the power to do what one should want to do and in no way being constrained to do what one should not want to do. (*SL*, 11.3)

Reference to "what one should want to do" here is disconcerting. As we will see in our discussion of Rousseau in the following chapter, this is central to one account of liberty—or freedom, terms we can use interchangeably—which is known as "positive freedom."[24] This centers upon belief in an objective good to which the laws direct one. But Montesquieu does not pursue this conception of liberty. What he actually has in mind is what is generally referred to as "negative liberty," and has been seen in our discussions of Hobbes and Locke. This focuses on an absence of coercive interference by other people. The main idea is a certain space within which one is able to do what one wants. This kind of freedom is manifested in important rights, such as the right to hold property, to worship as one pleases, and to say and think what one pleases. A person with the requisite liberty is able to do these things (within limits) without the interference of other people, especially government.

A definition of liberty along these lines is given at the beginning of the crucial Chapter 6 of Book 11, which contains Montesquieu's account of the English Constitution. Here Montesquieu writes:

> Political liberty in a citizen is that tranquility of spirit which comes from the opinion each one has of his security, and in order for him to have this liberty the government must be such that one citizen cannot fear another citizen. (*SL*, 11.6)

Once again, this is not as precise as we might like, and again indicates Montesquieu's lack of interest in conceptual analysis. Though this definition focuses on security from other people, it mentions only other citizens while omitting government. An adequate account of liberty should include security from both other people and government. In spite of its shortcomings, however, this conception of liberty is consistent with Montesquieu's main intentions. In analyzing its necessary conditions, Montesquieu makes an important contribution to liberal political theory, though he is not a liberal in other respects—especially his defense of the nobility and its privileges.

The central argument of Books 11 and 12 concerns two ways in which laws can illicitly interfere with people's liberty. (a) Government can violate the laws and so abuse its citizens. (b) The laws themselves can be unsatisfactory, so even if government scrupulously adheres to them, it can still trample on people's rights. Montesquieu addresses these two areas of difficulty in Books 11 and 12, respectively. The problems associated with (a) can be overcome through a proper constitution, like that of England, which he discusses in Book 11. The problems of (b) are encountered mainly in regard to the criminal laws, discussed in Book 12. We will examine constitutions in the remainder of this section, and criminal laws in the next.

The need for proper constitutional structure is rooted in human nature. Montesquieu believes people are generally self-interested and so liable to misuse their power: "[I]t has eternally been observed that any man who has power is led to abuse it; he continues until he finds limits" (*SL*, 11.4). This tendency must be checked. Montesquieu presents a fundamental distinction between two kinds of governments. In "moderate" governments power is properly checked and the people are secure (*SL* 3.10; 6.1–2). This is not the case in other governments, especially despotism, which is a major reason for this form's abuses.

Power is limited in different regimes in different ways. In the republic, as we have seen, power is in the hands of the people, who are prevented from abusing it by their virtue. The case is similar in aristocracy, where the moderation of the rulers prevents them from taking advantage of the citizens. In the monarchy, the power of the king is limited by fixed fundamental laws and the intermediate powers. Liberty is most secure in a particular form of monarchy, in which political power is divided between the different branches of government in such a way that the power of one man or group is always checked by the power of others. Montesquieu believed that this arrangement existed in the Constitution of England, and was responsible for the great liberty the English people enjoyed.

Previous theorists had argued for the need to separate powers in a constitution. For instance, Locke argues that there are three powers in a properly constituted government: the legislative, executive, and federative. Though he believes the latter two should generally be placed in the same hands, he sees the need to have an independent legislature able to check the monarch (see p. 108). But as we have seen, Locke pays relatively little attention to this point. He views the king as an essential participant in the legislature, with the power to call it into session. Because of the king's ability to prevent the legislature from opposing him, Locke is less interested in constitutional questions than in revolution.

The idea of a mixed constitution had been discussed by many theorists since the ancient Greeks. In the *Laws*, Plato shows some awareness of the importance of dividing political power between different bodies and giving them the ability to check one another.[25] But more important was the theory of Polybius, discussed above in connection with Machiavelli.[26] The main idea here is that in a properly drawn constitution, power should be divided between the one, the few, and the many, as in the constitutions of Rome and Sparta. However, as we have seen, this arrangement is not devised so that power will check power. It is drawn from a particular theory of historical cycles. Because each simple form of constitution suffers from an inherent defect and so is liable to decay, a combination of the three simple forms should last much longer.

In Montesquieu's presentation we encounter something more recognizable as modern constitutional theory. The resemblances between his account and the United States Constitution are strong—largely, of course, because of Montesquieu's influence on the American founders. Montesquieu argues that there are three powers: legislative, executive, and judicial. On the whole, these should be placed in separate hands. The reason for this is not a dubious historical theory but the observed fact that people tend to misuse power with which they are entrusted. Thus if a person attempts to misuse his office for his own ends, things must be arranged to allow other people to oppose him: "So that one cannot abuse power, power must check power by the arrangement of things" (*SL*, 11.4).

Because of the natural human tendency to abuse power, it is dangerous to place more than one branch of government in the same hands:

When legislative power is united with executive power in a single person or in a single body of the magistracy, there is no liberty, because one can fear that the same monarch or senate that makes tyrannical laws will execute them tyrannically.

Nor is there liberty if the power of judging is not separate from legislative power and from executive power. If it were joined to legislative power, the power over the life and liberty of the citizens would be arbitrary, for the judge would be the legislator. If it were joined to executive power, the judge could have the force of an oppressor. (*SL*, 11.6)

It follows that to combine all three powers in the same hands would be devastating:

All would be lost if the same man or the same body of principal men, either of nobles, or of the people, exercised these three powers: that of making the laws, that of executing public resolutions, and that of judging the crimes or the disputes of individuals. (*SL*, 11.6)

The union of all powers in the ruler's hands is one reason for the horrors of despotism: "Among the Turks where the three powers are united in the person of the sultan, an atrocious despotism reigns" (*SL*, 11.6).

The means through which powers should be distributed are seen in the Constitution of England. The legislative branch should be divided in two parts, one elected by the people, with the other given over to hereditary nobility. Election should be by all the people, by districts, subject to a minor property qualification. The elected house should be the major legislative body, and the other should have only the power to veto. Executive power should be in the hands of a monarch, who has the power to summon the legislature, and to veto its decisions, while the legislature in turn should be able to check the executive, by examining how laws are made and calling executive ministers to account, though it should not have power over the person of the monarch. In addition, the legislative body should exercise considerable control over the executive through the provision that only it can raise public revenues. The judiciary should be independent of the other powers, and judgments should be rigidly according to law: they should be "fixed to such a degree that they are never anything but a precise text of the law."

Other details are included. But from this survey, the main idea should be clear. With powers separated and able to check one another, the cooperation of different powers is necessary if the government is to act:

The form of these three powers should be rest or inaction. But as they are constrained to move by the necessary motion of things, they will be forced to move in concert. (*SL*, 11.6)

Thus in this system, one branch of government cannot work without the cooperation of others. Because of multiple ways legislation can be vetoed and through which one branch can check the actions of others, possible misuse of power should be minimized.

A classic description of the principles underlying constitutional checks and balances, heavily influenced by Montesquieu, is given in *The Federalist*. This series of eighty-five papers was written by James Madison, Alexander Hamilton, and John Jay, and published under the joint name Publius, in 1787–1788, to defend the United States Constitution during the ratification process. The papers present what is probably the most thorough and searching account of the Constitution and its underlying principles in the literature. I quote from *Federalist* 51:

> [T]he great security against a gradual concentration of the several powers in the same department consists in giving to those who administer each department the necessary constitutional means and personal motives to resist encroachments of the others. The provision for defence must in this, as in all other cases, be made commensurate to the danger of attack. Ambition must be made to counteract ambition. The interest of the man must be connected with the constitutional rights of the place. It may be a reflection on human nature, that such devices should be necessary to control the abuses of government. But what is government itself, but the greatest of all reflections on human nature? If men were angels, no government would be necessary. If angels were to govern men, neither external nor internal controls on government would be necessary. In framing a government which is to be administered by men over men, the great difficulty lies in this: you must first enable the government to control the governed; and in the next place oblige it to control itself. . . .
>
> The policy of supplying by opposite and rival interests, the defect of better motives, must be traced through the whole system of human affairs, private as well as public.[27]

The idea of checks and balances is closely related to Montesquieu's notion of honor. In a properly devised system, each person acts to advance his own good, and so contributes to the stability of the system as a whole. The properly constructed constitution is a complex creation. Montesquieu believes the great difficulty of creating such governments is one reason despotism, with all its horrors, continues to exist:

> [D]espite men's love of liberty, despite their hatred of violence, most peoples are subjected to this type of government. This is easy to understand. In order to form a moderate government, one must combine powers, regulate them, temper them, make them act; one must give one power a ballast, so to speak, to put it in a position to resist another; this is a masterpiece of legislation that chance rarely produces and prudence is rarely allowed to produce. By contrast, a despotic government leaps to view, so to speak; it is uniform throughout; as only passions are needed to establish it, everyone is good enough for that. (*SL*, 5.14)

Certain aspects of Montesquieu's discussion of the English Constitution are left unclear. At times the reader must supply connections between his somewhat oracular pronouncements. Other remarks are puzzling. For instance, after introducing the three separate powers, Montesquieu reduces the number to two, declaring that the power of judging "is in some fashion null." As we have seen, he argues that the legislative power should be divided between elected representatives of the people and hereditary nobility, and the executive power should be in the hands of a monarch. Though these precepts conform to the English system, it is not clear why they are preferable to other arrangements. Similarly, Montesquieu argues that the legislative power should not convene itself but should be summoned by a king. But again, exactly why is not carefully explained. A notably puzzling remark is: "This state will perish when legislative power is more corrupt than executive power." Exactly what Montesquieu means by this is difficult to say.

Considerable controversy has been stirred up by Montesquieu's opposition to a parliamentary system, in which executive power is lodged in a cabinet made up of members of the legislature. He writes:

> If there were no monarch and the executive power were entrusted to a certain number of persons drawn from the legislative body, there would no longer be liberty, because the two powers would be united, the same person sometimes belonging and always able to belong to both. (*SL*, 11.6)

In view of the large number of stable, nontyrannical parliamentary systems the world has seen since Montesquieu's time, it seems that his reasoning here has been proved incorrect. It could, perhaps, be argued that in a cabinet government the means through which power is wielded in the executive and legislative branches are significantly different, and so power is not really concentrated in the same hands.[28] Or perhaps there are features of modern parliamentary systems that prevent Montesquieu's logic from applying to them. In regard to this, as in other cases, more and clearer discussion on Montesquieu's part would be welcome.

In spite of these problems, Montesquieu's basic points are clear. The great success of the English Constitution lies in its separation of powers and checks and balances. Because of this arrangement, it is far more difficult for its powers to be abused than in other systems. Though arguments along these lines had been advanced by previous theorists, Montesquieu moves beyond them in clearly delineating the essential constitutional features and in explaining how they work. The American founders recognized his contribution:

> No political truth is certainly of greater intrinsic value, or is stamped with the authority of more enlightened patrons of liberty, than that on which the objection is founded. The accumulation of all powers, legislative, executive, and judiciary, in the same hands, whether of one, a few, or many, and whether hereditary, self-appointed, or elective, may justly be pronounced the very definition of tyranny. . . .
>
> The oracle who is always consulted and cited on this subject is the celebrated Montesquieu. If he be not the author of this invaluable precept in the science of politics, he has the merit at least of displaying and recommending it most effectually to the attention of mankind. (*Federalist* 47)

To close out this section, I will briefly discuss one other respect in which Montesquieu influenced basic principles of American constitutional doctrine.[29] This is in the negative sense that his analysis of the republic posed a significant problem the founders had to overcome. As we have seen, Montesquieu views the republic as necessarily small. Only within a confined area is it possible to generate the intense political virtue that is this state's principle. But the territory the American founders had to work with was of course large. If they had followed Montesquieu's precepts, they would have had to renounce republican forms.

This problem is tackled by Alexander Hamilton in *Federalist* 9. Addressing "the observations of Montesquieu on the necessity of a contracted territory for a republican government," Hamilton finds a ready response in the idea of a "confederate republic." In *Spirit of the Laws*, Montesquieu speaks of the advantages a confederacy has over a republic in terms of ability to defend itself:

> Composed of small republics, it enjoys the goodness of the internal government of each one; and with regard to the exterior, it has, by the force of the association, all the advantages of large monarchies. (*SL*, 9.1)

It is not clear exactly how much Montesquieu's reasoning in this regard influenced the founders. But it is possible to view the United States as a confederation of separate republics. Though the individual states are far larger than the units on which Montesquieu focused, his authority provided important support for a confederation of states. But we will return to points of difference between Montesquieu's conception and the United States below.

More important is the argument advanced by Madison in *Federalist* 10, defending a large republic over a small one. Though Montesquieu is not mentioned by name here, Madison is probably attempting a direct refutation of his position. Madison's argument—a version of which was originally developed by Hume[30]—concerns the evils of factions, self-interested groups that are liable to sacrifice the public good to advance their own ends. Factions form in regard to any important interest—religion, political beliefs, and so on. Most important generally are economic interests. The notion of factions, then, is closely related to the notorious "special interests" prevalent in modern Western politics.

Madison believes that the tendency to form factions is basic to human nature and so ineliminable. To avoid its effects, he argues, one must *extend* the territory. The relatively small number of interests found in a *small* republic can easily lead to extreme divisiveness:

> The smaller the society, the fewer probably will be the distinct parties and interests composing it; the fewer the distinct parties and the more frequently will a majority be found of the same party; and the smaller the number of individuals composing a majority, and the smaller the compass within which they are placed, the more easily will they concert and execute their plans of oppression. (*Federalist* 10)

The great danger of factions in small states stems from two circumstances. First, in a small state with few distinct interests, it is relatively easy for the state to be sharply divided over some issue or other. Second, because of the small number of interests, it is relatively easy for a single faction to represent a majority in the state, and so to be able to take control of the government and use it to suppress its opponents. If faction is undesirable, a single faction in control of the government is truly dangerous:

> [A] pure democracy, by which I mean a society consisting of a small number of citizens, who assemble and administer the government in person, can admit of no cure for the mischiefs of faction. A common passion or interest will in almost every case, be felt by a majority of the whole; a communication and concert result from the form of government itself; and there is nothing to check the inducements to sacrifice the weaker party or an obnoxious individual. Hence it is that such democracies have ever been spectacles of turbulence and contention; have ever been found incompatible with

personal security or the rights of property; and have in general been as short in their lives as they have been violent in their deaths. (*Federalist* 10)

By extending the sphere, one increases the number of interests. This makes it more difficult for a single group to gain majority control of the government:

> Extend the sphere and you take in a greater variety of parties and interests; you make it less probable that a majority of the whole will have a common motive to invade the rights of other citizens; or if such a common motive exists, it will be more difficult for all who feel it to discover their own strength, and to act in unison with each other. Besides other impediments, it may be remarked that, where there is a consciousness of unjust or dishonorable purposes, communications is always checked by distrust in proportion to the number whose concurrence is necessary.
>
> Hence, it clearly appears, that the same advantage which a republic has over a democracy, in controlling the effects of faction, is enjoyed by a large over a small republic—is enjoyed by the Union over the States composing it. (*Federalist* 10)

In *Federalist* 51 this argument is developed in relation to the conditions necessary for religious liberty. In a small state, it is far easier for a majority of the population to subscribe to one religion than in a large state, which encompasses diverse creeds and beliefs. Because of basic tendencies of human nature, the majority is likely to use its power to oppress different minorities. Religious liberty, then, is not easily attained in a small state. By extending the territory, one makes it less likely that a particular majority can control the government. The authors apply similar reasoning to support increasing the size of the American republic:

> In a free government the security for civil rights must be the same as that for religious rights. It consists in the one case in the multiplicity of interests, and in the other in the multiplicity of sects. The degree of security in both cases will depend on the number of interests and sects; and this may be presumed to depend on the extent of country and number of people comprehended under the same government. (*Federalist* 51)

The underlying logic of American democracy is sharply opposed to Montesquieu's account of the republic. In spite of the founders' desire to associate the United States with Montesquieu's conception of the confederate republic, there are enormous differences. Montesquieu's confederate republic is still composed of republics in his sense. The individual units must be small, austere, and devoted to the inculcation of civic virtue. These elements are not present in the American republic, which is based on elaborate balancing of self-interest. In view of the enormous time that passed between Montesquieu's main models of the ancient republic, Rome and Sparta, and the American founding, these differences are not surprising. However, though it is far removed from Montesquieu's small republics, the extended republic can be explained in his terms as a masterpiece of the legislative art. With power divided between a large number of sects, self-interested groups will cancel one another out. The result is a balance between opposing forces that will prevent any single group from controlling government and employing its power for untoward ends.

LIBERTY AND THE CRIMINAL LAW

As well as providing security against abuses of governmental power, the laws themselves must not be liable to abuse. Montesquieu's main concern in this regard is the criminal laws, which must possess certain characteristics if people are to be free. The subject of proper criminal laws is so important to liberty that Montesquieu says it is "of more concern to mankind than anything else in the world" (*SL*, 12.2).

A few basic principles are necessary for proper criminal laws. First and most obvious, the judiciary must be independent and so able to render fair decisions without interference. This principle is in accordance with the separation of powers, discussed in the previous section. Other important principles are that laws should be clear, and carefully applied. Montesquieu wishes to narrow the range of crimes that are punished, and to make penalties proportionate to crimes.

In a moderate government, each citizen is valued, and so punishment should be employed only after careful steps are taken to make sure it is needed. In these states, justice cannot be swift. In republics and monarchies, "where the head of even the lowest citizen is esteemed, his honor and goods are removed from him only after long examination." The slow pace of proceedings is a cost of liberty: "the penalties, expenses, delays, and even the dangers of justice are the price each citizen pays for his liberty." Thus "formalities increase in proportion to the importance given to the honor, fortune, life, and liberty of the citizens" (*SL*, 6.2). The practice of moderate governments is in contrast to a despotism, in which subjects are not valued, and justice can be immediate: "The manner of ending [disputes] is not important, provided that they are ended" (*SL*, 6.2). Not surprisingly, when a man achieves absolute power, he wishes to simplify the laws (*SL*, 6.2). Precise legal procedure is an essential protection against—and so a limitation upon—arbitrary rule.

Along with careful procedures comes the need for properly crafted laws. Crimes must be carefully specified:

> Vagueness in the crime of high treason is enough to make a government degenerate into despotism. (*SL*, 12.7)

Obviously, if the offenses that constitute capital crimes are not clearly defined, anyone can be accused at any time. Vague crimes amount to a grant of arbitrary power to government.

Similar reasoning leads Montesquieu to circumscribe the range of activities that should be viewed as criminal. On the whole, he favors penalizing only conduct that damages other people or the state. He opposes persecution on religious grounds. Actions against the divinity should be left between the perpetrator and God, who will exact appropriate revenge (*SL*, 12.4). Similarly, people should be penalized only for their actions; indiscreet speech alone is not a crime (*SL*, 12.12). The same is true of writing (*SL*, 12.13), and, obviously, thoughts (*SL*, 12.11). Along similar lines, Montesquieu worries about the abuse of procedures. To give a few people power to punish traitors gives them the opportunity to become tyrants (*SL*, 12.18). Thus he distrusts the practice of using spies (*SL*, 12.23), and believes that anonymous accusations can be tolerated only when the safety of the prince is threatened (*SL*, 12.24). Similarly: "laws that send a man to his death on the deposition of a single witness are fatal to liberty" (*SL*, 12.3).

Montesquieu bitterly opposes punishment when conduct is considered criminal because of popular ignorance or superstition:

> The emperor Theodore Lascaris attributed his illness to magic. Those who were accused of it had no other recourse but to handle a hot iron without burning themselves. It would have been a good thing, among these Greeks, to be a magician in order to vindicate oneself of the accusation of magic. Such was the excess of their ignorance that to the most dubious crime in the world, they joined the most dubious proofs. (*SL*, 12.5)

In all these cases, and others like them, Montesquieu opposes various practices that lend themselves to arbitrary power. If laws or legal procedures leave openings for governmental abuse, liberty is at risk. Given his conception of human nature, Montesquieu assumes that opportunities for such abuse will be realized. In these cases, constitutional protections such as checks and balances are of no help, because abuse of authority is in accordance with the law. Thus vague laws must be tightened up, and dubious crimes eliminated, along with suspect procedures.

Montesquieu also argues for reform of criminal penalties. They should not be arbitrary but in accordance with crimes. This is important on humanitarian grounds. Perhaps because of his own experience with torture, Montesquieu would like to limit the use of corporal punishments. For instance, crimes against property should be punished by loss of one's own property—if one has any. If not, corporal punishment is necessary. Crimes against mores should be punished through shame and public infamy. We have already noted that crimes against the divinity should be left to the divinity (*SL*, 12.4).

In each of these cases, Montesquieu has two concerns. First, obviously, is humanitarian. Corporal punishments are cruel and destructive of human dignity. Thus to curb them is desirable in itself. But more than this, attaching punishments to the nature of crimes removes an area of arbitrary powers. Improved policies in regard to penalties would make them certain, and not subject to the whims of judge or ruler:

> It is the triumph of liberty when criminal laws draw each penalty from the particular nature of the crime. All arbitrariness ends; the penalty does not ensue from the legislator's capriciousness but from the nature of the thing, and man does not do violence to man. (*SL*, 12.4)

In his discussion of criminal laws, as in his account of constitutional laws, Montesquieu wishes to establish the liberty of the citizen within the bounds of fixed legal procedures and institutions. One of his central teachings is that liberty is possible only within the confines of laws. This is true in the republic, where the laws are obeyed willingly, and in the different monarchies he describes, in which power checks power and rulers are compelled to obey the laws. It is obvious that Montesquieu's recommendations concerning criminal law are intended only for moderate governments, where human beings count for something. Because the principle of despotism is fear, most of what Montesquieu recommends would damage this form of state. In a despotism, as Montesquieu envisions it, nothing is fixed; all is subject to the ruler's whim. Vague crimes, irregular procedures, and savage penalties are in keeping with other aspects of the state. In such a state, of course, freedom is impossible. A citizen of a moderate government in which laws and penalties are fixed, "against whom proceedings had been brought and who was to be hung the next day would be freer than is a pasha in Turkey" (*SL*, 12.2).

NOTES

1. Biographical details are from R. Shackleton, *Montesquieu: A Critical Biography* (Oxford, 1961); this work is cited "Shackleton" in text.

2. *The Persian Letters* is abbreviated *PL* and cited according to letter number; *The Spirit of the Laws* is abbreviated *SL* and cited according to book and chapter number (e.g., 3.4 is Book 3, Chapter 4) (page numbers for this work are from the translation cited below); *Considerations on the Causes of the Greatness of the Romans and their Decline* is cited as *Considerations*, according to chapter number and page number in the translation of D. Lowenthal (Ithaca, NY, 1965). Montesquieu's *Pensées* are cited *P.* according to numbers in *Œuvres complètes de Montesquieu*, ed. A Masson, 3 vols. Other material in this edition is cited *Œuvres*. Full references for this edition and all translations are found below, under "Texts Cited." Unless otherwise indicated, all italics in quotations are from Montesquieu in "Texts Cited."

3. J. Shklar, *Montesquieu* (Oxford, 1987), p. 25.

4. See Vol. I, 11–14.

5. *PL*, 11–14, from which all quotations in the following paragraphs are taken.

6. See M. Dimoff, "Cicéron, Hobbes et Montesquieu," *Annales Universitatis Saravienis Philosophie Lettres*, 1 (1952); and A. Crissafulli, "Montesquieu's Story of the Troglodytes: Its Background, Meaning, and Significance," *Publications of the Modern Language Association of America*, 1943.

7. Shklar, *Montesquieu*, p. 27.

8. E. Durkheim, *Montesquieu and Rousseau: Forerunners of Sociology*, R. Mannheim, trans. (Ann Arbor, MI, 1970), p. 61. Other notable commentators sharing this view include R. Aron, *Main Currents in Sociological Thought*, R. Howard and H. Weaver, trans., 2 vols. (Garden City, NY, 1968), Vol. I, Chap. 2; L. Althusser, *Politics and History*, B. Brewster, trans. (London, 1972); F. Neumann, "Introduction" to *The Spirit of the Laws*, by Montesquieu, ed. Neumann (New York, 1949).

9. These are discussed in Volume I, 252.

10. See G. Lanson, "Le determinisme historique et l'idéalisme social dans l'*Esprit des loix*," *Revue de métaphysique et de morale*, 23 (1916).

11. J. Plamenatz, *Man and Society*, 2 vols. (New York, 1963), I, 297.

12. R. G. Collingwood, *The Idea of History* (Oxford, 1946), pp. 78–79.

13. Aron, *Main Currents*, I, 3.

14. See also, Vol. I, 160–165.

15. D. Hume, *An Enquiry Concerning the Principles of Morals*, in *Enquiries Concerning Human Understanding and Concerning the Principles of Morals*, ed. L. A. Selby-Bigge and P. H. Nidditch, 3rd ed. (Oxford, 1975), p. 197, n.1.

16. I. Berlin, "Montesquieu," *Proceedings of the British Academy*, 41 (1955), 293. For this problem, see G. Klosko, "Montesquieu's Science of Politics," *Studies on Voltaire and the Eighteenth Century*, 189 (1980).

17. Berlin, "Montesquieu," 290.

18. Berlin, "Montesquieu," 291.

19. See C. J. Beyer, "Montesquieu et l'esprit cartésien," in *Actes du Congrès Montesquieu, réuni à Bordeaux du 23 au 26 mai 1955* (Bordeaux, 1956); and Klosko, "Montesquieu's Science of Politics."

20. P. 1537; my trans.

21. See J. Brethe de la Gressaye, ed., *Montesquieu: De l'Esprit des loix*. 4 Vols. (Paris 1950–1961), I, cxvi–cxxi.

22. Shackleton, *Montesquieu*, p. 282.

23. F. Ford, *Robe and Sword* (Cambridge, 1952), p. viii; A. Mathiez, Review of E. Carcassone, *Montesquieu et le problème de la Constitution Française au XVIII siècle, Annales historiques de la Révolution français*, 4 (1927), 510 (my trans.).

24. See also, Vol. I, 92–93, 96–97.

25. *Laws* 691d–92c, 712d–14b; for discussion, see G. Klosko, *The Development of Plato's Political Theory* (New York, 1986), pp. 220–221.

26. See pp. 23–4; also, Vol. I, 160–165.

27. *The Federalist* 51. *Federalist* cited according to paper number, in text. Full reference below under "Texts Cited."

28. Plamenatz effectively makes this case (*Man and Society*, I, 283–293).

29. For evidence of discussion of Montesquieu's ideas during the founding period, see P. Spurlin, *Montesquieu in America: 1760–1801* (Baton Rouge, LA, 1940).

30. Hume, "That Politics May Be Reduced to a Science," in *Essays: Moral, Political, and Literary*, ed. E. Miller, revised ed. (Indianapolis, 1985); D. Adair, "'That Politics May Be Reduced to a Science': David Hume, James Madison, and the Tenth Federalist," in *Fame and the Founding Fathers* (New York, 1974).

TEXTS CITED

The Federalist: A Commentary on the Constitution of the United States. From the Original Text of Alexander Hamilton, John Jay, James Madison. New York, n.d.

Montesquieu. *Considerations on the Causes of the Greatness of the Romans and their Decline.* Trans. D. Lowenthal. New York, 1965.

Montesquieu. *Œuvres complètes de Montesquieu.* Ed. A. Masson. 3 vols. Paris, 1950–1955.

Montesquieu. *The Persian Letters.* Trans. J. R. Loy. Cleveland, 1961.

Montesquieu. *The Spirit of the Laws.* Ed. and trans. A. Cohler, B. Miller, H. Stone. Cambridge, 1989.

FURTHER READING

Althusser, L. *Politics and History*. B. Brewster trans. London, 1972.

Aron, R. 1968. *Main Currents in Sociological Thought*. R. Howard and H. Weaver, trans. 2 Vols. Garden City, NY, 1968. Vol. I, pp. 13–72.

Berlin, I. "Montesquieu." *Proceedings of the British Academy*, 41 (1955).

Beyer, C. J. "Montesquieu et l'esprit cartésien." In *Actes du Congrès Montesquieu, réuni à Bordeaux du 23 au 26 mai 1955*. Bordeaux, 1956.

Brethe de la Gressaye, J. Ed. *Montesquieu: De l'Esprit des loix*. 4 Vols. Paris, 1950–1961.

Congrès Montesquieu. *Actes du Congrès Montesquieu, réuni à Bordeaux du 23 au 26 mai 1955*. Bordeaux, 1956.

Durkheim. E. *Montesquieu and Rousseau: Forerunners of Sociology*. R. Mannheim, trans. Ann Arbor, MI, 1970.

Klosko, G. "Montesquieu's Science of Politics." *Studies on Voltaire and the Eighteenth Century*, 189 (1980).

Mathiez, A. "La place de Montesquieu dans l'histoire des doctrines politiques du XVIII siècle," *Annales historiques de la Révolution français*, 7 (1930).

Neumann, F. Introduction to *The Spirit of the Laws*, by Montesquieu. Ed. Neumann. New York, 1949.

Shackleton, R. *Montesquieu: A Critical Biography*. Oxford, 1961.

Shklar, J. *Montesquieu*. Oxford, 1987.

Chapter

6

Jean-Jacques Rousseau

Rousseau's Life and Intellectual Background

Jean-Jacques Rousseau was born in Geneva in 1712, the son of a watchmaker. Vastly talented in different fields, he wrote plays, operas, a dictionary of music, and devised a new system of musical notation. His epistolary novel, *The New Heloise*, was the most popular novel of the eighteenth century, while in *Emile*, he made profound and long-lasting contributions to educational theory. Rousseau's autobiography, appropriately called *Confessions*, helped launch the Romantic movement, which emphasized emotion and man's closeness to nature over reason and its accomplishments. The *Confessions* was original in being largely an account of Rousseau's "secret soul," of how he *felt*:

> I have displayed myself as I was, as vile and despicable when my behavior was such, as good, generous, and noble when I was so. I have bared my secret soul as Thou thyself has seen it, Eternal Being. So let the numberless legion of men gather round me and hear my confessions.[1]

Throughout the eighteenth and nineteenth centuries, Rousseau was viewed as the apostle of feeling and emotion, as epitomized in Romanticism. Today, this side of his thought is overshadowed by his political theory, which is of course our primary concern. In spite of their paradoxes and obscurities, his political ideas were probably the most influential of the eighteenth century.

To a large extent, Rousseau's opposition to then prevailing modes of thought can be attributed to his unusual life. His mother died nine days after his birth.[2] He was raised by an irresponsible father, then by relatives, given little formal education, and unhappily apprenticed to an engraver. At the age of sixteen, he left Geneva to wander through Europe.

The details of his experiences need not concern us, aside from the crucial fact of his discomfort with the sophisticated society of his day. Rousseau maintained uneasy relations with the Church and with major intellectual figures of the Enlightenment, including Voltaire and Diderot (see below). Another person with whom he had a famous quarrel was David Hume, after the latter, attempting to help him, took him to England under his protection.[3]

In 1745 Rousseau entered into a lifelong relationship with Thérèse Levasseur, a semi-literate servant girl.[4] They had five children, all of whom were turned over to foundling homes, which tormented Rousseau's conscience for the rest of his life. After the publication of his greatest political work, *The Social Contract*, and *Emile*, both in 1762, Rousseau was persecuted for religious reasons. His books were condemned and burned in both Paris and Geneva. Threatened with arrest, he went into hiding. Though Rousseau, notoriously, suspected many of his associates of plotting against him, his actual situation was often precarious. In his eyes, Hume was implicated in the plot, while the latter describes Rousseau as follows:

> He has reflected, properly speaking, and study'd very little; and has not indeed much Knowledge. He has only felt, during the whole Course of his Life; and in this Respect, his Sensibility rises to a Pitch beyond what I have seen any Example of: But it still gives him a more acute Feeling of Pain than of Pleasure. He is like a Man who were stript not only of his Cloaths but of his Skin, and turn'd out in that Situation to combat with the rude and boisterous Elements, such as perpetually disturb the lower World.[5]

Rousseau achieved literary celebrity in 1750, when he won an essay competition sponsored by the Academy of Dijon. The prize question was: "Whether the Restoration of the Sciences and the Arts Contributed to the Purification of Mores."[6] Rousseau argued in opposition to central Enlightenment convictions concerning the immense contribution the arts and sciences had made to civilization. The main theme of his essay is that "our souls have become corrupted in proportion as our sciences and our arts have advanced toward perfection" (*First Discourse*, Pt. I, p. 5). Progress in the sciences and arts has promoted luxury and idleness, dissipated our military abilities, and corrupted our morals. To support these claims, Rousseau argues mainly from historical examples, contrasting rude, uncultured peoples and weaker, corrupt "civilized" societies. Prominent examples of virtuous societies are Sparta and the Roman Republic. In his letter to Alembert, Rousseau describes Sparta, "which I have never cited enough," as "the example we ought to follow."[7]

On the title page of the *Discourse*, Rousseau identities himself as "A Citizen of Geneva." He viewed Geneva, "a free people, a small city, and a poor state" (*Lett. d'Alembert*, Pt. II, p. 15), as similar to Sparta and Rome, not only in these respects, but because of the resemblance between its Calvinist austerity and ancient virtue. Rousseau's condemnation of the arts and luxury throughout his life indicates a puritanical side to his character, which can perhaps be traced back to the influence of Geneva. As we will see below, the wish to resurrect a small, virtuous republic is a central theme in his political theory.

In looking backwards through history for his moral and political ideal, Rousseau placed himself in opposition to the major intellectual currents of his day. In the *Discourse*, he notes the incongruity of criticizing the sciences and arts in an essay written for a scientific society (Pt. I, p. 2). Emerging in the *First Discourse* is a rejection of central tendencies of Enlightenment thought.

The Enlightenment was the main intellectual current of the seventeenth and eighteenth centuries. It was a large and diverse movement, encompassing a range of different thinkers and doctrines. Though it is difficult to identify any particular beliefs as common to all its proponents, especially in this brief space, it seems safe to say that its outstanding characteristic was faith in reason and science, especially in opposition to forces of religion and superstition, which were viewed as responsible for the ills of mankind. Deeply impressed with recent accomplishments in the natural sciences, Enlightenment thinkers attempted to extend the bounds of knowledge in other areas, confident this would improve man's condition. In previous chapters we have seen a number of thinkers' attempts to apply scientific methods to a variety of fields. In different ways, Hobbes, Hume, and Montesquieu were involved in these efforts, while Locke's epistemological explorations in his *Essay Concerning Human Understanding* made him a central Enlightenment figure. Many of Rousseau's associates shared the Enlightenment faith in reason, including François-Marie Arouet de Voltaire (1694–1778) and Denis Diderot (1713–1784). According to Ernst Cassirer, the central tenet of the age was "the self-confidence of reason."[8] Enlightenment ideas are epitomized in the great *Encyclopedia*, edited by Diderot, which attempted to present the breadth of human accomplishments in the sciences and arts. In his *Preliminary Discourse to the Encyclopedia*, Jean le Rond d'Alembert (1717–1783) describes the *Encyclopedia*'s purpose as follows:

> [I]t is to contain the general principles that form the basis of each science and art, liberal or mechanical, and the most essential facts that make up the body and substance of each.[9]

Among the *Encyclopedia*'s many contributors was Rousseau, who wrote essays on musical subjects, and his *Discourse on Political Economy* (discussed below). The overall spirit of the Enlightenment is expressed by d'Alembert: "it is readily apparent that the sciences and the arts are mutually supporting, and that consequently there is a chain that binds them together."[10] Human knowledge is a single whole, growing steadily and extending its reach.

The intellectual turning point of Rousseau's life was his discovery that central beliefs of the Enlightenment were misguided. Enlightenment figures believed that with the advance of reason and defeat of religion, progress was assured. Civilization would develop; the lot of mankind would improve; and a bright future lay ahead. These beliefs were classically expressed by the Marquis de Condorcet (1743–1794), who popularized the concept of progress.[11] In contrast, the core of Rousseau's political theory arose from opposition between nature and civilization, the former of which is basically good, while the latter is a source of corruption. These ideas struck him as a revelation, which has been likened to that of St. Paul on the road to Damascus (Cranston, I, 227). In his *Confessions*, Rousseau describes how he first came upon the question posed by the Dijon Academy. Walking to visit Diderot, who had been imprisoned in Vincennes, Rousseau was resting beneath a tree when he read an advertisement for the prize competition:

> The moment I read this I beheld another universe and became another man. . . .
> What I remember quite distinctly about this occasion is that when I reached Vincennes I was in a state of agitation bordering on delirium. . . . All the rest of my life and of my misfortunes followed inevitably as a result of that moment's madness. (*Conf.*, Bk. 8, pp. 327–328)

In a famous letter, he elaborates:

> [I]f ever anything resembled a sudden inspiration, it is what that advertisement stimulated in me; all at once I felt my mind dazzled by a thousand lights, a crowd of

> splendid ideas presented themselves to me with such force and in such confusion, that I was thrown into a state of indescribable bewilderment. I felt my head seized by a dizziness that resembled intoxication.

He continues in a similar vein for several sentences and then indicates the thrust of his discovery:

> Ah, Monsieur, if ever I had been able to write down what I saw and felt as I sat under that tree, with what clarity would I have exposed the contradictions of our social system, with what force would I have demonstrated all the abuses of our institutions, with what simplicity would I have demonstrated that man is naturally good and has only become bad because of those institutions. (Quoted by Cranston, I, 228)

Rousseau says these ideas are "thinly scattered" in his "three principal works," the *First* and *Second Discourses*, and the *Emile*: "all three works are inseparable and form a single whole" (quoted by Cranston, I, 228). It is, however, curious that in this letter, written in 1762, Rousseau does not mention either *The Social Contract* or *The New Heloise*, both of which had also been completed by that time (Cranston, 228 n.).

As we will see throughout this chapter, the idea that man is naturally good but corrupted by society is central to Rousseau's political theory. A first account of this theme and its implications is presented in the prize-winning *Discourse on the Sciences and the Arts*, in which Rousseau attempts to show how developments in these areas contributed to corruption. In the *Confessions*, he expresses his eventual disappointment with this essay, which "though full of strength and fervour, is completely lacking in logic and order." He describes it as, of all his compositions, "the most feebly argued, the most deficient in proportion and harmony" (*Conf.*, Bk. 8, p. 329). But it clearly foreshadows central themes of his major political works.

Even with its shortcomings, the *Discourse on the Sciences and the Arts* created a sensation. Diderot reported, "'There has never been a success like it'" (*Conf.*, Bk. 8, p. 339). Its author achieved immediate celebrity. However, in spite of his assault upon the arts, he continued to write plays, operas, and novels.[12]

The opposition between nature and society posited in the *First Discourse* is fully worked out in the *Second Discourse*, on the foundations of inequality. This work was submitted to the same prize competition, in 1754. But though the *Discourse on Inequality* is incomparably greater than the *Discourse on the Sciences and the Arts*, it was less well received. It did not win the prize, perhaps because its radical political implications are closer to the surface.

Because it attacks the progress of civilization, the *Discourse on Inequality* breaks sharply with central themes of the Enlightenment. Opposition to Rousseau's ideas is seen in Voltaire's description of the work as Rousseau's "new book against the human race" (Cranston, I, 306). Such intellectual conflicts prefigured ruptured personal relationships between Rousseau and his former associates, and his later conviction that they were conspiring against him.

Scholars view the *Discourse on Inequality* as the most influential of all Rousseau's works (Cranston, I, 293). In addition to its high literary quality, this piece develops the opposition between man's natural goodness and the corrupting influence of civilization into a distinctive political position, opposed to liberal political theory as well as Enlightenment beliefs. According to Rousseau, the problems caused by civilization can be overcome only in a new form of political organization, along the lines of what he presents in *The Social Contract*. As Rousseau writes in the *Confessions*, "All that is challenging in *The Social Contract* had previously appeared in the *Essay on Inequality*" (*Conf.*, Bk. 9, p. 379).

Rousseau's political theory is complex, and has been interpreted in widely different ways. We will see some particular reasons for this below. Like Machiavelli and Montesquieu, he is a gifted literary stylist. His love of paradoxes and epigrams enlivens his writings, making them a delight to read. But he often writes *too* well. Apparently unable to resist a striking phrase, he presents particular ideas so vividly they take on exaggerated importance in his thought, often appearing to conflict with what he says elsewhere. But in spite of particular problems of interpretation, we will see that the *Discourse on Inequality* combines readily with *The Social Contract* to form a consistent political argument. This employs the familiar devices of the state of nature and the social contract. But in Rousseau's hands, these ideas take on radical, new implications.

Rousseau's State of Nature

In his *Discourse on the Origins of Inequality*, Rousseau presents a famous description of man in the state of nature. A representative passage is as follows:

> [W]hen I consider him, in a word, as he must have left the hands of nature, I see an animal less strong than some, less agile than others, but all in all, the most advanta- geously organized of all. I see him satisfying his hunger under an oak tree, quenching his thirst at the first stream, finding his bed at the foot of the same tree that supplied his meal; and thus all his needs are satisfied. (*Sec. Dis.*, Pt. I, p. 40)

Because of his hardy outdoor life, natural man is tougher than civilized man. He relies on physical abilities to satisfy his needs. Thus he must run faster, be stronger and better able to climb trees than his civilized successors. Having to live out of doors, he is far more robust and impervious to the weather. Similar characteristics can be observed in manlike apes, and natural man is likened by Rousseau to an orangutan (*See. Dis.*, n. 9, pp. 97–98).

It is obvious that there are enormous differences between Rousseau's "natural man" and man in the state of nature as depicted by Hobbes and Locke. Rousseau's man is obviously "natural" in the sense of unformed by civilization. But what does this say about the "state of nature" arguments basic to liberal political theory? As we will see, Rousseau's conception of "natural man" is bound up with wholesale rejection of liberal political ideas.

Rousseau's belief that man is naturally good and corrupted by civilization entails a conception of politics different from the liberal view. As we have seen, for liberal theorists, political institutions are instrumental, intended to serve as means to the attainment of preexisting ends. This view of politics is expressed in their accounts of the state of nature and the transition to political society made necessary by its problems. For Rousseau, in contrast, political institutions are not means to existing ends but are intended primarily to change people's ends. Like Hobbes and Locke, Rousseau posits a prepolitical state of nature and employs the device of the social contract. But because of his different conception of politics, his account of the state of nature departs sharply from previous presentations.

The instrumental view of politics presented by liberal theorists is bound up with a limited conception of what is politically possible. For these theorists, human nature is essentially stable. The state of nature and social contract are employed to justify specific political institutions by showing they are best suited to alleviate problems that would arise in their absence. The problems, in turn, result from flaws in human nature, which emerge in the absence of governmental restraint. This view posits significant continuities in man's nature between the state of nature and political society. Indeed, it is necessary that man's nature not change if the state of nature is to illustrate the problems that would arise without government.

Rousseau, in contrast, argues that human nature is malleable. The state of nature he postulates is intended to trace the changes man undergoes in moving from this condition to political society. Rousseau views this as essentially a process of corruption. In moving from the state of nature to civil society, man loses his initial innocence. The problems encountered in society are a result of this change and can be alleviated by reshaping people to recreate a semblance of their original situation. Rousseau's state of nature is a theoretical working out of the revelation he had on the road to Vincennes. In the *Discourse on Inequality*, he largely fulfills the ambition described in the letter, to demonstrate "that man is naturally good and has only become bad because of [social] institutions" (Quoted by Cranston, I, 228).

In previous chapters we have seen that the state of nature argument is generally comprised of two stages, movement from a state of nature to civil society. The two-stage model is not adequate for Rousseau's purposes. He distinguished between a state of natural innocence in which man is as he comes from the hand of nature, and a corrupt state, in which man's innocence has been lost, as he has fallen under society's sway. This second stage represents the situation of existing people, and so the political problem Rousseau wishes to solve. For Rousseau this is the condition people must leave in order to form a proper society. But in contrast to the problem situations described by Hobbes and Locke, Rousseau does not construct this corrupt stage by imagining what things would be like in the absence of government. Rather, corrupt existing government is a central feature of this condition—and a central part of the problem Rousseau addresses.

For ease of reference, we can refer to the two stages of Rousseau's analysis as the "original state of nature" and "existing society," respectively. Rousseau has a dim view of existing society. He believes it is thoroughly corrupt and its inhabitants miserable. But because he believes man is malleable, he posits a solution to this problem far more radical than anything envisioned by Hobbes or Locke. While they believe political institutions should *control* the defects of human nature, Rousseau's state is intended to *remove* them—to a large extent. His account of the original state of nature is intended to show it is possible to move beyond the sorry condition of existing society. Just as impure society has corrupted man's original innocence, so proper social conditions can largely restore this. Rousseau recognizes limits here. In crucial respects the movement to society brings about unalterable changes in man's nature, and there is no going back. But effects of some permanent changes can be counteracted. Accordingly, even with these limitations, Rousseau's contrast between the two stages of development presented in the *Discourse on Inequality* shows that man is not inevitably the corrupt creature we see around us.

Thus Rousseau's overall political argument is comprised of three stages:

A. the original state of nature, a situation of innocence;

B. corrupt existing society;

C. reformed society, based on proper moral and political principles.

The transition between A and B fulfills the essential function of describing the origin of man's present plight, and so also indicates what is possible by way of reform. The third stage is presented in *The Social Contract*.

The movement from A to B is reflected in the structure of the *Discourse on Inequality*. After a dedicatory letter to the Republic of Geneva, Rousseau presents a brief, theoretical preface. The bulk of the work is comprised of two parts. In Part I, Rousseau presents a description of life in the original state of nature. Part II presents the passage from this natural condition to the horrors of existing society in a series of stages, each of which introduces additional aspects of civilization and brings about increased corruption.

Rousseau makes no claim to historical accuracy. He is aware that his construction of the original state of nature, and so also the stages in the movement to existing society, are an imaginative reconstruction. He describes his state of nature as a condition "which no longer exists, which perhaps never existed, which probably never will exist, and yet about which it is necessary to have accurate notions in order to judge properly our own present state" (*Sec. Dis.*, Preface, p. 34). It is necessary to understand the progress from man's natural condition, because some semblance of this probably occurred. Proof that man is not naturally corrupt is the existence of societies in which he has been better, especially virtuous ancient republics such as Sparta and the Roman Republic. The prodigies of virtue who inhabited these states demonstrate that man is not without hope. As properly designed institutions have created good citizens in the past, so similar arrangements should have similar effects in the future. This indicates some raw material in man's nature that is capable of being shaped, yielding virtue or vice in accordance with its treatment. A central task of the *Discourse on Inequality* is to reconstruct this essential core. Though the details of the state of nature are speculative, Rousseau's overall endeavor is more securely grounded:

> Let us therefore begin by putting aside all the facts, for they have no bearing on the question. The investigations that may be undertaken concerning this subject should not be taken for historical truths, but only for hypothetical and conditional reasoning, better suited to shedding light on the nature of things than on pointing out their true origin, like those our physicists make everyday with regard to the formation of the world. . . .
>
> O man, whatever country you may be from, whatever your opinions may be, listen: here is your history, as I have thought to read it, not in the books of your fellowmen who are liars, but in nature, who never lies. (*Sec. Dis.*, pp. 38–39)

The makeup of natural man provides a moral standard against which existing societies can be measured. Good societies allow him to realize his potential; bad ones hinder this.

The Original State of Nature

As presented in Part I of the *Discourse on Inequality*, Rousseau's natural man is a limited being. Most striking is an absence of reason, leaving a creature as much animal as human.

Arguing that reason is not part of man's original endowment but develops in response to circumstances, Rousseau resists making "man a philosopher before making him a man" (*Sec. Dis.,* Pref., p. 35).

As we have seen, without reason, natural man is in many ways like other animals. In a note to the *Discourse,* Rousseau discusses the close relationship between natural man and "species of anthropomorphic animals," especially the orangutan (*Sec. Dis.,* n. 9, pp. 97–98; see pp. 95–101). Deprived of reason, natural man's existence is almost purely physical. He has few needs; he must eat and drink, find some modicum of shelter. He is also almost entirely solitary. Living alone, he has neither the need for language nor the capacity to develop it.

As we have seen, natural man is a hardy, apelike creature, as much animal as human, well-equipped to satisfy his simple needs. Living without a mate, he is able to reproduce because of purely physical urges. These lead men and women to meet, have sex, and part from each other. The female bears the child and cares for it until it is able to fend for itself. Then mother and child too part, and soon do not even recognize one another. In the natural condition there is no love. Love implies the focus of certain sentiments on an exclusive partner, whom the lover idealizes. Natural man does not have the psychological mechanisms necessary for this emotion. His conscious life as a whole is altogether limited. With little capacity for abstract thought, he focuses only on his immediate needs. His mind barely works at all:

> His imagination depicts nothing to him; his heart asks nothing of him. His modest needs are so easily found at hand, and he is so far from the degree of knowledge necessary to make him desire to acquire greater knowledge, that he can have neither foresight nor curiosity. (Pt. I, pp. 45–46)

When he is not moved by some need, he exists in a semiconscious state, between sleeping and waking, "like animals which do little thinking and, as it were, sleep the entire time they are not thinking" (Pt. I, p. 44).

In describing this semihuman creature as "natural," Rousseau uses the term in a particular way. What is natural is what develops, or would develop, without the intervention of human civilization. Thus we speak of "natural wilderness areas," by which we mean they are unaltered by man. "Natural foods" are grown without chemicals or other "artificial" substances. Rousseau also uses the term "natural" in a related but slightly different sense, which implies a moral standard. In this second sense, what is "natural" is what would develop without the *corrupting* influence of civilization. "Natural" in this sense implies some entity's *proper* development. Thus natural education, as described especially in *Emile,* is intended to allow the subject's capacities to achieve their full potential. This process is not "natural" in the previous sense, in that it requires human intervention. A proper understanding of nature can reveal man's potential and so guide us in an attempt to remold society to allow this to emerge. The society described in *The Social Contract* is natural in the second sense, as it is intended to develop people who lack the crippling difficulties of civilized men.

This second sense of "natural" illustrates how Rousseau views the goodness of nature. What is natural in this sense lacks the defects of society, which have turned man from his proper path. As described in the *Discourse on Inequality,* natural man is good primarily in a negative sense. Though not a moral being, he lacks the vices of civilization and so is innocent, and instinctively does what is right. Lacking reason, he has no access to natural law, and so cannot follow it. His psychology is dominated by two main urges. First is a form of self-love (*amour de soi*), centering on self-preservation. "Self-regard" or "self-concern" express what Rousseau has in mind. Natural man also feels compassion (*pitié*) for other creatures, which allows him to empathize with them and so experience something of their suffering. This leads him to avoid causing harm to other beings, especially fellow men (Pref., p. 35).

Natural man is interested in what he needs, but because of natural pity does not desire to harm other creatures. The combination of self-regard and compassion leads him to behave instinctively according to an ethic analogous to the golden rule: "*Do what is good for you with as little harm as possible to others*" (Pt. I, p. 55; Rousseau's emphasis). Because his psychological makeup leads him to follow this precept instinctively rather than consciously, he is not virtuous, properly speaking. With the development of reason, he can attain a higher moral condition, by reestablishing these rules "on other foundations" (Pref., p. 35). Though scholars have argued that Rousseau discards traditional notions of natural law, careful reading of his texts demonstrates a more complex view. Though the precepts are not accessible to natural man and are followed by no existing societies, natural law still provides an objective standard of right.[13]

As his innocence is comprised of an absence of motives to be otherwise, so natural man's happiness is mainly an absence of the misery found in society. Without the ability to think, he has few needs and is at peace. As a physical creature, he focuses on what is immediately at hand:

> For one can desire or fear things only by virtue of the ideas one can have of them, or from the simple impulse of nature; and savage man, deprived of every sort of enlightenment, feels only the passion of this latter sort. His desires do not go beyond his physical needs. The only goods he knows in the universe are nourishment, a woman and rest; the only evils he fears are pain and hunger. (Pt. I, p. 46)

He does not fear death, because he has no conception of it, and certainly does not live in its apprehension.

Natural man's happiness lies in a fit between his desires and ability to satisfy them. Rousseau believes satisfied desires are a source of contentment, while unsatisfied desires are the reverse. To attain happiness, then, one can limit one's desires or increase the ability to satisfy them. In general, Rousseau prefers the former course, because he believes increasing our abilities actually undermines our happiness. For, as we gain power, this stimulates the mind in such a way that our desires tend to grow as well, in fact outstripping our ability to satisfy them. As he says in *Emile*,

> It is only in this primitive condition that we find the equilibrium between desire and power, and then alone man is not unhappy. As soon as his potential powers of mind begin to function, imagination, more powerful than all the rest, awakes and precedes all the rest. It is imagination which enlarges the bounds of possibility for us, whether for good or ill, and therefore stimulates and feeds desires by the hope of satisfying them.[14]

In the primitive condition, man's powers are not developed, but neither are his needs. His desires are few, mainly physical. When these are satisfied, he is at peace. As we will see in the next section, man's decline from a condition of innocence and peace is precipitated by a growth in his powers which causes increasing desires he is never able to satisfy.

In addition to limiting his desires, natural man's absence of reason removes many possible sources of misery and conflict between people. In society, people are often unhappily in love, and battle other people over their chosen ones. Man's natural condition is without these evils. Rousseau distinguishes the physical and psychological aspects of love. Natural urges lead man to the opposite sex. But for his purposes, one partner is as good as another. There is no focus of sentiment on a single person who is viewed as the most beautiful or desirable possible lover. Rejected by one partner, natural man simply finds another and thinks no more about it.

Though the state of nature has sources of danger and harm, these are far less burdensome than those of society. In society, Mark slaps Ralph in the face. Though the physical injury is slight, Ralph is insulted and demands revenge. From an incident like this, severe conflict can result. A well-known example is described by Dostoyevsky in *Notes from Underground*. The underground man collides with a policeman. Though the underground man is not injured, he is enormously insulted. Plots for revenge come to dominate his life. This sort of morbidity is not possible for natural man. Once again, Rousseau distinguishes the moral and psychological sides of injury. If a tree falls on someone, injuring him slightly, he laments the injury but is not angry at the tree. Anger is a response to an offending agent's desire to cause one harm. Because the tree has no such desire, one regards the injury as a misfortune and thinks no more about it. The same is true if one is harmed by another person. Lacking the intellectual equipment to imagine the other's harmful intent, one deals only with the injury. The possibilities for conflict in such cases are thereby minimized.

All in all, as described in the *Discourse*, reason is a capacity we are well off without:

> If nature has destined us to be healthy, I almost dare to affirm that the state of reflection is a state contrary to nature and that the man who meditates is a depraved animal. (Part I, p. 42)

Because he does not think about anything beyond his immediate existence, natural man is happy. "I would very much like someone to explain to me what kind of misery there can be for a free being whose heart is at peace and whose body is in good health?" Though misery and even suicide abound in society, "I ask if anyone has ever heard tell of a savage who was living in liberty ever dreaming of complaining about his life and of killing himself" (Pt. I, p. 52).

In addition to being happy, natural man is naturally independent. For Rousseau, this condition is bound up with his ability to satisfy his own needs. Because these are minimal, he requires no one's assistance, and so cannot be subordinated to anyone else. "[I]t is impossible to enslave a man without having first put him in the position of being incapable of doing without another" (p. 59). Even if person A wishes to enslave person B, there is little way for him to do it. It would be more trouble for him to guard his captive than it would be worth. With the first opportunity, B would slip away into the woods, and A would never see him again (pp. 58–59). It would be much easier for A to fend for himself than to try to profit from another's labor.

Along similar lines, there is little inequality among natural men. One man can be taller or stronger or faster than another. But as with animals, there are few dimensions on which people differ. Men in the state of nature are as equal as dogs or cats or horses: "inequality is hardly observable in the state of nature, and . . . its influence there is almost nonexistent" (Pt. I, p. 59). The avowed subject of the *Discourse* is the origin of inequality. Rousseau argues that extensive inequality arises only with the differentiation of society.

THE DIALECTIC OF REASON

Though he is in many ways like other animals, natural man differs in having the crucial capacity to change. Rousseau refers to this as "perfectibility." One generation of cats is much like the one that came before it. The same is true of dogs and horses and other animals. But because of his reasoning capacity, man is able to progress. Rousseau's term *perfectibility* is perhaps ironic, as the consequences of developing reason destroy the harmony of the state of nature and initiate a series of profoundly corrupting developments.

As we have seen, Rousseau does not believe the ability to reason is innate. Rather, it lies dormant until a situation arises in which it is needed. If natural man is able to satisfy his needs without difficulty, then reason's contribution is minimal. If food is plentiful in the natural condition, then man simply picks it off trees or bushes. But if he must struggle to satisfy his wants, then he must begin to think. Imagine a hungry man finding fruit in a tree, but out of his reach. Desiring the fruit, he might come up with the idea of throwing something at it to knock it down. But presumably, even this amount of intellectual effort is unnecessary. If he cannot reach the fruit on one tree, there are others. In addition, far more agile than his civilized descendants, he might simply climb a high tree to pick its fruit. Thus as long as man's abilities are adequate to meet his needs, he will not have to think about satisfying them, and his reasoning capacity will not develop. Because, as we have seen, Rousseau views happiness as a condition in which one's needs are satisfied, the absence of developed reason is not only a source of happiness but a sign of it. When someone is content, he will not think much, and his ability to reason will lie dormant.

Rousseau does not claim to know how man evolved from his natural state. He imagines several possible transitions. Chance occurrences were necessary (Pt. I, p. 59), but Rousseau is unable to say exactly which actually took place. For instance, conditions might have changed, making subsistence harder to attain. This required the use of reason, and so brought about progressive developments. In Rousseau's words,

> Such was the condition of man in his nascent stage; such was the life of an animal limited at first to pure sensations, and scarcely profiting from the gifts nature offered him, far from dreaming of extracting anything from her. But difficulties soon presented themselves to him; it was necessary to learn to overcome them. The height of trees, which kept him from reaching their fruits, the competition of animals that sought to feed themselves on these same fruits, the ferocity of those animals that wanted to take his own life: everything obliged him to apply himself to bodily exercise. It was necessary to become agile, fleet-footed and vigorous in combat. Natural arms, which are tree branches and stones, were soon found ready at hand. He learned to surmount nature's obstacles, combat other animals when necessary, fight for his subsistence even with men, or compensate for what he had to yield to those stronger than himself. (Pt. II, p. 60)

In response to this account, one must wonder why these problems arose all of a sudden. Did trees suddenly become higher, or animals more ferocious? Throughout the bulk of his description of man's natural condition, Rousseau indicates that man easily satisfies his needs and therefore does not develop. Thus one wonders what occurs to alter this. In a few contexts Rousseau suggests that increasing population leads to new difficulties. Perhaps people spread to new territories, where conditions are less accommodating (p. 61). Or perhaps great floods or earthquakes cause the isolation of certain areas, creating new impediments to survival (p. 63). In any event, however these changes come about, the stability and ease of man's original existence are disrupted. He is forced to work harder to survive and as a result begins to rely more on his reason.

We will discuss specific stages of development in the following section. But first we should note the insidious dynamic Rousseau associates with reason. In certain respects, Rousseau views reason as an instrumental faculty. It is a means to the attainment of given ends, and as we have seen, as long as one's ends are satisfied easily, it does little. But as we have also noted, there is an additional dimension to reason: it dramatically affects desires. Natural man has a limited range of desires, mainly those associated with physical needs. But as he begins to reason, the range of his desires will increase, causing him to reason more and so further increasing his desires. Thus the appetites of a reasoning creature are unlimited. Because happiness centers on ability to satisfy one's desires, Rousseau holds that a reasoning creature is necessarily miserable.

The needs created by reason can be described as artificial or false.[15] They are distinct from the true needs of natural man in that they are not exclusively physical, such as, for instance, desires for increased physical comfort. More important is a range of desires associated with one's conception of oneself. These desires are not for specific objects, for example, food or drink, but to be a certain kind of person, especially one who is regarded by others in a certain way. Such needs are false in two ways. First, they are not "natural," in that they are produced only by human society and cannot arise in its absence. Second, these needs make people miserable. Because they cannot be satisfied, they are impediments to happiness, and as we will see, are viewed by Rousseau as the basic sources of civilized corruption.

The consequences of natural man's appeal to reason are accordingly immense. He evolves from a peaceful, unthinking creature to a thinking but miserable being, torn by needs he cannot satisfy. As further results of these changes, he loses his independence, his natural equality, and his innocence.

In constructing his original state of nature, Rousseau is aware of the enormous distance that separates it from the state of nature described by Hobbes. Hobbes's account, as we have seen, is one of unremitting horror. Conflict-torn, insecure, and brutish, the Hobbesian state of nature poses a stark contrast to Rousseau's idyllic condition. Rousseau believes his view is correct, and has a strong criticism of Hobbes.

Rousseau contends that Hobbes's state of nature is not "natural," that Hobbes constructs it by placing *social* man there. This is of course correct. Using the state of nature to illustrate sources of conflict that government must control, Hobbes places social man in a situation without government and describes the consequences. For this argument to work, the being placed in the state of nature must correspond closely to the being with whom political institutions must deal. In Rousseau's eyes, this procedure is flawed, because it does not explore man's true nature. In reading Hobbes, one can easily assume that man in this state of nature is natural man, in the sense of being this way because of inherent defects rather than human intervention. Accordingly, one would conclude that Hobbes views men as deeply flawed and liable to fall into conflict. But Rousseau believes Hobbes has "wrongly injected into the savage man's concern for self-preservation the need to satisfy a multitude of passions which are the product of society and which have made laws necessary" (Pt. I, p. 53).

The flaw in Hobbes's strategy is that he mistakes the men he finds in his society for mankind in general. This leads to unwarranted pessimism in regard to the possibility of political reform. If man is by nature—and so inevitably and necessarily—as Hobbes describes, the only plausible political arrangements are also as Hobbes describes, intended to check people's tendency toward violence. But because Rousseau believes natural man is actually as we have seen, a much better outcome is possible.

Hobbes's main mistake is in depicting man as by nature a reasoning creature. Rousseau believes that, because natural man is solitary and his reasoning capacity undeveloped, he is not prone to the sources of conflict Hobbes describes. As we saw in Chapter 2, Hobbes posits three main causes of conflict: scarcity, vainglory, and fear (see p. 45). To begin with the first, because there are not enough scarce goods to go around in Hobbes's state of nature, people fight over them. In Rousseau's state of nature, man's desires are extremely limited, and natural abundance is assumed. Thus this source of conflict is not a danger. Similarly, vainglory does not exist in Rousseau's state of nature. Natural man does not have the psychological resources to experience this. He is solitary rather than social, and not aware of how others view him. Similarly, the suspicion that one's neighbors might attack requires a degree of intellectual sophistication lacking in Rousseau's natural man. By making natural man a solitary creature and removing his ability to reason, Rousseau defuses the sources of conflict Hobbes describes. And so Rousseau's natural man should not fall into a war of all against all. In Rousseau's eyes, Hobbes is simply wrong; natural man is not the sorry creature he depicts. But as we will see, as natural man moves into society, develops the capacity to reason, and changes in other ways, he begins to engage in Hobbesian conflict. The peaceful state of nature becomes a war of all against all.

To close this section, we should note that the psychological model Rousseau sketches in the *Discourse on Inequality* is intended to describe the inner workings of social man as well. Rousseau believes the psychological mechanisms of natural man live on in developed society, but have been overgrown by additional attributes. Thus, as people become more civilized, they lose their natural repugnance at seeing others suffer. Though they still have natural compassion, this is drowned out by other capacities. "Reason is what engenders egocentrism, and reflection strengthens it. Reason is what turns man in upon himself. . . . Philosophy is what isolates him and what moves him to say in secret at the sight of a suffering man, 'Perish if you will; I am safe and sound'" (Pt. I, p. 54). Beneath the clamor of reason, however, the natural (i.e., potentially good) passions lie dormant. In *Emile*, Rousseau describes a process of education that allows a child to develop these passions in society. But because of the corrupting influences of society, proper education requires that the child be isolated. The young Emile is accordingly educated outside of society. In *The Social Contract*, Rousseau describes the kind of society in which the natural passions can develop to the fullest possible extent.

CORRUPT SOCIETY

The movement from the original state of nature to existing society, described in Part II of the *Discourse*, takes place in a series of stages. These can be counted in different ways, but it seems there are four main stages:

1. the village
2. the introduction of property
3. the formation of government
4. the degeneration of government into tyranny.

As we saw in the last section, for reasons about which Rousseau is not entirely clear, conditions changed in the state of nature. People were forced to struggle for subsistence, requiring development of their reasoning powers, and so giving rise to a spiral of transformation out of the state of nature.

The first stage emerged as people discovered the benefits of cooperation with one another. For example, a group of hunters is vastly more efficient at catching deer than a single hunter. As people came to associate, crude languages arose. Rousseau says these developments occurred only gradually, that he is "flying like an arrow over the multitude of centuries" (Pt. II, p. 62). But with each change, the next came more easily, and the pace of progress gained momentum. With each change came greater intellectual awakening, enabling more rapid advances, increased intellectual development, and so on. Gradually, people began to use tools and construct dwellings. Families began to live together. This brought about a fundamental emotional change:

> The first developments of the heart were the effect of a new situation that united the husbands and wives, fathers and children in one common habitation. The habit of living together gave rise to the sweetest sentiments known to men: conjugal love and paternal love. (Pt. II, pp. 62–63)

Living in society, people began to soften physically, and to lose some of their natural ferocity. Though individuals were less able to resist savage beasts, the combined efforts of the group made them more secure. With simple needs, people had considerable leisure, and devised conveniences. Rousseau has a highly negative view of comforts, which in time become necessities. We can see this in our own cases. Though there was in effect no television fifty years ago, it is now difficult to imagine how we would get along without it. The same is true of cars, and VCRs, to say nothing of personal computers. Unfortunately, in time each new convenience loses its novelty and ceases to be a source of pleasure, though losing it would be a privation. As people become used to having certain things, they give up some of their natural independence:

> [T]hat was the first yoke they imposed on themselves without realizing it, and the first source of evils they prepared for their descendants. For in addition to their continuing thus to soften body and mind (those conveniences having through habit lost almost all their pleasure, and being at the same time degenerated into true needs), being deprived of them became much more cruel than possessing them was sweet; and they were unhappy about losing them without being happy about possessing them. (Pt. II, p. 63)

In addition to man's increasing dependence on conveniences, problems emerged in his relationship with other people. Along with the tender sentiments of family life came other emotions, including jealousy: "Jealousy awakens with love; discord triumphs, and the sweetest passion receives sacrifices of human blood" (p. 64).

The most important change brought about by developing civilization concerned people's sense of themselves. As people became accustomed to seeing others, and with the advent of language, they began to make comparisons. With the development of ideas of beauty and merit, people wished to be viewed as having them and without faults:

> Each one began to look at the others and to want to be looked at himself, and public esteem had a value. The one who sang or danced the best, the handsomest, the strongest, the most adroit or the most eloquent became the most highly regarded. And this was the first step toward inequality and, at the same time, toward vice. From these first preferences were born vanity and contempt on the one hand, and shame and envy on the other. And the fermentation caused by these new leavens eventually produced compounds fatal to happiness and innocence. (p. 64)

Vanity (*amour propre*) is an outgrowth of self-regard (*amour de soi*). But whereas the latter is a natural sentiment, and also healthy, in causing people to be concerned with their own welfare, vanity emerges as the primary source of man's social ills.

The need to be esteemed is artificial in the two senses noted above. It not only grows through human interaction but represents a falling away from innocent drives and so causes unhappiness. Rousseau believes vanity cannot be satisfied:

> Vanity, which is always comparing oneself with others, is never satisfied and never can be; for this feeling, which prefers ourselves to others, requires that they should prefer us to themselves, which is impossible. (*Emile*, Book IV, p. 174)

We have seen Rousseau views happiness as a fit between desires and the ability to satisfy them, and this can be achieved either by increasing one's abilities or limiting one's needs. Man in the state of nature is happy because of the simplicity of his needs, which allow easy satisfaction. With the advent of vanity in civilization, however, people acquire a desire that resists satisfaction. Civilization necessarily causes unhappiness; the rise of vanity in the human psyche is an ineradicable ill.

In spite of its drawbacks, this first stage of civilization represented the happiest form of human life. Though it presented difficulties, these were on the whole outweighed by its new sources of satisfaction. Rousseau describes this as the "youth of the world," man's "happiest and most durable epoch," and says that man never should have left it. This is confirmed by the fact that primitive peoples throughout the world are generally found in this condition (Pt. II, p. 65).

The advantages of this condition are further confirmed by the fact that Europeans regularly defect to it—to live in some semblance of a tropical paradise. The reverse is never the case. Not only are there no instances of natives voluntarily leaving this for so-called civilization, but there are instances of natives who have been taken from their tribes and raised by Europeans under European conditions but have continued to prefer this way of life. "Nothing can overcome the invincible repugnance they have against appropriating our mores and living in our way" (n. 16, p. 106). Rousseau relates the story of a Hottentot raised from infancy by Dutch settlers in South Africa. He was given all the advantages of civilization, including rich clothing and education. But after visiting some Hottentot relatives, he returned in a sheepskin, gave back his European clothes, and vanished into the forest (n. 16, pp. 107–108).

In spite of the advantages of the village condition, it was unstable and eventually underwent changes. The discovery of metallurgy and other arts enabled the rise of agriculture. People began to cultivate the land, and along with an emerging division of labor came differences in wealth. With developing society, language too developed, and the mind assumed its present form. Living in close proximity, people assessed each other according to qualities of beauty, strength, skill, and talents. "And since these were the only ones that could attract consideration, [each man] was soon forced to have them or affect them." Vanity grew apace, and it became necessary for people to present themselves as something other than what they were. "Being something and appearing to be something became two completely different things; and from this distinction there arose grand ostentation, deceptive cunning, and all the vices that follow in their wake" (Pt. II, p. 67). Closer social interaction bred dependencies. While natural man could satisfy all his needs through his own efforts, people now had a plethora of needs for the satisfaction of which they had to depend on other people.

The most significant development at this stage was the rise of property. Rousseau is often viewed as a forerunner of socialism because of the ringing denunciation of property with which he opens Part II of the *Discourse*.

> The first person who, having enclosed a plot of land, took it into his head to say *this is mine* and found people simple enough to believe him, was the true founder of civil society. What crimes, wars, murders, what miseries and horrors would the human race have been spared, had someone pulled up the stakes or filled in the ditch and cried out to his fellow men: "Do not listen to this impostor. You are lost if you forget that the fruits of the earth belong to all and the earth to no one!" (p. 60)

In spite of the rhetoric, however, Rousseau was never a socialist in the strict sense; he never advocated public ownership of the means of production. In the *Discourse on Political Economy*, he says the right to property "is the most sacred of all the citizens' rights" (p. 127). As we will see below, in *The Social Contract* he advocates an economic system based on small farmers, each of whom owns his own land. On the whole, Rousseau is not opposed to property per se but to its effects, especially the problems that result from sharp divisions between the rich and poor. But though he is not a socialist in the strict sense, he is a spiritual father of socialism in that he believes the property system of existing society is responsible for enormous misery and must be reformed. He differs from socialists in the direction in which he would push reform—in this respect as in others, looking backward in time towards simple agricultural communities rather than forward. But his moral critique of the existing property system is an important feature he and socialists share.

With the introduction of property, a new source of distinction arose between rich and poor, and new ties of mutual dependence between the classes. The rich needed the poor's services; the poor needed the rich's help. As property fulfilled the essential function of increasing the esteem of the rich, inequalities inevitably grew as the rich became insatiable. They "had no sooner known the pleasure of domination, than before long they disdained all others, and using their old slaves to subdue new ones, they thought of nothing but the subjugation and enslavement of their neighbors, like those ravenous wolves which, on having once tasted human flesh, reject all other food and desire to devour only men" (p. 68).

The division between rich and poor created new difficulties. The poor coveted the property of the rich, and the rich feared to lose it. Conflict over property gave rise to "the most horrible state of war" (p. 68). It is at this point that people came to resemble the creatures who populate Hobbes's state of nature. One should probably regard Rousseau's language here as a direct allusion to Hobbes.[16] Now degenerated into a condition of conflict, society became insupportable, especially to the rich, who had the most to lose. Lacking means to justify their acquisitions, and conscious that what force had given them could also be taken away by force, the rich devised an ingenious plan to retain their goods. Rousseau calls this "the most thought-out project that ever entered the human mind." By instituting a government to protect the lives and goods of everyone, they could make sure their own fortunes were secure. Through this means, the greater strength of the poor could be enlisted on the side of the rich. Thus the rich approached the poor with the following proposition:

> Let us unite . . . in order to protect the weak from oppression, restrain the ambitious, and assure everyone of possessing what belongs to him. Let us institute rules of justice and peace to which all will be obliged to conform, which will make special exceptions for no one, and which will in some way compensate for the caprices of fortune by subjecting the strong and the weak to mutual obligations. (Pt. II, p. 69)

When the poor agreed to accept this arrangement, government was instituted, to protect all alike.

This contractual arrangement indicates Rousseau's fundamental rejection of liberal political theory. As we have seen especially in Locke, for liberal theorists government is instituted primarily to protect property. Though all are treated equally by such a policy, this is only formal equality. The rich benefit far more than the poor; they have greater resources and so more to protect. In fact, as Rousseau's discussion makes clear, the rich are primarily interested in protecting their property *from* the poor. Now, if the wealthy presented this bargain to the poor in its real terms, it would never be accepted. The poor would be foolish to agree to a set of rules designed to keep them away from the wealthy's goods. The wealthy overcome this problem by presenting the contract as in the poor's own interest. The purpose of government is to protect *them* from injustice, to make sure *their* property is secure. It is so important to protect the poor man's few miserable sticks of furniture that a sacred right to property must be established, which will guarantee the security of all property. The poor were taken in by this line of argument, not realizing the wealthy's ulterior motives. Of course a sacred right of property is most beneficial to those who own the most. Thus the poor "ran to chain themselves, in the belief that they secured their liberty" (p. 70).

Rousseau's criticism of the contract of government is of great importance, and will reverberate in the arguments of Karl Marx considered below. In the *Second Treatise of Government,* Locke presents the contractual mechanism through which government arises as between equals. All men are the workmanship of God and so equal in the fundamental respect of possessing natural rights. Though Locke is highly interested in the origin of property and well aware of unequal property in the state of nature, he does not relate these aspects of his theory to the contract. In fact, as we saw in Chapter 3, his argument is carefully crafted to justify an *unequal* distribution of property in civil society.

Rousseau's great advance here is to note respects in which people are unequal, and lay bare the contract's implications in regard to them:

> Such was, or should have been, the origin of society and laws, which gave new fetters to the weak and new forces to the rich, irretrievably destroyed natural liberty, established forever the law of property and or inequality, changed adroit usurpation into an irrevocable right, and for the profit of a few ambitious men henceforth subjected the entire human race to labor, servitude and misery. (Pt. II, p. 70)

It is not surprising that government, which was erected through the deviousness of the rich, was used by them to create additional inequalities. "For the vices that make social institutions necessary are the same ones that make their abuses inevitable" (p. 77). The power of the magistrate was misused, and a state of tyranny ensued.

Here, according to Rousseau, we have come full circle. While all people were equal, innocent, and independent in the original state of nature, at this point they were corrupt and dependent on one another, but restored to a new condition of equality. In the chaos that engulfed society, all were equal once again, but equal in being nothing:

> Here is the final state of inequality, and the extreme point that closes the circle and touches the point from which we started. Here all private individuals become equals again, because they are nothing. And since subjects no longer have any law other than the master's will, nor the master any rule other than his passions, the notions of good and the principles of justice again vanish. Here everything is returned solely to the law of the strongest, and consequently to a new state of nature different from the one with which we began, in that the one was the state of nature in its purity, and this last one is the fruit of an excess of corruption. (p. 79)

Rousseau indicates four dimensions along which inequality has developed. While in the original state of nature people differed only in their physical characteristics, in society they are unequal in regard to wealth, rank, power, and personal merit (p. 78). In developed society there are vast differences in all these respects. Given the desire for preeminence that drives people, the result is inevitably wholesale misery. Similarly, while the state of nature was one of independence, indeed, generally solitude, in society man has a litany of needs that cannot be satisfied without the help of other people. Thus people must live together, which is a source of pain because of insatiable desires for self-esteem.

In Rousseau's eyes, the major differences between the state of nature and corrupt, developed society are psychological. In moving from the former to the latter, natural man has lost his sense of self. Through alteration of his passions, the original makeup of his soul has been covered over with new drives. In the Preface to the *Discourse*, Rousseau compares social man to a statue of the sea god Glaucus, "which time, sea and storms had disfigured to such an extent that it looked less like a god than a wild beast." So man's soul, "altered in the midst of society by a thousand constantly recurring causes, by the acquisition of a multitude of bits of knowledge and of errors . . . by the constant impact of the passions, has, as it were, changed its appearance to the point of being nearly unrecognizable" (p. 33). The hypothetical course of development traced in the *Discourse* is intended to lay bare the nature of the transformation. This centers upon the effacement of all other drives by vanity. Social man is consumed by what others think of him. He is driven by a need for esteem he can never satisfy, and toward this end makes himself and those around him miserable.

Such, in fact, is the true cause of all these differences; the savage lives in himself; the man accustomed to the ways of society is always outside himself and knows how to live only in the opinion of others. And it is, as it were, from their judgment alone that he draws the sentiment of his own existence. (pp. 80–81)

For the sake of impressing others, civilized men have left nature behind. Society presents nothing but "an assemblage of artificial men and factious passions" (p. 80).

In spite of the grimness of Rousseau's account, there are grounds for hope. The problems we encounter in society are not rooted in man's nature but are caused by departure from this. The progress of man's passions traced in the *Discourse on Inequality* cannot be reversed. But because our problems are not inherent in man's original nature, under certain circumstances, they can be overcome.

THE SOCIAL CONTRACT

Rousseau's problem in *The Social Contract* is to find a form of political association that will restore as much of man's natural innocence as possible, allowing him to be as good as he can be. According to the famous first sentence of Book I, Chapter 1: "Man is born free, and everywhere he is in chains" (p. 141). The freedom Rousseau refers to regards man's potential, if he had not been corrupted by civilization. The sentence is of course rhetorical; since the advent of society, man's state of natural freedom has been left far behind. Thus addressing the great problem of political reform, Rousseau does not envision a society made up of people as they were before society transformed them. The development of reason cannot be reversed; man cannot be restored to his original, savage condition, with limited mental capacities and only physical needs. Beginning with "men as they are and laws as they might be" (Bk. I, p. 141), Rousseau believes proper completion of his task requires starting with human nature as it is in contemporary society.

Through proper laws, a semblance of man's original condition can be recaptured. Under certain circumstances, the progress of inequality can be reversed and people made equal citizens. Though society ordinarily places people in a situation of dependence, Rousseau hopes to make them independent. They will own their own land and so not be dependent on other people economically. In addition, a central feature of Rousseau's proposed political system is an absence of subordination. Though free citizens must obey the law, in doing so, Rousseau argues, they obey only themselves.

The Social Contract was originally intended to be part of a larger work, entitled *Political Institutions*, which Rousseau envisioned as a general treatise on government. In the *Confessions*, he writes:

I had seen that everything is rooted in politics and that, whatever might be attempted, no people would ever be other than the nature of their government made them. So the great question of the best possible government seemed to me to reduce itself to this: "What is the nature of the government best fitted to create the most virtuous, the most enlightened, the wisest, and, in fact, the best people, taking the word 'best' in its highest sense?" (Book 9, p. 377)

After working on *Political Institutions* for several years, Rousseau made little progress. He eventually decided to publish a portion of the work, "to extract what could be extracted and then to burn the rest." *The Social Contract* was published within two years (*Conf.*, Bk. 10, p. 479). In the Foreword to *The Social Contract*, Rousseau notes that it is "part of a longer work I undertook some time ago," which has been long since abandoned (*S.C.*, p. 140).

The Social Contract's origins are significant because the work is not a complete treatise. It discusses the question of the best form of government, and in that sense fulfills the intention noted in the *Confessions*. But missing is detailed attention to how government can make people virtuous. Though the question of education receives little direct attention in this work, it is central to Rousseau's overall design. *Emile* was published in 1762, the same year as *The Social Contract*, and Rousseau worked on the two books during the same period (*Conf.*, Bk. 10, p. 478). *Emile* contains a brief outline of the main political argument of *The Social Contract* (Bk. 5, pp. 422–430), and it seems reasonable to assume that the political forms presented in that work should be supplemented by some semblance of the system of education in *Emile*. Some caution is in order here, as education in *Emile* is of a single person within the confines of existing society. A system of public education would obviously be different in important respects.[17] But the close association of politics and education in Rousseau's thought is confirmed by the *Discourse on Political Economy*, in which the subject of political education is discussed in connection with the virtue necessary for government according to the general will.

In *The Social Contract* Rousseau pursues two supreme political values, freedom and equality. Both of these are present in the original state of nature and lost to the onslaught of civilization. The state described in this work maximizes its citizens' possession of both values. But because Rousseau pursues two different values, his precise position is often difficult to unravel. The fact that the two values often appear to conflict in part explains widespread controversy about his political theory. Rousseau has been viewed as both totalitarian and democratic—and much in between (see pp. 258FF).

NEGATIVE AND POSITIVE FREEDOM

The political institutions discussed in *The Social Contract* are intended to bring about freedom in a particular sense. Among the many paradoxes for which Rousseau is famous, one of the most notorious appears in Book I, Chapter 7 of the work. Rousseau writes that if a person refuses to abide by the "general will," he will be "forced to be free" (p. 150). We will discuss exactly what Rousseau means by the "general will" below. What concerns us here is the puzzling notion of forcing someone to be free, which raises fundamental issues concerning the nature of freedom. We will see that Rousseau's idea rests on a distinctive conception of freedom, different from that of the liberal tradition, encountered in our discussions of Hobbes, Locke, and Montesquieu.

In previous chapters we have seen that "freedom," as the term is generally used, is bound up with an absence of interference by other people, especially by government. Hobbes, for instance, defines freedom (or liberty, terms we can use interchangeably) as follows:

> Liberty, or Freedome, signifieth (properly) the absence of Opposition; (by Opposition, I mean externall Impediments of motion;) and may be applyed no lesse to Irrationall and inanimate creatures, than to Rationall. (*Leviathan*, Chap. 21, p. 145)[18]

According to Hobbes, inanimate objects can be impeded by obstacles. Thus the "freedom" of a rock to roll down a hill can be blocked by a wall. For people, the most important impediment is other people, who can prevent someone from doing what she wants to do. For example, if it is illegal to use cocaine, the government will penalize its use. Because of this interference, people are not "free" to use it. Thus Hobbes writes that in civil society the most important freedom depends on "the Silence of the Law": "In cases where the Sovereign has prescribed no rule, there the Subject hath the Liberty to do, or forbeare, according to his own discretion" (*Lev.*, Chap. 21, p. 152). In other words, the subject is free to do what she wants, as long as it is not against the law. When something is against the law, doing it raises the possibility of punishment by the sovereign, and so the subject is not free to do it.

A conception of freedom similar to Hobbes's is basic to the liberal tradition of political theory as seen in previous chapters, and also a familiar feature of many modern political systems. We describe the United States and Great Britain as "free countries," in opposition to other countries that are less fortunate. If we identify the point of contrast, we will probably say that in an "unfree" country, such as North Korea, the government is constantly interfering in people's lives, preventing them from doing what they would like. The United States is more "free" because the government allows people far more leeway. This is seen in many familiar "freedoms" American citizens enjoy. Freedom of religion centers on the fact that the government allows people to worship as they please, without punishing them. Freedom of speech means that people can say what they like, without interference. Freedom of the press means that people are able to print what they like, or broadcast their opinions using different media, without fear of government interference. The same is true of other freedoms, for example, freedom of movement and from arbitrary search and seizure, in short, the overall freedom to live as one likes. As we have seen in our discussions of Locke and Hobbes, securing freedoms of this sort is central to liberal political theory. We refer to political systems in which these freedoms exist, protected by constitutional governments, as "liberal" states.

Even in liberal states, the freedoms under discussion are of course limited. The nature of these limits is a difficult and controversial subject, which we cannot discuss in detail here.[19] Briefly, common sense tells us we are not free to do as we please if this causes harm to other people. I am not free to worship as I please, if doing so requires human sacrifice. I am not free to say what I please when this entails perjury, or slandering other people's reputations. Similarly, if I shout "Fire" in a crowded theater, the subsequent panic and scramble to escape could injure people, and so this sort of behavior is also forbidden. In each of these cases, exceptions to the freedom citizens generally enjoy are enforced by government. Citizens who violate these injunctions, and others like them, are subject to punishment. Thus we can say that I am not free to shout "Fire" in a crowded theater because the coercive interference of government prevents me from doing so.

On the whole, laws are the most significant restrictions on freedom in liberal societies. These prohibit certain modes of behavior and require punishment when they occur. Within the liberal tradition, then, we find general opposition between the spheres of freedom and government activity. Thus the force of Hobbes's phrase is clear: in general, freedom exists in the silence of the laws. But freedom can also be limited by other factors. For instance, the freedom of a four-year-old child is restricted by her parents. She is not free to stay up to all hours or to eat unlimited amounts of junk food, because of interference by her parents rather than government. Similarly, public opinion is often viewed as a limit on freedom. Especially in an intolerant society, people are not free to live as they like, or to worship as they like, because they would find resulting public disapproval unpleasant. Thus noncoercive interference can prevent people from doing what they like. We have repeatedly noted that government is often defined in reference to its monopoly of the legitimate use of force. Accordingly, governments tend to monopolize coercive limitations on freedom, while factors such as public opinion can limit freedom through other means.

As we saw in regard to "rights" in previous chapters, the liberal conception of freedom can be illustrated with spatial metaphors. The freedom someone enjoys can be viewed as a certain territory within which he is able to do as he likes, without fear of interference by other people, especially government. According to this view, the limits of this territory are most often justified by concerns that beyond a certain point the actions of one person intrude on the territory of others.

The conception of freedom we have been discussing, freedom as the absence of coercive interference by others, is frequently referred to as "negative" freedom.[20] We have noted in previous chapters that a negative conception of freedom is central to liberal political theory. But if we employ this conception, we can see why Rousseau's view is para-doxical. If freedom is an absence of coercive interference, of force, it appears to make little sense to speak of "forcing people to be free." How can we use force to bring about an absence of force? To take a concrete example, it appears odd to speak of forcing people to worship as they please, if worshipping as one pleases centers on making this choice without the threat of force.

In order to unravel Rousseau's view of freedom, we can begin with what he takes to be an important shortcoming of negative freedom. Rousseau focuses on an aspect of freedom about which liberal theorists are largely silent. As we have seen, negative freedom centers on a certain space within which people can do as they please. What is missing is attention to what people will do with their discretion. For instance, in liberal society a person is free to live as he likes—as long as he does not harm others. But what if he chooses to live in a worthless or self-destructive manner? Assume that Jake chooses to spend his time drinking large quantities of cheap wine, thereby damaging his health and causing unhap-piness to those around him. Conceivably, government could intervene to limit his freedom when he begins to threaten other people, for instance by driving under the influence of alcohol. But aside from these cases, it is his business what he does with his life. He is "free" to waste his life. But one can ask if an alcoholic is *really* free.[21]

If we answer this question in accordance with a negative conception of freedom, we must say that Jake is free in choosing to drink himself to death. After all, this is a choice he makes; it is not forced upon him by other people. But is it *really* a free choice? We recognize that alcoholism is an addiction, a disease. In this case, it is likely there is some-thing in Jake, his alcoholism, interfering with his choice of how to live. When we say that alcoholism limits *his* choice, we posit a part of him that is the seat of his identity, his real self, which would presumably behave reasonably if he did not suffer from the addiction. Because his addiction interferes with this, we can say *he* is not free in acting under the influence of alcoholism, because this prevents him from making the kind of choices sane, rational people ordinarily make. Though the factor impeding Jake's choice is something inside him, rather than external interference of other people, it is interference nonetheless. Before Jake is free to make rational choices, he must be purged of his harmful addiction to alcohol. A paradox similar to Rousseau's can emerge here. It might take the coercive interference of other people to get Jake to check into an alcoholism treatment center. In a sense, then, he can be forced to be free (of his addiction).

The main idea of what we refer to as "positive" freedom centers on *internal* impediments to people's ability to live as they like. The case of an alcoholic is a clear example. But as we will see, the concept becomes controversial in encompassing a wider range of cases. The notion of positive freedom requires an accepted standard of proper choice, that a person can be expected to do certain things, or to choose in a certain way, and that she would do so in the absence of constraint. Proponents of this view often appeal to the idea of a true self, and attempt to distinguish this from what is interfering with its operations. In the first volume of this work, we discussed the view of Plato, which clearly illustrates the relevant distinctions. According to Plato, the human soul is tripartite, possessing a reasoning part, what he calls a "spirited" part, and a part comprised of appetites, especially lower, physical appetites. Plato argues, basically, that when individuals choose on the basis of reason, they choose properly. They encounter problems when the appetitive part takes control and sacrifices the soul's overall good to the gratification of its own desires. In this sort of theory, it is natural to view the reasoning part of the soul as the "true" or "real" self, and the appetites as external factors that can interfere with this. It follows, then, that just as a person can be set free from external impediments, for example, from prison or slavery, so the reasoning part, the "true self," can be freed from the bondage of appetite. Plato argues along these lines, and a central concern of his political theory is rescuing people from the toils of appetite.[22]

In considering the case of a drug addict or alcoholic, we see that two important values can come into conflict. For ease of reference, we can refer to *what* a person chooses as the "content" of her choice, and the *way* the choice is made as its "form." In an ideal situation, a person left to her own devices will make the proper choice. In such a case, both form and content are consistent with important values. But an obvious problem arises if the person threatens to choose wrongly. One of the two conflicting values must be sacrificed, but which one? For proponents of positive freedom, this decision is frequently clear. In their eyes it is paramount that people behave properly. If they will not do so by themselves, then they must be made to through government interference. Positive freedom is a theory of "freedom," because its proponents generally argue that if a person is choosing wrongly, she is doing so because of the presence of internal impediments, analogous to addiction. Through government intervention, which can assume the form of counseling or education—or, more controversially, coercion—the subject can be rescued from this internal obstacle, and so allowed to behave properly. It is consistent with this conception of freedom that people can be forced to be free.

Though it is perhaps controversial to refer to intervention by external authorities as extending a person's "freedom," the network of ideas on which positive freedom is based is not entirely foreign to the liberal perspective. In certain extreme cases, the liberal tradition also recognizes that interference with people's liberty (negative liberty) is justified. The clearest cases concern people who suffer from mental handicaps and so are not able properly to control their own lives. Children too are properly placed under the supervision of their parents. But, as Locke notes, this is a temporary condition. When children attain the age of reason, they are ordinarily freed from parental domination and allowed to conduct their own lives. Because people who are mentally retarded or mentally ill are frequently unable to achieve the necessary degree of intellectual and emotional stability, they are placed under the custody of others. In severe cases, mentally ill people who are threats to themselves or others can be involuntarily confined to mental institutions.

Strictly speaking, the involuntary confinement of a dangerous schizophrenic is an infringement on that person's (negative) freedom. But even a strong proponent of negative freedom would surely view this as justified in many cases. Negative freedom is one value that must be accommodated to others. Supporters of negative freedom will defend a requirement that its possessor be able to use it effectively, at least to a minimal extent. A clear difference between upholders of negative and positive freedom is that proponents of the former view will minimize the conditions under which intervention is justified. One of the firmest convictions of the liberal tradition is that government intervention can be justified by people's incapacities only under extreme circumstances. Aside from these cases, people should be free (in the negative sense) to live their own lives in their own ways. Thus even if people are choosing wrongly (or in a way one views as wrongly), proponents of negative liberty generally believe they should be able to act without interference and suffer the consequences.

Proponents of positive freedom support intervention in a wider range of cases. They present stronger requirements individuals must satisfy before they can be allowed to choose for themselves. While traditional liberals recognize problems in allowing children, people with mental illness, and perhaps drug addicts or alcoholics, to be entirely free (in the negative sense), supporters of positive freedom expand the list of debilitating conditions. Most striking is the view of Rousseau and other thinkers that subordination to certain appetites precludes enjoyment of negative freedom. The core of Rousseau's view is that the corrupt urges that dominate civilized man prevent him from acting freely. Thus *most* inhabitants of existing societies are not free, regardless of the area of protected space afforded by government within which they are able to act.

Rousseau's espousal of positive freedom gives him an overall perspective sharply opposed to liberal political theory. The liberal theorist's main concern is placing limits on governmental power to maximize negative freedom. We have noted that liberals view politics as "instrumental." Political activity is not undertaken for its own sake, but to provide a framework of law and order which allows individuals to pursue goals they have prior to entering political society. For Rousseau and other proponents of positive freedom, the purpose of political institutions is primarily educative. It is to reshape people's characters so their "real" selves can predominate over offensive urges. In arguing along these lines, Rousseau presents a political theory that recalls central themes of classical political theory, especially the ideas of Plato, as discussed in Volume I.[23] Rousseau's resurrection of classical political ideas runs in tandem with his desire to restore political forms similar to the ancient city-states in which these ideas flourished.

Though to this point we have treated negative and positive freedom as different concepts, it is necessary to look more closely at the relationship between them. Scholars have questioned the distinction between the forms, arguing that they are actually variants of a single, broader conception of freedom.[24] Though to some extent the issue here is semantic, that is, what we mean by "freedom," exploring the relationship between the two forms is helpful in clarifying the nature of freedom and shedding light on both forms. The most notable discussion is by Gerald MacCallum, whose mode of analysis I will follow here.[25] According to this point of view, whenever we discuss a situation of freedom, three variables come under consideration. Freedom is a triadic relationship, which can be expressed as follows:

X *is free from* Y *to do or to become* Z.

In this formulation, X refers to a person or agent. Y refers to impediments to the agent's activity, while Z refers to the ends the agent can or should accomplish. In the standard situations of negative freedom discussed above, X is a person who is free from Y, governmental interference, Z, to say or to do what he pleases. This formula applies to freedom of worship: X, a person, is Y, free from governmental interference, Z, to worship as he pleases.

The main advantage of the triadic formula is that it also encompasses situations of positive freedom. For example, in saying that a drug addict is not free (in the positive sense) because of his addiction, we employ similar variables. In this case, X, the addict is not free because of Y, the interference of his addiction, which prevents him from Z, behaving responsibly or rationally. This analysis suggests that different conceptions of freedom are reducible to the basic triadic formula, with differences resulting from how the variables are employed in specific cases.

Though the triadic formula is able to cover cases of both negative and positive freedom, it does not eliminate the substantial differences between the two concepts. Negative and positive freedom differ in their treatment of the Y and Z terms. In a case of negative freedom, Y, the impediment to action, is generally coercive interference by other people. In a case of positive freedom, the impediment is often internal, for example, the drug addict's addiction. In regard to the Z term, the two concepts of freedom differ as well. In standard cases of negative freedom, the subject is free from the obstacles in question, Z, *to do as he pleases*, with little in the way of specified content. The situation is different in regard to positive freedom, as this provides a more precise account of Z, what or how the free person should choose. There is often a clear conception of proper conduct to which people should conform, and to which free people do conform. Thus the addict is not free because he does not behave as a rational person would. Though there are additional complexities involved in the relationship between the two kinds of freedom, this brief account should suffice here. The triadic relationship is admirably clear and so an important contribution to our understanding of freedom. But even though it encompasses the main variables in the two conceptions, their emphases are sufficiently different to justify regarding them as different kinds of freedom.

SELF-GOVERNMENT

For Rousseau, an additional sense of freedom must be considered. Though he is not always consistent in his use of moral language, he generally uses the term "freedom" (*liberté*) in a political sense. According to this usage, a people enjoys freedom if it makes its own laws, rather than having them made by others. An example of this sense is as follows:

The English people believes itself to be free (*libre*). It is greatly mistaken; it is free only during the election of the members of Parliament. Once they are elected, the populace is enslaved; it is nothing. Given the use made of these brief moments of freedom (*liberté*), the people certainly deserves to lose it. (Bk. III, Chap. 15, p. 198)[26]

Closely related to this is the notion of "moral freedom" (*liberté morale*). The idea here is that the morally free person governs himself, rather than being ruled by appetite:

[M]oral liberty (*liberté morale*) . . . alone makes man truly the master of himself. For to be driven by appetite alone is slavery, and obedience to the law one has prescribed for oneself is liberty (*liberté*). (Bk. I, Chap. 8, p. 151)

What Rousseau has in mind in this passage is clearly similar to positive freedom, as we have discussed it. The morally free person is not controlled by his appetites but rules himself (i.e., is controlled by his "true self"). The opposition between one's "self" and appetites has been discussed above. But moral freedom, as Rousseau uses the term, also encompasses the idea of ruling oneself. We can refer to this as "self-government."

Self-government is an important political idea, closely associated with democratic political forms. In a democracy, a people governs itself, rather than being governed by an external body, either monarch or nobility. We will see that Rousseau makes extreme demands in regard to self-government, that all citizens be able to vote directly (not through representatives) on every proposed law.

With the rise of liberal democratic states over the last few centuries, self-government, along with negative freedom, has become one of the central ideas in the Western tradition. These two values are central to many modern states. Because they are so closely linked in practice, it is possible to fail to distinguish their meanings, but they are easily distinguished. The main concern of self-government is who makes the rules according to which people must behave. In contrast, negative freedom centers on a space within which the subject is free to do as he pleases. The two concepts raise quite different questions: (i) What is the area within which subjects should be left to do as they please? (ii) What, or who, has control over defining this area?[27]

The differences between negative liberty and self-government are classically discussed in an essay by Benjamin Constant (1767–1830), "The Liberty of the Ancients Compared with that of the Moderns."[28] Constant's argument is largely in criticism of Rousseau and essential for understanding central difficulties of Rousseau's political thought. In looking at Constant's argument, we will see that he discusses self-government as a form of liberty, which he calls the "liberty of the ancients." His usage of this term is consistent with the way moral terms were employed in the ancient world. In the ancient world, a "free" people governs itself, in comparison to cities or states that are ruled by external powers. Similarly, a free person occupies a certain legal status. Especially important, he is not a slave. In the ancient world, being a free citizen was often closely associated with possessing certain political rights, especially the right to participate in the process through which laws were made.

Constant's main argument turns on distinguishing the liberty found in ancient city-states and that of the modern world. He argues that the modern conception of freedom is comprised mainly of freedom within the law, as found in France, England, and the United States. In these countries, freedom for each of their citizens "is the right to be subjected only to the laws, and to be neither arrested, detained, put to death or maltreated in any way by the arbitrary will of one or more individuals" (Constant, p. 310). This is clearly recognizable as negative freedom, as we have defined the term. In ancient city-states, what was referred to as "liberty" was, as we have noted, quite different, mainly rights of political participation (i.e., what we have called "self-government"). The free citizen enjoyed rights in this respect beyond any encountered in modern states. But Constant notes that this did not entail enjoyment of negative freedom:

> [A]mong the ancients the individual, almost always sovereign in public affairs, was a slave in all his private relations." (p. 311)

Constant contends that in these states, society's jurisdiction was unlimited. There was no area of privacy into which government could not intrude. The classic case was Sparta, in which the state took children away from their families at an early age to educate them. Citizens ate their meals at common tables. Husbands were not able openly to visit their wives until the age of thirty. The list could be extended.

Constant's main point is that the "liberty" of the ancients is compatible with an absence of negative freedom, with what we would regard as tyranny. Though extensive rights of self-government might give the individual some say in what the government decides, he has no real security against it. What Constant calls the aim of modern life, "the enjoyment of security in private pleasure" (p. 317), is not protected from state interference. The ancients believed "that everything should give way before collective will, and that all restrictions on individual rights would be amply compensated by participation in public power" (Constant, p. 320).

Thus it is possible for a state to be liberal but not democratic—or the reverse. For example, a nondemocratic system in which the individual's rights are protected, is a central aim of Montesquieu. As long as the individual enjoys an area of protected space, free from the interference of government or other individuals, he possesses negative freedom. To the extent provision of negative freedom is the central value of liberal political theory, such a state can be "liberal," even if government is not democratic and the people have no say in defining the boundaries of this protected space.

On the other hand, as the argument of Constant shows, democracy can be inconsistent with negative freedom and so a liberal state. Even if a given government is democratic, the system can provide individuals with little protected space. This was the case in the ancient world, where people had few rights against the state, and it could intrude into virtually all areas of life. As we will see, this also approximates the position of Rousseau. Negative freedom is not a central concern of his political theory. More important to him are positive freedom, that the individual be a certain kind of person, and self-government. Rousseau places great weight on this last, arguing that in a legitimate government all citizens must have extensive rights to participate in the political process. His reason for this is perhaps bound up with his great concern for equality and lack of dependence. Unless an individual rules himself, he must be ruled by others, and will be inferior to them in status and dependent on them for his well-being.

Rousseau believes the ideal of self-government can be realized only if all citizens vote on all laws. "Any law that the populace has not ratified in person is null; it is not a law at all" (S.C., Bk. III, Chap. 15, p. 198). He is aware that this limits the size of his proposed polity to something approximating an ancient city-state. In addition, it should be kept in mind that he assumes there will be relatively few laws. Rousseau believes that once a political system is enacted, it will change relatively little and hence need few new laws. A major reason for his view is that he wrote before the Industrial Revolution, as a result of which social conditions have been changing rapidly for more than two centuries. These have in turn necessitated extensive changes in the legal and political systems of modern countries.

Rousseau's main argument for requiring direct participation in legislation is that *will* cannot be represented. A person can authorize a representative to vote for her on a specific occasion. Let us assume Maria knows she is opposed to a specific water project and authorizes Pierre to cast her vote for her. But the situation is different if she authorizes Pierre to vote on a range of issues, some of which she might not yet even be aware of, over a period of time. A United States senator is elected for a six-year term, to represent the interests of his constituents in regard to all measures that come before the Senate. Rousseau does not view this as adequate representation. To appoint a representative in this fashion is not self-government, but rather to set up a master whom one promises to obey (*S.C.*, Bk. II, Chap. 1). For this reason, Rousseau criticizes the English system, which does not provide self-government. A portion of this passage was quoted above:

> The English people believes itself to be free. It is greatly mistaken; it is free only during the election of the members of Parliament. Once they are elected, the populace is enslaved; it is nothing. The use the English people makes of that freedom in the brief moments of its liberty certainly warrants their losing it. (Bk. III, Chap. 15, p. 198)

An immediate sense in which Rousseau regards the system he proposes as superior is that all citizens take part in the process through which each law is enacted. Because of his concern for self-government, Rousseau argues that sovereignty must be vested in the people, and so the only legitimate form of state is a republic. Rousseau's advocacy of self-government makes him one of the staunchest proponents of democracy in the history of political thought.

Rousseau is not consistent in his terminology in regard to freedom. Indeed, at one point he says "the philosophical meaning of the word *liberty*" is not one of his concerns (*S.C.*, Bk. I, Chap. 8, p. 151). But what we have called self-government is obviously central to his thought. What Rousseau calls moral liberty is based on extending the idea of self-government from the political to the personal sphere. One respect in which society is superior to the state of nature is that it allows a person to live according to rules she makes for herself. In the state of nature, one is innocent and free from both interference by other people and the promptings of corrupted appetite. But one is still governed by appetites one has not chosen and so by forces over which one has no control. Obviously, then, the ideal is to be governed by proper appetites one has chosen for oneself. This combines proper "form" (*how* rules are chosen) and proper "content" (that the rules are correct). These two ideas are present when Rousseau speaks of "the acquisition in the civil state of moral liberty, which alone makes man truly the master of himself. For to be driven by appetite alone is slavery, and obedience to the law one has prescribed for oneself is liberty" (*S.C.*, Bk. I, Chap. 8, p. 151). Though Rousseau does not draw the relevant connections, this account of moral liberty is based on positive freedom as well as self-government. Moral liberty is living according to laws one prescribes for oneself, when the laws in question are proper.

Throughout the remainder of this chapter, we will examine implications of Rousseau's desire that people not only govern themselves, but do so in a particular way.

Principles of Political Right

The subtitle of *The Social Contract* is "Principles of Political Right." In this, his greatest political work, Rousseau inquires into the moral conditions of a proper political order. Are there arrangements under which people can lead fully moral lives in society? If there are, then states must institute them in order to be legitimate.

The problem Rousseau poses in this work is as follows:

> "Find a form of association which defends and protects with all common forces the person and goods of each associate, and by means of which each one, while uniting with all, nevertheless obeys only himself and remains as free as before." This is the fundamental problem for which the social contract provides the solution. (*S.C.*, Bk. I, Chap. 6, p. 148)

Rousseau's question concerns what must be given up in order to live in society. The word "free" in the quotation refers to self-government. On the face of it, this must be sacrificed in society, unless some means can be devised through which all can live together cooperatively but still obey only laws each has prescribed for himself. In *The Social Contract*, Rousseau attempts to work out conditions under which this can be arranged.

He argues that the solution to the problem requires a particular relationship between citizens, expressed in a social contract. There is only one solution to the problem, and so only one possible contract: "The clauses of this contract are so determined by the nature of the act that the least modification renders them vain and ineffectual, that, although perhaps they have never been formally promulgated, they are everywhere the same, everywhere tacitly accepted and acknowledged" (p. 148). The contract consists of a single proviso: "the total alienation of each associate, together with all of his rights, to the entire community" (p. 148).

According to this contract all citizens turn over all their rights to the state. What they get in return is a share of sovereignty, the political body's decision mechanism. Rousseau believes this is an equal exchange and so entails no renunciation. Each citizen gets back exactly what he contributes, though in a different form. This can be illustrated with a simple example. Assume there are ten citizens and each possesses rights with a value of 1. Everyone's rights are turned over to the community, giving it rights with a value of 10, the disposition of which is to be determined by the community. Since each member is $\frac{1}{10}$ of the community, each has 10 percent control of rights valued at 10, which is equal to 1, what he started with. What is crucial to note is the citizens' transition from individuals to members of a community. Before entering the contract, each has his own rights valued at 1. After the contract, each controls a share of the community's total rights, though as an individual he controls nothing. He has renounced his individual status to become a part of the whole.

The contract gives each person two different statuses. In one capacity he is a decision-making member of the community, equal to all other members. In another, he is a subject, standing in a particular relationship to the community. Thus the contract creates a particular relationship between the individual and a public body of which he is a member.

It is central to this arrangement that citizens receive equal status. Because all turn over all their rights to the community, all are precisely equal: "since each person gives himself whole and entire, the condition is equal for everyone" (p. 148). Because this is so, each has an interest in making the condition all share as good as possible.

Rousseau presents the contract in highly paradoxical language. He argues that it entails no renunciation of freedom. After entering the contract, the citizens is as free as before:

> [I]n giving himself to all, each person gives himself to no one. And since there is no associate over whom he does not acquire the same right that he would grant others over himself, he gains the equivalent of everything he loses, along with a greater amount of force to preserve what he has. (*S.C.*, Bk. I, Chap. 6, p. 148)

To make sense of this, imagine that before the contract each individual has an acre of land. Because there is no state to protect the property of one individual from others, each is in a precarious situation. Through the contract they turn over all their land to the community in return for establishing a government to ensure the safety of all. The contract establishes a decision mechanism, and the citizens receive equal voting power. Each receives an equal share of control over the community's resources. Because Rousseau believes in private property, he believes the community will return its resources to individuals. Because of equal participation in the decision, these will be distributed equally, and so each citizen will receive his original acre back from the community. But his condition has improved enormously, because the community will now protect it. The individual need no longer fend for himself.

For Rousseau, freedom is attained by submerging oneself in the community. In this respect, the contract produces a gain in negative freedom. An individual's rights, now protected by the community, will be safe from outside interference. In this sense, Rousseau's argument appears similar to those of Locke and other liberal theorists. The liberal view is that security is attained by surrendering rights of self-government (in Locke's case, rights to interpret, judge, and enforce the law of nature) to government. But as we have seen, Locke views this surrender as a loss of freedom. After government is set up, I am no longer free to judge and punish cases as I see fit, though government results in an *overall* increase of freedom in comparison to the precarious state of nature.

Rousseau refuses to accept any lessening of freedom in this exchange. His great aim is to create a mechanism that will provide security without a loss of self-government. He believes this is possible through a closer combination of the individual and society than liberals envision. The great paradox at the heart of his political theory is that complete freedom is secured by complete surrender to the community.

Rousseau's contract departs from the liberal tradition in central respects. Complete submersion in the community entails a complete renunciation of negative freedom. Liberal theorists argue that, in order for a person to secure some of her rights, other rights must be surrendered to the state. The aim is to carve out an area, protected by government, within which the individual can safely pursue her ends. Rousseau's contract requires surrender of *all* rights to the state, and so does not provide for a protected area.

Rousseau tempers this doctrine by saying the surrender of rights is limited by considerations of public interest: "each person alienates by the social compact, only that portion of his power, his goods, and liberty whose use is of consequence to the community" (*S.C.*, II, 4, p. 157). But as he notes, "We must also grant that only the sovereign is the judge of what is of consequence" (p. 157). Thus the individual has no rights against the sovereign's opinion of what must be given up.

The liberal theorist will object that Rousseau's position is highly dangerous. The individual has no rights against the state and so is obviously subject to oppression. The surrender required by Rousseau is greater than that recommended by Hobbes. Hobbes's subjects retain rights of self-preservation, while Rousseau's surrender these along with all others. In order for Rousseau's position to make sense, we must explain how his citizens can safely enter this arrangement, without fear of governmental abuse.

Two main questions arise here. The first concerns the theoretical feasibility of what Rousseau proposes. In surrendering all rights to the state, the individual leaves nothing in reserve and places himself at the state's mercy. Thus we must ask why people can be confident this renunciation is safe. As we will see, Rousseau believes his contract will work under certain conditions, which we will attempt to identify. Our second question concerns the practicality of Rousseau's proposals. Having identified the conditions under which he believes true freedom is possible in society, we must ask if these conditions can be met in any actual societies.

THE GENERAL WILL

Rousseau believes the key to reconciling freedom and becoming part of the community is government according to the "general will." This is his term for the decision mechanism established by the contract. The general will is perhaps Rousseau's most famous (or notorious) political idea, and must be explored in detail.

A helpful preliminary account of the general will is found in the *Discourse on Political Economy*. Rousseau notes an analogy between the body politic and a human being, in that both can be presumed to have wills. The general will is that of a political body. It is analogous to the will of a person, which can be presumed to aim at its holder's good. Central to the idea of the general will is that this should be the only source of all laws in the state. If the general will actually wills the good of the whole, then all laws will be consistent with this. To be governed by the general will is to be governed by what is good for the entire political body. Rousseau writes:

> The body politic, therefore, is also a moral being which possesses a will; and this general will, *which always tends toward the conservation and well-being of the whole and of each part*, and which is the source of the laws, is for the members of the state in their relations both to one another and to the state, the rule of what is just and what is unjust. (*P.E.*, p. 114; my emphasis)

However, even if we grant the analogy between the will of a person and of a political body, it is not clear how much weight can be placed on it. Several questions occur immediately. Why should we believe such a will must tend toward the good of the whole? Is this simply an analogy, or does Rousseau have convincing arguments to support it? In addition, one will note that in the quotation Rousseau conflates the good of the whole and of its members. The general will is not only good for the whole but for each part, as what is good for a whole organism is also good for its parts. The "parts" of the body politic, we can assume, are the individuals who constitute the state. Thus we must ask if it is true that what is good for the entire political body is necessarily good for each individual member.

Rousseau believes the general will should work if it is general in two respects: generality of origin and of object. The former entails that laws must be made by all citizens alike. As we have noted in our discussion of self-government, Rousseau requires direct political participation by all citizens. All must have the right to vote on every law. This idea has been discussed above, and so we can move on to generality of object.

By this, Rousseau means that laws made by the sovereign must be in regard to general considerations, which concern all subjects. Rousseau makes an important distinction between the sovereign and the government. This is similar to a distinction between legislative and executive branches of government. The former makes the laws, while the latter puts them into effect. In Rousseau's government, however, the separation of powers and checks and balances in the ordinary sense do not obtain, as the legislative branch is superior to the executive, which serves at its pleasure. The sovereign legislature, as we have seen, is comprised of all citizens. Only this can make the laws, and these must pertain to general questions. The government, which can be democratic, aristocratic, or monarchical, applies the laws to particular cases. We will return to the distinction between sovereign and government below. For now, we should note that all particular questions must be addressed by the government. For instance, the sovereign will declare that it is illegal to commit murder, and murderers will be punished in such and such way. Whether a certain person is guilty of this crime is a matter for the government to decide, through procedures such as a trial.

Generality of object is important, because as long as the sovereign confines itself to general questions, it can make laws in the interest of everyone. If it deals with a particular issue, for example, a dispute between two people, it cannot possibly legislate in a way that benefits both. Thus the sovereign should dictate the procedures according to which disputes should be dealt with, while applying these to a given dispute is a task for the government. According to Rousseau, "just as a private will cannot represent the general will, the general will, for its part, alters its nature when it has a particular object" (Bk. II, Chap. 4, p. 157).

By confining its attention to matters that affect all subjects alike, the sovereign should be able to legislate in the general interest. The sovereign is comprised of all citizens. In their capacity as subjects, they are affected by the laws they make, and so cannot have an interest in making them onerous. As long as they address issues that concern the interests of all alike, they can be trusted to do what is good for everyone:

> [T]he sovereign cannot impose on the subjects any fetters that are of no use to the community. It cannot even will to do so, for under the law of reason nothing takes place without a cause. . . .
>
> The commitments that bind us to the body politic are obligatory only because they are mutual, and their nature is such that in fulfilling them one cannot work for someone else without also working for oneself. Why is the general will always right, and why do all constantly want the happiness of each of them, if not because everyone applies the word *each* to himself and thinks of himself as he votes for all. (Bk. II, Chap. 4, p. 157)

In order for the general will to advance the interests of all members of society, certain conditions must be satisfied. Two main ones concern the nature of society, and the moral character of the citizens.

Rousseau's arrangements can work successfully in only certain kinds of societies. From the requirement that all citizens vote on all laws, it is clear that the society in question must be small. (We can note, however, that some contemporary theorists argue that electronic means of communication now make direct participation possible in much larger societies.[29] A familiar recent example is Ross Perot's idea of the "electronic town meeting.") In addition, legislation can promote the interests of all, only if all have generally similar interests. Rousseau presupposes a highly homogeneous society. There cannot be significant differences in regard to economic status, religion, race, or cultural practices. Let us assume important religious differences in society, for example, a sharp division between believers and atheists. In any society, many overall questions of how religion is to be treated are sufficiently general to be dealt with by the sovereign. But because of religious divisions in many societies, all citizens cannot fare similarly as a result of any decision. Any decision will produce winners and losers.

Rousseau argues that society is founded on common interest. Without common interests it cannot exist, and so the sovereign should legislate in accordance with these:

> For if the opposition of private interests made necessary the establishment of societies, it is the accord of these same interests that made it possible. It is what these different interests have in common that forms the social bond, and, were there no point of agreement among all these interests, no society could exist. For it is utterly on the basis of this common interest that society ought to be governed. (Bk. II, Chap. 1, p. 153)

Rousseau realizes that a state with *only* common interests would not require a political system: "If there were no different interests, the common interest, which would never encounter any obstacle, would scarcely be felt. Everything would proceed on its own and politics would cease being an art" (Bk. II, Chap. 3, n. 4, p. 156). Thus the question of general suicide is not debated by the American government. No one has an interest in this, and so the matter never comes up. Questions come to the fore only when there are opposing interests. In the state Rousseau proposes, clashes of interests are dealt with in two stages. First, the legislature makes laws concerning general procedures for handling them. Then particular problems are dealt with by the government.

As long as society is generally homogeneous, conflicts between members should be relatively infrequent. As conditions do not change drastically, new problems should arise only infrequently, and mechanisms for handling them should be rarely needed. The kind of society Rousseau has in mind is similar to ancient city-states such as Rome or Sparta, which remained unchanged for many years. In his own time, the closest approximations were simple agricultural communities. This is indicated by the following passage:

> When among the happiest people in the world, bands of peasants are seen regulating their affairs of state under an oak tree, and always acting wisely, can one help scorning the refinements of other nations, which make themselves illustrious and miserable with so much art and mystery?

> A state thus governed needs very few laws; and in proportion as it becomes necessary to promulgate new ones, this necessity is universally understood. The first to propose them merely says what everybody has already felt. . . . (Bk. IV, Chap. 1, pp. 203–204)

The high demands Rousseau places on his intended society indicate the impossibility of imposing his ideas on modern nation-states, which are not only far too large to allow all citizens to participate in government but are generally divided by innumerable separate, competing interests. There is no possibility that a modern government could decide complex fiscal, military, or environmental questions in such a way that it would correspond to what everyone has already felt, and would meet with immediate, unanimous acceptance.

In addition to requiring a simple, homogeneous society, the proper working of Rousseau's principles requires that citizens be virtuous. Rousseau uses this term in a particular sense. In many cases, a question of public policy will affect an individual in different ways. He has his own particular interests which may conflict with the interest of society as a whole. Virtue is willingness to subordinate what is good for oneself to what is good for society (see esp. *P.E.*, p. 119).

Consider a simple example. In a small agricultural society, a stream floods on occasion, damaging the crops of some members but not of those who live on higher ground. The question debated by the legislature must be general—whether all members of society should pitch in and help prevent natural disasters, when this is possible. Let us assume that a policy of this sort will clearly be in the public interest. Now assume that Auguste lives on low ground which is periodically flooded, and Jean-Claude, who lives on higher ground, is out of danger. When this question is debated, they both know perfectly well how their particular interests will be affected by the outcome. Auguste, who will benefit from passage of the policy, will easily see that it benefits the public as a whole and will support it. The question is more difficult for Jean-Claude. Though the policy will benefit society, it will be costly to him. Perhaps his taxes will be raised, or there might be a requirement that he help construct a dam. Because he will not benefit personally from the construction measures, he can easily be tempted to vote against the proposal, not because he thinks it is bad for society, but because he does not think it is good for him. In such a case, he can put the question of how to vote in either of two ways, according to what is good for society or for himself. Rousseau believes virtue consists in voting in the first way rather than the second. The virtuous person thinks of society's interest rather than his own—though in practice, this is little more than another way of saying that virtue is willingness to subordinate what is good for oneself to the common good.

The stream example depicts a situation in which the general will can be counted on to yield the correct answer, as long as a sufficient percentage of the population is virtuous. It concerns a simple society, and we have assumed that the public interest is clear. Thus as soon as someone proposes flood control, the need will be universally felt and a law easily enacted. But when Rousseau thinks of virtue, he probably has more exalted cases in mind, in which citizens are willing to make greater sacrifices for the public good. Rousseau is deeply impressed with the virtue of the Romans and Spartans. This is illustrated by well-known examples, which he recounts in Book I of *Emile*. For instance,

> The Spartan Pedaretes presented himself for admission to the council of the Three Hundred and was rejected; he went away rejoicing that there were three hundred

Spartans better than himself. I suppose he was in earnest; there is no reason to doubt it. That was a citizen.

A Spartan mother had five sons with the army. A Helot arrived; trembling she asked the news. "Your five sons are slain." "Vile slave, was that what I asked thee?" "We have won the victory." She hastened to the temple to render thanks to the gods. That was a citizen. (*Emile*, Bk. I, p. 8)

Though this degree of virtue is not required for successful government by the general will, some semblance of it is. Citizens must be willing to set their own interests aside and vote according to what is good for society. Rousseau presents a fundamental distinction between the general will and what he calls the "will of all." The general will comes about, as we have seen, through the direct vote of all citizens—under the assumption that they vote virtuously and so in accordance with their view of society's good. The will of all is also the result of a vote. But in this case, citizens vote according to their own interests:

There is often a great deal of difference between the will of all and the general will. The latter considers only the general interest, whereas the former considers the private interest and is merely the sum of private wills. (Bk. II, Chap. 3, p. 155)

Government by the will of all is not freedom. Though each citizen participates in the vote, the result does not express the general will, but the interest of one portion of society, which it is able to impose on the other parts. Thus in Rousseau's eyes, self-government is not enough. In addition to direct participation in lawmaking, freedom in political society requires that the majority decide according to the interests of the whole. If the majority is motivated by virtue, then their vote will embody the general will. Unanimity is not necessary. Even in the most advantageous circumstances, people will perceive the public interest differently. Deviations from the majority's will can be canceled out; what is left is the general will (Bk. II, Chap. 3, pp. 155–156).

If the majority is virtuous, their decision represents the good of society. In following this, the individual behaves according to the general interest, for which he voted. Even if he voted against some course of action, to follow it (even if forced to do so) is still freedom. The fact that the policy he voted for did not prevail shows only that he was mistaken about society's good. If society had followed his view, no one would have been free, himself included. These apparently paradoxical ideas are discussed in Book IV:

The citizen consents to all the laws, even to those that pass in spite of his opposition, and even to those that punish him when he dares to violate any of them. The constant will of all the members of the state is the general will; through it they are citizens and free. When a law is proposed in the people's assembly, what is asked of them is not precisely whether they approve or reject, but whether or not it conforms to the general will that is theirs. Each man, in giving his vote, states his opinion on this matter, and declaration of the general will is drawn from the counting of votes. When, therefore, the opinion contrary to mine prevails, this proves merely that I was in error and that what I took to be the general will was not so. If my private opinion had prevailed, I would have done something other than what I had wanted. In that case I would not have been free. (*S.C.*, Bk. IV, Chap. 2, p. 206)

In the next sentence, Rousseau adds that this "presupposes, it is true, that all the characteristics of the general will are still in the majority." If this is not the case, then freedom in society is impossible (p. 206).

But as long as the majority (a) is virtuous and (b) successfully identifies what is good for all, all alike are free. All live according to laws they themselves support—or would support if they were better informed and/or virtuous. Though the necessary degree of agreement is possible only in small, homogeneous societies, under these conditions people are able to attain a degree of freedom otherwise impossible in either the state of nature or corrupt existing societies.

The requirement that citizens be virtuous shows that Rousseau's view of freedom requires a combination of self-government and what we have called positive freedom. In considering the good of society over his own good, the citizen is able to overcome the promptings of selfish appetites and do what is right. Given his conception of human nature, Rousseau believes the requisite virtue is possible under certain circumstances, but it requires intensive education. Though questions of education receive little attention in *The Social Contract*, they are the main subject of *Emile*, and are discussed in the *Discourse on Political Economy*. We can look briefly at the latter work, which expresses Rousseau's view in compact form. In regard to "the second essential rule of public economy," he writes:

> Do you want the general will to be accomplished: Make all private wills be in conformity with it. And since virtue is merely this conformity of the private to the general will, in a word, make virtue reign. (*P.E.*, p. 119)

The reign of virtue is accomplished through education. Ideal is the system of public education that existed in Sparta, which was intended to inculcate love of country. This is accomplished through patriotic public spirit, which pervades the entire state, and to which people are exposed from birth. An idea of what Rousseau has in mind is seen in the following passages:

> Public education under the rules prescribed by the government and under the magistrates put in place by the sovereign, is therefore one of the fundamental maxims of popular or legitimate government. If children are raised in common and in the bosom of equality, if they are imbued with the laws of the state and the maxims of the general will, if they are instructed to respect them above all things, if they are surrounded by examples of objects that constantly speak to them of the tender mother who nourishes them, of the love she bears for them, of the inestimable benefits they receive from her, and in turn of the debt they owe her, doubtlessly they thus will learn to cherish one another as brothers, never to want anything but what the society wants, never to substitute the actions of men and of citizens for the sterile and vain babbling of sophists, and to become one day the defenders and the fathers of the country whose children they will have been for so long. (*P.E.*, pp. 125–126)

> For wherever the lesson is unsupported by authority, or the precepts by example, instruction remains fruitless, and virtue itself loses its influence in the mouth of him who does not practice it. But let illustrious warriors bent under the weight of their laurels preach courage; let upright magistrates whitened in the wearing of purple and

in service at the tribunals, teach justice. Both of these groups will thus train virtuous successors and will transmit from age to age to the generations that follow the experience and talents of leaders, the courage and virtue of citizens and the emulation common to all of living and dying for one's country. (*P.E.*, p. 126)

Rousseau says he knows of only three peoples who practiced proper public education: The Spartans, Cretans, and ancient Persians. It is surprising that ancient Rome achieved great virtue without such a system (*P.E.*, p. 126). But whatever the details of the institutions through which virtue is taught, this is a necessary condition for government according to the general will, and so for freedom in society.

GOVERNMENT

Though all citizens participate in making the laws, all do not administer them. This task is turned over to a government which we must keep sharply distinct from the sovereign. Though it is conceivable that the government can be democratic, if the sovereign legislature in another capacity administers the laws, Rousseau does not believe this is a workable system: "Were there a people of gods, it would govern itself democratically. So perfect a government is not suited to man" (*S.C.*, Bk. III, Chap. 4, p. 180). But even if the government is turned over to a monarch or a small body of aristocrats, this does not alter the fact that sovereign power remains in the people's hands. As noted above, because of the requirement that all citizens vote on all proposed laws, the people are sovereign in all legitimate governments. All legitimate governments are republics.

Because sovereign power is in the hands of the people, the government is subordinate to them. The people appoint it. The agreement between people and government is not a contract: "It is absolutely nothing but a commission, an employment, which the rulers, as simple officials of the sovereign, exercise in its own name the power with which it has entrusted them" (*S.C.*, Bk. III, Chap. 1, p. 173). The sovereign cannot enter into a contract with the government, because it cannot cede it any power: "the supreme authority cannot be modified any more than it can be alienated; to limit it is to destroy it" (Bk. III, Chap. 16, p. 200). Thus the government is entirely a creature of the sovereign. Its power is derivative; it serves at the pleasure of the sovereign, which can modify or revoke its authority at will (Bk. III, Chap. 1, p. 174).

Rousseau's discussion of government and other matters bearing on practical politics is heavily influenced by Montesquieu. In *Emile*, he notes, surprisingly, the latter's contribution to the "vast and useless" science of politics. Though Montesquieu receives high praise in comparison to other practitioners in this area, Rousseau criticizes him for not being concerned with "the principles of political right; he was content to deal with the positive laws of settled governments; and nothing could be more different than these two branches of study" (Bk. V, pp. 422–423). But in spite of Rousseau's preference for examining what ought to be over what is, he realizes the latter subject's implications for the former.

Like Montesquieu, Rousseau believes all forms of government are not suited to all countries, but must be in accord with a country's character and that of its people. Thus a people must be given the best institutions possible for its particular circumstances, though these are not necessarily best in absolute terms (*S.C.*, Bk. II, Chap. 11, p. 171). Rousseau realizes that his preferred form of government is not possible everywhere: "Since liberty is not a fruit of every climate, it is not within the reach of all peoples. The more one meditates on this principle established by Montesquieu, the more one is aware of its truth" (Bk. III, Chap. 8, p. 187). We will return to the specific conditions necessary for Rousseau's free state in a subsequent section.

Even if a successful republic is established, Rousseau believes its existence will be threatened by its government. The people who constitute a government have interests of their own, opposed to those of the public. Political power, placed in their hands, will tend to be abused for their own ends. If the government does manage to seize sovereign power, the contract of government is ruptured. Citizens would then be forced to obey, but without moral reasons to do so (Book III, Chap. 10, p. 193). As a student of history, Rousseau believes degeneration is inevitable: "If Sparta and Rome perished, what state can hope to last forever?" (Bk. III, Chap. 11, p. 194).

To preserve the state for as long as possible, Rousseau proposes extraordinary assemblies of the sovereign populace. These must be held according to a regular schedule, over which the government has no control. Because the government's power is derived entirely from the people, when the people are assembled the former relinquishes its power:

> Once the populace is legitimately assembled as a sovereign body, all jurisdiction of the government ceases; the executive power is suspended, and the person of the humblest citizen is as sacred and inviolable as that of the first magistrate, for where those who are represented are found, there is no longer any representative. (Bk. III, Chap. 14, p. 197)

Once assembled, the people must vote on two questions: whether they wish to preserve the present form of government; and whether they wish to retain the people who are presently serving in the government (Bk. III, Chap. 17, p. 203). Rousseau believes such assemblies can postpone the inevitable degeneration of his free state.

CIVIL RELIGION

As part of the state's moral foundation, Rousseau requires the institution of a civil religion. This is not propounded for the sake of theological orthodoxy. Toleration is one of its central tenets. But like Machiavelli, he realizes the important role religion plays in public affairs. No state has ever been founded without a religious basis (Bk. IV, Chap. 8, p. 223). Dissatisfied with possible alternatives, he presents a suitable civic religion for his free state.

Rousseau objects to Catholicism because it divides citizens' loyalties. It is so unsuited to civil affairs that he regards discussing it as a "waste of time" (Bk. IV, Chap. 8, p. 223). It confronts citizens with conflicting obligations. They must obey the laws of the state, but the edicts of the Church can contradict these:

> [S]ince there has always been a prince and civil laws, this double power has given rise to a perpetual jurisdictional conflict that has made all good polity impossible in Christian states, and no one has ever been able to know whether it is the priest or the ruler whom one is obliged to obey. (Bk. IV, Chap. 8, p. 222)

In Christian states, there are always "two sets of legislation, two leaders, and two home-lands." These "contradictory duties" are an insuperable obstacle: "Whatever breaks up social unity is worthless. All institutions that place man in contradiction with himself are of no value" (p. 223).

The possibility of a pagan religion has advantages. This provides religious reinforcement for the laws, and increases love of the homeland. It makes dying for the state martyrdom, and disobeying the laws impiety. Its problems, however, outweigh these virtues. Its precepts, to begin with, are "based on error and lies." "[I]t deceives men, makes them credulous, and superstitious, and drowns the true cult of the divinity in an empty ceremony" (Bk. IV, Chap. 8, p. 224). In addition, it increases animosity between states, transforming wars into holy wars, thereby contributing to murder and massacre (p. 224).

This leaves Gospel Christianity, a religion of simple piety. This has the great advantages of being true and promoting the brotherhood of all men. But it is unsuitable because it turns people's interests away from the state. As a spiritual religion, it will have the effect of making people servile and dependent. "Its spirit is too favorable to tyranny for tyranny not to take advantage of it at all times. True Christians are made to be slaves. They know it and are hardly moved by this. This brief life has too little value in their eyes" (pp. 224–225).

Rousseau's preference is for a civil religion, that is, a religion of the citizen. Because having a religion will make citizens more likely to fulfill their duties, religious convictions promote the public interest. Rousseau refers to these as "sentiments of sociability," rather than religious dogmas. But they must be held by all citizens. Beyond a few simple precepts, citizens are free to believe what they will. A suitable civil religion will make people better citizens, but their salvation is their own business. The state does not have jurisdiction over the life to come. The core of the civil religion is as follows:

> The dogmas of the civil religion ought to be simple, few in number, precisely worded, without explanations or commentaries. The existence of a powerful, intelligent, benefi-cent divinity that foresees and provides; the life to come; the happiness of the just; the punishment of the wicked; the sanctity of the social contract and of the laws. These are the positive dogmas. As for the negative dogmas, I have limited them to just one, namely intolerance. It is part of the cults we have excluded. (Bk. IV, Chap. 8, p. 226)

The sovereign cannot obligate people to believe these precepts. But it can make belief a condition for membership in the community. Anyone who does not accept them can be banished, "not for being impious but for being unsociable, for being incapable of sincerely loving the laws and justice, and of sacrificing his life, if necessary, for his duty." Once someone has sworn fidelity to the precepts, he is bound to uphold them. The state can execute anyone who "acts as if he does not believe them." The transgression here, once again, is not impiety, but "the greatest of crimes," lying before the laws (Bk. IV, Chap. 8, p. 226).

THE STATUS OF WOMEN

A remarkable aspect of Rousseau's political theory is his view of the proper treatment of women. He is greatly concerned throughout his works with increasing freedom and equality. In *The Social Contract*, he describes these values as "the greatest good of all" (Bk. III, Chap. 11, p. 170). Closely associated with these ideals is independence. To be dependent on another person places one in a position of subordination, violating equality and limiting the possibility of self-government, which is essential to Rousseau's conception of freedom. We have seen the sharp contrast he draws between man's original freedom and equality in the state of nature and their loss in society, especially in the *Discourse on Inequality*. It is therefore surprising to realize that his sharp distinction between natural goodness and social corruption is all but lost in his treatment of women. Contradicting central themes of his political theory, Rousseau advocates a highly subordinate place for women in society and that their education should make them fit for this role.

In general, Rousseau views women in the context of family life. Throughout his works he accepts the family, headed by the father, as fulfilling human potential. Within the family, women are subordinate to men. Their main functions are producing legitimate heirs and attending to men's sexual desires. They are to have virtually no public existence and should live almost in seclusion.

Rousseau's view of women's proper role is seen most clearly in Book V of *Emile*, in which he discusses the education of Sophie, the woman who is to marry the young Emile. His main points can be illustrated with quotations. First, woman is made for man's pleasure:

> [W]oman is specially made for man's delight. If man in his turn ought to be pleasing in her eyes, the necessity is less urgent, his virtue is in his strength, he pleases because he is strong. I grant you this is not the law of love, but it is the law of nature, which is older than love itself.
>
> If woman is made to please and to be in subjection to man, she ought to make herself pleasing in his eyes and not provoke him to anger. . . . (p. 322)

In addition to her role in pleasing man, woman's main function is producing his children. Because of her great responsibility in this regard, Rousseau is a classic exponent of the "double standard," according to which sexual ethics for men and women differ. Thus women should not object to differential treatment in society. The transgression of the unfaithful wife "is not infidelity but treason." It is the source of every sort of crime. "Can any position be more wretched than that of the unhappy father who, when he clasps his child to his breast, is haunted by the suspicion that this is the child of another, the badge of his own dishonor, a thief who is robbing his own children of their inheritance" (p. 325).

Rousseau believes women are created for family life, and should be subordinate to their husbands. To render them fit for this role, they should be taught to be gentle and docile, necessary qualities if they are "to obey a creature so imperfect as man" (p. 333). The family should be the center of a woman's existence, and she should rarely leave her home. The mode of life Rousseau recommends is patterned on that of the ancient Greeks, in which women lived in almost Oriental seclusion, rarely going out or seeing men other than close family members. "When Greek women married, they disappeared from public life; within the four walls of their home they devoted themselves to the care of their household and family. This is the mode of life prescribed for women alike by nature and reason" (p. 330).

Women's subordinate position is justified by their nature. The position of modest wife is that to which they are naturally suited. They lack essential intellectual abilities: "The search for abstract and speculative truths, for principles and axioms in science, for all that tends to wide generalization, is beyond a woman's grasp; their studies should be thoroughly practical" (p. 349). Among other qualities Rousseau notes, women love finery (p. 329), are more talkative than men (p. 339), and naturally cunning (p. 334). His account of the nature of little girls would now be identified as demeaning sexual stereotypes:

> What the little girl most clearly desires is to dress her doll, to make its bows, its tippets, its sashes, and its tuckers . . . Little girls always dislike learning to read and write, but they are always ready to learn to sew. (p. 331)

In educating women, Rousseau recommends building on their natural propensities.[30] Through such a process, Sophie emerges as an ideal wife. She is devoted to serving God (p. 359), loves virtue (p. 359), has a pleasant singing voice (p. 357), and derives her greatest enjoyment from needlework (p. 357).

This brief account should indicate Rousseau's view of women's nature and proper role in society. As evidence that this characterization is not confined to *Emile*, we can look briefly at his *Letter to d'Alembert*. In this work Rousseau discusses women in connection with the effects that exposure to actresses in a proposed theater would have on the people of Geneva. He remarks on women's sexual power over men, to which he refers as "the empire of the fair sex" (Pt. 5, p. 47). Because he finds this threatening to the legitimacy of men's children, he holds that chastity is natural to women: "Nature wanted it so, and it would be a crime to stifle its voice. The man can be audacious, such is his vocation; someone has to declare. But every woman without chasteness is guilty and depraved, because she tramples on a sentiment natural to her sex" (Pt. 8, p. 85). All the duties of women are derived "from the single fact that a child ought to have a father" (p. 85). In this work, as in *Emile*, Rousseau argues that women should be treated as in his favored ancient societies: "their lot ought to be a domestic and retired life" (Pt. 8, p. 87). "Among all the ancient civilized peoples they led very retired lives; they appeared rarely in public; never with men . . ." (p. 88).

Rousseau's account of women's nature and proper role is disconcerting for several reasons. As we have seen, he leaves them subordinate to and dependent on men, arguing that this is nature's intention. Clearly, however, his acceptance of this status demeans women, and is inconsistent with the emphasis on liberty and equality that otherwise pervades his philosophy. To free women from domestic subordination would increase these values, and so Rousseau should recommend such policies. His reason for not pursuing this course is his unquestioning acceptance of the family, which entails a subordinate position for women within its confines. Though criticism of the family—and women's place in it— would appear to be consistent with, indeed, dictated by, the overall thrust of Rousseau's social and political theory, this is a path he does not pursue.

Throughout his political writings, Rousseau is concerned with distinguishing what is natural in man from changes brought about by society. Especially in the *Discourse on Inequality*, he argues that men are by nature innocent, equal, and independent. The opposites of these characteristics develop in society. It is therefore surprising that the same sort of analysis is not applied to the position of women in the family. On the basis of their subordinate positions in existing societies, Rousseau argues that they are intended by nature for this role. In this respect his analysis recalls that of Aristotle, who concludes from women's position of inferiority in existing societies that she is by nature inferior to men, lacking a developed reasoning capacity.[31] If Rousseau had attempted to distinguish between women's natural attributes and the effects of her treatment in society, he might well have come to different conclusions. But throughout the bulk of his writings, he shows little interest in this question. The freedom and equality he seeks are freedom and equality for men.[32]

Rousseau's failure to distinguish the effects of nature and nurture is especially surprising in view of his discussion of women in the *Discourse on Inequality*. In this work, as we recall, men *and women* are equal and independent in the state of nature. Women, like men, lead solitary existences, and enjoy the innocent happiness of the natural condition. Like men, they are driven by sexual urges to mate, and differ from men only in caring for young children until they are able to fend for themselves. According to this work, then, women are not by nature members of families or subordinate to men. Their position in society should be viewed as another aspect of the overall process of corruption that accompanies the development of civilization. But even with these points clearly made, Rousseau not only does not draw obvious implications in the *Discourse*, but contradicts this analysis of women's nature in other works.

In the *Discourse* itself, women's natural equality is soon forgotten. As society forms and the family first develops, women readily fall into inferior positions. Rousseau writes: "Women became more sedentary and grew accustomed to watch over the hut and the children, while the man went to seek their common subsistence" (*Sec. Dis.*, Pt. II, p. 63). Thus there is a natural division of labor between the sexes. The man works and the woman takes care of home and family. This transition from equality and independence in the original state of nature to sexual subordination passes without remark,[33] which is surprising in an essay devoted to the origin of inequality.

It is difficult to explain Rousseau's view of women and the family, and I will not attempt to do so here. According to one suggestive line of argument, Rousseau does not believe women are *naturally* inferior to men, but should be subordinate for the sake of the family, a value which he holds dear.[34] But this approach would only push the problem back one level. Because women's subordination in the family is not consistent with his overall values, Rousseau's willingness to sacrifice these values for the sake of maintaining the family—in this particular form—requires explanation. The absence of the family in the state of nature presented in the *Second Discourse* shows that the male-dominated family is not dictated by nature.

It is possible that the lack of a stable family during his childhood accounts for the deep attachment to the family in Rousseau's political works. It is also possible that matters were not helped by his favored examples. Throughout his political theory, Rousseau criticizes existing institutions by comparing them to idealized virtuous societies, mainly Sparta and Rome. In these societies women were subordinate, and so he accepts this as inevitable and applies it to his own situation. In the *Letter to d'Alembert* especially, he makes recommendations on the basis of ancient experience. Perhaps his treatment of women is one area in which his appreciation of ancient virtue prevented him from addressing ills of his own society.

It is likely that undesirable aspects of women's position escaped Rousseau's attention. Perhaps he would have noticed these problems if he were more concerned with logical consistency. But Rousseau's apparent blindness here shows how difficult it is for many thinkers to see past fundamental aspects of their own societies, because they take them for granted. In this respect, Rousseau is a less penetrating thinker than Montesquieu, whose comparative analysis of societies made him highly conscious of women's treatment in his own (see pp. 180–2).

ROUSSEAU AND PRACTICAL POLITICS

To this point we have discussed Rousseau's views concerning the state he would like to institute. But we have said little about whether, and to what extent, he believed actual states could be reformed after his model. As we will see, Rousseau's attitude towards practical politics provides important evidence about the overall character of his political theory, a subject to which we will return in the following section.

Though Rousseau believes desired political reforms are possible, he does not consider them likely. They confront two important obstacles: the exacting conditions a free state requires, and impediments to changing existing societies.

In spite of Rousseau's disparaging remarks about the science of politics (see p. 248), he is well acquainted with its discoveries, including the views of Montesquieu, for which he has high regard. As we saw in a previous chapter, Montesquieu bases his account of the republic primarily on ancient city-states, especially Rome and Sparta. Because Rousseau uses similar models, it is not surprising that his free state closely resembles Montesquieu's republic. The briefest reflection will make clear the close relationship between Rousseau's preferred state and the republics Montesquieu describes. In regard to political reform, then, Rousseau limits the applicability of his proposed state to conditions approximating those of successful city-states.

Rousseau's account of the conditions necessary for political reform recalls Machiavelli's (see pp. 25–6). A people must be fresh, vigorous, without firmly established laws and customs. "What makes the work of legislation trying is not so much what must be established as what must be destroyed" (*S.C.*, Bk. II, Chap. 10, p. 170). "Once customs are established and prejudices have become deeply rooted, it is a dangerous and vain undertaking to want to reform them" (Bk. II, Chap. 8, p. 166). A people must be reformed in its youth, while it is still docile. "Liberty can be acquired, but it can never be recovered" (p. 166).

In accordance with out previous discussion, we can see that a suitable territory must be relatively small. It must have sufficient resources to support the population, but should not be so large that governing it becomes a problem. There must be strong ties of common interest among the people (Bk. II, Chap. 10, p. 169). They must also not be overly divided in regard to wealth. Though property need not be equal, "no citizen should be so rich as to be capable of buying another citizen, and none so poor that he is forced to sell himself" (Chap. 11, p. 170). In addition, it is necessary that the state enjoy a period of peace while the new laws take effect. Rousseau realizes the collection of requisite factors is rarely encountered: "All these conditions, it is true, are hard to find in combination. Hence few well constituted states are to be seen." In his eyes, the only country in Europe capable of receiving proper laws is Corsica (Bk. II, Chap. 10, p. 170).

In this last regard, we should note that, in 1764, Rousseau was approached by Corsican officers "to trace the plan of a political system" for the island. Rousseau accepted the task, but his *Constitutional Project for Corsica* was left unfinished. His problems resulting from the publication of *The Social Contract* and *Emile* forced him to set it aside. Soon after he found time for it, the island's French rulers eliminated the possibility of significant reform, and he abandoned the project.[35]

Even with favorable geographical conditions, political reform remains improbable. Even under the best of circumstances, a people is unlikely to accept new institutions. The very fact that people require reform means they will probably resist it. Rousseau realizes the existence of a classic chicken-and-egg problem here. In order for people to be willing to accept proper laws, they must be virtuous. But the only way they would be in this condition, free from the corruption of existing societies, is if they had been brought up in a properly constituted state—which is of course impossible until good laws are accepted:

> For an emerging people to be capable of appreciating the sound maxims of politics and to follow the fundamental rules of statecraft, the effect would have to become the cause. The social spirit which ought to be the work of that institution, would have to preside over the institution itself. And men would be, prior to the advent of laws, what they ought to become by means of laws. (Bk. II, Chap. 7, p. 164)

Rousseau's solution to this intractable problem is the lawgiver.

The lawgiver's task is to remake men. Beginning with them as individuals, he must transform them into constituents of a societal whole:

> He who dares to undertake the establishment of a people should feel that he is, so to speak, in a position to change human nature, to transform each individual (who by himself is a perfect and solitary whole), into a part of a larger whole from which this individual receives, in a sense, his life and his being; to alter man's constitution in order to strengthen it; to substitute a partial and moral existence for the physical and independent existence we have all received from nature. (*S.C.*, Bk. II, Chap. 7, p. 163)

To accomplish this task, he must be intimately acquainted with the passions of men, but feel none of them. His happiness must be independent of the people's, but he must devote himself to their interests (pp. 162–163). In addition, he must achieve his goal without political power. Though the lawgiver is the central figure in the establishment of the state, he has no official role in it. Because of the requirement of self-government, the lawgiver cannot make the laws. What he proposes must be voted on and accepted by the people. Thus his major task is to persuade the people to accept his advice. Because the people are corrupt and self-interested, this promises to be no easy task. "Thus we find together in the work of legislation two things that seem incompatible: an undertaking that transcends human force, and, to execute it, an authority that is nil" (p. 164). "Gods would be needed to give men laws" (p. 163).

The obstacles to reform must be overcome by the lawgiver's extraordinary personality. He must convince the people that he speaks with religious authority, that the gods are responsible for his wisdom. Though he can resort to devices such as oracles or stone tablets, it is his "great soul" that must carry conviction (pp. 164–165). If he can somehow convince the people to accept his laws, then the state will be on its way.

Rousseau has some historical examples to support his faith in the lawgiver. Once again, his favored instances are from ancient city-states, especially Sparta and Rome. In his discussion of the lawgiver in *The Social Contract,* he mentions Lycurgus, lawgiver of Sparta (*S.C.,* Bk. II, Chap. 7, p. 163). In his *Considerations on the Government of Poland,* he identifies three outstanding lawgivers, Lycurgus, Numa (of Rome), and Moses (Chap. 2, p. 163).[36] But his list is not confined to ancient figures. In *The Social Contract,* Calvin is also mentioned as a lawgiver of genius (Bk. II, Chap. 7, n. 7).

In spite of these precedents, Rousseau's account of the lawgiver indicates the unlikelihood of his proposed reforms. As is also the case with Machiavelli—to whom he refers directly (Bk. II, Chap. 7, n. 8)—his examples are primarily quasi-mythological figures. Aside from Calvin, the historical reliability of testimony concerning the deeds of Lycurgus, Numa, and Moses is not necessarily strong, and they are hardly models an eighteenth-century politician could easily follow. It is notable that Rousseau, unlike Machiavelli, does not countenance violence as a means of reform. And so his hopes are left to rest on the intervention of miraculous forces.

We see, then, that though Rousseau's political ideas are extremely radical, they have little applicability to existing political affairs. In this sense, he is not unlike Montesquieu—whom he follows in much of his discussion of practical politics. Because of his strict requirement of self-government, Rousseau makes political demands that no state existing during his time could meet. But though his view implies that all existing governments—and all that have existed since—are illegitimate, he is unable to present a practical alternative. One must wonder if "the great soul of the lawgiver" is an adequate standard for revolutionaries to rally around. In spite of the incendiary quality of Rousseau's thought, it is not clear he would support many actual movements for wholesale political change.

Important evidence of Rousseau's views concerning practical political reform is provided by his proposals in regard to two actual situations, discussed in two of his works, the unfinished *Constitutional Project for Corsica* and *Considerations on the Government of Poland.* We will look briefly at the latter. The circumstances surrounding this piece need not concern us. It was Rousseau's last political work, completed in 1772. The work was occasioned by a request from the Polish government during a period of political crisis for advice about proposed reforms.[37] Rousseau's response is remarkable for its modesty.

Following the teachings of Montesquieu, Rousseau realizes that political reforms must be in accordance with a country's character. Thus reforms of the Polish state require detailed knowledge of the country. Though he is aware that Poland is a corrupt state with many undesirable features, Rousseau believes it is necessary to preserve what is good in the existing system: "Worthy Poles, beware! Beware lest, in your eagerness to improve, you may worsen your constitution" (*Govt. Pol.,* Chap. 1, p. 160). Thus his attitude towards reform is highly cautious: "I do not say that things must be left in their present state; but I do say that they must be touched only with extreme circumspection" (Chap. 1, p. 161).

At that time, the Polish political system was an elective monarchy. The population was divided into different statuses. The serfs, who constituted the lowest order, were without civil rights. Yet Rousseau is willing to accept the existing system of representative government as long as there are more frequent diets, and representatives more closely follow the instructions of their constituents. He does not propose to abolish the monarchy, but only to make sure it is actually elective. Even the condition of the serfs, whom he recognizes are "less than nothing" (Chap. 6, p. 183), should be left unaltered, until they are rendered fit to be free:

> To free the common people of Poland would be a great and worthy enterprise, but bold, perilous, and not to be attempted lightly. Among the precautions to be taken, there is one which is indispensable and requires time; it is, before everything else, to make the serfs who are to be free worthy of liberty and capable of enduring it. (Chap. 6, p. 186)

As C. E. Vaughan, an important scholar, writes: "When we take into account both what he did, and what he did not, say—both what he proposed and what he omitted—we may well be inclined to think that he left too much, rather than too little, of the existing fabric in its place."[38]

The area to which Rousseau devotes greatest attention is developing the Polish people's moral character. He says of education: "This is the important question. It is education that must give souls a national formation, and direct their opinions and tastes in such a way that they will be patriotic by inclination, by passion, by necessity" (Chap. 4, p. 176). He is greatly concerned with public education, public ceremonies for the conferral of honors, and other devices through which patriotic feelings can be inculcated. Children's games should be conducted under the public eye. Similarly, great attention should be given to signs of distinction through which honored citizens can be identified. Rousseau's overall approach is clear in the following passage:

> Work, therefore, without pause or relaxation, to bring patriotism to the highest pitch in every Polish heart. . . . [A]rrange things so that every citizen will feel himself to be constantly under the public eye; that no one will advance or succeed save by the favor of the public; that no office or position shall be filled save by the will of the nation; and finally that, from the lowliest nobleman, even from the lowliest peasant, up to the king, if possible, all shall be so dependent on public esteem that nothing can be done, nothing acquired, no success obtained without it. Out of the effervescence excited by this mutual emulation will arise that patriotic intoxication without which liberty is but an empty word, and laws but a chimera. (Chap. 11, p. 244)

In place of immediate institutional reform, Rousseau hopes to bring about moral reforms that will make proper institutions better able to succeed in the future.

The practicality of Rousseau's specific proposals for Poland need not concern us. What interests us is what these tell us about his overall political theory. In previous sections, we have seen the radicalism of his political ideas. All existing societies are thoroughly corrupt and crying for reform. But it seems that his ideas about possible or actual reforms are far more moderate. Though reform is desirable, he does not believe it is likely to succeed. In its absence, he proposes practical measures to improve existing situations. The teaching of Montesquieu is in evidence in Rousseau's discussions of practical politics—including those in *The Social Contract.* The reformer must realize the complexity of political reality. Unless circumstances are almost impossibly favorable, he must proceed with care. He should attempt to improve conditions as much as possible, without risking measures that might make them worse. Even the corrupt institutions of Poland are recognized as better than possible alternatives. To quote Vaughan once again: "[W]e are compelled to acknowledge that the popular image of Rousseau, as the fanatical champion of abstract rights, as the determined foe of all historic institutions 'which do not quadrate with his theories,' is a pure delusion."[39]

IMPLICATIONS

For more than two hundred years, Rousseau's political ideas have had enormous influence. They have been appealed to in support of causes of democracy and revolution throughout the world. Rousseau was the unofficial ideologue of the French Revolution, caustically described by Edmund Burke as "the insane *Socrates* of the National Assembly."[40] The Revolutionary government, the Constituent Assembly, erected a statue to him in 1790, with the inscription: "The free French nation, to Jean-Jacques Rousseau." In 1794, during the Reign of Terror, a measure was passed to disinter his body and bury it in the Pantheon, where it was placed later that year.[41] Rousseau's influence on Robespierre and other architects of the Reign of Terror is well known.[42] Robespierre not only invoked Rousseau's ideas, but recounted a meeting with Rousseau before the latter's death—which probably did not occur.[43] Even Vaughan, a sympathetic scholar, notes that during "the later and more terrible phases of the Revolution," fundamental ideas of *The Social Contract* were put into practice.[44]

Yet it is far from clear that Robespierre or others of Rousseau's self-proclaimed followers understood him. To some extent this is Rousseau's own fault. Many of his ideas are complex, and presented less clearly than one would like. It is also not certain they form a consistent whole, or are consistent through all his works. Depending on which passages one chooses to emphasize, one can make Rousseau say a great many things. To close this chapter, we will consider some dangers associated with Rousseau's ideas. We begin with a brief look at one particular interpretation, according to which Rousseau contributed to the rise of "totalitarian democracy."

Though Rousseau did not invariably support radical political change, his authority has been claimed by revolutionary movements, including those that gave rise to Fascist and Communist totalitarian states earlier this century. Detailed discussion of totalitarianism is not necessary here.[45] What we should note is the breakdown between private and public spheres such a system fosters, along with complete domination of private life by the state. Citizens of a totalitarian state have no rights against the government, which intrudes in all areas of life.

Clearly, from what we have seen in this chapter, there are respects in which Rousseau's ideas are similar. To begin with, he is not a liberal political theorist. His citizens surrender *all* rights to the state, the primary function of which is not to protect them from interference but to make them virtuous through educational means. While liberal political theory centers on individual rights and negative freedom, Rousseau advances a complex conception of freedom, the primary emphasis of which combines self-government and positive freedom. If the individual does not willingly support the laws, he can be forced to be free. Throughout *The Social Contract*, Rousseau argues that the interests of the community take precedence over those of its individual members. The totalitarian side of Rousseau is especially clear in his account of the lawgiver. This figure's task is to make the individual part of a social whole, so "each citizen is nothing except in concert with all the others" (*S.C.*, Bk. II, Chap. 7, p. 163). The unpalatable implications of Rousseau's view are forcefully expressed by Vaughan, who is, again, sympathetic to Rousseau:

> From the moment the Contract is concluded, the individual ceases to be his own master. His life, his will, his very individuality are merged in those of the community.

He is as much lost in the communal self as the member is in the body. He has no longer the independent value of an unity. He has become a mere fraction whose worth is determined solely by its relation to the whole.[46]

Arguably, Rousseau's most significant contribution to totalitarianism is in providing it with a sophisticated moral language. In his ideas of positive freedom, forcing people to be free, and complete subordination to the infallible general will, Rousseau gives totalitarian governments means to legitimate their actions, though in doing so they doubtless exaggerate one side of his ideas.

An influential critique of Rousseau's totalitarian tendencies is presented by J. L. Talmon, in his classic work, *The Origins of Totalitarian Democracy*.[47] Talmon argues that Rousseau's ideas exemplify a certain pattern, characterized by moral absolutism and a distinctive way in which this must be realized. According to this line of argument, Rousseau believes in the existence of an exclusive moral truth and that the state's task is to impose it on society, regardless of costs or other considerations. What sets totalitarian democracy apart from other doctrines is the central role all individuals must play in realizing moral truth through direct political participation:

> Modern totalitarian democracy is a dictatorship resting on popular enthusiasm, and is thus completely different from absolute power wielded by a divine-right King, or by a usurping tyrant. . . . Rousseau's "general will," an ambiguous concept, sometimes conceived as valid *a priori*, sometimes as immanent in the will of man, exclusive and implying unanimity, became the driving force of totalitarian democracy, and the source of all its contradictions and antinomies. (Talmon, p. 6)

This line of criticism focuses on an insidious combination of elements in Rousseau's thought. The general will is an objective standard of right, in accordance with which people must live. But what is distinctive in Rousseau's view is that people must rule themselves in accordance with the general will. It is not enough for people to have conformity imposed on them by an external force, such as a Platonic philosopher-king.[48] They must will it themselves. "In this way the general will is at the same time outside us and within us" (p. 41). "In marrying [the general will] with the principle of popular sovereignty, and popular self-expression, Rousseau gave rise to totalitarian democracy" (p. 43).

There is undoubtedly an element of truth to Talmon's criticism. Rousseau posits a standard of right to which people must conform. If they do not pursue this themselves, they can be forced to do so without violating their freedom. He holds that, along with self-government, freedom lies in choosing the proper course, in subordination to the will of the virtuous majority. If one chooses differently, one is simply wrong. But these points must be tempered by considerations of degree. Talmon clearly overstates the extent of Rousseau's citizens' participation in public affairs: "There is nothing that Rousseau insists on more than the active and ceaseless participation of the people and of every citizen in the affairs of the State" (Talmon, p. 47). This is not true; though the people must vote on all laws, and take part in the public assemblies discussed above, this represents only limited infringement on their activities. In discussing how citizens are to vote on proposed laws, Rousseau insists that they do this without public deliberation (*S.C.*, Bk. II, Chap. 3). Far from immersion in the group, Rousseau wishes for each citizen to consult himself alone, thereby escaping public pressures while voting.[49] In addition to retaining this area of privacy, the legislative process as a whole should not dominate the state. Because there are to be few laws, public participation is hardly "ceaseless." According to Talmon, "If a constant appeal to the people as a whole, not just to a small representative body, is kept up, and at the same time unanimity is postulated, there is no escape from dictatorship" (p. 46). The spirit of Talmon's critique is far removed from the simple peasant society Rousseau has in mind.

Rousseau's ideas are ambiguous and have been interpreted in widely different ways. Certain aspects of his thought perhaps support views like Talmon's, though once again, to a more limited extent. However, Talmon is clearly correct about Rousseau's influence. Even if subsequent proponents of tyrannical states *read* their ideas into Rousseau (see Talmon, p. 46), it must be admitted that aspects of his thought lend themselves to dangerous misinterpretation. Especially troublesome are his contentions that the general will is always correct, and that because individuals surrender all rights to the community, they have no moral claim against it.

We have seen that under certain conditions the general will accurately expresses the public interest and is not dangerous to individual citizens. The main conditions have been discussed. A question at issue must be general, and so concern everyone. If society is largely homogeneous and the public interest clear, and if all citizens vote according to the public interest rather than their own, then the vote of the majority should embody the general will, in accordance with which all citizens must act. If Alain refuses to go along with this, he can be compelled to do so by the majority. According to Rousseau, in such a case, Alain is forced to be free. What is troublesome here is the difficult position in which Alain is placed by his difference of opinion.

We have seen that, according to Rousseau, if Alain dissents from the general will, he is incorrect:

> When, therefore, the opinion contrary to mine prevails, this proves merely that I was in error, and that what I took to be the general will was not so. If my private opinion had prevailed, I would have done something other than what I had wanted. In that case I would not have been free. (S.C., Bk. IV, Chap. 2, p. 206)

The conception of freedom discussed in this passage is positive freedom. Rousseau's implication is that if Alain dissents from the vote of the majority, he must do so for a reason. Perhaps he has miscalculated and so is simply wrong about the public interest. Or perhaps he mistakenly asks himself what is good for himself rather than for society. But another explanation is that he asks the wrong question out of self-interest. In voting on the issue at hand, Alain displays a lack of virtue; he is not sufficiently interested in the public good. This is not necessarily the case, but it is a conclusion one can easily draw. The only real alternative is that Alain is simply in error. In either case, he can have little objection to being required to accept the majority opinion.

There are two sources of concern with these ideas. First is the fact that Rousseau's view tells against the possibility of honest disagreements over public policies. Perhaps this is because he assumes a simple society in which the public interest is apparent. Thus if someone votes otherwise, he is wrong and must be corrected. The fact that different people can interpret the public good differently is all but lost on Rousseau. Even if the kind of society he has in mind is so simple and homogeneous that disagreements will not occur, this would make his ideas utopian, unsuited for any society that could ever exist.

More ominously, Rousseau is extremely vague about the substance of the general will. In his favored examples of ancient societies, citizens display their virtue mainly in times of war. When the safety of the country is at stake and citizens bravely face the enemy, their public-spiritedness is hardly open to question. But in times of peace, the public good can often be more difficult to discern. This causes a severe problem for Rousseau. In regard to any issue of general concern, there will be a vote. Assuming that normal conditions obtain, the vote of the majority will embody the general will, and the minority will be compelled to accept this. In spite of the problems we have noted, this outcome is defensible as long as the majority is virtuous and the public interest is clear. But can one ever be sure these conditions are met?

Rousseau indicates a second possible outcome. Even in a corrupt state, the general will survives. Though it is not voted into law by an actual majority, he believes it remains in existence. The following passage is lengthy, but it is necessary to quote it in full:

> [W]hen the social bond begins to relax and the state to grow weak, when private interests begin to make themselves felt and small societies begin to influence the large one, the common interest changes and finds opponents. Unanimity no longer reigns in the votes; the general will is no longer the will of all. Contradictions and debates arise, and the best advice does not pass without disputes.
>
> Finally, when the state, on the verge of ruin, subsists only in an illusory and vain form, when the social bond of unity is broken in all hearts, when the meanest interest brazenly appropriates the sacred name of the public good, then the general will becomes mute. Everyone, guided by secret motives, no more express their opinions as citizens than if the state had never existed; and iniquitous decrees having their sole purpose the private interest are falsely passed under the name of laws.
>
> Does it follow that the general will is annihilated or corrupted? No, it is always constant, unalterable and pure; but it is subordinate to other wills that prevail over it. (Bk. IV, Chap. 1, p. 204)

Rousseau indicates that in such a case, people still want what is good for society. But this is overpowered by desires for their own good. In voting, people respond to the wrong question. In such a case, freedom does not lie in following the will of the majority. In voting this way, people are "driven by appetite."

In such a case, we can assume, *all people* are not lacking in virtue. Thus there will be a remnant who still vote according to the public good. Because the majority lacks virtue, this remnant will lose the vote. And so will be forced to go along with the majority, who will justify this by saying *they* are right and the remnant is wrong. In forcing them to conform to the outcome of the vote, the majority claims that it forces them to be free.

Thus we have two possible situations: either a virtuous majority forces a nonvirtuous minority to conform to their will; or a nonvirtuous majority forces a virtuous minority to conform. In either case, it is impossible to know whether the majority is right. There are certain signs that it is, especially if the vote is smooth and lacking in contention, and if only a few people dissent. But there is no *external* criterion against which a particular expression of the general will can be assessed. In the words of one commentator, Rousseau's "theory ends, therefore, with the rather unsatisfactory conclusion that no government is legitimate unless it rests on the general will, and that there is no reliable way of telling what the general will may be."[50]

In regard to the situation under discussion, in either case, the majority will presumably claim that its vote embodies the general will, that it has right on its side. Because Rousseau's overall ideas tell against the possibility of reasonable disagreement, in either case the minority will be suspect and forced to accept its decision. Thus whether or not the majority is actually virtuous, dissenters will be forced to conform. Rousseau argues that this is necessary for freedom. But one can easily see its more ominous implications.

Rousseau demands a great deal from his free state and its virtuous citizens. If his high expectations are not satisfied, great danger looms. An advantage of liberal political theory, then, is that it does not ask so much. In providing people with a safe area in which they can live free from coercive interference, it provides security against the imperfections of human nature. In having individuals surrender all rights to the state, and in abandoning negative freedom in favor of his own conception, Rousseau affords far less protection. Of course, from his point of view, this is necessary. Liberal theory should be faulted for not demanding enough, for leaving people as they are, corrupt and miserable. Whether it is possible—or prudent—to move beyond existing arrangements is a central political question, which will always be debated. This brings us back to the question of nature. Are things ordained by nature to be forever as they are? Or is nature more benign, fraught with unrealized possibilities? As we have seen, such questions are fundamental to Rousseau. How we respond to them will decisively affect our assessment of his political theory.

Rousseau's political theory is often difficult and has been interpreted in widely different ways. We have seen why he is often viewed as a great proponent of human liberation. But on the other hand, the insidious implications of some of his ideas have been developed by subsequent theorists in directions to which he undoubtedly would have objected.

NOTES

1. Rousseau, *Confession*, Bk. 8, pp. 328–329. This work is cited *Conf.*, in the text, according to book and page number; full reference, below under "Texts Cited."

2. For biographical details, see M. Cranston, *Jean-Jacques: The Early Life and Works of Jean-Jacques Rousseau* (New York, 1982) and *The Noble Savage: Jean Jacques Rousseau 1754–1762* (Chicago, 1991); these works are cited in parentheses in the text, as Cranston, Vols. I and II, respectively; see also L. Crocker, *Jean-Jacques Rousseau*, 2 vols. (New York, 1968–1973).

3. On the relationship between Hume and Rousseau, see E. Mossner, *The Life of David Hume*, 2nd ed. (Oxford, 1980), Chap. 35.

4. On Therese, see Cranston, I, 198–199.

5. Quoted by Mossner, *Life of David Hume*, p. 523.

6. Jean-Jacques Rousseau, *Basic Political Writings*, D. Cress, ed. and trans., p. xxi. *Discourse on the Sciences and the Arts* (the *First Discourse*); *Discourse on the Origin and*

Foundations of Inequality Among Men (the *Second Discourse*); the *Social Contract*, and *Discourse on Political Economy* are quoted from this edition. *Social Contract* (*S.C.*) is cited according to book and chapter number, and the *Second Discourse* (*Sec. Dis.*) is cited according to part number, both with page references to this edition. Notes to the *Second Discourse* are cited according to number and page number. The *First Discourse* and the *Discourse on Political Economy* (*P.E.*) are cited by page number. Translations are occasionally modified slightly; or I substitute other published translations, as indicated. References for additional translations used are found below under "Texts Cited." For original texts, I use Rousseau, *Œuvres complètes*, full reference below under "Texts Cited."

7. Rousseau, *Politics and the Arts: Letter to M. d'Alembert on the Theatre*, Pt. II, p. 15; complete reference below, under "Texts Cited." This work is cited in the text, according to part and page number, as *Lett. d'Alembert*.

8. E. Cassirer, *The Philosophy of the Enlightenment*, F. Koelln and J. Pettegrove, trans. (Princeton, 1951), p. 22.

9. J. d'Alembert, *Preliminary Discourse to the Encyclopedia of Diderot*, p. 4; full reference below, under "Texts Cited."

10. J. d'Alembert, *Preliminary Discourse*, p. 5

11. For a good brief discussion of Condorcet, see F. Manuel, *The Prophets of Paris* (Cambridge, MA, 1962; rpt. New York, 1965), Chap. 2.

12. Rousseau addresses this contradiction in the "Preface" to his play, *Narcisse*, in Rousseau, *The First and Second Discourses together with Replies to Critics and Essay on the Origin of Languages*, V. Gourevitch, ed. and trans. (New York, 1986), pp. 96–111.

13. R. Derathé, *Jean-Jacques Rousseau et la science politique de son temps* (Paris, 1950), pp. 155–156.

14. *Emile*, p. 44; *Emile* is cited according to book and page number; full reference below under "Texts Cited."

15. Here I am indebted to J. Charvet, *The Social Problem in the Philosophy of Rousseau* (Cambridge, 1974), Chap. 2.

16. This is the opinion of J. Starobinski, ed., *Discours sur l'origine et les fondements de l'inégalité*, in *Œuvres complètes*, III, 1349.

17. In reference to training a man and a citizen, Rousseau writes: "Two conflicting types of educational systems spring from these conflicting aims. One is public and common to many, the other private and domestic" (*Emile*, Book I, p. 9). On Rousseau's two moral ideals, see J. Shklar, *Men and Citizens* (Cambridge, 1969).

18. See pp. 71–2; for full reference, see below, under "Texts Cited."

19. For J. S. Mill's classic discussion of this problem in *On Liberty*, see below, Chapter 8.

20. Two important discussions are I. Berlin, "Two Concepts of Liberty," in *Four Essays on Liberty* (Oxford, 1969); and G. MacCallum, "Negative and Positive Freedom," *Philosophical Review*, 76 (1967).

21. This theme is discussed in connection with the main argument of Plato's *Republic*, in Volume I, 62–69.

22. For discussion, see G. Klosko, *The Development of Plato's Political Theory* (New York, 1986), pp. 149–157.

23. For the influence of Plato on Rousseau, see C. E. Vaughan, Introduction to *The Political Writings of Jean-Jacques Rousseau*, Vaughan, ed. 2 vols. (1915; rpt. New York, 1962), I, 2–4, 44, 54–56.

24. See especially MacCallum, "Negative and Positive Freedom"; a sophisticated recent analysis is C. Swanton, *Freedom: A Coherence Theory* (Indianapolis, 1992).

25. MacCallum, "Negative and Positive Freedom."

26. The final sentence from R. Masters's translation.

27. Berlin, "Two Concepts of Liberty," pp. 121-22; there is, however, some lack of clarity in Berlin's distinctions between the different forms of freedom.

28. In B. Constant, *Political Writings*; this work cited as Constant in text; full reference below under "Texts Cited." The essay was originally delivered as a speech, in 1819.

29. See R. P. Wolff, *In Defense of Anarchism* (New York, 1970), Chap. 2.

30. S. Okin, *Women in Western Political Thought* (Princeton, 1979), p. 114.

31. See Vol. I, 115–116.

32. Okin, *Women in Western Political Thought*, Chap. 7.

33. I am indebted to Okin, *Women in Western Political Thought*, pp. 112–113; for another view of Rousseau's treatment of women, see J. Schwartz, *The Sexual Politics of Jean-Jacques Rousseau* (Chicago, 1984).

34. P. Weiss, "Rousseau, Antifeminism, and Woman's Nature." *Political Theory*, 15 (1987).

35. For discussion, see Vaughan, *Political Writings*, II, 292–305. The *Constitutional Project for Corsica* appears in English translation in *Jean-Jacques Rousseau: Political Writings*, F. Watkins, trans. and ed. (1953; rpt. Madison, WI, 1986).

36. *Considerations on the Government of Poland* is cited as *Govt. Pol.*, according to chapter and page number; in Watkins, ed., Rousseau, *Political Writings*.

37. For discussion, see Vaughan, *Political Writings*, II, 369–395.

38. Vaughan, *Political Writings*, II, 377.

39. Vaughan, *Political Writings*, II, 377–378; the phrase in quotations is from E. Burke's *Reflections on the Revolution in France*.

40. Burke, *Letter to a Member of the National Assembly*, in *Further Reflections on the Revolution in France*, D. Ritchie, ed. (Indianapolis, 1992), p. 48.

41. Crocker, *Jean-Jacques Rousseau*, II, 354–355.

42. See J. L. Talmon, *The Origins of Totalitarian Democracy* (New York, 1970); a stimulating recent discussion is C. Blum, *Rousseau and the Politics of Virtue* (Ithaca, 1982).

43. N. Hampson, *The Life and Opinions of Maximilien Robespierre* (Oxford, 1974), pp. 15–16.

44. Vaughan, *Political Writings*, I, 21–22.

45. See C. Friedrich and Z. Brzenski, *Totalitarian Dictatorship and Autocracy*, 2nd ed. (New York, 1966).

46. Vaughan, *Political Writings*, I, 21.

47. This work is cited hereafter, in the text, as Talmon.

48. See Vol. I, Chap 3.

49. For calling my attention to the implications of this point in regard to the question of Rousseau's totalitarianism, I am indebted to Tim Collins.

50. F. Watkins, Introduction to Rousseau, *Political Writings*, p. xxx.

TEXTS CITED

D'Alembert, J. *Preliminary Discourse to the Encyclopedia of Diderot.* R. N. Schwab, trans. Indianapolis, 1963.

Constant, B. *Benjamin Constant: Political Writings.* B. Fontana, ed. and trans. Cambridge, 1988.

Hobbes, T. *Leviathan.* R. Tuck, ed. Cambridge, 1991.

Rousseau, J.-J. *Basic Political Writings.* D. Cress, ed. and trans. Indianapolis, 1987.

Rousseau, J.-J. *The Confessions.* J. M. Cohen, trans. Harmondsworth, England, 1953.

Rousseau, J.-J. *Considerations on the Government of Poland.* In *Political Writings.* F. Watkins, ed. and trans. Madison, WI, 1986.

Rousseau, J.-J. *Emile.* B. Foxley, trans. London, 1911.

Rousseau, J.-J. *Œuvres complètes.* B. Gagnebin and M. Raymond, eds. 4 vols. Paris, 1959–1969.

Rousseau, J.-J. *On the Social Contract, with Geneva Manuscript and Political Economy.* R. Masters, ed. J. Masters, trans. New York, 1978.

Rousseau, J.-J. *Political Writings.* F. Watkins, ed. and trans. Madison, WI, 1986.

Rousseau, J.-J. *Politics and the Arts: Letter to M. d'Alembert on the Theatre.* A. Bloom, trans. Ithaca, 1960.

FURTHER READING

Berlin, I. "Two Concepts of Liberty." In *Four Essays on Liberty.* Oxford, 1969.

Charvet, J. *The Social Problem in the Philosophy of Rousseau.* Cambridge, 1974.

Cobban, A. *Rousseau and the Modern State.* 2nd ed. London, 1964.

Cranston, M. *Jean-Jacques: The Early Life and Works of Jean-Jacques Rousseau.* New York, 1982.

Cranston, M. *The Noble Savage: Jean-Jacques Rousseau 1754–1762.* Chicago, 1991.

Derathé, R. *Jean-Jacques Rousseau et la science politique de son temps.* Paris, 1950.

MacCallum. G. "Negative and Positive Freedom." *Philosophical Review,* 76 (1967).

Masters, R. D. *The Political Philosophy of Rousseau.* Princeton, 1968.

Okin, S. *Women in Western Political Thought.* Princeton, 1979.

Shklar, J. *Men and Citizens.* Cambridge, 1969.

Starobinski, J. *Jean-Jacques Rousseau: Transparency and Obstruction.* A. Goldhammer, trans. Chicago, 1988.

Talmon, J. L. *The Origins of Totalitarian Democracy.* New York, 1970.

Vaughan, C. E., ed. *The Political Writings of Jean-Jacques Rousseau.* 2 vols. (1915; rpt. New York, 1962).

C h a p t e r
7

EDMUND BURKE AND CONSERVATIVE POLITICAL THEORY

CONSERVATIVE POLITICAL THEORY

EDMUND BURKE IS GENERALLY VIEWED as the greatest and most influential conservative political theorist. His book, *Reflections on the Revolution in France,* is widely considered the greatest work in conservative political theory. According to the *Dictionary of the History of Ideas,* he presented "the first (and to date most important) formulation of conservative political philosophy."[1] In *The Conservative Mind,* a well-known study, Russell Kirk identifies Burke's as "the true school of conservative principle." "Conscious conservatism in the modern sense did not manifest itself until 1790, with the publication of *Reflections on the Revolution in France.*"[2]

As a political philosophy, conservatism has existed in various forms. The word "conservative" began to be used as a political term after the French Revolution, to "signify a partisan of the maintenance of the established social and political order."[3] But numerous doctrines have been assigned this label, though they have differed in important respects— perhaps as important as their similarities. Thus J. G. A. Pocock writes, "a general history of 'conservative' doctrine" may never be written: "too many minds have been trying to 'conserve' too many things for too many reasons."[4] Probably the main characteristic uniting different variants of conservatism is support of the existing order and opposition to radical change. This is not to say conservatives resist all change or political reform. Rather, they hold that reforms must be undertaken with great care, to ensure that their results will not be inconsistent with what exists.

A helpful account of the main elements of English and American conservative thought is given by Kirk, who lists six key features.[5] First, conservatives generally have a religious bent. They believe "a divine intent rules society as well as conscience." Thus the existing order is somehow sanctioned by more than human forces. Second is attachment to traditional life, in spite of its variety and apparent disorder. Third, conservatives believe "civilized society requires orders and classes." Thus society cannot be levelled. Though all people are equal morally, they must be unequal in social terms. Fourth is a close relationship between freedom and private property. The former is made possible only by the existence of the latter, and so conservatives support the existing distribution of property, even with its inequalities. Fifth is faith in *prescription* and distrust of reason. (The precise nature of

266

prescription will be discussed below.) Reason is not an adequate guide to human conduct. Finally, though conservatives are willing to countenance a measure of reform, they distrust more substantial change: "innovation is a devouring conflagration more often than it is a torch of progress."

If we put this admittedly overly simple list of points together, we end up with a straightforward doctrine. It should not be misleading to glance at this briefly, bearing in mind its highly schematic character. According to this view, conservatives support the existing social and political order, in spite of its class system and inequalities of wealth and political power. Their support rests primarily on the fact that it exists and preserves important values, and perhaps also because it is somehow endorsed by divine forces. This sketch of conservatism is consistent with the view of Burke, as we will see throughout this chapter. But more than the details of Burke's view, we will be concerned with its theoretical underpinnings, important assumptions upon which it rests. Burke's political theory represents a distinctive approach to the analysis of political and social questions that is sharply opposed to the dominant tendencies in liberal political theory, as discussed in previous chapters.[6] Though Burke's overall approach is not common to all conservative political theorists, it is an important component of many variants. One reason for Burke's enduring influence is his supremely eloquent expression of this point of view and its implications.

If we return to the brief sketch of conservative political theory given above, we can note two important underlying features: the great complexity of existing society, and human beings' limited ability to understand it. To quote Kirk once again,

> A narrow rationality . . . cannot of itself satisfy human needs. 'Every Tory is a realist,' says Keith Feiling: 'he knows that there are great forces in heaven and earth that man's philosophy cannot plumb or fathom. We do wrong to deny it, when we are told that we do not trust human reason: we do not and we may not.'[7]

The connection between the complexity of society and the limited power of reason is along the following lines. Because of the interconnectedness of all aspects of society, its separate features cannot be extracted from their context and examined on their individual merits. Conservatives view society as a complex whole. Its parts are closely, perhaps organically, interconnected and so resist scrutiny in individual terms. Similarly, aspects of existing society should not be assessed against abstract moral standards. In these respects the conservative outlook is sharply opposed to Enlightenment views. Common sense, as epitomized in Enlightenment philosophy, suggests that all aspects of society should be examined and criticized, so they can be improved, if improvement is possible.

As we saw in previous chapters, the Enlightenment as a whole is committed to the extension of reason's domain and belief that as ignorance and superstition are overcome, the human condition can be improved. Enlightenment thinkers support people's equality and dignity and believe they have important rights which must be respected. Features of society that interfere with these values must be reformed. Demands for reform become pressing as, when measured against abstract standards, society is seen to be fraught with evils and injustice. At the time Burke approached the height of his powers, Jeremy Bentham (discussed in the next chapter) published his first book, *A Fragment of Government.*[8] In its opening paragraphs, Bentham expresses central aspects of the Enlightenment view: "The age we live in is a busy age; in which knowledge is rapidly advancing towards perfection." Bentham notes the great progress that has been made in the natural world, in which "every thing teems with discovery and improvement." Corresponding to these developments is Bentham's intention to advance "*reformation* in the moral." In *Fragment of Government*, Bentham addresses the shortcomings of English law—"the universal inaccuracy and confusion" which pervades the system—which he wishes to bring into accordance with his fundamental principle, the greatest happiness of the greatest number.

Demands for rational scrutiny and for moral reform go hand in hand. Society consists of innumerable institutions and features. If a specific institution exists, there must be a reason for it, and so the critic will ask what this is and how the institution contributes to the good of society. This is especially important if some features of the institution can be seen to have undesirable consequences, in which case the critic will examine these, to find out why they are necessary. Perhaps additional aspects of these features can be identified, which outweigh their apparent harms. Or perhaps the questionable aspects are necessary to maintain the institution as a whole, which is important to society. Obviously, there are numerous possibilities here, and the way things work can be ascertained only after careful examination of the institution in question. But in any given case, the clear demand of reason is that questionable aspects of society be justified, and reformed if they cannot be defended.

The central place of rational justification in liberal political theory has been seen in previous chapters. Fundamental questions of political justification are addressed through the social contract argument and the device of the state of nature. An existing government is not viewed as simply given, to be accepted on faith. In order to show that a specific form of government is justified, the theorist imagines what would happen if it did not exist. Through the employment of such arguments, government can be assessed according to its consequences for society.

Close connections between rational criticism and social utility have been seen especially clearly in our discussion of Hume. As part of his overall project, Hume subjects numerous aspects of morality and society to intense philosophical scrutiny. He casts aside indefensible systems of moral philosophy, leaving the simple fact that people are interested in what benefits them and promotes happiness. Because government survives scrutiny along these lines, Hume believes it should be obeyed, unless it becomes odiously oppressive and so more trouble than it is worth.

The demands of reason can assume different forms. But common to all is the requirement that specific aspects of society be justified. Defenders of a particular institution must explain why it is beneficial to society. Strong reasons are especially necessary to defend social practices that infringe on people's equality and rights. As it says in the French *Declaration of the Rights of Man and the Citizen* (1789),

> In respect of their rights men are born and remain free and equal. The only permissible basis for social distinctions is public utility.[9]

From this point of view, social distinctions need not be shown to benefit all members of society. But if they depart from commonsense principles of equality and the common good, then rational criticism demands good reasons for them. At the heart of liberal political theory is the demand for a certain form of moral *transparency*, that social institutions must be defensible at the bar of each person's reason. Jeremy Waldron identifies this imperative as the "theoretical foundations of liberalism." According to Waldron, the distinctively liberal standpoint toward social and political justification centers on "an impatience with tradition, mystery, awe and superstition as the basis of order, and of a determination to make authority answer at the tribunal of reason and convince us that it is entitled to respect."[10]

> Society should be a *transparent* order, in the sense that its workings and principles should be well-known and available for public apprehension and scrutiny. People should know and understand the reasons for the basic distribution of wealth, power, authority and freedom. Society should not be shrouded in mystery, and its workings should not have to depend on mythology, mystification, or a "noble lie." (Waldron, p. 146)

As Waldron says, the possibility of justifying social and political institutions to the members of society is central to the distinctively liberal conception of a "reasonable" society (Waldron, p. 145).

Conservatives, however, are less confident in the powers of reason. They believe that the maintenance of social order depends on "a degree of mystery, illusion and sentiment" (Waldron, p. 149). To support this claim, Waldron quotes Burke, and we will be concerned with this theme throughout this chapter. It was in response to what he viewed as the excessive demands of reason that Burke developed his own ideas, especially in *Reflections on the Revolution in France*. Because of their doubts about the power of reason, conservatives resist subjecting all of society to its scrutiny. As Burke writes in *A Vindication of Natural Society* (1757), "what would become of the World if the practice of all moral duties, and the foundations of society, rested on having their reasons made clear and demonstrative to every individual?"[11] A central imperative of Burke's political theory, then, is to explain circumstances under which reason *should not* be used. Though common sense demands that questionable aspects of society be justified, Burke attempts to show that in this respect common sense is wrong. Because of his opposition to rational scrutiny of society—and other tenets of the Enlightenment—one commentator describes Burke as in "revolt against the eighteenth century."[12]

In spite of their reservations, conservative theorists' attitude towards reason is necessarily two-sided. They must make use of reason in order to justify limiting it. One of Burke's greatest theoretical accomplishments is his forceful series of arguments along these lines. His reasoned assault on the overreaches of reason has been appealed to by opponents of wholesale political reform ever since.

Because of its distrust of reason, conservative political philosophy is to some extent inherently at odds with itself. Within conservative thought there is a strong streak of antirationalism. If, on the most basic level, conservatism is "largely a matter of temperament, of a disposition to preserve the tried and true ways of life,"[13] this end can be accomplished most effectively by *not* thinking about things too carefully. The "tried and true" ways of life are most secure when they are *not* called into question, and so do *not* require elaborate defense. To the extent defense is necessary, this can be provided most easily by religious doctrines, which counsel acceptance. As we have seen, the first of Kirk's points bears on religious sanctification of the existing order. In addition, if the way things are is somehow necessitated by divine decree, then it would be more than futile to attempt to change them; it would be sinful as well. Because acceptance of a strongly religious point of view can stop proposals for change in their tracks, it is not surprising that there is a strong religious streak in Burke's philosophy. But in the wake of Enlightenment rationalism, religion alone is not enough. A central tendency of the Enlightenment is criticism of religion, which is widely dismissed as ignorance and superstition. Not only does religion by its very nature resist rational scrutiny, but when expounded by those who benefit most from the existing order, it is obviously self-serving, whether or not it is true. Claims regarding the divine sanctification of the existing order are apt to strike people quite differently depending on where they stand in it and their feelings about it. The divine right of kings obviously benefits holders of political power far more than those who lack it.

Historically, the need for conservative political theory arose only when traditional and religious points of view came under attack. It was only when the existing order was questioned and appeals to religious acceptance were no longer convincing that reasoned justification became necessary.

As befits a conservative theorist, Burke's political thought did not arise from an attempt to develop abstract, systematic political theory. A sustained theoretical account of the limits of theory was far from his intention. During the bulk of his career, he was a member of the House of Commons, debating pressing issues of the day. His political theory is contained in the speeches and pamphlets he wrote to support his positions in particular disputes. The fact that Burke's works are generally polemical compositions causes problems in reconstructing his political theory, especially since his ideas must be extracted from particular contexts. But Burke possessed an unusual talent for drawing connections between general moral and political principles and specific political issues. This point is made by John Morley, one of Burke's biographers:

> [N]o one that ever lived used the general ideas of the thinker more successfully to judge the particular problems of the statesman. No one has ever come so close to the details of practical politics, and at the same time remembered that these can only be understood and only dealt with by the aid of the broad conceptions of political philosophy.[14]

Appeals to political principles fill Burke's works, though it is often difficult to know how far a principle put forth in one context is intended as a general rule, applicable to others as well. But on the whole, Burke's works present a consistent point of view. A set of related attitudes and themes characterize his major compositions, despite apparently conflicting positions he appears to espouse (most notably opposition to revolution in France in spite of his earlier support of the American Revolution; see pp. 282FF). Even Burke's greatest work, *Reflections on the Revolution in France*, was written in response to the early stages of the French Revolution. This work contains the most general and theoretical statement of Burke's view, because he believed the threat the revolution posed was so sweeping as to require a categorical response. Though, as we noted in a previous chapter, Hume's conservative political theory is in many ways similar to Burke's, the crisis Burke believed his society faced called forth a full conservative theory, both more systematically developed and more forcefully articulated than anything presented by Hume.

Throughout this chapter we will attempt to reconstruct the central elements of Burke's political theory, always bearing in mind the problems caused by the circumstances of his works' composition. Because they address particular political issues, a full under-standing of many of his works requires extensive knowledge of eighteenth-century British politics. For obvious reasons, I will avoid detailed discussion of these matters, preferring to concentrate on Burke's overall approach to political questions, and the important assump-tions on which this rests. Once again, central to this endeavor is Burke's striking attempt to develop a reasoned defense of existing society against an overly aggressive use of reason. In this as in many other respects, Burke mapped out philosophical territory conservative theorists have attempted to defend ever since.

BURKE'S LIFE AND POLITICAL CAREER

Burke was born in Dublin in 1729, into a middle-class family.[15] He was educated at a Quaker school, and then Trinity College, Dublin. Because his father, a lawyer, wanted him to study law, he moved to London, and enrolled in the Middle Temple in 1750. But within a few years, he decided to pursue a literary career. After a period of obscurity and poverty, he published two works in 1757, *A Vindication of Natural Society* and *A Philosophical Enquiry into the Origin of our Ideas of the Sublime and the Beautiful*. Among his other literary projects was editing the *Annual Register*, an important annual review of literary, social, and artistic events, which he continued to edit for thirty-two years (Ayling, p. 16).

Burke's future, however, lay in politics. In 1759 he secured employment as secretary to William Hamilton, a young member of Parliament. After falling out with Hamilton in 1764, he began a crucial association with the Marquis of Rockingham, one of the wealthiest and most influential political figures of the day. Rockingham's parliamentary faction, known as the "Rockingham-Whigs," was dominated by wealthy aristocrats, who claimed to be descendants of the Whigs of 1688 and the "balanced, aristocratic govern-ment that it produced" (Cone, I, 69; the "old Whigs" are discussed in the following section). Burke became secretary to Rockingham in 1765, and a seat was found for him in the House of Commons, representing Wendover. With this turn of events, he viewed himself "as raised to the highest dignity to which a creature of our species could aspire."[16] Burke served continuously in Parliament until 1794. With Rockingham's ascension to Prime Minister, in 1765, he found himself at the center of British politics. Though Rockingham's ministry lasted only a year, Burke was retained in a position of influence. It was said that the Rockingham party would have been "a set of uninspiring politicians" without him. One noble remarked that "Burke was not Rockingham's right hand, but both his hands" (Cone, I, 69).

In the House of Commons, Burke's talents were manifested in the speeches he delivered, and in a series of pamphlets which presented extended statements of his views. From 1774 to 1780 he represented the commercial seaport of Bristol and from 1780 to 1794 Lord Rockingham's borough of Malton. He did not hold governmental office until Rockingham's second ministry, in 1782, when he became Paymaster-General of the forces (see Cone, II, 18–32). Burke's association with the Rockingham Whigs causes problems in unraveling his political ideas. If his role was the faction's "spokesman and ideas man,"[17] then his pamphlets and speeches in Parliament cannot necessarily be assumed to represent his own point of view. But we will set this problem aside. Once again, the ideas Burke expressed throughout his thirty-year political career are generally consistent. Though detailed examination of particular utterances might raise problems, we can assume that his overall body of work represents his own ideas.

Burke achieved notoriety with his opposition to the French Revolution, most forcefully expressed in *Reflections on the Revolution in France*, which was published in 1790. This work, which is described as "the greatest and most influential political pamphlet ever written,"[18] was an enormous success. It sold 19,000 copies in its first six months. Among its many admirers was the English King, George III (Ayling, pp. 216–217). *Reflections* also inspired critical responses, the best known of which was Thomas Paine's *The Rights of Man* (published in 1791 and 1792). One scholar reports forty-eight different replies to Burke's work.[19] *Reflections* and Burke's subsequent works played a crucial role in turning European sentiment against the Revolution, and so helping to bring on war against France. But Burke's ferocious opposition to the French Revolution caused severe rifts within his party, leaving him at times an embattled, isolated figure (see Ayling, Chap. 16). He retired from Parliament in 1794. In *An Appeal from the New to the Old Whigs*, published in 1791, he defends his consistency, and lifelong adherence to the principles of the old Whigs of 1688.

Burke was obviously a man of enormous gifts. His continuing influence in political philosophy is due in large measure to the power and beauty of his language. He is widely viewed as one of the great masters of English prose (see Ayling, pp. 283–284). As for his personal qualities, these are nicely expressed by Samuel Johnson, a longtime friend:

> Yes sir, if a man were to be by chance at the same time with Burke under a shed to shun a shower, he would say—'This is an extraordinary man.' If Burke should go into a stable to see his horse drest, the ostler would say—'We have had an extraordinary man here.' (quoted by Ayling, p. 27)

In order to appreciate Burke's conservative philosophy, it is necessary to look briefly at exactly what he believed himself to be conserving. As we have noted, this was the constitutional settlement of 1688, which created a balanced, stable government. It was in the course of defending this conception of English government from various threats that Burke's political philosophy took shape. The following discussion will roam freely through Burke's different works in order to sketch his overall political theory. In doing this, I extract passages from their immediate contexts, and also combine passages written at different points in his life. But these procedures should be unobjectionable, as long as we are correct in assuming the overall consistency of Burke's political views.

BURKE AND BRITISH POLITICS

Throughout his life, Burke supported a set of principles which he identified with the victorious Whig party in the Glorious Revolution of 1688. As noted in our discussion of Locke, through the Glorious Revolution, the Catholic King of England, James II, was removed from the throne and replaced by his daughter Mary and her husband, William of Orange. As a result of these events, the "ancient rights and liberties" of the English people were affirmed.[20] Parliamentary supremacy was established. Frequent meetings of Parliament were mandated, and the King was forbidden to suspend the law, raise revenue, or keep a standing army without Parliamentary consent. In addition, individual rights were confirmed, including prohibitions on excessive bail and the right to trial by jury. It is this system of rights, protected by the English Constitution, that led Montesquieu to identify England as "the one nation in the world that has political liberty for its direct purpose."[21]

According to Burke, the principles established by the events of 1688 were longstanding. In *Reflections*, he refers to "the ancient fundamental principles of our government."[22] These existed *before* the Glorious Revolution, which was undertaken to counteract a threat to the Constitution, and so to *preserve* them. In an early, unfinished study of English history, Burke endorses a not uncommon view of the longstanding nature of English liberties, protected by the Constitution. Thus he notes that the barons who forced King John to sign the Magna Carta (in 1215) were moved by a desire to preserve "the liberties which *their* ancestors had received by the free concession of a former king."[23] Burke holds that English liberties constitute a legacy of the past, handed down from previous generations:

> [F]rom Magna Charta to the Declaration of Right it has been the uniform policy of our constitution to claim and assert our liberties as an *entailed inheritance* derived to us from our forefathers, and to be transmitted to our posterity. . . . By this means our constitution preserves a unity in so great a diversity of its parts. We have an inheritable crown, an inheritable peerage, and a House of Commons and a people inheriting privileges, franchises, and liberties from a long line of ancestors. (*Reflections*, p. 37)

Accordingly, Burke opens *Reflections* with a lengthy discussion of the Glorious Revolution, in order to distinguish its principles from those underlying the French Revolution. The principles defended in *Reflections* are those of "the ancient Whigs" (*Appeal*, p. 193), fidelity to which was maintained by the Rockingham Whigs. In *Appeal*, Burke notes that upon beginning his association with Rockingham, it was his wish "to form an eternal connexion" with these principles (*Appeal*, p. 120). Some twenty-five years after that time, he describes himself as "among the most forward in my zeal for maintaining that constitution and those principles in their utmost purity and vigor" (*Reflections*, pp. 4–5).

Burke's view of the British Constitution was widely held. It is related to what we have seen in our discussion of Montesquieu. In *Appeal*, he takes pride that Montesquieu, "a genius not born in every country, or in every time," preferred the British Constitution to any other he encountered in his research (pp. 198–199). Like Montesquieu, Burke views this constitution as possessing the benefits of separation of powers and checks and balances. Power is carefully divided between the Crown and the two houses of Parliament, so the power of each element is contained by the others. In *Appeal*, he quotes an old Whig's account of the principles underlying the Constitution, from the time of Queen Anne: "The nature of our constitution is that of a *limited monarchy*, wherein the supreme power is communicated and divided between Queen, Lords, and Commons . . ." (*Appeal*, p. 124). Burke's view of the crucial importance of constitutional balance was shared by other political thinkers of the time. Thus, according to Lord Bolingbroke, an important eighteenth-century political theorist: "nothing surely can be more evident than this; that in a constitution like ours the safety of the whole depends on the balance of the parts, and the balance of the parts on their mutual independency on one another."[24]

Like Montesquieu, Burke views the stable, settled character of the British Constitution as essential for the maintenance of liberty. Throughout his works, the conception of freedom he has in mind is negative (see pp. 231–6). Freedom centers on an absence of interference by other people. The necessary security can exist only in the confines of a stable government, which is constructed so it cannot abuse its citizens. This might not be liberty in a perfect philosophical sense, but Burke views it as "a manly, moral, regulated liberty" (*Reflections*, p. 8). Under this constitution, liberty exists in concrete form, not as "'the rights of men,' but as the rights of Englishmen, and as a patrimony derived from their forefathers" (*Reflections*, p. 36).

The British Constitution not only secures liberty but transmits it from generation to generation, linking all in a tradition of benefiting from and cherishing its fundamental principles. Thus the rights of Englishmen have been secured through time. They are supported by tradition and precedent, enjoyed by generations in the past, to be left to future generations. In expounding the British Constitution, Burke has the great advantage of describing something that exists. His theory illuminates "the principles of a constitution already made. It is a theory drawn from the *fact* of our government" (*Appeal*, p. 194). The security provided by an existing, stable constitution is eloquently described in Burke's 1784 speech on "the Representation of the Commons in Parliament":

> Our Constitution is like our island, which uses and restrains its subject sea; in vain the waves roar. In that Constitution, I know, and exultingly I feel, both that I am free, and that I am not free dangerously to myself or to others. I know that no power on earth, acting as I ought to do, can touch my life, my liberty, or my property. I have that inward and dignified consciousness of my own security and independence which constitutes, and is the only thing which does constitute, the proud and comfortable sentiment of freedom in the human breast.[25]

Burke's view of liberty, secured by a balanced, stable, and above all, existing constitution lies at the heart of his political theory. Many of the specific causes he undertook throughout his career were intended to counteract perceived threats to these important values. For example, in *Thoughts on the Causes of the Present Discontents* (1770), he presents a celebrated account of political parties and their role. Strong claims have been made for Burke's analysis. For instance, Carl Cone writes: "It was the first major attempt to explain the nature and the utility, even the necessity of political parties." Cone says portions of Burke's analysis "will remain relevant as long as political freedom exists. Burke's discussion of the political party marked a new era in political thought and practice, and when the lesson he taught eventually was learned, a new state of constitutional development began in England" (Cone, I, 195). But claims of this sort are overblown. As one might expect, Burke's analysis of political parties is not an abstract and general treatment of the subject but is addressed to a specific problem. His proposals concerning parties must be understood in the context of a particular threat to the existing constitutional balance.

The "present discontents" Burke observes bear on maintaining the separation of powers. Under the influence of Montesquieu,[26] he views monarchy as distinguished from despotism because the power of the monarch is restrained by fundamental, fixed laws. If the monarch is able to erode the institutions that contain him, he can establish a tyranny. Thus Burke notes it is the nature of despotism to oppose all power but its own, and so "to annihilate all intermediate situations between boundless strength on its own part, and total debility on the part of the people" (*Thoughts*, p. 125). Burke fears that in his own political situation the independence of Parliament is jeopardized by corruption, the King's ability to grant favors and so to influence members. In a letter, he describes his dismay on first coming to Parliament and seeing the House of Commons "surrendering itself to the guidance, not of an authority grown out of experience, wisdom, and integrity, but of the accidents of court favor. . . ."[27]

It is to counteract this situation that Burke puts forth his idea of party—one of the first developed accounts of political parties in the literature. According to Burke, a party is a group of people motivated by common principles. Because of their values, they are less likely to yield to temptations dangled by the King or his ministers. Burke's famous definition is as follows:

> Party is a body of men united for promoting by their joint endeavors the national interest upon some particular principle in which they are all agreed. (*Thoughts*, p. 187)

The "party" Burke has in mind conforms to the eighteenth-century model of a great man, or wealthy aristocrat, and his clients. His account is especially suited to the Rockingham Whigs, who at that time most clearly approximated this conception, as they were unwilling to take office except as a party.[28] But far from laying out the role of the modern party in a two-party parliamentary government, Burke is in essence appealing to the virtue of an exceptional class of men, who are uniquely able to resist temptation. The nature of this group and their special role in government will be discussed in more detail in the following section.

Commentators note problems with Burke's analysis of the present discontents. In particular, he is frequently too ready to believe his political opponents are conspiring against his forces, and against the public interest. Thus commentators believe his analysis of secret manipulation of Parliament by the Crown is "hopelessly exaggerated."[29] But in responding to the situation he perceives, in this case as in countless others, Burke reveals great ability to locate a kernel of political truth in the details of a particular situation. Once again, it is far from his purpose to develop universal principles. As he says in *Thoughts*:

> It is the business of the speculative philosopher to mark the proper ends of government. It is the business of the politician, who is the philosopher in action, to find out proper means toward these ends, and to employ them with effect. (*Thoughts*, p. 187)

In this quotation, Burke distinguishes himself from the speculative philosopher. The politician, who must act in the world, is concerned with concrete accomplishments, with getting things done, while the philosopher retreats to a realm of theory. But in addressing particular problems, Burke often verges on the latter role. Thus in his observations concerning the possibilities of principled bodies of politicians, he sheds important new light on how governments can work to attain their proper ends.

THE ROLE OF THE ARISTOCRACY

In his capacity as spokesman for the Rockingham Whigs, Burke defends the aristocracy's central role in the English political system. As we have seen, the men of principle and virtue upon whom he bases his conception of party are Rockingham and his associates.

In his writings, Burke frequently idealizes the aristocracy and their importance to the maintenance of a stable political order. A famous description of their role, in comparison to that of ordinary mortals, is contained in a letter he wrote to the Duke of Richmond in 1772:

> You people of great families and hereditary Trusts and fortunes are not like such as I am, who whatever we may be by the Rapidity of our growth and of the fruit we bear, flatter ourselves that while we creep on the Ground we belly into melons that are exquisite for size and flavor, yet still we are but annual plants that perish with our Season and leave no sort of Traces behind us. You if you are what you ought to be are the great Oaks that shade a Country and perpetuate your benefits from Generation to Generation.[30]

The comparison between annual plants that come and go and mighty oak trees is perhaps overstated. But the analogy expresses Burke's belief that the great noble families provide the stable pillars of the kingdom. They afford the secure, protected environment necessary for ordinary people's daily existence.

The nobility's privileged place is bound up with their wealth, passed from generation to generation. The great advantage of wealth is the independence it allows. As we have seen, Burke believes it is essential that the power of the monarch be held in check. Thus people with independent means are important, because they can resist blandishments to which others might succumb. People who cannot do without the Court's favor provide little check upon it, in comparison to an association of aristocrats, who can resist with impunity. Burke expresses his pride in belonging to a party of aristocrats, a party of wealth, in a letter written in 1792:

> The party with which I acted had, by the malevolent and unthinking, been reproached, and by the wise and good always esteemed and confided in—as an aristocratic party. Such I always understood it to be in the true sense of the word. I understood it to be a party, in its composition and in its principles, connected with the solid, permanent and long possessed property of the Country; a party, which, by a Temper derived from that Species of Property, and affording a security to it, was attached to the ancient tried usages of the Kingdom, a party therefore essentially constructed upon a Ground plot of stability and independence; a party therefore equally removed from servile court compliances, and from popular levity, presumption, and precipitation.[31]

As Burke writes in another context, "Independence of mind will ever be more or less influenced by independence of fortune."[32] The close connections between the nobility's privileged position and their substantial property entails that Burke's support of the aristocracy is closely tied to defense of the existing property system.

In addition to providing independence, the nobility's great wealth renders it particularly suited to positions of responsibility and power. Wealth allows leisure and opportunities for education denied those without its advantages. Burke believes that man is by nature reasonable. But in saying this, he uses the term "nature" in a particular way, in reference to an entity's most highly developed condition. A creature's nature is found in a fully formed, mature example of its species. Because reason is the highest human capacity, man achieves his nature only when this is completely developed. According to Burke: "Art is man's nature" (*Appeal*, p. 169). The "art" he has in mind is proper education, which alone is able to raise a human being to his full heights. As one commentator says, "Not 'natural' man, but civilized man, is the object of Burke's solicitude."[33] The nobility's position is privileged in innumerable ways. Not only do they receive a better education, but sheltered from much evil and misery, they avoid the coarsening effects of ordinary life and so develop a superior sensibility. A fully developed member of this group is aware his privileges also entail responsibilities. He will therefore be devoted to public service—virtuous in the sense in which Rousseau and Montesquieu use the term, willing to subordinate his own interest to what is good for society. The privileged position of the nobility, then, combined with their superior educational opportunities, makes them suited to their great responsibilities. Their superior upbringing is described in *Appeal*:

> To be bred in a place of estimation; to see nothing low and sordid from one's infancy; to be taught to respect one's self; to be habituated to the censorial inspection of the public eye; to look early to public opinion; to stand upon such elevated ground as to be enabled to take a large view for the wide-spread and infinitely diversified combinations of men and affairs in a large society; to have leisure to read, to reflect, to converse; to be enabled to draw the court and attention of the wise and learned, wherever they are to be found; to be habituated in armies to command and to obey; to be taught to despise danger in the pursuit of honor and duty; to be formed to the greatest degree of vigilance, foresight, and circumspection, in a state of things in which no fault is committed with impunity and the slightest mistakes draw on the most ruinous consequences; to be led to a guarded and regulated conduct from a sense that you are considered as an administrator of law and justice, and to be thereby amongst the first benefactors to mankind; to be a professor of high sciences, of liberal and ingenuous art; . . . These are the circumstances of men, that form what I should call a *natural* aristocracy, without which there is no nation." (*Appeal*, p. 168)

Members of this "natural" aristocracy achieve the full development of their nature. Because the advantages of their upbringing are reserved for members of this class, it could be argued that only aristocrats are fully developed human beings. Though Burke does not go this far, he clearly believes the great opportunities they enjoy make the aristocracy society's "proper chieftains" (*Appeal*, p. 169). Members of this class are uniquely positioned to rule.

It is notable that Burke's defense of the aristocracy is supported by a reasoned account of the public good. Rather than saying simply that they should rule because they have always done so, or because they have been put in their position by God—though he says these things too in various contexts—Burke argues that their unique qualities make them especially suited to rule. The aristocrats are "the wiser, the more expert, and the more opulent," rightly suited to lead and enlighten "the weaker, the less knowing, and the less provided with the goods of fortune" (*Appeal*, p. 167). Defending the entitlements of the aristocracy on the grounds of their superior qualities, Burke is able to argue that privilege has advantages. In opposition to the leveling tendencies of much Enlightenment thought, he spells out the benefits of a differentiated class structure.

Far from giving the aristocracy interests opposed to those of society, their privileged position renders them uniquely suited to represent society as a whole:

> A true natural aristocracy is not a separate interest in the state, or separable from it. It
> is an essential integrant part of any large people rightly constituted. (*Appeal*, p. 168)

The aristocracy's privileged position allows them to develop special, valuable qualities. Because of this, only they are suited to represent the good of all.

REPRESENTATION

Burke's account of the aristocracy and its special qualities provides the context for his important contribution to the theory of representation. As generally used, the concept of representation centers on the fact that one person acts on behalf of another, and is able to perform actions binding on the other. In a familiar case, American citizens are represented in the House of Representatives. Every two years, the citizens of a given district elect someone to cast votes in Congress on their behalf, with the votes of the representatives changing the rights and duties of the citizenry. For instance, if the representatives vote to raise the gasoline tax, then all citizens are required to pay, regardless of their feelings on this particular matter.

The concept of representation is used differently by different theorists, and there is no universally accepted definition. Burke provides what is generally viewed as the *locus classicus* for one particular account of the concept. As one commentator says, this is "without doubt one of his most important contributions to the history of political thought."[34] There is an important ambiguity in the concept of representation. Briefly, if Miguel represents Marie, he can cast his vote according to (a) what he views as the best solution to the problem under consideration, or (b) what Marie wants him to do, that is, what she perceives to be in her interest in this situation, and so what she has instructed him to do. To give an example, assume that Miguel is asked to vote on a gasoline tax, and he believes it is important that the tax be enacted to reduce the government's budget deficit. But Marie believes it is not in her interest to pay higher taxes and has instructed her representative to vote accordingly. In a case of this sort, the role of the representative is obviously important. If Marie were to vote in person, she would vote against the tax. But because all citizens cannot vote directly on every measure that is considered (or at least, cannot do so outside the narrow circumstances described by Rousseau), their representatives must act for them. But the question is, how does a representative act *for* someone? Does the representative merely carry out his constituents' wishes, or does he act according to his own judgment of the best alternative? Of course, many cases are more complex than this simple example. In general, the representative is required to vote on issues that arise during his term of office. In many cases, he has not received explicit instructions from his constituents. But even in these cases, he can attempt to discover their views, perhaps by taking a poll. Should the representative vote, then, according to the poll responses of his constituents or according to his own best judgment?

Burke supports the latter position. The clearest statement of his view is in a speech he made upon being elected to the House of Commons by the people of Bristol. He refers to his conception of the representative's role as "virtual representation." This is in contrast to what we can call the "mandate" view. According to this latter conception, the representative should vote according to his constituents' wishes, regardless of his own thoughts on some question. Burke's opponent in the election, Henry Cruger, had argued for the voters' right to instruct their representative. He held that the latter was their "Servant" not their "Master," and should be "subservient to their Will, not superior to it" (Cone, I, 274). Burke staunchly opposes this conception of representation. The wishes of his constituents, he says, "ought to have great weight" with the representative. Their business must have his "unremitted attention." "It is his duty to sacrifice his repose, his pleasure, his satisfactions, to theirs—and above all, ever, and in all cases, to prefer their interest to his own."[35] But he must not sacrifice his judgment:

> Your representative owes you, not his industry only, but his judgment, and he betrays, instead of serving you, if he sacrifices it to your opinion. ("Bristol Poll," p. 115)

In other words, the representative must follow his own judgment of what is right, regardless of the wishes of his constituents.

To defend this view of the representative's role Burke presents a distinctive view of the nature of government. The representative is sent to Parliament to deliberate about the country's good. Believing there is a rational solution to any given problem, Burke argues that the representative should attempt to find this: "government and legislation are matters of reason and judgment, not of inclination" ("Bristol Poll," p. 115). The representative's view of the good takes precedence over what his constituents want. What is more, his role is to ascertain what is good for the country as a whole, not only for his constituents, when these are in conflict:

> Parliament is not a *congress* of ambassadors from different and hostile interests, which interests each must maintain, as an agent and advocate, against other agents and advocates; but Parliament is a *deliberative* assembly of *one* nation, with *one* interest, that of the whole—where not local purposes, not local prejudices, ought to guide, but the general good, resulting from the general reason of the whole. You choose a member, indeed; but when you have chosen him, he is not a member of Bristol, but he is a member of *Parliament.* ("Bristol Poll," p. 116)

Burke's conception of representation is justly famous. The great eloquence with which he presents it makes it perhaps the clearest statement of this view in the literature. Thus the idea that the representative must act on his conception of the national interest is often referred to as "Burkean representation." This view rests on particular assumptions about the nature of politics, which we must examine.

What is distinctive of Burke's view is clearly seen in the light of James Madison's discussion of the extended republic in *Federalist* 10 (discussed in Chapter 5). According to Madison, a country is comprised of a collection of conflicting interests. For instance, he describes the conflict between different economic interests as follows:

> A landed interest, a manufacturing interest, a mercantile interest, a moneyed interest, with many lesser interests, grow up of necessity in civilized nations, and divide them into different classes, actuated by different sentiments and views.[36]

Madison argues that conflict between numerous interests makes it difficult for a single one to constitute a majority, and so to dominate government. The assumption here, we must note, is that the people who make up these different interests will support conflicting policies. For instance, a particular tariff might be good for the moneyed group but bad for manufacturers. Madison's expectation is that elected officials representing each group will act according to its interests and instructions. Thus government is viewed as a process through which the conflicting interests of different groups are weighed and balanced, until some reasonable compromise is worked out. On the mandate view, representatives contribute to this process by upholding the interests of their particular groups against others. Now on this view, if Jones, representing manufacturers, decides that his role is to represent the good of the nation as a whole, rather than that of the manufacturers, this could be damaging to his constituency. Unless *all other* representatives act in the same way, his constituents will be at a disadvantage in the bargaining between groups that constitutes the policy process. With all other representatives advocating the narrow interests of their groups, the manufacturers' particular interests will not be taken into account in the search for an acceptable compromise.

Burke's view is different in two respects. First, he assumes there is an identifiable national interest, beyond the compromise accommodation Madison posits. As one commentator puts this, "For Burke, political representation is the representation of interest, and interest has an objective, impersonal, unattached reality."[37] Thus government is a matter of reason, because its primary role is to discover this objectively real interest. Second, Burke also assumes that this conception of the representative's role will be shared by most if not all representatives. Because all will act in accordance with the national interest rather than narrow sectional interests, no one group will be advantaged or disadvantaged in the policy process. Unfortunately for his own political career, Burke was incorrect about this second assumption. In Parliament, he largely ignored the narrow interests of his Bristol constituency, not even visiting Bristol between 1776 and 1780. Finding it impossible to run for reelection in Bristol, he was returned to the House in a Malton district controlled by Rockingham (see Cone, I, 382–386; Ayling, pp. 98–101).

It follows from Burke's conception of representation that the proper representative for some group is the person best able to perceive its interests. In addition, because he acts on the people's real interests rather than their wishes, the representative need not be chosen by the people. As long as he does what he believes to be good for them—which is not necessarily what they *want* him to do—he is fulfilling his function. Virtual representation can be less democratic than a mandate view. According to the latter view, group *A*'s representative is supposed to follow their wishes on some question. This can be accomplished most easily if they are able to choose him and he is made accountable to them. If he votes against their wishes, they can vote him out of office at the next election—as happened to Burke himself. Burke's view of representation, on the other hand, does not necessarily entail democracy. If the representative's role is to do what is right, then he need not be accountable to the people. In fact, if the representative has a clearer understanding of the people's interest than they themselves do, it is actually counterproductive to make him so accountable. These points are made in a letter Burke wrote in 1792:

> Virtual representation is that in which there is a communion of interests and a sympathy in feelings and desires between those who act in the name of any description of people and the people in whose name they act, though the trustees are not actually chosen by them. This is virtual representation. Such a representation I think to be in many cases even better than the actual. It possesses most of its advantages, and is free

from many of its inconveniences; it corrects the irregularities in the literal representation, when the shifting currents of human affairs or the acting of public interests in different ways carry it obliquely from its first line of direction.[38]

Burke's view of virtual representation is central to his conception of the aristocracy's role in the political system. Briefly, he believes they are especially suited to represent the people, for the reasons discussed above. Well educated, leisured aristocrats are uniquely able to perceive the people's interests and to act on them. As indicated above, the aristocracy "is not a separate interest in the state, or separable from it" (*Appeal*, p. 168). Thus Burke supports aristocratic control of the political system, "government by an aristocratic clique," to use one commentator's words.[39]

As one would expect from Burke's support of the aristocracy, he also opposes electoral reforms, especially extending the right to vote to a larger section of the population. During Burke's time, a small percentage of the English people had the right to vote, and government was firmly in the hands of the landed elite. This suited Burke. When a political opponent proposed extending the franchise, Burke opposed this. In 1769, in *Observations on a Late State of the Nation*, in his first public pronouncement on parliamentary reform, Burke proposed further *limiting* the franchise. A narrower electorate would allow the representative greater freedom:

> I believe that most sober thinkers on this subject are rather of opinion, that our fault is on the other side; and that it would be more in the spirit of our constitution, and more agreeable to the pattern of our best laws, by lessening the number, to add to the weight and independency of our voters. (*Observations, Writings*, II, 177)

In addition, given the low moral quality of the majority of people, it would not be wise to allow them to vote:

> And truly, considering the immense and dangerous charge of elections; the prostitute and daring venality, the corruption of manners, the idleness and profligacy of the lower sort of voters, no prudent man would propose to increase such an evil. (*Observations, Writings*, II, 177)

In other contexts, Burke argues against electoral reforms for other reasons. When it was proposed that Parliament be elected more frequently, he opposed this idea because of "the horrible disorders among the people attending frequent elections." An additional consideration is financial. The vastly greater resources of the Crown give it a substantial advantage over gentlemen of independent means (*Thoughts*, pp. 178–179). Frequent elections could be extremely burdensome, especially to landed candidates.[40]

Though Burke's opposition to democratic reforms is consistent with the main tendencies of his political theory, it leaves him vulnerable to criticism. Clearly, his ideas stand in opposition to emerging doctrines that all people are equal and have important natural rights. For an age that is beginning to view democracy as a good in itself, aspects of his philosophy can appear as "propaganda to serve the cause of the aristocratic clique around Rockingham."[41] Burke could perhaps respond that his views are more democratic than they are often made out to be. Even in his speech at the Bristol Poll, which is his best-known defense of virtual representation, he makes strong concessions to the interests of his constituents. Though the representative must not surrender his judgment, Burke says the constituents' wishes "will have great weight with him." He resolves "to live in the strictest union, the closest correspondence, and the most unreserved communication" with his constituents ("Bristol Poll," p. 115). Though this is distinct from giving their wishes deter-minative force, Burke clearly views the representative as representing specific people.

The fact that this does not acquit him of the charge of being undemocratic would probably not concern Burke greatly. He would undoubtedly view this criticism as the application of an abstract standard, removed from the complexities of the political world. To apply conceptions such as natural rights to the world of politics with an aim to improve conditions is far more likely to do harm than good—as we will see especially in regard to Burke's criticism of the French Revolution. For reasons we have seen, a central impetus of his philosophy is to demonstrate that the people are better off if their representation is not fully democratic. If the representative knows more than his constituents, it is best that he not follow their opinions rather than his own—regardless of whether this is democratic, or consistent with constituents' natural rights.

A more severe criticism could be directed at Burke's claim that there is an objective natural interest which the aristocratic representative is best able to perceive. Opponents of the aristocracy would undoubtedly attack this contention. Far from seeing the interests of the aristocracy as intertwined with those of the nation as a whole, critics might perceive sharp conflict between them. An argument along these lines raises severe problems for Burke's position. If the relationship between aristocracy and common people is less harmonious than he envisions, then it becomes less evident that the former should have exclusive rights to represent the latter. In fact, if, as many people began to argue in the eighteenth century, there is a fundamental conflict of interest between the aristocracy and the remainder of the population, then the former's demand to monopolize political power will not seem benevolent. If this conflict of interests is widely believed to exist, then the aristocracy will face increasing demands for political reform. Arguments such as Burke's to oppose extending the franchise will be brushed aside. If the aristocracy does not make the requisite concessions voluntarily, the thoughts of many of their subjects will turn to revolution.

THE AMERICAN REVOLUTION

Burke's adherence to the principles we have seen led him to take very different views of the American and French Revolutions. His support of the former while condemning the latter is the basis for a widespread charge of inconsistency. Burke is unprincipled, so the argument goes; he shifts his views according to prevailing political winds, from self-interest, or perhaps the interest of his aristocratic party. But far from demonstrating his inconsistency, his views on these two great political crises represent applications of consistently held principles.[42] He supports different conclusions because of different circumstances. We will discuss his views in regard to the American Revolution in this section, to be followed by examination of the French Revolution in succeeding sections. Burke's major pronounce-ments on the American Revolution are contained in two great speeches, "On American Taxation," delivered in 1774, and "On Conciliation with America," delivered in 1775, and a letter to the Sheriffs of Bristol, written in 1777.[43] Serving in Parliament during the years leading up to the American Revolution and during the war itself and its aftermath, Burke made numerous other pronouncements on the issues involved, while the subject is also discussed in his correspondence. But we will look mainly at these three compositions, as in previous sections, moving readily between them.

Throughout, Burke argues for restraint in dealing with America. He does not view the colonists' aims as radical or revolutionary in the proper sense of the term (as discussed in succeeding sections). Rather, the colonists, of English descent, acted to protect the rights of Englishmen, to provide security to America's "*ancient* condition" (*Appeal*, p. 107). He likens their situation to that of the Old Whigs in 1688, whose rebellious actions were provoked. In *Appeal*, Burke describes the Americans "as standing at that time, and in that controversy, in the same relation to England, as England did to King James the Second, in 1688." He argues that the Americans took up arms for only one reason, the British attempt to tax them without their consent (*Appeal*, p. 107).

In approaching American affairs, Burke's end is similar to what we have seen. He is concerned with the preservation of ancient liberty, which is threatened, not by the zealotry of the colonists, but by the incompetence of the British government. To some extent Burke's complaints about the government's actions can be attributed to political motives. His disquisitions on American affairs are from the perspective of an opposition member of Parliament, naturally critical of political opponents. But throughout his discussions, he also expresses central themes of his conservative political philosophy. To a large extent, Burke believes, misguided policies result from an incorrect approach to political affairs. The government bases its policies on *theoretical* rather than practical concerns. It is deeply interested in the legal relationship between Britain and the colonies and Parliament's right to tax them, but does not pay adequate attention to the social and political circumstances within which its policies must be enacted. As Burke says in his letter to the Sheriffs of Bristol, "everything that has been done there has arisen from a total misconception of the object" ("Sheriffs of Bristol," p. 196).

Central to Burke's conservative philosophy is the need for a practical approach to political questions, and opposition to speculative approaches, which can be highly destructive. One of his favorite terms of opprobrium is "metaphysical." Misguided politicians are interested in theoretical speculations, in metaphysics, rather than in the actual factors at work in political situations and how they can be turned to one's maximum advantage. As noted above, Burke is deeply concerned with the *limits* of reason. As far back as 1757, in the Preface to *A Vindication of Natural Society*, he expresses his fear of "a mind which has no restraint from a sense of its own weakness, of its subordinate rank in the creation, and of the extreme danger of letting the imagination loose upon some subjects."[44]

Burke is opposed to theoretical speculation in two related respects. First, he demonstrates the importance of clearly analyzing the circumstances in which one must act, as opposed to considering problems in the abstract. Careful attention to the facts is necessary for drawing up a range of options and ascertaining the probable consequences of each. Second, in regard to crucial questions of choosing one's course of action, Burke is interested in securing what is possible. In deciding on one's proper object, one must choose realistic goals, in the light of the difficulty of attaining anything more. What one has a right to in theory is often at odds with the best one can realistically achieve. To pursue the former can often damage prospects of attaining the latter. Burke's sentiments are expressed in the familiar maxim (originally penned by Voltaire) that "the best is the enemy of the good." In regard to both means and ends, the successful politician must act in the real world rather than as he wishes things were or might turn out. In his letter to the Sheriffs of Bristol, Burke says that he does not "pretend to be an antiquary, a lawyer, or qualified for the chair of professor in metaphysics." He would not put his constituents' "solid interests upon speculative grounds" ("Sheriffs of Bristol," pp. 198–199). The contrast between practical analysis and what Burke derides as metaphysical speculation is central to his political philosophy—and to much subsequent conservative thought.

In addressing American affairs, Burke argues from careful attention to circumstances. As a student of Montesquieu, he begins by studying what is in effect the general spirit of the American colonists. Because of a range of factors, the Americans have a great love of liberty ("Conciliation," pp. 221–227). For instance, they are English by descent, and Protestant, which is a form of dissent. In addition, the possession of slaves in the Southern states makes their other inhabitants especially conscious of their freedom. The Americans are also heavily influenced by lawyers and possess democratic governments. Finally, they are separated from the English by three thousand miles of ocean. "[F]rom all these causes a fierce spirit of liberty has grown up" ("Conciliation," p. 227). This is a fact, which must be recognized and dealt with, whether one likes it or not: "[T]he question is not, whether their spirit deserves praise or blame—what in the name of God, shall we do with it?" ("Conciliation," p. 227).

The Americans' fierce attachment to liberty limits Britain's options. Any attempt to coerce the colonists will be resisted, and the more so the more they are pushed. Thus to insist on England's legal *right* to impose certain taxes will do no good, because the colonists will refuse to pay. "Obedience is what makes government, and not the names by which it is called . . ." ("Conciliation," p. 228). To make matters worse, the colonists are not attached to liberty in general or in the abstract, but to the rights of Englishmen, "to liberty according to English ideas and on English principles" ("Conciliation," p. 222).

The British recognize something similar in their own situation. In their system of government, Parliament is in a legal and theoretical sense omnipotent. However, over time, practical limits to Parliament's powers have emerged. What Parliament is theoretically or legally able to do does not correspond with what it can actually do—with what it can get away with, if you will ("Sheriffs of Bristol," pp. 199–200). To transcend these limits will provoke popular uproar, perhaps resistance. Thus the legal powers of Parliament are superseded by the attitudes and opinions of the people it must govern. Its *actual* rights are what the people will accept, and this can be ascertained only through careful study of British politics and culture. In the absence of such knowledge, theoretical speculation, and even careful analysis of English law, will be misleading. A legal right is not *real* unless it is consonant with the general spirit of the people. In dealing with the American colonies, however, British policy makers have not recognized this. They have also failed to recognize that the colonists are especially sensitive to questions of taxation, and view English policy in this area as intolerable.

Because of the colonists' fierce commitment to liberty, Burke believes the only reasonable approach is to devise policies that will allow them to retain their formerly close ties with the British. Only through conciliation can an acceptable outcome be achieved: "I propose, by removing the ground of the difference, and by restoring the *former unsuspecting confidence of the colonies in the mother country* to give permanent satisfaction to your people, and (far from a scheme of ruling by discord) to reconcile them to each other . . ." ("Conciliation," p. 210). This policy is not ideal, as it would mean that the British government must do without the revenue it hoped to raise. But Burke believes it is the best possible policy under the circumstances. As he says in his letter to the Bristol Sheriffs: "there is a difference between bad and the worst of all" ("Sheriffs of Bristol," p. 196). Not realizing the consequences of the policies it has pursued, the British government has backed the colonists against a wall, virtually forcing them to fight.

Burke believes conciliation is necessary because warfare benefits no one. While the consequences of losing the war would be loss of empire, and so of course dreadful, even if the British were to win, the outcome of a policy of coercion would be severe tension between themselves and their colonies, stretching into the future. Sober assessment of the facts will yield this conclusion:

> Will they be content in such a state of slavery? . . . Reflect how you are to govern a people who think they ought to be free, and think they are not. Your scheme yields no revenue; it yields nothing but discontent, disorder, disobedience; and such is the state of America, that, after wading up to your eyes in blood, you could only end just where you begun. . . . ("American Taxation," II, 459)

Burke also sees dangers to the carefully balanced British political system from a policy of force, even if war with America is successful. The effects of exercising tyrannical power abroad will be reflected in altered political relationships at home. In *Appeal* (describing himself in the third person), Burke reflects upon these consequences:

> He was fully persuaded, that if such should be the event, they must be held in that subdued state by a great body of standing forces, and perhaps of foreign forces. He was strongly of opinion, that such armies, first victorious over Englishmen, in a conflict for English constitutional rights and privileges, and afterwards habituated (though in America) to keep an English people in a state of abject subjection, would prove fatal in the end to the liberties of England itself. . . . (*Appeal*, p. 108)

If the consequences of the government's policies are self-defeating, one must wonder why they have been pursued. The government does not desire the ends Burke foresees, so why has it followed a course of action that will bring them about? To a large extent, Burke believes this results from an improper approach to political problems. Rather than examining the facts of the case, the government has been misled by abstract ideas, especially its legal sovereignty over the colonies. If it has the right to tax the colonies and it needs the money, why should it not do so? But the answer, as we have seen, is that this policy will have terrible effects. To be a successful politician, one must look past legal rights and other related notions to see the world as it is. In his speech, "American Taxation," Burke expresses his disdain for such lines of reasoning:

> I am not here going into the distinctions of rights, nor attempting to mark their boundaries. I do not enter into these metaphysical distinctions; I hate the very sound

of them. Leave the Americans as they anciently stood, and these distinctions, born of our unhappy contest, will die along with it. ("American Taxation," II, 458)

Reliance upon abstractions is misleading for a number of reasons which we will explore throughout the remainder of this chapter. In analyzing American affairs, Burke shows how concern with abstractions can distract political actors from studying the facts of their situation, and so also the likely outcomes of their actions. In concentrating on Britain's rights, its political leaders have undertaken policies that are not in its best interests. In the following sections, in discussing Burke's response to the French Revolution, we will see additional problems with a metaphysical approach to politics. To close this section, we will examine two additional objections to metaphysical politics which Burke expresses in his response to the American situation. These are, first, his view of the inescapably messy nature of political affairs, and the importance of emotions and sentimental ties in political relationships.

To begin with the former, in analyzing political affairs, Burke's perspective is that of a political actor. Practical experience, along with the influence of Montesquieu, has convinced him of the complex nature of political reality and the need to rough out the best possible solutions. Political experience has taught him the need to accept compromises, half measures, when these are all that can be had. Neat solutions that are possible in theory are often out of place in the actual world. This aspect of his political outlook is expressed eloquently throughout his corpus. For instance, in his speech on conciliation with America,

> All government, indeed every human benefit and enjoyment, every virtue and every prudent act, is founded on compromise and barter. We balance inconveniences; we give and take; we remit some rights, that we may enjoy others; and we choose rather to be happy citizens than subtle disputants. ("Conciliation," p. 257)

Burke expresses similar ideas in regard to the reality of civil freedom in his letter to the Sheriffs of Bristol:

> Civil freedom, Gentlemen, is not, as many have endeavored to persuade you, a thing that lies hid in the depth of abstruse science. It is a blessing and a benefit, not an abstract speculation; and all the just reasoning that can be upon it is of so coarse a texture as perfectly to suit the ordinary capacities of those who are to enjoy, and of those who are to defend it. Far from any resemblance to those propositions in geometry and metaphysics which admit no medium, but must be true or false in all their latitude, social and civil freedom, like all other things in common life, are variously mixed and modified, enjoyed in very different degrees, and shaped into an infinite diversity of forms, according to the temper and circumstances of every community. The *extreme* of liberty (which is its abstract perfection, but its real fault) obtains nowhere, nor ought to obtain anywhere; because extremes, as we all know, in every point which relates either to our duties or satisfactions in life, are destructive both to virtue and enjoyment. ("Sheriffs of Bristol," pp. 202–203)

Solutions to political questions are messy. They do not allow theoretical rigor, while pursuit of rigor distracts one from what can actually be achieved. In this sense, Burke's view is similar to that of Machiavelli. The statesman's standard is what is possible, whether it is theoretically elegant or even desirable according to absolute standards. Holding this attitude leads Burke to be resolutely antitheoretical at times. For instance, in regard to the question of what constitutes a free government in America, he responds: "I answer, that, for any practical purpose, it is what the people thinks so—and that they, and not I, are the natural, lawful, and competent judges of this matter" ("Sheriffs of Bristol," p. 202). A free government is one that will be accepted by the people and so will not have to be imposed by force. To find out what this is, one must inquire into the spirit of the American colonists, rather than abstruse reflections on the nature of freedom.

Like Machiavelli, Burke believes that in the political world, absolute standards of value are generally of little relevance. The merely bad is better than the worst of all. The standard according to which policies should be assessed is what is possible, comparison of their likely consequences with those of other policies. To strive for something more than the best of a bad lot will often doom one to less. Burke views politics as a *practical* science, "made for the happiness of mankind, and not to furnish out a spectacle of uniformity to gratify the schemes of visionary politicians" ("Sheriffs of Bristol," p. 201). Accordingly, in regard to America, the British government's task "was to rule, not to wrangle." It is poor policy to pursue a course that is theoretically elegant, at the cost of one's empire ("Sheriffs of Bristol," p. 201). As he says in favor of moderate policies in his speech on American taxation,

> These are the arguments of states and kingdoms. Leave the rest to the schools; for there only they may be discussed with safety. But if, intemperately, unwisely, fatally, you sophisticate and poison the very course of government, by urging subtle deductions, and consequences odious to those you govern, from the unlimited and illimitable nature of supreme sovereignty, you will teach them by these means to call that sovereignty itself into question. ("American Taxation," II, 458)

Burke believes an additional drawback of an abstract approach to politics is that it often omits the strong emotional side of political affairs. We have seen something of this already, in Burke's analysis of the Americans' fierce spirit of liberty. Lawyers might focus on the legal relationship between Britain and the colonies, but Burke believes ties of sentiment must also be considered. It is on the cultivation of these, and the allegiance that follows from sentimental attachments, that stable political relationships depend. In regard to Britain's relationship with its American colonies, Burke recommends policies that will strengthen sentimental ties, especially the two sides' shared commitment to liberty. In his speech on conciliation, he says: "Let the Colonies always keep the idea of their civil rights associated with your Government;—they will cling and grapple to you; and no force under heaven will be of power to tear them from their allegiance" ("Conciliation," p. 265). After all, he continues, ties of love and loyalty are responsible for the well-being of the British state as well. It is the attachment of its soldiers and sailors that makes for the nation's armed forces. Without this, "your army would be a base rabble, and your navy nothing but rotten timber." Burke is therefore contemptuous of politicians who recognize only "what is gross and material." People's feelings are of the utmost importance ("Conciliation," p. 266).

In his emphasis on the feelings and habits of political actors, Burke resembles Hume—with both men influenced by Montesquieu. Politics is less a matter of abstract standards, than of how political actors feel. Through long courses of repeated actions, practical relationships are established. Governments become legitimate as their citizens become accustomed to obey. Parameters of legitimacy are similarly set, as departures from established expectations result in friction. The British government's failure to realize this in its dealings with America is largely responsible for the avoidable catastrophe it has brought about.

In its emphasis on the power of custom and habit, Burke's view is closely akin to the conservatism of Hume. There is, however, another side to his thought, in that he idealizes the state and the existing order far more than Hume does. While Hume is resolutely anti-religious, Burke spreads a religious patina over existing social and political relationships. This leads to a depth of commitment to existing affairs—even when they do not promote the good of all—that is not in keeping with the more moderate attachments of Burke's skeptical Scottish predecessor.

THE FRENCH REVOLUTION

Opposition to a "metaphysical" approach to politics is central to Burke's greatest work, *Reflections on the Revolution in France*, and his other writings on the French Revolution. He is largely consistent in taking a conciliatory attitude toward the American Revolution and vigorously opposing the French, because in the former case it was the colonists who resisted metaphysical considerations in favor of their ancient liberties, while in the latter the revolutionaries appealed to abstract principles and so set liberty at risk.

Reflections is ostensibly written in the form of a letter to M. Charles DePont, a Frenchman with whom Burke corresponded. He had asked Burke for his opinion of events in France. Burke responded in November 1789, with a lengthy letter, in which central themes of *Reflections* are apparent.[45] Over the course of the next year, Burke's sentiments hardened into the fully developed form presented in his greatest work. The book's precipitating event is seen in its complete title: *Reflections on the Revolution in France and of the Proceedings in Certain Societies in London Relative to that Event, in a Letter Intended to have been sent to a Gentleman in Paris*. As this indicates, the work's immediate occasion was Burke's desire to respond to a sermon given by Richard Price before the Revolution Society, in 1789.[46] The Revolution Society had been founded to honor the Glorious Revolution. In his speech, Price praised the French Revolution and the principles it embodied:

> I have lived to see a diffusion of knowledge which has undermined superstition and error. I have lived to see the rights of men better understood than ever, and nations panting for liberty, which seemed to have lost the idea of it. I have lived to see thirty millions of people, indignant and resolute, spurning at slavery, and demanding liberty with an irresistible voice, their king led in triumph, and an arbitrary monarch surrendering himself to his subjects. After sharing in the benefits of one Revolution, I have been spared to be a witness to two other Revolutions, both glorious. And now, methinks, I see the ardor for liberty catching and spreading, a general amendment beginning in human affairs, the dominion of kings changed for the dominion of laws, and the dominion of priests giving way to the dominion of reason and conscience.
> (Price, p. 195)

The Revolution Society sent the French National Assembly a congratulatory message, encouraging other countries to affirm man's rights and to reform their governments (Cone, II, 300–301).

Price associates the French and Glorious Revolutions on the basis of common principles they embodied. According to him, the Glorious Revolution was founded on fundamental principles, which the Revolution Society presents in its report "as an instruction to the public." The three principles he notes are: liberty of conscience in religious matters; the right to resist the abuse of power; and "that civil authority is a delegation from the people" (Price, p. 190). Were it not for its adherence to these principles, the Glorious Revolution would have been "not an assertion but an invasion of rights, not a revolution but a rebellion" (Price, pp. 189–190).

Central to Burke's efforts in *Reflections* is distinguishing the French Revolution from the Glorious Revolution of 1688, which, he believes, was *not* made in support of man's abstract rights. Burke says Price's comparison between the two revolutions "gave me a considerable degree of uneasiness" (*Reflections*, p. 10). As is often the case, he approaches the French Revolution with concerns about England at the forefront of his thought, viewing events in France as a prelude to what could happen at home. As he says in *Reflections*, "Whenever our neighbor's house is on fire, it cannot be amiss for the engines to play a little on our own" (*Reflections*, p. 10).

Burke views the French Revolution as "the most astonishing thing that has hitherto happened in the world" (*Reflections*, p. 11). He believes the danger is great, and his tone is accordingly shrill. According to Thomas Paine, who responds to Burke in *The Rights of Man*, "There is scarcely an epithet of abuse to be found in the English language, with which Mr. Burke has not loaded the French nation and the National Assembly. Every thing which rancor, prejudice, ignorance, or knowledge could suggest, are poured forth in the copious fury of near four hundred pages."[47] It is therefore striking that *Reflections* was written early in the revolutionary period, before many of its radical aspects had emerged.

In the popular imagination, the French Revolution is indelibly associated with the Reign of Terror and the Paris mob; with Louis XVI and his Queen, Marie Antoinette, going to the guillotine; with the revolutionary wars that swept Europe, and the demonic figure of Robespierre, a fanatic in power, until he too went to the scaffold. Whether or not these images express the essence of the Revolution, it is important to realize that at the time Burke wrote, they all lay in the future. When *Reflections on the Revolution in France* was published, in 1790, the King was still on his throne, though his power had been limited by the National Assembly, the newly constituted legislative body. France had not yet declared itself a republic. Revolutionary war between France and England, Austria, and Prussia had not broken out. The emergency government of the Committee of Public Safety, and the Reign of Terror it eventually initiated, could hardly be foreseen. What had happened was of course significant. The power of the monarch had been limited, and the royal family forcibly brought from Versailles to Paris by a mob. The privileges of the nobility had been curbed, feudalism abolished, and the serfs freed.[48] Especially important to Burke, Church lands had been confiscated. But whether these measures amounted to "the most astonishing thing that has hitherto happened in the world" is open to question. In view of Burke's response to the Revolution's opening events, it is not surprising that, during subsequent years as it became more radical, his estimation of its dangers increased, and his rhetoric became even more heated.

Central to Burke's assessment of the Revolution is his belief that it represented the triumph of extreme ideas. Because of the attraction of these ideas—all too appealing in the abstract—Burke feared their spread, and believed they were so dangerous they had to be stamped out, or could not otherwise be contained. In 1791 he wrote:

> The present Revolution in France seems to me to be quite of another character and description, and to bear little resemblance or analogy to any of those which have been brought about in Europe, upon principles merely political. *It is a Revolution of doctrine and theoretic dogma.* It has much greater resemblance to those changes which have been made upon religious grounds, in which a spirit of proselytism makes an essential part. (*Thoughts on French Affairs*, Ritchie, p. 208)

Burke likens the Revolution to "the last revolution of doctrine and theory" which took place in Europe, the Reformation (*Thoughts on French Affairs*, Ritchie, p. 208). When war broke out between France and the other European powers, this too was distinctive: "We are in a war of a *peculiar* nature . . . It is with an *armed doctrine* that we are at war." Because of its unusual nature, he believed the Revolutionary regime was "inimical to all other governments."[49] "Never shall I think any country in Europe to be secure, whilst there is established in the very center of it a state (if so it may be called) founded on principles of anarchy, and which is in reality a college of armed fanatics, for the propagation of the principles of assassination, robbery, rebellion, fraud, faction, oppression, and impiety."[50] Burke feared that in the struggle against the Revolution, the fate of England too hung in the balance: "if it stands there, it *must* prevail here."[51] Because of the danger the Revolution posed, Burke devoted considerable space in *Reflections* and subsequent works to important differences between it and the English Revolution of 1688, and to refuting the arguments of those who linked them. Though Price's sermon itself might not merit the attention Burke accords it, he was deeply concerned with what the sermon represents.

In his works on the French Revolution, Burke presents classic pronouncements on important political issues: conditions that make for political stability, differences between reform and revolution, the proper role of ideas in politics, and the dangers when proper limits are transgressed. Like his other works, Burke's discussions of the French Revolution are occasional pieces, written in response to specific political events. But the events were of such magnitude that they drew forth from him something verging on a theory of politics. In the following sections, we will concentrate on central themes of Burke's political philosophy, paying less attention to his analysis of specific events and policies of the Revolution—though as always with Burke, these two sides of his writings are closely linked. Burke's important role in the history of political theory is as an oracle of conservatism. We will focus on his distinctive approach to the French Revolution, which became central to subsequent conservative political thought.

ABSTRACT AND CONCRETE RIGHTS

Burke opens *Reflections on the Revolution in France* by criticizing the views of Price and others who link the French and English Revolutions. As we have seen, Price believes the latter established the English people's rights to choose their own governors, to dismiss them for misconduct, and to frame their government for themselves. To readers of Locke, these rights are familiar. They are basic to liberal political theory, and to Locke's justification of the Glorious Revolution. But Burke will have none of this. One of his most important contributions to political theory is criticism of abstract rights of the Lockean kind, which he believes underlie the French Revolution. In order to defend his own view of the Glorious Revolution, Burke contrasts these with what we can call *concrete* rights, rights embedded in a stable political system.

Unlike concrete rights, abstract rights are not *real*. They can be likened to wishes or aspirations.[52] For instance, consider the *Universal Declaration of Human Rights*, drafted in 1948 and adopted by all member states of the United Nations. According to Article 24, "Everyone has the right to rest and leisure, including reasonable limitation of working hours and periodic holidays, with pay." About this, Burke would surely ask what it means to say everyone has a right to rest and leisure. This is merely a wish, a hope, unless there is some mechanism through which rest and leisure can be supplied to all mankind. In a world in which many millions live in hunger, paid holidays would doubtless seem a luxury. Compare the Bill of Rights of the United States Constitution. In part, the Fifth Amendment reads: "nor shall any person be subject for the same offense to be twice put in jeopardy of life or limb." In contrast to the universal right to leisure, this right is real for all Americans, because there is an established means through which it is enforced. If John Doe is acquitted of a specific crime, he cannot be tried for it again. If he is put on trial again and this time convicted, the case will undoubtedly be appealed to a higher court, which will reverse the conviction. Knowing this, members of the lower court will refuse to try him again. The right not to be tried more than once for a single crime is real because it is enforced by the predictable workings of institutions, which are parts of a stable system of government.

Burke is greatly taken by this contrast. He would undoubtedly prefer a system of government in which all people had all the rights granted by the Universal Declaration of Human Rights. But he would be skeptical of them until he saw them put into practice by an existing political system. A strong supporter of these rights might go so far as to say that any government that does not grant them is illegitimate and should rightfully be overthrown. We have seen this pattern of argument in previous chapters. The demand that government conform to central tenets of natural law is central to liberal political theory, classically enshrined in the thought of Locke and the Declaration of Independence. But one must realize what this claim entails. According to a strong supporter of human rights, government X is not legitimate because it does not guarantee all its inhabitants paid holidays. To make a revolution for this reason would probably be costly. In spite of its shortcomings, government X does have its virtues. To the extent it is stable, it provides its inhabitants with a measure of freedom, with actual rights that are enforced. To make a revolution for the sake of extending these rights to include leisure and paid holidays would jeopardize the existing structure. Faced with the choice of whether to make a revolution in such a situation, Burke emphasizes the fact that the rights guaranteed by the existing structure are real in a way the others are not.

Burke eloquently makes this point in his original letter to Depont. He expresses his great support of the principle of liberty:

> You hope, Sir, that I think the French deserving of liberty? I certainly do. I certainly think that all men who desire it, deserve it. . . . It is the birthright of our species. (Letter to Charles DePont, November 1789, Mansfield, p. 256)

But Burke does not love liberty in the abstract:

> The Liberty I mean is *social* freedom. It is that state of things in which liberty is secured by the equality of restraint; A constitution of things in which the liberty of no one man, and no body of men and no number of men can find means to trespass on the liberty of any person or any description of persons in the society. This kind of liberty is indeed but another name for justice, ascertained by wise laws, and secured by well constructed institutions. (p. 256)

Accordingly, he withholds judgment as to whether the French Revolution actually means an increase of liberty. He will congratulate the French in this regard only when he sees they have a constitutional order in which liberty is secured by stable institutions:

> When therefore I shall learn, that in France, the Citizen, by whatever description he is qualified, is in a perfect state of legal security, with regard to his life, to his property, to the uncontrolled disposal of his person, to the free use of his industry and his faculties;—When I hear that he is protected in the beneficial enjoyment of the estates, to which, by the course of settled law, he was born, or is provided with a fair compensation for them;—that he is maintain'd in the full fruition of the advantages belonging to the state and condition of life, in which he had lawfully engaged himself, or is supplied with a substantial, equitable equivalent;—When I am assured that a simple citizen may decently express his sentiments upon public affairs, without hazard to his life or safety, even tho' against a predominant and fashionable opinion. . . . (p. 258)

When he knows all this of France, then he will congratulate its citizens for their liberty. To give freedom, he writes in *Reflections*, is easy. One must only release the reins of authority. But to create an ordered structure in which liberty is secured is another matter altogether, requiring "much thought, deep reflection, a sagacious, powerful, and combining mind" (pp. 288–289).

HISTORICAL PROCESSES

The real liberty Burke cherishes is not easily achieved. In fact, he believes it can be attained only by accident, as it were, rather than through conscious effort. Central to Burke's political theory is belief that human affairs cannot be directed by human agency. Perhaps a suitable metaphor is a storm. We can take shelter from a storm, perhaps ride it out, or even profit from it—for instance, by making use of its rain for irrigation—but we cannot hope to control or direct it. In Burke's eyes, human history is analogous, simply too powerful and complex for man to manage. There is a strongly religious side to Burke's political theory. His view of man's near helplessness in the face of ineluctable history recalls the medieval Christian view that Providential forces are at work in the world, guided by the hand of God, and that human reason is too feeble to grasp divine intentions. Burke's strikingly written reflections on this view of history and its relationship to human reason are perhaps the best-known passages in all his writings, and probably the *locus classicus* for these ideas in the history of political theory. His elaborate imagery weaves together a number of different themes, which are not easy to disentangle. We will concentrate on three: the complexity of human affairs; some implications of the relationship between nonrational and rational aspects of human nature; and the disproportionate weakness of the individual's reason, in comparison to that of mankind.

As we have noted, because of the great complexity of human affairs, men cannot hope to control them. Burke's view can perhaps be expressed as the law of unanticipated consequences. Throughout history people act, with statesmen acting on a grand scale, on a world stage. Though most actions are undertaken for specific purposes, they are often unsuccessful. Chance or circumstances intervene to thwart human designs. Because the vagaries of chance are beyond the powers of human prediction, people are often surprised by the results of their actions.

A simple case of unanticipated consequences is income tax laws.[53] Government passes certain provisos to the effect that people must pay some percentage of their earnings. Preferring not to pay, many people find ways around the law—loopholes. Once these come to light, government passes additional laws to close them. Prospective payers find dodges around these too, and so government must act again. Over a long period of time the process continues, and the tax code takes on byzantine complexity. The point here is that the original legislators could not possibly have foreseen the results of the overall process of tax legislation. The eventual code is the product of years of tinkering with and improving things, with the activity of many different people involved.

The tax code is only a small part of government. Combine this with the similar institutional histories of all other aspects of government, and one can see the enormous complexity of the result. Countless other considerations must also be dealt with, especially the ways in which developments in one area affect others. For example, with the introduction of certain taxes, donations to charities might fall. So exceptions can be passed to deal with this. But the exceptions can be abused, requiring additional tinkering. What is important to note here is that the tax code is not an entity unto itself. It affects countless other aspects of government and society, and is in turn affected by them. Innumerable other aspects of government affect and are affected by many others. The intricacy of all these interconnections is beyond human powers to foresee. Accordingly, in a successful state, changes and improvements take time. Reforms are made. As their effects become apparent, further improvements are attempted. Some work; others don't. Human society proceeds through a process of trial and error, through the course of many years, many centuries. The result of this process of growth is a set of arrangements superior to any that could have been constructed initially.

In arguing along these lines, Burke shows the influence of Montesquieu. Viewing society as infinitely complex, he also takes a view of political reform similar to Montesquieu's,[54] though in his case the implications receive greater emphasis. If society works through a process of trial and error, then what survives must fulfill some useful function. We may not always be able to identify this; it may have been lost long in the past. But the very fact that a given measure was instituted at some point, and then retained while innumerable other measures have been cast aside, creates a strong presumption in its favor. Burke uses the term "prejudice" in a nonderogatory manner. Prejudices, "untaught feelings" are not bad but good. If we have certain beliefs or habits, then we do so for a reason. The longer they have survived, the stronger the evidence in their favor. Such beliefs cannot be abandoned just because we are unable fully to understand them now. Burke believes we should cherish our prejudices, "and the longer they have lasted and the more generally they have prevailed, the more we cherish them" (*Reflections*, p. 99). This is because prejudices reflect the wisdom of previous generations, "latent wisdom," as he calls it. Accumulated in this way, prejudices outweigh the wisdom of a single man, or a single generation. They are like family money, an inheritance from previous generations:

> We are afraid to put men to live and trade each on his own private stock of reason, because we suspect that this stock in each man is small, and that the individuals would do better to avail themselves of the general bank and capital of nations and of ages. (*Reflections*, p. 99)

What is true of specific beliefs and practices holds more strongly for matters of greater significance, such as the choice of government. Related to Burke's idea of prejudice is his view of "prescription." This is a legal term, the technical sense of which concerns "the way in which an adverse possession of property and authority may be legitimated by virtue of use and enjoyment during a long passage of time."[55] The idea here is that, over time, possessions come to attain legal force, even if they were not acquired rightfully initially. As Burke says in a letter written in 1790, prescription "gives right and title," even when estates are acquired by violence. The point is that this is *old violence*.[56] Over time, even possessions gained by violence become the holders' rightful property. Once again, this view is supported by Burke's conception of historical progress proceeding through trial and error. Even if a given government came into existence through violence—as, Hume notes, all governments have—its continued existence through time makes it legitimate. Through continued obedience to their government, generations of people show they choose it:

> [T]his is a choice not of one day or one set of people, not a tumultuary and giddy choice; it is a deliberate election of ages and of generations; it is a constitution made by what is ten thousand times better than choice; it is made by the peculiar circumstances, occasions, tempers, dispositions, and moral, civil, and social habitudes of the people, which disclose themselves only in a long space of time.[57]

This process involves nonrational factors as well as rational. As institutions do not arise solely through choices, they affect and are affected by people's entire personalities. Men are not only creatures of reason. They are motivated by habit and feeling, and their institutions must be compatible with these aspects of their personalities. Like Montesquieu, Burke conceives of a people's *spirit*, with which their institutions must be in accord. We have seen arguments along these lines in regard to Britain's policies concerning America, which he believed would not succeed because they were out of keeping with the temper of the American people.

Habits and customs exercise strong influence throughout society, because they are pervasive, affecting all areas of life. Like society itself, these elements grow up gradually over time, shaped by other factors and shaping them in turn. Ultimately, these factors constitute a determinate framework into which laws and institutions must fit:

> Manners are of more importance than laws. Upon them, in a great measure the laws depend. The law touches us but here and there, and now and then. Manners are what

vex or soothe, corrupt or purify, exalt or debase, barbarize or refine us, by a constant, steady, uniform, insensible operation, like that of the air we breathe in. . . . According to their quality, they aid morals, they supply them, or they totally destroy them. (*First Letter on a Regicide Peace*, *Writings*, IX, 242)

Because of the force of factors other than laws, altering laws can have limited effects. Government actions must be in accord with a people's spirit, which necessarily limits them. Through historical selection, these psychological factors play a significant role, determining which institutions will work and so will be maintained and which do not and must be discarded.

The relative obduracy of customs and habits reinforces Burke's view of the limited ability of reason to control historical processes. Psychological complexity and institutional complexity are mutually supporting, limiting individuals' ability fully to grasp historical processes and their ability to change them.

In both these respects Burke stands sharply opposed to rationalistic tendencies of liberal thought. Liberals envision man as primarily a rational creature, determining his actions by his interests. According to their view, collective human actions are the basis of social institutions, indeed of society as a whole. For Burke, however, historical processes transcend human rationality because of limits to what man can know, and the ability of nonrational forces to influence the rational. Over the course of time, historical forces overawe the power of conscious human intentions. Central political institutions result from these factors, largely beyond conscious control. Through the actions and interactions of the community as a whole, society assumes its overall shape, within the parameters of which human actions are performed.

Thus the historical process is not subject to neat calculations. Its core darkly resists efforts at human comprehension. But in spite of Burke's generally dark view of man and society, there is an element of optimism in his view of history. Though the individual is not competent to judge the historical process, through its actions, the community as a whole passes judgment. Though the opinions of individuals are subject to question, the community's judgment, exercised through trial and error, tends in the right direction, over generations. "For man is a most unwise and a most wise being. The individual is foolish; the multitude, for the moment is foolish, when they act without deliberation; but the species is wise, and, when time is given to it, as a species, it almost always acts right" ("Representation," p. 331).

Burke is often said to have an "organic" view of society, that it grows and develops like some mysterious form of life. There is an element of truth to this description. The analogy holds in two important respects. Consider, for example, a form of plant. Like a plant, society is a closely intertwined system of elements, each of which has developed as part of a system, involved with all others. The intricacy of interconnection is so great that no individual can grasp it entirely. In addition, like a form of organic life, society develops and changes over time. It cannot be created at a single stroke, but must result from a lengthy process of growth. But the analogy does not hold in other respects. In particular, Burke does not view society as a "super-organism," over and above the people of whom it is composed. He certainly does not believe society has interests of its own, beyond those of the individuals who constitute it. Though society grows and changes over time, the process of development is driven by people as they pursue their interests. There is a strongly religious side to Burke's political theory, as we will see in a subsequent section, and he clearly sanctifies the historical process. But to a large extent, this merely represents acceptance of the direction in which things move, while the mechanisms behind the process of development itself can be understood in purely human terms.

Burke's view of historical development sets him apart from many liberal and Enlightenment political theorists. Whereas these theorists view the individual as the building block of society and discuss the individual on his own terms and in regard to his own interests, Burke views the individual in relationship groups to which he belongs—up to and including the human species. As we have seen in previous chapters, proponents of abstract rights postulate a hypothetical state of nature and argue that political society comes into existence as individuals contract to leave this. Taking a more historical view, Burke sees society developing over time. Men do not come into society voluntarily but are born into it. Its "social ties and ligaments" are not created by individuals through their conscious choices but exist independently of them; society "consists, in a great measure, in the ancient order into which we are born" (*Appeal*, p. 161). Only by coming to terms with this ancient order can people find their place in the world. Not to do so would entail great loss: "the whole chain and continuity of the commonwealth would be broken. No one generation could link with the other. Men would become little better than the flies of a summer" (*Reflections*, p. 108).

But men are more than creatures of a season. Though society does rest on a contract, this contract is not, as liberal theorists would have it, generated by individuals through acts of deliberate choice. We have seen that the concepts of the social contract and contract of government were originally taken over from the private law of corporations (see pp. 55–7). For Burke, an analogy between the state and private agreements is fundamentally flawed. The state has an element of transhistorical reality absent from all voluntary agree-ments. Its ends transcend those of private individuals, while its existence surpasses individual activity. In perhaps the best-known passage in all his works, Burke describes the superiority of the contract of government to those intentionally entered into by individuals, and indeed, to the individuals themselves:

> Society is indeed a contract. Subordinate contracts for objects of mere occasional interest may be dissolved at pleasure—but the state ought not to be considered as nothing better than a partnership agreement in a trade of pepper and coffee, calico, or tobacco, or some other such low concern, to be taken up for a temporary interest, and to be dissolved by the fancy of the parties. It is to be looked on with other reverence, because it is not a partnership in things subservient only to the gross animal existence of a temporary and perishable nature. It is a partnership in all science; a partnership in all art; a partnership in every virtue and in all perfection. As the ends of such a partnership cannot be obtained in many generations, it becomes a partnership not only between those who are living, but between those who are living, those who are dead, and those who are to be born. Each contract of each particular state is but a clause in the great primeval contract of eternal society, linking the lower with the higher natures, connecting the visible and invisible world, according to a fixed compact sanctioned by the inviolable oath which holds all physical and all moral natures, each in their appointed place. (*Reflections*, p. 110)

Reference to "the great primeval contract" is religious in nature, and we will return to this aspect of Burke's thought below. But to close this section, we can retrace the connections between essential elements of his political theory. Throughout this and the previous sections, we have been pursuing different aspects of his conception of historical development. As we have seen, Burke views the human species at work in history as moving forward through an extended process of trial and error. It is only within the confines of institutions that develop in such a way, not only standing the test of time but improving through time, that concrete liberty can exist. When placed alongside the wisdom of the species, the wisdom of isolated individuals pales by comparison. Individuals do not create society; they are born into it and take their places in its rightful order. The process of historical development gives rise to a pattern of institutions too complex for men fully to understand, let alone to create through an act of will. Because the species is wise, we must defer to its judgments, and so prescription justifies existing governments. This does not mean we must accept all that exists as inevitable and wise. Reform is possible, but only within limits, and in accordance with the spirit of what exists. Central to Burke's political philosophy, then, is a distinctive view of history and the individual's place in it.

REFORM AND REVOLUTION

The view of history and government discussed in previous sections places severe limits on Burke's conception of allowable political reform. A system of ordered liberty grows up over time, and is beyond the capacity of any individual to construct or even to comprehend. In spite of the enormous advantages such a system possesses, Burke never claims it is perfect. But that is not the standard. Governments should not be assessed against standards of abstract perfection but against possible alternatives. It is essential to be able to accept an existing system of government in spite of its faults:

> It is no inconsiderable part of wisdom, to know how much of an evil ought to be tolerated lest, by attempting a degree of purity impracticable in degenerate time and manners, instead of cutting off the subsisting ill-practices, new corruptions might be produced for the concealment and security of the old. (*Thoughts*, p. 180)

If one peruses the existing system in the proper frame of mind, one will accept its advantages and attempt to alleviate its faults through a gradual process of reform, knowing that only a gradual process can succeed. In attempting to improve things, one must work with what is given. Burke at one point says his "leading principle" is "in a reformation of the state, to make use of existing materials" (*Letter to a Member of the National Assembly*, Ritchie, p. 67). "A man full of warm, speculative benevolence may wish his society otherwise constituted than he finds it, but a good patriot and a true politician always considers how he shall make the most of the existing materials of his country. A disposition to preserve and an ability to improve, taken together, would be my standard of a statesman" (*Reflections*, p. 181).

Considerations along these lines are central to Burke's distinction between the Glorious and French Revolutions. Though Richard Price and others view the two events as embodying similar principles, the former was not undertaken for the sake of fundamental change. There was no thought of uprooting existing society in order to replace it with something better. Instead, action was taken to preserve the existing system. Though the king was removed, "the stable, fundamental parts" of the British Constitution were not affected:

The nation kept the same ranks, the same orders, the same privileges, the same franchises, the same rules for property, the same subordinations, the same order in the law, in the revenue, and in the magistracy,—the same lords, the same commons, the same corporations, the same electors.

The Church was not impaired; Her estates, her majesty, her splendor, her order and gradations, continued the same. She was preserved in her full efficiency, and cleared only of a certain intolerance, which was her weakness and disgrace. The Church and the State were the same after the Revolution that they were before, but better secured in every part. ("Speech on the Army Estimates," Harrison, p. 318)

The English government was essentially sound before the Revolution and was left intact by it. This is a far cry from France, in which, in Burke's eyes, all was overturned, and without justification. Though Burke recognizes problems in the French system of government, he feels these could have been corrected through gradual reforms, along the lines of what had taken place over a lengthy period of time in Britain. He believes the King was willing to make substantial reforms. Similarly, in *A Letter to a Member of the National Assembly*, in 1791, he says the Estates-General were capable of being reformed. However, the revolutionaries would have none of this. Their aim was "wholly to destroy conditions, to dissolve relations, to change the state of the nation, and to subvert property, in order to fit their country to their theory of a Constitution."[58]

One can, however, take a view of things very different from Burke's. The fact that some existing institution is ridden with faults can lead one to wish to change it. If the faults are viewed as sufficiently severe, then one might not be too scrupulous about preserving what exists while doing so. Revolutionaries hold extreme views in this regard. Believing the existing order is hopelessly corrupt, they are willing to cast it aside in its entirety in order to create a better society. In regard to prerevolutionary France, it is possible to hold such a view. In *The Rights of Man*, Paine refers to its "despotic principles," and its "Augean stable of parasites and plunderers too abominably filthy to be cleansed, by anything short of a complete and universal revolution" (*Rights of Man*, p. 283). Burke of course holds a different view. Much of *Reflections* is devoted to showing the *ancien régime* was not all that bad, and so worth preserving in spite of its faults.

At this point one might conclude that the conservative and the revolutionary are divided by a difference of opinion. The latter views existing society in a much dimmer light and so is less careful about the means he will use to change it. It is notorious that people with different backgrounds and points of view differ in regard to questions of political judgment, especially in regard to such enormous, complex questions as a fair assessment of the faults of prerevolutionary France. But though we might appear to be at an impasse, Burke has a response.

Though he is less critical of the French monarchy than Paine or other political radicals, Burke still recognizes its shortcomings and wishes to improve things. But in regard to the process of reform, he insists on invoking a standard of common sense: will proposed reforms actually make things better? In principle, Burke could imagine accepting even the French Revolution if it would bring about a better state of affairs. As he writes in *Appeal*:

The subversion of a government, to deserve any praise, must be considered but as a step preparatory to the formation of something better, either in the scheme of the government itself, or in the persons who administer in it, or in both. These events cannot in reason be separated. (*Appeal*, p. 90)

This test, however, is not easy to pass. To rend an existing government to pieces in the expectation of replacing it with something better is a prospect likely to fail. It is especially damaging to cast aside the hard-won advantages of an existing government for the sake of abstract principles. This is to sacrifice something real for the sake of speculations.

Let us return to an example used in a previous section. Proponents of human rights can complain of some existing government that it denies important rights to leisure and paid holidays. I do not wish to trivialize these rights. But Burke would probably be unimpressed by such a complaint, as long as the government as a whole was reasonably stable and supplied most of the other rights necessary for civilized life. But if this response can be attributed to Burke, then he is open to criticism for being against human rights. We have seen that he has antidemocratic sentiments. Is he also against granting all people rights to leisure and paid holidays? Burke would undoubtedly respond that he is a great proponent of these values. But when one talks of granting them, one must also look at what this entails. What are the circumstances under which they would be granted? What are the costs? Discussing the value of liberty, in *Reflections*, Burke writes: "Circumstances (which some gentlemen pass for nothing) give in reality to every political principle its distinguishing color and discriminating effect. The circumstances are what render every civil and political scheme beneficial or noxious to mankind" (*Reflections*, p. 8). Thus, he would ask about the costs of supplying the rights in question. If one contended these rights are so important that they justify revolution against a government that does not supply them, Burke would dismiss that idea out of hand. Though rights are important values, they cannot be considered in the abstract alone. In regard to liberty, he asks, if this is so great a value, should we congratulate a murderer who has escaped from prison? (*Reflections*, p. 8). In his letter to DePont, Burke expresses his basic rule of political prudence. Actions have costs as well as benefits; before one performs the actions, one must consider the costs and make sure the benefits outweigh them: "all I recommend is, that whenever the sacrifice of any subordinate point of morality, or of honor, or even of common liberal sentiment and feeling is called for, one ought to be tolerably sure, that the object is worth it. Nothing is good, but in proportion, and with reference" (Letter to Charles DePont, November 1789, Mansfield, p. 262).

Lovers of liberty, however, do not consider the costs. They are deeply committed to men's rights and so wish to extend them. Impediments to their goals are brushed aside. Burke likens lovers of abstract values to religious zealots, and as we have seen, views the French Revolution as a religious movement.

While prudent reformers carefully calculate the costs and benefits of their actions, reforming zealots are characterized by single-minded attention to their goals. They assess existing society according to standards of abstract perfection, specific rights, which have never been fully implemented anywhere. Because no existing society adequately measures up, their call for reform is universal. Societies without the requisite rights are not worth saving, and revolutionary zealots attempt to pull them down. "They have 'the rights of men.' Against these there can be no prescription, against these no agreement is binding; these admit no temperament and no compromise; anything withheld from their full demands is so much fraud and injustice" (*Reflections*, p. 66). "These teachers profess to scorn all mediocrity—to engage for perfection—to proceed by the simplest and shortest course. They build their politics, not on convenience, but on truth; they profess to conduct men to certain happiness by the assertion of their undoubted rights. With them there is no compromise. All other governments are usurpations, which justify and even demand resistance" (*Appeal*, p. 193).

Burke assails such an approach. The study of morals is not like mathematics. The former admits of clarity and exactitude. The mathematician keeps a single end in view and brushes all else aside. But in morals and politics, one must keep "the greatest number and variety of consideration in one view before him." The aim is to find a middle way between them ("Speech on the Duration of Parliament," Stanlis, p. 321). Once again, the standard is not perfection, but the best possible course under the circumstances. Burke believes it is an important part of political wisdom to be able to judge the degree of evil that is acceptable in a state of affairs, lest by trying to make things better one actually makes them worse (*Thoughts*, p. 180).

In a previous section, we noted Burke's distinction between the "speculative philosopher" who studies the proper end of government and the politician, the "philosopher in action," whose task is to find the best means to desired ends (see p. 275). To determine this, one must examine circumstances, and weigh the myriad considerations involved. A great danger of the French Revolution is that the roles of the speculative philosopher and the politician have been merged. Lovers of abstract truth are dictating means as well as ends. But the philosophic habit of mind does not lend itself to careful weighing of circumstances. When this disposition sets the course of public affairs, the result is a form of madness:

> A statesman differs from a professor in an university; the latter has only the general view of society; the former, the statesman, has a number of circumstances to combine with those general ideas, and to take into his considerations. Circumstances are infinite, are infinitely combined, are variable and transient: he who does not take them into consideration is not erroneous, but stark mad . . . metaphysically mad. ("Speech on the Petition of Unitarian Society," Stanlis, p. 313)

The results of philosophic politics are all too apparent in France. Assessing the existing order against their standard of abstract perfection, revolutionaries have found it entirely lacking and attempted to wipe it away. According to Burke, to hear them describing France, one would suppose they were discussing "the barbarous anarchic despotism of Turkey," where in spite of natural advantages, arts, manufacture, and science languish, the country is wracked by war, and "the human race itself melts away and perishes under the eye of the observer" (*Reflections*, p. 146). Such an assessment is entirely lacking in perspective, in judgment. One of Burke's important tasks in *Reflections* is to present a fair assessment of the old regime. Of course he recognizes abuses, but population was growing; national wealth was increasing; the cultural level was improving (*Reflections*, pp. 146–151). Was the whole fabric of society, he asks, so decrepit that it had to be ripped apart in favor of a "theoretic, experimental edifice" to be put in its place? (*Reflections*, p. 145).

Not only do the revolutionaries' criticisms of existing society lack perspective, but for reasons we have seen, they cannot hope to replace it with anything better. A successful society cannot be built on a blueprint produced by one man or group of men. Things are too complex. According to the principles of unanticipated consequences we have noted, plans go awry. Reforms in one area of society necessarily clash with reforms in others. The entire fabric of society is too intricately interwoven to be recreated through a single act. An attempt to recreate the British Constitution in this way would be ruinous. Such an edifice "is the result of the thoughts of many minds in many ages" (*Appeal*, p. 196). For a single group of men to attempt to replicate the work of history would be "to deprive men of the benefit of the collected wisdom of mankind, and to make them blind disciples of their own particular presumption" (*Appeal*, p. 197).

Of course, the revolutionaries pay scant attention to the thoughts and minds of many ages. Motivated by fanatical zeal, they aim to destroy the old to make way for the new. All other considerations are brushed aside. Early in 1790, Burke says: "The French had shown themselves the ablest architects of ruin that had hitherto existed in the world. In that very short space of time they had completely pulled down to the ground their monarchy, their church, their nobility, their law, their revenue, their army, their navy, their commerce, their arts, and their manufactures" ("Speech on the Army Estimates," Harrison, p. 309). It takes a rare sort of mind to be willing to sacrifice so much for a speculative return. But this is the signature attitude of the "metaphysician." The metaphysician *knows* his own ideas express eternal truths, and against them no other claims have merit: "Nothing can be conceived more hard than the heart of a thorough-bred metaphysician. It comes nearer to the cold malignity of a wicked spirit than to the frailty and passion of a man. It is like that of the principle of Evil himself, incorporeal, pure, unmixed, dephlegmated, defecated evil" (*Letter to a Noble Lord*, Ritchie, pp. 314–315).

To make matters worse, metaphysicians intent on reforming society come to discover the efficacy of a certain means—power. We have seen that Burke viewed war with France as combatting an *armed doctrine*. The force of arms is as important as revolutionary doctrine itself, as the revolutionaries discover that resistance to their ideas can be overcome through force alone. The aim to remake society according to a plan entails the need to concentrate power in the reformers' hands. In place of the wreckage wrought by revolution in France, what has emerged is an all-powerful state. As this is the means to revolutionary ends, all other values are sacrificed to it:

> What now stands as government in France is struck out at a heat. The design is wicked, immoral, impious, oppressive: but it is spirited and daring; it is systematic; it is simple in its principle; it has unity and consistency in perfection; . . . To them the will, the wish, the want, the liberty, the toil, the blood of individuals is nothing. Individuality is left out of their scheme of government. The state is all in all. Everything is referred to the production of force; afterwards, everything is trusted to the use of it. It is military in its principle, in its maxims, in its spirit, and in all its movements. The state has dominion and conquest for its sole objects,—dominion over minds by proselytism, over bodies by arms. (*Second Letter on Regicide Peace*, *Writings*, IX, 288)

The fate of the French Revolution shows that the aim to remake society in order to increase liberty results in a system in which liberty disappears. Though Burke is not averse to necessary political reforms, he expounds the virtues of prudence and moderation. Since politics is concerned with means as well as ends, the costs of actions must be considered.

It is not enough to posit supreme values and demand their instantiation. The probable consequences of attempting to realize them must be calculated. Central to Burke's political philosophy is the belief that attempts to make enormous changes inevitably result in enormous harm. What is valuable in society depends on balance, harmony, moderation. The intricate interconnection of parts necessary for concrete liberty in a just society must grow over time. It is not the work of one generation, let alone of one man. To attempt to replicate all the advantages of a just constitution from whole cloth, on a clean slate, is a recipe for disaster, made all the worse by inevitable abuse of power, as plans for reform go awry.

RELIGION AND THE LIMITS OF REASON

To this point we have concentrated on Burke's response to Enlightenment critiques of existing society. As noted at the outset of this chapter, we have examined his reasoned account of the limits of reason. There is little doubt that his most important contributions to the history of political thought lie in this direction. But there is another side to Burke's political theory that remains to be discussed. Though in many respects the conservatism of Burke resembles that of Hume, one great difference between the two thinkers is that Burke was a genuinely religious man.[59] This colors his political philosophy in a number of important ways.

In previous sections, we have traced the main strands of Burke's opposition to wholesale political reform. The existing order is the fruit of generations of wisdom and experience. This cannot possibly be replicated by a single group of reformers. For them to tear down the existing edifice in hope of replacing it with something better is the height of irresponsibility. Burke advises would-be reformers carefully to calculate the costs and benefits of their actions before undertaking their work of destruction. Now, one can share Burke's views concerning the process through which governments have come into existence while disagreeing with him about the advisability of revolution. Though it took time for an existing constitution to achieve its present form, one will believe it deserves our reverence and respect only if one also accepts Burke's highly favorable judgment of it. One could perhaps concede that his assessment of Great Britain is fair while disagreeing with his view of France. Burke tends to assimilate the constitutional history of prerevolutionary France to that of Britain. As the latter is a highly valuable political system, the result of the efforts and wisdom of past generations, so must be the former. But it is equally reasonable to distinguish the two states, according France much lower esteem.

Burke's condemnation of the French Revolution rests heavily on his assessment of the *ancien régime*. If, like Paine, one were to view it as an Augean stable of poverty, filth, and corruption, one would be less reluctant to tear it down in the hope of building something better. It is at this juncture that the religious side of Burke's thought becomes important. To put the matter quite simply, Burke has a religious faith in historical progress, at least when things are allowed to develop properly. Though God works in history only through the actions of men, God provides for improvement through time. A strong statement of Burke's view is found in his *Second Letter on a Regicide Peace*. Burke refers to the course of history as "the known march of the ordinary providence of God" (*Writings*, IX, 269).

Burke believes in the divine basis of existing society. One reason he is reluctant to rearrange things is that God has overseen their development, through the process of trial and error that we have noted. Though things are not perfect according to absolute standards, tampering with them will only make them worse. Burke has an almost Stoic acceptance of the given order of society, of the need to stay in one's place and perform one's tasks to the best of one's ability: "I know that there is an order that keeps things fast in their place: it is made to us, and we are made to it. Why not ask another wife, other children, another body, another mind?" ("Representation," p. 334). Along similar lines, in *Appeal*,

> I may assume that the awful author of our being is the author of our place in the order of existence; and that having disposed and marshalled us by a divine tactic, not according to our will, but according to his, he has, in and by that disposition, virtually subjected us to act the part which belongs to the place assigned us. (*Appeal*, p. 160)

In his famous passage on the contract of society quoted above, Burke writes: "Each contract of each particular state is but a clause in the great primeval contract of eternal society, linking the lower with the higher natures, connecting the visible and invisible world, according to a fixed compact sanctioned by the inviolable oath which holds all physical and all moral natures, each in their appointed place" (*Reflections*, p. 110). The "great primeval contract" refers to God's governance of the world. The contracts underlying different governments are connected with this, as part of a divine, ineluctable plan. Thus Burke supplements his rational assessment of the benefits of existing society with faith that things are as they are for a reason, and so should be preserved.

If one disagrees with Burke's faith in historical development, one might assess political circumstances differently. Burke says it is an important part of wisdom to accept the evil unavoidably connected with institutions. His general assumption is that what exists has been brought forth for a reason and should be accepted in spite of its imperfections. Accordingly, Burke emphasizes the benefits of the *ancien régime*, including the stability of the property system and the chivalrous spirit of the age. He implies that the existing power structure was voluntarily acting to correct its abuses, that the nobility, though understandably attached to its privileges (*Reflections*, p. 159), were willing to make much-needed concessions. Few historians would accept this assessment. The fact that the crisis from which the Revolution emerged was precipitated by the nobility's resistance to proposed reforms is never mentioned by Burke.[60] Throughout *Reflections* and his other writings, he uses the full resources of his rhetorical arsenal to evoke sympathy for what the Revolution cost, while paying scant attention to the abuses it was intended to alleviate. Among the losses Burke associates with the Revolution is the *ancien régime's* chivalrous attitude, "the spirit of a gentleman" (*Reflections*, p. 89). The classic response to Burke in this regard was given by Paine: "He pities the plumage, but forgets the dying bird" (*Rights of Man*, p. 288).

If the abuses of society are intolerable, then revolution can be justified. According to Burke's maxims of prudence, this course can be taken only when prospective benefits outweigh the costs. But in the case of France, one could argue that all other roads to reform were closed. The nobility steadfastly refused to make concessions, regardless of the consequences for society as a whole. If reforms do not work, then one may have to take up arms. This is the position of Hume, and perhaps Burke's as well. In his original letter to DePont, he writes: "A positively vicious and abusive government ought to be chang'd, and if necessary, by violence, if it cannot be (as sometimes it is the case) reformed"

(Mansfield, p. 263). He notes that this should be done only to combat evils, rather than to achieve perfection. But one could argue that this is precisely what was attempted in the early stages of the French Revolution. According to the rules of political prudence, the ends must justify the means. Once again, Burke writes to DePont: "all I recommend is, that whenever the sacrifice of any subordinate point of morality, or of honor, or even of common liberal sentiment and feeling is called for, one ought to be tolerably sure, that the object is worth it. Nothing is good, but in proportion, and with reference" (Mansfield, p. 262). Whether or not an object is worth it depends heavily on one's assessment of existing abuses. Believing in the presumptive value of what exists, Burke defends the existing property distribution in society. He argues against democratic political reforms, and favors a highly differentiated class system. This is what has emerged; it fulfills important functions, and so must be accepted. Aspects of Burke's account are mere celebrations of the *ancien régime*. Among the most famous is his outraged account of the indignities heaped on the royal family (*Reflections*, pp. 81–84), and his depiction of Marie Antoinette:

> It is now sixteen or seventeen years since I saw the queen of France, then the dauphiness, at Versailles, and surely never lighted on this orb, which she hardly seemed to touch, a more delightful vision. I saw her just above the horizon, decorating and cheering the elevated sphere she just began to move in—glittering like the morning star, full of life and splendor and joy. Oh! what a revolution! and what a heart must I have to contemplate without emotion that elevation and that fall. (*Reflections*, pp. 85–86)

This description was dismissed by one of Burke's correspondents as "pure foppery."[61] Once again, in reading it, one should keep in mind that at the time the passage was written, Marie Antoinette had not only not gone to the guillotine; she was still queen of France.

There is an additional aspect of Burke's religion that is important to his political theory. In addition to viewing the state as justified by religious forces, he believes propagation of religion is one of its central tasks. One part of the greatness of the English regime was the established Church, through which the state supported religion and propagated religious teaching. Though Burke took different sides in political struggles in regard to religion throughout his career,[62] on the whole he viewed religious functions as essential to the state. Thus he wrote in 1792:

> [I]n a Christian commonwealth the Church and the State are one and the same thing, being different integral parts of the same whole. . . Religion is so far, in my opinion, from being out of the province of the duty of a Christian magistrate, that it is, and it ought to be, not only his care, but the principal thing in his care; because it is one of the great bonds of human society, and its object the supreme good, the ultimate end and object of man himself. ("Speech on the Petition of the Unitarian Society," Stanlis, pp. 314–315)

Similar sentiments are voiced in *Reflections* (e.g., p. 113), as one of Burke's main objections to the French Revolution is its hostility to religion. This is seen in the confiscation of Church lands, to which Burke devotes enormous space. Even more serious in his eyes is the Revolution's atheism. He believes the revolutionaries place great stock in their opposition to religion. Their "one predominant object" is "the utter extirpation of religion" (*Second*

Letter on a Regicide Peace, Writings, IX, 278). Their "fanatical fury" in this regard gives them the attributes of a religious movement, and their struggles with the other powers of Europe the character of a religious war. "*It is a religious war.* It includes in its object, undoubtedly, every other interest of society as well as this; but this is the principal and leading feature. It is through this destruction of religion that our enemies propose the accomplishment of all their other views" (*Remarks on the Policy of the Allies, Writings*, VIII, 485). We have seen that Burke likens the French Revolution to the last great struggle of ideas that tore through Europe, the Reformation. But while that was a struggle to transform religious faith, the French Revolution is intended to eliminate it: "I call it *Atheism by Establishment*" (*First Letter on a Regicide Peace, Writings*, IX, 241).

In addition to his religiously tinged view of history and belief in the importance of politically supporting religion, Burke holds a view of human nature that is essentially religious. By this I refer to the fact that in Burke's eyes, man is essentially a sinful creature, who requires the resources of society in order to be controlled. Burke views history as fraught with "the miseries brought upon the world by pride, ambition, avarice, revenge, lust, sedition, hypocrisy, ungoverned zeal, and all the train of the disorderly appetites which shake the public with the same" (*Reflections*, p. 162). Accordingly, controlling man's undesirable passions is a central purpose of government, and one reason it is dangerous to tamper with existing institutions. The maintenance of society requires that passions be restrained. This is one reason Burke is against democracy. Means of restraint must be beyond people's control. It is inconsistent with human nature to ask the people to restrain themselves in a democratic government. Political power in the hands of the multitude "admits of no control, no regulation, no steady direction whatsoever." To turn power over to the people is "to subject the sovereign reason of the world to the caprices of weak and giddy men" (*Appeal*, p. 158). This is also one reason Burke is opposed to atheism. He believes it is essential that those exercising political power believe they are accountable to some higher authority (*Reflections*, pp. 105–106).

Burke believes an important means through which passions are controlled is by being channelled into social forms and customs. We have noted the important role he ascribes to manners. These grow up gradually over time, are not easily changed, and form a framework within which laws must function. Burke's analysis is especially striking as it touches on the role of aesthetic factors in channeling passions and so working to stabilize institutions. Aesthetic sentiments are analyzed by Burke in his first work, *A Philosophical Enquiry into the Origin of Our Ideas of the Sublime and Beautiful.*[63] Especially interesting to Burke is the style of conduct that dominates his society, the code of chivalry, or of the gentleman. The components of this code are prejudices in the sense discussed above. They have evolved through the passage of time, without necessarily being open to rational scrutiny. But they play a crucial social role. Through a mixture of sentiment and opinion that has taken shape over the centuries, people have been brought to soften their passions. But in recent times, the age of chivalry has given way to rational scrutiny. It has been overtaken by reason, an age "of sophisters, economists, and calculators" (*Reflections*, p. 86).

The spirit of honor not only smooths the ordinary interactions of life, but plays an important political role, as a complement to political authority: "These public affections, combined with manners, are required sometimes as supplements, sometimes as correctives, always as aids to law" (*Reflections*, pp. 86–88). This works in regard to rulers as well as subjects. Properly conditioned passions mitigate the fierceness of the former, forcing "sovereigns to submit to the soft collar of social esteem" and elegance (*Reflections*, p. 87). The chivalrous code of the nobility promotes a spirit of *noblesse oblige*, of honor and service. Such sentiments are still more important for subjects. As Burke argues in 1791, men are fit for liberty only if they can control their passions. If the necessary control does not exist within them, then it must be imposed from without (*Letter to a Member of the National Assembly*, Ritchie, p. 69). Essentially aesthetic passions play an important role in political stability. In the words of one commentator, "these sentiments come to constitute, for [Burke], the deepest anchors of a legitimate politics, or at least they do when properly cultivated."[64]

Dissolved by reason's critical scrutiny, this spirit represents a considerable loss. In the absence of chivalry's myths, relationships between rulers and subjects stand bare before the viewer. If people cannot be brought to obey through aesthetic passions, then they will be brought along by other means. In regard to the French Revolution, nothing remains "which engages the affections on the part of the commonwealth," and so rule is by force alone: "at the end of every vista, you see nothing but the gallows" (*Reflections*, p. 88).

Thus we see another respect in which reason is a destructive force. It dissolves the manners and prejudices of society, which are better left intact. Having grown up over time, these sentiments have proved their value. But confronted with cold, critical scrutiny, they show themselves "ridiculous, absurd, and antiquated fashion" (*Reflections*, p. 87). Deprived of the veil of prejudices, men in society directly confront "the defects of our naked, shivering nature." "All the pleasing illusions which made power gentle and obedience liberal, which harmonized the different shades of life, and which, by a bland assimilation, incorporated into politics the sentiments which beautify and soften private society, are to be dissolved by this new conquering empire of light and reason. All the decent drapery of life is to be rudely torn off" (*Reflections*, p. 87).

BURKE'S CONSERVATISM

In his classic work, *Ideology and Utopia*, Karl Mannheim explores distinctive patterns of thought associated with different political views. Of what he calls "historical conservatism" he writes:

> Historical conservatism is characterized by the fact that it is aware of that irrational realm in the life of the state which cannot be managed by administration. It recognizes that there is an unorganized and incalculable realm which is the proper sphere of politics. Indeed it focuses its attention almost exclusively on the impulsive, irrational factors which furnish the real basis for the further development of state and society. It regards these forces as entirely beyond comprehension and infers that, as such, human reason is impotent to understand or to control them.[65]

Mannheim cites Burke as the prime example of this sort of attitude and notes that he was the model for most German conservatives.

Throughout this chapter, we have explored this aspect of Burke's thought. Connections between reason's lack of power and the desire not to make wholesale political change are at the center of his political philosophy. In discussing this theme, I have noted its similarity to a religious view of social development, which can suggest similar political implications. If God's will is behind historical events, and also resists comprehension by the mind of man, then people must step back and allow history to unfold, rather than attempting to manage it. An extreme form of historical passivity is the doctrine of the divine right of kings. According to this view, God places rulers on their thrones. A bad ruler must be accepted as part of God's plan, perhaps as punishment for the sins of the ruled. The crucial political implication is that an unjust ruler must be accepted. Though citizens can refuse to obey commands that directly contravene their religious obligations, they can never resist.[66] In the last section we have seen the strongly religious side of Burke's political philosophy. But though his position resembles the divine right of kings in certain respects, it also differs in important ways.

First, though religion is an element of Burke's political philosophy, he moves beyond a religious view of history to provide a rational explanation of the process. Strongly influenced by Montesquieu's study of society, Burke presents a basically sociological view of historical development and change. Through both his literary career and experience of practical politics, he was immersed in political facts, and his writings display an impressive mastery of the details of a wide range of public issues. In approaching political questions, Burke realizes the importance of ascertaining the facts, and is deeply critical of political actors who place reliance on their theories above mastery of their subject matter. One great conclusion Burke drew from his study of politics is the overwhelming complexity of events, and so man's inability to understand them fully, let alone to manage them. As a gifted politician, Burke himself was unusually successful at predicting the course events would take. This is apparent in his writings on the American Revolution, and also in his forebodings about the future course of France. Already, in *Reflections*, published in 1790, Burke predicts the rise of military dictatorship in France (p. 258)—which did not come about for several years. But in spite of his own abilities in this respect, Burke comes away from his study of politics and history with a strong conviction of their intractability to human reason. Though the species may be wise, the individual has little power in the face of historical events. As we have seen, Burke's view resembles religious faith that God is at work in the world and human beings can only accept this without full understanding. Strengthening this conviction by providing a rational basis for it is one of his crucial contributions to conservative political philosophy. As noted at the beginning of this chapter, the Enlightenment rejected religion, placing great reliance on the powers of man's reason. To this, Burke offers a powerful response: a reasoned account of the limits of reason.

In his analysis of society, Burke takes a view of political reform similar to Montesquieu's. Both men are impressed by organic interconnection throughout society, which develops over time and cannot easily be reworked. In comparison to Montesquieu, Burke accords resistance to reform greater emphasis, as his most noted writings are in opposition to the French Revolution. But on the whole his position is generally similar to Montesquieu's. It is therefore interesting to note that both men were partisans of the nobility, and defended the interests of this class in their works. Montesquieu, of course, was an hereditary member of the nobility. Burke, though of middle-class origin, attained political prominence through service to aristocratic patrons. The enormous disparity between his own abilities and those of the men he served clearly grated on Burke. Fascinatingly, several of his works, especially

A Letter to a Noble Lord (1796), reveal deep ambivalence towards the British aristocracy.[67] But in spite of the complexity of his feelings, throughout the bulk of his works, Burke supports the aristocracy. Their position depends on tradition—prescription. Their wealth and power are theirs by inheritance, rather than the free choice of members of society. In justifying the course of historical development, in spite of its objectionable aspects, Burke provides a powerful defense of aristocratic prerogatives.

Like Montesquieu, Burke is a liberal in important respects, without being a democrat. We have noted his opposition to Parliamentary reforms for a variety of prudential reasons. He did not believe the masses were really capable of self-government, and thought a wider franchise and more frequent elections would have undesirable consequences. His theory of virtual representation (see pp. 278–82) is in large part an attempt to explain how the interests of all would be defended in spite of their lack of political participation. Because of their superior qualities, the nobility can represent the interests of all, and need not be held accountable to the people to do so. The strongest liberal aspect of Burke's political theory is his concern for the value of liberty. In this respect, too, he resembles Montesquieu. Both men celebrated the virtues of the British Constitution, for similar reasons. Both believed real liberty—what we have called "concrete" liberty—can exist only within the confines of working political institutions. Burke's account of the conditions necessary for political liberty is one of his classic contributions to political theory. As Rousseau describes the unusual conditions under which the kind of freedom that interests him can exist in society, Burke presents a compelling account of the conditions necessary for the "rights of Englishmen"—rights to which liberal political theory accords enormous value.

Though Burke is perhaps the greatest figure in the history of conservative political theory, he was not averse to all political reform. His attitude in this regard was eminently practical. Reforms can be undertaken to alleviate undesirable conditions. But in every case the reformer must be confident the results will be better than what he started with. In *Spirit of the Laws*, Montesquieu says the work was written "only to prove [that] the spirit of moderation should be that of the legislator." In *The Persian Letters*, he writes: "the laws should be touched only with trembling hand."[68] The attitude of Burke is of course similar, though he goes beyond Montesquieu in exploring the historical dimension to political change and reform in far greater detail, and in his classic expostulations against wholesale reform, attempting to remake society from the ground up, on the basis of abstract ideas. But in spite of his opposition to wholesale reform, Burke did not oppose more modest attempts to make things better. In this sense his political views fall well within the liberal tradition.

Burke broke with traditional liberal political theory in regard to theoretical underpinnings. Because of his historical sense, he was able to view the individual only as a member of society, which was itself the product of generations past, stretching into time immemorial. This leaves Burke with the intriguing position of defending individual freedom on a nonindividualist basis. While Locke posits the individual as the basic building block of society and argues that political society rests on individual consent, Burke is closer to Filmer in seeing the individual as born into a society he has played no part in choosing. "Men without their choice derive benefits from that association; without their choice they are subject to duties in consequence of these benefits; and without their choice they enter into a virtual obligation as binding as any that is actual" (*Appeal*, p. 160). Though Burke displays little of the great Enlightenment faith in historical progress, at the core of his theory is a strong desire to accept what history has brought forth. Throughout his life Burke shared the central conviction of his aristocratic party that history has given rise to the great values of British civilization and the British Constitution. Though exactly how this has come about cannot be known, it represents the inspired choice of past generations. Ever conscious of the great legacy of this system, Burke devoted himself to its preservation.

NOTES

1. R. Vierhaus, "Conservatism," *Dictionary of the History of Ideas*, P. Wiener, ed., 4 vols. (New York, 1968), I, 481.

2. R. Kirk, *The Conservative Mind* (Chicago, 1953), p. 5.

3. Vierhaus, "Conservatism," I, 477; use of the term in this sense is attributed to F. R. Chateaubriand's weekly newspaper, *Le Conservateur*, which was started in 1818.

4. J. G. A. Pocock, Introduction to Burke, *Reflections on the Revolution in France* (Indianapolis, 1987), p. xlix.

5. Kirk, *Conservative Mind*, pp. 7–9, from which quotations are taken.

6. An important exception is Montesquieu, who strongly influenced Burke; see C. P. Courtney, *Montesquieu and Burke* (Oxford, 1963).

7. Kirk, *Conservative Mind*, pp. 7–8.

8. J. Bentham, *A Fragment of Government*, J. H. Burns and H. L. A. Hart, eds. (Cambridge, 1988); quotations are from pp. 3–4. The comparison with Bentham is suggested by A. Cobban, *Edmund Burke and the Revolt Against the Eighteenth Century*, 2nd ed. (London, 1960).

9. Reprinted in J. Waldron, ed., *"Nonsense Upon Stilts"* (London, 1987), p. 27.

10. Waldron, "The Theoretical Foundations of Liberalism," *Philosophical Quarterly*, 37 (1987), 134; this work cited hereafter in the text as Waldron.

11. Burke, *A Vindication of Natural Society*, in *Prerevolutionary Writings*, I. Harrison, ed. (Cambridge, 1993), p. 11. Unless indicated otherwise, Burke's individual works are cited according to title or short title and the collection in which they are found. The following collections are used; full references for all are found below, under "Texts Cited": *Prerevolutionary Writings*, Harrison, ed. (cited as Harrison); *Burke's Politics*, R. Hoffman and P. Levack, eds. (cited as Hoffman and Levack); Burke, *Further Reflections on the Revolution in France*, D. Ritchie, ed. (cited as Ritchie); *Edmund Burke: Selected Writings and Speeches*, P. Stanlis, ed. (cited as Stanlis); Burke, *The Writings and Speeches of Edmund Burke*, P. Langford, ed. (cited as *Writings*). At the present time, five volumes of this collection have appeared: vols. 2, 5, 6, 8, and 9. Two works cited frequently are *An Appeal from the New to the Old Whigs*, from Ritchie, cited as *Appeal*; and *Thoughts on the Causes of the Present Discontents*, from Harrison, cited as *Thoughts*. In quotations from Burke, I occasionally regularize spelling and punctuation, to facilitate movement between different editions, without being distracted by preferences of different editors. Throughout, unless otherwise noted, all italics used are Burke's.

12. Cobban, *Edmund Burke and the Revolt Against the Eighteenth Century*.

13. T. Ball and R. Dagger, *Political Ideologies and the Democratic Ideal* (New York, 1991), p. 93.

14. J. Morley, quoted by C. B. Macpherson, *Burke* (Oxford, 1980), p. 14.

15. For biographical details, I follow S. Ayling, *Edmund Burke: His Life and Opinions* (New York, 1988) (cited as Ayling, in parentheses in the text); and the more detailed account of C. Cone, *Burke and the Nature of Politics*, 2 vols. (Lexington, KY, 1957, 1964) (cited as Cone, in text).

16. Burke, Letter to T. Burgh, Jan. 1, 1780, *Writings*, IX, 561.

17. Macpherson, *Burke*, p. 19.

18. Cobban, *The Debate on the French Revolution: 1789–1800*, 2nd ed. (London, 1960), p. 4.

19. Stanlis, *Edmund Burke and the Natural Law* (Ann Arbor, 1965), p. 71 and 269 n. 94.

20. *The Declaration of Rights*, Feb. 13, 1689; for discussion, see M. Ashley, *The Glorious Revolution of 1688* (London, 1966).

21. Montesquieu, *The Spirit of the Laws*, Bk. 11, Chap. 5, p. 156; full reference below, under "Texts Cited."

22. *Reflections on the Revolution in France*, p. 28; full reference below, under "Texts Cited" (cited hereafter in the text as *Reflections*).

23. Burke, *Essay Towards an Abridgement of the English History*, Stanlis, pp. 82–83; my emphasis.

24. Bolingbroke, quoted by Courtney, *Montesquieu and Burke*, p. 64.

25. Burke, Speech on "Representation of the Commons in Parliament," Stanlis, p. 334.

26. See Courtney, *Montesquieu and Burke*, pp. 76-82.

27. Burke, Letter to T. Burgh, Jan. 1, 1780, *Writings*, IX, 561.

28. Macpherson, *Burke*, p. 23.

29. F. O'Gorman, *Edmund Burke: His Political Philosophy* (Bloomington, IN, 1973), p. 41.

30. Burke, Letter to Duke of Richmond, Nov. 15, 1772; in *The Selected Letters of Edmund Burke*, H. Mansfield, ed. (Chicago, 1984), p. 184; this edition cited hereafter as Mansfield.

31. Burke, Letter to William Weddell, January 31, 1792, in Mansfield, p. 472.

32. "Speech on the Duration of Parliaments," Stanlis, p. 324.

33. Kirk, *Conservative Mind*, p. 45.

34. I. Kramnick, *The Rage of Edmund Burke* (New York, 1977), p. 123.

35. "Speech at the Conclusion of the Poll in Bristol," November 3, 1774, Hoffman and Levack, p. 115; this work cited hereafter as "Bristol Poll."

36. *Federalist*, 10, p. 56; full reference below, under "Texts Cited."

37. H. Pitkin, *The Concept of Representation* (Berkeley, 1967), p. 168.

38. Burke, Letter to H. Langrishe, January 3, 1792, Hoffman and Levack, pp. 494–495.

39. Courtney, *Montesquieu and Burke*, p. 81.

40. "Speech on a Bill for Shortening the Duration of Parliament," Stanlis, pp. 324–325.

41. Kramnick, *Rage of Edmund Burke*, p. 111.

42. The same can be said of the two other great cases in which Burke was involved, concerning Ireland and India. For good brief discussion, see O'Gorman, *Edmund Burke*.

43. References for the three works are as follows: "Letter to the Sheriffs of Bristol," in Stanlis (cited in text as "Sheriffs of Bristol"); "Speech on Conciliation with America," in Harrison (cited as "Conciliation"); "Speech on American Taxation," in *Writings*, II (cited as "American Taxation").

44. *Vindication of Natural Society*, Harrison, pp. 10–11.

45. This is included in Mansfield, 255–268.

46. This was later published as *A Discourse on the Love of Our Country* (in Price, *Political Writings*, cited in text as Price; full reference below, under "Texts Cited"). For an excellent brief discussion of Price's views and Burke's strategy in responding to them, see Pocock, Introduction to *Reflections*; also Cobban, ed., *The Debate on the French Revolution*.

47. Paine, *The Rights of Man*, p. 275; cited hereafter as Paine; full reference below, under "Texts Cited."

48. See W. Doyle, *Origins of the French Revolution* (Oxford, 1980), pp. 200–203.

49. *First Letter on a Regicide Peace*, *Writings*, IX, 199.

50. *A Letter to a Member of the National Assembly*, Ritchie, p. 40.

51. Burke, Letter to Henry Dundas, September 30, 1791, in Mansfield, p. 305.

52. I am indebted to Kirk here, *Conservative Mind*, pp. 42ff., from whom I quote Article 24 of *The Universal Declaration of Human Rights* (p. 42).

53. As Pocock argues, Burke's view of historical development was heavily influenced by his knowledge of legal history; "Burke and the Ancient Constitution—A Problem in the History of Ideas," *Historical Journal*, 3 (1960).

54. See pp. 197–8; see pp. 297–302.

55. P. Lucas, "On Edmund Burke's Doctrine of Prescription; Or, An Appeal from the New to the Old Lawyers," *Historical Journal*, 11 (1968), 36.

56. Burke, Letter to Thomas Mercer, February 26, 1790; in Mansfield, p. 277.

57. "Speech on Representation of the Commons in Parliament," Stanlis, pp. 330–331 (cited hereafter as "Representation").

58. *Letter to a Member of the National Assembly*, Ritchie, p. 69.

59. See F. Dreyer, "Burke's Religion," *Studies in Burke and His Time*, 17 (1976); Cone, II, 324–327.

60. For discussion, see Doyle, *Origins of the French Revolution*, Chaps. 6–10.

61. Letter of Philip Francis to Burke, February 19, 1790, in Mansfield, p. 270.

62. See above, n. 59.

63. *A Philosophical Enquiry into the Origin of Our Ideas of the Sublime and Beautiful*, T. Boulton, ed. (New York, 1958).

64. S. White, "Burke on Politics, Aesthetics, and the Dangers of Modernity," *Political Theory*, 21 (1993), 213–214; see also N. Wood, "The Aesthetic Dimension of Burke's Political Thought," *Journal of British Studies*, 4 (1964).

65. K. Mannheim, *Ideology and Utopia*, L. Wirth and E. Shils, trans. (New York, 1936), p. 120.

66. See Vol. I, 190–191, 223–224.

67. See Kramnick, *Rage of Edmund Burke.*

68. *Spirit of the Laws*, Bk. 29, Chap. 1; *Persian Letters*, Letter 129; full references below, under "Texts Cited."

TEXTS CITED

Burke, E. *Burke's Politics.* R. Hoffman and P. Levack, eds. New York, 1949.

Burke, E. *Edmund Burke: Selected Writings and Speeches.* P. Stanlis, ed. Gloucester, MA, 1968.

Burke, E. *Further Reflections on the Revolution in France.* D. Ritchie, ed. Indianapolis, 1992.

Burke, E. *Prerevolutionary Writings.* I. Harrison, ed. Cambridge, 1993.

Burke, E. *Reflections on the Revolution in France.* T. Mahoney, ed. Indianapolis, 1955.

Burke, E. *The Selected Letters of Edmund Burke.* H. Mansfield, ed. Chicago, 1984.

Burke, E. *The Writings and Speeches of Edmund Burke.* P. Langford, ed. 5 vols (to date). Oxford; 1981–1991.

The Federalist: A Commentary on the Constitution of the United States. From the Original Text of Alexander Hamilton, John Jay, James Madison. New York, n.d.

Montesquieu. *The Persian Letters.* J. R. Loy, trans. Cleveland, 1961.

Montesquieu. *The Spirit of the Laws.* A. Cohler, B. Miller, H. Stone, eds. and trans. Cambridge, 1989.

Paine, T. *The Rights of Man.* In Burke, *Reflections on the Revolution in France*, and Paine, *The Rights of Man.* Garden City, NY, 1973.

Price, R. *Political Writings.* D. O. Thomas, ed. Cambridge, 1991.

FURTHER READING

Ayling, S. *Edmund Burke: His Life and Opinions.* New York, 1988.

Cobban, A. *Edmund Burke and the Revolt Against the Eighteenth Century.* 2nd ed. London, 1960.

Cone, C. B. *Burke and the Nature of Politics.* 2 vols. Lexington, KY, 1957, 1964.

Courtney, C. P. *Montesquieu and Burke.* Oxford, 1963.

Kirk, R. *The Conservative Mind.* Chicago, 1953.

Kramnick, I. *The Rage of Edmund Burke.* New York, 1977.

Macpherson, C. B. *Burke.* Oxford, 1980.

O'Brien, C. C. *The Great Melody.* Chicago, 1993.

O'Gorman, F. *Edmund Burke: His Political Philosophy.* Bloomington, IN, 1973.

Pocock, J. G. A. "Burke and the Ancient Constitution—A Problem in the History of Ideas." *Historical Journal,* 3 (1960).

Pocock, J. G. A. Introduction, to Burke, *Reflections on the Revolution in France.* Indianapolis, 1987.

White, S. "Burke on Politics, Aesthetics, and the Dangers of Modernity." *Political Theory,* 21 (1993).

Wood, N. "The Aesthetic Dimension of Burke's Political Thought." *Journal of British Studies,* 4 (1964).

C h a p t e r
8

UTILITARIAN LIBERALISM:
JEREMY BENTHAM, JAMES MILL, JOHN STUART MILL

IN THIS CHAPTER, UNLIKE THE others in this volume, the focus is not a single work or a single political theorist. We will concentrate on a broader theme, a certain approach to liberal political theory rooted in utilitarianism. Though anticipations of utilitarianism have been seen in previous chapters—in our discussions of Hobbes and Hume—only in the works of Jeremy Bentham does it appear in a fully developed form. The first sections of this chapter are devoted to a brief account of Bentham's utilitarianism and to the distinctive utilitarian approach to problems of public policy, especially criminal law. Then we turn to a utilitarian defense of democracy, focusing on James Mill's *Essay on Government.* James Mill was Bentham's most important disciple and the father of John Stuart Mill. Finally, we consider John Stuart Mill's attempt to shore up weaknesses in utilitarianism, especially his great defense of individual liberty in *On Liberty.* The closing section discusses Mill's defense of equal treatment of women in *The Subjection of Women.*

BENTHAM'S EXPERIENCE AND REPUTATION

Though Hobbes and Hume are important figures in the utilitarian tradition, Bentham is generally viewed as the school's founder.[1] Bentham is not as sophisticated philosophically as Hume—whose influence he acknowledges. In reading Hume, Bentham says, he "felt as if scales had fallen from my eyes."[2] But Bentham went beyond Hume. Not only did he present a much clearer account of utilitarian ethics—in large part because it is less sophisticated than Hume's—but he made a monumental contribution in applying utilitarian principles to the reform of social and political institutions. As J. S. Mill says, if Bentham had simply followed the work of Hume, he would never have been heard of, because he lacked Hume's philosophical talents. His genius lay in "the field of practical abuses": "This was Bentham's peculiar province; to this he was called by the whole bent of his disposition: to carry the warfare against absurdity into things practical."[3] Because Bentham helped lay the groundwork for rational or scientific public policy, he deserves a prominent place "among the great intellectual benefactors of mankind" (Mill, "Bentham," p. 98).

Like many theorists discussed in previous chapters, Bentham was deeply impressed with the accomplishments of the natural sciences and wished to shed comparable light on the social world. We have identified this attitude as the spirit of the Enlightenment, and

Bentham was an Enlightenment figure par excellence. He was born in London in 1748 to a prosperous family.[4] Intellectually precocious, he began to study Latin at the age of three and enrolled at Queen's College, Oxford, at the age of twelve. In accordance with the wishes of his father, an attorney, he studied law. But he disliked practicing law. Bentham decried "the universal inaccuracy and confusion" which pervaded the law (*Fragment*, Preface, p. 4), and assailed this in his first book, *A Fragment of Government*, published in 1776. By the early 1770s Bentham had resolved that studying and reforming legislation was to be the central vocation of his life.

Two aspects of Bentham's life are of special concern in this chapter. First are his indefatigable efforts to put his proposed reforms into practice. Throughout his life, it was not enough for Bentham to criticize existing practices; he wanted to bring about concrete changes, and offered his services to a remarkable range of rulers and countries. While in Russia, visiting his brother who was working there, he attempted to secure the post of "legislator in residence" at the court of Catherine the Great.[5] With the outbreak of the French Revolution, he proposed possible reforms to the new government, in the form of a *Draught of a New Plan for the Organization of the Judicial Establishment in France* (1790) and other proposals. Though some of these attracted interest, none was enacted.[6] He devoted several years to attempting to put into practice, in England, a new design for prisons he had devised, and later worked on proposed changes in public means of maintaining the poor. His interests extended to Spain and Portugal, Mexico, and several countries in South America. At one time he entertained the idea of going to live in Mexico in association with Aaron Burr, who would set up an empire there with Bentham as his legislator.[7] During the Greek war of independence, in 1823–1824, he sent draft installments of his *Constitutional Code* to Greece, as he had earlier written to President Madison in 1811, offering his legislative services to the young United States government. In 1822, he issued a *Codification Proposal*, which was addressed "to all nations professing liberal opinions," which proposed an "all-comprehensive body of law," which he was to draft.[8]

Bentham's forays into political reform are significant for two reasons. First, by working on practical political issues, he gained detailed knowledge of the actual workings of government. His talent for systematic analysis and inexhaustible capacity for work allowed him to combine detailed critiques of existing institutions with similarly detailed proposals for reformed alternatives. The result was a vast—an almost unmanageable—body of work. Other thinkers had criticized aspects of the English government. Bentham proposed systematically developed improvements. Examples are his 502-page *Constitutional Code* and his 1,031-page *Rationale of Judicial Evidence*.[9] Among specific aspects of the British legal system he examined are criminal law, the prison system, rules of evidence, and judicial procedure—all worked out according to a core set of philosophical principles. In *Fragment of Government*, Bentham distinguishes the roles of "expositor" and "censor." The former describes what the law actually is; the latter addresses "what he thinks it ought to be" (*Fragment*, Preface, p. 7). Bentham's role was ever the latter. But he differed from other would-be philosophic-reformers in his concrete knowledge of actual institutions. As a result of his combination of talents, Bentham exerted significant influence on the development of modern government in the early nineteenth century. Details are discussed below.

Bentham's early lack of success in enacting his ideas was also important, because this taught him fundamental lessons in practical political reform. Rebuffed in his attempts to approach monarchs and purportedly benevolent despots, Bentham was driven in the direction of democracy. In order for the government to enact reforms in the public interest, it must be accountable to the public. This is the basis for a utilitarian defense of democracy developed by Bentham and James Mill, which is not only a distinctive argument, different from other defenses of democracy we have encountered, but which had significant practical effects in the extension of democratic governments throughout the nineteenth century. To this subject, too, we will return in subsequent sections.

In addition to Bentham's political activity, we must consider his contributions as a theorist and writer. He lived a long, active life, and wrote prodigiously on a wide range of subjects. In addition to his published writings, he left a great mass of manuscripts which have remained unpublished, stored in University College, London. (A comprehensive edition of his writings is currently being prepared for publication.) Bentham's reputation as a political theorist rests primarily on two works, *Fragment of Government* and *An Introduction to the Principles of Morals and Legislation*. The latter, which was written in 1780 but remained unpublished until 1789, is the best known of his writings. Its first four chapters present a vigorous account of Bentham's utilitarian philosophy. In the opening chapter he declares his intention to provide "an explicit and determinate account" of the principle of utility (*Principles*, Chap. 1, p. 2). Thus these chapters are widely quoted as representing his philosophical views. But there is a problem here. The views contained in these chapters are notably crude and vulnerable to criticisms. It is therefore not surprising that Bentham is widely believed to be a poor philosopher. This opinion is forcefully expressed in J. S. Mill's two classic essays on Bentham, and in an influential historical study of utilitarianism, *The Growth of Philosophical Radicalism*, by Elie Halévy, among other sources.[10] According to Mill, "We must not look for subtlety, or the power of recondite analysis, among his intellectual characteristics. In the former quality, few great thinkers have ever been so deficient," while the same is also true of the latter ("Bentham," p. 44). Mill argues that Bentham's achievements lay in the "business part" of human affairs, in people's social and political interactions. But because Bentham made the mistake of viewing this side of life as the whole of life, the principles he developed are not applicable beyond this sphere ("Bentham," pp. 73–74). As we will see, Mill believes the simplicity and one-sidedness of Bentham's philosophy require the corrections to which he devoted his own efforts.

Like Mill, Halévy emphasizes Bentham's achievement in the practical sphere, at the expense of his philosophical accomplishments. He says that, in developing his philosophy, Bentham employed utilitarian precepts he did not fully understand: "for the whole force of his criticism is concentrated not on the principles of metaphysics but on established institutions, as a source of corruption and oppression" (Halévy, pp. 33–34). According to this common view, the inadequacies of Bentham's philosophy were in a way a strength. Though deficient in certain respects, Bentham's principles possessed great virtues of simplicity and clarity, which made them especially powerful weapons of reform. In the realm of practical politics, the principles were adequate. They dealt effectively with the large-scale interactions of the population as a whole that are the primary concern of legislation, though they contributed little to moral subjects beyond this domain.

However, although the view that Bentham lacks philosophical talent is widely held, it is clearly overly simple and may not be true. Not only were the works generally cited to support this view written early in Bentham's career, but this opinion takes no account of his massive unpublished output. A series of scholars who have examined this material dismiss the common opinion as caricature and present a more nuanced, sophisticated thinker in their analyses.[11] But in spite of this body of research, in this chapter we will concentrate on Bentham the reformer rather than the philosopher. The utilitarianism we will discuss is mainly that of *Principles of Morals and Legislation*, as it has been generally understood. Though there is an element of historical injustice in ignoring qualifications of this view Bentham presents in other works, our primary concern is utilitarianism as a moral and political philosophy, rather than assessing the philosophical merits of Bentham himself. A great deal can be learned about utilitarianism by examining the problems in the crude view often attributed to Bentham, and various resources utilitarianism has to circumvent them.

TELEOLOGICAL AND DEONTOLOGICAL MORAL THEORIES

Regardless of exactly how we interpret Bentham's utilitarianism, it is clear that he was led to this position largely by his interest in science. Halévy describes utilitarianism as "nothing but an attempt to apply the principles of Newton to the affairs of politics and of morals" (p. 6). Bentham was impressed with the French philosopher Helvetius (1715–1771), whose accomplishment was to "treat morals like any other science and to make an experimental morality like an experimental physics" (Halévy, p. 19). In an appendix to *Of Laws in General*, Bentham writes:

> The present work as well as every other work of mine that has been or will be published on the subject of legislation or any other branch of moral science is an attempt to extend the experimental method of reasoning from the physical branch/department/world to the moral. What Bacon was to the physical world, Helvetius was to the moral. The moral world has therefore had its Bacon; but its Newton is yet to come.[12]

Bentham envisions himself in this role. As we saw in the last chapter, in *Fragment of Government*, he notes great advances in the natural sciences and his desire to extend the benefits of this knowledge to the moral world (Preface, p. 3).

The key to Bentham's scientific analysis is the attractive force of pleasure. As Newton laid bare the workings of nature on the basis of gravitational attraction, Bentham believes pleasure plays a similar role in the moral and political spheres. Pleasure functions in his philosophy in two distinguishable ways: as the force responsible for how people do behave; and as the standard according to which their behavior should be evaluated. The famous opening paragraph of *Principles of Morals and Legislation* is as follows:

> Nature has placed mankind under the governance of two sovereign masters, *pain* and *pleasure*. It is for them alone to point out what we ought to do, as well as to determine what we shall do. On the one hand the standard of right and wrong, on the other the chain of causes and effects, are fastened to their throne. They govern us in all we do, in all we say, in all we think: every effort we can make to throw off our subjection, will serve but to demonstrate and confirm it. In words a man may pretend to abjure their empire: but in reality he will remain subject to it all the while. (Chap. 1, p. 1)

In this passage, one will note, Bentham says two quite different things about pleasure: it is what people *do* seek in their actions and what they *should* seek. We will return to the implications of Bentham's failure clearly to distinguish these two notions. We can begin our examination of his political philosophy by looking into the great scientific advantages of his utilitarian philosophy.

An immediate strength of utilitarianism is its simplicity and clarity. Philosophers today commonly divide moral theories into two categories, to which they refer as "teleological" and "deontological."[13] (The terms are derived from the Greek *telos*, which means "end" or "aim," and *to deon*, which means "the necessary.") The basic moral concept in theories of the former kind is "good." If some quality is identified as the good, the right action is one that will bring about the greatest possible amount of good. Utilitarianism is a teleological moral theory that identifies the good with the satisfaction of desire, or more commonly, with pleasure. Like other teleological theories, it focuses on the consequences of actions. If Elena can perform two actions and the consequences of one will be more pleasurable than those of the other, then the first is the right action, and utilitarians hold that she would do wrong to perform the second. The reader will note that, according to this logic, "rightness" or the "right action" has no independent definition. It is identified solely in reference to the amount of good brought about by different actions. Bentham writes:

> He who adopts the *principle of utility* esteems virtue to be a good only on account of the pleasures which result from it; he regards vice as an evil only because of the pains which it produces. Moral good is *good* only by its tendency to produce physical good. Moral evil is *evil* only by its tendency to produce physical evil; but when I say *physical*, I mean the pains and pleasures of the soul as well as the pains and pleasures of sense. (*Theory*, Chap. 1, p. 3)

One will note Bentham's repeated use of the word "only" in this quotation.

Perhaps an example will clarify matters. Assume that Elena can either kick Hans or give him a piece of cake. Because the second action would produce more pleasure than the first, it is the right action under the circumstances. The distinctive utilitarian analysis of this situation is that giving Hans the cake is right *only* because of the greater pleasure it produces. Kicking him is wrong *only* because this produces less pleasure (or more pain, on which, more below) than the alternative action.

In a deontological theory, in contrast, the right is defined independently of the good. There are numerous possibilities here, some of which have been encountered in previous chapters. Some examples are moral theories based on natural law, or on moral relations that are rooted in the "nature of things," and are detectable by reason (see pp. 152–3). In these cases, the right action under some circumstances is one that is consistent with natural law or these relationships. Immediate reference is not made to the consequences of different actions, or to the amount of goodness they bring about. Another example of a deontological theory is one that is religiously based. According to such a view, the right action might be defined as one that is in accordance with God's will. Once again, in this case there need not be immediate reference to the goodness of an action's consequences in assessing its rightness.

To return to our example of Elena and Hans, there are various possible deontological analyses of the situation. Her kicking him might be judged wrong because it is inconsistent with rationally detectable moral relationships, with natural law, or with God's will. To take another example, assume Elena steals Hans's wallet. A common deontological critique of this action is that it violates the Biblical injunction, "Thou shalt not steal." Contrariwise, it could be declared wrong because it is inconsistent with moral relationships rooted in the nature of things. Though in cases of these sorts, the consequences of the actions in question are not excluded from consideration, the rightness or wrongness of a given action is *not* assessed solely in reference to the amount of goodness it brings about.

As we can see from this comparison, utilitarianism allows considerable rigor in moral questions. In turning away from abstruse matters such as God's will, natural law, and moral relations rooted in the nature and reason of things to concentrate on the observable consequences of actions, utilitarianism makes it possible to approach moral subjects with scientific precision. The consequences of actions possess tangible—indeed, quantifiable—properties that are not found in other moral notions.

CRITIQUE OF ENGLISH LAW

Throughout his life, the most important target of Bentham's criticism is the English legal system, which he assails on a number of fronts. He assesses it according to the standard of pleasure; the gist of his critique is that it does not do what it should, which is to advance the interest of society, or "the greatest good of the greatest number." As he writes in *Theory:* "The sole object of the legislator is to increase pleasures and to prevent pains" (Chap. 8, p. 31). Bentham displays remarkable tenacity in uncovering different ways in which English law falls short of this goal.

Bentham views English law as a tangled mass of doctrines, based on different principles, that have evolved haphazardly over the centuries. He describes this as rights and duties "jumbled together in one immense and unsorted heap . . . a labyrinth without a clew."[14] Bentham believes many laws have outgrown their usefulness, for instance, laws concerning torture and other extreme punishments. But more fundamental is his assault on the philosophical foundations of the legal system as a whole, as classically expressed by William Blackstone in his *Commentaries on the Laws of England* (1765–1769). *Fragment of Government* is a withering criticism of Blackstone's Introduction to the *Commentaries.* Believing that the only suitable basis for a law is its tendency to promote the public good, Bentham views all other bases as unacceptable. Towards this end, he criticizes a range of legal notions as irrational in basis or effect. In his works, moral and scientific criticisms proceed in tandem. One of his central tasks is to uncover the actual bases of laws—as opposed to the claims of their adherents. Once it is clear how laws have actually been established, they can be criticized on moral grounds.

Bentham's aim in *Fragment* is to "cleanse the Augean stable," "to pour in a body of severe and steady criticism . . . in one unbroken tide."[15] Accordingly, he attacks traditional mainstays of English law dating back to the time of Locke. For instance, he dismisses the idea of the social contract as a fiction, never entered into. The "notion of an actually existing unconnected *state of nature* is too wild to be seriously admitted" (*Fragment,* Chap. 1, p. 36). Following Hume, Bentham casts aside the contract itself as a "chimera" and a "fiction" (*Fragment,* Chap. 1, pp. 51–52).

Closely related to these arguments is Bentham's famous criticism of the moral side of social contract theory. He dismisses the law of nature as "nothing but a phrase" (*Fragment,*

Chap. 4, p. 95). Natural law lacks substance. The edicts presented by great natural law theorists—Grotius, Puffendorf, and Burlamaqui—point "sometimes to *manners*, sometimes to *laws*" (*Principles*, Chap. 17, p. 329, n. 1) Bentham believes these are mere expressions of theorists' preferences, dressed up in legal language. In contrast to these fictions, Bentham espouses a doctrine that is now known as "legal positivism," that laws are commands issued by the appropriate authorities: "whatever is given for law by the person or persons recognized as possessing the power of making laws, is *law*" (*Principles*, Chap. 17, p. 330, n. 1).[16]

Bentham links the notions of law and sovereignty. The sovereign is the body in society that is recognized as having the authority to make law. The sovereign can be identified by the people's habit of obeying it: "of the power of the sovereign himself the constituent cause is the submission and obedience of the people."[17] In contrast to doctrines of natural law, which espouse the existence of binding rules accessible to reason, legal positivism limits law to the sovereign's commands: "*every law is a command or its opposite*" (*Principles*, Chap. 17, p. 332, n.). As is the case with utilitarian moral philosophy, a great advantage of legal positivism is its tangibility. Because law is created, put into effect through the actions of actual persons on specific occasions, it has a public, objective quality, absent from natural law. Natural law is purported to be directly accessible to man's reason. But as we have seen in previous chapters, people disagree about its interpretation, and there is no easy way to clear up such disputes. In Bentham's eyes, natural law is no more than a persuasive device used to mask people's preferences. Rather than saying, "I wish you wouldn't steal," the proponent of natural law says, "It is against the law of nature for you to steal." But these utterances amount to the same thing.

Though moral rules, unlike laws or legal rules, are not backed by the sovereign's force, they too should increase pleasure and reduce pain. Utilitarian reasoning allows clear assessment of such rules. For instance, the rule that promises should be kept is justified because violating it causes observable disappointment, which is a form of pain. Contrast this with alternative approaches to moral reasoning, for instance "the principle of sympathy and antipathy" (*Principles*, Chap. 2, pp. 14–16). According to this view, an action is assessed according to one's feelings about it, "holding up that approbation or disapprobation as a sufficient reason for itself," and not believing it is necessary to determine the action's effects. Bentham criticizes this as pure subjectivism; he refers to it as "the principle of *caprice*" (p. 13, n. 1). Like natural law, this is no more than people's feelings supported by appeals to mysterious, fictive notions:

> When a man disapproves of a mode of conduct considered independently of any actual system of jurisprudence he says there is a Law of Nature against it. . . . If he cannot tell why he disapproves of it he begins talking of a Rule of Right, a Fitness of Things, a Moral Sense or some other imaginary standard which howsoever varied in description, is from first to last nothing but his own private opinion in disguise.[18]

"It is manifest, that this is rather a principle in name than in reality: it is not a positive principle of itself, so much as a term employed to signify the negation of all principle" (*Principles*, Chap. 2, p. 16).

According to Bentham, rights as well as laws must be grounded on observable political facts. Employing reasoning like that of Burke discussed in the last chapter, he contends that rights are real only if they are supported by laws in a concrete legal system.

Accordingly, "right and legal right are the same thing"; a right not created by a law is a contradiction in terms, like a "round square" or "cold heat."[19] Bentham contemptuously dismisses natural rights. The rights to life, liberty, and the pursuit of happiness, presented in the Declaration of Independence, are "a cloud of words" enunciated by the colonists "to cover (veil) the enormity of their crimes" in invading Canada during the Revolutionary War.[20] Bentham is similarly critical of the claims in the French Declaration of the Rights of Man and Citizen: "*Natural rights* is simple nonsense: natural and imprescriptible rights, rhetorical nonsense—nonsense upon stilts."[21] The reason for this is clear. Rights cannot exist without a legal system in which they are encased. The existence of such a system implies the existence of a government that has made the laws. Rights are not natural, created by God. Rather, they are created, along with laws, by the commands of a sovereign authority. Bentham describes the *Declaration of the Rights of Man* as "a perpetual vein of nonsense, flowing from a perpetual abuse of words."[22]

Though Bentham is similar to Burke in believing that rights must be protected by existing laws, his view of British law is quite different from Burke's. In Bentham's England all law was grounded on "common law," and so viewed as stemming from "an ancient collection of unwritten maxims and customs" (Postema, p. 4). In practice, this body of law had grown up over time largely through judicial decisions, which were viewed as precedents for further decisions. Because of the absence of a systematic, written code of law, judges had great latitude in deciding cases. The result of hundreds of years of the accumulation of law, through both judicial action and Parliamentary statutes, was a tangled mass of decisions, many of which had to be reinterpreted in order to be applied to new circumstances as they arose. In opposition to Burke, who viewed this process as an accumulation of centuries of wisdom, Bentham is overcome by its irrationality. He criticizes the so-called fallacy of the "wisdom of our ancestors." Though among people who are alive at the same time, an older person might have more experience—and so wisdom—than a younger person, this is not true of different generations. If anything, a later generation can profit from the experience of, and so become wiser than, an earlier generation. Of the argument that we should defer to the judgment of our forebears, he says: "An absurdity so glaring carries in itself its own refutation" (*Fallacies*, Chap. 11, p. 43). Bentham believes a law's age is relevant to assessing it only because time makes its consequences more readily apparent: "If the law in question has contributed to the public good, the older it is, the easier it will be to enumerate its good effects, and to prove its utility by a direct process" (*Theory*, Chap. 13, p. 67).

We have seen Burke's argument that social and political institutions would not have survived unless they promoted the public good. To this Bentham has a response. Existing laws can serve the interests of particular individuals while being harmful to others, perhaps to society as a whole. Those who benefit from existing laws attempt to preserve them, frequently having the power to do so. Bentham believes the impenetrability of the English legal system is not accidental. This serves to obscure the effects of harmful laws, while it makes it easier for people with access to the system to manipulate it to their advantage. Because of law's tangled development, no one but a trained lawyer can understand it. This situation is exacerbated by legal language, and devices used to render a law made during one period applicable to quite different circumstances centuries later. In spite of its manifest lack of logic, the system is defended by lawyers, who love "the source of their power, of their reputation, of their fortune." They approve of the common law "for the same reason that the Egyptian priest loved hieroglyphics."[23]

Accordingly, Bentham believes it is necessary to codify the law, to render it systematic and logical, which in turn means tracing all rules back to a simple and clear principle, "the greatest good of the greatest number." All laws should advance this end; those that do not should be stricken from the books. Bentham's view is supported by legal positivism. The requirement that laws be made by identifiable authorities can help eliminate elements of custom and tradition from common law. Burke, once again, defends these elements of the legal system because of their great complexity and man's limited ability to comprehend them. Bentham views complexity as an enemy to be wiped away. For similar reasons, he turns his attention to judicial procedure and other aspects of the legal system. The public good demands that these too be rationalized and simplified. Among subjects he considers are rules of evidence. His efforts to bring about needed legal reforms took up much of his energy throughout his life. His end was always intended to be a system of laws that benefitted society as a whole, rather than narrow privileged interests.

BENTHAM'S UTILITARIANISM

In opposition to the tangled conceptions of existing legal systems, utilitarianism poses a scientific alternative. It is not rooted in fictions, chimeras, or the uncontrolled growth of centuries of statutes and precedents. Rather, its basis is the scientifically observable fact that people pursue pleasure and so pleasure should ground morality. The object of legislation should be "the greatest happiness of the greatest number." This phrase, immortalized by Bentham, was not originally coined by him. In the Introduction to *On Crimes and Punishments*, a pioneering work on reform of criminal law, Cesare Beccaria (1738–1794) describes his aim as "*the greatest happiness shared by the greatest number.*"[24] Other possible sources for the idea were Helvetius and Frances Hutcheson (1694–1746) (Halévy, pp. 13–14, 19). But wherever Bentham discovered the "greatest happiness principle," it became fundamental to his thought. It is expounded on the first page of his first published book: "*it is the greatest happiness of the greatest number that is the measure of right and wrong*" (*Fragment*, Pref., p. 3).

The greatest happiness principle affords moral deliberations a measure of certitude otherwise unattainable. Actions should be judged according to their tendency to increase or diminish pleasure. In accordance with what we have identified as the core of teleological moral theories, Bentham assesses the rightness or wrongness of moral actions *exclusively* in these terms: "When thus interpreted, the words *ought*, and *right* and *wrong*, and others of that stamp, have a meaning: when otherwise, they have none" (*Principles*, Chap. 1, p. 4).

In order to make this standard clearly applicable, Bentham makes a number of simplifying assumptions. First, he views the interest of the community as "the sum of the interests of the several members who compose it" (*Principles*, Chap. 1, p. 3). Thus the community is no more than the people who constitute it. The greatest good of the greatest number can be ascertained by examining proposed policies' effects on the people involved. Bentham pays little attention to problems in moving between the pleasures and pains of different people, or different activities. Two people who are hit on the head might experience different amounts of pain, because of their physical constitutions, or perhaps other reasons. Bentham tends to ignore such factors. He appears to view pleasures as *things*—with tangible, measurable properties that are readily compared with one another.

At one point he refers to pleasures and pains as "homogeneous real entities" (*Principles*, Chap. 6, p. 45, n. 1). The root of pleasure appears to be physical sensations, in the words of one commentator, "particular types of sensations, directly comparable with each other."[25] The problems with this are seen if one considers the pleasures of eating ice cream, reading a great novel, listening to a symphony, taking a walk, finishing a job, and lying on the grass on a beautiful day and doing nothing. In one of his works, Bentham himself lists the pleasures of sympathy, sex, power, religion, and others (Harrison, pp. 148–149). A moment's reflection will show that the pleasures of these activities are not easily compared, and that different people will enjoy some more than others. But Bentham sets such complexities aside. Because he views all pleasures as alike, he notoriously remarks, "the quantity of pleasure being equal, push-pin is as good as poetry" (quoted by Mill, "Bentham," p. 95). The problem, of course, is assessing the precise quantities of pleasure involved in push-pin (an early form of bowling) and poetry, while once again, people might find different degrees of enjoyment in the two activities. For some people push-pin will be better than poetry; for others the reverse will hold. Demonstrating that the quantities of pleasure involved are equal would be no easy task. Bentham also views happiness and pleasure as basically synonymous and pleasures and pains as convertible. Because units of one cancel the other out, to increase pleasure and to diminish pain (or vice versa) are interchangeable.

Granted these assumptions, Bentham believes one can *calculate* the effects of possible actions in terms of the pleasures and pains of their consequences, and so determine with assurance their moral worth. He presents a series of variables attached to different pleasures, which allow one to assess their magnitudes with precision. These are as follows (*Principles*, Chap. 4): *intensity, certainty* or *uncertainty, propinquity* or *remoteness, fecundity,* or the chance a pleasure has of being followed by similar sensations; *purity,* or the chance of not being followed by the opposite sensations; and *extent.* By this last, Bentham refers to the number of people affected by a specific action. Through the use of these variables, as Bentham writes in *Theory of Legislation,* legislation "becomes a matter of arithmetic" (Chap. 8, p. 33).

The variables themselves are relatively clear. Even if they do not actually offer great quantitative precision, they are strongly rooted in common sense. For example, by drinking a great deal of alcohol, one risks a hangover. This can consist of relatively severe pains, which last for a good period of time, perhaps several hours. The pains are fairly certain if one drinks a great deal, but their remoteness is a factor in inducing one to drink. The perceived pleasures of drinking are in the immediate future, while the hangover will not be encountered until several hours later. A hangover is not fecund but can be considered pure, in that it is not likely to be followed by similar pains, or to give rise to pleasures. In this sense it differs from the impure pleasures of drinking, in that this will likely be followed by sensations of the opposite sort, the pains of the hangover. Applying Bentham's variables should give one a clear idea of the pain of the hangover. By comparing this with the expected pleasures of drinking, one can ascertain whether it is worthwhile to drink. In this case, however, things are probably more complicated, in that drinking can have additional, more remote, undesirable consequences.

Precise assessment of the consequences of different courses of action is possible only if each of the variables can be measured exactly, and can also be added and subtracted to yield precise scores. Bentham's view that these assumptions hold is referred to as his "felicific calculus." This view is often criticized because of the obvious absurdity of attaching precise quantitative measures to the different dimensions of pleasures and pains. The problem is seen immediately if one attempts to identify exact pleasure scores for going bowling as opposed to getting an *A* in an organic chemistry course. However, if we assume that the variables are clearly understood, we can see they are helpful in assessing courses of action, regardless of whether they yield exact measurements. Setting aside the demand for mathematical precision, we can see that there is a great deal of sense to what Bentham says. As he writes in *Principles*: "In all this there is nothing but what the practice of mankind, wheresoever they have a clear view of their own interest, is perfectly conformable to" (Chap. 4, p. 32). People regularly perform quantitative analysis of the consequences of different courses of action in their daily lives. Why do people go to the dentist? Many people believe this is a painful experience. It can also be inconvenient and expensive. However, though these pains are relatively certain and imminent, they are also of relatively short duration, though on occasion the pains involved can be intense. Most important, these pains are impure; going to the dentist makes it more likely that other pains will not be encountered in the future. The consequences of not going to the dentist can be much greater, though they are less certain and more remote. But because of the immensely greater duration of living with bad teeth—or without teeth—many people are willing to undergo the short-run pains of going to the dentist in order to avoid the long-run pains that can result from not going. Though it would be difficult to produce precise numerical expressions for the different factors involved in these calculations, the overall principle is clear, and rough quantitative assessments of the variables are readily supplied by common sense. Similar examples can be multiplied without end. For instance, why do people go to work instead of staying home and taking it easy? Why do students study for examinations instead of going out with the gang? Why do people diet and exercise, and remain faithful to their spouses, though there are short-run pleasures associated with the opposite courses? In each of these cases, the near and perhaps intense pleasures associated with indulgence are outweighed by remote pains which are relatively certain and of far greater duration. What is to be noted, however, is that all these cases concern assessing the pleasures and pains of one person's possible courses of action. Though Bentham does not clearly distinguish the logic of cases of this sort and cases that involve the pleasures and pains of many different people, the latter obviously involve a range of problems not encountered in the former. Bentham has long been criticized for paying insufficient attention to the fact that different people may assess given courses of action differently. Problems of interpersonal comparisons make utilitarianism far more complex than Bentham envisions.

Even granted these complexities, however, in the areas of life of most concern to Bentham, much can be said for his method. Bentham's greatest concern is with public affairs, the activities of large numbers of people. His main idea is that public policies should be assessed according to their consequences for the people affected, with the desired aim the greatest good of the greatest number. Though he perhaps errs in the degree of precision consequences will admit, his position is easily translated into the common sense demand that consequences be assessed with the greatest possible precision. His recommendations constitute the basis for a rational approach to problems of public policy.

The strengths of the method can be seen if we consider an example. Consider a controversial issue, whether to require that handguns be registered. Strong arguments have been advanced on both sides of this question. Proponents of registration say such a requirement will cut down on the number of guns in circulation. Consequently, there will be less crime. Fewer people will be shot in domestic disputes; there will be fewer accidents and fewer successful suicides. In short, according to their assessment, the result of a registration policy will be a happier, safer society. Opponents of this policy advance countervailing considerations. They believe the requirement will keep guns from law-abiding citizens, while criminals will still get them. Because honest citizens will have a harder time defending themselves, the result will be more rather than less crime. In addition, opponents of registration are suspicious of government. They believe restricting handguns is only a first step. Once this is accomplished, government will move to restrict rifles and shotguns as well. Not only will this limit the great pleasure people take in gun ownership and use, but when things have run their course, citizens will be disarmed and so more susceptible to government tyranny. Interestingly enough, opponents of handgun registration also claim their policy will eventuate in a safer, happier society. They also include in their vision of a desirable society the enjoyment to be derived from guns, but in the final analysis they realize that this pales in comparison to large-scale concerns of public safety, which accordingly dominate debate.

What is striking about this debate is its rationality. As we have seen in previous chapters, rational analysis concerns determining the most effective means to the attainment of given ends. In this case, proponents of each handgun policy argue that their preferred course is the most effective means to a happier, safer society—or in Bentham's terms, the greatest good of the greatest number. Though we lack the full resources of Bentham's felicific calculus, common sense gives clear guidance for distinguishing happier and less happy societies. Obviously, the crucial question in regard to handgun policy is the amount of handgun violence in society. At least in principle, disagreements in a debate of this sort can be settled through careful examination of the issue, collection of relevant data, etc. If it can be shown convincingly that requiring or not requiring handgun registration will significantly reduce violence, the debate could in principle be settled—though whether die-hard proponents of either side would be convinced by even overwhelming evidence is an open question.

To see the rationality of this debate, consider other courses it could take. Jack says handguns should not be restricted because he has a natural right to bear arms. June says this is not true; she has a natural right to be safe, and there is no natural right to bear arms. Or perhaps Jack says the customs of the United States over the past fifty years give him a right to bear arms, which overrides other considerations. To this June replies that fifty years of practice cannot confer rights. In these cases, one will note the intractability of the debate. How does one go about finding out if there is a natural right to bear arms, or if custom confers rights? These are deeply philosophical questions, which not only defy easy reso-lution but have no accepted means for resolving them. Things could be worse. Jack says it is against his religion to restrict handguns. In response, June scoffs at his religious beliefs. Once again, how does one even begin to deal with this disagreement? To make matters even worse, in a large and diverse society, all three of Jack's arguments could be put forth, along with all three of June's counters, and one would have to determine the relative weights of these different considerations. Though the range of possible disagreements presented in this paragraph might strike us as far-fetched, Bentham believed the situation he encountered in the English legal system was along these lines. Different laws, based on different and not easily compatible principles, had grown up over time and stood jumbled together in no rational order.

In presenting issues of public policy as concerned with (and only with) the consequences of different possible courses of action, Bentham cuts through accumulated irrationality. If his method is accepted, everyone knows, first, what policy debates are about. Everyone's concern is promoting a safer, happier society; different policies must be assessed in regard to this end. The need to examine controversial philosophical claims is eliminated, as is also the requirement to weigh different kinds of claims against one another. Proponents of the two sides of the handgun debate (and other debates) may well still disagree. But this is because they believe specific policies will work differently. In other words, they have conflicting predictions as to how people will respond to the policies in question. As a result of important differences in people's overall views of the nature of man and government, they see the future differently. But in spite of this range of problems, Bentham's method makes an enormous contribution. Even an issue as intractable as gun control is far easier to resolve when it is put in these terms rather than in those of Jack and June.

Less intractable issues obviously lend themselves to utilitarian analysis. Should the government build a bypass around some city? What are the costs and benefits involved? To begin with, is such a bypass necessary? To answer this, one must assess the amount of time people spend tied up in traffic on existing roads and what this costs them. If the existing situation is intolerable, then alternatives should be considered. How much time will a bypass save? What will it cost? Will taxes have to be raised to pay for it? By how much? Whom will construction inconvenience, and for how long? Presumably, land will have to be acquired, and some people will be forced to give up their homes. How many people will be affected? How will a new bypass affect the beauty of the surrounding countryside, which everyone enjoys? Along similar lines, if a bypass should be built, where should it be located? Obviously, the answer to this question is where it will benefit the most people and inconvenience the fewest. Presumably, information bearing on this question and all the others can be found. The decision whether to build the bypass can then be made in the light of hard evidence about its future. Once again, all parties agree about the aims of the policy disagreement; all want minimal time spent in traffic with as little expense and inconvenience as possible. Issues bearing on the interpersonal comparison of utilities are bound to arise here. Some people might not mind the extra time driving if the bypass means higher taxes. Others might be more willing to pay the taxes. The fact that the bypass would detract from the beauty of the surrounding countryside might concern some people—perhaps those most directly affected. But once again, the utilitarian approach is far more manageable than others that might take religious or metaphysical turns, or veer off into customary law. Many other issues lend themselves to similar analysis. Thus in spite of its weaknesses, Benthamite utilitarianism is a valuable tool for tackling issues of public policy—in regard to what Mill calls the "business part" of life.

ANALYSIS OF CRIMINAL LAW

Perhaps Bentham's most striking contribution to reforming the English legal system lay in the area of criminal law. This subject is classically discussed in the *Principles of Morals and*

Legislation, and practices like those Bentham recommends have been widely implemented. The situation he encountered in English criminal law was similar to other aspects of the legal system. Laws were based on a jumble of different principles, untidily arranged. A wide range of conduct was prohibited by law, and so was to be punished. But the reasons for criminality varied. Some actions were prohibited for customary or religious reasons. Other laws were based on superstition, such as those against witchcraft. Penalties bore no clear relationship to the seriousness of crimes, while many penalties were unnecessarily severe. Hanging was the penalty for innumerable offenses, mainly crimes against property.[26] But this was inconsistently applied. For instance, while it was a felony to damage the bridges at Brantford and Blackfriars, damaging the London or Westminster bridges carried a sentence of death. Stealing a sheep or horse, and picking a man's pocket, were capital crimes, while attempting to kill one's father was a misdemeanor. According to Bentham, "the cobweb of ancient barbarism," with its gaps and loopholes, "had to be destroyed."[27]

In approaching this situation, Bentham not only pointed out the existing system's shortcomings but proposed detailed, preferable alternatives. For instance, we have just noted that many existing penalties were unnecessarily severe. Demonstrating this presupposes a clear means of determining how severe a given penalty should actually be. One of Bentham's great contributions lay in his ability to answer this questions and others like it. By working from clearly developed principles on which an acceptable legal system should be based, Bentham was able to present categorical criticisms of the existing system and provide a coherent alternative. Bentham's underlying principle, of course, was the principle of utility. The analysis of criminal law he pioneered can be reformulated along the following lines.

The rationale behind criminal law is that people are generally self-interested and so should be left alone as much as possible. They can be trusted to do what is in their best interests, and will be more successful at this without than with government guidance. As Bentham says in *Theory*,

> As a general rule, the greatest possible latitude should be left to individuals, in all cases in which they can injure none but themselves, for they are the best judges of their own interests. If they deceive themselves, it is to be supposed that the moment they discover their error they will alter their conduct. (Chap. 12, p. 63)

Though the rule against government interference holds in most cases, this is not true in all. People's interests are not always compatible. It can easily be in my interest to steal from other people. Provided I can get away with this, I will reap the benefits of money without the pain of earning it. In other familiar cases, it can be in the interest of one person to prey on others. Such behavior must be discouraged. The above quotation continues as follows:

> The power of the law need interfere only to prevent them from injuring each other. It is there that restraint is necessary; it is there that the application of punishments is truly useful because the rigor exercised upon an individual becomes in such a case the security of all. (Chap. 12, p. 63)

In certain cases government should intervene to prevent behavior that injures other people. Such behavior is identified as criminal and so subject to penalties.

The utilitarian theory of punishment is referred to as a "deterrence" view. The purpose of punishment is to discourage, or deter, certain kinds of conduct. Thus, if Phil is caught stealing, he is punished to set an example to other people. Stealing can obviously be construed as beneficial to the perpetrator. By punishing Phil, the government attempts to convey the message that crime does not pay, and so to prevent other people from stealing as well. This is distinguished from other views of punishment. The two most common are a rehabilitation view, according to which the purpose of punishment is to improve the moral condition of the malefactor, so he will be a better person, and presumably will not commit further crimes in the future. According to a "retributive" view, the purpose of punishment is essentially revenge. "An eye for an eye, a tooth for a tooth" expresses this view. Its proponents argue that the commission of certain acts somehow upsets the moral order, and that the perpetrator must pay in order to make things right again. Many people adhere to such a view, as is seen especially clearly in cases of horrible crimes, for example, mass murders or the murder of children. Proponents of capital punishment argue that such acts are so loathsome the perpetrator deserves to be punished with death, whether or not this will deter similar acts in the future.

The utilitarian view is less dramatic, but firmly rooted in Bentham's desire to achieve the greatest good of the greatest number. There are some acts that should be prevented. Obviously, these diminish the happiness of society. Thus, eating ice cream is easily distinguished from stealing or murdering. The latter acts are harmful and so must be discouraged, while the former is not. In order to discourage commission of such acts, government resolves to punish them. This is done through infliction of penalties. Thus if captured thieves are publicly boiled in oil, this should have the effect of discouraging other people who might wish to steal.

Utilitarian reasoning is far more sophisticated. The end of legislation, as we recall, is society's greatest good. There is an apparent paradox in regard to punishment, because it is the infliction of pain, and so should be discouraged. Punishment not only lessens the happiness of the apprehended perpetrator, but it causes worry among the populace as a whole, as people fear the same thing could happen to them. According to Bentham, "all punishment is mischief: all punishment in itself is evil" (*Principles*, Chap. 13, p. 170). But though punishment itself lowers the public happiness, it is sometimes necessary, because it prevents greater evils. There is no denying that punishing a thief causes pain. But this pain is less than if thieves were not punished, in which case more people would steal, and the welfare of society would be affected more adversely than it is through punishments. A particular punishment is justified if it will prevent greater evils than it produces, or in Bentham's words, "in as far as it promises to exclude some greater evil" (*Principles*, Chap. 13, p. 170). The clear rule is that if punishment must be employed, it must be as little as possible, so it causes as little mischief as possible.

In keeping with his fondness for moral arithmetic, Bentham provides rules punishment should follow. As we have seen, it should be used only when it will deter greater evils. Thus actions should not be punished if they have been committed already, before the law was instituted. The actions in question must be intentional. They must not be accidental, and must be performed by people capable of committing them willingly. This last condition, for instance, rules out punishing young children and people with mental defects. To punish such people would be useless pain, for other, similar people lack the understanding to be deterred by these examples from similar conduct in the future (*Principles*, Chap. 13).

Punishments should also bear a clear relationship to offenses. If a certain act is greatly harmful to society, it can justify severe punishment and still be in the public interest. Because it is more important to deter severe crimes than lesser crimes, their punishments can be greater. But in these cases as in all others, we want to punish people as little as possible. Therefore the proper punishment for a crime should be the *least* pain that will actually deter it. Bentham believes this can be calculated with precision. Consider an example. If we assume John will gain 1,000 units of pleasure by stealing, we must provide a penalty of at least 1,001 units of pain to deter him. Because John can be presumed to be a rational agent, he will not steal if it does not pay to do so. The purpose of penal legislation is to make it not pay. Of course, a greater penalty, say 1,000,000 units of pain (e.g., boiling him in oil), would deter him as well. But because this would represent useless evil, the proper course is to impose the lowest possible penalty still able to do the job.

There are additional complications. John knows he might not be caught. If there is roughly a 50 percent chance of being caught stealing and the penalty is 1,001 units of pain, he will not be deterred. The rewards of crime outweigh the penalty, if we discount for the possibility of not being caught. To compensate for this, penalties must be increased accordingly. Thus, if there is a 50 percent chance of being caught, the penalty must be at least 2,001 units of pain, so that even taking this into account, it will not be in John's interest to steal.

Though precise mathematical calculations are unlikely in these cases, once again, Bentham's basic principles are not only sensible but have been put into practice in many modern states. The reason for this is clear if we compare the situation Bentham encountered with his recommended changes. If his principles are adopted, then criminal law will be rationalized. Similar crimes will be treated similarly—with clear utilitarian principles provided to identify them. Barbaric penalties will be eliminated, while still preserving the central purpose of the criminal justice system, that people be dissuaded from committing acts that are damaging to society. In place of an impenetrable jungle of rules and principles redounding to no one's interest, Bentham's principles are clearly directed toward the public good.

Bentham's principles also provide a clear means for distinguishing between matters of law and morals. He believes morality, like law, is constituted of rules that promote the public interest. We have rules against lying and breaking promises, because such behavior causes more harm than good. The same is true of other aspects of morality, for instance, rules of sexual behavior. What distinguishes the domain of law from morality is that *coercive enforcement* of only certain rules will redound to the public good. Because the use of force always detracts from the public good, enforcement of a rule is not always beneficial, even if the public would benefit from general adherence to it. Punishment is not justified when it would be "unprofitable" (*Principles*, Chap. 17, pp. 315–316). There are two main kinds of cases here: when the cost of punishing the guilty would outweigh the benefit; and when there is danger that the innocent might be punished. An example of the first kind Bentham provides is fornication. Because detection is difficult, punishments must be enormously severe to be effective. Moreover, in order to detect people committing this act, it is necessary to intrude on their privacy. Sustained effort to root out fornication by punishment would result in wholesale violations of privacy. In addition, cases in which people are caught and punished would be so unusual they would have little deterrent effect. Bentham writes:

> With what chance of success, for example, would a legislator go about to extirpate drunkenness and fornication by dint of legal punishment? Not all the tortures which ingenuity could invent would compass it: and, before he had made any progress worth regarding, such a mass of evil would be produced by the punishment, as would exceed, a thousand-fold, the utmost possible mischief of the offense. (*Principles*, Chap. 17, p. 320)

On the whole then, it is better to attach condemnation to this behavior, and so to attempt to discourage it through the influence of public opinion than to employ the criminal law.

Among cases of the second type are offenses that resist clear identification. Ingratitude is undesirable behavior, sometimes the cause of considerable pain. But exactly what constitutes ingratitude is so difficult to determine that, if one attempted to punish instances of it, a large percentage of the population would be subject to punishment at any time. The same is true of rudeness and treachery.

Instead of employing coercion, the legislator should attempt to discourage both sorts of acts through moral disapproval. But both kinds of undesirable behavior can be tolerated to some extent without significant damage to society. This is one difference between fornication or rudeness and murder. The consequences of murder are so serious that it must be rooted out and punished—to discourage similar conduct in the future—with less regard for the costs involved.

UTILITARIANISM AND DEMOCRACY

Throughout much of his life, Bentham was notably unsuccessful at having his ideas put into practice. As we have seen, he approached numerous rulers and governments, including Catherine the Great of Russia, South American governments, revolutionary France, and the young United States of America. However, more frustrating than these endeavors were his repeated failures in England. Legal reform lay at the center of Bentham's interests. But his efforts in this direction were repeatedly thwarted. The British government of the late eighteenth and early nineteenth centuries was far from democratic. The franchise was tightly restricted and the political system controlled by the landed aristocracy. Bentham came to believe his reforms were resisted because Parliament favored narrow, special interests over those of society as a whole. In particular, the legal profession, a "confederated sinister interest," profited from the existing state of affairs, was reluctant to change things, and exerted great influence on Parliament. As a result, the country as a whole suffered from a "mountain of abuse and injustice which the fraternity of lawyers were so constantly employed in raising up as they pursued their own sinister ends."[28] Bentham's repeated failures at political reform, especially reform of the English legal system, turned him into a staunch adherent of democracy.

Bentham developed a powerful utilitarian defense of democracy. If the purpose of legislation is to promote society's greatest good, then government must have a strong incentive to do so. If it lacks this incentive, it will not only produce bad laws but resist attempts at political reform. Utilitarians claim human behavior is governed by self-interest. Rulers will not improve conditions in their societies unless it is in *their own interest* to do so. For a monarch like Catherine the Great, this is clearly not the case. Her main interest is to stay in power, and so it is not clear that the interests of monarch and subjects coincide. The same is true of parliamentary government, if, for example, the members of Parliament have more to gain from supporting the legal profession than from advancing society's overall good. Democratization of the political process provides a way around this problem. The clearest way to make sure the ruler gains by governing in the public interest is to make him directly accountable to the public. Because government officials benefit from being in office, it is in their interest to promote the good of society if society is able to control them. In 1790 Bentham wrote: "The stricter the dependence of the governors on the governed, the better will the government be."[29] In order to make governors dependent, Bentham advocated extending the franchise, to dilute the landed nobility's power. In 1809 he argued that extending the franchise was crucial to ensure that "the greatest happiness of the greatest possible number shall be the object really and constantly aimed at" by the state (Bentham, quoted by Dinwiddy, "Transition," p. 691). Additional measures he proposed were annual elections, publication of parliamentary debates, regulations to ensure members' attendance, and various electoral reforms. These included secret ballots, and redistricting to even out the population of electoral districts (Dinwiddy, "Transition," p. 690). With the publication of his writings on parliamentary reform in 1817, Bentham became an important figure in the movement for democratic reform in England, which achieved a major victory with the passage of the Great Reform Bill in 1832, the year of Bentham's death.

Thus the utilitarian defense of democracy is strongly rooted in common sense. According to Bentham: "In this there is no jargon, no obscurity. It is founded on the universal, necessary, and undisputed, and not even to be lamented property in human nature, the predominance of the self-regarding affections over the social" (Bentham, quoted in Mack, p. 455).

This defense of democracy is different from others we have encountered. Perhaps the most familiar argument for democracy in the Western tradition is one from natural rights, similar to what we have seen in Locke (though the extent of Locke's adherence to what we now regard as meaningful democracy is questionable). The main claim here is that among people's natural (or human) rights is a right to consent to one's governors. Taking this one step farther, proponents of this view claim people have a right to consent to the laws under which they are bound. Because direct participation in the legislative process is not possible for all citizens, representative institutions provide the most logical means through which people can express their consent. Thus according to this line of argument, representative institutions are necessary in a just political system so people can consent to the laws. Rousseau takes this line of argument one step farther, arguing that a person's will cannot be represented. To be bound by laws in the making of which one has not directly participated is a violation of freedom. Thus Rousseau rejects representative democracy in favor of participatory democracy. However, his overall argument is similar to the Lockean one we have noted.[30]

Bentham's argument is significantly different. As we have seen, he has no use for natural rights, and little interest in citizens' consent to government. Democratic institutions are necessary, he argues, solely as a means to control the actions of government, to make sure it serves the public interest. If this could be accomplished more effectively without democracy, Bentham would no doubt support this other form of government. But the need for democracy is firmly rooted in human nature. The fact that people are self-interested holds for people who serve in political office. They will legislate in their own interest rather than that of society unless they are prevented from doing so. The clearest way to accomplish this is to make them accountable to the group in society that is most deeply concerned with the public good, the people as a whole, whose good it is.

Given his concern with the public good, Bentham naturally supports extending the franchise as widely as possible. Unless some group is included in the body to which government is accountable, its interest will not be considered. An important reason for the shortcomings of the existing political system in England was the narrow franchise, which ensured that government would serve the interest of a small portion of the population. In our own time we have seen a clear application of this principle in connection with the civil rights struggle in the American South. One reason racial segregation was able to persist was the exclusion of blacks from the electoral system. Because they were not accountable to blacks, public officials did little to advance their interests. Thus the extension of real political rights to black citizens—through voting rights legislation and important Supreme Court decisions—was a crucial element in the civil rights revolution. In view of these considerations, we can appreciate utilitarian reformers' support for extending the franchise, though there are some complexities to their views, to which we will return.

Though common opinion closely associates support of natural rights and support of democratic government, the examples of Bentham and other utilitarians show that this association is by no means necessary. Because he rejects natural rights but upholds democracy for other reasons, Bentham presents an interesting contrast with Burke. We have noted that Bentham and Burke present similar criticisms of natural rights. As we saw in the last chapter, Burke argues that, in order for a right to have substance, it must be embodied in an existing legal system. Thus he dismisses appeals to abstract moral principles, including natural rights, as "metaphysical" arguments—language not unlike Bentham's "nonsense upon stilts." But Burke's assessment of the political system of his day led him away from democracy. In order to preserve concrete rights, he argued, it was necessary to maintain the stability of the British political system. For reasons we have seen, he believed the landed aristocracy was uniquely suited to represent the interests of the country as a whole. Fearing the disorders associated with greater political participation by the mob, Burke favored further restricting the franchise—within only a few years of Bentham's initial conversion to democracy during the time of the French Revolution. The case of Burke—and Montesquieu as well—demonstrates there is no necessary connection between concern with individual rights and democracy. Burke clearly supports the former, as does Montesquieu. Both thinkers believe individual security rests upon maintenance of the existing political system, and that this task is best entrusted to only a portion of the population, the nobility.

Bentham presents a fundamental critique of this line of argument. Though he too argues that rights become real only in a stable political system, he is deeply suspicious of the nobility's claim to govern in the interest of society as a whole. In spite of all their privileges, the nobility are still human beings, and so driven by self-interest. Rather than pursuing the good of society, they will govern in their own interest, unless they are prevented from doing so. Bentham's low opinion of the English legal system and the frustration of unsuccessfully attempting to improve it led him to become suspicious of the nobility. Skeptical of their claim to rule, he subjects their arguments to withering critical scrutiny. Throughout his works Bentham takes great pleasure in unmasking the "fictions"— whether conscious or unconscious—through which social groups deceive one another. Thus in spite of the protestations of the nobility and their defense of the existing political system, Bentham believes it is necessary to make government accountable to the people, to ensure that it actually governs in their interest.

Bentham's conversion to democracy was at least partially due to the influence of James Mill.[31] The utilitarian defense of democracy receives classic expression in the latter's *Essay on Government*, which was originally published in 1820, in a supplement to the *Encyclopedia Britannica*. Though Mill's position is similar to Bentham's, there are also important differences, which we will point out.

James Mill was born in Scotland in 1773. After working as a journalist and writer for some years, he met Bentham in 1808 and became his disciple. For many years Mill and his family lived in a house owned by Bentham, and spent long periods of time at Bentham's country house. With the publication of his *History of British India*, in 1817, Mill achieved literary success. But for historians of political thought he is mainly interesting as a publicist for Bentham's ideas. Much of Bentham's voluminous output remained unpublished, and what was published often made difficult reading. With a clearer prose style and highly logical mind, Mill was ideally suited to communicate utilitarian ideas to a wider public. In the words of Halévy: "Bentham gave Mill a doctrine, and Mill gave Bentham a school" (p. 251). Mill's best-known contribution to political theory is his *Essay on Government*, which provides perhaps the clearest statement of the utilitarian position.

Mill's task in the essay is to explain what the end of government is and how it can be achieved most effectively. He upholds the usual liberal position that politics is instrumental. It is not an end in itself, but valuable as a means to an end. As one can expect from a disciple of Bentham, he argues that the desired end is "the happiness of the greatest number."[32] Mill views the happiness of the greatest number as a composite of the happiness of individual people, which they in turn secure largely through their labor. Government promotes happiness by protecting private property, thereby securing an essential incentive people require in order to labor. Like many liberal theorists we have discussed, Mill holds that government's most important function is protecting property.

Like other liberal theorists, Mill considers two different dangers with which government must deal. In order to protect a person's property from other people, government requires a certain amount of power. But erecting a powerful institution makes it possible for the people who constitute government to abuse their power, and so advance their own interests rather than society's. The problem, then, as we saw with Madison (pp. 76–7), is to arrange government in such a way that this will not happen: "All the difficult questions of government relate to the means of restraining those in whose hands are lodged the powers necessary for the protection of all from making bad use of it" (*Essay*, p. 50).

Because of his conception of human nature, Mill believes the problem of controlling government is especially acute. We can assume that the people who constitute government will be self-interested, because all people are self-interested. It is in their interest, moreover, totally to dominate and plunder their subjects, if they can get away with this. Mill criticizes Hobbes's view that it is safe to surrender all power to an absolute ruler. Anticipating the dictum (of Lord Acton) that "power corrupts, and absolute power corrupts absolutely," he argues that an absolute ruler will have a limitless desire to subordinate all others to his will. This desire is "boundless in two ways: boundless in the number of persons to whom he would extend it, and boundless in its degree over the actions of each" (p. 57).

It follows, then, that governmental power must be checked. In the British Constitution, the power of the monarch is checked by the House of Commons. But this raises an additional problem, making sure the checking body does not abuse *its* power. This can be accomplished, in turn, by making this body accountable to a group in society that is interested in promoting the public good. The only such group is the public: "there is no individual or combination of individuals, except the community itself, who would not have an interest in bad government, if entrusted with its powers" (p. 67). Accordingly, the checking body, Parliament, must be made accountable to the community. This is most effectively accomplished by requiring that members be elected to their seats, and limiting the duration of their terms to enable regular review by the community.

To this point, Mill's logic seems unassailable. To ensure that government pursues the community's interest, it must be made accountable to the community. In his words: "It is very evident that, if the community itself were the choosing body, the interest of the community and that of the choosing body would be the same" (p. 73). Interesting questions are raised, however, in regard to the composition of the choosing body. Though one would expect Mill to endorse the widest possible franchise, he retreats from this conclusion, arguing for significant restrictions.

Utilitarian logic does not demand that everyone be represented; people do not have *rights* to be represented. Rather, representation is to ensure that people's interests are considered. Thus if some portion of the community could adequately represent the interests of all members, the franchise could be restricted to it. If Miguel's interests would be considered as well as Amy's, if she were given the vote, he need not receive the vote as well. The most significant implication Mill draws from this line of argument is denying women the vote. He writes:

> One thing is pretty clear, that all those individuals whose interests are indisputably included in those of other individuals may be struck off without inconvenience. In this light may be viewed all children, up to a certain age, whose interests are involved in those of their parents. In this light, also, women may be regarded, the interest of almost all of whom is involved either in that of their fathers or in that of their husbands. (pp. 73–74)

Mill also discusses the interests of the propertyless and propertied classes, opting for a very low or no property qualification for voting.

It is not surprising that Mill argues against giving women the vote. Women were not able to vote in most democratic countries until the late nineteenth or early twentieth centuries. It was not until the Nineteenth Amendment to the United States Constitution (1920) that they were granted the vote throughout the United States, and many other countries lagged behind this pace of reform. Mill was a practical politician as well as a theorist, and expediency clearly dictated that his proposals not be overly far-reaching. There is also philosophical support for his position, if the interests of women are in fact "indisputably included in those of" their husbands. This factual premise, however, is controversial. As a result of struggles for women's rights—in many ways paralleling those for civil rights—in the United States and other countries, it has become clear that women's interests often diverge from those of men, that if women are denied political rights, they will suffer from oppression and exploitation. The same facts of human nature that Mill pursues throughout his *Essay* support these conclusions. A moment's reflection indicates that women have interests that are not included in those of their husbands—and what of women who do not have husbands? As Thomas Macaulay wrote in a famous response to Mill's *Essay* (in 1829):

> Is then the interest of a Turk the same with that of the girls who compose his harem? Is the interest of a Chinese the same with that of the woman whom he harnesses to his plough?[33]

As William Thompson wrote in his *Appeal of One Half the Human Race* in 1825, also in response to the *Essay*, Mill's premises rightfully entail extending the franchise, rather than excluding "one half of the human race."[34] The consequences of denying women the vote, and other forms of political power, are familiar in the kinds of cases Macaulay notes. Situations along these lines exist in the present day, most clearly in various Muslim countries, in which women have few rights and live in conditions verging on domestic slavery.

It is in regard to the question of women's suffrage that Bentham's democratic theory differs most sharply from Mill's. Though Bentham's support for giving women the vote is not unequivocal,[35] he realizes that women's interests often diverge from men's, and generally favors enfranchising them. In unpublished comments on Mill's *Essay*, he wrote that it would not be easy to find "positions pregnant with greater evil" than Mill's recommendations concerning women:

> In the . . . situation in question, a selfish and tyrannical husband, how eagerly will he be apt to catch at it, and make out of it a pretense for aggravating the already universally existing tyranny of the male sex over the female.[36]

Elsewhere Bentham notes that "a practical consequence that could be expected from the granting of votes to women" would be improved relations between the sexes.[37] But fearing resistance such proposals would encounter, he did not aggressively push the idea.[38]

On the whole, Bentham and James Mill are like other theorists in the liberal tradition in concentrating on the negative functions of government, especially protection of property. Their conception of what government should do corresponds to the primary purpose governments actually served during the period in which they formulated their ideas. However, the same utilitarian reasoning that supports representative democracy can be developed to support extending state functions into numerous additional areas. The purpose of government of course is to promote the public good. Accordingly, if a particular program would do more good than harm, then government would be justified in taking on this function. For example, if poor people are on the brink of starvation, the overall happiness of society would be increased significantly by slightly taxing better-off members to provide for them. The poor would take far greater pleasure from this money—which keeps them alive—than would the rich, who might leave it in the bank, or perhaps purchase luxuries. It is not surprising, then, that Bentham was deeply involved in schemes to improve the lot of the poor.

During the nineteenth century, European governments underwent enormous changes, broadening their functions to promote public health, education, safety and other important goals. The state itself changed dramatically, enlarging its administrative structures to be able to accomplish these ends. The state that emerged from this process of growth (which has continued into the twentieth century, and is still continuing in important areas, for example, consideration of national health policies in the United States, as I write) is recognizably similar to the modern governments of the Western democracies, which have responsibilities vastly greater than protecting property.

Among additional tasks modern governments perform are providing public education, regulating food and drugs to ensure their safety, essential public health measures such as ensuring safe drinking water, and old age, accident, and unemployment insurance. The list could be extended. What is important for our concerns is that each of these programs can be supported by utilitarian reasoning. Throughout the nineteenth century, the growth of government was associated with the enfranchisement of increasingly large sections of the population. As the middle class and then the working class received the vote, they demanded government services to improve the quality of their lives. Because these people constituted the bulk of the population, what was good for them was good for the public as a whole, and there is little doubt that many new government programs served the greatest good of the greatest number. Bentham was an inveterate reformer, and the movement he began, known as the "philosophical radicals," was deeply involved in the extension of state services.

Specific reforms undertaken by the English government in the first half of the nineteenth century include the following. In 1834, the Poor Law Commission was established to care for the indigent. In 1834 an Education Committee was established, and in 1848 a Board of Health. In the 1830s and 1840s measures were passed to provide for the inspection of factories, prisons, and mines. In 1841 a Railway Board was established, and in 1845 a Lunacy Commission. In 1850 a Merchant Marine Department was created, and in 1853 a Charity Commission and a Department of Science and Art. Each of these reforms had been recommended by Bentham—though it is not clear they came about as a result of his direct influence. But regardless of the degree to which Bentham can claim responsibility for specific changes, as one scholar says, by the mid-nineteenth century, "Bentham's blueprint for an administrative state had been translated, albeit very roughly, into the reality of the mid-Victorian administrative state."[39]

Because the growth of government administration brings about new problems, Bentham worked to develop means to ensure that growing bureaucracies served the public interest. His basic principle is that people are self-interested; they will do what is good for themselves rather than for the public, unless they are prevented from doing so. This holds for government employees as well, who are susceptible to the "influence" of special interests. Therefore, Bentham worked out principles of bureaucratic efficiency and accountability to make sure government employees, like elected officials, would be answerable to the public. Once again, the measures he recommended reflect common sense, for example, that officials have carefully prescribed duties, that detailed records be kept, and officials' actions be open to public scrutiny. Taken together these measures give public officials strong incentives to pursue the public good. Bentham's ability to understand and to improve the functioning of bureaucratic bodies was altogether rare for a political philosopher. Combining clear moral principles that all branches of government should pursue and detailed understanding of different branches, Bentham made fundamental contributions to "a theory of organization and management."[40]

UTILITARIAN LIBERALISM

At this point, we have discussed the main features of Bentham's political theory and the case for democratic government it supports. We have also noted substantial differences between the utilitarian argument for democracy and more familiar arguments based on natural rights. Though he rejects natural rights, Bentham is able to ground the need for democratic government on important factual claims about human nature. If we grant that the end of government should be to promote the greatest possible happiness of society, then ultimate political responsibility must be placed in the hands of the people as a whole—or a narrower segment of the population that still represents the interests of the whole. Because people are self-interested, they will promote their own interests at the expense of those of other people, unless they are prevented from doing so. The only group that can be trusted to further the interest of the public as a whole is the public itself. Though the conclusion of this argument, support for representative democracy, is obviously similar to the conclusion of an argument from natural rights, there are also important differences. These can be seen if we assess Bentham's and James Mill's political theories against the criteria of liberal political theory discussed in earlier chapters. (For ease of reference, in this section I will refer to this as Bentham's political theory, giving him credit for views in Mill's *Essay*, in spite of differences between the two thinkers.)

As we have seen in previous chapters, liberal political theory can be viewed as having five main features: (a) Its centerpiece is the individual, who is assumed to be rational and self-interested. The individual is the building block of society. He has rights prior to entering into society, and does so primarily to protect them. (b) The community is regarded as nothing more than a collection of individuals. (c) Politics is viewed as instrumental. It is undertaken as a means to advance interests beyond itself, rather than as an end in itself. (d) The (classical) liberal conception of the state, including its functions and institutions, is negative and minimal. The state exists primarily to protect property, which it does through coercive means, especially by punishing people who violate others' property. The state's main institutions are coercive, including police, judicial, and prison systems, and a military establishment to provide national defense. Finally, (e) the liberal conception of freedom is negative (see pp. 231–6). This centers on an absence of coercive interference by other people, which allows the individual to pursue her own interests in her own way.

From what we have seen in this chapter, it is clear that Bentham's political theory satisfies these requirements in most respects. He of course sees the individual as the basic unit of society, and argues that society is nothing but a collection of individuals. This is explicitly stated in Chapter 1 of *Principles*: "The community is a fictitious *body*, composed of the individual persons who are considered as constituting as it were its *members*. The interest of the community then is, what? —the sum of the interests of the several members who compose it" (p. 3).

Though he does not support the idea of rights, Bentham believes politics is instrumental, intended to promote people's happiness. The greatest good of the greatest number is not only a composite of the happiness of different individuals but consists of the satisfaction of desires Bentham views as, in essence, existing prior to entry into society. Bentham tends to view people's desires as fully formed and shows little interest in how they develop. In his eyes, desires are generally regarded as given, while government's end is to promote their satisfaction.

Bentham's view of the state is essentially coercive, intended to protect property. In the last section we noted exceptions to this rule. One respect in which utilitarian liberalism differs from classical liberalism is in its easy support of wider governmental functions, and so bigger government. For ease of reference, I will refer to the political philosophy outlined in this section and discussed in previous chapters as traditional liberalism, to distinguish it from both utilitarian liberalism and later liberal theories associated with the welfare state.[41]

Finally, though Bentham does not uphold the idea of rights, his view is similar to traditional liberalism in supporting an idea of negative freedom. Bentham presents a powerful argument for allowing individuals to lead their own lives, free from coercive interference by other people, including government. As we have seen (p. 327), he argues that individuals are the best judges of their own interests. Thus it is best to leave them alone to pursue their happiness as they see fit. Government interference diminishes happiness, when people are forced to do things they would prefer not to, in addition to the evils of coercion used to alter behavior. Thus all things being equal, government should stay out of people's lives. The main exception, as we have seen, concerns conduct that is clearly harmful to society at large, such as stealing and killing. Government must use coercion to prevent this, according to principles we have noted. Bentham's advocacy of limited government and strong commitment to individual freedom are to some extent tempered by his support of additional government functions that are in the public interest. How these additional programs affect individual freedom raises difficult philosophical problems which cannot be discussed here. To a certain extent they will be addressed in our discussion of John Stuart Mill in the following sections. But let us set this problem aside for now and view Bentham as generally supporting the widest possible freedom for individuals, which in his case is negative freedom.

In spite of this close correspondence between Bentham's theory and traditional liberalism, Bentham's view suffers from a series of important defects, which we must examine. We will look at three main problems, concerning (i) Bentham's view of human motivation; (ii) the relationship between the good of the individual and of society; (iii) protection of individuals and minorities from the threat of majority tyranny.

To begin with (i), as we have seen in previous sections, Bentham defends utilitarianism as the standard of right and wrong actions on the basis of the fact that people naturally pursue pleasure. He says the principle of utility cannot be directly proven, "for that which is used to prove everything else cannot itself be proved: a chain of proofs must have their commencement somewhere" (*Principles*, Chap. 1, p. 4). It appears his reasoning is that the fact that all people pursue pleasure proves it is good and should be the object of individual and government action.

The claim that people always pursue pleasure (commonly referred to as "psychological hedonism") raises numerous problems for Bentham, as commentators have long pointed out. A moment's reflection will indicate that people do many things that do not appear to be intended to increase their pleasure. People make sacrifices for others all the time. But, one can respond, when Jane goes hungry so her baby can eat, she is doing this to increase her happiness, for she would be less happy if the baby were hungry. Consider another example: the male passengers on the sinking ship Titanic allowed the women and children to evacuate in lifeboats while they stayed on board and died. Surely this behavior was not intended to increase their pleasure. However, one can respond that the male passengers would have been miserable with guilt if they had survived at the cost of others' lives. The problem with this kind of response is that it makes Bentham's psychological claim true by definition. It allows one to *interpret* any action whatsoever as performed to increase pleasure—or why else would the person do it? The point is trenchantly made by Macaulay, in his response to James Mill:

> What proposition is there respecting human nature which is absolutely and universally true? We know of only one: and that is not only true but identical; that men always act from self-interest. This truism the Utilitarians proclaim with as much pride as if it were new, and as much zeal as if it were important. But in fact, when explained, it means only that men, if they can, will do as they choose. When we see the action of a man we know with certainty what he thinks his interest to be. But it is impossible to reason with certainty from what *we* take to be his interest to his action. One man goes without a dinner that he may add a shilling to a hundred thousand pounds; another runs in debt to give balls and masquerades. One man cuts his father's throat to get possession of his old clothes; another hazards his own life to save that of an enemy. . . . Each of these men has, no doubt, acted from self-interest. But we gain nothing by knowing this, except the pleasure, if it be one, of multiplying useless words. In fact, this principle is just as recondite and just as important as the great truth that whatever is, is. . . . And it is equally idle to attribute any importance to a proposition which, when interpreted, means only that a man had rather do what he had rather do. (Macaulay, p. 299)

In outlining his psychological principle, Bentham says:

> I use the words *pain* and *pleasure* in their ordinary signification, without inventing any arbitrary definition for the sake of excluding certain pleasures or denying the existence of certain pains. In this matter we want no refinement, no metaphysics. . . . *Pain* and *pleasure* are what everybody feels to be such—the peasant and the prince, the unlearned as well as the philosopher. (*Theory*, Chap. 1, p. 3)

Not only is Bentham's notion of pleasure intended to be that of typical common sense, but, as we have seen, he believes quantities of pleasure can be measured according to precise variables. Thus his version of psychological hedonism is that, when faced with different possible courses of action, people always pursue the greater quantity of pleasure. But this contention is simply wrong. By any normal reckoning, the male passengers on the Titanic would have been happier living than dying, as would other people who sacrifice their own interest to benefit others. The fact that human motivation is far more complicated than Bentham allows has important consequences for his moral and political theories. The principle of utility is ostensibly supported by universal facts of human conduct. "Nature has placed mankind under the governance of two sovereign masters, *pain* and *pleasure*." Thus it undermines the theory to call into question these universal facts. Without the support of invariable nature, it is not clear how Bentham could defend his position.

Bentham's problems here are compounded by a fundamental difficulty in his conception of utilitarianism. This is the second problem. If, as we have just seen, he defends utilitarianism according to people's natural tendencies to pursue pleasure, then it would follow that the right thing for Sam to do under given circumstances is to perform the action that brings about the greatest possible pleasure. It is important to realize that there are two different ways in which one can calculate the consequences of Sam's actions. One can calculate the consequences *for Sam himself* or *for everyone affected by the action*. In most cases, Bentham believes, there will be little difference between the two, and so it does not matter how one counts. For instance, should Sam stay in and study for a physics exam or go out with the boys? If he does the former, then he will probably gain greater pleasure over the long run, thereby benefitting himself. Society would also benefit from this course of action. Its good is nothing but the sum of the goods of its members. By increasing his own pleasure (while not diminishing that of anyone else), Sam would increase the happiness of society.

Things become more complicated when the two methods of counting yield different results. Important cases involve conflicts between what is good for an individual and for society. Assume that Stefanie can rob a bank and not get caught. On utilitarian grounds— if we assume she does not suffer enormous pangs of conscience—she should rob it, as this increases her happiness much more than not robbing it. But this conclusion holds only if we consider the calculations for Stefanie alone. (In fact, because robbing the bank is the right thing to do in this way of counting, Stefanie has no reason to feel guilty. Rather, she should feel guilty if she chooses *not* to rob the bank. This would decrease her pleasure and therefore be wrong.)

If we step back and examine this conclusion, we will probably see a problem. It contravenes our notions of right and wrong to conclude that robbing a bank is right. Or consider someone who enjoys murdering children. Because doing this increases his happiness, it is right to do. Obviously, this sort of analysis is unacceptable. When assessing an action according to its consequences, we should consider everyone it affects. Proceeding in this way, we would conclude that robbing the bank is wrong, as is also of course murdering children. Thus, it is not surprising that, in presenting the principle of utility, Bentham generally couches it in terms of the consequences for everyone affected by actions. His general standpoint is that of the legislator. Because of his interest in reforming social institutions, he looks at how society as a whole is affected by present conditions and would be affected by his proposed remedies. Thus he naturally tends to calculate in terms of the interests of all affected parties. However, though this gives what appear to be correct answers to moral questions, it raises a different problem.

If we decide whether an action is good or not according to how it affects everyone involved, then the consequences for the person who performs the act count no more than those of everyone else. Calculating in this way, we will say Stephanie's robbing the bank would be wrong. Because this accords with our overall moral views, we are likely to accept this conclusion. But the problem is explaining why she would want to perform the right act. We have seen that Stefanie benefits from robbing the bank. If people are, as Bentham says, self-interested, we can understand why she would want to rob it. But we have a much harder time explaining why she would prefer to do the right thing.

The intervention of the legislator helps Bentham with this problem. By passing laws against certain behavior and severely punishing violators, the legislator alters the costs and benefits of criminal behavior to make crime not pay. Once again, Bentham's reasoning makes sense from the community's point of view. As long as we concentrate on the community's good and how legislators can promote this, utilitarian calculations are a valuable tool—as we have seen in previous sections. Thus J. S. Mill is correct in praising Bentham's contributions to the "business part" of life: "There is the field of his greatness, and there he is indeed great" ("Bentham," p. 74). But these contributions are not without costs. We have noted that utilitarianism is grounded on the universal fact that people seek pleasure and shun pain. This is obviously in reference to their own pleasure and pain. Thus, the demand that the consequences of actions be calculated in terms of the interests of all affected people clashes with the purported psychological fact that people are always moved by what is good for themselves. There is a fundamental conflict between Bentham's observations of human behavior and the moral recommendations he grounds on these. In regard to Bentham's basic principles, John Stuart Mill remarks: "Mr. Bentham does not appear to have entered very deeply into the metaphysical grounds of these doctrines."[42] This appears to be a fair assessment, and we will see that an important element of J. S. Mill's utilitarian philosophy is filling holes Bentham left. Mill says unequivocally that, according to utilitarian principles, actions should be considered right or wrong according to their consequences for all concerned. But he realizes this principle conflicts with people's self-interest. To defuse this and other similar difficulties, J. S. Mill carefully explores the philosophical basis of utilitarianism and how it can be reformulated to make it a consistent theory.

I have saved the most important problem for last. We have noted that Bentham discards the concept of rights while developing a political theory that is otherwise similar to traditional liberalism. But discarding rights has important consequences.

According to utilitarian principles, social policies should promote society's greater good. The problem is this can often mean restricting the freedom of various individuals, especially members of minority groups. Let us assume that most members of society X are of one religion and object strongly to adherents of other faiths. They find religious practices other than their own offensive and disturbing. As long as a large majority feels this way, society would be justified in preventing the adherents of a small sect from worshipping in their preferred way. Restricting the minority's freedom of worship would cause them considerable pain. But since they are few and the large majority would be demonstrably happier, utilitarian calculations support suppression. Faced with this situation, we are likely to respond unfavorably. The minority should be allowed to worship as they please, we might say. It is their natural right. A response of this sort, however, is not open to adherents of utilitarianism, for they have discarded rights as empty verbiage.

Similar problems arise in other areas. If publication of a certain book would offend a large percentage of society, then utilitarian logic can support censorship. If certain modes of life are deeply offensive to the majority, for example, unmarried couples living together, then utilitarian logic can support laws against these practices. Innumerable other cases can be adduced.

These cases indicate an advantage of traditional liberalism that utilitarianism has trouble replicating. As we saw in our discussion of Locke, doctrines of rights are tightly bound up with the sanctity of the individual. Declaring that everyone has natural, inalienable rights expresses the fact that each person is important and occupies a protected space. His independence cannot be sacrificed for the convenience or happiness of other people, even if society would benefit from this sacrifice. Discarding rights, then, leaves the individual far more vulnerable to interference by the community. Especially if we assume that most people are strongly set in their ways and take exception to people different from themselves, utilitarianism threatens to submerge the individual in a mass, homogeneous society. Without a doctrine of rights to fall back on, the individual who wishes to be different is left vulnerable.

JOHN STUART MILL'S EDUCATION AND "ENLARGEMENT"

John Stuart Mill was born in 1806 in London. He received an "unusual and remarkable" education at the hands of his father.[43] Brought up to be the intellectual leader of the philosophical radicals, he began studying Greek at age three and Latin at eight. By the time he was ten years old, he was reading Plato (in Greek). Each day, walking with his father, he recounted what he had read the day before. He was especially fond of reading books in history, and while still a young boy began writing histories. His father, "one of the most impatient of men," was extremely stern, demanding "not only the utmost that I could do, but much that I could by no possibility have done" (*Autobiography*, p. 28). Mill had eight younger siblings, all of whom were also educated at home. Early on, he was involved in their education, and held almost as responsible for their lessons as his own (p. 31).

At the age of thirteen, Mill began studying political economy with David Ricardo's *Principles of Political Economy*. Each day he prepared a written summary of the lesson his father had delivered the previous day. These pieces served as notes for his father's *Elements of Political Economy*, which was published in 1821 (*Autobiography*, pp. 42–43).

As a result of this education, which Mill describes in fascinating detail in his *Autobiography*, he became "a mere reasoning machine" (*Autobiography*, p. 96). Mill attributes his remarkable intellectual development far more to nurture than to nature: "what I could do, could assuredly be done by any boy or girl of average capacity and healthy physical constitution: and if I have accomplished anything, I owe it all to the early training bestowed on me by my father" (*Autobiography*, p. 44). Faith in the transformative power of education is an important theme throughout Mill's works. In this regard, he follows in his father's footsteps. He notes that his father's fundamental conviction was "the formation of all human character by circumstances . . . and the consequent unlimited possibility of improving the moral and intellectual condition of mankind by education" (*Autobiography*, p. 95).

Among the tasks Mill was assigned was editing the manuscripts of Bentham's *Rationale of Judicial Evidence*, which he saw through the press in five large volumes (*Autobiography*, p. 100). He describes first reading Bentham, at age fifteen, as "an epoch in my life; one of the turning points in my mental history" (*Autobiography*, p. 66). Having been trained in "a course of Benthamism," Mill was strongly attracted to the greatest happiness principle (*Autobiography*, p. 67). Through reading Bentham, he discovered "what might truly be called an object in life; to be a reformer of the world," "a theoretical reformer of the opinions and institutions of my time" (*Autobiography*, pp. 111, 80). Mill became a philosophical adherent of Bentham's utilitarianism, around which he organized his beliefs:

> The 'principle of utility' understood as Bentham understood it, and applied in the manner in which he applied it . . . fell exactly into its place as the keystone which held together the detached and fragmentary component parts of my knowledge and beliefs. It gave unity to my conceptions of things. I now had opinions; a creed, a doctrine, a philosophy; in one among the best senses of the word, a religion; the inculcation and diffusion of which could be made the principal outward purpose of a life. (*Autobiography*, p. 68)

The intention to turn Mill into a Benthamite reformer had apparently succeeded.

When Mill was seventeen, his father secured him a position as a clerk for the East India Company. He eventually came to exercise considerable power in Indian affairs, until the dissolution of the Company in 1858 led to his retirement. Mill enjoyed his work for the Company, which also provided an ideal situation for his "private intellectual pursuits" (*Autobiography*, p. 79).

Mill's plans were thrown off course by what he calls a "mental crisis," which he experienced in 1826. He found that he had lost all joy in life, and wondered if he had entirely lost the capacity to feel. Aside from the fact that he was deeply depressed, the nature of Mill's affliction remains unclear.[44] One scholar notes that the term "mental crisis" has more serious connotations in our day than Mill intended (Robson, p. 21). Though it is frequently described as a nervous breakdown, what Mill experienced appears actually to be more the beginning of an "enlargement" of his worldview (Packe, p. 81). During his period of crisis, Mill maintained his normal routine in his post at the East India Company, in his personal relationships, and in Benthamite societies, of which he was a member. Though he functioned joylessly, he still managed to function, until he began to recover from depression with the discovery of poetry, especially the romantic poetry of Wordsworth, and the philosophy of Coleridge.

It seems that Mill's crisis was largely an *intellectual* crisis bound up with his growing realization that what he had been taught was not entirely true—or not the entire truth. His attempts to move beyond this philosophy were complicated by his relationship with his father. He still lived at home and worked beside his father at the East India Company. He also wished to spare his father the knowledge that his educational endeavors had failed (*Autobiography*, p. 113). What Mill had been taught, he now realized, was incomplete. He notes that his father's teaching "tended to the undervaluing of feeling" (*Autobiography*, p. 97). "For passionate emotions of all sorts, and for everything which has been said or written in exaltation of them, he professed the greatest contempt. He regarded them as a form of madness" (p. 56). Though aware of the great strengths of his training, Mill also became aware of having been shortchanged in important respects. His training to be a thinking machine had created distortions. As Mill came to discover his own feelings, this led to new appreciation of the emotional side of life and set before him the daunting task of integrating this into his overall philosophy. "The cultivation of the feelings became one of the cardinal points in my ethical and philosophical creed" (*Autobiography*, p. 118).

In his essay on Coleridge (published in 1840), Mill notes that the most common shortcoming of social philosophies is not that they are incorrect but that they are incomplete:

> [T]he besetting danger is not so much of embracing falsehood for truth, as of mistaking part of the truth for the whole. It might be plausibly maintained that in almost every one of the leading controversies, past or present, in social philosophy, both sides were in the right in what they affirmed, though wrong in what they denied; and that if either could have been made to take the other's views in addition to its own, little more would have been needed to make its doctrine correct.[45]

Though commentators have provided various explanations for Mill's crisis (see Packe, pp. 79–80), it is indisputable that during this period he became aware of entire areas of human experience which Benthamite philosophy, "professing to be a theory of government in general, ought to have made room for, and did not" (*Autobiography*, p. 127).

In his essay on Bentham, Mill attributes the one-sidedness of Bentham's philosophy to Bentham's lack of experience and imagination. Throughout his life, Mill argues, Bentham never knew prosperity or adversity, passion or satiety. "He knew no dejection, no heaviness of heart. He never felt life a sore and a weary burthen. He was a boy to the last" ("Bentham," p. 62). In these sentences, one can perhaps detect a comparison between Mill himself, who had passed through an emotional crisis, and Bentham, who had not.

Bentham's limitations are manifested in the view of human nature upon which his philosophy is founded: "Knowing so little of human feelings, he knew still less of the influences by which those feelings are formed; all the more subtle workings both of the mind upon itself, and of external things upon the mind, escaped him; and no one, probably, who, in a highly instructed age, ever attempted to give a rule to all human conduct, set out with a more limited conception either of the agencies by which human conduct *is*, or those by which it *should* be, influenced" ("Bentham," p. 63).

Mill believed there was little false in Bentham's philosophy. The problem was its one-sidedness. Among the principles Bentham treats inadequately are conscience, sympathy, honor, and the desire for spiritual perfection. "If he thought at all of any of the deeper feelings of human nature, it was but as idiosyncrasies of taste, with which the moralist no more than the legislator had any concern" ("Bentham," pp. 66–68).

In the poets, Coleridge, and other philosophers, Mill found what was missing in Bentham. In his essay on Coleridge, he points out the direct contrast between Coleridge's philosophy, which concentrates heavily on the emotions, and Bentham's:

> In every respect the two men are each other's 'completing counterpart': the strong points of each correspond to the weak points of the other. Whoever could master the premises and combine the methods of both, would possess the entire English philosophy of his age. ("Coleridge," p. 102)

Though it is overly simple to read Mill's future philosophical program into this quotation, something along these lines is probably at its heart. Drawing from different sources, he attempts to construct an eclectic philosophy that encompasses more of the truth than any of its constituent parts.

Thus as a result of his emotional experiences, Mill undertook an arduous process of moving beyond the philosophy of Bentham and his father. His goal was to broaden his horizons to make room for his new awareness of sentiment and emotion, the aesthetic and spiritual realms. In regard to fundamental points of Benthamism, Mill never wavered. These include emphasis on pursuing the public good through involvement in political reform and a broadly utilitarian conception of society's good. But as we will see, Mill's conception of utilitarianism is both broader and more diffuse than Bentham's.

Mill's attempt to combine the antagonistic approaches of Bentham and Coleridge is especially clear in his social and political philosophy, in which great weight is placed on the sentiments' capacity to develop. Mill believes Bentham ignored the question of *character*. With his highly limited conception of human nature, Bentham concentrated on institutions that would manage people as they are. Mill believes it is also necessary to consider processes through which people have achieved their present state—and might be led beyond it.

Thus Mill's resultant philosophy is more wide-ranging and eclectic than Bentham's. We will see this has important consequences for his political theory, in allowing him to deal with shortcomings of Bentham's more limited point of view, though it also causes difficulties in his own thought. We will concentrate on problems discussed in the previous section, especially defending individual liberty and reconciling the interests of the individual and society. We will examine the main argument in *On Liberty* in the following four sections, and then Mill's modification of utilitarian premises in the next.

ON LIBERTY

On Liberty, Mill's most enduring contribution to political theory, was published in 1859. Its epigraph is a remarkable tribute to his wife, Harriet, who had died the year before. In addition to extolling her memory, he says:

> Like all that I have written for many years, it belongs as much to her as to me; but the work as it stands has had in a very insufficient degree, the inestimable advantage of her revisions . . . Were I but capable of interpreting to the world one half the great thoughts and noble feelings which are buried in her grave, I should be the medium of a greater benefit to it, than is ever likely to arise from anything that I can write, unprompted and unassisted by her all but unrivaled wisdom.[46]

Mill met and fell in love with Harriet Taylor in 1830, when she was the wife of John Taylor. The two maintained an intense but chaste friendship for the next nineteen years, until John Taylor died in 1849. They were married two years later, and worked in collaboration until Harriet's death. In his *Autobiography*, Mill, again, speaks of her in rapturous terms. For instance, he calls her "the honor and chief blessing of my existence, as well as the source of a great part of all that I have attempted to do, or hope to effect hereafter, for human improvement" (*Autobiography*, p. 145). He notes that if she had lived during a time in which women had more opportunities, her talents would "have made her eminent among the rulers of mankind" (p. 147).

Mill describes *On Liberty* as a "joint production": "for there was not a sentence of it that was not several times gone through by us together, turned over in many ways, and carefully weeded of any faults, either in thought or expression, that we detected in it"

(*Autobiography*, p. 188). However, though there is no reason to doubt Mill's description of his wife's influence on his thinking, scholars generally believe he overestimates her intellectual gifts. In the words of Mill's brother George, who knew her well, Harriet Mill was a "clever and remarkable woman, but nothing like what John took her to be."[47] Thus in spite of the unquestioned influence of Harriet, we are probably safe in viewing *On Liberty* as essentially an expression of Mill's views and so integrally connected with his other works—though he also claimed her influence for many of these as well.

The main object of *On Liberty* is to defend a strong principle of what we have called negative freedom. We have seen that utilitarian reasoning leaves the individual, especially the member of a minority group, vulnerable to abuse at the hands of the majority—allowing this to be justified in the name of the greatest good of the greatest number. Mill argues in opposition to this possibility that the individual should always enjoy an area of protected space. The subject of the work is "the nature and limits of the power which can be legitimately exercised by society over the individual" (Chap. 1, p. 1). One will notice here that Mill is concerned with the power *society* can wield. Writing during what he viewed as a period of stifling conformism, he was as concerned with society's power to oppress as government's.

The problem, as he perceives it, is the tyranny of the majority. Though the triumph of democracy is in the process of coming about, Mill believes this will not solve the problem of individual oppression. In past ages, when the people stood opposed to the abusive power of their rulers, theorists believed that once the latter were overthrown, the people would be able to govern themselves without difficulty. But along with democratic governments, a new range of problems has emerged:

> It was now perceived that such phrases as 'self-government,' and the 'power of the people over themselves,' do not express the true state of the case. The 'people' who exercise the power are not always the same people with those over whom it is exercised; and the 'self-government' spoken of is not the government of each by himself, but of each by all the rest. . . . 'the tyranny of the majority' is now generally included among the evils against which society requires to be on its guard. (Chap. 1, p. 4)

But protection from governmental tyranny is not enough. Mill also fears the ability of the "prevailing opinion and feeling," society's tendency "to impose, by other means than civil penalties, its own ideas and practices as rules of conduct on those who dissent from them" (p. 4). Society as a whole is naturally opposed to individuality, to any mode of thought or conduct that departs from what is common. Mill holds that people are naturally bigoted and intolerant: "The practical principle which guides [people] to their opinions on the regulation of human conduct is the feeling in each person's mind that everybody should be required to act as he, and those with whom he sympathizes, would like them to act" (Chap. 1, p. 5).

In order to protect individuality from society and government, Mill attempts to establish a limit to justifiable interference. "All that makes existence valuable to anyone depends on the enforcement of restraints upon the actions of other people" (p. 5). The result is his great attempt to establish the dividing line between what is the individual's and what is society's. The result is "one very simple principle," which Mill classically expresses in the following terms:

> The object of this essay is to assert one very simple principle, as entitled to govern absolutely the dealings of society with the individual in the way of compulsion and control, whether the means used be physical force in the form of legal penalties or the moral coercion of public opinion. That principle is that the sole end for which mankind are warranted, individually or collectively, in interfering with the liberty of action of any of their number is self-protection. That the only purpose for which power can be rightfully exercised over any member of a civilized community, against his will, is to prevent harm to others. His own good, either physical or moral, is not sufficient warrant. (Chap. 1, p. 9)

Mill's aim is to distinguish two spheres. There is an area of activity that pertains solely to the individual. In this space of privacy, he should be left free from coercive interference by other people. Again, this can take either the form of government coercion or the more elusive but equally harmful coercion of public opinion. There is another part of life that pertains to society or is public. In this area society is justified in using coercion in order to make an individual conform to some standard of conduct. The distinction between the two spheres is stated again, as follows:

> The only part of the conduct of anyone for which he is amenable to society is that which concerns others. In the part which merely concerns himself, his independence is, of right, absolute. Over himself, over his own body and mind, the individual is sovereign. (p. 9)

As a utilitarian, Mill attempts to justify his principle in terms of the best interests of society. For a nonutilitarian a similar distinction between what pertains to the individual and to society can be developed on the basis of a doctrine of rights. If someone has inalienable rights in regard to some aspect of life, then his independence in this area is established. Thus if Edward has a right to the free exercise of his religion, he should be able to do this without the interference of government or society. Accordingly, the philosophical work done by a doctrine of rights is similar to what Mill attempts to accomplish through his principle. However, Mill does not wish to argue from a doctrine of rights—doubtless because of the great difficulty of establishing such a doctrine. His strategy is to support his principle on utilitarian grounds:

> It is proper to state that I forego any advantage which could be derived to my argument from the idea of abstract right as a thing independent of utility. I regard utility as the ultimate appeal on all ethical questions. (p. 10)

What is crucial, however, is that the utilitarianism he appeals to departs from the position of Bentham: "it must be utilitarianism in the largest sense, grounded on the permanent interests of man as a progressive being" (p. 10). Mill's departure from Bentham's conception of the greatest good of the greatest number is clear in this formulation. This is a subject to which we will return.

If we step back from Mill's project, we can see that it encompasses two stages. First, he must draw the necessary distinction between the spheres, between the "self-regarding" and "other-regarding," or private and public, areas of life. Then having done this, he must defend the distinction. As we have just seen, his defense is in terms of utility. He must show it is in the permanent interests of man as a progressive being that the border between the two spheres, once drawn, be respected.

Though Mill apparently assumes that the distinction between actions that are self-regarding and other-regarding is relatively clear, a moment's reflection will suggest its actual complexity. Merely by breathing Helga diminishes the amount of oxygen in a room available for other people to breathe. If her breathing affects other people, is it then other-regarding? Mill clearly wishes to exclude such cases, but where do we draw the line? If Helga takes a rifle and shoots Simone, this is clearly other-regarding behavior. But there is an enormous range of actions between breathing and shooting.

As a utilitarian, Mill looks to the consequences of acts to locate the line. Behavior is self-regarding if it does not harm other people. Other-regarding behavior is open for governmental or societal intervention because it does harm others. To protect some of its members from harm, society can limit the liberty of others. This account of the distinction between the spheres is clear in Mill's statement of the simple principle, quoted on the previous page. His claim that society can limit liberty to prevent harm and only for this reason is often referred to as the "harm principle."

To a certain extent the harm principle is grounded in common sense. If Smith is going to murder Brown, we are obviously justified in stopping him. The reason for doing so is evident. The same is true if he is going to assault Brown, to rob him, or to destroy his property. In all these cases, his actions are normally prohibited by law, and punished when they are performed. These actions are different from others, for example, taking a walk, reading a book, or sitting at home. We do not ordinarily believe it is justified to interfere with these activities. Clearly the basis for viewing the two kinds of actions differently is the need to protect people from others.

It is central to Mill's argument that the prevention of harm that justifies interference with liberty is limited to harm to *other* people. He is especially concerned with moralistic interference. If Daphne is living in a manner different from most people and these others take exception to her activities—because, in Mill's eyes, they prefer that she be like them—then they might wish to force her to conform. Toward this end, they might use either the coercive mechanisms of the state or the moral force of public opinion. In either case, Daphne will be stifled into conformity, even if she is not harming anyone else. But if she is doing no harm, how can they justify forcing her to conform? The answer to this question is often that the many believe—sincerely believe—Daphne would be better off behaving in a different way. This sort of justification has been seen throughout history, perhaps most familiarly in cases of religious persecution. Luigi is not practicing the religion of everyone else. His soul is therefore in jeopardy, and so people are justified in forcing him to worship as they do. This argument can go so far as to justify Luigi's death—killing his body to save his soul. But Mill will have none of this: a person's "own good, either physical or moral," is not a sufficient justification for interfering with his liberty (p. 9). Unless he is threatening to harm other people, Luigi must be left alone.

This rule holds regardless of what we think of people's activities. If someone appears to be living a wasteful or even self-destructive life, that is essentially his or her own business. There are unavoidable complexities here. For instance, Mill's principle implies that Brown should be let alone to drink himself into a stupor every night. Brown should not be allowed to drive when drunk—as this would constitute a danger, a potential harm, to other people.

Similarly, if he is a police officer or in the army, he should be penalized for drinking on duty because of the danger this entails (Chap. 4, p. 80). But aside from such exceptions, we should not penalize Brown's disreputable conduct. Such conduct gives us good reason to argue with him, to criticize him (Chap. 1, p. 9), and to shun his society (Chap. 4, p. 75). But compulsion is not permitted. One must note, however, that the sort of censure and general opprobrium Mill endorses in these cases is obviously closely related to the influence of public opinion he claims he wishes to combat elsewhere in the book and which he describes as the chief danger to individuality in his society. But we can set this problem aside. A case in which a person harms himself obviously calls for a different response than one in which he harms others. In the former case the evil consequences fall on himself alone, and so should be viewed as self-regarding.

Mill recognizes that a person's dissolute life-style can cause problems for others:

> When by conduct of this sort, a person is led to violate a distinct and assignable obligation to any other person or persons, the case is taken out of the self-regarding class and becomes amenable to moral disapprobation in the proper sense of the term. (Chap. 4, p. 79)

For example, if because of his drunkenness Smith is unable to pay his creditors, then he is subject not only to disapproval but to punishment. But the basis for this is not the harm he does to himself but his failure to fulfill a legal obligation. Punishment in a case of this sort is not for drunkenness but for breaking the laws of contract.

These examples suggest the complexity of attempting to draw a precise line between self- and other-regarding spheres. Generations of commentators have savaged Mill's handling of the details of the distinction. But though these considerations are of great philosophical interest, we will set them too aside temporarily. In its broad outlines, Mill's principle is reasonably clear and supported by common sense.

Mill's arguments for his principle are distinctive in requiring defense on utilitarian grounds. Consider the following case. We believe Sharon would be better off practicing religion X rather than Y. With all the goodwill in the world, we therefore wish to force her to conform to X. In response to this line of argument, many people would argue that this would violate Sharon's right to worship as she pleases. But as we have seen, Mill wishes to make his case without appeal to rights. Rather, he attempts to show it is in the best interest of society to leave Sharon alone to worship in her own way. As noted above, this promises to be no easy task. If most people are as bigoted as Mill suggests, then they will take exception to Sharon's practice of a different religion. Sharon is only one person; forcing her to conform would therefore cause relatively little pain—and would also be better for her in the long run (or so the many believe). More importantly, by forcing her to conform, they would eliminate adverse feelings of large numbers of people. Clearly, in having to defend the self-regarding sphere on utilitarian grounds, Mill has his work cut out for him.

FREEDOM OF THOUGHT AND DISCUSSION

In order to defend his distinction between the spheres, Mill attempts to demonstrate that it holds in two areas. These are liberty of conscience, which he closely associates with liberty to express and publish one's opinions, and liberty to live as one pleases. Mill also mentions but does not discuss freedom of association. He believes these liberties are essential to meaningful life: "The only freedom which deserves the name is that of pursuing our own good in our own way, so long as we do not attempt to deprive others of theirs or impede their efforts to obtain it" (Chap. 1, p. 12). These three liberties must be respected if people are to pursue their own good.

Mill's defense of freedom of thought and expression is widely viewed as one of the most forceful and eloquent in the Western tradition. He expresses its importance in powerful terms:

> If all mankind minus one were of one opinion, mankind would be no more justified in silencing that one person than he, if he had the power, would be justified in silencing mankind. (Chap. 2, p. 16)

To make his case, Mill presents three different situations, and argues that respecting freedom is better in each. The three circumstances are: (i) when the opinion society wishes to suppress is correct; (ii) when this opinion is incorrect; (iii) when the situation is complex, in that the opinion in question is partly correct and partly incorrect.

To begin with cases of the first kind, Mill supports his position with examples. Two clear instances in which persecuting a person for his opinions did not benefit society were the executions of Jesus and Socrates. In each case, the mob was convinced of the correctness of its opinion and that the views it suppressed were incorrect. But as these examples clearly illustrate, people are not infallible. Even when they are *certain* they are right, they can be wrong, and are therefore not justified in suppressing opinions opposed to their own, which after all may turn out to be true.

An even more striking case is that of Marcus Aurelius. This Emperor of the Romans was one of the wisest and most virtuous men who ever lived. But Marcus Aurelius committed the great crime of persecuting Christianity. The fact that so fine a man could be guilty of this heinous act indicates the danger inherent in all persecution. "Unless anyone who approves of punishment for the promulgation of opinions flatters himself that he is a wiser and better man than Marcus Aurelius—more deeply versed in the wisdom of his time, more elevated in his intellect above it, more earnest in his search for truth, or more singleminded in his devotion to it when found—let him abstain from that assumption of the joint infallibility of himself and the multitude which the great [Aurelius] made with so unfortunate a result" (Chap. 2, pp. 25–26).

These cases involve the persecution of truth. Perhaps it will be argued that they pose little danger to the fortunes of mankind, because in the long run truth always triumphs over persecution. Mill finds little solace in this argument. "History teems with instances of truth put down by persecution." This has been illustrated repeatedly in the history of religion. The Reformation broke out numerous times but was suppressed, before Luther eventually triumphed. Fra Dolcino, Arnold of Brescia, the Hussites, the Lollards, Savonarola, were all put down by persecution, to name only a few. Even after the time of Luther, persistent persecution was often successful. In fact, persecution has always been successful, unless the heretics were too strong to be suppressed. The one great advantage truth enjoys over error is that, being true, it may be rediscovered. Even after it is defeated by persecution, it can be found again, until it arises in circumstances propitious for its propagation (pp. 27–28).

The most celebrated portion of Mill's defense of free thought and discussion concerns the persecution of error. Even if a doctrine is incorrect, he argues, we do well to allow it to be expressed. Unless our own opinions are constantly engaged in struggle with opposing points of view, they will lose their vital force and become dead dogmas. Thus we must subject our ideas to critical scrutiny from other points of view. It is not enough to borrow the arguments of our adversaries for this purpose. In order for opposing views to be put as forcefully as possible, their actual adherents must be allowed to advance them. Famously, Mill argues: "He who knows only his own side of the case knows little of that." Even if someone has a theory that others have not been able to refute, his knowledge is thin unless supported by clear awareness of the reasoning for opposing points of view (p. 35). The fact that staunch adherents of a doctrine cease defending it against opponents helps explain why doctrines ossify into dogmas as they are passed from their discoverers—who had to defend their merits against opponents—to successors, who view them as evident truth (p. 38). Intellectual vitality depends on the clash of competing doctrines. Even if our views express the truth, we benefit from arguing their merits against people who do not accept them.

Finally, Mill argues that in the majority of cases, what is at issue is not the persecution of simple truth or simple error but a more complex state of affairs in which both sides of the argument possess some truth and some error. Through the clash of ideas in open discussion, truth is sorted from error and emerges in purified, more forceful form. "Truth in the great practical concerns of life, is so much a question of the reconciling and combining of opposites that very few have minds sufficiently capacious and impartial to make the adjustment with an approach to correctness, and it has to be made by the rough process of a struggle between combatants fighting under hostile banners" (pp. 45–46).

Mill's three cases constitute a powerful defense of freedom of thought and expression. He presents good reasons to believe allowing all comers to enter the intellectual arena will promote important values. Not only will truth be sorted from error through the open interchange of ideas, but people will lead more active intellectual lives, as they think through their theories anew to meet the challenge of forceful opponents. Contrasting his vision of an intellectually vital society with one in which the dead hand of state power stifles intellectual initiative, Mill makes a strong case for the advantages of the former.

In spite of his advocacy of free thought and discussion, Mill recognizes necessary exceptions. Under some circumstances, forms of speech can lead to immediate public harm and must be prevented:

> [E]ven opinions lose their immunity when the circumstances in which they are expressed are such as to constitute their expression a positive instigation to some mischievous act. An opinion that corn dealers are starvers of the poor, or that private property is robbery, ought to be unmolested when simply circulated through the press, but may justly incur punishment when delivered orally to an excited mob assembled before the house of a corn dealer, or when handed about among the same mob in the form of a placard. (Chap. 3, p. 53)

What distinguishes this case from the others Mill discusses is the direct harm to which speech would contribute. This is not merely a matter of expressing opinion but of harming others. The opinion to which Mill objects is voiced to an angry mob and helps incite it to riot. It follows from Mill's principles that other sorts of speech should also be prevented.

These include false advertising, libel, and perjury. In each of these cases, specific persons are directly harmed by the speech in question. But absent the clear harms associated with this range of cases, Mill presents an eloquent defense of free thought and discussion.

INDIVIDUALITY

In the same way that a proliferation of competing doctrines benefits society, people also gain from a wide variety of modes of life. Mill argues that "free scope should be given to varieties of character." A range of different "experiments of living," is therefore desirable, once again, as long as this is not injurious to others (Chap. 3, p. 54). We can refer to the value under discussion here as "individuality." What Mill has in mind is people's ability to live and act as they please, as long as they do not harm others in doing so.

Mill has two main arguments to support individuality. First, great advances in society generally come about through the efforts of exceptional, creative individuals. Mill's estimation of the general run of men is not high. In intellectual matters most people must be led. "There is always need of persons not only to discover new truths and point out when what were once truths are true no longer, but also to commence new practices and set the example of more enlightened conduct and better taste and sense in human life" (Chap. 3, p. 61). Though people with the requisite potential are few and far between, they are "the salt of the earth; without them, human life would become a stagnant pool" (p. 61). The ability to develop in interesting ways is beyond the reach of most people. Their "glory" is ability to follow the lead of the guiding few, "to respond internally to wise and noble things, and be led to them" willingly (p. 64).

In order for exceptional individuals to arise in society, they must be insulated from the stifling effects of public opinion. They must be allowed to live as they like, even if this is different from the way most people live. "Genius can only breathe freely in an *atmosphere* of freedom. Persons of genius are [by definition] more individual than any other people— less capable, consequently, of fitting themselves, without hurtful compression, into any of the small number of molds which society provides in order to save its members the trouble of forming their own character" (p. 62).

This argument is straightforward, but we should realize it depends on questionable factual assertions. Once again, because he is not able to appeal to people's right to be left alone, Mill must show that leaving them alone benefits society. Thus he argues that important innovations come from exceptional people, and that in order to do their work, these people must be allowed to live as they please. If we think about these assertions, it will become clear that the evidence for them is not overpowering. In regard to scientific advances, for instance, it is not clear that allowing potential inventors to practice unusual lifestyles is necessary for their work. For instance, many scientists appear to be quite ordinary members of society, without interesting habits or styles of life. Because we can presume highly intolerant members of society experience some discomfort at being exposed to alternative life-styles, the burden is upon Mill to show that allowing these is necessary for important innovations. In addition, even if an area of freedom is necessary for exceptional people, this does little to justify freedom for people who are not exceptional. A stronger case for unusual life-styles could perhaps be made on the basis of the benefits of "experiments in living," the life-styles themselves. But to do this Mill must show that alternative ways of living significantly benefit society. People who live on communes or practice bohemian styles of life are certainly different from average middle-class citizens. But it is not clear that these differences benefit many people other than those who practice them.

Mill's second argument is that allowing people to live as they please is necessary for their own development. In order for a person to develop fully, to achieve her complete potential, she must be able to make her own choices. To "conform to custom merely *as* custom" does not help an individual develop any of the endowments distinctive of a human being (p. 56). Mill's argument here is teleological in the Aristotelian sense.[48] Man has attributes and capacities that are distinctively human and have the potential to develop. "Human nature is not a machine to be built after a model, and set to do exactly the work prescribed for it, but a tree, which requires to grow and develop itself on all sides, according to the tendency of the inward forces which make it a living thing" (pp. 56–57).

In order for human capacities to attain their full development, they must be exercised. The moral faculties are like muscles which develop only through being used. Thus if someone is to achieve his full potential, he must be left alone to exercise his capacity to choose. His choices may be incorrect according to some standard or other, but even in making undesirable choices, people develop important parts of themselves. A person who blindly follows choices other people make might do the right thing (whatever we mean by that) but will not achieve his full potential. In addition to what people do, Mill is concerned with the kind of people they are:

> It really is of importance, not only what men do, but also what manner of men they are that do it. Among the works of man which human life is rightly employed in perfecting and beautifying, the first in importance is surely man himself. (p. 56)

Mill presents a distinctive view of human life as a process of self-development. If development is indeed a human imperative, then people must have the opportunity to strike out on their own. If self-development requires exercising the capacity to choose, then there are strong grounds for leaving people alone to make their own choices.

An argument of this kind is familiar in regard to raising children. In order for children to develop properly, it is often said, they must be allowed the opportunity to try new things, to make their own choices, and unfortunately to fail. From the experience of failure, people are able to learn and to improve, and so to achieve a higher standard in the future. The alternative to allowing children to fend for themselves is cultivating unhealthy dependency. The sheltered child grows up unable to think for himself, to do things for himself. In cowering before the world, he leads a less exalted life than the person who achieves the ability to stand on his own as an autonomous being.

Though an argument like this is familiar, and doubtless persuasive, we must realize that it rests on the controversial claim that human beings have somehow been assigned a certain potential which they are intended to achieve. Mill realizes this is an essentially religious assumption:

> [I]f it be any part of religion to believe that man was made by a good Being, it is more consistent with that faith to believe that this Being gave all human faculties that they might be cultivated and unfolded, not rooted out and consumed, and that he takes delight in every nearer approach made by his creatures to the ideal conception

embodied in them, every increase in any of their capabilities of comprehension, of action, or of enjoyment. (Chap. 3, p. 59)

The distance Mill has traveled from his Benthamite starting point is evident in his appeal to religion to shore up his argument.

SOCIETY AND THE INDIVIDUAL

Setting aside for now the religious aspects of Mill's thought, we can see the powerful implications of his argument. Once the line between self- and other-regarding conduct has been established, Mill presents strong grounds for respecting individuals' privacy within the self-regarding sphere. This is essential if they are to develop their full potential and will contribute to the overall vibrancy and tenor of society. In many cases, however, the distinction between spheres is not hard and fast, and important problems arise. Some of these are raised by Mill in *On Liberty*. I will briefly touch on a few examples to illustrate these problems and how he deals with them.

To begin with, we have seen that liberty cannot be infringed for a person's own good. But is this rule inviolable? Clearly, we cannot force Carlos to stop smoking out of concern for his health. But Mill employs a famous example to indicate circumstances under which interference is warranted:

> [I]t is a proper office of public authority to guard against accidents. If either a public officer or anyone else saw a person attempting to cross a bridge which had been ascertained to be unsafe, and there were no time to warn him of his danger, they might seize him and turn him back, without any real infringement of his liberty; for liberty consists in doing what one desires, and he does not desire to fall into the river. (Chap. 5, p. 95)

In this case, we should interfere with the bridge-crosser's liberty in order to comply with his presumed wishes. Under the assumption he does not wish to fall into the river, we can tackle him to prevent this. Similar reasoning would support administering CPR to an unconscious accident victim. Presumably, she would like to live. In a more complex case, this kind of reasoning would justify treating a mentally deranged patient, even if at the present time he does not wish to be tampered with. Presumably, his rational self (or recovered self) would wish to be treated. Like the bridge-crosser, he would probably be grateful to his rescuers once he had recovered.

Related cases cause problems in existing society. Many countries have laws requiring use of automobile seatbelts and motorcycle helmets. Perhaps if Smith knew the facts about the life-saving potential of seatbelts, he would wear them. Thus requiring him to wear them is arguably consistent with his wishes, in this case the wishes he would have if he were fully informed. Unfortunately, however, it is not clear Smith would change his mind if he had this information. Many people who are aware of the facts still prefer not to wear seatbelts. Since they are subject to legal penalties for this behavior, does this violate Mill's strictures?

Another of Mill's well-known examples concerns a person who wishes to use his liberty to put an end to it:

> In this and most other civilized countries . . . an engagement by which a person should sell himself, or allow himself to be sold, as a slave would be null and void, neither enforced by law nor by opinion. The ground for thus limiting his power of voluntarily disposing of his own lot in life is apparent, and is very clearly seen in this extreme case. (Chap. 5, p. 101)

In this case too, Mill argues for interference:

> The reason for not interfering, unless for the sake of others, with a person's voluntary acts is consideration for his liberty. . . . But by selling himself for a slave, he abdicates his liberty; he forgoes any future use of it beyond that single act. He therefore defeats, in his own case, the very purpose which is the justification of allowing him to dispose of himself. (p. 101)

Mill's reasoning here is not entirely clear. Perhaps the problem is that the man sells himself into slavery. Mill is apparently bothered by the fact that, through one use of autonomy, the subject surrenders it for all time. Thus this contract must be disallowed, not only because it is an abdication of liberty but because of its permanence. Presumably, Mill would not object to a transaction through which someone abdicated his liberty temporarily, for example, for a five-year period. According to Mill's principles, it might seem that a series of five-year contracts through which Alice sells herself into slavery would be acceptable, even if the effect is lifelong slavery. However, according to an alternative interpretation, what Mill objects to in the passage is not that Alice sells herself into slavery, but that the transaction is a contract, in other words, an agreement enforceable by law. Thus in this case, the state assists Alice in renouncing her liberty.[49]

The overall thrust of these and other cases is clear-cut, though particular cases raise troublesome issues.[50] It is not clear that all Mill's arguments in regard to difficult cases are consistent, or supportable from his distinctive utilitarian point of view. But clearly, the overall thrust of his arguments is to create a strong presumption against the state's or the community's interference in individual liberty. Mill's great effort to carve out an inviolable private sphere of life and his eloquent defense of it in various troublesome cases have provided starting points for informed discussion of many of these issues to the present day.

MILL'S *UTILITARIANISM*

Powerful and persuasive as Mill's argument in *On Liberty* is, it is also beset with a hornet's nest of problems. His defense of the self-regarding area rests on controversial assumptions, some of which he would have trouble defending in detail. Other points raise theoretical issues, especially concerning the overall consistency of his philosophy. Important problems can be seen if we compare Mill's view and a more straightforward Benthamite mode of analysis.

In arguing that people should be free to live as they please, Mill, like Bentham, defends liberty because of its consequences, rather than as good in itself. But these consequences are in terms of "utility in the largest sense, grounded on the permanent interests of man as a progressive being" (*On Liberty*, Chap. 1, p. 10). Mill's defense of free thought and expression and individuality depends on this interpretation of utility. On a Benthamite understanding of utility, his argument would be in jeopardy. Certain problem cases have been noted. If people are as fiercely intolerant as Mill avers, they will object strenuously when others practice different life-styles—modes of living that depart from "community standards." Assume that Jones is a polygamist, living with six wives. People will be deeply offended by this, and will find it distressing to have Jones living among them. The same would be true if Grey pursued unusual sexual practices, or Green propagated beliefs widely at variance with those of her neighbors. For instance, suppose she strenuously maintained that the Holocaust never took place, even though some of her neighbors and their families were victims of it? Her propaganda would infuriate her neighbors and perhaps cause significant distress. On any usual understanding of "pain," people in the community would find the activities of Jones, Grey, and Green painful. On Benthamite grounds, then, their behavior can be prevented, as long as the additional pleasure they gain from their activities is outweighed by the distress they cause. To defend liberty in these cases, Mill must develop a mode of analysis different from Bentham's.

Mill of course believes Bentham's approach is flawed. These cases are exactly the kind he wishes to protect. As long as the self-regarding/other-regarding distinction is respected, he has no trouble deriving the proper conclusions. In Chapter 4 of *On Liberty*, he notes that certain people are pained when others act differently: "There are many who consider as an injury to themselves any conduct which they have a distaste for, and resent it as an outrage to their feelings; as a religious bigot, when charged with disregarding the religious feelings of others, has been known to retort that they disregard his feelings by persisting in their abominable worship or creed" (pp. 81–82). As examples, Mill discusses Moslems who are repelled at the sight of Christians eating pork, Spaniards who are pained by the practice of any religion other than Roman Catholicism, and New England Puritans, who object to public amusement, for example, dancing, music, theater. Another example is the intense reaction called forth by Mormons, especially in regard to their practice of polygamy, "which, though permitted to Mohammedans, and Hindus, and Chinese, seems to excite unquenchable animosity when practiced by persons who speak English and pro-fess to be a kind of Christian" (Chap. 4, p. 89). Mill believes these examples show the need for his distinction. Because people generally feel that what they think is right is right, they will often suppress conduct different from their own.

In approaching these cases, Mill does not attempt to compare the consequences of tolerating and suppressing offensive practices. Rather, applying his distinction, he argues that the feelings of the offended majority should not count:

> [T]here is no parity between the feelings of a person for his own opinion and the feelings of another who is offended at his holding it, no more than between the desire of a thief to take a purse and the desire of the right owner to keep it. (Chap. 4, p. 82)

Along similar lines, the offending practices cannot be prohibited for the practitioners' own good. The desire to make others religious must be guarded against, as this has justified religious persecution throughout history (Chap. 4, p. 84). Thus Mill's arguments strongly support freedom of religion in these troublesome cases.

It is interesting, however, that Mill presents a range of cases in which majority sentiment should prevail. These concern offenses against public decency:

> [T]here are many acts which, being directly injurious only to the agents themselves, ought not to be legally interdicted, but which if done publicly are a violation of good manners and, coming thus within the category of offenses against others, may rightly be prohibited. Of this kind are offenses against decency; on which it is unnecessary to dwell, the rather as they are only connected indirectly with our subject, the objection to publicity being equally strong in the case of many actions not in themselves condemnable, nor supposed to be so. (p. 97)

Presumably, among acts not condemnable unless performed in public, Mill would include various sexual acts and nudity. He believes these should be subject to legal penalty if done in public.

Mill's discussion here raises a series of problems. To begin with, one must wonder why he is more solicitous of community sentiments in regard to public decency than other matters such as religion. The reason to penalize public nudity is because it makes people uncomfortable. But many people are equally uncomfortable at the sight of others eating pork. In the former case Mill views community standards as important enough to justify coercive sanctions, while in the latter he does not. Exactly why this is true remains unclear. Perhaps the problem with public nudity is that it is thrust on people in an unavoidable way. Jones's nudity at home is his own business; if Green looks into his window and is made uncomfortable, that is the latter's fault. But when Jones carries his nudity into public areas, people simply going about their business are confronted with it and feel uncomfortable.[51] But if the publicness of offensive behavior is the problem, one must wonder why offensive religious practices should not be similarly driven underground. If Moslems object to Christians eating pork, one could see good grounds for allowing them to do this only in private. Or to take another case, if a majority in society are made uncomfortable by polygamy, should this be allowed? Or should it be permitted as long as it is practiced only in private? These are sticky issues; because Mill does not present his reasoning in detail, we are left to wonder how he could defend his position.

Aside from cases of public decency, Mill argues strenuously in favor of granting minorities freedom of thought and expression and to live as they please. His resulting vision of society is thus quite different from Bentham's. While Bentham argues in terms of increasing people's pleasure, with little regard for different kinds of pleasure or the sources from which it derives, Mill believes some values are clearly preferable to others. Looking back on his defense of freedom of thought and expression, we can see that this is largely in terms of the preservation of intellectual vitality and the propagation of truth. Protecting each person's rights to think and say what she wishes leads to a society in which these values are in greater supply than they would be otherwise. Mill's defense of individuality is largely in terms of allowing people to develop their intellectual faculties as much as possible. Clearly, these values correspond to the "permanent interests of man as a progressive being." To make sense of the distinction between protecting the public practice of religion, but not such things as nudity, Mill would probably appeal to the far greater significance of the former values. In basing his position on what he views as important values, rather than simple Benthamite calculations of how people feel, Mill clearly departs from Bentham's utilitarianism. Though the philosophical implications of Mill's new position are not developed in *On Liberty*, they are spelled out in his work *Utilitarianism*, first published in 1861.

Two arguments of *Utilitarianism* are of special concern to us here. First, Mill introduces an important innovation into his moral theory. He complains that utilitarianism is commonly viewed as a crude philosophy which, in postulating pleasure as the end of life, likens human existence to that of animals, for example, swine. Mill argues for the qualitative superiority of some pleasures to others. While many utilitarians favor mental pleasures over physical, they generally support this superiority in terms of the former's greater permanence, security, and lower cost. Mill believes a case can also be made for their higher *quality*. "It is quite compatible with the principle of utility to recognize the fact that some kinds of pleasure are more desirable and more valuable than others. It would be absurd that, while in estimating all other things quality is considered as well as quantity, the estimation of pleasure should be supposed to depend on quantity alone" (*Utilitarianism*, Chap. 2, p. 8).

Mill believes some pleasures are better than others if they involve the employment of higher faculties. Thus mental pleasures are higher than the physical. Mill is especially interested in the pleasures of a cultivated mind, which can appreciate "the objects of nature, the achievements of art, the imaginations of poetry, the incidents of history, the ways of man-kind, past and present, and their prospects in the future" (p. 14). His proof that these pleasures are qualitatively superior to those of the lower faculties is that people who have experienced both kinds of pleasures invariably prefer the former. However, though Mill claims this is an "unquestionable fact" (p. 9), his argument is widely criticized. According to John Plamenatz, Mill's argument "carries no conviction at all."[52] It is not clear people who have experienced both physical and mental pleasures always prefer the former. What is more, even if people who have experienced both pleasures claim to prefer the former, we can ask if they have *really* experienced the latter in the same way as other people. Mill's argument depends on the assumption that pleasures possess objective inherent qualities and so strike all who experience them in exactly the same way. Thus if ten people are asked if a six-foot man is taller than a three-foot child, they are likely to agree. But preferences notoriously vary. As Plamenatz says, "No man has ever known the pleasures experienced by another." If Socrates preferred philosophy to sensuality, how do we know this was not merely because of the sort of man he was, because of distinctive characteristics of his nervous system?[53] Even if all people who have experienced both kinds of pleasures prefer the mental, it is not clear what this proves. Arguably, this would merely show that it takes a certain kind of person to ascend to the intellectual realm and experience its pleasures. Even if people who make this ascent prefer these pleasures to others, one must ask why other people, who are so constituted that they do not enjoy intellectual activities, should set aside their own preferences to pursue these. This is especially clear if they are so constituted that they enjoy physical pleasures more. Mill has not established the crucial premise that all human beings are alike and so what one group enjoys all other people will as well.

The qualitative superiority of higher to lower pleasures is essential to many of Mill's arguments in *On Liberty*. If some pleasures are better than others, then the life of a person who pursues them is qualitatively superior to that of someone who does not. "Thus it is better to be a human being dissatisfied than a pig satisfied; better to be Socrates dissatisfied than a fool satisfied." The pig and the fool might not agree with these assessments. But that is because "they only know their own side of the question. The other party knows both sides" (*Utilitarianism*, Chap. 2, p. 10). The only true judge is someone who has experience with the entire range of entities being judged. The fact that the man and Socrates prefer *failing* to gain the intellectual pleasures to attaining the physical indicate how far Mill has come from the position of Bentham. Caring only for greater quantities of happiness, Bentham declares: "Call them soldiers, call them monks, call them machines, so long as they be happy ones, I shall not care."[54]

In spite of its problems, Mill's distinction between qualitative and quantitative aspects of pleasures allows him to demonstrate the superiority of certain activities to others. Because cultivating the intellectual faculties leads to a superior life, the connection with *On Liberty* should be clear. If liberty is necessary for the development of higher faculties, it must be protected. Self-regarding activities must be defended for the sake of higher pleasures. Even if a society in which the distinction is not respected and a stifling conformity is enforced on all inhabitants is happier in strictly quantitative terms, this is not true superiority. Its people lead a lower form of life and so enjoy a lesser form of happiness than they could otherwise achieve. As we saw above,

> It really is of importance, not only what men do, but also what manner of men they are that do it. Among the works of man which human life is rightly employed in perfecting and beautifying, the first in importance surely is man himself. (*On Liberty*, Chap. 3, p. 56)

Once again, the extent of Mill's departure from Bentham's view is striking. As we see from this quotation, he substitutes an essentially aesthetic account of human happiness for the greatest good of the greatest number.

A second aspect of utilitarianism worth noting is Mill's attempt to reconcile the interests of the individual and society. This is a further problem in Bentham's position, which we have discussed (see pp. 340–41). Mill believes the higher pleasures are not confined to the intellect. Among the higher faculties he also includes what he calls "noble" sentiments, which center on concern for other people. We saw above that Bentham has trouble deciding in which of the two possible ways utilitarian agents should count pleasures. In assessing the value of a particular act, should the agent consider only the consequences for himself alone, or those for everyone involved? Mill answers unequivocally that the "standard is not the agent's own greatest happiness, but the greatest happiness altogether." In calculating the consequences of an action, the utilitarian agent should not ignore how it affects his own welfare, but he should give this no more weight than the consequences for anyone else (*Utilitarianism*, Chap. 2, pp. 11, 16). In discussing Bentham, we encountered a problem with this sort of standard. Bentham's utilitarianism is grounded on fundamental laws of human nature. Because the laws in question depict behavior as self-interested, Bentham is hard-pressed to explain why a person with the characteristics he envisions would be willing to set aside his own good in favor of the public good.

Mill's more complex view of pleasure provides an answer. Nobility of character, as he uses the term, is closely related to altruism. Among the higher pursuits that constitute the life of qualitatively superior pleasure Mill includes development of the noble sentiments. With the cultivation of these, people become willing to do what is good for society rather than for themselves alone. Because the pleasures they derive are superior to those of self-indulgence, they lead more exalted lives and so are happier. Among the psychological attributes to which Mill appeals are the social feelings and conscience. He argues that the social state "is at once so natural, so necessary, and so habitual to man, that, except in some unusual circumstances or by an effort of voluntary abstraction, he never conceives himself otherwise than as a member of a body" (Chap. 3, p. 37). As these attitudes are intensified in society and become increasingly widespread, private good and public good are reconciled, and all are better off.

In spite of the great advantages of Mill's version of utilitarianism, it has important weaknesses. We can briefly examine some of these, to close this section.

To begin with, introducing distinctions between higher and lower pleasures and emphasizing the development of human capacities greatly complicates the tasks utilitarianism was originally intended to accomplish. It is obvious that Mill's utilitarianism departs from the rigors of Bentham's social science. We have seen that Bentham wished to purge moral discourse, and especially the reasoning behind public policies, of imprecise and arbitrary notions. As examples, we have examined his assaults on natural law and natural rights, custom, and related conceptions, such as moral judgments based on sentiments of approval and disapproval. In order to establish a rigorous science of legislation, Bentham requires a moral theory that admits of precision and so excludes such things. Accordingly, Mill's distinctions between higher and lower pleasures and higher and lower human faculties threaten to muddy the waters. Consider the striking passage with which we closed a previous section:

> [I]f it be any part of religion to believe that man was made by a good Being, it is more consistent with that faith to believe that this Being gave all human faculties that they might be cultivated and unfolded, not rooted out and consumed, and that he takes delight in every nearer approach made by his creatures to the ideal conception embodied in them, every increase in any of their capabilities of comprehension, of action, or of enjoyment. (*On Liberty*, Chap. 3, p. 59)

In opening the doors of utilitarianism to metaphysical and religious conceptions, Mill threatens to reintroduce into morality the entire range of abstract notions against which Bentham fought. Religious notions are inherently imprecise and subjective. Mill would have a difficult time demonstrating the truth of his religious view to people who were inclined to doubt it. As we have seen, moreover, language of this sort cannot be attributed to inadvertence. The points expressed in the passage are central to the argument of *On Liberty*, which depends on the superior worth of the higher faculties.

Along similar lines, introducing the distinction between higher and lower pleasures into utilitarianism makes it a far less effective means for deciding issues of public policy. In addition to some policy's effects on the people involved, one must also consider questions of quality. The simple calculus Bentham recommends is no longer so simple. Consider once again the question of where to place the bypass that is to be built around a city. In addition to the considerations noted above—how much time will be saved with different routes, how many people will be inconvenienced by construction, for how long, and so on—we must also worry about questions of quality. In this case, perhaps, different bypass routes will affect the scenic environment differently. According to Mill's criteria, we might argue that the pleasures of beauty are qualitatively higher than those associated with commuting less each day. Thus a case can be made for building the bypass where it damages the surroundings less, or perhaps where it will provide the most beautiful ride for people who travel it. What is especially troublesome about introducing this new variable is having to weigh it against other factors. Because it is qualitatively different from other factors, it cannot be weighed directly against them, as other aspects of Bentham's variables can be. What is more, different people are likely to disagree about the importance of natural beauty in a case such as this, and so will weight them differently. In providing the basis for new and intractable disagreements, Mill's distinction between higher and lower pleasures threatens to undermine the scientific method of resolving questions of policy to the establishment of which Bentham devoted much of his life.

MILL'S LIBERALISM

As a way of reviewing the aspects of Mill's political theory we have discussed so far, we can look briefly at the extent to which his position conforms to classical liberalism. The essence of liberal theory has been discussed above. To begin with, we can see that Mill departs from the initial claim. According to liberal theory, the individual is the building block of society. The individual is also taken to be rational and self-interested. In arguing that the individual is prior to society, liberal theorists commonly fill this out to mean that the individual's goals and interests exist without extensive input from society. Thus Hobbes's individual wishes to preserve himself; Locke's has rights and property he wishes to protect; Bentham's pursues pleasure. Mill's case is more complex. In arguing that the individual has the potential to develop in society, and in supporting this position with the distinction between higher and lower pleasures, Mill has society play an important role in shaping individual ends. Thus the strong separation between individual and society commonly found in liberal theory is largely eroded by Mill. In order to develop properly, Mill's individual is a social creature. In addition, in *Utilitarianism* especially, Mill argues that the individual is naturally bound to other people through his social feelings. While classical liberals view society as a sum of individuals, and its interests as a numerical sum of the interests of its members, Mill once again presents a more complex picture, with the individual and society closely bound. There is, however, no hint in Mill's thought that the interests of society can be anything other than the interests of its inhabitants, regardless of the differences between Mill and classical liberals in regard to how these are conceived.

The third claim of classical liberals is that the state is instrumental; that is, people regard it as a means to the attainment of preexisting ends. Here too, Mill departs from the standard view. Once again, people's higher faculties require society in order to develop. Thus society is clearly not instrumental. If we grant Mill a strong separation between society and the state, we could perhaps argue that he still views politics as instrumental. However, in his work *Considerations on Representative Government*, which we have not discussed in this chapter, he argues that participation in political activity can have valuable educational effects.[55]

The state as Mill envisions it is in a process of transformation. To some extent, this is a result of the time at which he wrote. But because of his interest in education, which is once again necessary if the higher faculties are to develop, he departs from the standard liberal view here as well.

The final point, in regard to freedom, is more straightforward. Classical liberals uphold the values of negative freedom, of an absence of coercive interference by other people. Mill's *On Liberty* is of course a great classic in propagating this value. Though he abjures arguments from natural rights, Mill presents a classic account and a classic defense of the distinction between what is the individual's alone and what can properly be claimed by the state. The situation is perhaps complicated by the fact that his emphasis on education and the development of human potential could justify interference for these purposes. But aside from this, and in spite of the complexities of his position in regard to the first four points discussed above, Mill's eloquent defense of a sphere of private life free from interference by state and society makes him a major figure in the liberal tradition.

THE SUBJECTION OF WOMEN

Mill wrote *The Subjection of Women* in the winter of 1860–1861, two years after Harriet Taylor's death. Waiting for a more favorable climate of public opinion, he did not publish it until 1869. The work has been largely overlooked by scholars. It is mentioned only once by John Robson, in his fine book on Mill's social and political thought (Robson, p. 55). In his general book on Mill, Alan Ryan has a chapter called "*Liberty* and *The Subjection of Women*." But of its thirty-four pages, the former work receives about twenty-nine pages and the latter only five. In his general treatment of Mill's philosophy, R. P. Anschutz never mentions the work,[56] while this was the only one of Mill's books on which his publisher lost money (Packe, p. 497). The work is, however, worthy of note. Aside from the great interest in issues concerning the treatment of women that has arisen in recent years, *Subjection* sets Mill apart from other important figures in the history of political theory, including Hobbes and Locke, who drew back from the individualistic implications of their theories in regard to the status of women.[57] Earlier in this chapter, we encountered the similar failing of James Mill. Even Rousseau, highly radical as he is, upholds a traditional view of women's rightful subordination to men (see pp. 250–4). In *Subjection*, Mill develops his main moral and political principles to uphold women's equality. The fact that he pursues the implications of his principles in this area is itself worthy of note. In her important study, *Women in Western Political Thought*, Susan Okin writes: "John Stuart Mill is the only major liberal political philosopher to have set out explicitly to apply the principles of liberalism to women" (Okin, p. 197).

Subjection of Women is the product of Mill's longstanding opposition to the unequal treatment of women. As part of his program of political reform, he supported giving women the vote, and thus viewed his father's retreat in this area as a great error (*Autobiography*, p. 93). One reason he was attracted to the writings of various socialist authors was their espousal of the "perfect equality of men and women, and an entirely new order of things in regard to their relations." Mill believed these views earned these authors "the grateful remembrance of future generations" (*Autobiography*, p. 134). In his brief career in electoral politics, Mill acted on his convictions. While representing Westminster in Parliament, to which he was elected in 1865, he attempted to amend the second Reform Act of 1867 to include women's suffrage. This was the first time the question of women's right to vote was debated in the legislature of a modern country. Though Mill's motion failed, it attracted seventy-three votes (Packe, p. 492). In his *Autobiography*, Mill describes this as "the only really important public service I performed in the capacity of a Member of Parliament" (p. 222). Mill's wife, Harriet Taylor, was also a strong supporter of women's emancipation. Her pamphlet, *The Enfranchisement of Women*, which was published under Mill's name, presents views that are more radical than those expressed in *Subjection* (Okin, pp. 229–230). However, Mill's own ideas were actually more radical than *Subjection* indicates. To avoid causing a sensation, he omitted his ideas on divorce and birth control from the work (Okin, p. 203).

In *Subjection*, Mill criticizes the treatment of women in his society on a variety of grounds. The core of his case is that existing arrangements stifle women, causing both them and men to lead far less happy lives than they might otherwise. In his words, "the legal subordination of one sex to the other" is both "wrong in itself, and now one of the chief hindrances to human improvement." He believes this should be replaced by "perfect equality, admitting no power or privilege on the one side, nor disability on the other" (*Subjection*, Chap. 1, p. 119).

As presented by Mill, the situation of women in his society is clearly dire. A woman's legal position is likened to that of a "bondservant" (Chap. 2, p. 147). When married, she has no rights to property. Her property belongs to her husband, including property she inherits. Husband and wife are "one person in law" (Chap. 2, p. 148). Children are the husband's, not the wife's; by law they are *his* children (p. 148). Women have few rights against their husbands. Divorce is extremely difficult to attain. If physically abused, women are returned to the custody of the abuser, though Mill notes some slight progress toward protecting women in recent years (p. 152). According to old English law, the husband was referred to as the wife's *lord*, literally her sovereign. Accordingly, murdering one's husband was treason, and more cruelly punished, by burning, than other murders (p. 147). Women have few political rights, and notably lack the right to vote. Not having opportunities for gainful employment, they are induced to marry for lack of alternatives. The only choice women have is Hobson's choice: that or nothing (Chap. 1, p. 145). Because of their dependence on men, women must learn to please them. The main object of their education and training is how to be attractive to men and to gain a secure place in their affections.

Because of women's subordinate position, Mill refers to the family as a "school of despotism" (Chap. 2, p. 160). In order to account for existing domestic relations, he turns to history. In the distant past, the normal rule of human life was force. "People are not aware how entirely, in former ages, the law of superior strength was the rule of life; how publicly and openly it was avowed" (Chap. 1, p. 125). Physically weaker than men, women were placed in a "state of bondage" to them (Chap. 1, p. 123). Over the course of centuries, the dominance of force has been removed from successive areas of life. Slavery has been abolished—though in some countries only recently. Political relationships have retreated from the absolute rule of divinely appointed monarchs, and are coming to be viewed as between equals. Only in relationships between men and women is this not the case. Women's subordination to men "is the primitive state of slavery lasting on, through successive mitigations and modifications" (Chap. 1, p. 123). "The social subordination of women thus stands out an isolated fact in modern social institutions; a solitary breach of what has become their fundamental law; a single relic of an old world of thought and practice exploded in everything else but retained in the one thing of most universal interest" (Chap. 1, p. 137).

Because this is the way things have always been, people view it as natural. Existing subordination of women is justified by the belief that nature has made men masters and women their virtual servants. Thus nature has shaped the sexes differently, fitting them to their roles. It is not surprising that men easily accept this view: "Was there ever any domination which did not appear natural to those who possessed it?" (Chap. 1, p. 129). Mill refers to "all the fanaticism with which men cling to their theories that justify their passions and legitimate their personal interests" (p. 128). But because of the power of education and indoctrination, existing relationships are generally accepted by women as well. Though there are exceptions, women's vulnerable position has heavily influenced their thinking. Instead of railing against the injustice of the existing relationships, each complains about her own husband—without understanding the wider implications (Chap. 1, p. 132).

Central to *Subjection* is Mill's deflation of popular prejudice. To the claim that existing arrangements are natural, Mill responds they are only customary. "The subjection of women to men being a universal custom, any departure from it quite naturally appears unnatural" (Chap. 1, p. 130). Because of the pervasive power of education and cultural forces, Mill argues that women's *nature* cannot be known in existing society. Existing relationships between men and women, and those witnessed in past societies, do not reflect necessities of nature but the results of social arrangements:

> I deny that any one knows, or can know, the nature of the two sexes, as long as they have only been seen in their present relation to one another . . . What is now called the nature of women is an eminently artificial thing—the result of forced repression in some directions, unnatural stimulation in others. (Chap. 1, p. 138)

All senses in which women are different from and inferior to men have resulted from their being denied the same education and experiences men have had. In addition, women have acquired a range of personality traits needed to make the best of their bad situation. Most important is submissiveness: "All women are brought up from the very earliest years in the belief that their ideal of character is the very opposite to that of men; not self-will, and government by self-control, but submission, and yielding to the control of others" (Chap. 1, p. 132).

Rejecting the claims of invariable nature, Mill argues that the treatment of women should be assessed according to its consequences for society. The fact that women are so universally subordinate would carry more weight if other arrangements had been tried, and found less beneficial. But the way things are is not the result of comparative investigation but a residue of primitive rule by force (Chap. 1, pp. 122–123). Application of utilitarian standards clearly indicates the preferability of other arrangements. As things stand, the subordination of women is a source of great evils, analogous to those associated with slavery. "The sufferings, immoralities, evils of all sorts, produced in innumerable cases by the subjection of individual women to individual men, are far too terrible to be overlooked" (Chap. 4, p. 195). Thus an overpowering reason for emancipating women is that this will alleviate their suffering and so benefit society. Mill also claims this would produce greater happiness. Appealing to a principle similar to that enunciated in *On Liberty*, he argues against unnecessary social restrictions. Each person is the best judge of her interests and what will make her happy. Society benefits by allowing her to pursue it (Chap. 1, p. 135).

The foregoing are powerful arguments, but Mill has others as well. Society as a whole will gain in freeing women. This will double the pool of talent available for "the higher services of humanity" (Chap. 4, p. 199). Affording additional outlets for their talents will also benefit women, who endure enforced idleness after their children are grown. The lack of opportunities to employ one's faculties is a source of considerable unhappiness (Chap. 4, p. 214). Altering relationships within the family will also transform society's moral tenor. As things stand, the family is a corrupting environment, teaching values of domination and subjection. The male, born to a life of unjustified privilege, comes to believe he deserves this. Mill views the effects on his character as analogous to those of hereditary nobility. Family relations are the principal cause of "all the selfish propensities, the self-worship, the unjust self-preference," that proliferate in the modern world (Chap. 4, p. 196). By making marriage a relationship between equals, these baneful effects can be reversed; this will do much to weaken unscrupulous urges for power throughout society (pp. 213–214). In addition to all these considerations is the enormously increased happiness of domestic unions:

> What marriage may be in the case of two persons of cultivated faculties, identical in opinions and purposes, between whom there exists that best kind of equality, similarity of powers and capacities with reciprocal superiority in them—so that each can enjoy the luxury of looking up to the other, and can have alternatively the pleasure of leading and of being led in the path of development—I will not attempt to describe. (Chap. 4, p. 211)

Mill experienced a happy marriage of equals, and believes the results of allowing others similar relationships would be substantial. "The moral regeneration of mankind will only really commence, when the most fundamental of the social relations is placed under the rule of equal justice, and when human beings learn to cultivate their strongest sympathy with an equal in rights and in cultivation" (p. 211).

Powerfully argued as *Subjection* is, it falls short of the standards of contemporary feminism in various ways. Though Mill is a strong supporter of women's rights in society, he has more trouble freeing himself from conventional opinions in regard to relationships within the family. He not only accepts the existence of the family as inevitably given, but unquestioningly accepts a natural division of labor within the family. The man should work and the woman should stay home to care for the house and children (Chap. 2, p. 164). He believes women should not work outside of the home, and naturally prefer to stay at home (Chap. 3, p. 167). In this sense, Mill is less radical than Harriet Taylor who had realized women's difficulty achieving true equality in society unless they had independent economic status (see Okin, pp. 226–230). In addition, in spite of his strictures against attempting to ascertain the nature of women from the evidence of existing society, Mill attempts to do just this, mainly on the basis of individual women who had exceptional opportunities. Though he defends women's abilities from various prejudices and stereotypes, much of his analysis supports what one commentator calls "the oldest cliché in the book," that women are intuitive and emotional while men are less passionate and better able to reason.[58] There is an obvious inconsistency between Mill's strong dismissal of the evidence of society on the one hand, and his attempt to argue from this—albeit in defense of women's abilities—on the other. This portion of the argument is conducted mainly in Chapter 3, parts of which are not of high quality (see Annas, pp. 184–186). But aside from these difficulties, *Subjection* is a powerful polemical tract.

As is the case in *On Liberty*, Mill's defense of women's equality departs from the strictures of Benthamite utilitarianism. In this regard, one can see how strongly the work is shaped by application of principles presented in *On Liberty* and *Utilitarianism*. In *Subjection*, Mill forecasts great gains in happiness that wait upon the reordering of social relationships. This is consistent with his general faith in human nature's potential to develop under proper circumstances. Through the beneficial effects of education, higher faculties will emerge; the satisfaction of new desires will provide a form of happiness greater than presently known. From a Benthamite point of view, however, this argument is problematic, because it does not pay adequate attention to the satisfaction or dissatisfaction of existing desires. One of Mill's main themes in *Subjection* is how existing arrangements have perverted the self-understandings of both women and men. Though there are great miseries associated with existing relationships, there is also considerable joy—or what people regard as joy because they have been taught to do so. Mill tends to brush this aside. He would probably argue that people who experienced relationships between the sexes in both existing society and a reformed society would greatly prefer the latter. But it might not be easy to convince people of this.

Because of the degree of people's *satisfaction* with existing arrangements, extensive state interference would be necessary for the cultivation of higher faculties (see Annas, pp. 191–192). This is especially true of men, who obviously benefit from existing affairs. Though existing arrangements coarsen men and give rise to desires that are lower than those of which human nature is capable, these desires are a source of considerable enjoyment. The effects of centuries of miseducation will not be changed easily. Though Mill believes men too would be happier in a society with improved domestic relationships, they would probably resist attempts to change things. Even setting aside problems of how the envisioned political reforms could possibly take place, one can see that enormous state interference in areas such as education and protecting women in their homes and in the labor market would be necessary to change consciousness. Such measures are obviously difficult to reconcile with limits on coercion defended in *On Liberty*.

Perhaps Mill would attempt to reconcile these conflicting aspects of his philosophy through appeal to his faith in the transformative powers of education and culture, and the tremendous effect of open discussion and "experiments in living." Though Mill views the effects of culture as pervasive, he has a relatively benign view of what constitutes culture. In spite of his attraction to Romantic thinkers who emphasize the role of the passions and sentiments in shaping society, Mill is still largely a rationalist at heart, in believing people's conduct is governed by ideas. As a result of centuries of ignorance and prejudice, many dominant ideas are incorrect. Accordingly, the theoretical reformer must combat these, as Mill himself did throughout his life.

There are significant theoretical problems in Mill's works, especially the difficulty of reconciling their conflicting strands. However, through the combined force of their eloquence and moral seriousness, they have attained enormous influence and have perhaps achieved much of what they were intended to do. Mill not only preaches the virtue of open discussion, but his works provide an ongoing attempt to shape disparate ideas into an adequately consistent point of view. In departing from the narrow consistency of his

Benthamite origins, Mill achieved the rarer feat of a political philosophy that is not overly neat but is adequate to far more of the facts of human experience.

NOTES

1. For discussion, see J. Plamenatz, *The English Utilitarians*, 2nd ed. (Oxford, 1958); a good brief account is A. Quinton, *Utilitarian Ethics*, 2nd ed. (La Salle, IL, 1988).

2. Bentham, *A Fragment of Government*, Chap. 1, p. 51, n. 2. The following of Bentham's works are cited in the text by short titles: *A Fragment of Government* (*Fragment*), *The Theory of Legislation* (*Theory*), *An Introduction to the Principles of Morals and Legislation* (*Principles*), and *Handbook of Political Fallacies* (*Fallacies*), according to chapter and page number in the editions used; full references are found below under "Texts Cited." Unless otherwise noted, all italics in quotations from Bentham are his.

3. J. S. Mill, "Bentham," in *On Bentham and Coleridge*, F. R. Leavis, ed. (New York, 1950), p. 44; this work cited hereafter, in parentheses in the text, as "Bentham."

4. Biographical details are from J. Dinwiddy, *Bentham* (Oxford, 1989), Chap. 1.

5. D. Lieberman, "From Bentham to Benthamism," *Historical Journal*, 28 (1985), 206.

6. See J. H. Burns, "Bentham and the French Revolution," *Transactions of the Royal Historical Society*, 16 (1966).

7. Dinwiddy, "Bentham's Transition to Political Radicalism," *Journal of the History of Ideas*, 36 (1975), 686. This work is cited hereafter as Dinwiddy, "Transition," in the text.

8. Lieberman, "From Bentham to Benthamism," 219.

9. Lieberman, "From Bentham to Benthamism," 206.

10. Trans. M. Morris (1928; rpt. London, 1972); this work cited hereafter "Halévy," in parentheses in the text.

11. For example, J. Steintrager, *Bentham* (Ithaca, NY, 1977); M. Mack, *Jeremy Bentham: An Odyssey of Ideas* (New York, 1963).

12. Bentham, quoted by D. Long, *Bentham on Liberty* (Toronto, 1977), p. 164.

13. Discussion here is indebted to J. Rawls, *A Theory of Justice* (Cambridge, MA, 1971), Sec. 5.

14. Bentham, quoted by R. Harrison, in Introduction to *A Fragment of Government*, J. H. Burns and H. L. A. Hart, eds. (Cambridge, 1988), p. vi.

15. Bentham, quoted by Harrison, Introduction to *Fragment*, p. vi.

16. For discussion of legal positivism and its opposition to natural law doctrines, see Vol. I, 283–286.

17. Bentham, quoted by G. Postema, *Bentham and the Common Law Tradition* (Oxford, 1986), p. 233; this work cited, hereafter, as "Postema," in the text.

18. Bentham, quoted by Postema, *Bentham*, p. 269.

19. H. L. A. Hart, *Essays on Bentham* (Oxford, 1982), p. 82, with quotations from Bentham.

20. Bentham, letter to John Lind, September 2, 1776, in *Correspondence*, Vol. I, 342 (slightly altered); full reference below, under "Texts Cited."

21. Bentham, *Anarchical Fallacies*, in J. Waldron, ed. *'Nonsense Upon Stilts'* (London, 1987), p. 53.

22. *Anarchical Fallacies*, in Waldron, ed., *'Nonsense Upon Stilts'*, p. 48.

23. Bentham, quoted by Dinwiddy, *Bentham*, p. 58.

24. C. Beccaria, *On Crimes and Punishments*, H. Paolucci, trans. (Indianapolis, 1963), p. 8.

25. R. Harrison, *Bentham* (London, 1983), p. 148; this work cited hereafter as Harrison, in text.

26. Postema, *Bentham*, p. 264; details of the English system in the remainder of this paragraph are drawn from Postema, pp. 264–265.

27. Postema, *Bentham*, p. 266.

28. Bentham, quoted by Dinwiddy, "Transition," 687, 688. My account of Bentham's transition to democracy follows this piece.

29. Bentham, quoted by Mack, *Bentham*, p. 455 (this work is cited hereafter in the text as Mack).

30. An additional defense of democracy, which I will not discuss in the text, centers on the beneficial effects of participating in democratic institutions. A notable proponent of this view is Aristotle, who extols the virtues of "ruling and being ruled in turn" in the Greek *polis* (see *Politics*, Bk. II, Chap. 2; Book III, Chap. 6; for discussion, see Vol. I, 110–112). Another important thinker who expresses a similar view is John Stuart Mill, in his *Considerations on Representative Government*. For reasons of space, this work is not discussed in this chapter.

31. See Dinwiddy, "Transition"; cf. Mack, *Bentham*, 17, 432–440.

32. J. S. Mill, *An Essay on Government*, p. 47; this work cited hereafter as *Essay* in the text; full reference below under "Texts Cited."

33. T. Macaulay, "Mill on Government," p. 291 (cited hereafter as Macaulay, in text); full reference below, under "Texts Cited."

34. Quoted by T. Ball, Introduction to *James Mill: Political Writings* (Cambridge, 1992), p. xxii.

35. See F. Rosen, *Jeremy Bentham and Representative Democracy* (Oxford, 1983), pp. 131–132, 184, 191; and the exchange between T. Ball and L. Boralevi, in *The Bentham Newsletter*, 4 (1980).

36. Bentham, in B. Parekh, ed., *Bentham's Political Thought* (London, 1973), p. 312.

37. Bentham, quoted in Dinwiddy, *Bentham*, p. 110.

38. Dinwiddy, *Bentham*, p. 82.

39. D. Roberts, "Jeremy Bentham and the Victorian Administrative State," *Victorian Studies*, 2 (1959), 196; the list of reforms is taken from Roberts, p. 195.

40. L. J. Hume, *Bentham and Bureaucracy* (Cambridge, 1981), pp. 163, 251.

41. When the need for wider government functions became apparent in the nineteenth and twentieth centuries, liberal theorists responded by extending the range of individual rights government must protect to include such things as rights to economic subsistence, education, a healthy environment, and in most of the Western democracies, to basic health care. These are provided by an enlarged state, the welfare state. In the Western democracies,

"liberalism" is now associated with the policies of the welfare state. In the United States, these are most closely associated with the left (or liberal) wing of the Democratic Party. More limited, traditional liberalism, which centers on the protection of a more limited, traditional set of rights, is associated with the views of the Republican Party, especially its conservative wing.

42. Mill, "Remarks on Bentham's Philosophy," p. 5; full reference below, under "Texts Cited."

43. Mill, *Autobiography*, p. 25; this work cited hereafter as *Autobiography*, in text. Full reference below, under "Texts Cited."

44. On this see M. S. Packe, *The Life of John Stuart Mill* (London, 1954), pp. 77–81; J. M. Robson, *The Improvement of Mankind: The Social and Political Thought of John Stuart Mill* (Toronto, 1968), pp. 21–27; these works cited hereafter by authors' names in the text.

45. Mill, "Coleridge," p. 105; full reference below, under "Texts Cited;" this work cited hereafter as "Coleridge" in text.

46. Mill's *On Liberty, Utilitarianism,* and *Subjection of Women* are cited according to chapter and page number, in the editions listed below under "Texts Cited."

47. Quoted by Robson, *Improvement of Mankind,* p. 54.

48. See Vol. I, 105-10.

49. C. L. Ten, *Mill on Liberty* (Oxford, 1980), pp. 117–179; see also J. Gray, *Mill on Liberty: A Defense* (London, 1983), pp. 90–97.

50. For the complexities involved in detailed working out of a principle similar to Mill's, see J. Feinberg's four-volume work, *The Moral Limits of the Criminal Law* (Oxford, 1984–1987).

51. For discussion, see Ten, *Mill on Liberty*, pp. 102–107.

52. Plamenatz, *English Utilitarians*, p. 136.

53. Ibid.

54. Bentham, quoted by A. Ryan, *J. S. Mill* (London, 1974), p. 133.

55. *Considerations on Representative Government*, Chaps. 2–3; in *On Liberty, Utilitarianism,* and *Considerations on Representative Government*, H. Acton, ed. (London, 1972).

56. Ryan, *J. S. Mill*, Chap. 5; R. P. Anschutz. *The Philosophy of J. S. Mill*, 2nd Impression (Oxford, 1963).

57. See S. M. Okin, *Women in Western Political Thought* (Princeton, 1979), pp. 197–202; this work cited hereafter as Okin, in text.

58. J. Annas, "Mill and the Subjection of Women," *Philosophy*, 52 (1977), 184; this work cited hereafter as Annas, in text.

Texts Cited

Bentham, J. *Anarchical Fallacies*. In *'Nonsense Upon Stilt's*. J. Waldron, ed. London, 1987.

Bentham, J. *Bentham's Political Thought*. B. Parekh, ed. London, 1973.

Bentham, J. *The Correspondence of Jeremy Bentham*. T. L. S. Sprigge, ed. Vol. I: 1752–1776. London, 1968.

Bentham, J. *A Fragment of Government.* R. Harrison, ed. Cambridge, 1988.

Bentham, J. *Handbook of Political Fallacies.* H. Larrabee, ed. Baltimore, 1952.

Bentham, J. *An Introduction to the Principles of Morals and Legislation.* New York, 1948.

Bentham, J. *The Theory of Legislation.* C. K. Ogden, ed. R. Hildreth, trans. London, 1931.

Macaulay, T. B. "Mill on Government." In James Mill, *Political Writings.* T. Ball, ed. Cambridge, 1992.

Mill, J. *An Essay on Government.* C. Shields, ed. Indianapolis, 1955.

Mill, J. S. *Autobiography.* J. Robson, ed. Harmondsworth, England, 1989.

Mill, J. S. *On Bentham and Coleridge,* F. R. Leavis, ed. New York, 1950.

Mill, J. S. *On Liberty.* E. Rappaport, ed. Indianapolis, 1978.

Mill, J. S. "Remarks on Bentham's Philosophy." In Mill, *Essays on Ethics, Religion and Society,* J. M. Robson, ed. Toronto, 1969.

Mill, J. S. *The Subjection of Women.* In *On Liberty with The Subjection of Women and Chapters on Socialism.* S. Collini. ed. Cambridge, 1989.

Mill, J. S. *Utilitarianism.* G. Sher, ed. Indianapolis, 1979.

FURTHER READING

Annas, J. "Mill and the Subjection of Women." *Philosophy,* 52 (1977).

Anschutz, R. P. *The Philosophy of J. S. Mill,* 2nd Impression. Oxford, 1963.

Brock, D. "Recent Work in Utilitarianism." *American Philosophical Quarterly,* 10 (1973).

Dinwiddy, J. *Bentham.* Oxford, 1989.

Dinwiddy, J. "Bentham's Transition to Political Radicalism." *Journal of the History of Ideas,* 36 (1975).

Gray, J. *Mill on Liberty: A Defense.* London, 1983.

Halévy, E. *The Growth of Philosophical Radicalism.* M. Morris. trans. 1928; rpt. London, 1972.

Harrison, R. *Bentham.* London, 1983.

Lieberman, D. "From Bentham to Benthamism." *Historical Journal,* 28 (1985).

Okin, S. M. *Women in Western Political Thought.* Princeton, 1979.

Packe, M. S. *The Life of John Stuart Mill.* London, 1954.

Postema, G. *Bentham and the Common Law Tradition.* Oxford, 1986.

Robson, J. M. *The Improvement of Mankind: The Social and Political Thought of John Stuart Mill.* Toronto, 1968.

Ryan, A. *J. S. Mill.* New York, 1970.

Ryan, A. *J. S. Mill.* London, 1974.

Ten, C. L. *Mill on Liberty.* Oxford, 1980.

C h a p t e r

9

G. W. F. HEGEL

HEGEL'S LIFE AND WORKS

G. W. F. HEGEL WAS BORN in Stuttgart in 1770.[1] While attending the University of Tübingen, he became close friends with major figures of the German Romantic movement, including the poet Friedrich Holderlin and the philosopher Friedrich Wilhelm Schelling. After university, he secured a position as a tutor in a private household, before beginning to teach philosophy at the University of Jena. Hegel was on the verge of completing his first major work, *Phenomenology of Spirit*, in 1807, when Napoleon smashed the armies of Prussia at the Battle of Jena, thereby putting an end to the Holy Roman Empire, which dated back a thousand years to the time of Charlemagne. With the university closed, as Napoleon occupied the city, Hegel left Jena and was forced to edit a newspaper for a year before securing a position as rector of a boys' school in Nuremburg. He remained in this position until 1816, when he received a professorship in philosophy at the University of Heidelberg. His most important work during this period was his *Logic*, published in 1812–1813. At Heidelberg he published his *Encyclopedia*, before moving to the University of Berlin, in 1818, where he remained for the rest of his life. *Philosophy of Right* (1821), the most important work published during this period, is Hegel's main work in political philosophy and the last book published during his lifetime. While at Berlin, Hegel was generally viewed as the greatest philosopher in Germany. For reasons we will discuss, *Philosophy of Right* was widely considered the all but official political philosophy of the Prussian state.

The two works on which we will concentrate in this chapter are *Philosophy of Right* and *Lectures on the Philosophy of World History*, which was assembled from Hegel's lecture notes and some taken by students who attended his lectures and published after his death.[2] *Philosophy of Right* was also delivered in the form of lectures, and Hegel's text is supplemented with "Additions" from his students, which illuminate many obscure points.[3]

Hegel is a notoriously difficult thinker, clearly the most difficult encountered in this book and one of the most difficult in the history of political theory. To a certain extent, the obscurity of his prose can be explained as what was expected of a philosopher writing in Germany at that time. Hegel's language is often impossibly vague and abstract. A representative passage from the *Phenomenology* is as follows:

> The spiritual alone is the *actual*; it is essence, or that which has *being in itself*; it is that
> which *relates itself to itself* and is *determinate*, it is *other-being* and *being-for-self*, and in

371

this determinateness, or in its self-externality, abides within itself; in other words, it is *in and for itself.*—But this being-in-and-for-itself is at first only for us, or *in itself,* it is spiritual *Substance.* It must also be this *for itself,* it must be the knowledge of the spiritual, and the knowledge of itself as Spirit, i.e., it must be an *object* to itself, but just as immediately a sublated object, reflected into itself. It is *for itself* only for *us,* in so far as its spiritual content is generated by itself. But in so far as it is also for itself for its own self, this self-generation, this pure Notion, is for it the objective element in which it has its existence, and it is in this way, in its existence for itself, an object reflected into itself.[4]

As one can see from this perhaps unusual but by no means extreme example, Hegel's writing is riddled with forbidding technical jargon. When a number of such terms appear in a single sentence, or even a single paragraph, obscurity can thicken into impenetrability. It is not surprising that J. N. Findlay, a distinguished Hegel scholar and editor of the *Phenomenology,* says that in reading the work Hegel's style "makes one at times only sure that he is saying something immeasurably profound and important, but not exactly what it is."[5] According to (untrue) legend, Hegel's last words on his deathbed were: "Only one man has understood me, and he has not understood me either" (Kaufmann, p. 108).

In the case of the *Phenomenology,* Hegel's obscurity is to some extent explained by external factors. Not only does the work contain difficult and complex ideas, which Hegel was presenting in developed form for the first time, but it was written under tremendous pressure. Victorious in the Battle of Jena, Napoleon occupied the city on October 13, 1807, the very day Hegel completed his manuscript. In order to secure Hegel a badly needed advance, one of his friends had offered to pay a severe penalty if Hegel did not meet a firm deadline, and so Hegel was forced to mail the manuscript to his publisher under these tumultuous circumstances, with no guarantee it would not be lost in the mail (Kaufmann, pp. 90–91).[6] In order to finish on time, Hegel wrote the work in a rush. Simply to copy it would take almost as long as it took him to write it (Kaufmann, p. 90 n. 5). To make matters worse, during the time Hegel was completing the *Phenomenology,* he discovered he had impregnated the abandoned wife of a servant, who had already produced two illegitimate children (Kaufmann, pp. 91–94). (Hegel's illegitimate child, Ludwig, was born in February 1808.) As Kaufmann remarks, the circumstances under which Hegel wrote what many regard as his greatest work were akin to those in a Dostoyevsky novel (pp. 90–91).

There is a more important reason for Hegel's obscurity, which also helps explain his jargon-ridden language. Hegel believed philosophical truth could be expressed only in the form of a developed system, which encompassed literally everything. As he says in the *Phenomenology,* "The True is the whole" (Pref., p. 11). Hegel expresses this idea more fully as follows:

> Among the various consequences that follow from what has just been said, this one in particular can be stressed, that knowledge is only actual, and can only be expounded, as Science or as a *system;* and furthermore, that a so-called basic proposition or principle of philosophy, if true, is also false, just because it is *only* a principle. It is, therefore, easy to refute it. (*Phenomenology,* Pref., p. 13)

Hegel believes a statement can be fully true only if it is integrated into a complete system. The implication is that all truth is organically bound up in a single system that encompasses everything. A statement that has the appearance of truth, which we would be likely to accept as true, cannot be *entirely* true unless it is part of such a philosophical system. In saying such a statement is partly false, Hegel means it is necessarily one-sided. To refute it, one can show this, thereby demonstrating its incompleteness.

The system Hegel produced is one of the great undertakings in the history of philosophy, encompassing logic and metaphysics, the natural world, and the human world, including art, religion, philosophy, political and social forms, and the history of each of these subjects. Hegel contends that the different parts of his system are necessarily inter-connected, so each is presupposed by the system as a whole and can be understood only in its light. It follows that proper appreciation of any aspect of one of Hegel's works presupposes comprehension of the entire system. An attempt to browse through one of his works at random is not likely to succeed—as the above passage illustrates. The jargon that riddles his philosophical works is the language of his system, which is constantly drawn upon in exposition of its parts. It is reported that when someone asked Hegel for a concise statement of his philosophy, he replied that some things cannot be explained succinctly.[7]

Because Hegel's political philosophy is also part of his system, it too is often obscure, its language riddled with technical jargon. On first encountering the *Philosophy of Right*, the reader is often at a loss. Hegel opens the work by noting that "philosophy's mode of progression from one topic to another and its mode of scientific proof—this whole speculative way of knowing—is essentially distinct from any other way of knowing" (Preface, pp. 1–2). He notes that the method he follows is that expounded in his *Logic*, acquaintance with which is presupposed (p. 2). Exactly what this distinctive way of knowing is is a complex subject into which we will enter only as necessary. On the whole, I will attempt to present important themes in Hegel's political theory in remove from his overall system—though Hegel would not accept these ideas as entirely true expounded in this way.

In his masterful study of Hegel's philosophy, Charles Taylor notes that commentators generally approach Hegel's thought in two basic ways. Some put a premium on intelligi-bility, and so attempt to be terribly clear. But this risks oversimplification; oftentimes, the result does not *sound* like Hegel. The alternative, as Taylor says, is that the commentator "can remain faithful but impenetrable, so that in the end readers will turn with relief to the text in order to understand the commentary."[8]

In regard to Hegel's political philosophy, the first alternative amounts to abstracting the political ideas from their place in the system and examining them on their own.[9] The other possibility is tackling the system head-on and attempting the daunting task of presenting Hegel's political philosophy in its place in the system, which it presupposes. The problem with this, of course, is that, presented in this fashion, Hegel's political theory is forbiddingly abstract and obscure. Accordingly, the approach pursued in this chapter is the former. We will examine central themes in Hegel's political philosophy with relatively little attention to other aspects of his philosophy. The one unavoidable exception is his philosophy of world history, with which his political philosophy is intimately connected. Thus we will discuss the *Philosophy of History* as well as the *Philosophy of Right*. Fortunately, the former is among the most accessible of Hegel's works.

In spite of the difficulty of Hegel's thought, it is arguable that no philosopher has been more influential in shaping our understanding of the modern world, and so also the world itself. Major nineteenth- and twentieth-century philosophical movements were deeply influenced by Hegel, including existentialism, phenomenology, and, most obviously, Marxism. In *Capital*, Marx openly proclaims himself "the pupil of that mighty thinker."[10] In regard to political philosophy, we will see that Hegel presents important critiques of central elements of liberal political theory, especially the closely linked liberal conceptions of freedom and the state. In many ways Hegel builds on themes presented by Rousseau and Burke—in spite of the dissimilarities between these two thinkers and the fact that Hegel goes much further than either of them. The resulting doctrine is widely believed to lay the groundwork for modern theories of the totalitarian state. The validity of this assessment will be discussed in the concluding section of this chapter.

HEGEL'S ORIENTATION

Throughout his life, a central aim of Hegel's philosophy was to recreate the possibility of meaningful life. Believing religion was no longer able to accomplish this, he attempted to solve this problem through reconceptualization of the state. Hegel sought a situation in which individuals could be reintegrated into the state, achieving a semblance of the fulfilled life that existed in the Greek *polis*. His concerns along these lines were common to many figures of his time, for instance the poet Friedrich Schiller, who contrasted the harmonious life of the classical Greeks with fractured existence in modern society (see Kaufmann, Chap. 1). For Hegel, the *polis* was a political community that provided a unified focus for man's highest aspirations. In the words of one commentator,

> Hegel never for a moment forgot or abandoned his view that the ideal of human existence was the life achieved in the Greek cities, and especially in Periclean Athens. . . . He knew it was through the work of his older contemporaries, Rousseau, Lessing, Mendelssohn, Kant, Fichte, and Schiller that he had been placed in a position to appreciate the Greek achievement as he did; and he believed that through the right 'application' of their theories the wholeness of life could be restored.[11]

Aristotle had captured the essence of Greek political life in describing man as a "political animal," because a person's moral and intellectual faculties can be developed fully only as a member of a *polis*.[12] Hegel was well aware that the age of the *polis* had passed, and that reintegration into a modern state must be on somewhat different lines. But throughout his political writings, recapturing a *semblance* of what life was like in a Greek *polis* was one of his central goals.

In view of his concern to reintegrate the individual into society, Hegel's standpoint is immediately different from that of classical liberal theorists, whose main concern is protecting the individual from encroachments of society. Classical liberals wish to preserve an area of freedom (negative freedom) in which the individual will be able to pursue his own ends without worrying about other people. Instead of protecting individuals from the state, Hegel wishes to draw them into it. Thus it is not surprising that he has been criticized for being a "totalitarian," for wishing to erode the essential zone of private life that classical liberalism defends. To this criticism we will return.

To appreciate Hegel's view, we can note some important differences between his conception of the state and the liberal state. As we have seen in previous chapters, for liberal theorists, the state is nothing more than a collection of individuals, united in pursuit of their interests. Hegel views the state differently; like the Greeks, he believes the political community is a moral association. In order to refer to this, I will generally use the term "ethical order," though for reasons of convenience, I will also use "state" and "society" on occasion. In *Philosophy of Right*, Hegel refers to "the strictly political state and its constitution" (Par. 267, p. 163). This sense, which is narrower than his general usage, is in reference to the political institutions that constitute government and coincides roughly with the "state" as discussed by liberal theorists. But in general, in discussing the "state," Hegel means much more than this. It encompasses not only political institutions but the moral, religious, and cultural life these institutions protect and make possible. In attempting to reintegrate the individual into this broader conception of the state, Hegel is obviously doing something quite different from subordinating the individual to the state (in its narrow, institutional sense). It is more correct to say that he wishes for individuals to realize themselves as members of their civilizations.

Hegel's broader conception of politics shows up in the title of his major political work. *Philosophy of Right* is the usual translation of the German *Philosophie des Rechts. Recht*, like the French *droit*, can be translated as both "right" and "law." Carl Friedrich, a distinguished historian of political theory, translates the title of the work as *Philosophy of Right and Law* in his edition of selections from Hegel's works.[13] While judging from its title, *Philosophy of Right* might seem to be a book about morality, that is, the right thing to do, *Recht* has legal as well as moral connotations, in keeping with Hegel's belief that a person can lead a truly ethical life only by participating in a political community. In an early work, Hegel quotes a remark of an unnamed Pythagorean philosopher. Upon being asked what was the best education for one's son, the philosopher replied: "Making him the citizen of a people with good institutions" (Kaufmann, pp. 82–83).

Hegel's break with the liberal view of politics is seen in his fundamental distinction between the state and what he calls "civil society." The latter is comprised mainly of economic relationships. Throughout much of society, people interact in the economic marketplace out of mutual self-interest. In *Wealth of Nations*, Adam Smith classically writes:

> It is not from the benevolence of the butcher, the brewer, or the baker that we expect our dinner, but from their regard to their own interest. We address ourselves, not to their humanity but to their self-love, and never talk to them of our own necessities but of their advantages. Nobody but a beggar chooses to depend chiefly upon the benevolence of his fellow citizens.[14]

In the marketplace, people attempt to make exchanges that are mutually beneficial. I give you what you want in return for what I want: "it is by treaty, by barter, and by purchase that we obtain from one another the greater part of those mutual good offices which we stand in need of."[15]

Relationships such as these are prototypically instrumental. I view other people as means to satisfy my own needs; they view me in a similar light. Because an association comprised of such relationships is not an end in itself, Hegel refers to civil society as a "system of needs":

> In the course of the actual attainment of selfish ends . . . there is formed a system of complete interdependence, wherein the livelihood, happiness, and legal status of one

man is interwoven with the livelihood, happiness, and rights of all. On this system, individual happiness, &c., depend, and only in this connected system are they actualized and secured. (*Philosophy of Right*, Par. 183, p. 123)

This set of relationships, "the state based on need" (p. 123), is closely related to the instrumental state as envisioned by liberal theorists. The liberal state exists to aid in the satisfaction of preexisting aims. For Hegel, once again, the state is far more than this. Though civil society performs the essential task of moving people beyond their family spheres and so relating them to one another, the selfish relationships it establishes are based on an undeveloped moral principle. Self-interest divides people while it brings them together. In a properly constituted state, in contrast, instrumental relationships are overcome and people reintegrated. Hegel views such a state as a moral community, the concrete embodiment of the ethical order.

Hegel's view of the state as the ethical whole leads him beyond liberal theory's emphasis on the individual. His philosophy makes an important contribution to the concepts of the nation and nationalism, which became increasingly important in Europe in the years following the French Revolution. In viewing a civilization as the focus of people's aspirations, Hegel calls attention to phenomena such as culture and traditions that classical liberal theorists tend not to discuss—though these matters receive considerable attention from Montesquieu and Burke, whom Hegel acknowledges as predecessors. To use Friedrich's words, Hegel is "the philosopher of the French revolutionary goals of a secular nation state in which the citizen is the loyal participant."[16] Hegel's belief in the need for immersion in the culture and traditions of one's nation helps account for his influence on a wide variety of political movements that exalt the state, including both Fascism and Communism—though he undoubtedly would have abhorred both of these.

The great wealth of Hegel's philosophy confronts the commentator with the need to choose a limited set of central themes on which to concentrate. I will focus on his closely linked conceptions of freedom, the individual, and the state, which are central to his political philosophy. In view of significant differences between Hegel's goals and those of liberal theory, it is only natural that his analyses of these concepts differ as well. We can begin with Hegel's fundamental criticisms of the liberal perspective that led him to work out his own position.

HEGEL AND LIBERAL POLITICAL THEORY

As we have noted, liberal political theory conceives of the state primarily in instrumental terms. Political activity is not good in itself but is a means to the attainment of other goods. Several theorists we have examined argue that people have goals or projects which they are not able to satisfy without the state's assistance. For instance, Locke argues that man in the state of nature is plagued by inconveniences. Though he has natural rights, these are threatened by the lack of a neutral judge to settle disputes and by the threat of unscrupulous others. Thus people are willing to cede certain rights to political authority in order to protect others. However, they do not do this because they view the state as good in itself but because it is necessary for attaining ends they already have. To be as clear as possible, we can say the state is instrumental when the ends it is intended to achieve exist apart from it and are not brought into being through its agency. This is clearly true in the case of Locke, as natural rights are given by God. In the case of Bentham, people desire to maximize their pleasure. Neither the desire for pleasure nor the form this desire assumes is determined by the state. Rather, the state helps people satisfy specific desires for pleasure they already have without reference to it. As we saw in the last section, Hegel views civil society in similar terms. People enter into social relationships in order to satisfy preexisting needs.

As we have also seen, the liberal conception of freedom is negative freedom, freedom from coercive interference by other people. In general, liberal theorists hold that people can effectively attain their ends only if they are protected from others. According to Hobbes and Locke, the state is erected to protect people from others in the state of nature. Mill states this idea especially clearly: "All that makes existence valuable to anyone, depends on the enforcement of restraints upon the actions of other people."[17] Because the state also threatens to impinge on people's liberty, it must be limited as well. Carving out a protected sphere for people's activities, into which neither other people nor the state can enter, is a central concern of liberal theorists.

In concentrating on a protected sphere for individual activity, liberal theorists leave themselves open to an important line of criticism. Though the questions they address are obviously significant, there are others to which they pay insufficient attention, especially the nature of the individual and how he will use his freedom, in other words, the ends he will choose to pursue. In placing the individual and his aims, *whatever they happen to be*, at the center of their theory, liberal theorists accord great weight to the satisfaction of desires, without making sure these will not be arbitrary or unworthy. In spite of its obvious merits, the liberal conception of freedom can promote unworthy ends.

As we have seen (see p. 236) the concept of freedom centers on a *three-part* relationship:

A *is free from* X *to do* Y.

Liberals concentrate on the X term, making sure the individual, A, is not interfered with as she pursues her ends. But the Y term, the nature of the ends in question, is not adequately explored. On the whole, liberal theorists leave this to the individual to decide for herself. As we have seen, Bentham argues that the individual is the best judge of her own interests. Government interference is likely to be either useless or harmful. Though Mill, unlike Bentham, distinguishes between pleasures in terms of higher and lower quality, he too is against government interference: "The only freedom which deserves the name, is that of pursuing our own good in our own way."[18]

The main problem with noninterference is that individuals can use their liberty to choose wrongly. We have discussed Rousseau's argument that people in existing societies have corrupt, artificial desires and so will use their liberty to pursue harmful ends. Hegel's view is similar, though he is less concerned with people making incorrect choices than with providing a framework of political and social institutions within which they can choose properly and so be truly free. Thus in addition to being concerned with noninterference (that A is free from X), Hegel is deeply concerned with the question of how this negative freedom will be used (ensuring A will choose the proper Y).

Hegel criticizes the liberal conception of freedom in *Philosophy of Right*. Liberal theorists argue that, by removing constraints upon the individual's ability to choose what he wants, we make him free. Hegel rejects this idea out of hand: "If we hear it said that the definition of freedom is ability to do what we please, such an idea can only be taken to reveal an utter immaturity of thought" (Par. 15, p. 27). Left to his own devices, the individual is likely to choose on the basis of desire or caprice. Because these are not proper bases of choice, this is not true freedom. Though the individual will choose according to his own desires, rather than being forced to conform to those of arbitrary rulers or other people, this is not an overwhelming improvement, because his own desires are likely to be similarly arbitrary and irrational.

Hegel believes the essence of freedom is self-determination, an absence of dependence on factors outside one's self: "For if I am dependent, I am beholden to something other than myself, and cannot exist without this external point of reference. If, however, I am self-sufficient, I am also free" (*Reason in History*, p. 48). To be self-determined, to act on the basis of one's own will, entails an absence of dependence on irrational elements within oneself as well as on other people. "Only in freedom of this kind is the will by itself without qualification, because then it is related to nothing except itself and so is released from every tie of dependence on anything else" (*Philosophy of Right*, Par. 23, p. 30). The central claim of Hegel's doctrine of freedom, and of his political philosophy as a whole, is that the all-important self-determination can be attained only in a properly organized state: "The state is the actuality of concrete freedom" (*Philosophy of Right*, Par. 260, p. 160). It is to the network of ideas underlying this formidable conception that we turn.

Hegel's View of Freedom

We saw in the last section that Hegel views freedom as self-determination, as an absence of dependence on anything outside the self. In order to understand his view, we must look into what it is to be determined by one's self and how this differs from determination by other factors. In exploring this topic, we will see that Hegel displays greater interest in the nature of the *self* than one finds in liberal theories.

We can begin with the liberal conception of the self. If one thinks about the liberal theories discussed in previous chapters, one will note that relatively little attention is paid to the choosing agent. Because of their concern with negative freedom, liberal theorists focus on ensuring that individuals are protected from coercive pressures. But in regard to how this freedom will be used, they are generally content simply to say that people should be free to choose what they want, to pursue their own good in their own way. Bentham is striking in this respect. He holds that it really does not matter what a person chooses, as long as it gives him pleasure, and does not unduly lessen the pleasures of other people. Though more extreme than the views of other liberal thinkers, Bentham's position does not differ greatly in its overall thrust. Criticisms of this view have been noted. Failure to discriminate among different ways individual discretion can be used opens the possibility that people will choose badly, whether from the corrupt, artificial values excoriated by Rousseau, or from momentary whims that are not integral parts of people's characters. This last concern exercises Hegel. We can call a desire that is not integrated into the overall structure of an individual's personality a whim or impulse. In Hegel's eyes, liberal theory allows choices to be made on the basis of whims. In other words, liberal theory does not distinguish between important, stable desires that are central to an individual's personality, to his self, and mere whims or impulses. When a person chooses from desires of the latter sort, he is determined by factors external to his *self* and so is not truly free.

Obviously, to become clear about Hegel's meaning, we must examine his view of the self. Hegel's preferred method of approaching such questions is genetically. He traces the series of steps—whether temporal or logical—through which the concept in question comes into existence. Accordingly, we can examine the process through which a person's conception of herself develops. We begin with an infant, completely dominated by impulses and appetites. This view of the infant is familiar and need not be discussed in detail. During her first days, the infant is entirely dominated by appetites, for nourishment, for warmth, sleep, and so on. When she requires satisfaction, she signifies discomfort by crying until what she wants is provided. As the infant progresses through childhood she is taught to suppress certain appetites and to schedule satisfaction of others. She must eat at certain times, and not between meals. Her parents do not allow her to eat bags of candy but insist that what she eats be nourishing. Toilet training is a clear case, as the child is taught to use the toilet and not to soil her diapers. At this stage, the process of ordering the child's desires is imposed from without, by her parents or other authorities. But as the child develops, she increasingly takes over this responsibility herself. At first, her parents prevent her from eating between meals. At this stage, she is clearly not free in Hegel's sense, as her will is determined by factors outside of her, that is, by other people. As time passes and she assumes control of her own appetites, she moves closer to the ideal of self-determination.

A crucial stage in the process of development is when the person—probably no longer a young child—is able to pursue complex, long-range goals, which involve detailed balancing of desires. Perhaps she decides to become a doctor, which entails rigorous studying, and so must deny satisfaction to certain urges. For example, on a nice day, she might like to go for a walk, but she stays in and works on a report. She carefully develops a strategy according to which she will take the courses required for admission to medical school, and subordinates her other interests to doing well in them.

The need to arrange one's desires in an ordered structure is familiar. People do this all the time, whenever they go to work, or get out of bed in the morning though they would prefer to sleep in. For Hegel, there is an important distinction between different ways in which a person can schedule desires. Most simply, a person can do this to maximize her happiness. After receiving three pieces of candy, she can decide the order in which to eat them for greatest enjoyment. Thus the urge to cram all three pieces into her mouth at once is fought off for the sake of overall pleasure. Or perhaps she knows that eating all three pieces at once will give her a stomach ache, and so she decides to wait between pieces. A more sophisticated form of arranging desires is when a person does this in order to advance some conception of *herself*. Our example of the aspiring doctor is a case in point. This person does not merely schedule her desires to increase happiness (though on a more advanced level, something like this is involved). She does this in order to realize a particular conception of herself; in other words, she sees herself as a doctor and arranges her life in order to make this vision a reality. Desires and inclinations that do not fit into this overall plan are necessarily thrust aside.

If we consider such a person's overall goals, we can distinguish between desires that are consistent with her plan to be a physician and others that are not. Obvious examples of desires that are central to her plans are those to work hard, to keep her appointments, to get along with her fellow-students and teachers. Not to do any of these things could damage her plans. Thus desires to do them are necessary components of her overall desire to be a doctor. Desires that do not fall inside her overall plan are what we have referred to as whims. These can be harmless. Perhaps she is feeling down and decides to buy a book or a picture for her wall. Whether or not she makes this purchase will not affect her plan to become a doctor. Other whims can be less innocuous. Perhaps she feels like purchasing an expensive car that has caught her eye but she cannot afford. To make the payments, she would have to take on a part-time job which would interfere with her studies. This sort of whim is inconsistent with her overall plans and must be combatted if she is to succeed. For ease of reference, we can refer to whims of the first sort as "harmless whims," and those that are damaging to a person's long-term goals as "harmful whims." Deciding to buy an inexpensive book is ordinarily a harmless whim; deciding to buy a Porsche can often be a harmful whim.

In our case of the aspiring doctor, then, we can distinguish desires that are consistent with her conception of herself, which she intends to realize in her actions, and others that fall outside this self-conception. If, as Hegel argues, freedom is self-determination, then in order to be free, a person's choices must be dictated by desires that are bound up with her self-conception, rather than by whims, which fall outside this. To keep things relatively simple, we can set aside harmless whims and concentrate on the harmful. Clearly, Hegel believes that to give in to desires of this kind is to make choices that are not determined by one's self, which are in fact (by definition) damaging to one's self. When one chooses on the basis of these desires, one is not self-determined and so not free.

Accordingly, as we noted in the last section, it is overly simple to believe freedom is *mere* noninterference. The simple absence of restrictions allows domination by whims as well as by the more important desires of one's self. Hegel believes freedom requires restrictions on whims:

> To regard freedom in a purely formal and subjective sense, abstracted from its absolutely essential objects and aims, is a perennial misunderstanding; for it means that impulses, desires, and passions—which pertain by their nature exclusively to the particular individual—and arbitrariness and random inclinations are identified with freedom, and that any restrictions imposed upon these are seen as restrictions on freedom itself. On the contrary, such restrictions are the indispensable conditions of liberation. . . . (*Reason in History*, p. 99)

As this passage continues, Hegel argues for a source of preferred desires higher than the self. But this additional theme depends on additional points we must develop.

Having looked briefly at Hegel's view of the self, and so the distinction between desires consistent and inconsistent with one's self, we can examine how this is tied in with freedom in more detail. We have seen that Hegel views self-determination as the essence of freedom. But the nature of self-determination can be further developed. Hegel believes there are two immediate conditions that must be satisfied if an individual is to be self-determined, and so free. These bear on *how* a person chooses and *what* he chooses; the free person must choose in a certain way, and must make choices with particular contents. In accordance with longstanding usage, we can refer to the former as the *form* of a given choice and the latter as its *content* (see p. 234). The former concerns qualities of the person—or his will—as he makes a given choice. The latter concerns the nature of what he chooses.

To begin with the former, there are clear restrictions on how free choices are made. In accordance with what we have seen, whims are desires that a person happens to have, in contrast with desires that are central to his self-conception. Desires of the latter sort are results of deliberation, not only about the nature of the overall end in question but about how particular desires are consistent and inconsistent with this. In order to achieve a complex, long-term goal, a person's life must be subjected to a certain order, which can be described as rational. In previous chapters we have seen that the concept of rationality is bound up with selecting the most appropriate means to attain a given end. Clearly, at minimum, if a person is to be self-determined, other aims and projects must be subordinated to the more important aspirations that are central to his self-conception. If the overall goal is complex, this can require achieving a series of lesser, subsidiary goals, which are means to it. For example, to become a doctor, one must complete medical school. This in turn requires that one be admitted to medical school, and so one must do well in certain courses in college. Accomplishing any or all of these goals requires that certain desires be cast aside and the satisfaction of others postponed. Thus the raw material of a person's motivations must be shaped by the agency of reason if her goals are to be accomplished and her self is to emerge. Though this is clear if the goals in question are complex and long-term, it is equally true of simpler goals. In any given case, reason must exercise a supervisory capacity over the person's aims and desires to make sure those that are acted on are consistent with her sense of self. Desires themselves are unable to determine this: "An impulse is simply a uni-directional urge and thus has no measuring-rod in itself" (*Philosophy of Right*, Par. 17, p. 29). Deciding whether or not a desire is to be satisfied falls to a faculty outside of it, the person's rational or deliberative capacities: "When reflection is brought to bear on impulses, they are imaged, estimated, compared with one another, with their means of satisfaction and their consequences, &c., and with a sum of satisfaction (i. e., with happiness). In this way reflection invests this material with abstract universality and in this external manner purifies it from its crudity and barbarity" (Par. 20, p. 29).

There are clear requirements reason must satisfy in assessing desires. Obviously, it must do this in a deliberate, careful way. Desires must be examined to see if they are consistent with one's sense of self. Desires that do not fit in must be suppressed, while others must be assigned appropriate satisfaction. As choices that proceed from impulses or arbitrary desires are not free, so self-determination requires that choices not be arbitrary or capricious. Careful, deliberate choices, however, are not enough. Not all senses of self are equally appropriate bases for self-determination. The particular example on which we have focused appears a suitable case. Choosing to be a doctor is a sensible, respectable thing to do. But is this also true of choosing to be a gambler, or a drug dealer, or an axe murderer? In each case, successful realization of a certain conception of the self requires suppressing desires and scheduling the satisfaction of others. But in these cases, the plans themselves are based on the satisfaction of obviously questionable desires. Can one pursue a course of life devoted to the satisfaction of such aims and still be· free?

It appears that certain conceptions of the self are inherently flawed and so disqualified from being bases of actions that are self-determined and so free. But unacceptable conceptions cannot be weeded out simply on the basis of their lack of rationality. It is entirely possible that a person can choose to be a drug dealer after carefully weighing his options, fully aware of what this entails. In accordance with this aim, he will suppress certain desires and rearrange others. The resulting structure of purposes and desires will have qualities of rationality and deliberateness similar to those associated with the choice to become a doctor. Accordingly, we must go beyond the consistency of a person's aims and the care with which they are chosen in order to determine if they are a suitable basis for freedom.

Hegel argues along these lines in *Philosophy of Right*, in criticizing the moral views of his great predecessor, Immanuel Kant (1724–1804). Briefly and simply, Kant argues that the essence of a moral action is its rationality. Kant attempts to move from the requirement of rationality to a developed moral system solely on the basis of rationality's demand for consistency. He argues that, if Jones is to act rationally, he must follow a rule or principle he is willing to have consistently applied, and so one he would allow others—all others— to use as a basis for their actions as well. Not to do so would be inconsistent and so irrational. Thus when Jones acts, he in effect represents all people. In choosing a maxim of action for himself, he also chooses it for everyone else. Therefore, he should not choose to do *X* unless he is willing to have all other people do *X* as well. Kant's basic moral precept, his "categorical imperative," is as follows:

> I ought never to act except in such a way *that I can also will that my maxim should become a universal law.*[19]

Arguing that rationality alone is an adequate basis for morality, Kant is unwilling to appeal to the consequences of acts. For example, assume that Jones borrows money, promising to pay it back, though he knows he will not be able to do so. In performing this action, Jones declares his willingness to allow everyone else to break their promises as well. Kant believes this is obviously absurd, and so Jones's action is irrational. But in regard to why this is irrational, Kant is not entirely convincing.[20] Obviously, Kant believes it is a contradiction for Jones to act on the basis of a rule he would not allow for others. However, it is not clear exactly why Jones would not permit others to act on this rule.

Confronted with an example of this sort, we would probably say that Jones is unwilling to allow everyone to break their promises because he recognizes the importance of the institution of promising and so would not allow it to be undermined. If everyone broke promises, it would be impossible to rely on other people; contracts would not exist, to say nothing of informal agreements between people and such things as marriage vows. The result would be a more difficult life for everyone. In contrast with Kant's view, we would attribute Jones's inconsistency not to inherent self-contradiction but to his concern for the maintenance of important social rules.

In criticizing Kant, Hegel builds on this line of argument. Very briefly, he argues that consistency alone is not an adequate basis for moral rules. He believes Kant's arguments appear to go through only because Kant *covertly* appeals to consequences in demonstrating the impossibility of irrational behavior. According to Hegel, *any* principle can be acceptable as a universal maxim for action, if one does not care about the consequences. In the example we have noted, Kant argues for the absurdity of the false promise as follows:

> For the universality of a law that every one believing himself to be in need can make any promise he pleases with intention not to keep it would make promising, and the

very purpose of promising, itself impossible, since no one would believe he was being promised anything, but would laugh at utterances of this kind as empty shams. (*Groundwork*, Chap. 2, p. 90)

While Kant apparently views this situation as involving a logical absurdity, Hegel believes the absurdity of the promise stems from our unwillingness to accept the severe consequences involved. If Jones were willing to live without the institution of promising, he would allow other people to follow the same moral rule he assigns to himself and so would not be inconsistent.

Hegel criticizes Kant's view in the second part of *Philosophy of Right*, which he calls "Morality." He believes a great advantage of Kant's view is its ability to establish the morality of actions solely on the basis of the individual's own will. What any one of us is able to will rationally and so consistently is moral, without reference to any further standard. However, Hegel characterizes Kant's view as "the pure unconditioned self-determination of the will," and dismisses it as "empty formalism" (*Philosophy of Right*, Par. 135, pp. 89–90), because Kant gives substantial guidance as to *how* we should will, but is less helpful in regard to *what* we should will. Because *any* maxim can be acted upon as long as one is willing to accept the consequences of allowing everyone else to follow it, Hegel argues that moral actions must rest on something beyond the individual's will. While he agrees with Kant's claim that moral actions must be rational in form, he believes rationality alone cannot provide their content. In order to explain why a given action is unacceptable, we must appeal to social rules and institutions we are unwilling to do without:

> The absence of property contains in itself just as little contradiction as the nonexistence of this or that nation, family, &c., or the death of the whole human race. But if it is already established on other grounds and presupposed that property and human life are to exist and be respected, then indeed it is a contradiction to commit theft or murder; a contradiction must be a contradiction of something, i.e., of some content presupposed from the start as a fixed principle. It is to a principle of that kind alone, therefore, that an action can be related either by correspondence or contradiction. (*Philosophy of Right*, Par. 135, p. 90)

Hegel's distinctive position is that the necessary content of moral actions must be supplied by an existing society and state. He refers to the network of rules established in a given society as the "ethical order" or "ethical life." The German word he uses is *Sittlichkeit*, which derives from *Sitte*, which means "custom." In using the term *Sittlichkeit*, Hegel does not refer to customs alone. Rather, he means "the laws and institutions of a social, cultural, and legal nature that inform the life of a people."[21] In Charles Taylor's words, "*Sittlichkeit* refers to the moral obligations I have to an ongoing community of which I am part. These obligations are based on established norms and uses" (Taylor, p. 376). The need to conform to an existing ethical order is the heart of Hegel's argument that full freedom can be attained only through the agency of the state.

There is something strongly counter-intuitive in the claim that freedom consists in the requirement, the duty, to conform to the dictates of an ethical order. Because freedom is self-determination, this appears not to exist if the individual must submit to rules and institutions external to himself. But in accordance with what we have seen in this section, we can make sense of Hegel's view. To act in accordance with the ethical order is to be governed by rational norms, which are chosen rationally. Hegel's view of the substantive rationality of existing norms is a subject to which we will return. But it is clear immediately that behaving in this way liberates the individual from two impediments to freedom: the dictates of whims and impulses, and the empty formalism of trying to ground one's actions solely on one's own will. To choose the norms of one's society is a self-conscious act, while these rules give content to one's choices. In Hegel's words,

> The bond of duty can appear as a restriction only on indeterminate subjectivity or abstract freedom, and on the impulses either of the natural will or of the moral will which determines its indeterminate good arbitrarily. The truth is, however, that in duty the individual finds his liberation; first, liberation from dependence on mere natural impulse and from the depression which as a particular subject he cannot escape in his moral reflections on what ought to be and what might be; secondly, liberation from the indeterminate subjectivity which, never reaching reality or the objective determinacy of action, remains self-enclosed and devoid of actuality. In duty the individual acquires his substantive freedom. (*Philosophy of Right*, Par. 149, p. 107)

However, even if we grant that acceptance of the ethical order liberates the individual from these impediments to freedom, it is not clear that this submission is an improvement. The ethical order still appears to be external to the individual. It is not clear how submission to such rules can be reconciled with self-determination. We will examine this claim in the following section.

To close this section, we can note that Hegel's realization of the distance between his own and the traditional liberal conception of freedom, which he calls "abstract freedom," is clear in his embrace of "positive freedom":

> Duty is a restriction only on the self-will of subjectivity. It stands in the way only of that abstract good to which subjectivity adheres. When we say: 'We want to be free,' the primary meaning of the word is simply: 'We want abstract freedom,' and every institution and every organ of the state passes as a restriction on freedom of that kind. Thus duty is not a restriction on freedom, but only on freedom in the abstract, i.e., on unfreedom. Duty is the attainment of our essence, the winning of *positive* freedom. (*Philosophy of Right*, Par. 149A, pp. 259–260)

SOCIAL CONSTITUTION OF THE SELF

Hegel is able to argue that freedom lies in acting in accordance with the rules of the ethical order, because he does not view this as standing in opposition to the individual inhabitants of the state. Hegel's view, which can be described as *the social constitution of the self*, stands in sharp opposition to major currents in liberal political theory. The liberal theorists we have examined posit a separation between the individual and society. Society is generally viewed as nothing but a collection of individuals, who come together out of self-interest, in order to achieve ends they have prior to entering it. The distance between the individual and society is most apparent in the state of nature theories of Hobbes and Locke. Though Rousseau criticizes Hobbes for reading qualities of social man back into the state of nature, the Hobbesian individual is in important respects an asocial creature, intent on satisfying his own desires. For Hobbes and Locke, and other liberal theorists, the individual attains his identity from sources other than society. The views of liberal theorists concerning the source of identity parallel those concerning desires and interests discussed in the previous section.

Hegel's far-reaching inquiry into the nature of the self gives rise to a more searching account of the relationship between the individual and society. His view of the social constitution of the self centers on the close relationship between the individual and the society to which he belongs. In our discussion of Montesquieu in Chapter 5, we saw that each culture has distinctive characteristics, and so individuals who are raised in different cultures differ as well. Hegel believes Montesquieu's analysis is "thorough and profound" (*Reason in History*, p. 27). He takes this line of analysis much farther, exploring just how the institutions and practices of a society shape individual identity. Hegel believes the abstract individual in the state of nature discussed by liberal theorists has no basis in reality. We have noted repeatedly that the individual is necessarily born into a society—and so the claim that political relationships rest on voluntary choices is a myth. More than this, the individual does not create his identity out of whole cloth, but becomes the person he is through the agency of society. In his Introduction to the *Philosophy of History*, Hegel writes: "Each individual is the son of his own nation at a specific stage in this nation's development. No one can escape from the spirit of his nation, any more than he can escape from the earth itself" (*Reason in History*, p. 81). Hegel's claim is obviously true in regard to language. According to liberal theory, the individual is above all a rational, thinking being. But the language in which he thinks is that of his society, which he learns by living in it. There can be no thought without language—the particular language of a particular society. Thus individual identity is not chosen in the abstract. "The individual does not invent his content, but merely activates the substantial content which is already present within him" (*Reason in History*, p. 81). Taylor makes this point clearly:

> We can think that the individual is what he is in abstraction from his community only if we are thinking of him qua organism. But when we think of a human being, we do not simply mean a living organism, but a being who can think, feel, decide, be moved, respond, enter into relations with others; and all this implies a language, a related set of ways of experiencing the world, of interpreting his feelings, understanding his relation to others, to the past, the future, the absolute, and so on. It is the particular way he situates himself within this cultural world that we call his identity. (p. 380)

To carry this line of thought an additional step farther, Hegel also believes individual identity is built up from a series of roles provided by society.

It is possible for an individual to minimize his contact with society, most obviously by living reclusively. But a life of this sort is limiting. An individual living outside society is unlikely to develop all his capacities. As Aristotle says in the *Politics*, the individual who can realize all his powers apart from society must be either more than or less than human, either a beast or a god.[22] Outside society, the individual "is like the war-mad man condemned in Homer's words as 'having no family, no law, no home.'"[23] In discussing freedom, Hegel speaks of "indeterminate subjectivity which, never reaching reality or the objective determinacy of action, remains self-enclosed and devoid of actuality" (*Philosophy of Right*, Par. 149, p. 107). In order to avoid this undeveloped condition, a person must live as a member of his society. Not to do so is to remain indeterminate, self-enclosed, and devoid of reality. The crucial connection between individual and society lies in the fact that the range of options from which one can choose is provided by society. Just as the words and concepts with which one thinks are those of the language of one's culture, so one creates his identity by assuming a series of roles that are similarly supplied. An individual is able to develop his full potential—and so to become fully human—only by entering into specific relationships with other members of society. These relationships are conducted according to socially defined rules, which the individual must internalize. As he takes these into himself, they become constitutive of his identity.

Hegel's point can be illustrated by examining the identity of a typical (or, at least, not atypical) member of society. Let us imagine Smith, who is a married man with children. He works as a teacher, and has been employed in that capacity for many years. There are of course other aspects of his identity, but we can concentrate on these. Let us assume Smith is having an extremely bad day. He yells at his students and storms out of the lecture hall. His students are likely to think *he is not himself* today. Similarly, upon arriving at home, he ignores his children to go work on some hobby. When the children seek his attention, he yells at them too. They too are likely to think *he is not himself* today, as will his wife if he picks a fight with her.

The point here is that people with whom Smith regularly interacts build up expectations in regard to his behavior. When he behaves in an unusual or abnormal manner, they respond—that is not like him; he is not being *himself*. When Smith is being himself, he behaves in accordance with the expectations of other people. But more than this, he also behaves according to the established rules of social roles he occupies. The expectations he fails to meet on an especially bad day bear on his usual conduct according to these rules.

The expectations held by the people with whom Smith interacts are not simply dreamed up by them. They are built into the fabric of society. For example, Smith's students expect competent instruction from him. But teaching them properly is not something he just happens to do. He has not invented his repertoire of pedagogical techniques. Rather, these had to be learned, through both training and experience. Over the years, he has acquired a collection of techniques which he has found to be especially effective. Not surprisingly, these are similar to techniques other teachers have learned or discovered, which are common throughout the teaching profession.

Now, contrast Smith's normal, carefully rehearsed classroom performance with how he would behave in the throes of some mental illness or other circumstance that affected his ability to function. He would not be able to lecture or control his class; rather, he might behave irrationally, raving and carrying on. Or he might not be able to stand before his class at all and run out of the room. We have noted that in engaging in these aberrant forms of behavior, Smith is not being himself. What is crucial to note is that he *is* himself in following the norms of the teaching profession. Because many people have been teaching for centuries, a store of knowledge has been built up about what works and does not work, and this knowledge has been incorporated into society's expectations about teachers' performance. A good teacher stays within established guidelines—though perhaps deviating in particular respects in accordance with his own proclivities. Thus as Smith conducts himself in accordance with the carefully rehearsed rules he has learned through experience, he occupies the socially defined role of effective teacher. In doing so, he realizes his professional ambitions and so a central aspect of himself.

What is true of Smith's behavior as a teacher also holds in other aspects of his life, in regard to his activities as husband, father, and so on. In each case, effective performance of the role requires behavior according to a textured framework of rules that define normal performance. In choosing to occupy a given role, Smith also accepts these rules. When he gets married, he assumes duties to love, honor, and cherish his wife, as behavior of this kind is necessary to a successful marriage. Rules of this sort, though not always easy to formulate explicitly, ground moral duties, because success in an area of life depends on them.

Hegel believes the substance of a person's life is the set of roles he occupies. His life is built upon such roles, with each particular role in turn structured according to the traditions of his society and the expectations grown up around them. In occupying each of his major roles, a person's behavior is largely in conformity with societal norms. But this does not make it less central to his identity—just as the fact that his thoughts are in his society's language does not make them less his own. The set of roles a person occupies gives structure to his life, defining his identity in the eyes of other people, and his own as well. Thus Hegel writes of the rules of the ethical order:

> [T]hey are not something alien to the subject. On the contrary, his spirit bears witness to them as to its own essence, the essence in which he has a feeling of his selfhood, and in which he lives as in his own element which is not distinguished from himself. The subject is thus directly linked to the ethical order by a relation which is more like an identity than even the relation of faith or trust. (*Philosophy of Right*, Par. 147, p. 106)

Hegel's close association of the individual and society runs counter to common liberal convictions. To people with liberal political ideas, it seems odd to speak of freedom as conformity to social rules, which one has had no part in making. Deeply imbedded in the liberal tradition are values of individualism and spontaneity. Freedom, according to the liberal conception, includes the notion of doing as one pleases. This in turn is widely viewed as including ability to act against stodgy traditions. Hegel's response to this claim has been seen in the previous section. He would of course argue that acting from momentary feelings or inclinations is not consistent with self-determination. As for conforming to traditions, this is an important component of most people's lives. A life of opposition to existing society, like that of a recluse, is largely devoid of substance, in comparison to full participation in different aspects of society. Someone who only opposes the practices of others without creating his own alternative way of life will lead a life of "indeterminacy."

Though indeterminacy preserves the possibility of spontaneity, it precludes significant action. Every time a person chooses, something is lost. At one point, a young man is free to marry any woman in the world. Then he chooses a particular woman, and all other options are closed. In choosing a single woman, he renounces innumerable others. But the implication here is that the freedom to marry whomever one chooses survives only as long as it is not exercised. Hegel believes the individual is truly free only when he exercises the freedom to choose, and so takes on a network of social rules and customs. In the words of one commentator, "Then and only then is his will free not merely potentially, and free not merely in the abstract and negative sense of pure indeterminateness, but free actually and in a concrete and positive sense."[24] To preserve the freedom to choose—by not exercising it—is to retain only the illusion of freedom.

Though freedom requires assuming a range of preexisting social roles, individual choice is not eliminated entirely. This is true most obviously in modern societies. Such a society offers a range of options in regard to career, family, and other aspects of life. In the example discussed above, Smith is himself and self-determined when he acts according to the rules that dictate the conduct of teachers. But he might have chosen to be a lawyer, a pharmacist, or an engineer. In each of these cases, he would have chosen to assume a range of established rules along with his choice of profession. Though there is an element of discretion in regard to which norms he will assume, even in this case it is clear that a person's options are limited by the range of possible careers offered in his society. Smith cannot choose to be a nuclear physicist unless the study of nuclear physics has been established. The rules and customs of modern society are such that he cannot choose to be an alchemist. Though the individual has some discretion in choosing particular social roles, this does not alter the fact that he comes to be defined by existing norms in his society.

We can see why Hegel believes established social rules have greater substance than what an individual can create for himself by looking briefly at the institution of marriage. According to the popular view, marriage is a relationship built on love. This view emerged relatively recently along with the practice of voluntary marriage, according to which a man and woman could marry because they wished to do so, rather than because their parents or other people believed they made a good match. The popular view of marriage places emotion at its center. People should not get married unless they are in love, with the unhappy implication that if they fall out of love or otherwise grow apart, they can divorce. This view of marriage is obviously closely related to the liberal conception of the state as a union of individuals, joined out of self-interest. According to liberal political theory, when political relationships no longer serve their function—when the contract of government is broken, or the state does more harm than good—they too can be dissolved.

Hegel believes emotion, caprice, is not a sufficient basis for a substantial moral relationship. If marriage is based on love, this has the potential of leaving the individual hostage to his emotions. Dependence on how one feels, as we have seen, is not self-determination, and so not freedom. Hegel believes the marriage relationship becomes fully real only through its connection with the ethical order. While sentiment, even love, is subject to change, the ethical order is permanent. In taking their wedding vows, a man and woman unite their wills with the will of the state. In Hegel's words, "the spiritual bond of union secures its rights as the substance of marriage and thus rises, inherently indissoluble, to a plane above the contingency of passion and the transience of particular caprice" (*Philosophy of Right*, Par. 163, p. 112). After the wedding vows have been taken, the rights and obligations of marriage are placed beyond the feelings of the people involved. The responsibilities of each partner are spelled out in the norms of society, which exist in the ethical order, in permanent, concrete form. To fulfill one's ethical obligations in marriage, one has only to follow these rules. Both life and literature are replete with tales of married people whose feelings change, often with tragic results. This possibility is foreclosed as man and woman solidify their relationship in the ethical order, becoming husband and wife, and achieving security from the tyranny of feeling. This "eliminates from marriage the transient, fickle, and purely subjective aspects of love" (*Philosophy of Right*, Par. 161A, p. 262). The ceremonial aspects of marriage signify its ethical reality:

> [T]he solemn declaration by the parties of their consent to enter the ethical bond of marriage, and its corresponding recognition and confirmation by their family and community, constitutes the formal completion and actuality of marriage. The knot is tied and made ethical only after this ceremony, whereby . . . the substantial thing in the marriage is brought completely into being. As a result, the sensuous moment, the one proper to physical life, is put into its ethical place as something only consequential and accidental, belonging to the external embodiment of the ethical bond, which indeed can subsist exclusively in reciprocal love and support. (*Philosophy of Right*, Par. 164, p. 113)

If marriage is taken so seriously, it follows that divorce must be difficult to obtain. One implication of the popular view of marriage is that people should not be forced to stay married if they are no longer in love. Because he elevates marriage above the realm of feelings, Hegel does not believe feelings should justify ending a marriage: "Marriage is not to be dissolved because of passion, since passion is subordinate to it." In making divorce as difficult as possible, lawgivers preserve marriage's sacred character, and so "uphold the right of the ethical order against caprice" (Par. 163A, pp. 262–263).

As depicted here, marriage is representative of the ethical order as a whole. As husband and wife fulfill their moral obligations through this institution, the same is true in other spheres of life. Rather than following one's own will or inclinations, one should be guided by the rules of the existing ethical order. "In an *ethical* community, it is easy to say what man must do, what are the duties he has to fulfill in order to be virtuous: he has simply to follow the well-known and explicit rules of his own situation" (*Philosophy of Right*, Par. 150, p. 107). In adhering to social norms, a person does not subordinate himself to something outside himself; he becomes himself.

Though Hegel views adherence to social norms as rational life, this does not rule out other aspects of one's personality, for example, feelings, spontaneity. Adherence to social norms takes precedence over these elements; it is within the structure of defined roles that these other factors should take shape. Whims, impulses, emotions should not stand apart from one's social identity but be focused by it. In attempting to harmonize reason and feeling in this way, Hegel stands opposed to common liberal conceptions. According to him, the liberal view unduly emphasizes discretion, the ability to choose what one wants. Hegel of course rejects this view because he sees feeling as an inadequate basis for action. But in spite of his opposition to feeling in this respect, a central theme of his philosophy is the need to integrate feeling and reason harmoniously. This is accomplished in the ethical order. In pursuing his career as a teacher, Smith should not act rationally *rather than* passionately in following the norms of his profession, which are grounded in reason. His passion should be invested in the stable framework of his role as a teacher—instead of being the sole basis for his conduct. Similarly, though his relationship with his wife should not have feeling for its main support, Hegel of course does not believe Smith should *not* love his wife. Rather, love should grow within the stable framework provided by the institution of marriage. Instead of wishing to eliminate feeling from ethical life—which is an error he attributes to Kant—Hegel wishes to situate it properly within the ethical order. Only in this way, he believes, can all human faculties be integrated in fully harmonious lives.

WORLD HISTORY AND THE STATE

Hegel's claim that freedom is union with the ethical order of an existing society is plausible only if the ethical order is in fact rational. If the institutions of one's society are grossly evil or immoral, one could hardly behave rationally in accepting them. Fortunately, as far as Hegel is concerned, the situation in his society is not of this kind. He views the Germanic world as essentially rational. In the Preface to *Philosophy of Right*, he expresses the conviction: "*What is rational is actual and what is actual is rational*" (p. 10). By this he means that what exists is inherently rational, because it is the product of purposive historical development. In this respect, Hegel's view is similar to those of Burke and Montesquieu, who explain existing conditions as produced by fundamental underlying processes. Hegel's view, however, is more complex. He not only sees what is as the result of rational processes, but also believes these processes are impelled to realize themselves in the world—to give rise to something actual. Hegel believes the Germanic realm represents the culmination of the overall process that constitutes world history. This realm's privileged place in world history is central to his *Philosophy of History*.

The main theme of the *Philosophy of History* is the process of world history as progressive, moving in the direction of increasing rationality and freedom. This is fairly straightforward, and Hegel illustrates this theme with a wealth of supporting material. His reasons for viewing history in this light, however, are complicated, and will be only touched on here. Hegel's belief in the rationality of the ethical order depends on his understanding of the modern state's place in world history. His distinctive view is that world history is not only rational but the unfolding of divine Reason.

Hegel's conception of world history is essentially a religious view. But in his thought, theology and philosophy are one. While religion studies God through images and representations, philosophy apprehends God's nature by means of concepts, through the medium of rational thought. Thus Hegel argues that "the distinction between faith and knowledge is in fact an empty one" (*Reason in History*, p. 41). In the same way God reveals himself in the form of the Christian religion, wherein he can be apprehended by faith, he also reveals himself to human reason through his works in the world. There is an inner logic to the course of history, which can be rationally understood. But more than this, Hegel believes the historical process discloses not only God's plan but his essence.

Hegel's idea of God is unusual. He does not believe God is, from the beginning, perfect and transcendent; rather, God requires the opposition of the external world to realize these attributes. In other words, it is only through history that God becomes God. As Plant says, Hegel's God "is not to be conceived as in the Judaic religion as the perfect, self-sufficient sovereign lord of the Universe, but rather in a deep sense dependent on his creation as the medium of his own development, a development which by taking place in the world can be comprehended by the philosopher" (p. 137). If God were perfect, he would have had no reason to create the world. "If God is all-sufficient and lacks nothing, why does he disclose himself in the sheer other of Himself?" (Hegel, quoted by Plant, p. 136).

Hegel believes God requires the world so that, in overcoming its opposition to himself, he can achieve self-knowledge. The essence of God—otherwise identified as Spirit, the Idea, or the World Spirit—is freedom. We have seen that Hegel views freedom as self-determination. Because God is a perfect being, he cannot be dependent on anything outside himself. But because all knowledge requires an object, God's self-knowledge can be gained only by reflecting on his apprehension of some object. For God this purpose is served by the world. Hegel accepts the Aristotelian teaching that God is thought which has itself as its object. God can only have himself as an object of knowledge by reflecting on the process through which he apprehends an object outside himself, the world, which he creates for this purpose, through an act of self-externalization. God's self-knowledge, then, develops over time through the process by which he apprehends the world, which is history. At the beginning of time, God stands opposed to the world. The vehicle through which the world is apprehended and God's self-knowledge progresses is the consciousness of human beings. "The world spirit is the spirit of the world as it reveals itself through the human consciousness; the relationship of men to it is that of single parts to the whole which is their substance" (*Reason in History*, p. 52).

Hegel's notion of "Spirit" is elusive. As he argues in the *Phenomenology*, this should be understood as the consciousness of human beings, in a collective sense. He describes Spirit as "this absolute substance which is the unity of the different independent self-consciousnesses . . . 'I' that is 'We' and 'We' that is I" (*Phenomenology*, B. IV, p. 110).[25] Briefly, an important implication of his view of Spirit is identification of the consciousness of human beings and of God. Throughout the course of history, human beings attain self-knowledge. In coming to know themselves as beings whose purpose it is to know themselves, they achieve self-determination and so freedom in Hegel's sense. Through this process, God attains self-knowledge and realizes himself as God. In world history freedom and consciousness develop in tandem: "World history is the progress of the consciousness of freedom—a progress whose necessity it is our business to comprehend" (*Reason in History*, p. 54).

Regardless of the extent to which this complex web of ideas can be clearly grasped, the overall direction of history is, again, straightforward. Civilizations are the vehicles through which history develops. Hegel depicts these as links in a chain, reaching toward the full flowering of freedom realized in his own society. The main civilizations he discusses are the Oriental world, Greece, Rome, and the Germanic world, by which he means Protestant Northern Europe since the Reformation. His basic position is that the consciousness of freedom develops to a certain point in a given civilization. At that point, having exhausted the possibilities of that stage of development, the spirit of freedom leaves it behind to move on to the next stage. The process is cruel, as innumerable individuals are ruthlessly sacrificed to the demands of the evolving World Spirit. History is a "slaughter-bench," on which "the happiness of nations, the wisdom of states, and the virtue of individuals" meet their end (*Phil. Hist.*, p. 21; *Reason in History*, p. 69). Though the growth of reason cannot pause to consider the welfare of individuals, Hegel's overall vision is a theodicy, a justification of the evils of the world. The suffering of single individuals is compensated by the growth of freedom produced by the historical process as a whole.

Hegel believes the main civilizations that arose in world history represent different stages of progress toward freedom. He describes the stages as follows:

> The East knew and the present day knows only that *One* is Free; the Greek and Roman world, that *some* are free; the German World knows that *All* are free. The first political form therefore which we observe in History, is *Despotism*, the second *Democracy* and *Aristocracy*, the third *Monarchy*. (*Phil. Hist.*, p. 104)

Hegel's depiction of monarchy (rather than democracy) as the highest form of state in which all are free must strike us as surprising. Though he has in mind a specific form of monarchy, akin to that of Prussia in his own day, this still raises the question whether his political theory is skewed to justify the Prussian state. We will return to this important question in our final section.

There is an obvious logic to history's overall pattern. Freedom, as we have seen, is self-determination. In Oriental society, all people live under the brutal sway of a despot's will. Only the despot himself is determined by his own will, and so can be considered free. "The glory of Oriental conception is the One Individual as that substantial being to which all belongs, so that no other individual has a separate existence, or mirrors himself in his subjective freedom" (*Phil. Hist.*, p. 105). In a larger sense, however, even the despot is not free, as his will is dominated by brutal passions rather than reason. Hegel discusses various Oriental despotisms—China, India, Egypt, Persia—but all are relatively undeveloped in regard to freedom. Comparing the development of Spirit in different societies to the stages of a person's life, Hegel describes the Oriental stage as "the childhood of History" (*Phil. Hist.*, p. 105).

In Greek society, the "adolescence" of History (p. 108), a higher stage is achieved, as people are able to live according to their own wills. But this is a right reserved for the few, because the institution of slavery precludes freedom for all men (*Reason in History*, p. 54). In addition, the freedom of the privileged few is not fully realized. In the Greek mind, individual wills are united with important abstract moral norms such as justice, but the union is unconscious:

> Of the Greeks in the first and genuine form of their Freedom, we may assert, that they had no conscience; the habit of living for their country without further reflection, was the principle dominant among them. (*Phil. Hist.*, p. 253)

Thus when Socrates inaugurated the practice of questioning one's moral convictions and so getting people to think critically about them, this was a significant threat to Greek morality. In condemning Socrates to death, the Athenians were justified: "the sentence bears on the one hand the aspect of unimpeachable rectitude—inasmuch as the Athenian people condemns its deadliest foe." But simply stopping Socrates could not halt the rising historical tide of individualism that had begun to sweep the Greek world. The essence of Greek morality, full integration into society and acceptance of its norms, was irrevocably changed by the emergence of self-conscious thought. "Spirit had acquired the propensity to gain satisfaction for itself—to reflect" (*Phil. Hist.*, pp. 269–270).

The Roman stage is the manhood of History (p. 107). This surpasses the Greek level in extent; in the Roman state, individuals unite with something universal, and are rewarded with legal rights. These represent a development past the Greek stage, as they are secured by positive law, and so distinct from morality (p. 289). But here too government is according to the whims of a single despot.

Finally, the German phase represents the full flowering of Spirit, its old age. But Hegel adds that this is not a debilitated condition, as Spirit, unlike the individual, does not perish. Rather, it is old age as increased maturity. The key to this stage is freedom of conscience, won by the Reformation. This established subjectivity as "the common property of *all mankind*." The subject himself judges religious truth, choosing the principles to which he will surrender, and in the process making the truth his own: "the banner of *Free Spirit*, independent, though finding its life in the Truth, and enjoying independence only in it. This is the banner under which we serve, and which we bear." The Reformation declares its essential principle: "Man is in his very nature destined to be free" (*Phil. Hist.*, pp. 416–417).

Hegel describes the different stages of history in considerable detail. Though the vehicle of historical progress is the state, at each stage an entire civilization is built up around it. Especially important are the components of what Hegel calls Absolute Spirit, each civilization's art, religion, and philosophy. These elements are organically connected; all represent a particular point in the development of Spirit, which is visible in all of its aspects. For instance, the stage of development represented by the Greek mind is evident in its anthropomorphic conception of the gods, which indicates the value the Greeks place on the human individual. This obviously contrasts with the Oriental world, which associated the gods with forces of nature. But though the Greek conception moves beyond the Oriental, it is still imperfect: "the divinity of the Greeks is not yet the *absolute*, free Spirit, but Spirit in a particular mode, fettered by the limitations of humanity—still dependent as a determinate individuality on external conditions." The limitations of this conception are apparent if we look forward to the bodiless, universal God of Christianity. Thus the Greeks' lack of self-consciousness about themselves shows up in their religion: "since they did not yet realize Spirit in its Universality—[they] had not the idea of man and the essential unity of the divine and human nature according to the Christian view" (*Phil. Hist.*, pp. 244, 250). The relatively undeveloped consciousness of the Oriental stage is apparent throughout its culture. In different areas, one can literally see Spirit just beginning to emerge from nature:

> Of the representations which Egyptian Antiquity presents us with, one figure must be especially noticed, viz. *the Sphinx*—in itself a riddle—an ambiguous form, half brute, half human. The Sphinx may be regarded as a symbol of the Egyptian Spirit. The human head looking out from the brute body, exhibits Spirit as it begins to emerge from the merely Natural—to tear itself loose therefrom and already to look more freely around it; without, however, entirely freeing itself from the fetters Nature had imposed. The innumerable edifices of the Egyptians are half below the ground, and half rise above it into the air. The whole land is divided into a kingdom of life and a kingdom of death . . . Written language is still a hieroglyphic; and its basis is only the sensuous image, not the letter itself. (*Phil. Hist.*, p. 199)[26]

More than the details of the specific stages of historical development, Hegel is concerned to demonstrate the progress of Spirit towards self-consciousness and freedom. Though human societies are the vehicles through which Spirit develops, its progress follows its own logic, which is beyond the capacity of historical actors to grasp. It is only in retrospect, looking backward after the development of a specific stage is complete, that one can make out its role in the course of world history's "long and laborious journey"

(*Phenomenology*, Pref., p. 88, Baillie trans.). Hegel describes philosophy as "its own time apprehended in thoughts" (*Philosophy of Right*, Pref., p. 11). Philosophy cannot move beyond the confines of the society in which it exists in order to predict the future or to make moral recommendations that outstrip the development of its place in the progress of civilization. Philosophy's task is to grasp what the process of history has brought forth: "To comprehend what is, this is the task of philosophy, because what is is reason" (*Philosophy of Right*, Pref., p. 11). But to understand what is, one must examine how it came to be. Looking back over the development of world history, the philosopher is able to grasp its inevitable path, in a way that transcends the understanding of people who were involved in historical events. Just as philosophy cannot project itself beyond the framework of its own time into the future, so historical actors are bound by their own time. This is true even of the great men who are responsible for the epochal events through which history moves forward.

Hegel's account of the role of great men in history is one of the best-known aspects of his theory. He refers to important actors as "world historical individuals." Examples are Alexander the Great and Julius Caesar, men whose actions brought about monumental changes in their civilizations. During Hegel's own time, the most striking example was Napoleon. Hegel, who supported the spread of the ideals of the French Revolution, which Napoleon facilitated, was greatly impressed at seeing Napoleon ride through Jena after his great victory in the battle of Jena. In a famous letter, he wrote:

> The Emperor—this world soul—I saw riding through the city to a review of his troops; it is indeed a wonderful feeling to see such an individual who, here concentrated in a single point, sitting on a horse, reaches out over the world and dominates it. (in Kaufmann, pp. 318–319)

Similarly important individuals who have emerged since Hegel's time are Lenin, Hitler, Gandhi, and Mao Tse-tung. As a rule, such people are not outstanding from a moral point of view (though Gandhi would be an exception). In fact, one of their vital functions is to burst the constraints of the moral systems of their societies—in order to help inaugurate new ones. Their actions bring about widespread suffering: "A mighty figure must trample many an innocent flower underfoot, and destroy much that lies in its path" (*Reason in History*, p. 89). By seizing upon the historical potential present in a given moment, they are able to move the process forward.

> The great individuals of world history, therefore, are those who seize upon this higher universal and make it their own end. It is they who realize the end appropriate to the higher concept of the spirit. (*Reason in History*, pp. 82–83)

In their actions, however, these people do not have the goals of world history in view. Rather, they are men of passion, moved by their own particular interests. Because of their political acumen and power, they are able to accomplish great deeds. But in spite of their own designs, the ends they accomplish are not the ones they set for themselves, but the purposes of the World Spirit, which unbeknownst to them, governs their situation: "Caesar had to do what was necessary to overthrow the decaying freedom of Rome; he himself met his end in the struggle, but necessity triumphed . . ." (p. 89).

Hegel refers to the World Spirit's ability to use the passions of people towards its own ends as "the cunning of reason." Through this means, history "sets the passions to work in its service, so that the agent by which it gives itself existence must pay the penalty and suffer the loss" (p. 89). Thus history works through a law of unanticipated consequences. Great men act to achieve specific purposes, to which they dedicate and with which they identify themselves (p. 86). Through their actions, great things are indeed brought about, but not the ones conceived by their limited vision. History sees farther than any individual actor. Though great men are necessary for historical movement, they occupy the stage only until history is done with them, at which point "they fall aside like empty husks" (p. 85).

Because of the limitations inherent at each stage of historical development, the inhabitants of a given civilization can see no farther than its horizons. In one of his most famous pronouncements, in the Preface to the *Philosophy of Right*, Hegel describes this limitation:

> One word more about giving instruction as to what the world ought to be. Philosophy in any case always comes on the scene too late to give it. As the thought of the world, it appears only when actuality is already there cut and dried after its process of formation has been completed. The teaching of the concept, which is also history's inescapable lesson, is that it is only when actuality is mature that the ideal first appears over against the real and that the ideal apprehends this same real world in its substance and builds it up for itself into the shape of an intellectual realm. When philosophy paints its grey in grey, then has a shape of life grown old. By philosophy's grey in grey it cannot be rejuvenated but only understood. The owl of Minerva spreads its wings only with the falling of the dusk. (pp. 12–13)

The reference to "grey in grey" is to Goethe; Hegel is referring to the idea that philosophy paints the grey of theory against the background of a greying—or aging—world.[27] The owl is the symbol of the goddess Minerva (Athena), goddess of wisdom. Thus Hegel holds that philosophy can describe only what exists before it at a particular time, in the light of the past events that have brought it about. Limited by the perspective of his time, the philosopher can theorize only upon the development of civilization up until his time. It follows that the full import of an historical stage can be understood and captured in a philosophical system only when it has realized its full potential and so exhausted its capacity for further progress. Hegel believes his own position is privileged. Obviously he has the great advantage over previous philosophers of coming after them and so being able to see farther ahead. But he also believes history has reached its culmination in his own stage of civilization. In the civilization of Germany (again, Protestant Northern Europe), the World Spirit has realized its full potential. Through the media of Germanic art, religion, and philosophy it has come to understand the reason for its long travails; in understanding itself, it is now self-conscious and free. In Germany, as we have seen, all are free. Hegel believes he is the philosopher of Germanic freedom, and so of the full development of Spirit. In his philosophy, Spirit has achieved self-consciousness and is able to look back on the great distance it has had to travel in order to realize itself.

Through its historical journey, Spirit has refashioned the world after its own image. The world no longer stands opposed to Spirit as something external to it, but in the external world, Spirit is able to recognize itself. Because the vehicle through which Spirit moves forward is human consciousness, man now recognizes himself in the ethical order, and so is at home in what was once external to him. Hegel notes that in earlier stages of historical development, before human beings achieved full self-consciousness, moral norms were accepted without self-consciousness. As we have seen, this was a crucial feature of Greek society. Though the Greeks achieved a level of significant moral development, the norms to which they adhered were regarded as given and were accepted without criticism. Hegel illustrates this point with reference to Sophocles' play *Antigone*. "If we consider ethical life from the objective standpoint, we may say that in it we are ethical unselfconsciously. In this sense, Antigone proclaims that 'no one know whence the laws come; they are everlasting'. . ." (*Philosophy of Right*, Par. 144A, p. 259).

In Germanic society, Spirit has moved to a higher level. For full freedom to be realized, moral norms must be rational, so that in obeying them, the individual behaves rationally, as opposed to following the caprice of appetite. In addition, if complete freedom is self-determination, in obeying the rules of the ethical order, the individual must obey only himself. In one sense, this condition is met, as long as the ethical order is rational. For the essence of man is rationality; in obeying the ethical order, the individual adheres to principles that embody his own essential nature. Hegel takes this line of argument an additional stage farther. The fully self-conscious individual recognizes that the rules of the ethical order are rational and so not only consistent with his nature, but because they were created by Spirit, they are a projection of his nature. The rules of the ethical order do not stand opposed to the self-conscious man; they are a part of him. To repeat a passage quoted above:

> [T]hey are not something alien to the subject. On the contrary, his spirit bears witness to them as to its own essence, the essence in which he has a feeling of his selfhood, and in which he lives as in his own element which is not distinguished from himself. The subject is thus directly linked to the ethical order by a relation which is more like an identity than even the relation of faith or trust. (*Philosophy of Right*, Par. 147, p. 106)

The completion of history is the creation of an ethical order which is fully rational and recognized as such. Since rationality is the essence of human nature, the fully conscious man can subject the rules and norms of his society to critical scrutiny and accept them. In comporting his conduct in accordance with them, he obeys only what is rational and so only himself. In Taylor's words,

> There is nothing in it which is not transparently dictated by reason itself. It is thus not an order beyond man which he must simply accept. Rather it is one which flows from his own nature properly understood. Hence it is centered on autonomy, since to be governed by a law which emanates from oneself is to be free. (Taylor, p. 374)

For self-consciousness to emerge, both the process of history and the rationality of the moral order it has brought forth must be understood. In expounding on these matters in his philosophical works, Hegel is moved by a conviction that rational necessity rules the world. The course of world history is laid bare in his *Philosophy of History*, while the rationality of the ethical order is a central theme of his political theory. As he says at the outset of *Philosophy of Right*, his aim in the work is "to apprehend and portray the state as something inherently rational" (Pref., p. 11).

THE PRUSSIAN STATE

Hegel believes freedom can be achieved in a state along the lines of Prussia, which is the highest stage yet reached. For the most part, his discussion corresponds to the Prussian state of his own time, which he describes as the inevitable product of the World Spirit's development. There are, however, significant departures from the Prussian state, which we will discuss.

We can identify three main principles of Hegel's state. First, it is what Germans call a *Rechtsstaat*, a state ruled by fixed laws, within the confines of which individual rights are securely established. Second, though the state is intended to preserve individual liberty, it is also anti-individualistic and antidemocratic in important respects. Finally, the state is intended to have important functions that are absent from liberal political theory—or from the liberal theories of Hegel's day. In the same sense Hegel's conceptions of freedom and the self carry him beyond the confines of liberal political theory, his view of the state departs from liberal assumptions.

We can begin with the first point. The constitution Hegel posits is based on familiar principles of separation of powers and checks and balances. He envisions a constitutional monarchy. There is a king and a legislature. The legislative body, which has the power to make the laws, is to be divided between two houses. The upper, like the English House of Lords, is hereditary, given over to large landowners. The lower is elected, though as we will see, not by direct popular vote. The powers of the monarch, like those of the contemporary Queen of England, are largely ceremonial. The third major feature of the constitution is the bureaucracy or civil service. No doubt influenced by the strong tradition of Prussian bureaucratic administration, Hegel accords the bureaucracy considerable power.

Though Hegel's state is a monarchy, it differs sharply from despotic, one-man rule. The monarch holds authority by hereditary right, according to the laws of primogeniture (Par. 286), but he has little discretionary authority. In fact, he verges on being a symbol. Hegel insists on the need for a monarch, as the visible embodiment of the will of the state. A law obtains binding force only when it is willed, which comes about when the monarch says, "I will" (Par. 279). But in affixing the stamp of his will to a piece of legislation the monarch cannot resist the decision of his counsellors, the chief officials of the executive departments (Par. 279A). "In a completely organized state, it is only a question of the culminating point of formal decision . . . he has only to say 'yes' and dot the 'i,' because the throne should be such that the significant thing in its holder is not his particular make-up" (Par. 280A, pp. 288–289).

The legislative body, the Estates, stands as a mediating link between the government and society, which is broken into individual people and associations (Par. 302). Member-ship of the first house is based on hereditary landed property. This has the advantage of freeing its members from ties of dependence, from having to rely on either payment by the state or the uncertainty of the business world. Its members are also freed from the temptation to misuse their own property, as this must be handed down to their children. Because of these advantages, members of this class hold their seats by right: "this class is

summoned and entitled to its political vocation by birth without the hazards of election"
(Par. 307, p. 199; Pars. 305–307). Members of the lower house come from the business
world. They are elected, but not by citizens voting as individuals. Rather, they represent the
corporations or associations into which society is divided, which naturally grow up around
different economic and social interests. Selecting members in this way ensures direct
representation of the main branches of society (e.g., trade, manufacture) (Par. 311).
Dividing the legislature between two chambers has an important checking function, in
making bad decisions more difficult to put into law. In addition, with the upper chamber
like the monarch holding power from heredity, divisiveness between monarch and legislature will be lessened (Par. 313). The legislature's main function is of course making laws.
But it does this primarily by drawing on the expertise of the civil service, whose work it
supervises (Par. 301). The Estates also perform an important function by debating public
issues. This helps bring these matters to public attention, while public concern with affairs
of state integrates individuals and the community as a whole (Pars. 314–318).

The third major component of the constitution is the bureaucracy. Hegel calls this
the "universal class," because it is especially well positioned to promote the interest of
society as a whole. "The universal class, or, more precisely, the class of civil servants, must,
purely in virtue of its character as universal, have the universal as the end of its essential
activity" (Par. 303). Its primary function is to apply the law to particular cases. Because the
laws are made by others, it can perform this function with an element of objectivity, and
Hegel provides means to ensure impartial decisions. Officials are to be appointed on the
basis of merit, rather than birth or "native personal gifts" (Par. 291, p. 190), and guaranteed
a secure livelihood. Freed from concern with their own particular interests, they will be able
to concentrate on the good of the state (Par. 294).

More important than the details of Hegel's constitution is the state's regular, legal
character. The stability of the whole and the freedom of the citizens are guaranteed by the
institutions of a rational constitution. Hegel refers to these as "mutually conditioning
moments, organically interconnected" (Par. 286). We have noted the separation of powers
between monarch, bureaucracy, and Estates, with the last in turn divided between two
bodies. The legislature is explicitly enjoined to oversee the bureaucracy, while the independence of the landed upper house frees it from possible sources of temptation and influence.
Within this framework individuals are guaranteed essential rights. Though Hegel does not
believe negative freedom should be the state's main goal, he does not overlook its
importance. He says "the right of subjective freedom" is the chief difference between
antiquity and modern times (*Philosophy of Right*, Par. 124, p. 84). Subjective freedom, what
we refer to as negative freedom, is an essential product of history's development, which
Hegel wishes to preserve. Like Burke, he believes this is best accomplished in the form of
rights guaranteed by the institutions of a stable political system: "[I]f I have a right, it must
at the same time be a right posited in law. I must be able to explain and prove it, and its
validity can only be recognized in society if its rightness in principle is also made a posited
rightness in law" (Par. 222A, p. 274). Hegel believes in a series of inalienable rights. These
include "my personality as such, my universal freedom of will, my ethical life, my religion"
(Par. 66, p. 53). Accordingly, institutions such as slavery and serfdom, which require that
one person be in another's possession, are illegitimate (Par. 66). Along similar lines, moral
freedom requires that religious freedom be respected:

> A religious feeling which is partly in control of someone else is no proper religious feeling at all. The spirit is always one and single and should dwell in me. I am entitled to the union of my potential and my actual being. (Par. 66A, p. 241)

Government is by law, and people have the right to have their cases judged according to precise procedures. This is necessary because "a trial is implicitly an event of universal validity, and although the particular content of the action affects the interests of the parties alone, its universal content, i.e., the right at issue and the judgment thereon, affects the interests of everybody" (Par. 224, p. 142). Other important rights include those to trial by jury (Par. 228), freedom of the press, and freedom to say and think what one pleases. These liberties are, however, restricted by strong laws against libel and falsely criticizing the government and the monarch (Pars. 318–319). The laws of the state are to be administered impartially, and all people stand before them as equals: "A man counts as a man in virtue of his manhood alone, not because he is a Jew, Catholic, Protestant, German, Italian, &c." (Par. 209, p. 134).

Though Hegel upholds important rights, protected by law and constitutional government, he does not support democracy, if we include in this notion direct popular participation in government. In this sense he is like two other conservative thinkers we have discussed, Montesquieu and Burke. His reasons for opposing the extension of democracy are similar to Burke's, mainly fear of its disruptive potential. But in Hegel's case, this position is somewhat surprising. We have noted his belief that history moves in the direction of increasing freedom. One might expect that progress from Oriental despotism, in which one is free, to the modern state in which all are free, would be realized in democracy, government by all. However, Hegel retreats from this view, arguing that all are free under monarchy, which is the culminating political form. Nondemocratic elements of the state include the hereditary positions of the monarch and upper house of the Estates. More important, Hegel resists democracy because he believes it entails the breakdown of society into isolated, atomistic individuals. He views the state as naturally built up from lesser groups, first the family, then economic and other associations. The people as they exist outside such groups are cause for alarm:

> The Many, as units—a congenial interpretation of 'people,' are of course something connected, but they are connected only as an aggregate, a formless mass whose commotion and activity could therefore only be elementary, irrational, barbarous, and frightful. (Par. 303, p. 198)

This view justifies appointing members of the upper house without elections. Though the lower house is elected, this is not by direct popular vote. Instead, members of this house represent particular groups, which Hegel calls "corporations" or "organizations," and are to be chosen by them. Corporations are described by Shlomo Avineri as "voluntary organizations into which persons organize themselves according to their professions, trades and interests."[28] Members thus represent specific organized interests, and are thoroughly conversant with their concerns. Ensuring all organized interests are represented is too important to leave to chance (Par. 311). Hegel also believes that choosing the lower house through these groups is preferable to allowing "the democratic element without any rational form" to take part in political affairs (Par. 308, p. 200). He views popular suffrage as counterproductive. To allow people to vote directly "leads inevitably to electoral indifference, since the casting of a single vote is of no significance where there is a multitude of electors" (Par. 311, pp. 202–203). Voting through organized groups overcomes this problem; the associations perform a mediating function between the isolated individual and the distant, abstract state.

Closely related to his rejection of direct democracy is Hegel's opposition to individualism in other respects. He believes the basic units of society are not individuals but the groups they naturally fall into, first the family, then corporations: "Unless he is a member of an authorized Corporation . . . an individual is without rank or dignity, his isolation reduces his business to mere self-seeking, and his livelihood and satisfaction become insecure" (Par. 253, p. 153). Hegel describes the corporation as a "second family for its members." Among its responsibilities are providing education for its members and protecting them against misfortune, including poverty (Par. 252, p. 153). Within the corporation, economic assistance "loses its accidental character and the humiliation wrongfully associated with it." The wealthy take care of the poor because it is their duty to do so (Par. 253, p. 154). Group membership gives people identity, and unites them in a common endeavor. Membership in a corporation differs from membership in the state mainly in that the former encompasses only certain people, while the latter includes everyone—and so also all organizations in the state—within its domain.

As in liberal political theory, Hegel's state is the ultimate form of association. It has the functions ascribed to the liberal state, protecting citizens and their rights, and national defense. Hegel goes beyond liberal political theory in requiring that it protect its inhabitants in additional ways, especially from the unpredictable ravages of the emerging modern economy.

The problem of economic instability arose with complex market societies. In a complex economy, people do not produce in order to satisfy their own needs. They work on specialized products, often in large factories, along with large numbers of similarly placed others, while their products are often sold to distant customers. Disruptions in the marketplace, though no fault of their own, can have severe consequences for large numbers of workers. The clearest cases concern the obsolescence of a product on which large numbers work. For instance, though the electric typewriter is not completely outmoded at the present time, the emergence of the personal computer has severely lessened demand for it. To cite a more striking case, because of the invention of cassette tapes and then compact discs, few vinyl records are now produced. Under circumstances such as these, people working on the old product are suddenly uprooted. Because of forces beyond their control, they are laid off as demand for their products falls. Or entire factories close, throwing hundreds or thousands of workers onto the street.

Circumstances along these lines first began to arise on a large scale in Europe in the late eighteenth century, along with the incipient Industrial Revolution. Thus it is not surprising that Hobbes and Locke are not concerned with them. By the beginning of the nineteenth century, their effects were visible, especially in Britain, and Hegel takes them into account in drawing up the functions of his state. A typical passage follows:

> Not only caprice, however but also contingencies, physical conditions, and factors grounded in external circumstances . . . may reduce men to poverty. The poor still have the needs common to civil society, and yet since society has withdrawn from them the

natural means of acquisition . . . their poverty leaves them more or less deprived of all the advantages of society, of the opportunity of acquiring skill or education of any kind, as well as of the administration of justice, the public health services, and often even of the consolations of religion, and so forth. (Par. 241, pp. 148–149)

Though charitable giving can remedy this condition to an extent, it is not sufficiently reliable. Alleviating the effects of economic upheavals is a task for the state. This is necessary, not only for humanitarian reasons, but because poverty has deleterious social effects. People thrown into poverty are often deprived of more than their livelihoods. They can lose all sense of right and wrong, becoming a "rabble of paupers" (Par. 244, p. 150). Poverty alone does not necessarily make people a rabble, but must be accompanied by certain attitudes. Membership in corporations plays an important role in shielding people from harmful psychological effects. Thus corporations provide moral as well as economic assistance, but they cannot do enough. Understanding and alleviating the causes of impoverishment is a crucial function of the state.

As Hegel confronts the modern world, he moves beyond the liberal conception of the state. Not only does the state provide the moral arena necessary for the rise of freedom, but it fulfills functions beyond those typically assigned to the liberal state. We have seen that the state envisioned by liberal theorists is intended to provide two sources of protection: from other people and from the misuse of governmental power. But with the rise of complex economies, the need for protection from impersonal economic forces also becomes apparent. Hegel assigns this task to the state, in full awareness of its complexity. He recognizes that relieving the misery of impoverished masses can be assigned to the wealthy, or to public sources of wealth. Corporations can also contribute, as we have noted. Another means of dealing with poverty is to set people to work. But there is a problem with this remedy, as overproduction is the immediate cause of economic dislocations, and so poverty. "In this event the volume of production would be increased, but the evil consists precisely in an excess of production and in the lack of a proportionate number of consumers who are themselves also producers, and thus it is simply intensified" by the methods sought to deal with it (Par. 245, p. 150). In order to alleviate the pressure of poverty, the state can be driven to expand overseas: "to push beyond its own limits and seek markets, and so its necessary means of subsistence, in other lands which are either deficient in the good it has overproduced, or else generally backward in industry, &c." (Par. 246, p. 151).

The connections Hegel draws between economic conditions at home and the need for expansion abroad are remarkably farsighted. As Avineri says, "Few people around 1820 grasped in such depth the predicament of modern industrial society and the future course of nineteenth-century European history" (p. 154). But in spite of his attempt to find solutions to emerging economic problems, Hegel clearly perceives their complexity. "The important question of how poverty is to be abolished is one of the most disturbing problems which agitate modern society" (Par. 244A, p. 278). But he does not have ready answers. As Avineri notes, Hegel leaves no other problem so open (p. 154).

WAR

Hegel's analysis of politics carries him beyond the purview of the state into the arena of international affairs, where states confront each other as individuals. One might suppose that the development of the World Spirit would culminate in a situation in which all states were finally joined together in a single world-state, in which everyone could be free. But Hegel pursues quite a different course, extolling the value of conflict between states: "War is not to be regarded as an absolute evil and a purely external accident" (Par. 324, p. 209). Rather, it is necessary for the progress of the World Spirit. Hegel makes two main points in favor of war: that it tests a country's mettle, and that it is a means through which rising states, which represent the progress of the World Spirit, are able to push aside others, whose time has passed. These arguments are among the most notorious features of Hegel's philosophy.

Hegel believes war invigorates the patriotism and virtue of a country's population. It forces people to turn aside from their usual care for life and property, "the vanity of temporal goods and concerns," to focus on what is really important, the survival of the state (Par. 324, pp. 209–210). When the safety of the state is threatened, all other considerations must give way:

> It is the moment wherein the substance of the state—i.e., its absolute power against everything individual and particular, against life, property, and their rights, even against societies and associations—makes the nullity of these finite things an accomplished fact and brings it home to consciousness. (*Philosophy of Right*, Par. 323, p. 209)

Clearly, warfare requires enormous sacrifice. People must subordinate their own concerns to the good of the state, recapturing the virtuous spirit extolled by Rousseau and other proponents of the virtue of ancient republics. Thus the shock of war can prevent people from becoming morally stagnant. As "the blowing of the winds preserves the sea from the foulness which would be the result of prolonged calm, so also corruption in nations" would result from prolonged peace (Par. 324, p. 210). In his work, *Perpetual Peace*, Kant looks forward to peaceful relations between states as they become democracies. But Hegel rejects this idea as morally enervating.

In the light of modern warfare and its horrors, Hegel's arguments may strike us as both intellectually and morally dubious. To some extent this can be explained by the simpler time in which he wrote. Warfare at the end of the eighteenth century was on a much smaller scale, and tended to involve combatants alone, sparing civilian populations. This sort of warfare has been described as "limited conflict between rival professional armies of states that were allied at least by common conceptions of 'civilized' warfare and in general were conscious of being part of a larger European or Western Civilization."[29] But it should be noted that the French Revolution inaugurated the modern era of total war. Hegel was not only familiar with this, but he had been directly affected by the Napoleonic wars. However, innovations in warfare between the eighteenth and nineteenth centuries seem not to have affected his philosophy. His account of the extent of the nation's moral claim upon its citizens during war must strike us as harsh:

> The intrinsic worth of courage as a disposition of mind is to be found in the genuine, absolute, final end, the sovereignty of the state. The work of courage is to actualize this final end, and the means to this is the sacrifice of personal actuality. This form of experience thus contains the harshness of extreme contradictions: a self-sacrifice which yet is the real existence of one's freedom; the maximum self-subsistence of individuality,

yet only as a cog playing its part in the mechanism of an external organization; absolute obedience, renunciation of personal opinions and reasonings, in fact complete *absence* of mind, coupled with the most intense and comprehensive *presence* of mind and decision in the moment of acting; the most hostile and so most personal action against individuals, coupled with an attitude of complete indifference or even liking towards them as individuals. (Par. 328, p. 211)

Hegel recognizes that states may be able to settle their differences through international law. But the possibilities here are limited. The main principle of international law is that agreements between states should be kept (Par. 333). However, in the absence of a sovereign authority to enforce obedience, when states disagree and cannot be brought to agree, their controversies can be settled only by war (Par. 334).

Hegel believes wars advance the course of world history. Once again, the consequences of wars are justified by the overall logic of the historical process he discusses in his *Philosophy of History*, while *Philosophy of Right* ends with a capsule summary of important themes of that work. We saw in *Philosophy of History* that Hegel views his philosophy as a theodicy, a justification of the suffering apparent throughout history as in accordance with God's plan. War plays a crucial role in this. States enjoy moments of historical prominence during their life cycles. After they have risen and exhausted the possibilities latent in their times, the World Spirit casts them aside. This can be done through warfare, which expresses History's judgment of the finitude of states. Hegel remarks upon "'the history of the world, which is the world's court of judgment'" (Par. 341, p. 216, quoting Schiller).

When history is through with a particular state, defeat in war is the means through which it is passed over. Though great suffering can be incurred, this is a necessary consequence of the rise of a new state:

> In contrast with this . . . present stage in the World Spirit's development, the spirits of other nations are without rights (*rechtlos*), and they, along with those whose hour has struck already, count no longer in world history. (Par. 347, p. 218)

Though warfare between states is a Darwinian struggle through which the stronger states advance and the weaker are left behind, the process accords with the ends of the World Spirit. More than brute force is involved: "world history is not the verdict of mere might, i.e., the abstract and non-rational inevitability of a blind destiny" (Par. 342, p. 216). The course of war, as part of the overall course of historical development, is guided by providential reason and so is part of the World Spirit's march to self-consciousness.

ASSESSMENT

Since Hegel's own time, his political theory has been the subject of enormous controversy. A wide variety of opinions have been advanced, depicting Hegel as everything from an important critic of liberalism to the intellectual godfather of Nazism. As Avineri says, "almost everyone writing on modern intellectual life has his own image of Hegel."[30] Disagreements arose during Hegel's lifetime. While he was widely viewed as the greatest philosopher of his time, he was also accused of being a paid agent of the Prussian state, hired to provide a theoretical justification for the regime.[31] In his edition of the *Philosophy of Right*, Allen Wood characterizes the traditional view of Hegel as "reactionary, absolutist, totalitarian."[32] A typical expression of this point of view is given by Bertrand Russell:

> It follows from his metaphysics that true liberty consists in obedience to an arbitrary authority, that free speech is an evil, that absolute monarchy is good, that the Prussian state was the best existing at the time when he wrote, that war is good, and that an international organization for the peaceful settlement of disputes would be a misfortune . . . What he admired were . . . order, system, regulation and intensity of governmental control.[33]

It would be possible endlessly to multiply quotations and authorities in support of this view. Its most important recent proponent is probably Karl Popper, in his influential book, *The Open Society and Its Enemies*.[34]

The gist of Popper's argument is that Hegel not only provided the intellectual justification for twentieth-century totalitarianism but did so for ulterior reasons, because he had been hired to do so (Popper, pp. 32–33). The latter charge need not be taken seriously, but the former is important. We can identify three distinct claims here, that Hegel is a totalitarian, a reactionary, and extols the values of war and conquest. We can begin with the charge that Hegel glorifies war.

There is no doubt that language in *Philosophy of Right* appears to glorify war. Especially troubling is Hegel's view that during any given historical period, certain civilizations are rising and others falling, and that the latter have no rights against the tide of history (*Philosophy of Right*, Par. 347; see p. 403). As one would expect, Popper makes much of this, arguing that Hegel's view amounts to historical justification of the existing order: "History is our judge. Since History and Providence have brought the existing powers into being, their might must be right, even Divine right" (Popper, p. 49). The implication one might draw from this is that if country *A* conquers and destroys country *B*, this is acceptable as willed by the World Spirit. From this, it is a short step to allowing leaders in country *A* who covet the riches of country *B*, and believe *A* is stronger than *B*, to justify attacking *B* on the grounds that this is acceptable to history. The fact that they are able to destroy *B* means that history intends for them to do so. After they have invaded and conquered, their victory justifies their aggression. Hegel would undoubtedly dispute this interpretation. Not only does he say "world history is not the verdict of mere might" (*Philosophy of Right*, Par. 342, p. 216), but he explicitly attacks the view that might makes right. He harshly criticizes Ludwig Von Haller (1768–1854), who did uphold such a view. Hegel dismisses Haller's theory as a "welter of incredible crudity" (*Philosophy of Right*, Par. 258, p. 160 n.). But in spite of Hegel's protestations, it remains to be seen how his view can avoid such implications. This will become clear as we proceed.

The core of the claim that Hegel is a totalitarian is that his extollation of the state and the importance he ascribes to its historical role justify denying individuals all rights and negative freedom. There is no question that Hegel criticizes traditional liberal values. Much of this chapter has explored aspects of his critique. Unlike liberal individualists, Hegel sees the individual as constituted by the society to which he belongs, and argues that true freedom lies in adherence to the practices of an ongoing community. We have discussed reasons for Hegel's high opinion of the state in previous sections. But one is still startled to read statements such as the following:

> The march of God in the world, that is what the state is. (*Philosophy of Right*, Par. 258A, p. 279)

> The state is the world which mind has made for itself; its march, therefore, is on lines that are fixed and absolute. . . . Man must therefore venerate the state as a secular deity, and observe that if it is difficult to comprehend nature, it is infinitely harder to understand the state. (Par. 272A, p. 285)

Similarly, in the *Philosophy of History*,

> The State is the Divine Idea as it exists on Earth. (*Phil. Hist.*, p. 39)

This language, however, is suspect. The first quotation, which is the most notorious, is an obvious mistranslation. The translation Popper presents is similar: "The state is the march of God through the world" (p. 31). In spite of the similarities between this rendering and the standard translation of Knox, the proper translation is actually: "It is the way of God with the world that there should be the state."[35] It must also be noted that this passage, along with the others Popper presents from *Philosophy of Right* and *Philosophy of History* (on p. 31), are all from notes on Hegel's lectures taken by his students. (The Additions in *Philosophy of Right*, as one will recall, are taken from Hegel's students' notes to his lectures.) None is in Hegel's own words.[36]

More important than Hegel's inflammatory language in particular passages, whether or not it reflects his fully considered views, are his views themselves. From a liberal perspective, totalitarian theory is objectionable because it supports erosion of the dividing line between the individual and the state, between private and public. Individual rights are disregarded in the face of the supreme moral claims of the state. The main question, then, is whether Hegel holds such a view. Does he deny individual rights and so improperly subordinate the individual to the state? We have seen clear language to this effect in regard to times of war (see pp. 402–3), and Hegel makes similar statements in other contexts. For instance:

> The state does not exist for the sake of the citizens; it might rather be said that the state is the end and the citizens are its instruments. (*Reason in History*, pp. 94–95)

However, Hegel continues that "this relation of ends and means is not at all appropriate in the present context." There is no opposition between individuals and the community, because individuals are organic constituents of the whole (p. 95). In *Philosophy of Right* we find the following:

> This substantial unity [the state] is an absolute unmoved end in itself, in which freedom comes into its supreme right. On the other hand this final end has supreme right over the individual, whose supreme duty is to be a member of the state. (*Philosophy of Right*, Par. 258, p. 156)

> Whether the individual exists or not is all one to the objective ethical order. It alone is permanent and is the power regulating the life of individuals. (Par. 145A, p. 259)

> Mind has actuality, and individuals are accidents of this actuality. Thus in dealing with ethical life, only two views are possible: either we start from the substantiality of the ethical order, or else we proceed atomistically and build on the basis of single individuals. This second point of view excludes mind because it leads only to a juxtaposition. (Par. 156A, p. 261)

Similar passages from both Hegel himself and his students' notes could be added. Clearly, such language supports the view that Hegel believes the state is everything and the individual is nothing. But this interpretation must be strongly qualified.

Though Hegel is not a liberal theorist, he does not entirely reject liberal values. Rather, he believes these can be secured only in a stable political system. As we saw above, though Hegel departs from strict democracy, negative freedom, in the form of a sphere of protected rights, is a central feature of his political order. Individuals in Hegel's preferred state enjoy freedom of religion, thought, and speech; they cannot be subjected to serfdom or slavery; all people stand equal before the law, and legal actions against individuals must be conducted according to strict procedures. Though Hegel places great weight on non-individualist aspects of society, especially corporations, among important functions he assigns these are caring for needy individuals and mediating between isolated individuals and the state. As we have seen, Hegel believes the value accorded individual rights is a crucial respect in which modern society differs from ancient society.

Now we have also seen that Hegel criticizes negative freedom as insufficient to guarantee true freedom and a moral life. Like Rousseau, he believes true freedom can be attained only in unity with society as a whole. We have explored his reasons for this position at length. But this important theme in his philosophy should not blind us to the fact that even in union with society, the individual enjoys an area of protected space.

There is also strong evidence against the view that Hegel is a reactionary or a simple ideologue of the Prussian state. The claim that Hegel is a reactionary is based on his attempt to justify the existing order as the product of rational necessity. To quote a crucial sentence once again, "*What is rational is actual and what is actual is rational*" (*Philosophy of Right*, Pref., p. 10). According to a longstanding interpretation, Hegel believes the historical process, which is governed by rational necessity, has borne fruit in the Germanic state. It follows that if the existing Prussian regime is the product of divine reason, then attempts to reform it cannot be justified. Obviously, this is why the Prussian state would support his views and regard him as its official spokesperson. Hegel is often interpreted along these lines. For instance, his philosophy was denounced as "the scientific domicile of the spirit of Prussian reaction" by the important nineteenth-century scholar Rudolf Haym:

> As far as I can see, in comparison with the famous saying about the rationality of the actual in the sense of Hegel's Preface, everything Hobbes and Filmer, Haller or Stahl, have taught is relatively liberal doctrine. The theory of God's grace and the theory of absolute obedience are innocent and harmless in comparison with that frightful dogma *pronouncing the existing as existing to be holy.*

Haym contends that Hegel's view, correctly understood, leads to "the absolute formula of political conservatism."[37]

There is, however, a fundamental problem with this interpretation—and with the related claim that, because the state is divine, the individual has no rights against it. These conclusions hold only if Hegel intended to identify an existing state, Prussia, with the realization of the divine plan. This is a question upon which scholars have held different views. But the strong consensus of recent scholars is that Hegel did not believe the Prussian state that existed during his time was rationally justified in all its aspects.

In *Philosophy of Right*, Hegel makes a crucial distinction between actual or existing states and the *Idea* of the state, by which he means the state as an instrument of the World Spirit in its progress towards freedom. It is not entirely clear how the Idea of the state relates to actual states. But it seems this refers to actual states viewed in the perspective of long-term historical developments. We know the state is an instrument of progress, but exactly how it functions in this regard can be understood only from the perspective of world history. In the Introduction to the *Philosophy of History*, Hegel writes:

> The sole aim of philosophical enquiry is to eliminate the contingent. Contingency is the same as external necessity, that is, a necessity which originates in causes which are themselves no more than external circumstances. (*Reason in History*, p. 28)

At any given time, the political order combines the contingent and the necessary. Obviously, what is rationally necessary cannot be tampered with. But Hegel offers no guidance for distinguishing the necessary and contingent. It seems that he believes this determination can be made only in retrospect, from the perspective of the historian, once a civilization's time has passed. In *Philosophy of Right*, he says philosophy does not give instruction as to what the world ought to be (Pref., p. 12). This includes instruction that the world ought to be exactly as it is. In this work he says his pronouncements apply only to the Idea of the state and not to any existing state:

> In considering the Idea of the state, we must not have our eyes on particular states or on particular institutions. Instead we must consider the Idea, this actual God, by itself. (Par. 258A, p. 279)

> . . . all these questions are no concern of the state. We are here dealing exclusively with the philosophic science of the state, and from that point of view all these things are mere appearance and therefore matters for history. (Par. 258, p. 156)

It is interesting that the first of these passages follows Hegel's notorious language concerning the state and the march of God in the world discussed above (after the intervention of one sentence).

Strong evidence that Hegel wishes to distinguish the existing Prussian state from the Idea of the state is a series of discrepancies between the state described in *Philosophy of Right* and the Prussian state of his time. Four important differences can be noted.[38] First, while Hegel's monarch has little power and is to rubber-stamp laws put before him, Frederick William III of Prussia had considerable power and discretion. Second, though the Estates is an essential feature of Hegel's state, Prussia had no functioning parliament. Third, while Hegel's state guarantees freedom of the press, this right had been removed by reactionary forces in the Prussian government. Finally, while Hegel's state has trial by jury, this was absent from the Prussian state. These differences prove that Haym and other critics of Hegel's reactionary politics are simply wrong. As T. M. Knox says, though *Philosophy of Right* is often interpreted as a defense of the existing Prussian order, "the differences are so striking . . . that no contemporary of Hegel's could reasonably have made such an assertion."[39]

It appears that Hegel's state is intended to serve as a standard against which the Prussian state should be assessed. Rather than preaching reaction, *Philosophy of Right* actually preaches reform. This interpretation is supported by the facts of Hegel's life. As is seen in numerous political writings outside *Philosophy of Right*, throughout his life, Hegel was not a reactionary. He criticized aspects of his society and was a proponent of "peaceful, gradual, and constitutional reform."[40] In Hegel's early political writings, reform is a recurrent theme, while he was a staunch supporter of the French Revolution throughout his life. Each year, he drank a toast to the French Revolution.[41] In *Philosophy of History*, he writes of it in rapturous terms:

> The conception, the idea of Right asserted its authority *all at once*, and the old framework of injustice could offer no resistance to its onslaught. A constitution, therefore, was established in harmony with the conception of Right, and on this foundation all future legislation was to be based. Never since the sun had stood in the firmament and the planets revolved around him had it been perceived that man's existence centers in his head, i.e., in Thought, inspired by which he builds up the world of reality . . . This was accordingly a glorious mental dawn. All thinking beings shared in the jubilation of this epoch. (p. 447)

The allegation that *Philosophy of Right* was written from the perspective of Hegel's official chair in Berlin, in order to support the government he represented, is proved false by the fact that many of the work's ideas are recurrent themes in Hegel's political writings and are present in his early works.[42] A further indication that *Philosophy of Right* was not intended to extol the existing Prussian state is that Hegel withheld the manuscript from publication for a time, because of fear of official censorship.[43]

The fact that Hegel does not support all aspects of the existing political order suggests a different interpretation of his claim that the rational is the actual and the actual is the rational. We have seen that influential scholars view this as a statement of *fact* about the identity of these two orders, and so infer the requirement to submit to the existing order, which is rationally necessary. This is the basis for the reactionary political implications drawn by Haym and other scholars. However, if we equate the rational order with the *Idea of the state*, rather than an existing state, the identification of the actual and the rational becomes a *demand* to bring the existing political order into closer accord with the Idea of the state, and so with what is rational. Within the existing order at any given time, the rational and the contingent exist together. Through reform, the latter can be weeded out. It is likely Hegel viewed his political theory in this light. However, though he supported political reform, his profound appreciation of world history and the organic interconnectedness of the political world steered him in the direction of cautious, gradual reform, and the strong requirement that changes be in accord with a country's overall spirit. Not surprisingly, these views are similar to those of other great conservative thinkers we have discussed—Montesquieu and Burke.

There are additional reasons why Hegel limited his aspirations to moderate change. Anything beyond this entails looking into the future, and this philosophy cannot do. As the product of its time, philosophy always comes upon the scene too late to offer guidance—including guidance that a particular state would be justified in historical terms in waging war against some other. Philosophy gives forth its meaning over the long run, in retrospect.

Though Hegel is often viewed as a reactionary, it is of great importance for the history of political theory that his demand that the existing order be brought into accord with reason lends itself to quite a different interpretation. If reason's requirements can somehow be known, this will create a moral imperative to overturn the existing order in the interest of rationality. Setting aside the question of how we can know what reason commands, if we can discover this, it will constitute a standard with absolute moral force. Against the claims of reason, no other claims can stand. In the hands of Hegel's most influential follower, this line of interpretation gave rise to a demand for revolutionary change, for "a ruthless criticism of everything existing."[44]

NOTES

1. For biographical information, I follow W. Kaufmann, *Hegel: A Reinterpretation* (Garden City, NY, 1965); this work is cited hereafter in the text as Kaufmann.

2. For the composition of this work, see J. Hoffmeister, Preface to *Lectures on the Philosophy of World History: Introduction: Reason in History*, H. Nisbet, trans. (Cambridge, 1975). This work will be cited in the text as *Reason in History*, according to page number. Hegel's *Philosophy of History* is cited in the text as *Phil. Hist.*, according to page number; full reference below under "Texts Cited."

3. See T. M. Knox, ed. and trans., *Hegel's Philosophy of Right* (Oxford, 1952), p. v; along with "Additions," *Philosophy of Right* also contains "remarks," which Hegel himself appended to the text, and are printed by Knox in smaller type. This work will be cited in parentheses in the text according to paragraph number and page number in this edition. Remarks will not be identified as such, but for additions, paragraph numbers will be followed by "A." Knox's translations are occasionally slightly altered. Additional translations of *Philosophy of Right* and others of Hegel's works that are used will be indicated; full references are found below under "Texts Cited."

4. Hegel, *Phenomenology of Spirit*, Preface, p. 14; this work is cited hereafter as *Phenomenology* in parentheses in the text, according to paragraph and page number; full reference below under "Texts Cited." All italics in this passage and other quotations from Hegel are his, unless otherwise noted.

5. J. N. Findlay, Foreword to *Phenomenology of Spirit*, by Hegel, p. xiii; full reference below, under "Texts Cited."

6. Though this is true of the *Phenomenology* as a whole, the Preface, from which the above quotation is taken, was written under less pressing circumstances a few months later (Kaufmann, p. 90). But again, the difficulty of the quoted passage is typical of much of the work.

7. R. Plant, *Hegel* (London, 1973), p. 124, n.1; this work is cited in parentheses in the text, by author's name.

8. C. Taylor, *Hegel* (Cambridge, 1975), p. vii; this work is cited in parentheses in the text, by author's name.

9. In discussing Hegel's political theory, this approach is followed by S. Avineri, *Hegel's Theory of the Modern State* (Cambridge, 1972); in regard to his philosophy as a whole, Kaufmann pursues a similar course.

10. K. Marx, *Capital*, 3 vols., S. Moore and E. Aveling, trans. (New York, 1967), I, 20 (Afterword to the Second German Edition).

11. H. S. Harris, *Hegel's Development* (Oxford, 1972), p. 231.

12. For the *polis*, see Vol. I, 2–6, 110–112; for Aristotle, see esp. Vol. I, 105–112. For fuller discussions of Hegel's concern with integration, see Plant, *Hegel*, and Kaufmann, *Hegel*, to both of which I am indebted.

13. C. Friedrich, ed., *The Philosophy of Hegel* (New York, 1953).

14. A. Smith, *An Inquiry into the Nature and Causes of the Wealth of Nations*, E. Cannan, ed. (New York, 1937), Bk. I, Chap. 2, p. 14.

15. Smith, *Wealth of Nations*, Bk. I, Chap. 2, p. 15.

16. Friedrich, ed. *Philosophy of Hegel*, p. xv.

17. J. S. Mill, *On Liberty* (Indianapolis, 1978), Chap. 1, p. 5.

18. Mill, *On Liberty*. Chap. 1, p. 12.

19. I. Kant, *Groundwork of the Metaphysic of Morals*, Chap. 1, p. 70; full reference below under "Texts Cited." This work is cited hereafter in the text as *Groundwork*.

20. For Kant's discussion of this example, see *Groundwork*, Chap. 2, pp. 89–90.

21. R. Schacht, "Hegel on Freedom," in *Hegel: A Collection of Critical Essays*, A. MacIntyre, ed. (Garden City, NY, 1972), p. 317.

22. Aristotle, *Politics*, Bk. I, Chap. 2 (1253a1–4); revised ed., T. Sinclair and T. Saunders, trans. (Harmondsworth, England, 1981). For discussion, see Vol. I, 110–112.

23. Aristotle, *Politics*, Bk. I, Chap. 2 (1253a5–6)

24. Schacht, "Hegel on Freedom," p. 311.

25. For a good brief discussion of Spirit, see J. N. Findlay, *Hegel: A Re-examination* (Oxford, 1958), Chap. 2.

26. The illustrative value of this passage is suggested by G. A. Cohen, *Marx's Concept of History: A Defence* (Princeton, 1979), p. 11; I am indebted to Cohen's excellent, brief account of Hegel's view of history (Chap. 1).

27. Knox, ed., *Philosophy of Right*, note, p. 304.

28. Avineri, *Hegel's Theory of the Modern State*, p. 164; this work cited hereafter by author's name, in text.

29. D. Germino, *Machiavelli to Marx* (Chicago, 1972), p. 339. My points in this paragraph follow Germino's discussion.

30. Avineri, "Hegel Revisited," in *Hegel*, MacIntyre, ed., p. 329.

31. The view of Hegel as paid agent was held by Arthur Schopenhauer, who was Hegel's philosophical rival and detested him (K. Popper, *The Open Society and Its Enemies*, 2 vols. 5th ed. [Princeton, 1966], II, p. 33; on Schopenhauer's competition with Hegel, see

Kaufmann, pp. 229–230). For assessments of Hegel by his contemporaries and immediate successors, see Avineri, "Hegel Revisited."

32. A. Wood, Introduction to Hegel, *Elements of the Philosophy of Right* (Cambridge, 1991), p. xxvii.

33. Quoted by Avineri, *Hegel's Theory of the Modern State*, p. 239.

34. Popper, *Open Society*, Vol. II; cited hereafter in text as Popper. For a withering critique of Popper's interpretation of Hegel, see Kaufmann, "The Hegel Myth and Its Method," in *Hegel*, MacIntyre, ed.

35. The original reads: "*Es ist der Gang Gottes in der Welt, dass der Staat ist.*" For the translation, see Kaufmann, Introduction to *Hegel's Political Philosophy*, Kaufmann, ed. (New York, 1970), p. 4. Surprisingly, Nisbet's recent translation in Wood, ed., *Elements of the Philosophy of Right*, is similar to Knox's: "The state consists in the march of God in the world . . ." (p. 279).

36. Kaufmann, Introduction, *Hegel's Political Philosophy*, p. 4.

37. Quoted by Wood, Introduction to *Elements of the Philosophy of Right*, p. xxx, n. 5.

38. Knox, "Hegel and Prussianism," in Kaufmann, ed., *Hegel's Political Philosophy*, pp. 21–22; see also the exchange between Knox and E. F. Carritt in the same volume.

39. Knox, "Hegel's Prussianism," p. 18.

40. Z. A. Pelczynski, Introduction to *Hegel's Political Writings*, Pelczynski, ed. (Oxford, 1964), p. 53. See the writings collected here, and Pelczynski's valuable introduction.

41. Knox, "Hegel's Prussianism," p. 20.

42. Pelczynski, Introduction to *Hegel's Political Writings*.

43. Knox, "Hegel's Prussianism," p. 16.

44. K. Marx, in R. Tucker, ed. *The Marx-Engels Reader*, 2nd ed. (New York, 1978), pp. 12–15.

Texts Cited

Hegel, G. W. F. *Elements of the Philosophy of Right*. A. Wood, ed. H. B. Nisbet, trans. Cambridge, 1991.

Hegel, G. W. F. *Grundlinien des Philosophie des Rechts*. J. Hoffmeister, ed. Hamburg, 1955.

Hegel, G. W. F. *Lectures on the Philosophy of World History: Introduction: Reason in History*. Translated from the German edition of J. Hoffmeister by H. Nisbet. Cambridge, 1975.

Hegel, G. W. F. *The Phenomenology of Mind*. J. B. Baillie, trans. New York, 1967.

Hegel, G. W. F. *Phenomenology of Spirit*. A. V. Miller, trans. Analysis of the Text and Foreword by J. N. Findlay. Oxford, 1977.

Hegel, G. W. F. *The Philosophy of History*. J. Sibree, trans. New York, 1956.

Hegel, G. W. F. *Philosophy of Right*. T. M. Knox, ed. and trans. Oxford, 1952.

Kant, I. *Groundwork of the Metaphysic of Morals*. H. J. Paton, ed. and trans. 3rd ed. New York, 1964.

FURTHER READING

Avineri, S. *Hegel's Theory of the Modern State*. Cambridge, 1972.

Copleston, F. *A History of Philosophy*. Vol. VII: *Modern Philosophy*. Part I: *Fichte to Hegel*. Garden City, NY, 1963.

Findlay, J. N. *Hegel: A Re-examination*. Oxford, 1958.

Hegel, G. W. F. *Early Theological Writings*. T. M. Knox, trans. Chicago, 1948.

Hegel, G. W. F. *Hegel's Political Writings*. Z. A. Pelczynski, ed. T. M. Knox, trans. Oxford, 1964.

Kaufmann, W. *Hegel: A Reinterpretation*. Garden City, NY, 1965.

Kaufmann, W., ed. *Hegel's Political Philosophy*. New York, 1970.

Marcuse, H. *Reason and Revolution: Hegel and the Rise of Social Theory*. 2nd ed. Boston, 1955.

Pelczynski, Z. A., ed. *Hegel's Political Philosophy: Problems and Perspectives*. Cambridge, 1971.

Plant, R. *Hegel*. London, 1973.

Popper, K. *The Open Society and Its Enemies*. Vol. II: *The High Tide of Prophecy: Hegel, Marx, and the Aftermath*. 5th ed. Princeton, 1966.

Reyburn, H. *The Ethical Theory of Hegel*. Oxford, 1921.

Schacht, R. "Hegel on Freedom." In *Hegel: A Collection of Critical Essays*, A. MacIntyre, ed. Garden City, NY, 1972.

Singer, P. *Hegel*. Oxford, 1983.

Smith, S. *Hegel's Critique of Liberalism*. Chicago, 1989.

Taylor, C. *Hegel*. Cambridge, 1975.

Karl Marx

Marx's Life and Works

Karl Marx was born in Trier, in the Rhineland, in 1818.[1] While studying law at the University of Berlin, he became intensely interested in philosophy and the possibilities of political reform, then widely discussed in Hegelian philosophical circles. He received a doctoral degree in philosophy in 1841, writing his dissertation on *The Difference Between the Democritean and Epicurean Philosophies of Nature*. When his hopes for an academic career were blocked by objections to his political views, he turned to journalism. He began writing for the *Rheinische Zeitung* in 1842, becoming its editor in 1842. In 1843, Marx also worked on his first major philosophical composition, a critique of Hegel's *Philosophy of Right*. After the *Rheinische Zeitung* was censored by the Prussian government, Marx resigned and eventually moved to Paris, where he wrote the *Economic and Philosophical Manuscripts* of 1844. This work, along with his critique of Hegel and numerous later compositions, was left incomplete, and not published until some fifty years after his death. In response to Marx's continuing criticism, the Prussian government accused him of treason, and used its influence to force him to leave Paris. Marx moved to Brussels, and was active in the Revolutions of 1848. In 1849 he moved with his family to London, where he lived for the rest of his life.

In 1844, Marx began a lifelong collaboration with Friedrich Engels, the son of a German textile producer. Their continuing intellectual and literary partnership is perhaps the most successful on record of two such important thinkers. Between 1845 and 1848, the two men jointly authored a number of important works, including *The German Ideology, The Holy Family*, and *The Communist Manifesto*. While Marx lived in London, Engels moved to Manchester in 1850 to work in the family business. The two men maintained a voluminous correspondence over the next twenty years, which provides an invaluable record of the development of their ideas and their relationship during this period.

During the late 1840s and 1850s, Marx worked out the main lines of his critique of the capitalist economic system, which will be our main focus in this chapter. Along with his theoretical works in political economy, Marx also wrote acute journalistic analyses of contemporary social and political affairs, and was active in a series of revolutionary political organizations. These included the Communist League, and the International Working Men's Association, which he helped found, in 1864.

In England, Marx and his family lived in grinding poverty. Though he and his wife struggled to keep up bourgeois appearances, three of their children died in early childhood. The death of his eight-year-old son, Edgar, in 1855, was an especially severe blow to Marx:

> The house is naturally desolate and empty since the death of the dear child, who was its animated soul. It is indescribable how we miss the child everywhere. I have already experienced all kinds of ill luck, but only now do I know what real misfortune is. I feel myself broken down. Luckily, I have had such wild headaches since the burial that I have lost the power of thinking, hearing, and seeing. (*Letters*, April 12, 1855, pp. 97–98).

The family survived through a combination of Marx's work as a journalist and the generosity of Engels. An idea of their living conditions is as follows:

> My wife is ill . . . I cannot and could not call the doctor because I have no money for medicine. For the past eight to ten days I have been feeding the family on bread and potatoes, and it is questionable whether I can get any more today. (*Letters*, September 8, 1852, p. 84)

In October of that year, Marx pawned his coat to buy paper. In December he said of one of his compositions: "You will be able to appreciate the humor of the book when you consider that its author, through lack of sufficient covering for his back and feet, is as good as interned and also was and is threatened with seeing really nauseating poverty overwhelm his family at any moment" (quoted by McLellan, p. 263). In 1859, he wrote: "I don't believe that anybody had ever written about 'money' while suffering such a lack of money" (*Letters*, January 21, 1859, p. 129). The passion with which Marx assails the condition of the working class is readily explained by his own circumstances. Through years of such misery, Marx toiled away at his analysis of capitalist society, spending much of his time in the reading room at the British Museum.

After years of delays, the first volume of Marx's greatest work, *Capital*, was published in 1867. Marx continued to work on the additional volumes until his death, in 1883. Volumes II and III of *Capital* were edited by Engels and published two years after Marx's death. Engels lived for another ten years. He developed Marx's ideas into a complete philosophical system and used his considerable talents as a popularizer to forge these into the ideology of the German Social Democratic Party.

Engels' contribution to the subsequent development of Marxist thought was immense. In addition to the works he wrote with Marx, he advised Marx on many others, and edited volumes II and III of *Capital*. Engels also wrote works of his own. Especially notable is his extension of Marx's methods into additional fields, especially the natural sciences, in *Anti-Dühring* (1878) and *Dialectics of Nature* (published posthumously, in 1927). The extent to which Marx would have agreed with these developments is a difficult question— and one I will avoid as largely peripheral to Marx's main political and social ideas. For our purposes, their joint compositions will be viewed as expressing Marx's ideas and for ease of reference will not be carefully distinguished from works authored by Marx alone. For example, in referring to the *Communist Manifesto*, which was written by both men, I will frequently use language such as, "in this work Marx says. . . ." Throughout this chapter we will also draw on works written by Engels alone, which will be identified as such. Regardless of what Marx thought (or would have thought) of Engels' original ideas, these were enormously influential in the subsequent history of the doctrine. Thus in the standard three-volume edition of Marx's and Engels' *Selected Works*, published in Moscow (and used heavily in this chapter), some 50 percent of the selections are by Engels.

Though Engels was a person of many talents, there was never any doubt that Marx had the more powerful intellect. In 1888, after Marx had been dead for five years, Engels described their relationship in the following terms:

> [B]oth before and during my forty years' collaboration with Marx I had a certain independent share in laying the foundations of the theory, and more particularly in its elaboration. But the greater part of its leading basic principles—especially in the realm of economics and history, and above all, their final trenchant formulation, belong to Marx. For all that I contributed—at any rate with the exception of my work in a few special fields—Marx could very well have done without me. What Marx accomplished I would not have achieved. Marx stood higher, saw farther, and took a wider and quicker view than all the rest of us. Marx was a genius; we others were at best talented. Without him the theory would not, by a long way, be what it is today. It therefore rightly bears his name.[2]

The ideas of Marx and Engels of course exerted tremendous influence after their deaths. Adapted to the distinctive conditions in Russia at the end of the nineteenth century by Vladimir Ulyanov (Lenin) and other Russian Marxists, they constituted the intellectual foundations of twentieth-century Communism. But the extent to which Russian Marxism—and applications to other countries in later years—departed from the thought of Marx himself is seen in its identification as "Marxism-Leninism."

ANALYSIS OF SOCIETIES

Though not a systematic writer, Marx was a systematic thinker. His literary output was enormous. A projected edition of his and Engels' complete works, begun in 1975, is scheduled to run to fifty volumes (large volumes with small print).[3] But through this vast outpouring of analysis and criticism there is a fairly straightforward argument, central elements of which we will attempt to reconstruct in this chapter. There is a problem here in that Marx's works give a strong appearance of inconsistency. Within the vast corpus, he appears to say different things in different places about innumerable questions. Depending on which themes one chooses to emphasize, or which specific passages one chooses to quote, Marx can be made to hold virtually any position on any issue. In regard to important political questions, he has been interpreted as everything from a social-democratic supporter of essentially peaceful reform to an insistent proponent of violent revolution.[4] There is no easy way around this problem, and scholars will probably always disagree about basic aspects of Marx's thought. The reader should be advised that, though the interpretation offered here is quite conventional and falls between these two poles, many of my claims would be disputed by scholars from different camps.[5] In this chapter, we will concentrate on Marx's overall approach to the analysis of society and important political aspects of his system, including his analyses of the state, ideology, the capitalist system, the unity of theory and practice, and the revolution. Throughout, a major theme will be Marx's critique of liberal political theory, as discussed in previous chapters.

Like any thinker, Marx should be understood in the context of his times. The problems he addresses are those of his immediate intellectual milieu. In particular, he should be understood in relationship to basic assumptions of the Enlightenment. Like other thinkers we have discussed, Marx was impressed by the progress made in the natural sciences, and wished to extend similar methods to the political and social realms. We should note that concern with a full-fledged science of society is a central theme in the works of Engels; his greater emphasis on this is one respect in which he differs from Marx. But a clear indication of Marx's own interests along these lines is his wish to dedicate *Capital* to Charles Darwin, though the latter declined (McLellan, p. 424).

The particular conception of science that interests Marx is essentially twofold. First, it is an *historical* science. Marx traces the processes through which history moves, the forces responsible for societies' rise and fall, which cause them to come into existence and pass away. Marx's historical investigations are inextricably linked to a second science, the study of individual societies, or *sociology*. In this regard, he is interested in explaining the specific factors that make societies the way they are and generate their major features. The connection between the two sciences—or the two aspects of what can be viewed as a single science—lies in the fact that the same elements that account for a society's major features eventually cause it to cease to function properly, and so lead the society to pass over into another social form, or a new stage in its development. To understand the processes through which societies work and cease to work is to understand the forces responsible for the movement of history.

Marx believes society has gone through four basic stages. From earliest to latest, these are: *tribal, communal, feudal,* and *bourgeois.* Tribal society is ancient society, before civilization was highly developed. Communal society corresponds to the ancient world, including the Greek *polis* and the Roman Empire. Feudal society is that of Europe in the Middle Ages, while bourgeois or capitalist society is what existed in Marx's own day. This last is arguably what exists in much of the world at the present time. It is not clear whether Marx's view is that all societies must go through these four stages, or only the ones in Western Europe in which he is most interested.[6] On this, as on many issues, Marx appears to say somewhat different things in different contexts. Regardless of where we come down on this issue, Marx undoubtedly believes that, after going through these stages of development, the societies in question will pass over into communism, which is a higher form, qualitatively different from anything that has been seen before.

Marx believes historical movement takes place according to laws, somewhat analogous to those encountered in the natural world. In the Preface to *Capital,* he speaks of the "natural laws of capitalist production" (I, 8); "it is the ultimate aim of this work, to lay bare the economic law of motion of modern society" (I, 10). By studying the workings of the most developed society then in existence, England, he hopes to chart the path other societies will follow:

> Intrinsically, it is not a question of the higher or lower degree of development of the social antagonisms that result from the natural laws of capitalist production. It is a question of these laws themselves, of these tendencies working with iron necessity towards inevitable results. The country that is more developed industrially only shows, to the less developed, the image of its own future. (*Capital,* I, 8–9)

Probably the single clearest statement of Marx's central themes is contained in the Preface to *A Contribution to the Critique of Political Economy* (1859). In order to begin to unravel his system, we can examine some basic concepts Marx introduces here. In the crucial paragraphs of the Preface, Marx writes:

> The general result at which I arrived and which, once won, served as a guiding thread for my studies, can be briefly formulated as follows: In the social production of their life, men enter into definite relations that are indispensable and independent of their will, relations of production which correspond to a definite stage of development of their material productive forces. The sum total of these relations of production constitutes the economic structure of society, the real foundation, on which rises a legal and political superstructure and to which correspond definite forms of social consciousness. The mode of production of material life conditions the social, political and intellectual life process in general. It is not the consciousness of men that determines their being, but, on the contrary, their social being that determines their consciousness. (Preface to *A Contribution to the Critique of Political Economy, Works*, I, 503)

These sentences are compressed and appear to employ a form of jargon. But Marx's meaning can be made clear. He believes societies function in a particular way, which can be understood through the analysis of certain categories. In the quotation he introduces four elements of a given society. These are:

1. forces of production
2. relations of production
3. political forms
4. ideas

His basic claim is that (1) and (2), which are commonly referred to as a society's "base" or "economic base," influence (3) and (4), which are commonly referred to as its "superstructure." In addition, within the base, (1) influences (2). Though these lines of influence are clear, the precise relationship between the elements is a difficult subject, to which we will return in the following section.

The four categories are understood most easily by looking at their workings in specific societies. Marx generally avoids discussing his main concepts in the abstract. He believes categories take on different meanings and implications as they are employed in different contexts. The main thrust of these four categories is seen most clearly if we look briefly at the last three stages of society, beginning with communal society. On the whole, Marx pays little attention to tribal society, and I will generally ignore it. The accounts of the societies given here are obviously highly simplified, but they should serve for purposes of illustration.

By productive forces, Marx means what people use in order to satisfy their daily needs. Productive forces are applied to nature, most obviously in order to satisfy people's need for food, clothing, and shelter. Marx is often said to be a "technological determinist," by which it is claimed he believes everything follows from the kind of technology employed in a given society, most clearly things like tools, machinery, and implements. But this view is too simple, as forces of production encompass more than these things. Also included are raw materials, for example, the wool from which clothes are made and the wood and clay used in houses. More important, the identity of productive forces depends on relationships within which they are used and changes according to circumstances. Thus a rifle in the hands of a hunter is a force of production, as he uses this in order to acquire food, while a rifle in the hands of a target shooter is not a force of production. In communal society, the ancient world, the main forces of production were agricultural, as people grew what they ate. Productive forces in this society also included such things as the tools and implements people used in agriculture and to make their clothing and houses. We can refer to the productive forces in general in a society as its "means of production."

Relations of production are the social relations within which production is carried out. For Marx, these are relationships of ownership, or property relations. Forces of production are employed in different societies in different ways, which depend on the means through which they are owned. Tools are not always owned by the workers who use them. More important, the people engaged in productive activity do not always own the fruits of their labor. Marx believes a central fact of human history is the existence of social relations through which workers have been exploited by other people who owned the means of production. The key to production in communal society was the existence of slavery. Not only were tools possessed as means of production, but people were as well. They were forced to work for their owners and received little reward for their labor.

Relations of production are, to use Marx's more familiar term, *class* relations. Marx makes little effort to say exactly what he means by the term (see p. 442), but it is safe to say that a class is a group of people who stand in similar relationships to the means of production. We will add additional elements to this account below. In Marx's view, class antagonisms are central to the workings of all societies, including communal society. In the *Manifesto of the Communist Party*, he writes: "The history of all hitherto existing society is the history of class struggles" (*Works*, I, 109). In each society there has existed a fundamental division between rich and poor. The former have owned the means of production, enjoyed the benefits of society's production, and lived lives of relative ease. The latter have owned little or nothing, lived in poverty, and had to work extremely hard. These two fundamental classes have gone by different names and stood in different legal relations to one another. In the *Communist Manifesto*, Marx says: "Freeman and slave, patrician and plebeian, lord and serf, guild-master and journeyman, in a word, oppressor and oppressed, stood in constant opposition to one another . . ." (*Works*, I, 108–109). Regardless of the names by which members of the opposed classes have gone, the reality of their situation has been exploitation of the weaker by the stronger.

The fundamental class antagonism in communal society was between masters and slaves. Marx refers to this society as "communal," because the citizens held power over their slaves only as a community, rather than through individual ownership of them (*The German Ideology*, p. 9). It is apparent that in this society, as in all others, the exploited class objected to its situation and attempted to resist, when this was possible. In this society as in all others, the remaining two elements of society, political forms and ideas, came into existence in order to keep the lower class in check. Political forms in the different stages of society are closely related to what we know as the state, though states, properly speaking, arose in Europe only in the sixteenth century (see pp. 4–6). The main political forms in the ancient world, the *polis* and the Roman city-state, were organizations developed by the masters to suppress their slaves. If the slaves attempted to resist, the organized force of the exploiting classes was used against them. An example of the function of the state, and the lengths to which the masters were prepared to go in order to preserve their position, was seen in Rome, in the first century B.C. Around the year 70 B.C., there was a revolt of slaves and gladiators, led by Spartacus. Interestingly, Spartacus was one of Marx's two favorite heroes (the other was Kepler) (McLellan, p. 457), but his revolution was not successful. After winning a number of victories, Spartacus's army was defeated by the Romans, and he himself was killed in the battle. Six thousand captured slaves were crucified along the Appian Way, between Capua and Rome, as both punishment and example to others that there are things worse than slavery.

Ideas are necessary because force alone is an inefficient means of controlling the oppressed class. A far better situation occurs when the slaves can be brought to believe they are somehow naturally fitted to their position as slaves, and so will not rebel against it. The masters too require justification of their position. We can assume they are ordinary human beings; they do not enjoy making other people suffer or profiting from their suffering. They are far more comfortable with their situation if they can believe they are somehow entitled to their privileged position, as the slaves are suited to theirs. A set of ideas that fulfills these important functions, thereby supporting the existing class structure, is referred to by Marx as an "ideology."

The main doctrine that fulfilled these functions in the ancient world was the idea of natural slavery. (We encountered a variant of this doctrine in our discussion of Aristotle, in Volume I.)[7] According to this point of view, some people are naturally smart, and others stupid. The intelligent are destined by nature to be masters and the others slaves. It is important to note that these ideas explain how slaves *benefit* from the existing order. Because they are not fully rational, they profit from incorporation into the masters' civilization. Through exposure to the masters' rationality, they are able to achieve the highest development of which they are capable. Thus the notion of natural slavery smooths class conflicts by convincing members of both classes that the class structure of society is not accidental or arbitrary. It is, rather, consistent with natural processes that benefit all members of society.

In this example, we can see the main features of an ideology. As Marx envisions these ideas, they have three main features. First, they depict the existing order as rooted in forces that are beyond human control. The way things are is not arbitrary, or instituted by people solely for their own advantage. Rather, it stems from God's will, or nature, or some other, similar force. In communal society, the division between masters and slaves is a result of their different biological natures.

Second, ideologies explain how the existing order benefits everyone in society. At first glance, the division between exploiting masters and exploited slaves would obviously appear to be in the former's interests and against the latter's. But this appearance is deceiving. Because the slaves are naturally suited to be slaves, it is actually in their interest to be in this position, as it is in the masters' interests to be in theirs. Finally, ideologies depict the existing order as beneficial in a particular way. Again, at first glance it appears that one class benefits while others are exploited. In depicting this situation as beneficial to all members of society, an ideology passes off the interest of one class as in the interest of all. Marx believes that, in reality, the way society is ordered is not arbitrary. The social order has been set up in a particular way to promote the interests of the dominant class. Thus what is good for this class must be made to *appear* to be in the interests of everyone. We have seen that this is done by appealing to more than human forces, which somehow place their stamp of approval on the existing order.

Because of the existence of a society's ideology, its actual workings are hidden from its members. Within the Marxian tradition, this notion is described as "false consciousness." Members of a society do not see it for what it is. The exploited class views its position as necessary and inevitable; the exploiting class sees itself as fulfilling a role that benefits all members of society, not themselves alone. An essential aspect of Marx's role as theoretician is to unmask the false appearance of his society—bourgeois society. Looking back over history, we can easily see how specific ideas fulfilled ideological roles in justifying different social orders. But because our thoughts too are controlled by ideologies, we do not detect this phenomenon in our own societies. Marx criticizes the ruling class in bourgeois society in the following terms:

> The selfish misconception that induces you to transform into eternal laws of nature and of reason, the social forms springing from your present mode of production and form of property—historical relations that rise and disappear in the progress of production— this misconception you share with every ruling class that has preceded you. What you see clearly in the case of ancient property, what you admit in the case of feudal property, you are of course forbidden to admit in the case of your own bourgeois form of property. (*Communist Manifesto, Works,* I, 123)

From the example of communal society, we can understand basic relationships between different societal factors. We can see that the lines of causation run from economic factors to others—though the complexities here will be discussed in the following section. Clearly, the most important factor is the forces of production. These give rise to specific relations of production, which political and ideological factors work to reinforce. Society is divided into dominating and oppressed classes. If it is to function effectively, means must be devised to keep the lower classes in their places, doing their work and not causing severe disruptions. Through a combination of force and fraud, they are kept under control, and the exploiting classes are able to enjoy the benefits of exploitation. In some obvious sense, economic structures are primary; political and ideological forms are brought about by them in order to preserve them. Thus Marx says men's social being determines their consciousness, rather than the other way around.

Having discussed the workings of communal society, we can look at the other stages briefly. In regard to forces of production, feudal society, like the communal stage, is essentially agricultural. In this stage, however, the main relations of production are not slavery but serfdom. Rather than a situation in which people are owned by others, as in a slave system, some people are attached to the land, as serfs, while this is owned by the dominant class. Under one typical arrangement, the serf farms two plots of land. He keeps the produce of one but must turn over that of the other to his master, who owns both plots. The essential fact of exploitation is visible in this form of ownership as well. While serfs work endlessly, own nothing, and enjoy few fruits of their labor, their masters own all the land, live in leisure, and partake of society's benefits. Naturally, the serfs are unhappy with their lot and will rise in rebellion—as they did periodically throughout medieval history. To keep them in line, the masters have organized political force in the form of the feudal state, though once again the word "state" is anachronistic here. Regardless of what we call this institution, however, its essence is organized violence intended to keep the serfs in line. To justify the overall system, an ideology is appealed to, in this case the Christian religion. In deemphasizing the value of this world and stressing the importance of salvation in the next, Christianity resigns the oppressed to their fate. It also teaches obedience to higher authorities, and that God is responsible for whether people are free or slave, rich or poor. Distinctions such as these mean nothing in God's eyes; God views all people as equal in regard to the fundamental matter of eternal salvation.[8] Thus both masters and serfs can accept the existing order as in accordance with God's will.

Similar arrangements are seen in bourgeois society. But while Marx's analyses of communal and feudal society are relatively uncontroversial, we are likely to be more troubled by what he says of this stage, because it corresponds to existing society, the society in which we live. Marx believes the reality of exploitation is as palpable here as in the earlier forms, but that it is veiled from us by bourgeois ideology.

The forces of production in bourgeois society are industrial. Central to all Marx's works is analysis of the Industrial Revolution. He recounts in great detail the rise of industry in the womb of feudal society (Marx frequently uses the language of birth) and the subsequent transformation of all aspects of feudal society this brought about. Industrial production is carried on within the structure of a two-class system: the bourgeoisie own the means of production; the workers, or proletariat, own only their labor (their labor power, to use the technical term) and so work in factories for wages, to earn their keep. The working and living conditions of the proletariat during the period when Marx developed his system were horrific. These are documented in Engels' classic *The Condition of the Working Class in England* (1845), and in many of Marx's works, especially *Capital*. If we penetrate beneath the surface of capitalist society, we can see the fundamental fact of class exploitation here as well. The bourgeoisie own the means of production, live in relative ease, and enjoy all society's benefits. The proletariat work long hours in horrendous conditions, own little, and live in poverty and squalor. Once again, the oppressed class is not content with its lot and would rise in revolt, if it could. To keep them in line, the bourgeoisie have organized means of force, the liberal state. To justify the existing order, they have concocted a powerful set of ideas, especially the basic liberal notions of natural rights and the free market. These have been central components of Western consciousness for hundreds of years. Thus Marx's account of their ideological role is highly interesting and will be a central theme of this chapter.

In all stages of society, then, we see similar structures at work. A dominant class exploits a lower class, reinforcing its position with political and intellectual constructions. As Marx continues to set forth his main ideas in the Preface, he moves from the factors that account for the workings of a society to those that cause its downfall:

> At a certain stage of their development, the material productive forces of society come in conflict with the existing relations of production or—what is but a legal expression for the same thing—with the property relations within which they have been at work hitherto. From forms of development of the productive forces these relations turn into their fetters. Then begins an epoch of social revolution. (Preface to *A Contribution to the Critique of Political Economy, Works*, I, 503–504)

Just as a harmonious relationship between an economic structure and the other elements that come into existence to maintain it allows a society to function smoothly, conflict between these elements causes the society to collapse. In this passage, we see that Marx focuses on a specific conflict, a clash between changing forces of production and the existing relations of production, which are in harmony with older forces of production. We will return to the nature and implications of economic conflict in the following sections.

Marx notes that the existing stage of society is the fourth in an historical sequence:

> In broad outlines Asiatic, ancient, feudal, and modern bourgeois modes of production can be designated as progressive epochs in the economic formation of society. (*Works*, I, 504)

As he continues, however, he passes from analysis of existing circumstances to predicting the future course of development. After the existing stage of society passes away, a qualitatively new form of society will arise:

> The bourgeois relations of production are the last antagonistic form of the social process of production—antagonistic not in the sense of individual antagonism, but of one arising from the social conditions of life of the individuals; at the same time the productive forces developing in the womb of bourgeois society create the material conditions for the solution of that antagonism. This social formation brings, therefore, the prehistory of human society to a close. (Preface to *A Contribution to the Critique of Political Economy*, *Works*, I, 504)

Marx's science of society is more than an analysis of what has happened in the past. It also contains an essential apocalyptic element. Existing society will not only go the way of all past societies, but its transition will be the last. Upon the downfall of bourgeois society, communism will arise. This society will lack the conflicts seen in past stages, thereby inaugurating a higher form of existence.

Marx's prediction of the end of society as we have known it is one of his theory's most distinctive features. Human history up to this point is only "prehistory," and is coming to a close. Marx's proclamation of the inevitability of social change is the basis for his call to political action. In the nexus between historical and sociological analysis and political struggle lies the essential Marxian idea of the "unity of theory and practice," to which we will return.

Before moving on to discuss particular aspects of Marx's system, we should note two important questions it raises. First is the uniformity of the sequence of stages. Does Marx believe all societies must pass through all four, and in this particular order, before arriving at communism? Or is communism possible without completing the entire progression? This question assumed great political importance in debates concerning the possibilities of socialism in the late nineteenth and early twentieth centuries. A number of countries have undergone revolutionary transformations to what their new rulers identified as communism. In addition to Russia, this has been seen in China, Cuba, and Viet Nam, while other countries could perhaps also be named. What is striking about all these examples is that the revolutions in question took place *before* the countries had passed through a capitalist stage. For a potential revolutionary in a preindustrial society, whether or not his society must go through a capitalist stage before arriving at communism is a crucial question. If one's country is just beginning the process of industrialization, this could mean having to delay a communist revolution for decades, or centuries. It is clear Marx believed that the first countries to move to a communist stage would be those that were most highly industrialized during his time, especially England. We have noted his remark in the Preface to *Capital* that England is marking a path that other countries will follow. But whether this is the *only* path to communism is a difficult question. A crucial difference between Marx's own thought and Marxism-Leninism is that the latter is applicable mainly to preindustrial countries—as all countries that underwent Marxist-Leninist revolutions were preindustrial. And so an important question in the history of Marxian political theory is whether Marx would have allowed these developments of his theory.

A related question concerns the uniformity of the transitions between stages of society. As we will see below, the main subject of Marx's study throughout his life was the Industrial Revolution in Western Europe and its social and political implications. Marx believed these profound economic changes brought about corresponding political changes, to which he refers as the "bourgeois revolution." The bourgeois revolution in England took place in the seventeenth century; Marx focuses on the English Civil War and the Glorious Revolution, through which divine rights monarchy was replaced with parliamentary democracy. In France, the bourgeois revolution was the French Revolution. These two revolutions—revolutions in important countries—were violent affairs. Does this mean transitions from one stage of society to another are necessarily violent? This question has immediate implications in regard to questions of revolutionary strategy. In particular, is it possible for capitalism to develop peacefully into communism, or is violent revolution necessary? Obviously, the position one takes in regard to this question will profoundly affect the shape of the revolutionary political movement one supports.

MATERIALISM

The general framework of analysis discussed in the previous section raises a number of important questions. Several of these concern the relationship between different aspects of society, especially between economic and other factors. Marx's belief that economic factors exert important causal influence on other aspects of society is referred to as his belief in "materialism," or "historical materialism," though the latter term was used more frequently by Engels than by Marx. This aspect of Marx's thought profoundly influences all aspects of his system and is necessary for understanding any of its parts.

Marx's materialism is, to begin with, largely negative in content, formulated in opposition to the dominant Hegelian ideas of his time. As we saw in the last chapter, Hegel viewed Spirit, or consciousness, as the primary causal force in human history. Spirit manifests itself in the philosophy, religion, and art of a society, which are that society's determining forces. Marx believes this view is precisely backwards. Though, as noted in the last chapter, he proclaims himself a pupil of Hegel, whom he characterizes as a "mighty thinker," he believes Hegel has gotten things upside down:

> The mystification which dialectic suffers in Hegel's hands, by no means prevents him
> from being the first to present its general form of working in a comprehensive and

conscious manner. With him it is standing on its head. It must be turned right side up again, if you would discover the rational kernel within the mystical shell. (*Capital*, I, 20).

In addition to Hegel's concentration on the historical role of Spirit, before Marx's time, many historians concentrated on political events. History was the story of kings and emperors, their struggles, wars, and battles. Dramatic as this material is, however, in Marx's eyes it is not the whole historical story. History is incomplete if it does not include central economic factors. More important, the cornerstone of Marx's materialist outlook is that economic factors are not one interesting subject matter among others. Rather, they are the ultimately moving forces of all history. According to Marx, the one great constant in all human history is that people must be able to live before they can perform historical acts. They have bodily needs they must fulfill as a necessary condition for being able to do anything else. As Marx and Engels write in *The German Ideology*:

> [W]e must begin by stating the first premise of all human existence, and therefore of all history, the premise namely that men must be in a position to live in order to be able to "make history." But life involves before everything else eating and drinking, a habitation, clothing and many other things. The first historical act is thus the pro- duction of the means to satisfy these needs, the production of material life itself. And indeed this is an historical act, a fundamental condition of all history, which today as thousands of years ago, must daily and hourly be fulfilled merely in order to sustain human life. (*German Ideology*, p. 16)

In order to satisfy these needs, men must engage in production. More than a constant factor in all societies, Marx believes production determines other factors. Thus in opposition to German thinkers (Hegel and certain of his followers) who study the history of conscious- ness, Marx believes consciousness has no independent history. Philosophy is always the philosophy of particular people who are engaged in particular productive activities through which they satisfy their physical needs. Once again, as Marx and Engels write in *German Ideology*,

> In direct contrast to German philosophy which descends from heaven to earth, here we ascend from earth to heaven. That is to say, we do not set out from what men say, imagine, conceive, nor from men as narrated, thought of, imagined, conceived, in order to arrive at men in the flesh. We set out from real, active men, and on the basis of their real life-process we demonstrate the development of the ideological reflexes and echoes of this life-process. . . . Morality, religion, metaphysics, all the rest of ideology and their corresponding forms of consciousness thus no longer retain the semblance of indepen- dence. They have no history, no development; but men, developing their material production and their material intercourse, alter, along with this their real existence, their thinking and the products of their thinking. Life is not determined by conscious- ness, but consciousness by life. (*German Ideology*, pp. 14–15)

Clearly, Marx and Engels view the need to produce in order to live as fundamental to human existence and the cornerstone of their analysis of society. In the speech he delivered at Marx's funeral, Engels gives this pride of place as the first of Marx's great discoveries:

Just as Darwin discovered the law of development of organic nature, so Marx discovered the law of development of human history: the simple fact, hitherto concealed by an overgrowth of ideology, that mankind must first of all eat, drink, have shelter and clothing, before it can pursue politics, science, art, religion, etc.; that therefore the production of the immediate material means of subsistence and consequently the degree of economic development attained by a given people or during a given epoch form the foundation upon which the state institution, the legal conceptions, art, and even the ideas on religion, of the people concerned have been evolved, and in the light of which they must, therefore, be explained, instead of *vice versa* as had hitherto been the case. (*Works*, III, 162)

More than a content of history, production plays an essential role in determining the form assumed by other elements of society. In the last section we discussed basic connections between economic elements and other aspects of society. In assessing the causal role of production, we must address two distinct questions: the nature of the relationship between economic and other factors; and the strength of this connection.

In regard to the nature of the connection, once again, there are two distinct questions. As noted in the last section, Marx believes the forces of production somehow determine the form of the relations of production in a given society. Then also, these two elements in combination, which constitute the economic "base," determine the form of society's political and ideological "superstructure." In both cases, the relationships are based on facilitation.[9] Marx is unclear on specific causal mechanisms, but the thrust of his thought is that, granted the existence of specific forces of production, a class structure will grow up around them that is able to exploit their full potential. The causal process can be viewed as a Darwinian struggle for survival between competing possible class structures, with the winner the one that is best adapted to the forces of production. This process is seen most clearly in the rise of bourgeois society within the womb of feudal society. Briefly, the bourgeoisie felt stifled by the existing class structure and the severe restrictions it placed on economic activity. These restrictions had been put in place by the feudal nobility, who benefitted from and so were reluctant to change them. The emerging bourgeoisie came to realize how much they could gain from altering these economic conditions, and began to struggle to change them. As new forces of production continued to develop, other people made similar discoveries and became similarly committed to change. Eventually, the struggle between these classes led to the overthrow of the existing relations of production and a new class structure, which allowed fuller development of the new forces of production. Thus changing forces of production eventually lead to changes in the existing relations of production, and so to fundamental changes throughout society, which Marx identifies as the emergence of a new stage of society. Throughout his works, Marx describes the specific source of change as conflict between evolving forces of production and constricting relations of production. A representative passage, from the Preface to the *Contribution to the Critique of Political Economy*, is quoted in the last section:

At a certain stage of their development, the material productive forces of society come in conflict with the existing relations of production or—what is but a legal expression for the same thing—with the property relations within which they have been at work hitherto. From forms of development of the productive forces these relations turn into their fetters. Then begins an epoch of social revolution. (*Works*, I, 503–504)

As Marx continues, he indicates the implications of this conflict throughout society:

> With the change of the economic foundation the entire immense superstructure is more or less rapidly transformed. (I, 504)

Marx uses the language of "fetters" frequently. For instance, in the *Communist Manifesto*, he describes the conflict between the rising bourgeoisie and the class structure of feudal society in the following terms:

> At a certain stage in the development of these means of production and of exchange, the conditions under which feudal society produced and exchanged, the feudal organization of agriculture and manufacturing industry, in one word, the feudal relations of property became no longer compatible with the already developed productive forces; they became so many fetters. They had to be burst asunder; they were burst asunder. (*Works*, I, 113)[10]

The fundamental relationship between the economic base and the noneconomic superstructure is similar. Just as relations of production must be compatible with the forces of production, so must the superstructure be with the base. Once again, compatibility here refers to the ability of the superstructure to allow the full development of productive forces. The overall relationship between base and superstructure is as indicated in the last section. Given the reality of class conflict, the oppressed class must be kept in its place through a combination of direct force and false consciousness. The political forms in a given society are the means through which the ruling class employs force. The main social and political ideas are similarly intended to keep the lower classes down. Though these aspects of society are not directly involved in the productive process, they are essential to its proper working. As part of the movement from one set of productive forces to the next, new political and intellectual forms must come into existence. The existing political and intellectual forms have been created by and serve the interests of the dominant class. When a new class arises that is better able to utilize emerging forces of production, it must replace the existing political and intellectual structure with one that serves its interests. The struggle between the old and the new political and intellectual forms is the essence of political revolutions, such as the French Revolution.

The nature of the relationships between the forces and relations of production, and between these two elements and the political and ideological superstructure, are difficult questions. Do the forces of production "influence" the relations of production, and so political and intellectual factors? Or do they "determine" these factors? The former is a relatively weak term, but the latter runs the risk of being too strong. In the first passage from the Preface to the *Contribution to the Critique of Political Economy* quoted in the last section, Marx uses different terms to specify the relationship. In successive sentences, he indicates different relationships. In the second to last sentence in the passage, he says that the base "conditions" (*bedingt*) the superstructure, but in the next sentence he indicates that the base "determines" (*bestimmt*) it. The fact that these terms indicate quite different relationships is not noted by Marx, while throughout their voluminous corpus, Marx and Engels describe these relationships in different terms. It is not surprising that various interpretations of their view have been advanced.

According to strict or "vulgar" Marxism, there is a direct causal relationship between changes in the forces of production and all other aspects of society. What is distinctive of this view is the absence of reciprocal interaction between elements. This is a form of technological determinism. The productive forces cause all else, while their movement is caused solely by factors internal to them. The great advantage of this interpretation in the eyes of its adherents is that it makes it relatively easy to predict changes in other aspects of society. If all that happens is caused directly and only by changes in the forces of production, then in order to predict the future development of society as a whole, one must study only these. The problem with this view, however, is it is improbable. Beyond a certain point, it makes little sense to say *everything* follows from changes in the forces of production, and both Marx and Engels repudiate this view. Engels forcefully criticizes it in a series of letters he wrote towards the end of his life.[11] For instance, in 1890, he wrote to Joseph Bloch as follows:

> According to the materialist conception of history, the *ultimately* determining element in history is the production and reproduction of real life. More than this neither Marx nor I have ever asserted. Hence if somebody twists this into saying that the economic element is the *only* determining one, he transforms that proposition into a meaningless, abstract, senseless phrase. (*Works*, III, 487)

By distinguishing between the view that economic forces are the *ultimate* determinant of historical events and the *only* determinant, Engels admits the possibility of reciprocal interaction. According to the view expressed in his letters, a variety of economic, social, and political factors interact to determine the course of some event, with the economic factors exerting the greatest influence. This view is strongly supported by common sense:

> Without making oneself ridiculous it would be a difficult thing to explain in terms of economics the existence of every small state in Germany, past and present, or the origin of the High German consonant permutations, which widened the geographic partition formed by the mountains from the Sudetic range to the Taunus to form a regular fissure across all Germany. (*Works*, III, 487–488)

It would be absurd to explain *all* historical events solely on the basis of economics. Did economic factors alone cause the North to win the Battle of Gettysburg but lose at Chancellorsville? Did economic factors cause the Miami Dolphins to win successive Super Bowls in the 1970s? Obviously, a wide range of factors were involved in these events—and countless others like them. Engels insists that he and Marx hold the more flexible causal view. In a letter to Conrad Schmidt, also in 1890, he reports that Marx himself used to say, if "Marxism" requires adherence to narrow economic determinism, "'All I know is that I am not a Marxist'" (*Works*, III, 484). In spite of Marx and Engels' dismissal of strict economic determinism, Engels notes that they were largely responsible for this construal of their doctrine. Because of the prevalence of historical views that paid insufficient attention to economics, they were forced to emphasize this against their opponents. Their words, then, removed from specific polemical contexts, could lead to misinterpretation of their position (*Works*, III, 488–489).

Much of Marx's corpus is consistent with the flexible causal view Engels espouses in these letters. This view has the considerable advantage of being a reasonable explanation of historical change, and to some extent is subscribed to by most social scientists currently doing research in the Western world. In spite of the many problems with his theory, Marx has probably exerted a more profound influence on twentieth-century social science than any other thinker.[12] To a large extent, this is because of the power of a flexible economic view of historical causation, to which he called widespread attention. A flexible causal view, according to which historical events result from the interaction of economic, political, social, and intellectual factors, is employed in many of Marx's journalistic writings, notably his classic analyses of French politics during the mid-nineteenth century: *The Class Struggles in France*, *The Eighteenth Brumaire of Louis Bonaparte*, and *The Civil War in France*.

The essence of such a view is that economic factors provide a kind of framework within which the particulars of historical events work themselves out. They *limit* the possible forms political and social events can take, without determining their details. As noted above, it is silly to believe economic forces alone explain the victories of Northern armies at Gettysburg and Southern armies at Chancellorsville. But the overall outcome of the Civil War was heavily influenced by the North's enormous superiority in industrial capacity. Because of its lack of productive capacity, Southern victory was highly improbable and would have had to depend on numerous unlikely occurrences.

We can flesh out this historical view by saying economic factors provide the *necessary conditions* for great historical events. It is often noted that the ideas of Martin Luther were not notably different from those of previous reformers—for example, Wycliffe in England and Hus in Bohemia. Why, then, did the Reformation break out in Germany and not in these other countries? The answer suggested by Marx's flexible account of historical causation is that circumstances were ripe in Germany during Luther's time, while they were not elsewhere in previous centuries. If the requisite factors had been present in Bohemia in the fifteenth century, then the Reformation would have broken out there, and Luther would be at best a minor figure. Thus Engels argues that specific individuals do not bring about important historical changes. Hegel had argued for the importance of "world-historical individuals," who are the catalysts of great historical transformations.[13] But according to Marx and Engels, individuals have only limited power to influence events. The conditions within which people work are "independent of their will" (*Works*, I, 503; I, 24). Within these parameters they are able to act, but the parameters are set. More than this, if a set of circumstances will allow particular events to unfold, then it is likely that specific agents of change will arrive on the scene to realize what is possible. In a letter to H. Starkenburg written in 1894, Engels says:

> That such and such a man and precisely that man arises at a particular time in a particular country is, of course, pure chance. But cut him out and there will be a demand for a substitute, and this substitute will be found, good or bad, but in the long run he will be found. That Napoleon, just that particular Corsican, should have been the military dictator whom the French Republic, exhausted by its own warfare had rendered necessary, was chance, but that, if a Napoleon had been lacking, another would have filled the place, is proved by the fact that the man was always found as soon as he became necessary: Caesar, Augustus, Cromwell, etc. While Marx discovered the materialist conception of history, Thierry, Mignet, Guizot and all the English historians

up to 1850 are evidence that it was being striven for, and the discovery of the same conception by Morgan proves that the time was ripe for it and that it simply *had* to be discovered. (Tucker, pp. 767–768)

If Marx had not made his discoveries, because circumstances were ripe, someone else would have made similar discoveries. This analysis is supported by the history of science. For example, calculus was discovered more or less simultaneously, by two men, Newton and Leibniz. Oxygen was discovered more or less simultaneously by three, Priestly, Lavoisier, and Scheele. The fact that different researchers came upon the same discoveries at roughly the same times indicates that conditions were ready for the discoveries to be made, and so they were made. The same is true of great historical events. Because the time was ripe for the ideas of the French Revolution to be spread throughout Europe, a great man arose to spread them. Engels' analysis is similar to Hegel's view of the great man, whose particular aspirations are used by the "cunning of reason," as an agent of historical development.[14] Along similar lines, Montesquieu pioneered sophisticated historical analysis in the *Spirit of Laws* and his *Considerations on the Causes of the Greatness of the Romans and their Decline*. In reference to the fall of the Roman Republic, he wrote: "If Caesar and Pompey had thought like Cato, others would have thought like Caesar and Pompey; and the republic, destined to perish, would have been dragged to the precipice by another hand."[15] Marx goes beyond Hegel and Montesquieu primarily in carefully analyzing the economic nature of the causal factors involved.

In his letter to Starkenburg, Engels presents a clear, overall characterization of the materialist conception of history. Economic factors are ultimate causes, not sole causes. Though their influence cannot be traced in the short term, in day-to-day events, it clearly manifests itself over the course of history. Over the long run, the influence of economic factors is apparent:

> The further the particular sphere which we are investigating is removed from the economic sphere and approaches that of pure abstract ideology, the more shall we find it exhibiting accidents in its development, the more will its curve run zigzag. But if you plot the average axis of the curve, you will find that this axis will run more and more nearly parallel to the axis of economic development the longer the period considered and the wider the field dealt with. (Tucker, p. 768)

If one considers the course of world history over the last two hundred years, the overwhelming influence of the Industrial Revolution is everywhere apparent. Though it is difficult to explain the contours of particular events, or to make short-term predictions on the basis of one's understanding of developments in the forces of production, the overall shape of historical change is clearly determined *in the final analysis* by economic factors. Marx devotes a substantial part of his works to analyzing the Industrial Revolution and its influences. I believe one of his claims to fame is as perhaps the greatest historian of this period. Once again, his analysis has exerted substantial influence on historians and social scientists ever since.

In spite of the great attractions of Marx's flexible, multicausal understanding of historical change, he frequently departs from this view and favors a narrower, more deterministic approach. To my mind, the fact that Marx presents different accounts of the relationship between economic and other factors in society is difficult to deny. Nor is it difficult to understand why he falls into this trap. To the extent Marx is interested in political change, the narrower view serves his purpose. For Marx is not *only* a dispassionate social scientist. The scientific analysis of society he pursues is in his eyes the "unity of theory and practice." It is a political as well as a theoretical endeavor.

In his funeral speech, Engels duly notes this side of Marx. After summarizing what he views as Marx's two greatest contributions to science—the materialist conception of history (p. 425), and his specific analysis of the workings of capitalist society—Engels continues:

> Such was the man of science. But this was not even half the man. Science was for Marx a historically dynamic, revolutionary force. However great the joy with which he welcomed a new discovery in some theoretical science whose practical application perhaps it was as yet quite impossible to envisage, he experienced quite another kind of joy when the discovery involved immediate revolutionary changes in industry, and in historical development in general. . . .
>
> For Marx was before all else a revolutionist. His real mission in life was to contribute, in one way or another, to the overthrow of capitalist society and of the state institutions which it had brought into being, to contribute to the liberation of the modern proletariat, which *he* was the first to make conscious of its own position and its needs, conscious of the conditions of its emancipation. (*Works*, III, 162–163)

The essence of Marx's theory of revolution—and so his hope for actual revolution—is its inevitability. This in turn is brought about by revolutionary changes in the developing forces of production in capitalist society, to the tracing of which he devoted much of his work. Because of the importance of proving the inevitability of revolution, Marx naturally gravitates toward a simpler understanding of history, which makes this more feasible. Accordingly, though in his analysis of particular political events, he shows great understanding of the multiplicity of factors involved, when he turns to the overall course of social and political development, he tends to fall into simpler, more deterministic patterns of historical analysis. This lends a discordant character to Marx's political writings. The sophisticated, nuanced analyses of his journalistic works, also found in Engels' statements of his and Marx's overall point of view, are contradicted by aspects of Marx's view, especially in regard to the future course of capitalist society. A simpler causal relationship is especially clear in Marx's view of the state as generally reflecting economic forces, without independent power to act—as we will see in the next section. It is perhaps most apparent in Marx's view of the "withering away of the state" after the communist revolution. Because of changes in the forces of production, communism will be a classless society, and so also without political institutions (on which also, more below).

Because Marx analyzes political forms in the context of the overall economic and social systems of which they are parts, it is difficult to discuss his view of politics in isolation from these other elements. In working through his analysis of bourgeois society, we will see that his account of the bourgeois state is inseparably connected with liberal ideology and the capitalist economic order. Regardless of where we begin, discussion of any one element of this overall system necessarily leads into the others. This makes a certain amount of repetition unavoidable in disentangling Marx's system. We will begin with his view of the state before moving on to other elements.

THE STATE

It is remarkable that Marx is one of the most important figures in the history of political theory although, in his major theoretical writings, he devotes relatively little attention to the state or other political institutions. Things are somewhat different in regard to his political journalism, but as we will see, important aspects of these works do not rest well with his theoretical works. The reason Marx devotes relatively little direct attention to politics is clear. He believes political phenomena have little independent reality. In keeping with his materialist approach to social and historical explanation, he views them as essentially reflections of more significant economic factors.

The main tenets of materialism have been discussed in previous sections. Marx believes political forms exist in a "superstructure" that rests upon an economic "base." As we saw in our discussion of the different stages of society, he believes political forms arise in order to reinforce an existing class system. Once again, I generally use terms such as "political forms" and "political institutions" rather than "states," because institutionalized violence has existed in different forms throughout history. What we know as the state appeared relatively recently, in the sixteenth century. But regardless of the extent to which the political institutions of a given stage of society correspond to the state, they have existed in all past stages of society and always followed the interests of the dominant class. In order to maintain its privileged position, the ruling class must employ means of organized violence to keep the lower class in its place. In Marx's eyes, the essence of political forms is agencies of class oppression. This view is seen in countless passages in his works. For instance, in the *Communist Manifesto*, he says: "Political power, properly so called, is merely the organized power of one class for oppressing another" (*Works*, I, 127). Similarly, in regard to the state in capitalist society: "The executive of the modern State is but a committee for managing the common affairs of the whole bourgeoisie" (*Works*, I, 110–111). Of the legal system of this society, he says (addressing the bourgeoisie): "your jurisprudence is but the will of your class made into a law for all, a will, whose essential character and direction are determined by the economical conditions of existence of your class" (*Works*, I, 123).

A more explicit statement of this view is in the *German Ideology*.

> Through the emancipation of private property from the community, the State has become a separate entity, beside and outside civil society; but it is nothing more than the form of organization which the bourgeois necessarily adopt both for internal and external purposes, for the mutual guarantee of their property and interests. . . .
>
> Since the state is the form in which the individuals of a ruling class assert their common interests, and in which the whole civil society of an epoch is epitomized, it follows that in the formation of all communal institutions the state acts as intermediary, that these institutions receive a political form. (*German Ideology*, pp. 59–60)

Marx's view of the state as an agency of class oppression is one reason he believes it will die out under communism. In Marx's eyes, communism will be a classless society. If the existence of classes is a necessary condition for the existence of political institutions, it follows that communism will be without political forms. Thus he writes in *The Poverty of Philosophy*:

The working class, in the course of its development, will substitute for the old civil society an association which will exclude classes and their antagonism, and there will be no more political power properly so called, since political power is precisely the official expression of antagonism in civil society. (*Poverty of Philosophy*, p. 174)

Engels' famous discussion of this subject is found in his work, *Socialism: Utopian and Scientific*:

> As soon as there is no longer any social class to be held in subjection; as soon as class rule, and the individual struggle for existence based upon our present anarchy in production, with the collisions and excesses arising from these, are removed, nothing more remains to be repressed, and a special repressive force, a state, is no longer necessary. The first act by virtue of which the state really constitutes itself the representative of the whole of society . . . this is, at the same time, its last independent act as a state. State interference in social relations becomes, in one domain after another, superfluous, and then dies out of itself; the government of persons is replaced by the administration of things, and by the conduct of processes of production. The state is not 'abolished.' *It dies out.* (*Works*, III, 147)

One well-known translation of the last phrase (*er stirt ab*) is that the state "withers away." The implication of Engels' argument, and the similar statements by Marx, is that after the revolution, with an end to the domination of one class by others, the state, as a particular kind of repressive agency, will pass out of existence. This does not necessarily mean there will be no repression after the revolution; rather the specific kind of repression associated with class conflict—that is, of other classes by the ruling class through the agency of the state—will be a thing of the past. It is likely that in the future force will be exercised by the community as a whole; separate state agencies will not be needed. Marx argues along these lines in responding to a critique of his theory presented by the anarchist Mikhail Bakunin. He clarifies one of his points in regard to future communist society as follows:

> This means only: when class domination ends, there will be no state in the present political sense of the word. (Tucker, p. 545)[16]

There is more to Marx's belief that communist society will be without a state than a verbal point. The state is a distinctive institution. It is comprised of people separated from the normal division of labor, whose business is delivering violence. People who serve in the state staff its police force and army, jails, and judicial system. Marx describes existing states in these terms in his *Critique of the Gotha Program*:

> [I]n fact by the word 'state' is meant the government machine, or the state in so far as it forms a special organism separated from society through the division of labor. (*Critique of the Gotha Program*, *Works*, III, 27)

In all previous instances of class domination, institutions such as these were necessary because the dominant class was a minority, having to hold power against a majority. The only way it could do this was through institutionalized violence. In future communist society, for the first time, the majority will be in charge and separate state organizations will no longer be necessary.

Marx's analysis of the state indicates fundamental differences between his view and liberal political theory. As we have seen in previous chapters, liberal theorists argue for an instrumental view of the state. Individuals require it in order to accomplish their ends. This is seen most clearly in the state of nature arguments of Locke and Hobbes. The individual in the state of nature is threatened by other people and therefore surrenders some of his rights to the state in order to protect the rest. The major institutions of the state are the coercive institutions we have just noted: police, army, courts, jails. Its major functions are also coercive. The agreement between Marx and liberal theorists in these matters is because they were commenting upon existing political institutions, which were of that form.

Marx and liberal theorists also agree about the state's instrumental nature. Like the liberals, Marx believes political institutions are not good in themselves but exist to contribute to other ends. For liberal theorists, the ends in question are those individuals hold "prior to" entering political society. In order to achieve their projects, individuals require protection from others, and so the state's main function is protecting their rights and property. The central role of protecting property has been seen in our discussions of Locke, Hume, James Mill, and other theorists. In addition, liberal theorists believe the state itself poses a threat, and so protection is needed against abuse of governmental power. Thus liberal theorists emphasize constitutional government, separation of powers and checks and balances, which prevent government from behaving tyrannically. In protecting individuals from one another and from the abuse of political authority, the liberal state maximizes freedom (negative freedom), the absence of coercive interference by other people. Liberal theorists closely link the notions of rights and freedom, and argue that the state exists to protect both.

Throughout liberal theory, a basic assumption is that *all* people benefit from political authority. According to Locke, the state is a neutral umpire, providing security for all alike. Since the state does not favor anyone, all benefit from it, and so willingly leave the state of nature for civil society. Similarly, for J. S. Mill, all individuals enjoy an area of protected space within which to pursue their self-regarding activities. Faith that the political order benefits all alike is closely bound up with liberal beliefs that all people are equal and possess natural rights.[17]

In our discussion of Rousseau, we have seen respects in which this political argument can be criticized. Liberals argue for the need to protect the property of everyone alike. The obvious counter, however, is that all people do not have equal property, and so protection of property does not benefit all alike. Rousseau argues that this justification of the state in fact rests on deception. The rich, feeling threatened, convince the poor it is necessary to protect the property *of everyone*. Not realizing how little they stand to gain—and how much to lose—the poor rush to join political society, which becomes an additional means of oppressing them.[18] Marx carries this line of argument much farther and develops it into a systematic critique of the liberal order.

According to Marx, the basic building block of society is not the individual but the class. As we have seen, he believes each stage of society centers upon conflict between fundamental classes: a dominant class which owns everything, and exploited classes that are forced to work for it. In protecting the property of all alike, the state benefits the dominant class at the expense of the exploited. We will return to the idea that the state protects everyone's rights in the next section, in reference to the concept of ideology. Like liberal theorists, Marx views the state as instrumental. But it is not neutral; the ends it serves are those of the dominant class. In actuality, protecting the property of all classes amounts to protecting the property of the dominant class *against members of the other classes*. If one sees through liberal rhetoric, one will discover that protection of property, far from furthering the interests of all alike, is actually a means of oppressing the lower classes.

Marx believes the job of oppressing and exploiting the lower classes is accomplished especially efficiently in bourgeois society. As in other forms of society, it is essential that the lower class be kept in its place, but this stage is distinctive in that political forms play only an indirect role. In communal society, organized violence directly subjugates the slaves; in feudal society, similar violence is directed at the serfs. But in bourgeois society, the major work of oppression is performed by economic rather than political forces.

The class structure of bourgeois society centers on division between two classes. The bourgeoisie own the means of production and control the state—and, as we will see, the intellectual means of production as well. The proletariat own only their ability to labor. The existence of a class of "free" laborers (on which, more below) is a necessary condition for the capitalist economy: "Thus capital presupposes wage labor; wage labor presupposes capital. They reciprocally condition the existence of each other; they reciprocally bring forth each other" (*Wage Labor and Capital, Works*, I, 162; Marx's italics removed). Because they are without property, members of the proletariat must work for the bourgeoisie in order to live. They have no other alternative as long as this is their only means to subsistence. To make things worse, because of economic circumstances we will discuss, the proletariat are in a weak bargaining position; they are forced to work under conditions in many ways worse than those of serfs and slaves. Protecting the property of the bourgeoisie against the proletariat forces the latter to labor in this fashion. In reality, then, in protecting the property of all alike, the state does not treat people equally. Because the bourgeoisie own all the property and the proletariat only their ability to labor, protection of property ensures the subordination of the latter to the former.

Marx's analysis of the state as an agency of class oppression makes it appear epiphenomenal, as a reflection of more fundamental economic realities, instead of an independent force. For the most part, this is how he views the state. For instance, he writes in the *German Ideology*:

> It follows from this that all struggles within the State, the struggle between democracy, aristocracy, and monarchy, the struggle for the franchise, etc., etc., are merely the illusory forms in which the real struggles of the different classes are fought out among one another. (*German Ideology*, p. 23)

In interpreting Marx, however, quoting isolated passages proves little, because within his vast corpus quotations can be found to support virtually any position. In regard to the question of the state's independence from economic forces, strong evidence Marx views it as far more than epiphenomenal is found in his journalistic writings, especially his analyses of French politics. The most notable text is *The Eighteenth Brumaire of Louis Bonaparte*, which discusses the coup d'état against the French republic engineered by Louis Napoleon in 1851. In this work Marx analyzes the specific constellation of forces that allowed the state to rise above and rule all classes of society as an independent agency.[19] But analyses along these lines go against the overall thrust of Marx's political theory.

The situation here is analogous to what we saw in the last section in regard to Marx's materialism. Though there are places in his works in which he presents a more sophisticated view, Marx requires a strict doctrine of economic determinism in order to demonstrate the inevitability of communism. The same is true of his view of the state. Though there are places in his works where Marx presents a more nuanced view of the state, on the whole he views it as a reflection of economic circumstances. As we have seen, to do away with class antagonisms is to eliminate the state. Though Marx says little about the shape of future society after the revolution, one thing he is clear about is that there will be no state. Future society will, in other words, be anarchism. Once again, one reason Marx is able to hold this view is because he does not view the state as an independent entity. Because it reflects more fundamental economic factors, when these evolve in the direction of communal ownership, the state will wither away. Power will be lodged in the community as a whole, and distinct institutions for class oppression will no longer exist.

IDEOLOGY

In addition to political forms, Marx believes the work of domination is also performed by political and social ideas. His account of the nature of ideologies and how they function is one of his most original contributions to political theory. We have noted his view that in communal society the main ideology was belief in natural slavery, and that in feudal society religion fulfilled this function. While we have little trouble seeing how these ideas worked in their particular societies, things become more interesting and controversial in regard to the main ideology of bourgeois society, belief in natural rights and the free market. These ideas are among our deepest convictions.

In order to unmask the ideology of liberal society, Marx contrasts an idealized view of the way things are supposed to work and how things actually work. Thus in order to understand bourgeois ideology, one must understand the central workings of bourgeois society. As noted above, an ideology has three main features. It depicts the arrangements of a given society as somehow natural, rooted in more than human forces, and so beyond man's capacity to change. It also justifies the existing order by showing how all members of society benefit. Finally, in connection with his view that societies are constructed around class domination, Marx believes that, while the dominant class might benefit from existing arrangements, oppressed classes do not. An ideology passes off the interest of one class as in the interest of all.

Marx analyzes ideologies historically. He traces the process through which they come into existence, created by specific classes in order to advance their interests. Part of the process through which a class comes to dominate society is by imposing its own ideas on all other classes. In *The German Ideology*, he writes:

> The ideas of the ruling class are in every epoch the ruling ideas: i.e., the class which is the ruling material force of society, is at the same time its ruling intellectual force. The class which has the means of material production at its disposal, has control at the same time over the means of mental production, so that thereby, generally speaking, the ideas of those who lack the means of mental production are subject to it. The ruling

ideas are nothing more than the ideal expression of the dominant material relationships, the dominant material relationships grasped as ideas; hence of the relationships which make the one class the ruling one, therefore the ideas of its dominance. (*German Ideology*, p. 39)

The consciousness of all members of society is dominated by ideas propagated by the ruling class. The ruling class not only owns the means of production and controls political forces, but its members "rule also as thinkers, as producers of ideas, and regulate the production and distribution of the ideas of their age: thus their ideas are the ruling ideas of the epoch" (*German Ideology*, p. 39).

In generating the ideology of a given class, intellectuals play an important role. They formulate their class's ideas with a degree of abstract complexity beyond the power of most members of the class. Marx refers to the "thinkers" of a class as "its active, conceptive ideologist, who make the perfecting of the illusion of the class about itself their chief source of livelihood" (*German Ideology*, p. 40). In previous chapters we have discussed "the active conceptive ideologists" who developed the main ideas of bourgeois society, figures such as Locke, Hume, Bentham, James Mill, and John Stuart Mill. We could add important political economists, especially Adam Smith and David Ricardo. A central aspect of Marx's theoretical project was showing the ideological role of theorists such as these. He was especially concerned with political economists and spent years reading everything they wrote and attempting to demonstrate how it was wrong.

In Marx's eyes, bourgeois society is divided into two classes, the bourgeoisie, who own the means of production, and the proletariat, who own only their ability to labor, which they sell to the bourgeoisie. Important aspects of Marx's theoretical writings which we cannot discuss in this chapter include his detailed account of the historical process through which this particular class structure came into existence. Within capitalist society, the bourgeoisie's control of the means of production gives it tremendous power over the proletariat. Proletarians can acquire their subsistence only by working for the bourgeoisie. What is more, the terms under which they labor are dictated by the bourgeoisie and are highly disadvantageous. Central to Marx's analysis of capitalist society is the fact of unemployment. Under capitalism, there is furious competition among individual factory owners. They are constantly forced to introduce new technology in order to gain a competitive edge, or merely to remain competitive. As a result, machinery constantly replaces workers, who become unemployed. According to Marx, a central "contradiction" of capitalism is its tendency to generate higher productivity on the one hand and unemployment, and so misery, on the other. In *Capital*, he writes:

> The greater the social wealth, the functioning capital, the extent and energy of its growth, and, therefore, also the absolute mass of the proletariat and the productiveness of its labor, the greater is the industrial reserve army [Marx's term for the unemployed]. The same causes which develop the expansive power of capital, develop also the labor-power at its disposal. The relative mass of the industrial reserve army increases therefore with the potential energy of wealth. But the greater this reserve army in proportion to the active labor-army, the greater is the mass of a consolidated surplus-population, whose misery is in inverse ratio to its torment of labor. The more extensive, finally, the lazarus-layers of the working-class, and the industrial reserve army, the greater is official

pauperism. *This is the absolute general law of capitalist accumulation.* Like all other laws it is modified in its working by many circumstances, the analysis of which does not concern us here. (*Capital,* I, 644)

A combination of this insidious dialectic and an absence of alternative means of subsistence for the growing ranks of the unemployed constitutes the reality of capitalist society in Marx's eyes, and so the backdrop against which he assesses the claims advanced in capitalist ideology.

During Marx's day, the effects of unemployment were especially severe. Between the state that existed during his time and twentieth-century social welfare states with which modern citizens are familiar there looms a great gap. During his day, there were few social services to help people who had lost their jobs. There was no unemployment insurance— or such related forms of social security as compensation for injuries, or old age insurance. There were also few programs to deal with the needy. Aside from minimal public relief and private charity, people were on their own, and starvation was not uncommon. This was especially true during the 1840s, which was an extremely severe time, as is reflected in Marx's descriptions of capitalist society and in Engels' *The Condition of the Working Class in England.* In this decade, during which Marx first developed his theory, potato famine caused widespread starvation in Ireland, while conditions were similarly harsh elsewhere.

Given this social situation, the only real choice for a member of the working class is between working and starving. If there are more potential workers than available jobs, workers must accept whatever terms the capitalists dictate. Under these circumstances, workers' pay will be subsistence, what is needed to keep them alive from day to day. They will not be paid more than this, because employers do not have to pay more. If Alejandro refuses to work for subsistence, Albert will. He too faces starvation and so would accept the job. The only reason workers are not paid less than subsistence is this would not keep them alive. Even if a specific capitalist took pity on his workers and wished to pay them more, he would be unable to, because this would put him at a disadvantage in competing with other capitalists, who pay their workers subsistence. Given the coercive competition that dominates the capitalist economy, if only one employer in an industry pays subsistence, all others must follow suit, or they could not compete.

Under these circumstances, workers are subject to brutal exploitation. The fruit of their labor is not owned by them but by the capitalists for whom they work, who use profits wrung from their labor to consolidate the economic and political system that holds them in thrall. Believing that all value is created by human labor (i.e., in what is commonly called the "labor theory of value"), Marx describes the specific form of exploitation central to capitalist society as "surplus value." Briefly, by this Marx means that workers create more value than is returned to them in the form of wages. Assume that Jackson's labor adds 50 cents an hour of value to the products on which he works. Because he is at the mercy of the capitalist who employs him, he might be paid 25 cents an hour, with the capitalist pocketing the rest. Marx explains all profit as resulting from surplus value extracted from workers' labor. Thus even if workers were paid more than subsistence, the exploitation central to capitalism would still be objectionable on moral grounds.

But subsistence and exploitation go hand in hand. If Jackson's subsistence costs $2.00 a day, he is able to produce this amount of value in four hours. If he were paid the full value of his labor, he would earn his daily bread in four hours and be free to leave—or work additional hours to raise his standard of living. But because the terms of his employment are set by his employer, he will be forced to work longer hours for subsistence. Regardless of how long he works, he still needs $2.00 a day to survive. Thus if he is paid 25 cents an hour, he will have to work eight hours. But it is in the capitalist's interest to pay him even less and force him to work longer still, as many hours as human endurance allows. Because Jackson's only other alternative is starvation, he must accept this arrangement, while if he decides not to, other workers will take his place—so they don't starve. Though this situation is clearly appalling to Marx, he does not hold individual capitalists responsible. Again, because of coercive competition, they have no choice about how to treat their workers. If a given employer decides to ease up on them, perhaps to pay them more or allow them to work fewer hours, he will not be able to compete. His factory might have to close. Ironically, this would be even worse for his workers, who would be thrown onto the streets to starve.

Thus the inner logic of capitalism requires exploitation. Workers must work ever harder, ever longer hours. The economic system is a vise, squeezing out their life blood. In the absence of some means to regulate workers' hours, exploitation is virtually without limit. Marx's discussion of the working day in different industries is among the most horrific aspects of his depiction of capitalism. When he first formulated his theory, there was virtually no maximum hour legislation. (This began to emerge in England in the 1830s and 1840s, and given the logic of Marx's view of the bourgeois state, he has no easy time explaining it.) An idea of resulting conditions can be seen in the lace industry, in which, a meeting was held to *limit* the number of hours a day a man could work to eighteen. Before that time, the working day was longer. And this industry was not alone.[20] Moreover, it bears repeating that a worker's pay for his eighteen-plus hours was subsistence, regardless of how much value he actually produced.

The proletariat also worked under horrible conditions. With the advent of machinery, workers spent all their time performing a few simple operations. Work was not only endless, but also unsafe. Factories were dark, and there was little effort to protect workers from dangerous machinery or unsafe substances. Marx recounts in graphic detail the results of industrial accidents. He views injuries to and deformities of workers as tangible manifestations of the spiritual deadening that results from long hours of mind-numbing work. Once again, for an individual capitalist to attempt to improve conditions would place him at a competitive disadvantage, possibly forcing his business to close.

Finally, the proletariat's living conditions were abominable. Their wages were enough to keep them alive, but little more. They lived in darkness and filth, while women and children worked long hours alongside men. Much of Marx's account of the proletariat's life is familiar to readers of English literature. The conditions he describes are similar to those Dickens depicts in his novels. In the *Economic and Philosophical Manuscripts* of 1844, Marx describes the living conditions of the proletariat as follows:

> For the worker even the need for fresh air ceases to be a need. Man returns to the cave dwelling again, but it is now poisoned by the pestilential breath of civilization. The worker has only a *precarious* right to inhabit it, for it has become an alien dwelling which may suddenly not be available, or from which he may be evicted if he does not pay the rent. He has to *pay* for this mortuary. The dwelling full of light which

Prometheus, in Aeschylus, indicates as one of the great gifts by which he has changed savages into men, ceases to exist for the worker. Light, air, and the simplest *animal* cleanliness cease to be human needs. *Filth*, this corruption and putrefaction which runs in the sewage of civilization (this is to be taken literally) become the *element in which man lives*. Total and *unnatural* neglect, petrified nature, becomes the *element in which he lives*. . . . It is not enough that man should lose his human needs; even animal needs disappear. The Irish no longer have any need but that of *eating—eating potatoes*, and then only the worst kind, *moldy potatoes*.[21]

In order to be able to live in these conditions—described at length throughout Marx and Engels' works—workers were forced to labor long hours, in unclean, unsafe factories, at endlessly repetitive tasks.

According to Marx, the ability to produce, to perform creative labor, is a distinctive attribute of man's nature, central to what makes human beings human. Under the conditions of capitalist society, the capacity to labor ceases to be a source of fulfillment, to which other aspects of man's nature are subordinated. It becomes instead a means to satisfy his barest animal needs. In order to stay alive, people must sell their capacity to labor, and work under the conditions we have noted. For Marx, then, in capitalist society, man's distinctively human attributes become means to preserve physical existence: "We arrive at the result that man (the worker) feels himself to be freely active only in his animal functions—eating, drinking, and procreating, or at most also in his dwelling and in personal adornment—while in his human function he is reduced to an animal. The animal becomes human and the human becomes animal" (*Manuscripts*, p. 99). "If the silk worm were to spin in order to continue its existence as a caterpillar, it would be a complete wage-worker" (*Wage Labor and Capital, Works*, I, 153). It is arguable that in no earlier stage of society did human beings live and work in such deplorable conditions. The rise of productivity brought about by the Industrial Revolution came at a terrible price.

In spite of the appalling depiction of capitalist society Marx presents, there is little doubt about his accuracy. Conditions among the working class at that time were truly grim. Interestingly, much of Marx's information about working and living conditions was derived from investigative reports commissioned by the English government. In the Preface to *Capital*, Marx praises the factory inspectors for their competence and lack of partisanship (I, 9). Exactly why the state would investigate working conditions is a difficult question for Marx. Investigative reports were but one step in an involved process of reform that led from the conditions Marx describes to the more benign conditions in present-day capitalist societies. But regardless of how things have changed in subsequent decades, the plight of the proletariat in the mid-nineteenth century was dire, and is a central theme in Marx's works.

If we keep the proletariat's circumstances in mind, we can understand why Marx is skeptical of the basic ideas of bourgeois society and views them as ideological. The two main ideas on which we will focus are rights and the free market. We have seen something of his critique of rights in the previous section. According to liberal political theory, all people have rights—to life, liberty, and property. But without the guarantee of an adequate standard of living and freedom from the slavery of factory labor, these rights amount to very little. The right to one's property is especially meaningless for the proletariat, which is without property, and no matter how hard workers work, they achieve no more than subsistence and so can never acquire significant property. In reality, the right of property amounts to the right of the property-owning class to protect its property *against* the mass of the population. The sanctity of private property has long been a familiar argument against socialism. In the *Communist Manifesto* Marx replies:

> You are horrified at our intending to do away with private property. But in your existing society, private property is already done away with for nine-tenths of the population; its existence for the few is solely due to its non-existence in the hands of those nine-tenths. You reproach us, therefore, with intending to do ways with a form of property, the necessary condition for whose existence is the non-existence of any property for the immense majority of society. (*Communist Manifesto, Works,* I, 122)

Along similar lines, it is argued that capitalist society grants workers freedom to choose for whom to work. This is in contrast to slavery in communal society and serfdom in feudal society. In these systems, workers were bound to specific masters. The importance of being free to work for whom one pleases is widely discussed in present society in regard to "right-to-work" laws, according to which workers cannot be forced to join unions as a condition for employment. Once again, this freedom is at first sight attractive, but Marx assesses it against the reality of capitalist society. The worker does not have a choice whether or not to work. If he does not work he will starve. So the only real choice is whom to work for. But in this regard, he must work for a member of the capitalist class. Only owners of the means of production offer employment. Thus for a given worker, freedom to choose his employer amounts to freedom to choose which capitalist to sell his labor to, and on the terms we have discussed. Accordingly, the worker "belongs not to this or that capitalist but to the *capitalist class*" (*Wage Labor and Capital, Works,* I, 154). Because all other workers are in the same position, the proletariat as a whole belongs to the capitalist class as a whole. In light of the reality of subordination of one class to another, freedom to choose one's employer amounts to very little.

It is interesting that Marx's critique of rights is similar to a conservative argument advanced by Burke. As we saw in Chapter 7, Burke is skeptical of rights in the abstract. The declaration of a particular right means little, unless there exist political and social institutions to make it real. Thus rights are meaningful only within the context of a political system that will enforce them (see pp. 290–2). Marx takes this line of argument one step further. The existence of the requisite institutions is not enough. People require a certain level of economic well-being before they can enjoy their rights. Within the liberal tradition, people are granted a litany of rights to protect them from unjust arrest and imprisonment. But as Marx's line of argument demonstrates, even though these rights exist and are enforced, for people who are forced to work fourteen or sixteen hours a day in miserable conditions, they are essentially meaningless. The condition of a prisoner might be an improvement.

Marx's criticism of rights in liberal society is of course in reference to the specific rights that existed during his time. As we can see from the examples discussed, these were essentially political rights. At the time Marx wrote, there were few economic rights ("entitlements") in liberal societies. But as a response to the conditions he discusses—and to some extent to his works as well—the retinue of rights granted by the state expanded during the late nineteenth and early twentieth centuries in all the liberal democracies, in realization of the fact that political rights alone are not sufficient to protect the values they are intended to advance.

The other side of Marx's critique of liberal ideology concerns central claims of liberal political economy. Issues of considerable complexity are raised here, but we will concentrate on the core of Marx's analysis. According to the central arguments of classical economic theory, as epitomized in the writings of Adam Smith, under certain conditions, there is a harmony of interests throughout society. The gist of Smith's "invisible hand" argument is that it is in the interest of a merchant to employ his money as effectively as possible, thereby investing it as capital. By investing his money in the most profitable enterprise, and then reinvesting the returns, the merchant achieves his end, which is to make the largest possible amount of money. As all merchants behave in this way, the overall amount of capital in society increases. This in turn increases the employment possibilities for workers. Capital can realize profits only if it is used to employ workers. Beyond a certain point, the demand for workers outstrips supply, and so merchants are forced to pay them more than sub-sistence. Under these circumstances, then, increasing profits for merchants also mean better pay and so living conditions for workers. As long as the overall capital pool is growing—that is, along the lines of what is now referred to as a growing economy, or good economic growth—the interests of all members of society are effectively realized.

Once again, Marx unmasks this line of argument by assessing it against actual conditions in society. As he sees things, the main flaw in Smith's argument is that it does not take into account the effects of automation. The reason for this is clear. Smith published *Wealth of Nations* in 1776, which was at the beginning of the Industrial Revolution, when machinery was just beginning to be employed. Thus while Smith discusses the effects of the division of labor, he has little to say about machinery. For Marx, of course, the problem with machinery is that it displaces workers. As productivity increases, according to "the absolute general law of capitalist accumulation," unemployment and misery do so as well. Coercive competition forces individual capitalists to seek out new machinery in their search for competitive advantages. But any such advantage is only temporary, as other capitalists, faced with the specter of being unable to compete, are forced to purchase similar machines:

> That is the law which again and again throws bourgeois production out of its old course and which compels capital to intensify the productive forces of labor, *because* it has intensified them, it, the law which gives capital no rest and continually whispers in its ear: 'Go on! Go on!' (*Wage Labor and Capital, Works*, I, 170)

As a result of new technology, productivity increases, but at the cost of increased un-employment. Marx describes this as "the industrial war of the capitalists among themselves; this war has the peculiarity that its battles are won less by recruiting than by discharging the army of labor. The generals, the capitalists, compete with one another as to who can discharge the most soldiers of industry" (*Wage Labor and Capital, Works*, I, 172; Marx's italics removed).

Increased productivity has additional untoward effects. There is not always a market for the greater quantity of goods produced. This can eventuate in economic crisis. Unable to sell their products, capitalists cut costs and so discharge even more workers, but still they may not be able to sell their products. Working harder, producing more, simply exacerbates the situation. When business enterprises fail, their workers too are thrown out of their jobs, and left to fend for themselves. Unemployed workers are unable to purchase what the economy produces, and so demand falls farther still. To make matters worse for the workers, with the introduction of machinery, work becomes simpler. Unskilled workers replace the skilled; women and children replace men. As entire families go to work, the father's wages need no longer feed his entire family and fall accordingly. Increased reliance on women and children throws men out of jobs, further swelling the ranks of the unemployed. "Thus the forest of uplifted arms demanding work becomes ever thicker, while the arms themselves become ever thinner" (*Wage Labor and Capital, Works*, I, 173). As Marx mordantly notes, all this takes place when the economy is expanding, which is supposed to be the best situation for both proletarian and capitalist classes (*Wage Labor and Capital, Works*, I, 174).

Once again, if we compare the reality of the capitalist economy with its theoretical justification, the glaring shortcomings of the latter emerge. The exploitation and misery of the proletariat are justified by economic and political ideas according to which its situation not only benefits it but is in harmony with natural forces, the rights of man and the laws of political economy. For Marx, these more-than-human forces are nothing of the sort. Like ancient ideas of natural slavery and medieval religious ideas, liberal ideas are human constructions, devised to support a particular economic and political order. An economic order that is claimed to benefit all classes actually benefits only one, at the expense of all others. But as we will see in the next section, bourgeois civilization too is only temporary. Within its womb are maturing forces that will inevitably cause it to fall, and so to pass into a new stage of society, as happened to all societies that preceded the present age.

THE UNITY OF THEORY AND PRACTICE

Marx's concept of ideology is closely bound up with his notion of class. It is striking that nowhere in his vast corpus does Marx provide a detailed account of exactly what constitutes a class. The subject is discussed most explicitly at the end of Volume III of *Capital*. But after Marx distinguishes the classes in capitalist society according to the source of their income and raises a few complexities, the manuscript breaks off (*Capital*, III, 886). We have seen that a class is a group of people who stand in similar relationships to the forces of production. In capitalist society, the capitalists of course own the forces of production, and the proletariat is forced to sell its labor power and work for them. But a class also involves an element of consciousness.

Following Hegelian terminology, Marx distinguishes a class "in itself" and "for itself." The former term can be translated as a group of people that is *potentially* a class; the latter is a group that is *actually* a class. They have realized their potential and are able to pursue their common interests. For Marx, a class is always one member of a relationship that involves at least two members. A group of people who stand in similar relationships to the means of production do not discover their common interests unless these are threatened. When this happens, they band together and struggle against their opponents. Marx believes struggle between classes has been a constant factor in every society that has existed. As a result of struggle with other classes, people develop a fuller understanding of their interests. This in turn intensifies their conflict with other classes and so leads to renewed struggle and greater consciousness. Marx believes class consciousness develops only from conflict between classes and intensifies that conflict. Thus qualities of awareness and activity in pursuit of its interests against other classes distinguish a class "for itself" and a class "in itself." These interconnected ideas can be illustrated by two passages. The first is from *The Poverty of Philosophy*:

> Economic conditions had first transformed the mass of the people of the country into workers. The combination of capital has created for this mass a common situation, common interests. This mass is thus already a class as against capital, but not yet for itself. In the struggle, of which we have noted only a few phases, this mass becomes united, and constitutes itself as a class for itself. The interests it defends become class interests. But the struggle of class against class is a political struggle. (*Poverty of Philosophy*, p. 173)

A famous description of the lack of class consciousness among the French peasantry in the mid-nineteenth century is found in the *Eighteenth Brumaire of Louis Bonaparte*:

> A small holding, a peasant and his family; alongside them another small holding, another peasant and another family. A few score of these make up a village, and a few score of villages make up a Department. In this way, the great mass of the French nation is formed by simple addition of homologous magnitudes, much as potatoes in a sack form a sack of potatoes. In so far as millions of families live under economic conditions of existence that separate their mode of life, their interests and their culture from those of the other classes, and put them in hostile opposition to the latter, they form a class. In so far as there is merely a local interconnection among these small-holding peasants, and the identity of their interests begets no community, no national bond and no political organization among them, they do not form a class. They are consequently incapable of enforcing their class interest in their own name, whether through a parliament or through a convention. (*Works*, I, 478–479)

Though the terminology is not used here, according to this description, the peasantry are a class "in itself" but not yet "for itself," because they lack full awareness of their interests. Such awareness impels a class to organize and engage in struggle with other classes.

Through conflict with members of other classes, people begin to understand their grievances as class grievances. Rather than arising from their particular situations, people realize their problems stem from factors common to all members of their class, and so can be dealt with only through class action. As Marx writes in the *German Ideology*: "The separate individuals form a class only in so far as they have to carry on a common battle against another class . . ." (pp. 48–49).

This process is of great interest to Marx as it concerns the proletariat. Forced to work and live under the conditions we have noted, individual workers at first believe they are victims of particular misfortunes, that their problems are rooted in local circumstances. Perhaps a worker thinks he is suffering because of the ill temper of his employer. But as he discovers that other workers are suffering similarly, and not only in his factory but elsewhere as well, he begins to grasp the true nature of his plight. By bringing large numbers of workers together in factories, capitalists unwittingly contribute to the workers' developing class consciousness. The discovery that their grievances are class grievances inspires workers to combine and act against their oppressors. By retaliating, the capitalists further harden class lines. This further contributes to the growth of class consciousness, and so to further struggle, further consciousness, etc. Marx describes this dynamic in the *Communist Manifesto*:

> [W]ith the development of industry the proletariat not only increases in number; it becomes concentrated in greater masses, its strength grows, and it feels that strength more. . . . The growing competition among the bourgeois, and the resulting commercial crises, make the wages of the workers ever more fluctuating. The unceasing improvement of machinery, ever more rapidly developing, makes their livelihood more and more precarious; the collisions between individual workmen and individual bourgeois take more and more the character of collisions between two classes. (*Works*, I, 116)

A similar dynamic was observed in the rise of the bourgeoisie within feudal society. The bourgeoisie started out as urban merchants. In order to protect their interests against the landed nobility, they were forced to unite, first within towns and then between towns. Their circumstances and grievances were similar, as were their struggles against interference by the nobility. Similarity of situation gave rise to consciousness of common interests and common grievances against the nobility. Through struggle with the nobility, consciousness developed further; this encouraged further struggle, which eventually took political form. Eventually, the bourgeoisie were successful; they overthrew the nobility and established their own dominance in society, with their consolidation setting the stage for the next act in the historical drama, the proletariat's revolution against them.

The view that class consciousness develops gradually through conflict between classes, and that this inspires further struggle and further conflict, is central to Marx's important idea of "the unity of theory and practice." The essence of Marx's view is that political ideas grow from material circumstances, and that as people act from their ideas and so change circumstances, their ideas also change. As these inspire new action, circumstances are further altered, and so on. Thus Marx posits a relationship of reciprocal interaction between ideas and circumstances. In regard to the possibilities for political action at any given time, the unity of theory and practice implies that circumstances provide parameters within which ideas must work. Only certain ideas can be effective at any particular time. This is in keeping with Marx's view of history as discussed above, especially his belief that material circumstances constitute necessary conditions for the effectiveness of political ideas.

Marx's belief in the unity of theory and practice sets him apart from other proponents of political reform. He believes that, under specific circumstances, the possibilities for political change are limited. Before wholesale change is possible, objective circumstances necessary for it must exist. Accordingly, in *Socialism: Utopian and Scientific*, Engels derisively criticizes "utopian socialists" (especially, Robert Owen, Charles Fourier, and Henri de St. Simon), would-be universal reformers who believed they had discovered plans of society, which, if implemented, were capable of putting an end to all human problems:

> If pure reason and justice have not, hitherto, ruled the world, this has been the case only because men have not rightly understood them. What was wanted was the individual man of genius, who has now arisen and who understands the truth. That he has now arisen, that the truth has now been clearly understood, is not an inevitable

event, following of necessity in the chain of historical development, but a mere happy accident. He might just as well have been born 500 years earlier, and might then have spared humanity 500 years of error, strife, and suffering. (*Works*, III, 117)[22]

To some extent, Marx and Engels agree that the dawn of a new age of pure reason and justice waits upon the discovery of ideas that will make this possible. But these ideas are not discovered by an individual man of genius. Rather, they grow out of an historical situation that makes the relevant changes possible. This is not to say individual men of genius do not arise and propagate ideas with far-reaching consequences. However, if the times are not ripe for the *proper reception* of their ideas, they will fall on deaf ears and have little influence. As noted above, ideas strikingly similar to Luther's were propagated earlier by a series of religious reformers. But because times were not ripe, none of these people was successful. The reason Luther succeeded was not because of the superior quality of his ideas but because the times were right to receive them. The same is true of the communist revolution Marx and Engels expound. Would-be reformers have ex-pressed similar ideas in the past, but because objective circumstances were not ready, these ideas did not have far-reaching repercussions. In the *German Ideology*, Marx writes: "The existence of revolutionary ideas in a particular period presupposes the existence of a revolutionary class" (p. 40). His meaning is not that ideas similar to his own have not *existed* in past ages, but they were without influence, because the circumstances for their proper reception did not exist.

As we see in the last quotation, the circumstances necessary for a set of ideas to have real implications center on a class able to receive them. This will happen when the ideas express the objective interests of class members. Ideas become important historical forces when they encapsulate the material interests of a class. The economic and social circum-stances of the class are thus primary; ideas that express these are secondary. But ideas are nevertheless important. We have seen that a class is more than a group of people with similar interests. Unless members of the group become aware of their interests, they remain a class "in itself," only potentially a class; they become an actual class, a class "for itself," when they become aware of their interests, and so begin to struggle with other classes in order to realize them. This has the effect of further increasing their struggle, and so their consciousness, etc. Under certain circumstances, ideas can become "material weapons." As Marx writes in his (early 1843) Introduction to his *Contribution to the Critique of Hegel's Philosophy of Right*:

> It is clear that the arm of criticism cannot replace the criticism of arms. Material force can only be overthrown by material force; but theory itself becomes a material force when it has seized the masses. (Tucker, p. 60)

With greater awareness of their common interests, members of a class are better able to engage in the activity necessary to achieve them. In the passage quoted above on this page a revolutionary class is a group of people whose material interests can be achieved only through revolution against the existing order. As the members of this class become aware of their situation, they express this in the form of revolutionary ideas. Thus active expression of revolutionary ideas presupposes circumstances in which they can have real effects, and so the existence of a revolutionary class.

Marx's understanding of his theory and his activity as a theorist should be interpreted in this context. Theorists play an essential role in helping a class articulate its interests. He believes his theory is superior to other socialist theories because it more accurately expresses the class interests of the rising proletariat. Only insofar as it corresponds to the interests of this class, can his theory be effective, and its effectiveness is limited by the obduracy of existing circumstances. Nevertheless, the expression of theoretical ideas can make a difference. As Marx writes in *Capital*, a society "can neither clear by bold leaps, nor remove by legal enactments, the obstacles offered by the successive phases of its normal development. But it can shorten and lessen the birth-pangs" (*Capital*, I, 10). Societies follow an objectively determined course of development. But within these parameters, the articulation of proper ideas can speed-up the process of transition from one stage to the next.

Revolutionary ideas can facilitate the movement between historical stages if they accurately reflect the interests of the rising class. The theory in question should express conclusions to which members of the class are being driven by the circumstances of their lives. Accordingly, the standard to be used in assessing revolutionary ideas is whether or not they are adopted by the revolutionary class. In the case of Marx's ideas, the standard is whether they represent the proletariat's needs, and so discoveries members of this class are making because of the harshness of their lives. Marx describes the important relationship between communist ideas and the circumstances of the revolutionary class in the *Communist Manifesto*:

> The theoretical conclusions of the Communists are in no way based on ideas or principles that have been invented, or discovered, by this or that would-be universal reformer.
>
>   They merely express, in general terms, actual relations springing from an existing class struggle, from a historical movement going on under our very eyes. (*Works*, I, 120)

Revolutionary ideas must be adopted by the class whose interests they express. Because Marx believes they cannot be *imposed* upon the class, he is an apostle of essentially spontaneous revolution. The proletariat will act in concert to bring about revolutionary change, because it is being driven to take this action by its actual circumstances. As its condition deteriorates, its members are becoming aware of the faults of the existing order and the need for revolution. This pattern is in contrast to one in which the proletariat is *led* to espouse revolutionary ideas by an organization of revolutionary ideologues or a vanguard party. Marx classically expresses the idea that the workers must make their own revolution in the "General Rules of the International Working Men's Association": "the emancipation of the working classes must be conquered by the working classes themselves" (*Works*, II, 19).

The idea of spontaneous revolution does not prevent a revolutionary party from playing a significant role. Its role, however, must be secondary to the developing consciousness of class members brought about by their material conditions. A classic expression of the party's role is given in the *Communist Manifesto*:

> Finally, in times when the class struggle nears the decisive hour, the process of dissolution going on within the ruling class, in fact within the whole range of old society, assumes such a violent, glaring character, that a small section of the ruling class

cuts itself adrift, and joins the revolutionary class, the class that holds the future in its hands. Just as, therefore, at an earlier period, a section of the nobility went over to the bourgeoisie, so now a portion of the bourgeoisie goes over to the proletariat, and in particular, a portion of the bourgeois ideologists, who have raised themselves to the level of comprehending theoretically the historical movement as a whole. (*Works*, I, 117)

When circumstances are reaching a climax, the propagation of revolutionary ideas can help the rising class achieve full awareness and so take necessary action. As happened during the French Revolution, the necessary ideologist will be from the ruling class—as is the case with Marx and Engels themselves, both members of the bourgeoisie. The proletariat's need for bourgeois ideologists is clear, in that members of this class do not have the education necessary to develop a theoretically sophisticated account of present and future conditions. But regardless of their philosophical power, a group of ideologists can contribute to the growing consciousness of the revolutionary class only if their theories are closely related to conclusions the class is spontaneously coming to of its own accord.

Marx's view of the relationship between revolutionary ideologues and the revolutionary class should be understood in opposition to "Jacobinism," or "Blanquism," terms which can be used interchangeably. These are revolutionary theories according to which a party of revolutionaries, who possess true consciousness, should impose their ideas on the masses. The Jacobins were radical clubs during the French Revolution, which supported the extreme actions in the pursuit of revolutionary virtue associated with Robespierre and the Reign of Terror. Louis-Auguste Blanqui (1805–1881) was a French socialist, who advocated achieving socialism through conspiratorial political activity.[23] Extreme Jacobins advocate a conspiratorial party that will seize control of the state, and then use this to educate the masses. For a time, during the late 1840s, Marx was associated with Blanquist organizations, though he never subscribed to their ideas.[24] Criticizing Blanquist organizations, in 1850, Marx writes:

> It goes without saying that these conspirators do not restrict themselves simply to organizing the revolutionary proletariat. Their business consists precisely in forestalling the process of revolutionary development, spurring it into artificial crises, making revolutions extempore without the conditions of revolution. For them the only condition required for revolution is the sufficient organization of their own conspiracy. They are the alchemists of revolution, and they share in every way the deranged notions and narrow-minded fixed ideas of the alchemists of old. They grasp eagerly at new contraptions to achieve the revolutionary miracle: incendiary bombs, explosive devices with magical powers, and rioting that is supposed to have effects all the more wondrous and astonishing the less it has any rational basis. Busy with such plot-mongering, they have no further aim than the next assault on the existing regime and look with deepest disdain upon a more theoretical enlightenment of the workers as to their class interests. . . . (quoted in Hunt, I, 252)

Blanquists and Jacobins are like utopian socialists in that they overlook the central truth of the unity of theory and practice. Revolutionary ideas must wait upon revolutionary conditions. They cannot be created by the propagation of universal truths, or through conspiratorial organizations that are able to seize political power. Should such a conspiracy succeed, this would merely inaugurate a period of political dictatorship, rather than the desired socialism. Socialism must wait upon the existence of the necessary objective conditions. The existence of these will be signalled by the organization of a class that is forced by its material interests to pursue a socialist program. In Marx's eyes the class in question was the proletariat, and he believed he lived in a privileged time, in that the emergence of the proletariat had made communism, which was otherwise impossible, not only possible but inevitable. Thus his theory is not a *theory* in the ordinary sense of the term. It is rather a set of ideas growing out of the objective conditions of the proletariat's existence, merely a more articulate expression of ideas they have been driven to discover for themselves. Thus in an Introduction he wrote to Marx's *Class Struggles in France*, in 1895, Engels describes the ideas that will win over the proletariat as follows:

> If, in all the longer revolutionary periods, it was so easy to win the great masses of the people by the merely plausible false representations of the forward-thrusting minorities, why should they be less susceptible to ideas which were the truest reflection of their economic condition, which were nothing but the clear, rational expression of their needs, of needs not yet understood but merely vaguely felt by them?[25]

Similarly, in *Socialism: Utopian and Scientific*, Engels says of the clash between the productive forces and class structure in capitalist society: "Modern socialism is nothing but the reflex, in thought, of this conflict in fact; its ideal reflection in the minds, first, of the class directly suffering under it, the working class" (*Works*, III, 134–135).

Because the rising consciousness of the proletariat depends on economic conditions that are beyond people's immediate power to bring about, the revolutionary party must play a secondary role. This is one respect in which Marx's own thought diverges sharply from Marxism-Leninism, which places enormous weight upon the party and its tasks. In the *Communist Manifesto*, Marx argues that the revolutionary party must be closely connected with the revolutionary class:

> The Communists do not form a separate party opposed to other working-class parties.
> They have no interests separate and apart from those of the proletariat as a whole.
> They do not set up any sectarian principles of their own, by which to shape and mold the proletarian movement. (*Works*, I, 119)

The major respect in which the party stands above the class is in its superior understanding of the latter's interests. But this merely constitutes understanding the direction in which the proletariat as a whole will necessarily develop:

> The Communists . . . have over the great mass of the proletariat the advantage of clearly understanding the line of march, the conditions, and the ultimate general results of the proletarian movement. (*Works*, I, 484)

In all his works, Marx never advocates having the party seize political power and then use this to educate the masses. Among revolutionary socialists of his day, he stands out in rejecting this approach. If the proletariat achieves revolutionary consciousness, domination by an elite party is unnecessary. If the proletariat does not develop, elite domination is no substitute for objective conditions that make revolution possible. In his detailed study of Marx and Engels' political thought through all stages of their development, R. N. Hunt concludes:

> Perhaps the key distinguishing feature of Marx and Engels' thinking, among the diverse currents of early socialism, was precisely their conviction, their ultimate democratic faith, that the masses could and would educate *themselves*, organize *themselves*, liberate *themselves*, and rule *themselves*. No external agent, no *deus ex machina* in the form of an enlightened elite, was required in their vision, although of course they never denied the incidental helpfulness of intellectuals like themselves.[26]

Because of the predominant role of material condition in shaping class consciousness, Marx believes the party's role is necessarily limited to helping to "shorten the birth-pangs" of the new society.

BOURGEOISIE AND PROLETARIAT

As the bourgeoisie rose within feudal society and brought it down, the proletariat is being formed within the womb of capitalist society. Parallels between the development of the two classes are central to Marx's theory. He believes his ideas are a theoretical expression of the class interests of the proletariat, as liberal economic and political ideas express the class interests of the bourgeoisie.

Though Marx was a revolutionary and spent his life fighting against the bourgeoisie, he believes this class has been in many ways a progressive force. Without the bourgeoisie, the proletariat would never have developed, and so socialism would not be possible. The bourgeoisie have created the objective conditions necessary for socialism, especially through the Industrial Revolution, which it initiated. The enormous increase of productivity in modern society is the work of the bourgeoisie:

> The bourgeoisie, during its rule of scarce one hundred years, has created more massive and more colossal productive force than have all preceding generations together. Subjection of Nature's force to man, machinery, application of chemistry to industry and agriculture, steam-navigation, railways, electric telegraphs, clearing of whole continents for cultivation, canalization of rivers, whole populations conjured out of the ground—what earlier century had even a presentiment that such productive forces slumbered in the lap of social labor? (*Communist Manifesto, Works*, I, 113)

The problem, of course, is that the relations of production in bourgeois society are not compatible with revolutionary developments in the forces of production. As a result, increase of productive power has been accompanied by increased misery on the part of the large majority of the population. This discord can be overcome only through the introduction of a new economic order based on communism, or public ownership of the means of production. But without the industrialization the bourgeoisie developed, this next stage would not be possible.

We see something similar in the political sphere. Though the bourgeoisie are the proletariat's opponents, and their overthrow is necessary for the advent of communism, without the aid of the bourgeoisie, the proletariat could not have become a revolutionary force capable of instituting a new order. This follows from Marx's view of the unity of theory and practice. The revolutionary program of the proletariat could not emerge until the bourgeoisie had led a revolution against the feudal order. As we have seen, at any given time, the possibilities for political change are limited by objective circumstances. Under feudal society, the economic and political practices of the nobility created demands for change among the bourgeoisie. Over the course of time, what were at first perceived as personal grievances by individual merchants came to be understood as common or class grievances. The bourgeoisie began to organize and so to emerge as a class "for itself." But circumstances at that time did not allow *more* change than what the bourgeoisie supported. The revolutionary program of the proletariat was not yet possible; at that time, the proletariat was only beginning to come into existence.

The proletariat was created by the bourgeoisie as they constructed the capitalist system. Marx calls the process through which the bourgeoisie began to industrialize and to bring into existence a force of workers who owned nothing but their labor power "primitive accumulation." In *Capital,* he recounts how the bourgeoisie kicked peasants off their land, which could be put to more profitable use in other ways. Over the course of time, an army of wage workers was created, "suddenly and forcibly torn from their means of subsistence, and hurled as free and 'unattached' proletarians on the labor-market," (I, 716). He describes this process in horrifying detail: "[T]he history of this, their expropriation, is written in the annals of mankind in letters of blood and fire" (*Capital,* I, 715); "it is notorious that conquest, enslavement, robbery, murder, briefly force, play the great part" (I, 714). Marx details legislative and other means that were used to effect this process. Eventually, with nowhere else to turn, uprooted peasants were forced to sell their labor in order to live, and went to work in emerging bourgeois factories.

Wage laborers, living and working under the conditions we have noted, constituted a class "in itself." Standing in similar relationships to the means of production, proletarians had similar interests. But it was not until they began to become aware of these and so to struggle against their bourgeois oppressors that they began to emerge as an actual class, a class "for itself." Throughout his works, Marx charts this course of development, in which he sees the salvation of mankind. Thus both politically and economically, the bourgeoisie create in the form of the proletariat the agency of their own undoing. The means through which they overthrew the feudal nobility are now being turned against them.

It is in this context that Marx assesses both the strengths and weaknesses of liberal political theory. The emerging proletariat and bourgeoisie were not always opponents. At one point, they fought together against the feudal lords. It was only with the overthrow of that system that their differences began to emerge. Marx's ideas here are complex. In order to untangle them, we can examine a lengthy passage in the *German Ideology*.

> For each new class which puts itself in the place of one ruling before it, is compelled, merely in order to carry through its aim, to represent its interest as the common interest of all members of society, put in an ideal form; it will give its ideas the form of universality, and represent them as the only rational, universally valid ones. The class making a revolution appears from the very start, merely because it is opposed to a *class*, not as a class but as the representative of the whole of society; it appears as the whole mass of society confronting the one ruling class. It can do this because, to start with,

its interest really is more connected with the common interest of all other non-ruling classes, because under the pressure of conditions its interest has not yet been able to develop as the particular interest of a particular class . . . Every new class, therefore, achieves its hegemony only on a broader basis than that of the class ruling previously, in return for which the opposition of the non-ruling class against the new ruling class later develops all the more sharply and profoundly. Both these things determine the fact that the struggle to be waged against this new ruling class, in its turn, aims at a more decided and radical negation of the previous conditions of society than could all previous classes which sought to rule. (*German Ideology*, pp. 40–41)

Marx believes the bourgeoisie came to oppose the nobility because of specific grievances. As is generally the case with political action, the revolutionary activity of the bourgeoisie grew out of their social and economic circumstances. The nobility were objectionable because of their systematic interference in economic affairs. For instance, the medieval guild system enforced monopolistic control over many areas of the economy, severely stifling the bourgeoisie's economic initiatives. Because the regulations of the guild system adversely affected merchants' economic interests, they came to oppose this system in the name of "free trade." Smith's *Wealth of Nations* is a full-scale assault on the restricted trade practices of the mercantile system. Smith argues that unrestricted trade will greatly increase national wealth and benefit all members of society. During medieval times, government was absolute and arbitrary. Objections to this system called attention to the importance of the natural rights of all people, which should be enforced by regular constitutional procedures. Thus the core of the program of the rising bourgeoisie, espousal of the free market and natural rights, was developed in opposition to the perceived abuses of feudal society. This is the origin of the political and economic components of what came to be known as classical liberalism. For Marx, any significant social or political doctrine must be the doctrine of a class. Liberal theory is the philosophy of the bourgeoisie.

At the time liberal ideas were formulated, they were not opposed to the interests of the proletariat. Liberal theory, like the theory of any emerging class, was formulated in opposition to the class then in power, the nobility. To the extent the incipient proletariat was also victimized by the economic and political practices of the nobility, liberal ideas supported their interests as well. The incipient proletariat fought alongside the bourgeoisie against the nobility, until the feudal order was overthrown. In England, as we have noted, this occurred in the seventeenth-century struggles between King and Parliament; in France, this was accomplished by the French Revolution. Marx identifies these events as instances of the "bourgeois revolution," which is necessary for the successful movement from feudal to bourgeois society.

The bourgeois revolution was not confined to England and France. At a particular stage of its development, every country should go through this transition. Thus at the conclusion of the *Communist Manifesto*, Marx writes:

The Communists turn their attention chiefly to Germany, because that country is on the eve of a bourgeois revolution that is bound to be carried out under more advanced conditions of European civilization, and with a much more developed proletariat, than that of England was in the seventeenth and of France in the eighteenth century. . . . (*Works*, I, 137)

To some extent, Marx's prediction was correct. The *Communist Manifesto* was written on the eve of the wave of revolutions that swept Europe in 1848, which he identified as bourgeois revolutions. In Germany, however, the revolution was repulsed, and Germany undertook a course of subsequent development rather different from those of England and France. The complications this entailed for Marxist theory are of great interest to political theorists, but cannot be discussed here.[27]

In any event, the bourgeois revolution is a political struggle in which incipient proletariat fight alongside the bourgeoisie, because overthrowing the nobility is in the interests of both classes. At first sight, this is surprising, because we have repeatedly noted the great suffering of the proletariat in bourgeois society. The explanation, of course, is that bourgeois society had not yet developed. It is only with the overthrow of the nobility that the bourgeoisie can bring forth full-fledged capitalism and the Industrial Revolution, through which the modern proletariat is brought fully into being. From their vantage point at the outset of the bourgeois revolution, it is not possible for the proletariat to perceive that their ultimate interest lies in opposition to the bourgeoisie and the introduction of communism. According to Marx's fundamental idea of the unity of theory and practice, it is necessary for revolutionary activity to change economic and political circumstances before this realization can emerge.

Only when the nobility have been vanquished as a common opponent does the proletariat begin to understand the extent of the differences between their interests and those of the bourgeoisie. The bourgeoisie, as we have seen, proclaim the fundamental right of private property. When the proletariat realize this does them little good because they have no property, they demand further changes, but the bourgeoisie resist. After the *political* side of the bourgeois revolution is accomplished, the proletariat begin to realize they have enormously important economic demands. But when they try to implement these, they are opposed by the bourgeoisie. As the proletariat begin to engage in political activity in favor of their interests, the bourgeoisie suppress them, turning the might of the liberal state which they now control against them. This is clearly symbolized in the "Terrible June Days" of the French Revolution of 1848. The Revolution of 1848 was initially successful. The King, Louis Philippe, was driven from the throne and a republic declared. But when the Parisian workers demanded economic reforms as well, the state was used against them, and they were shot down in the streets.[28]

The bourgeois revolution is thus *two-sided*. It is a revolution against the feudal nobility for the sake of implementing a capitalist economy and the liberal state. It is also a revolution against the proletariat. For as both classes begin to realize their different interests and so come into conflict, the bourgeoisie use their newfound political power to suppress the proletariat. This sets the stage for a new revolution, a revolution of the proletariat against the bourgeoisie, which will achieve the reforms that were blocked during the bourgeois revolution, and much more. Suppressed politically and exploited economically in bourgeois society, the proletariat are beginning to discover the hollowness of bourgeois ideology and the fact that their own class interests lie in further revolutionary change. It is this realization that Marx expresses in his theoretical writings, which are intended to be nothing more than a highly articulate expression of the class interests and growing class consciousness of the proletariat.

It is in this context that Marx criticizes liberal political theory. As we have noted, this is both an ideology and the revolutionary program of the rising bourgeoisie. Liberal theory came into existence in the bourgeoisie's struggle against the nobility and it is this struggle that grounds its main ideas. For instance, the personal and political rights the bourgeoisie discuss should be understood in opposition to the arbitrary rule of the nobility. Free trade, free labor, and other economic freedoms have their meaning in opposition to the practices of the nobility: "This talk about free selling and buying, and all the other 'brave words' of our bourgeoisie about freedom in general, have a meaning, if any, only in contrast with restricted selling and buying, with the fettered traders of the Middle Ages . . ." (*Communist Manifesto, Works,* I, 122). We have seen something similar in regard to "free" labor. Members of the proletarian class have the right to work for whomever they please. Though this has some meaning in contrast to the conditions of slaves and serfs in previous stages of society, it means little in the context of the capitalist economic system. "Freedom" to work for whomever one pleases is freedom to sell one's labor to one particular capitalist rather than another, under conditions that oftentimes make the situation of a medieval serf appear idyllic.

The origin of liberal ideas explains their limitations and the nature of the bourgeoisie's self-deception in regard to them. We have noted that an ideology passes off the interest of one class in society as the interest of all. The fact that the bourgeoisie do this is easily accounted for. At one time their ideas *were* in the interests of all members of society. The arbitrary and inefficient rule of the nobility was harmful to everyone, and so the incipient proletariat pursued its own good too in allying with the bourgeoisie against them. However, what the bourgeoisie do not realize is that circumstances have changed. Though their ideas were at one time beneficial to all classes, with the advent of industrial society, the proletariat have been thrust into terrible circumstances. But the same ideas that allowed the bourgeoisie to see through the nobility's claim of divine rights prevent them from perceiving the full depth of the proletariat's suffering. Presumably, the bourgeoisie blame this on the proletariat themselves. If they would only work harder, they too could be employers rather than employees. But isolated success stories mean little when an entire class of people are working eighteen hours a day in order to survive.

Just as their economic and political circumstances forced the bourgeoisie to penetrate the veil of feudal ideology, a similar process is taking place in capitalist society. The bourgeoisie justify their rule according to time-honored slogans of natural rights and the benefits of the free market. But the proletariat's impossible living conditions are forcing them to see the hollowness of these ideas and the need for radical change. Other socialist thinkers were presenting similar critiques of bourgeois society and similar demands for radical reform at the time Marx was writing. Striking examples are the utopian socialists, notably Fourier, St. Simon, and Owen. But Marx believes he differs from these figures, because their ideas were merely invented, thought up by individual men of genius. His ideas, in contrast, are not his inventions but reflect actual economic circumstances. Once again, they are merely a more articulate expression of discoveries the proletariat are making for themselves: "They merely express, in general terms, actual relations springing from an existing class struggle, from a historical movement going on under our very eyes" (*Communist Manifesto, Works,* I, 120). Marx believes revolutionary reform must wait upon the proletariat, who will be driven to revolution by fundamental economic conditions. Thus, while the "alchemists of revolution" dream of conspiracies through which existing society will be overthrown, Marx believes true revolutionaries must "restrict themselves simply to organizing the revolutionary proletariat," as this activity can "shorten the birth-pangs" of a new society. The proletariat are inspired by actual conditions rather than by abstract theory. But in the pursuit of their particular aims, they will unleash elements of the new, communist, society growing within the womb of the old:

> The [working class] have no ready made utopias to introduce *par décret du peuple* [by decree of the people]. They know that in order to work out their own emancipation, and along with it that higher form to which present society is irresistibly tending by its own economical agencies, they will have to pass through long struggles, through a series of historic processes, transforming circumstances and men. They have no ideals to realize, but to set free the elements of the new society with which collapsing bourgeois society itself is pregnant. (*The Civil War in France, Works*, II, 224)

Marx's theory, as "scientific socialism," is distinct from other socialist theories in not being a *theory*, but an expression of the revolutionary class consciousness of the rising proletariat. In his eyes, this class has before it a radical historical mission, which he sees his role as facilitating. In the Introduction to his *Contribution to the Critique of Hegel's Philosophy of Right*, he describes the proletariat's radical nature. The possibility of revolutionary reform in Germany depends on the emergence of a new kind of class:

> A class must be formed which has *radical chains*, a class in civil society which is not a class of civil society, a class which is the dissolution of all classes, a sphere of society which has a universal character because its sufferings are universal, and which . . . cannot emancipate itself without emancipating itself from all the other spheres of society, without, therefore, emancipating all these other spheres, which is, in short, a *total loss* of humanity and which can only redeem itself by a *total redemption of humanity*. This dissolution of society, as a particular class is the *proletariat*. (Tucker, p. 64)

As the mass of suffering humanity, the proletariat occupies a privileged historical position. In freeing itself from its subjection, it will free society as a whole, humanity as a whole. We have seen the bourgeois revolution is two-sided, against the lower classes after the higher classes have been vanquished. This has been the pattern in all previous revolutions; each of these struggles has resulted in the domination of a new class. The proletariat's act of liberation will differ, because there will be no one left to suppress. In overthrowing the bourgeoisie, it will realize itself as a universal class, a class encompassing all orders of society. Without additional classes with which to struggle, it will cease to be a *class*, in the proper sense of the term, and communism will be a classless and stateless society.

THE REVOLUTION

To bring our account of Marx to a close, we will discuss his view of the revolution that is to bring bourgeois society to an end and inaugurate the new stage of communist society. Throughout his vast corpus Marx presents little detailed description of communist society. He says he is reluctant to write recipes for the cook-shops of the future (*Capital*, I, 17). Other thinkers—for instance, Fourier—described future society in tremendous detail. But this is absurd, according to Marx. Communist society will be brought into existence through the revolutionary activity of the proletariat. It is possible to analyze the material conditions driving the capitalist economy to collapse and causing the proletariat to achieve class consciousness and to organize politically. This is what Marx spent the better part of his life doing in his works. But one cannot forecast the details of what will come about. Marx provides broad outlines concerning the coming revolution and the shape of future society. As is generally the case, he describes these in somewhat different terms in different contexts. We will discuss two main subjects: the political form the revolution will assume and basic conditions in communist society.

The fundamental dynamic leading to communism is the collapse of the capitalist economic system. Marx argues that this is coming about because of conflict between forces and relations of production. The new productive powers unleashed during the Industrial Revolution are incompatible with the system of private property in which they have arisen. Capitalists are forced to compete with one another, leading to overproduction, and so industrial crises. As we have seen, their competition leads to incessant attempts to replace workers with new machinery. This creates wholesale unemployment and incalculable misery for the proletariat, thereby transforming them into an agency of revolutionary change. Marx's analyses of the precise nature of the contradictions in capitalism have been widely discussed and are a source of continuing difficulty among scholars. We will set this subject aside to look at the activity of the proletariat.

As we have seen, the overall thrust of Marx's theory is in the direction of spontaneous revolution. Material conditions force the proletariat to rise in revolution. Organized political parties play a relatively small role in revolutionary politics, though they make an essential contribution in helping the proletariat develop class consciousness. Probably the greatest blow Marx's theory suffered was when things did not work out as he had foreseen. Capitalism proved far more resilient than he had imagined. Throughout Western Europe and North America, the nineteenth and twentieth centuries witnessed explosive economic growth. It is commonly said that Marx mistook the birth pangs of capitalism for its death throes. Throughout the history of capitalist society, there have been significant periods of economic panic and depression, with severe consequences for millions of people. But these have been isolated periods. The state has proved resilient as well, developing the institutions to provide an essential economic and social safety net for virtually all citizens. In regard to the rising proletariat, better economic conditions have reversed the developments Marx predicted. The working class, politically enfranchised and relatively prosperous, has ceased to be a revolutionary force. This overall course of development was apparent in Western Europe by the end of the nineteenth century, and socialist parties generally moved in the direction of democratic reform. Within the Marxian tradition, these developments were clearly recognized by the "revisionist" theorist Eduard Bernstein, who was a close associate of Engels and an important figure in the German Social Democratic Party. Bernstein argued that Marx's major predictions were incorrect. On the basis of abundant empirical evidence, he contended that the working class was no longer revolutionary. Its members wished to become middle class. Socialism, a political system in which their needs were addressed by the government, did not entail overthrowing the liberal order but *extending* it. According to Bernstein, extensive social welfare programs would be implemented by the state as the working class came increasingly to control it. In order to achieve socialism, the "liberal institutions of modern society . . . do not need to be destroyed; they need only to be further developed."[29]

Regardless of the details of Bernstein's analysis, there is little question that the overall course of events has confirmed his forecast. In 1895, looking back on the development of capitalism since the Revolutions of 1848, Engels himself questioned his earlier analysis:

History has proved us, and all who thought like us, wrong. It has made it clear that the state of economic development on the Continent at that time was not, by a long way, ripe for the elimination of capitalist production; it has proved this by the economic revolution which, since 1848, has seized the whole of the Continent, and has caused big industry to take real root in France, Austria, Hungary, Poland and recently, in Russia, while it has made Germany positively an industrial country of the first rank— all on a capitalist basis, which in the year 1848, therefore, still had great capacity for expansion. ("Introduction," *Works*, I, 191–192)

In the face of these changes, Engels also criticized the idea of a revolutionary insurrection by the proletariat: "[History] has also completely transformed the conditions under which the proletariat has to fight. The mode of struggle of 1848 is today obsolete in every respect" ("Introduction," *Works*, I, 190).

In spite of these difficulties, the great gains made by the German and other socialist parties at the ballot box opened up another possible path to political power. Working within the existing political system, socialist parties have won national elections and been in and out of power in most Western democracies throughout the twentieth century. The welfare state is indelibly planted in most industrial countries, its programs now all but irreversible. Antisocialist governments have done little more than trim around the edges.

It is open to question what Marx would have thought of these developments. There is no doubt that he had an extremely dim view of capitalist society and believed the way to socialism led through economic crisis and chaos. But though Marx predicted the collapse of capitalism and the revolutionary transition to a new society through the agency of the class-conscious proletariat, he said little about the details of this process, contenting himself with exploring the overall economic developments from which it would flow. Whether, or to what extent, the social welfare state and greatly improved standards of living now enjoyed by the working class in the industrial countries is a confirmation of Marx's forecasts is subject to debate. It is clear, however, that Marx foresaw a *moral* transformation of society, which has not come about.

In any event, we will close this chapter by looking at what Marx does say about the movement to communist society. Once again, however, his reluctance to provide detailed forecasts of events holds in regard to central issues of his political theory. For instance, he does not take a firm stand on the form the revolution will assume. We have noted that past revolutions have been violent, notably the French Revolution of 1789. But whether the Communist Revolution must also be violent is not discussed in detail. As is often the case with Marx, the textual evidence is ambiguous. In the *Communist Manifesto*, he mentions "the violent overthrow of the bourgeoisie (*den gewaltsamen Sturz der Bourgeoisie*)" (*Works*, I, 118–119), but then, more famously, the need for the proletariat to become the ruling class, and "win the battle of democracy (*die Erkampfung der Demokratie*)" (*Works*, I, 126). But this last clearly means winning the right to vote. As Engels explains this phrase, many years later, "The *Communist Manifesto* had already proclaimed the winning of universal suffrage, of democracy, as one of the first and most important tasks of the militant proletariat" ("Introduction," *Works*, I, 195).

The connection between violent revolution and democracy can be understood in light of the fact that, when the *Communist Manifesto* was written, the proletariat was not fully enfranchised anywhere in Europe. Because they outnumbered the bourgeoisie and were gaining class-consciousness, enfranchising the proletariat would be a revolutionary step.[30] Granted the right to vote, the proletariat could take power legally, and so extending the franchise was resisted by the ruling classes. An analogous situation existed in recent years in South Africa, in which the ruling white minority resisted the practice of "one man one vote" as clearly granting the black majority the ability to take power.

Perhaps the clearest statement Marx made in regard to whether or not the revolution would be violent was in a speech he delivered to a congress of the International Working Men's Association, in Amsterdam in 1872. Marx's position here is that political tactics should be adapted to circumstances. Under certain conditions, peaceful change is possible. But because these cases will be rare, violent revolution will be the rule:

> We know of the allowance we must make for the institutions, customs and traditions of the various countries; and we do not deny that there are countries such as America, England, and I would add Holland if I knew your institutions better, where the working people may achieve their goal by peaceful means. If that is true, we must also recognize that in most of the continental countries it is force that will have to be the lever of our revolutions; it is force that we shall some day have to resort to in order to establish a reign of labor. (*Works*, II, 293)

Thus Marx believes that, if conditions warrant, the proletariat can take power through peaceful means. This and other passages in his works lend support to the idea that, in spite of his general support for violent revolution, at least for certain countries, he was essentially a social democrat rather than a revolutionary,[31] and would have supported the movement toward gaining political power within the political system.

Marx has little to say about the political form of the transition to Communism. It seems clear that he believes in the need for a transitional political organization, a state controlled by the victorious proletariat. He refers to this as "the dictatorship of the proletariat." This is one of the most celebrated of Marx's ideas, referred to by Lenin as the "touchstone on which the *real* understanding and recognition of Marxism should be tested."[32] But Marx discusses it remarkably infrequently in his works. In his entire corpus, the idea of dictatorship is linked with the working class only some sixteen times, in eleven separate writings.[33] Only one of these, *Class Struggles in France*, can be considered a major work—and even this should be classified as journalism rather than a theoretical statement. Probably, the idea's clearest expression is in the *Critique of the Gotha Program* (1875). Marx wrote this work in the form of a private letter to leaders of the German Socialist movement. It was not written for publication, and Engels published it after Marx's death. Marx writes:

> Between capitalist and communist society lies the period of the revolutionary transformation of the one into the other. Corresponding to this is also a political transition period in which the state can be nothing but *the revolutionary dictatorship of the proletariat.* (*Works*, III, 26)

Though this notion is not found in Marx's major statements of his theory, it seems that he viewed it as an important part of his theory. This is seen in another famous passage, contained in a letter he wrote in 1852:

> Insofar as I am concerned, the merit of having discovered either the existence of classes in modern society or the class struggle does not belong to me. Bourgeois historians have

presented the historic development of this struggle of classes, and bourgeois economists the economic anatomy of the same, long before I did. What was new in what I did was: (1) to demonstrate that the *existence of classes* is tied only to *definite historical phases of development of production*; (2) that the class struggle necessarily leads to the *dictatorship of the proletariat*; (3) that this dictatorship is only a transition to the *dissolution of all classes* and leads to the formation of a *classless society*. (Marx to Joseph Weydemeyer, March 5, 1852; *Letters*, p. 81)

As these passages indicate, Marx believes in the necessity of a state during the period after the revolution, before the transformation to communist society is complete. Belief in the necessity of a transitional state distinguishes Marx's view from that of anarchists such as Bakunin, who hold that the state can be abolished immediately. But Marx views the dictatorship of the proletariat as only a transitional form. After an interim period, it will pass out of existence and yield a stateless society. Communism, which will be a classless society, will also be without political institutions wielded by a ruling class in order to suppress other classes.

Marx does not say exactly what the dictatorship of the proletariat will do during the transitional period. It is likely that it will be exercised against recalcitrant elements of the bourgeoisie, who, having been overthrown, must still be reincorporated into the new society.[34] But again, too much should not be made of this institution. At the time Marx wrote, the idea of dictatorship connoted a temporary period of emergency rule not bound by law, along the lines of what existed in the Roman Republic. The horrors of twentieth-century dictatorship were as yet unknown, and Marx undoubtedly would have been strongly opposed to a regime such as Stalin's. Once again, because Marx believes the revolution will be made by the class-conscious proletariat, there is no hint in his theory that a transitional period is required to allow a party of ideologues to employ state power in order to educate the masses. This idea, central to Jacobinism and Blanquism—and then, in the twentieth century, to Marxism-Leninism—is completely absent from Marx's thought.

Though Marx is similarly vague about the economic side of communism, he clearly sees it as a regime of abundance. There will be a transitional period during which the means of production will be publicly appropriated, and people will work for the state rather than themselves. No longer exploited, they will be rewarded according to their contributions. During this stage, inequalities will exist because of differences in people's ability to labor, while the means of production, freed from the shackles of capitalist private ownership, increase in productive power. Eventually, in a final stage of abundance, inequalities will cease. A glowing description of the final stage of communism is found in the *Critique of the Gotha Program*:

In a higher phase of communist society, after the enslaving subordination of the individual to the division of labor, and therewith also the antithesis between mental and physical labor, has vanished; after labor has become not only a means of life but life's prime want; after the productive forces have also increased with the all round development of the individual, and all the springs of cooperative wealth flow more abundantly—only then can the narrow horizon of bourgeois right be crossed in its entirety and society inscribe on its banner: From each according to his ability, to each according to his needs! (*Works*, III, 19)

In different contexts, Marx describes aspects of this system differently. Though it is without a state, there will be a central agency to run the economy. In Engels' famous words: "the government of persons is replaced by the administration of things" (*Works*, III, 147). In *German Ideology*, Marx indicates that under Communism, labor will lose its harshness; the division of labor will be done away with, and people will change jobs at their pleasure:

> [I]n communist society, where nobody has one exclusive sphere of activity but each can become accomplished in any branch he wishes, society regulates the general production and thus makes it possible for me to do one thing to-day and another to-morrow, to hunt in the morning, fish in the afternoon, rear cattle in the evening, criticize after dinner, just as I have a mind, without ever becoming hunter, fisherman, shepherd or critic. (*German Ideology*, p. 22)

In *Capital*, Marx is more restrained. He admits the need to labor under communism, as in all stages of society. But in a rationalized economy, with massive productive forces directed towards the good of society rather than individual capitalists, exploitation will end, and people will have to labor less:

> Just as the savage must wrestle with Nature to satisfy his wants, to maintain and reproduce life, so must civilized man, and he must do so in all social formations and under all possible modes of production. With his development this realm of physical necessity expands as a result of his wants; but, at the same time, the forces of production which satisfy these wants also increase. Freedom in this field can only consist in socialized man, the associated producers, rationally regulating their interchange with Nature, bringing it under their common control, instead of being ruled by it as by the blind forces of Nature and achieving this with the least expenditure of energy and under conditions most favorable to, and worthy of, their human nature. But it nonetheless still remains a realm of necessity. Beyond it begins that development of human energy which is an end in itself, the true realm of freedom, which, however, can blossom forth only with this realm of necessity as its basis. The shortening of the working day is its basic prerequisite. (*Capital*, III, 820)

This is a more reasonable depiction of a communist economy, and carries us back to themes with which we began this chapter. As we have noted, essential to all past stages of society has been a fundamental division between people who perform unpleasant labor and live badly and people who are exempt from unpleasant work and live well. Communism will end this disparity. Though some unpleasant labor will remain, because we must always wrestle with nature in order to attain what we need, the amount of such labor will diminish. The great odyssey of human history has been necessary in order to develop powerful forces of production that can be used to satisfy human needs with a minimum of effort. We have noted the great contribution the bourgeoisie have made to amassing the requisite productive forces. Without powerful means of production, better lives would not be possible for all members of society:

> [I]t is only possible to achieve real liberation in the real world and by employing real means . . . slavery cannot be abolished without the steam engine and the mule and spinning-jenny, serfdom cannot be abolished without improved agriculture, and . . .

in general, people cannot be liberated as long as they are unable to obtain food and drink, housing and clothing in adequate quality and quantity. (*German Ideology*, in Tucker, p. 169)

Without developed means of production, public ownership of the means of production would simply redistribute poverty: "without it only *want* is made general, and with *want* the struggle for necessities and all the old filthy business would necessarily be reproduced" (*German Ideology*, p. 24).

Only the development of productive powers has made liberation possible. People are naturally creative, productive beings. Freed from the need to do unpleasant labor in order to live, they would find fulfillment in their work and lead meaningful lives. With the great advances in technology that history has brought forth, the need to labor can be sharply lessened. But as things presently stand, private ownership of the means of production under capitalist society prevents this possibility from being realized. Along with increased productivity, capitalism brings forth increased unemployment and misery.

In the final analysis, Marx probably views communism as inevitable and necessary because it reconciles this conflict and so rights a great historical wrong. Like Hegel, Marx sees history as a rational process tending towards human freedom. His conception of freedom is more prosaic than Hegel's: freedom from enslaving subordination to the division of labor, and from other people who own the means of production. With the elimination of the capitalist system, this goal is in sight. Under communism, everyone will contribute according to his abilities and receive according to his needs. "It is the solution of the riddle of history, and knows itself to be this solution" (*Manuscripts*, p. 127).

NOTES

1. For biographical information, I rely on D. McLellan, *Karl Marx: His Life and Thought* (New York, 1973) (cited as McLellan, in parentheses in text); and M. Rubel and M. Manale, *Marx Without Myth: A Chronological Study of his Life and Work* (New York, 1975). *The Letters of Karl Marx* is cited as *Letters*, according to date and page number; *Marx-Engels: Selected Correspondence* is cited as *Correspondence*, according to author, date and page number; full references below, under "Texts Cited."

2. F. Engels, *Ludwig Feuerbach and the End of Classical German Philosophy*, *Works*, III, 361 n. Many works of Marx and Engels are quoted from *Karl Marx and Frederick Engels: Selected Works*, 3 vols., cited hereafter as *Works*. Citations are by individual works and volume and page in this edition. Works not contained in this edition are quoted from R. Tucker, ed., *The Marx-Engels Reader*, 2nd ed. (cited as Tucker, in the text) and individual texts. Full references are found below, under "Texts Cited." Unless otherwise indicated, all italics in quotations are from texts. For a good brief assessment of the relationship between Marx and Engels, see D. McLellan, *Engels* (Glasgow, 1977), Chap. 5; a more detailed account is T. Carver, *Marx and Engels: The Intellectual Relationship* (Bloomington, IN, 1983).

3. K. Marx and F. Engels, *Collected Works* (London, 1975–   ).

4. The former is the view of S. Avineri, *The Social and Political Thought of Karl Marx* (Cambridge, 1968), esp. Chap. 8; the latter is Lenin's, and those of subsequent figures in

the Communist tradition; see G. Lichtheim, *Marxism: A Historical and Critical Study*, 2nd ed. (New York, 1961); L. Kolakowski, *Main Currents in Marxism*, 3 vols. P. S. Falla, trans. (Oxford, 1978), Vols. II and III.

5. Of the works listed below under "Further Reading," I have been especially influenced by those of Lichtheim, Avineri, Kolakowski, Hunt, and Lenin's *State and Revolution*. I should note, however, that on many points, these scholars hold conflicting interpretations.

6. Marx addresses the question most clearly in regard to political possibilities in Russia; see his 1881 letter to Vera Zasulich (*Works*, III, 152–161; *Correspondence*, 319–320); his 1877 letter to the Editorial Board of the Russian publication, *Otechestvenniye Zapiski* (*Correspondence*, 291–294); and the Preface to the 1882 Russian edition of the *Communist Manifesto* (*Works*, I, 99–101). The thrust of these passages is that his theory is applicable mainly to Western Europe and that other countries could find other paths to socialism. But there is some reason to believe that in these pieces Marx speaks more as a political actor than as a theorist. Regardless of Marx's own view on this question, his theory was widely interpreted as applying outside of Western Europe, most importantly, to Russia; see Lenin, *Two Tactics of Social Democracy*, in *Selected Works*, 3 vols. (Moscow, 1970), Vol. I.

7. See Vol. I, 112–116.

8. For these themes in medieval political thought, see esp. Vol. I, Chap. 7.

9. See esp. G. A. Cohen, *Marx's Theory of History: A Defence* (Princeton, 1978).

10. For similar language, see *German Ideology*, pp. 71–72; *Capital*, I, 763. For problems reconciling these general statements with Marx's detailed historical accounts of the rise of the bourgeoisie, see R. Miller, *Analyzing Marx* (Princeton, 1984), Chap. 5.

11. The main ones are in *Works*, III, 483–504; see also his 1894 letter to H. Starkenburg, in Tucker, 767–768.

12. McLellan, "Karl Marx," in *The Blackwell Encyclopedia of Political Thought*, D. Miller, ed. (Oxford, 1987), 322.

13. See pp. 394–5; compare J. S. Mill's somewhat different use of the example of the Reformation in *On Liberty* (Indianapolis, 1978), Chap. 2, p. 27; see p. 350.

14. See p. 395.

15. Montesquieu, *Considerations on the Causes of the Greatness of the Romans and Their Decline*, D. Lowenthal, trans. (New York, 1965), Chap. 11, p. 108; see pp. 183–4.

16. The classic account of the political forms that will exist after the revolution is given in Lenin's explication of Marx and Engels's theory of the state in *State and Revolution*, *Selected Works*, Vol. II.

17. The harmony of interests in political society is closely related to liberal faith in the harmony of economic interests. This is seen most clearly in Adam Smith's famous claim that, as each person pursues his own interests, through an "invisible hand," the interests of society as a whole are advanced. See Smith, *The Wealth of Nations*, esp. Book II; this argument will not be discussed in this chapter. It is interesting to note, however, that much of Marx's economic theorizing is devoted to showing it is incorrect. This is central to the argument of *Capital*; it is advanced briefly and clearly in Marx's 1849 pamphlet, *Wage Labor and Capital* (see pp. 441–2).

18. See Chap. 6, p. 228.

19. Esp. *The Eighteenth Brumaire of Louis Bonaparte*, Sec. VII; in *Works*, I, 474–487; for discussion, see R. N. Hunt, *The Political Ideas of Marx and Engels*, 2 vols. (Pittsburgh, 1974, 1985), II, 49–60. This work is cited hereafter in text as Hunt.

20. *Capital*, I, 244; see *Capital*, Vol. I, Chap. 10.

21. Marx, *Economic and Philosophical Manuscripts*, pp. 142–143; full reference below, under "Texts Cited," cited hereafter as *Manuscripts*.

22. On the utopian socialists, see G. Lichtheim, *The Origins of Socialism* (New York, 1969); Marx and Engels, *Communist Manifesto*, *Works*, I, 134–136; Engels, *Socialism: Utopian and Scientific*, *Works*, III, 114–126.

23. On Blanqui, see Lichtheim, *Origins*, Chap. 4; for Jacobinism, see J. L. Talmon, *The Origins of Totalitarian Democracy* (New York, 1970).

24. See McLellan, *Life*, Chaps. 3–4; Hunt, *Political Ideas*, I, Chaps. 7, 10.

25. Engels, Introduction to Marx, *The Class Struggles in France*, *Works*, I, 191; this introduction cited hereafter as "Introduction."

26. Hunt, *Political Ideas*, I, 341; his emphasis. Within the Marxian tradition, the classic work on the need for an enlightened party is Lenin's *What Is To Be Done?* in *Selected Works*, Vol. I. On Lenin's view concerning the spontaneous development of the working class, and so the reason for his shift, see I, 146–153; on this, see L. Kolakowski, *Main Currents in Marxism*, 3 vols., P. S. Falla, trans. (Oxford, 1978), II, 389–390.

27. See Lichtheim, *Marxism*, pp. 65–75; C. Schorske, *German Social Democracy, 1905–17: The Development of the Great Schism* (Cambridge, MA, 1955).

28. See Marx, *The Class Struggles in France*, *Works*, I, 225–230; *Eighteenth Brumaire*, I, 404–406.

29. E. Bernstein, *The Preconditions of Socialism*, H. Tudor, ed. and trans. (Cambridge, 1993), p. 158; see Chap. 4.

30. See Lichtheim, *Marxism*, pp. 268–272.

31. See Avineri, *Social and Political Thought of Karl Marx*, Chap. 8; see above, n. 4.

32. Lenin, *State and Revolution*, *Selected Works*, II, 311.

33. Hunt, *Political Ideas*, I, 297; see Chap. 9.

34. As Lenin argues in *State and Revolution*, Chaps. 1 and 5.

TEXTS CITED

Bernstein, E. *The Preconditions of Socialism*. H. Tudor, ed. and trans. Cambridge, 1993.

Lenin, V. I. *State and Revolution*. In *Selected Works in Three Volumes*. No trans. Moscow, 1970.

Marx, K. *Capital*. 3 vols. F. Engels, ed. S. Moore and E. Aveling, trans. New York, 1967.

Marx, K. *Economic and Philosophical Manuscripts*. T. B. Bottomore, trans. In *Marx's Concept of Man*. E. Fromm, ed. New York, 1961.

Marx, K. *The Letters of Karl Marx.* S. Padover, ed. and trans. Englewood Cliffs, NJ, 1979.

Marx, K. *The Poverty of Philosophy.* No trans. New York, 1963.

Marx, K. and Engels, F. *The German Ideology.* R. Pascal, ed. No trans. New York, 1947.

Marx, K. and Engels, F. *The Marx-Engels Reader.* 2nd ed. R. Tucker, ed. New York, 1978.

Marx, K. and Engels, F. *Selected Correspondence.* S. W. Ryazanskaya, ed. I. Lasker, trans. 3rd ed. Moscow, 1975.

Marx, K. and Engels, F. *Selected Works in Three Volumes.* No trans. Moscow, 1966.

Marx, K. and Engels, F. *Werke.* 39 vols. Berlin, 1972–1978.

Further Reading

Avineri, S. *The Social and Political Thought of Karl Marx.* Cambridge, 1968.

Carver, T. *Marx and Engels: The Intellectual Relationship.* Bloomington, IN, 1983.

Cohen, G. A. *Marx's Theory of History: A Defence.* Princeton, 1978.

Hunt, R. *The Political Ideas of Marx and Engels.* 2 vols. Pittsburgh, 1974, 1985.

Kolakowski, L. *Main Currents in Marxism.* 3 vols. P. S. Falla, trans. Oxford, 1978.

Lenin, V. I. *The State and Revolution. Two Tactics of Social Democracy. What Is To Be Done?* In *Selected Works in Three Volumes.* No trans. Moscow, 1970.

Lichtheim, G. *Marxism: A Historical and Critical Study.* 2nd ed. New York, 1961.

Lichtheim, G. *The Origins of Socialism.* New York, 1969.

Lichtheim, G. *A Short History of Socialism.* New York, 1970.

McLellan, D. *Karl Marx: His Life and Thought.* New York, 1973.

Mandel, R. *The Formation of the Economic Thought of Karl Marx.* New York, 1971.

Miliband, R. *Marxism and Politics.* London, 1977.

Miller, R. *Analyzing Marx.* Princeton, 1984.

Rubel, M. and Manale, M. *Marx Without Myth.* New York, 1975.

Ulam, A. *The Unfinished Revolution.* Revised ed. Boulder, CO, 1979.

Epilogue

The history of Western political theory does not come to an end with Marx. The revolutionary transformation to an entirely new era that Marx forecast has not come about. As human history has continued to unfold, problems of political life have stayed with us, along with theoretical attempts to deal with them. In the *Philosophy of History*, Hegel remarks that one thing history teaches is that no one ever learns from history: "nations and governments have never learned anything from history or acted upon any lessons they might have drawn from it."[1] But even if we accept Hegel's observation in regard to nations and governments, the history of political theory is an exception. It provides the basis for subsequent attempts to address political questions. Because of the essential continuity of political affairs, the ideas recounted in this volume continue to dominate our conceptualization of politics. In the works of the great political theorists, we encounter developed presentations of different approaches to the political world, including those that ground contemporary understanding.

As we have seen throughout this work, political philosophy is not abstract speculation, removed from pressing concerns. Rather, it is above all an attempt to deal with critical problems. It is, in Aristotle's sense, a "practical" subject, aiming not at knowledge for its own sake, but to guide action. We study ethics, Aristotle writes, "not to know what goodness is, but how to become good men," since otherwise moral knowledge would not be of use.[2] The problems with which political theory deals are those of political life, which must be addressed if human societies are to continue.

In the Introduction to Volume I of this work, I quoted another remark of Hegel's—that philosophy is "its own time apprehended in thoughts."[3] The problems with which political philosophers deal are those that arise in their specific historical circumstances. Though these problems are in a sense perennial, they also vary over time, as essential underlying political circumstances evolve. Accordingly, there is no such thing as "man" or "society" as such, let alone the "state." Human institutions, and indeed, human beings, differ over time, shaped by the conditions in which they emerge. We have seen this in regard to political institutions, the evolution of which we have traced. As central political institutions have developed, political theory has as well. The terms with which a great political theorist addresses his situation are mediated by his political experience, while the institutions he considers are those of his civilization. To some extent, this accounts for great differences between the political theories we have examined, based in turn on the Greek *polis*, Hellenistic empire, medieval monarchy, and modern nation-state. In addition, the conceptual language of any political theory arises in a specific historical setting and is rooted in its overall mode of thought. Once again, this is clear throughout these volumes, as we have traversed enormous distances between classical, medieval, and modern modes of thought.

In spite of the great differences we have seen, the history of modern political theory, as recounted in this volume, is one of essential continuity. The nation-state that began to emerge during Machiavelli's time is with us still, as are problems it brings in its wake. Within the liberal paradigm, the individual and society are conceptualized apart from one another; the great task of political theory is to explain their relationship. Though it has evolved considerably during the period spanned in this volume, liberal theory and its problems continue to occupy contemporary theorists.

Over the last century, liberal political theory has, if anything, solidified its hold on the political world. Marx's faith in revolution was in a certain sense realized by Communist revolutions in Russia and several developing countries, notably China, Viet Nam, and Cuba—though the philosophy of revolutionary activism propounded by Lenin, Stalin, and Mao Tse-tung was in many ways alien to Marx's vision. Hence its designation: "Marxism-Leninism." From our present perspective, it is safe to say that the Marxian episode in political theory was a miserable failure, which contributed to the deaths of millions of people. As revolutionary Communism has fallen into the dustbin of history—to lie alongside Italian and German Fascism, which fell earlier this century—the theoretical landscape has come increasingly to be dominated by liberal ideas. At the present time, liberalism's most robust competition is provided by extreme nationalism and varieties of religious fundamentalism. But classical liberalism and its outgrowths reign supreme as heirs of the Western Enlightenment tradition of rational political thought.

At the present time, much political theory is concerned with extending and defending the great values of individual freedom and limited political authority that are at liberalism's heart. Battles rage concerning the nature and meaning of freedom and the rights the state must protect. Throughout the late nineteenth and twentieth centuries, the industrial democracies have moved from the limited, negative states of classical liberalism to far more extensive institutions, providing services in the areas of public health, welfare, and education. Questions concerning the legitimacy of state intervention in these areas, and exactly what the state should—and should not—do in regard to them, divide contemporary "Liberals" and "Conservatives," though adherents of these positions bear different names in different countries. Conservatives of the order of Ronald Reagan wish to roll back the state to an approximation of what existed under classical liberalism. Liberals, like Edward Kennedy, wish to extend state services. For example, most industrial democracies now guarantee health care to their members. The right to health care is obviously far removed in important respects from the right not to be harmed by other people. Justification of an extended concept of rights, and the redistribution of income from the wealthy to the poor that extensive state services require, ground current theoretical debates. Liberals support an expansive conception of rights, while Conservatives oppose this. With individual rights hotly contested, justifying these is a crucial concern. In this area, the skepticism of Hume has left a permanent mark. The triumph of reason and science has pushed aside the essentially theological defense of rights presented by Locke, and called into question other, related religious and metaphysical notions, such as John Stuart Mill's view of human nature's capacity to develop. As we saw in our discussion of Burke, conservative theorists are wont to turn to religious notions, not only to ground their arguments, but to support their view of the state's religious responsibilities as well. But in spite of their profound differences, contemporary Liberals and Conservatives agree on far more than they disagree. In most areas, the two groups share fundamental beliefs about the nature and purpose of political authority, and the need to ensure freedom to all alike. Many of their disagreements are over means to their shared ends.

Other debates in contemporary political theory concern extending liberal values. Theorists argue for the need to protect the rights of minority groups—racial, religious, cultural minorities—from forces of society as well as the state. In recent years, much attention has been paid to the situation of women, and the need to protect individual rights within the family as well as the public sphere. But on the other hand, as modern societies have extended benefits of freedom to an unprecedented degree, the need to limit this has been widely felt. Because liberal theory begins with the individual, accounting for his obligations to society, and so limits on his freedom, has not been easy. In keeping with the great liberal value of reasoned justification, the need to develop a convincing explanation of political and social obligations is now a pressing concern. Complicating matters further in increasingly diverse societies is the need to find a common theoretical language in which to discuss essential issues.

Throughout the twentieth century, the liberal tradition has evolved along with rapid changes throughout society. At times, its central tenets have been called into question—especially by Fascist and Communist movements. But these challenges it has withstood. In the world of political theory, fundamental questions must have answers. In spite of its many faults and shortcomings, liberal theory will probably dominate discussion for the foreseeable future. The values it expresses are central to the Western tradition, and likely substitutes are nowhere on the horizon.

In spite of Hegel's view of history as ordered by divine forces, the meaning of history is imposed upon it by the observer. All observation is selective, and in these volumes we have concentrated on the series of stages through which liberal ideas arose throughout the ancient and medieval periods, and were then developed and criticized by great thinkers in the liberal tradition. There is little reason to believe history was ordained to move in this direction. Other views are possible; other scholars would doubtless locate the fruit of historical development elsewhere. But at the present time, with liberal ideas ascendant, there is much to be gained in looking back over the series of stages through which they evolved. As the product of specific political and social occurrences, liberal theory bears the stamp of its origin. In no small degree, its strengths and weaknesses stand out more clearly against this backdrop.

But even on this approach, the history of political theory is more than a prehistory of liberal ideas. The political theorists who preceded liberalism, as well as those who criticize it, provide alternative visions of the political world. The great thinkers have distinctive conceptions of political life; their works call attention to various features. In keeping with its great values of open-mindedness and free debate, liberal theory will always need its critics as well as its proponents. As Mill says, of any controversy, "He who knows only his own side of the case knows little of that."[4] In tracing the rise of modern political theory, and then liberalism's main adherents and opponents, we have examined many different sides of the case. A clearer view of the past can help us understand our present situation, and so to grapple with what is to come.

Notes

1. G. W. F. Hegel, *Lectures on the Philosophy of World History: Introduction: Reason in History*, H. Nisbet, trans. (Cambridge, 1975), p. 21.

2. Aristotle, *Nicomachean Ethics*, II, 2 (1103b27–29); *The Ethics of Aristotle*, J. Thompson, trans., revised ed. (Harmondsworth, England, 1976). For Aristotle's conception of practical wisdom, see Vol. I, 103–105.

3. Hegel, *Philosophy of Right*, T. M. Knox, ed. and trans. (Oxford, 1952), p. 11.

4. J. S. Mill, *On Liberty* (Indianapolis, 1978), Chap. 2, p. 35.

Copyright Acknowledgments

INDEX